Intelligent Database Systems

ACM Press Books

This book is published as part of the ACM Press Books – a collaboration between the Association for Computing Machinery and Addison-Wesley. ACM is the oldest and largest education and scientific society in the information technology field. Through its high quality publications and services, ACM is a major force in advancing the skills and knowledge of IT professionals throughout the world. For further information about ACM contact:

ACM Member Services
1515 Broadway, 17th Floor
New York NY 10036-5701
Phone: +1 212 626 0500
Fax: +1 212 944 1318
Email: *acmhelp@acm.org*

ACM European Service Center
108 Cowley Road
Oxford OX4 1JF
United Kingdom
Phone: +44 1865 382338
Fax: +44 1865 381338
Email: *acm-europe@acm.org*
URL: *http://www.acm.org*

Selected ACM titles:

Software Requirements and Specifications: A Lexicon of Software Practice, Principles and Prejudices
Michael Jackson

Software Test Automation: Effective Use of Text Execution Tools
Mark Fewster and Dorothy Graham

Test Process Improvement: A Practical Step-by-step Guide to Structured Testing
Tim Koomen and Martin Pol

Mastering the Requirements Process
Suzanne Robertson and James Robertson

Bringing Design to Software: Expanding Software Development to Include Design
Terry Winograd, John Bennett, Laura de Young, Bradley Hartfield

Software for Use: A Practical Guide to the Models and Methods of Usage Centered Design
Larry L. Constantine and Lucy A. D Lockwood

Use Cases: Requirements in Context
Daryl Kulak and Eamonn Guiney

Software Blueprints: Lightweight Uses of Logic in Conceptual Modelling
David Robertson and Jaume Agusti

Intelligent Database Systems

Elisa Bertino, Barbara Catania and Gian Piero Zarri

An imprint of Pearson Education

Harlow, England · London · New York · Reading, Massachusetts · San Francisco
Toronto · Don Mills, Ontario · Sydney · Tokyo · Singapore · Hong Kong · Seoul
Taipei · Cape Town · Madrid · Mexico City · Amsterdam · Munich · Paris · Milan

PEARSON EDUCATION LIMITED

Head Office:
Edinburgh Gate
Harlow CM20 2JE
Tel: +44 (0)1279 623623
Fax: +44 (0)1279 431059

London Office:
128 Long Acre, London WC2E 9AN
Tel: +44 (0)20 7447 2000
Fax: +44 (0)20 7240 5771
Website: www.aw.com/cseng/

First published in Great Britain in 2001

ISBN 0-201-87736-8

British Library Cataloguing in Publication Data
A CIP catalogue record for this book can be obtained from the British Library

Library of Congress Cataloging in Publication Data
Applied for.

10 9 8 7 6 5 4 3 2 1

Typeset by Pantek Arts Ltd, Kent
Printed and bound in Great Britain by Biddles Ltd, Guildford and King's Lynn

The Publishers' policy is to use paper manufactured from sustainable forests.

1 Introduction

1.1 Informal definition of the domain

Intelligent database systems (IDBSs) derive from the integration of database (DB) technology with techniques developed in the field of artificial intelligence (AI). The main motivations that drove the development of the IDBS technology in the late 70s and early 80s can be summarized as follows:

- From a DB point of view, there was an urgent need to address the problems caused by the limited modelling capabilities of database systems, in particular relational database systems. Such limitations implied the impossibility of developing, in a pure DB context, certain facilities for reasoning, problem solving, and question answering. These were needed to take into account the requirements from the new data management applications, such as industrial automation, computer-aided design and manufacturing (CAD/CAM), office applications, computer-aided software engineering (CASE), military command and control, information retrieval from textual data, and cartography.
- From an AI point of view, it was necessary to transcend the era of the first 'intelligent' systems – very often toy systems running only in main memory and operating on very limited sets of *ad hoc* data – to achieve real information management systems able to deal with large amounts of information. This exigency entailed integrating in the AI systems at least some typical DB capacities for dealing efficiently with large amounts of data to be stored in online secondary storage, such as concurrency control, error recovery, distributed processing, and security.

To be even more concise, we can say that, at least until recently, traditional DBs lacked *semantic support*, while AI systems were limited in their capacity to supply and maintain *large amounts of factual data*. This book relates the solutions that the IDBS scholars have developed in the past two decades in order to use AI techniques to provide semantic support to a DB system, and DB techniques to aid an AI system to deal with large amounts of information. In discussing these topics, we have adopted a point of view characterized by the two following aspects:

- Our approach to the AI/DB integration conforms to the belief that one of the key factors for this integration resides in the exploitation of the equivalence between the *data models* developed in the DB field and the *knowledge repre-*

sentation systems of AI. To the extent that data models include relationships between data and procedures on the one hand, and the management of data on the other, they show in fact important similarities with knowledge representation systems, characterized by a strong interest in inferencing (management of information) as supported by their own modelling capabilities. The modelling aspects therefore have a high priority in the context of this book.

- The second point concerns the fact that we have conceived this book in a real didactic spirit. We have then tried to evidence the concrete ins and outs of the different architectural solutions adopted for the set-up of real IDBSs and their importance and practical value. Mainly, we have tried to contribute to a better understanding of the AI principles by the DB practitioners wishing to add some 'intelligence' to their usual DB applications, and to a better understanding of the DB principles by the AI practitioners aspiring to develop real-world applications. This implies, among other things, that the formal, theoretical developments have been limited as much as possible, and introduced, always to a limited extent, only when strictly necessary to enlighten the genesis and the modalities of use of very important IDBS concepts.

1.2 General characteristics of IDBSs

Even if there is no longer any consensus about the size of a 'normal' IDBS, we can say that, in general, such systems are characterized by the presence of several thousand 'rules', encoding 'intensional' domain knowledge and stored in the rule base (RLB), and several millions of 'facts' included in the fact database (FDB). In broad terms, intensional knowledge represents the knowledge – including both directly stored data and virtual data inferred from it – that is necessary for the reasoning activities of the IDBS. Note that this differentiation between RLB and FDB is sometimes only a didactic facility given that, in some of the more advanced systems (*see* Section 3.4, for example), the differentiation between knowledge and data is blurred. Note also that, to end up at the dimensions introduced above, rules and facts are taken at their simplest meaning, i.e. they correspond here to i) simple 'production rules' in the expert systems (ES) style of the form 'if ... then', and ii) elementary data equivalent to a single pair 'attribute-value' in a relational database.

For both rules and facts, persistency is crucial. In ordinary AI expert systems, for example, data needed for an application are normally introduced by the user at the system's requests, i.e. in small quantities and only when necessary. They reside in volatile memory and therefore they disappear as soon as the particular application using them is completed. The same happens to the intermediate results deduced during the reasoning process. Such an approach is not viable for the facts of an IDBS: as with data in an ordinary database, it must be possible to make use of those facts again, i.e. 'facts' must be permanently maintained independently of any application, even when the fact database is not being accessed. Because of this, and because of its huge dimensions, normally the fact database of an IDBS cannot reside in volatile storage but must be organized on secondary storage. Thus we can say that IDBSs are characterized by the following general properties:

- use, to various extents, of artificial intelligence techniques supporting various forms of reasoning;
- architectures that, at least implicitly, are based on an organization in the expert systems style. Such architectures consist then of a fact database and a rule base;
- persistency of the FDB.

This means that an IDBS is endowed with a data management system able to manage large quantities of persistent data to which various forms of reasoning can be applied to infer additional data and information. This includes knowledge representation techniques, inference techniques, and 'intelligent' user interfaces – interfaces which extend beyond the traditional query language approach by making use, typically, of natural language (NL) facilities. Note that, in agreement with our model-centred approach, we will allude only occasionally to these advanced – and, by the way, still almost limited – 'intelligent' interfaces. Those techniques play different roles in enhancing database systems: knowledge representation techniques allow one to represent better in the DB the semantics of the application domains; inference techniques allow one to reason about the data to extract additional data and information; and intelligent user interfaces help users to make requests and receive the replies.

1.3 Data models and the relational data model

As already stated, an important notion on which the layout of this book is based is that of the data model. A data model can be defined as a logical organization expressed in terms of some data structures, of the real-world objects (entities) of interest to a particular application, of the constraints on them and their relationships. Data models represent the basis on which database management systems (DBMSs) are built, in that each DBMS implements a specific data model. In particular, each data model has a number of operations for defining the data structures that represent the objects of interest, and for querying and manipulating such data structures. These operations are expressed through one or more languages, such as the Data Definition Language (DDL) for defining data, and the Data Manipulation Language (DML) for manipulating the data. Very often, the operations dealing with data retrieval are referred to as the query language.

Several 'generations' of data models have been developed over the years. We can say that the history of database technology is marked by the advancements in data models. Traditional data models in the DB domain include the hierarchical model, based on a tree-structured organization of data; the network model, based on a graph organization of data; and the relational model, based on set-oriented organization of data. It is important to point out that the relational model represented an important advancement with respect to the other two models. It introduced some relevant principles, such as declarative query and data manipulation languages, and was based on very simple and high-level data-structuring constructs. Most of today's applications use DBMSs based on this model.

We will look here at some well-known characteristics of the relational data model (a full section, Section 3.1, is devoted to the AI data models, i.e. knowledge representation systems). These are as follows:

- Information is represented as a collection of tables called 'relations'. Each relation may correspond to an 'entity type' (e.g. 'students' or 'course' for the traditional 'university' example used here) or to a 'relationship type' (e.g. 'grades', describing the relationships between students and courses).
- The 'rows' of a table are called 'tuples' and represent concrete 'instances' or 'occurrences' of the particular entity or relationship represented by the table (e.g. a particular student). The 'columns' of a table represent the 'attributes' ('properties') of the relation (e.g. for the entity student, the 'identification number' (ID), the 'student name' (SNAME), and the 'major' (MAJOR)).
- The set of all possible values that can be inserted in a column is called the 'domain' of the attribute represented by the column. Two relations are associated when they share a particular domain (e.g. if the relations 'students' and 'grades' are both characterized by the presence of the attribute ID, then we can say that 'students are related to grades' via the common (shared) domain of the attribute ID).

Figure 1.1 illustrates these characteristics.

Data manipulation in the relational model is based on the concepts of:

1. relational algebra, consisting of set operators, such as union, plus some special, derived operators, like 'join';
2. relational calculus, based on first-order logic.

The SQL language, which is the actual language used in most relational DBMSs, is an expression of the two above formalisms, and includes many practical features and functions. As an example, let us consider the query 'Retrieve the names of the students who received a C grade for the courses they have taken'. This query is expressed in SQL as follows:

```
SELECT SNAME
      FROM STUDENTS, GRADES
      WHERE STUDENTS.ID=GRADES.ID AND LGRADE='C'.
```

Even though the relational model represented a key milestone in the DBMS history, it has many drawbacks. This model, like the other traditional data models, is basically record-oriented. The reason is that the development of such models was initially influenced by the need for correspondence with the physical implementations of the early file systems, i.e. in a relational DBMS the tuples correspond to

Figure 1.1 An example of a relational database

Students		
ID	**SNAME**	**MAJOR**
S1	Peter	Computer Science
S2	Jane	Mathematics
S3	Bill	Computer Science
S4	Tom	Electrical Engineering

Courses		
CCODE	**CNAME**	**TEACHER**
CS101	Compliers	Smith
MA220	Calculus	Jones
CS210	Databases	Brown
EE220	Computer Architecture	Smith

Grades		
ID	**CCODE**	**LGRADE**
S1	CS101	B
S1	MA220	A
S2	CS210	B
S2	MA220	C
S2	EE220	B
S3	CS210	C

the records in a file. As a result, the model is too rigid. In particular, being forced to model everything as 'flat tables' like those in the example above often leads to awkward database designs and to unnecessarily complicated queries.

Another restriction that stems from the record-oriented paradigm is that relational DBMSs force the user to specify the 'schema' of the database, i.e. in the design phase of the database, before any tuple can be inserted, the user must specify exactly which relations contain which attributes. No data can be entered in the database that do not satisfy the format described by the schema. In particular, no additional attributes can be stored. From a knowledge representation point of view, the relational model is not fully adequate. It makes use of only one primitive modelling construct, the table. Furthermore, among other things, attributes in relations can be represented only in an atomic form because of the so-called 'first normal form restriction'. Trying to represent a large range of potentially extremely different application situations with only one modelling construct typically results in:

- a proliferation of the basic blocks, i.e. the tables, in the global database representation;
- the loss of the exact meaning to be associated with that modelling construct.

1.4 A taxonomy of intelligent database systems

There have been several research and development efforts to overcome the shortcomings of traditional data models and DBMSs. In this book we classify the efforts towards devising better ways of dealing in an intelligent manner with large quantities of information into two categories:

1. efforts originated in a prevailing DB context;
2. efforts originated in a prevailing AI context.

The efforts in the first category represent mainly extensions to DBMS technology. Such efforts can in turn be categorized as:

- extensions concerning primarily the increase of the expressive power of data models, i.e. *static extensions*;
- extensions related mainly to attempts to introduce some (limited) reasoning capabilities in DBMSs, i.e. *dynamic extensions*.

The 'DB part' of the book (Chapter 2) includes two sections about static extensions. The first, Section 2.1, is devoted to the presentation of nested relations, semantic and hyper-semantic data models. The models presented in this section are quite relevant because they were defined with the goal of supporting conceptual modelling activities, one of the most relevant tasks in the process of database design. Their goal was thus to increase in various ways the expressive power of data models. Current database design methodologies are still based on those models, or extensions of them. They are also relevant as theoretical background for more recent data models. This section finishes with a short introduction to UML, which is the most representative descendant of such models.

Section 2.2 describes the main concepts underlying the object-oriented data model and relevant aspects of object-oriented database management systems. Since there is a large number of variations among object models supported by the available object-oriented database management systems, the section also describes relevant aspects of those systems with special focus on the languages they provide for data definition and manipulation. Such a description is essential to make more concrete the presentation on object models. Section 2.2 also briefly discusses recent object-relational models and approaches to extend Java so that persistent objects are supported.

Chapter 2 concludes with a look at dynamic extensions with active databases and rule-based systems, Section 2.3.

Chapter 3 begins with a section (3.1) devoted to an introduction to the knowledge-based systems, mainly for the benefit of the DB scholars. This introduction is centred on the AI knowledge representation problems that are the equivalent of the DB data model problems. The chapter continues by describing two 'classical' approaches to the construction of IDBSs – the deductive databases (3.2) and the coupling of ES and DB systems (3.3). Section 3.4 is devoted to some of the most recent developments in the IDBS domain, the so-called 'integral AI approach systems' (IASs). This chapter includes, in particular, a very detailed examination of one of the most well-known and more controversial endeavours in this 'integral' domain, the CYC system by Doug Lenat.

By way of a conclusion, we have added a last chapter devoted to supplying a general overview of some very 'hot' topics, such as ontologies, data mining, semi-structured data, mediators and wrappers, etc. that are influencing deeply both the AI and the DB fields. Even if these topics depart, at least partly, from the traditional problems of the AI/DB integration, they still offer some interesting and 'modern' contributions to the problem of developing more 'intelligent' and flexible systems for the management of very important amounts of data which can sometimes be very 'unstructured'.

1.5 Guidelines for using intelligent database systems

This book can be read by different types of readers with varying backgrounds and interests. In particular, it will be of interest to readers with a database background who wish to get acquainted with knowledge-based systems, or to readers with an AI background who are interested in getting to know advanced database systems.

Readers with a database background may focus on Chapter 3, where they can find extensive material on knowledge-based systems (3.1), on the integration of knowledge-based systems with database systems (3.3), and on more advanced solutions such as TELOS, CYC, conceptual graphs and NKRL (3.4). These three sections, together with Section 3.2 discussing deductive databases, can also be used as the basis for a graduate course on knowledge-based systems that can be taken by students after a course on database systems. Section 3.1 contains, among other things, an extensive introduction to the basic concepts of the logic programming paradigm, such as the resolution principle. Also, at the end of Section 2.2, readers with a database background can find a short comparison between object-oriented models developed in the database context, and object models developed in the AI context. Section 2.3 contains a similar comparison between active database systems and AI production rule systems.

Readers with an AI background can focus on Chapter 2, where they can find extensive material on nested and semantics data models (2.1), object-oriented database systems (2.2) and active database systems (2.3). Such topics are not often familiar to readers with an AI background. These readers will also be interested in Section 3.2, discussing deductive database systems. These four sections can also form the basis of an advanced course on database models that can be taken by students after a course on the basics of database systems. We also strongly recommend that researchers in the AI field who are specifically interested in the areas of advanced data models read these four sections, together with Section 4.1 on the lastest developments, for a complete and up-to-date overview of the state of the art on such topics.

The book also contains relevant material for **practitioners**. Apart from using this book to get up to date on the state of the art on database systems, knowledge-based systems and integration efforts between these two technologies, they can find material on practical solutions and systems that are used today in several applications. Readers should focus in particular on Section 2.2, which discusses object-oriented and object-relational database systems used in several advanced applications, including multimedia applications; Section 3.1, which discusses frame systems used in many expert system applications; and Section 3.3, which discusses how to couple knowledge-based systems with standard database systems. This section is particularly relevant for practitioners since it covers approaches that are frequently used in advanced intelligent applications that need to support various forms of reasoning on large amounts of data. Such data are usually stored by traditional DBMSs from which it is not feasible to migrate 'as they are' to more advanced DBMSs/KBMSs (knowledge-based management systems). For those readers interested in modelling methodologies, we would recommend reading Section 2.15, on OMT and UML, two approaches that are widely used for modelling data, processes, and functions.

Finally, Chapter 4, with its overview of recent developments, will be of interest to all readers since it provides extensive coverage of recent trends on intelligent handling of data and knowledge. We believe that those trends will result – indeed many have already resulted – in increasingly intelligent systems, enabling a wider use of data and knowledge.

2 Efforts originated in a prevailing DB context

2.1 Nested and semantic data models

2.11 Introduction

The success of the relational model has been due mainly to two things: simplicity of the data structure and existence of a formal definition, providing a theoretical framework for the formal investigation of several database management system aspects. Unfortunately, simplicity became a severe limitation very early on when designing real database applications since in several contexts real data cannot be easily modelled by using the relational model, thus resulting in the definition of unclear and non-natural schemas.

To overcome this limitation, new models have been proposed with the aim of modelling real applications more naturally, providing at the same time the formal background that partially made the success of the relational model.

The aim of this section is to survey some of the first models proposed in order to increase the expressive power in data representation and querying. Most of these models were defined several years ago. However, they remain a reference point for several developments.

The section starts by surveying the nested relational model, providing sets and tuple representation inside the relational model. We then introduce semantic models, i.e. those data models that have been proposed in order to overcome the semantic limitations of the relational model in modelling real-world applications. Such models are used mainly during conceptual database design. A short description of hyper-semantic data models is then presented, as an example of approaches that have been defined for increasing the expressive power of semantic data models. We conclude the section by presenting some object-oriented models that have been proposed recently for the analysis and design of software applications and that can be used successfully during conceptual database design.

2.12 The nested relational model

A database, in the relational model, consists of a collection of relations. Each relation is a flat table, i.e. a table in which all entries are atomic data, belonging to some atomic type such as number, string, date, and so on. Thus, in the relational model, relations are in *first normal form*. It is therefore not possible to associate a set of values with any single table entry. To model sets, two different approaches can be considered:

- one new tuple is generated for each element in the set;
- two relations, instead of one, are defined, representing the 1:N relationship existing between the atomic value and the set.

Both solutions are of course not always adequate to represent complex applications, the first because it introduces redundancy and produces non-third normal form relations [Ullm89], the second because it often leads to the generation of unreadable schemas.

In order to avoid these problems, the *nested relational model* has been defined [Maki77]. Under the nested relational model, a relation is no longer a flat table. Rather, relation attributes can themselves be relations, thus reducing redundancy and increasing readability. In order to understand the differences between the relational and the nested relational model, consider the following example.

Example 1. Suppose you have to model information about (a) mothers together with the name of their children and their birthdate. Table 2.1 presents a relational table representing such information. If a mother has more than one child (as Mary does), more than one tuple will contain information about this mother. On the other hand, the nested relational model (See Table 2.1 (b)) provides a more intuitive representation by inserting information about each mother just once. Thus, the relation contains four tuples whereas the nested relation contains just two tuples, one for each mother.

Table 2.1 (a) a relation; (b) a corresponding nested relation

(a)		
Mother	**Child**	**Birthdate**
Mary	John	16 March 1976
Mary	Bill	1 September 1982
Mary	July	22 May 1980
Carolyn	Susan	12 June 1985

(b)

Mother	Child	Birthdate
Mary	John	16 March 1976
	Bill	1 September 1982
	July	22 May 1980
Carolyn	Susan	12 June 1985

In order to manipulate nested relational databases, relational languages have to be extended to deal with non-flat relations. In the following, we formally introduce the nested relational model, then briefly describe nested relational languages, before finally discussing some issues concerning the equivalence between the nested relational model and languages, and relational ones.

2.121 *The model*

Here the nested relational model will be presented according to what has been proposed in [Gyss91]. Suppose we have an infinitely enumerable set $\mathcal{U}$ of *atomic attributes* and an infinitely enumerable set $\mathcal{V}$ of *atomic values*. The set of *nested attributes* is the smallest set U such that $U \subseteq \mathcal{U}$ and for each finite subset X of U in which no atomic attribute appears more than once, $X \in U$. Attributes that are not atomic are called *composite*. For example, if $A, B, C \in \mathcal{U}$, then {C,{A,B}} is a composite attribute; {B,{A,B}} is not because B occurs twice.

Starting from the definition of nested attributes, a *nested relation scheme* can be defined as a composite attribute. If an attribute belonging to the schema is atomic, atomic values will be associated with those attributes in the instances of that schema. On the other hand, if the attribute is composite, the instances are nested relation instances whose schema is the composite attribute of which they are an instance. Consider Example 1. The schema of the nested relation presented in Table 2.1(b) is {Mother, {Child, Birthdate}}. Such a schema contains two attributes: the first, Mother, is an atomic attribute and its instances are atomic values (Mary and Carolyn in the example). On the other hand, {Child, Birthdate} is a composite attribute and its instances are flat relations over the schema {Child, Birthdate}.

Starting from the previous definitions, it is now possible to define nested values, nested tuples, and nested instances as follows. The set V of all nested values, the set I_X of all nested relation instances over a composite attribute X, the set T_X of all nested tuples over X, and the set $\mathcal{I}$ of all nested relation instances are the smallest sets satisfying the following properties:

1 $V = \mathcal{V} \cup I$, i.e. nested values are either atomic values or nested relation instances (values for composite attributes).

2 $I = \cup_{X \in U - \mathcal{U}} I_X$, i.e. nested relation instances are obtained as the union of all nested relation instances over a composite attribute X.

3 I_X consists of all finite subsets of T_X.

4 T_X consists of all mappings t from X into V, called *nested tuples*, satisfying t(A) $\in V$ for all atomic attributes $A \in X \cap U$ and $t(Y) \in I_Y$ for all composed attributes $Y \in X - U$.

A *nested relation* can now be defined as a pair (Ω,ω) where Ω is a nested relation scheme (called the *scheme* of the relation) and ω is a nested relation instance (called the *instance* of the relation). If $\Omega \subseteq U$, then (Ω,ω) is a *flat* relation.

2.122 The languages

The formalization introduced above can be used to define nested relational languages. As with the relational model, an algebra and an equivalent calculus have been defined for the nested relational model. In an attempt to provide some intuition on how such languages are defined, we provide in the following the basic definitions of the nested relational algebra. The formalization has been taken from [Gyss91]. For the definition of a nested relational calculus, see [Abit95], for example.

All the operators that have been defined for the relational algebra (union, difference, Cartesian product, projection, selection, renaming) have to be adapted to the new framework. Moreover, new operators have to be defined to deal with the nested structure of the relations. Such operators are defined as follows.

1 The union of $(\Omega,\omega1) \cup (\Omega,\omega2)$ equals $(\Omega,\omega1 \cup \omega2)$. Note that the schemes of the two input relations have to coincide.

2 The difference of $(\Omega,\omega1) - (\Omega,\omega2)$ equals $(\Omega,\omega1 - \omega2)$. Note that the schemes of the two input relations have to coincide.

3 The Cartesian product $(\Omega1,\omega1)$ X $(\Omega2,\omega2)$ equals $(\Omega1\cup \Omega2, \omega')$ where $\omega' = \{t \in T_{\Omega1\cup\Omega2} \mid t|_{\Omega1} \in \omega1$ and $t|_{\Omega2} \in \omega2\}$ where $t|_{\Omega1}$ represents the projection of t on to attributes in Ω1.

4 Let $\Omega1 \subseteq \Omega$. The projection $\pi_{\Omega1}(\Omega,\omega)$ equals $(\Omega1,\omega1)$ where $\omega1 = \{ t|_{\Omega1} \mid t \in \omega\}$.

5 Let (Ω,ω) be a relation scheme. A *selection condition* for (Ω,ω) is defined as follows:

- for all $X,Y,Z \in \Omega$ and for every atomic value d, X = d, X = Y, $X \in Y$, X = Y.Z, where d is a constant and Y.Z means that Y is a composite attribute containing Z, are selection conditions (with obvious restrictions on type attributes).

  Let φ be a selection condition. The *selection* $\sigma_\varphi(\Omega,\omega)$ equals (Ω,ω1) where $\omega1 = \{t \in T_\Omega \mid t$ satisfies $\varphi\}$.
  $t \in T_\Omega$ satisfies φ if the following conditions hold:

  - φ equals X = d and t(X) = d;
  - φ equals X = Y and t(X) = t(Y);
  - φ equals $X \in Y$ and $t(X) \in t(Y)$;
  - φ equals X = Y.Z and t(X) = t(Y).Z.

6 Let $X \subseteq \Omega$. The *nesting* $\nu_X(\Omega,\omega)$ equals $(\Omega1,\omega1)$ where $\Omega1 = (\Omega - X) \cup \{X\}$ and $\omega1 = \{t \in T_{\Omega1} \mid \exists\, t' \in \omega: t|_{\Omega - X} = t'|_{\Omega - X}$ and

$$t(X) = \{t''|_X \mid t'' \in \omega \text{ and } t'|_{\Omega - X} = t''|_{\Omega - X}\}\} .$$

Thus, the nesting operator replaces a set of attributes X with a composite attribute, whose composing elements are exactly the attributes contained in X.

7 Let $X \in \Omega - U$. The *unnesting* $u_X(\Omega,\omega)$ equals $(\Omega1,\omega1)$ where $\Omega1 = (\Omega - \{X\}) \cup X$ and $\omega1 = \{t \in T_{\Omega1} \mid \exists\, t' \in \omega: t|_{\Omega - \{X\}} = t'|_{\Omega - \{X\}}$ and $t|_X \in t'(X)\}$.

Thus, the unnesting operator flattens a composite attribute by replacing it with the set of attributes composing it.

8 Let (Ω,ω) be a relation scheme. Let φ be a permutation over *U*. φ is extended in the natural way to U, to I, and to V. The *renaming* $\rho^{\varphi}(\Omega,\omega)$ equals $(\varphi(\Omega), \varphi(\omega))$.

Example 2. Consider the nested relation presented in Table 2.1(b). Thus, $\Omega = \{\text{Mother}, \{\text{Child}, \text{Birthdate}\}\}$ and ω is the instance presented. Then:

- $\pi_{\{\{\text{Child, Birthdate}\}\}}(\Omega,\omega)$ coincides with the following nested relation, having just one composite attribute:

Child	Birthdate
John	16 March 1976
Bill	1 September 1982
July	22 May 1980
Susan	12 June 1985

- $\sigma_{\text{Mother} = \text{'Mary'}}(\Omega,\omega)$ coincides with the following nested relation, having just one tuple:

Mother	Child	Birthdate
Mary	John	16 March 1976
	Bill	1 September 1982
	July	22 May 1980

- Let $\Omega1 = \{\text{Mother, Child, Birthdate}\}$ and $\omega1$ be the instance presented in Table 2.1(a). Then, $\nu_{\{\text{Child,Birthdate}\}}(\Omega1,\omega1)$ equals the instance presented in (b).
- Let $(\Omega1,\omega1)$ as before. Then, $u_{\{\{\text{Child,Birthdate}\}\}}(\Omega,\omega)$ equals $(\Omega1,\omega1)$.

Besides the algebraic operators that have already been introduced, other nested operators have been presented in the literature. The most important one is certainly the *powerset operator* [Gyss91]. Such an operator is defined as follows. Let $(\Omega1,\omega1)$ be a nested relation. Let 2^{ω} denote the set of all subsets of ω. Then, the powerset operation $\Pi(\Omega,\omega)$ equals $(\{\Omega\}, 2^{\omega})$.

Besides the algebraic language, a nested relational calculus has been proposed. In this calculus, variables may denote sets, therefore the calculus permits quantification over sets [Gyss91]. Thus, it supports some second-order features, compared with the traditional relational calculus which is based on first-order logic. As in the relational context, a domain-independence notion has been proposed for the nested relational calculus. Such a notion is sufficient to prove that the nested algebra with or without the powerset operator is equivalent to the domain-independent nested calculus with or without the powerset operator. Thus, in a manner similar to that in the relational context, the nested calculus can be seen as the declarative counterpart of the nested (and procedural) algebra, which is used by the system mainly for optimization purposes and not for user query specification.

Concerning the relationships between nested languages with and without the powerset operator, it is possible to prove that the powerset operator strictly increases the expressive power of nested languages [Gyss91]. Moreover, it is possible to show that the algebraic operators, without the powerset operator, are non-redundant. However, in the powerset algebra, the nesting operator is redundant and can be eliminated without reducing the expressive power of the language. A similar consideration holds for the difference operator.

2.123 Relationships between the relational and the nested relational model

It has been shown that even if nested languages, also without the powerset operator, seem more powerful than corresponding relational languages (as we have seen, the nested calculus provides some second-order features different to those of the relational calculus), they can be proved to be equivalent to their corresponding relational languages [Gyss91], [Pare92]. Formally, this means that, given a nested database NDB and a nested query NQ, there exists a relational database DB and a relational query Q such that the evaluation of NQ against NDB produces the same result as the evaluation of Q against DB. This also means that, given a nested relation, it is always possible to obtain a set of flat relations equivalent to it, i.e. representing the same data and the same relationships among data. Thus, the nested model and languages, without the powerset operator, are just a way to increase schema readability but they do not increase the relational expressive power. On the other hand, the use of the powerset operator strictly increases the expressive power of relational languages.

2.13 Semantic models

The aim of semantic data models is to introduce more semantic features to the relational model. Their definition has been motivated by the fact that several applications cannot be easily modelled as a simple set of tables. Rather, a more complex modelling is often required, which is closer to the user perception than the relational modelling.

Semantic data models were defined starting from three significant papers – [ChenP76], [SchmH75], [SmitJ77], – that addressed two important issues in data modelling (*see also* [Peck88]):

- Users should be able to model data without considering the physical structure but rather based on their perception of the application. This is not true in the first data models that were defined, such as the hierarchical [Tsic76] and the network data model [Tayl76], which provided a record-level representation and navigation inside data. The relational model was the first model to overcome this approach, providing a logical representation of data that is independent from the physical structure.
- The data model should provide enough semantics. The relational model provides some semantics. For example, by using functional dependencies it is possible to specify some semantic relationships existing inside data [Ullm89]. However, additional semantic relationships could be useful in modelling a given application. For example, it could be quite useful to specify that a given set of data is obtained by generalizing another set. This fact cannot be represented by using the relational model.

Motivated by such considerations, semantic data models have been introduced to overcome the previous limitations. Besides the differences listed above, semantic data models differ from the relational model since the latter provides an immediate approach for mapping the model (which is logical) to the physical structure. On the other hand, semantic data models provide a *conceptual* representation of the real world, since the main aim is that of providing the user with some modelling tools for presenting in a convenient and expressive way objects and relationships among objects. Thus, they mainly help the design of a database more than the actual implementation.

Almost all semantic models represent the entities of a real-world application and provide constructs for generating new entities starting from the original ones. This is possible by using *abstractions* [SmitJ77]. Abstractions were first introduced by psychologists and AI researchers. By abstraction we mean the process by which, starting from some entities, it is possible to obtain new entities by applying some specific reasoning. Four main abstractions have been proposed:

- *Generalization* represents the process by which, starting from two or more entities, a new entity is constructed, forgetting the differences among the starting entities and emphasizing their similiarities. For example, a STUDENT entity in a school database can be seen as the generalization of other entities, such as GOOD_STUDENT, representing all students having good average rates, and BAD_STUDENT.
- *Aggregation* provides an easy way to define a new entity starting from a set of entities that represent the components of the entity being defined. For example, the STUDENT entity can be seen as the aggregation of other entities, such as NAME and ADDRESS. In the relational model, each tuple is obtained by aggregating a set of values.

- *Classification* is the abstraction that provides the definition of a new entity starting from a set of objects having similar properties. For example, the student John Ross can be seen as a specific instance of the STUDENT entity. Thus, the STUDENT entity is obtained by classification from a set of the student instances. In the relational model, a relation instance is obtained by classification starting from a set of tuples.
- *Association* defines a new entity starting from the relationships between two or more existing entities. For example, starting from the entities STUDENT and COURSES, we can generate a new entity STUDENT_COURSES that represents which courses are followed by each student.

In general, each semantic data model represents entities (objects) – any interesting concept of the considered application domain – attributes, i.e. object properties, relationships existing among entities, integrity constraints, some abstraction mechanisms, and some query and manipulation languages.

Modelling objects includes representing low-level or primitive types, such as strings, integers, and so on, as well as more complex entities, obtained by applying abstraction mechanisms to simpler entities. Relationships can be represented in several ways, in particular as attributes, entities, distinct objects, or functions.

In general, semantic data models easily represent some important types of constraints: key dependencies and inclusion dependencies. On the other hand, referential integrity constraints are generally modelled in an implicit manner. Thus, no specific formalism is provided to represent this type of constraint. A similar situation arises for multi-valued dependencies that are usually directly modelled by using multi-valued attributes.

The most important difference between languages for traditional models and those used for the semantic ones is that in the latter the language must be able to query abstract data types. Often, semantic manipulation languages resemble relational languages, providing additional constructs for navigating inside the semantic data structure. One negative characteristic of semantic languages is that often they are not closed, i.e. the result of a semantic query is not always a semantic database. Thus queries cannot be easily composed. Other languages do not have this drawback and therefore provide more flexibility. This is the case for FQL (functional query language) [Bune82].

Based on the previous considerations, semantic data models can be classified in three main classes:

- The first class uses abstraction mechanisms, especially aggregation, to construct new entities. The entity-relationship model (ERM) is the most prominent model belonging to this class [ChenP76].
- The second class stresses the use of attributes to interrelate objects. The functional data model (FDM) is the most representative model of this class [Ship81].
- The third class provides both types of representation. The semantic database model (SDM) is the most representative model of this class [Hamm81].

We will now look at the three models, pointing out their main characteristics with some examples related to the design of a database for a school. In this school we have students, teachers and courses. Each student takes one or more courses and each course is taken by an arbitrary number of students. Each teacher teaches exactly one course and each course is taught by exactly one teacher. Students are characterized by their name, address, age, and one or more telephone numbers. Teachers are characterized by their name, address, and one or more telephone numbers. Finally, each course is characterized by a name and the total number of required hours.

2.131 *The entity-relationship model (ERM)*

The *entity-relationship model* was defined by Chen in 1976. The fundamental modelling constructs supported by the model, as the name suggests, are *entities* and *relationships*. Thus, under such a model each application domain is seen as a set of entities, whose structure is described by a set of attributes and relationships connecting such entities. Both entities and relationships can be graphically represented. At the representational level, the information structures for entities and relationships strongly resemble relations.

The graphical representation of an ERM schema is quite simple. Rectangles represent entities, diamonds represent relationships, and ovals represent attributes. Key attributes are represented by shaded ovals. From the point of view of abstraction mechanisms, relationships represent associations whereas entities are obtained from attributes by aggregation. In the original definition, no generalization construct was provided. Such abstraction was incorporated later in the model [Bati86].

It is possible to point out the multiplicity of each relationship by using the so-called *cardinality constraints*. In particular, each binary relationship can be 1:1, 1:N or N:N – 1:1 means that each instance of the leftmost entity is associated with exactly one instance of the rightmost entity and vice versa; 1:N means that each instance of the leftmost entity is associated with an arbitrary number of instances of the rightmost entity. On the other hand, each instance of the rightmost entity is associated with exactly one instance of the leftmost entity; finally, N:N means that each instance of the leftmost entity is associated with an arbitrary number of instances of the rightmost entity and vice versa.

As we have already pointed out, relationships can be seen as new entities obtained by applying the association abstraction. For this reason, attributes can also be associated with relationships and not only with entities. In the original definition, only single-valued attributes were admitted. In such a definition, multi-valued attributes can only be represented by using relationships. An extension of the ER model able to represent multi-valued attributes has been presented in [Bati86], [Teor86].

In order to present an example of an ER schema, suppose we have to design the school database previously mentioned. Figure 2.1 presents the corresponding ER schema, which contains four entities: STUDENT, TEACHER, COURSE, and

TELEPHONE. The entity TELEPHONE has been introduced in order to model the fact that students and teachers may have more than one telephone number. In this case, the telephone number represents a multi-valued attribute that can be represented only by using an additional relationship. The schema also contains four relationships: one associating STUDENT with COURSE, one associating TEACHER with COURSE, and two associating STUDENT and TEACHER with TELEPHONE.

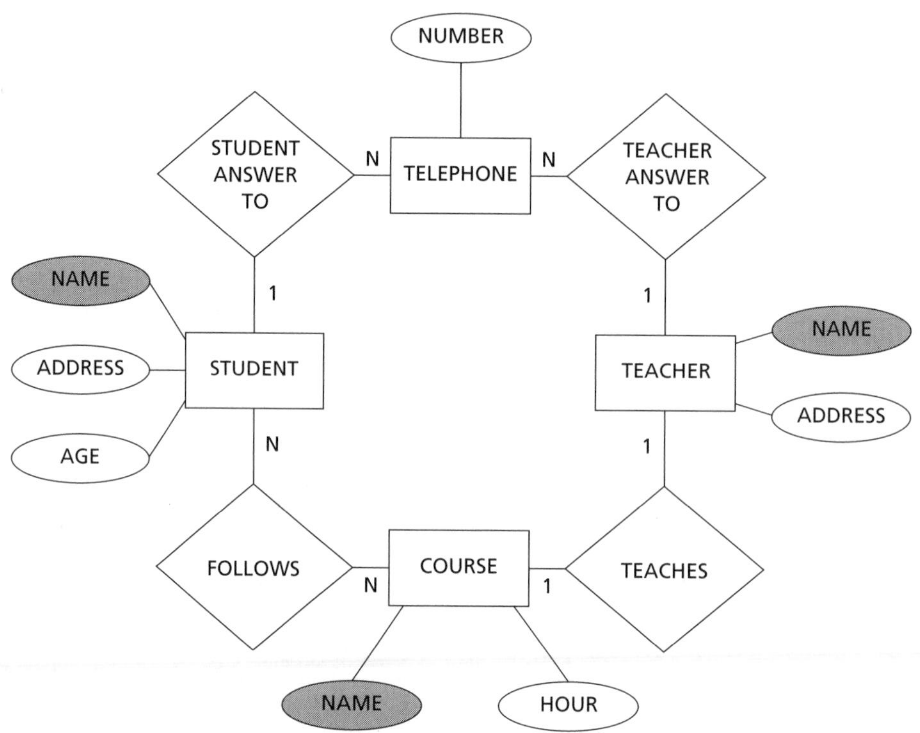

Figure 2.1 An entity-relationship schema for the school database

2.132 *The functional data model (FDM)*

The *functional data model* (FDM) [Ship81] was defined in conjunction with the data definition language DAPLEX. The basic elements of this model are *entities* and *functions*. In particular, functions can be used to define attribute aggregation, which is then used to form an entity and to specify relationships. The model does not provide explicit constructs for representing generalization and classification, but functions can be easily used to specify these abstractions. Functions can be single-valued or multi-valued. This means that, from a formal point of view, functions supported by the model are indeed relationships. By using functions, everything can be represented. For example:

- Each entity is represented as a 0-ary function, e.g. the declaration:

  `DECLARE STUDENT () ==>> Entity`

  specifies that STUDENT is an entity. The function STUDENT () returns the set of instances for the STUDENT entity. TEACHER and COURSE can be defined in a similar way. The double '>>' means that the function is multi-valued (i.e. it is a relation).
- Attributes can be specified by using unary functions from the entity to which they are related to the type of the considered values. For example, the declaration:

  `DECLARE Name (STUDENT) ==> String`

  specifies that Name is a single-valued attribute (just one '>' is used) for the entity STUDENT. On the other hand, the declaration:

  `DECLARE Telephone(STUDENT) ==>> Number`

  specifies that Telephone is a multi-valued attribute for the entity STUDENT.
- Relationships can be specified as n-ary functions. For example, the declaration:

  `DECLARE teaches (TEACHER) ==> COURSE`

  specifies that TEACHES is a relationship (seen as a new entity) between TEACHER and COURSE. The single arrow specifies that the relationship is 1:1.

From the previous examples it follows that the functional model supports three abstractions by using functions with different arity:

- classification (by means of 0-ary functions);
- aggregation (by means of 1-ary functions);
- association (by means of n-ary functions).

No direct support is provided for generalization. Two different languages have been defined for the FDM: DAPLEX and FQL. DAPLEX [Ship81] is the first integrated language for both data definition and data access. In particular it can be seen as an extension of the relational calculus, supporting query specification, schema definition, simple update specification, and some general-purpose language constructs. DAPLEX has been embedded in the programming language ADA in the ADAPLEX semantic database system [ChanA82]. Functional query language (FQL) is based on a functional programming style and supports just query specification [Bune82].

2.133 *The semantic database model (SDM)*

The main characteristic of the semantic database model (SDM) is that of incorporating a wide range of modelling constructs into a single abstraction, the class. Thus, it offers a full set of modelling facilities [Hamm81].

More precisely, an SDM database is a collection of entities organised into classes, or types. The emphasis is therefore on class definition and not on relationships among classes (or entities) as in the entity relationship model. Thus, SDM uses class abstraction as the primary modelling mechanism. Classes represent entities in such an approach. On the other hand, relationships among entities are embodied in the interclass connections included in the class definitions. The class abstraction offers inheritance, multiple inheritance (thus, modelling generalization), constraints, and derivation options (thus, modelling aggregation).

Consider the school database again. STUDENT becomes a class and the class attributes describe the properties of the class as a whole, including the relationships in which this class is involved. In particular, the N:N relationship with the entity COURSE is translated into a multi-valued attribute Course, having COURSE as the value class. On the other hand, the 1:N relationship with TELEPHONE, that in the entity relationship model has been artificially introduced in order to model a multi-valued attribute, here is directly replaced by a multi-valued attribute, having STRING as the value class. Table 2.2 presents the corresponding representation in SDM.

Table 2.2 An SDM representation of the STUDENT entity

```
STUDENT
    Description: all students of the considered school:
        Name
            Value class: STRING
        Address
            Value class: STRING
        Telephone
            Value class: STRING
            multi-valued
        Course
            Value class: COURSE
            multi-valued
    Identifiers
        Name
```

It is important to note that the main difference between SDM, ERM and FDM is that SDM provides a large set of modelling facilities from which the user can choose to model a given application domain. The same facilities may not be available in the ERM and FDM models, even if the basic constructs can usually be combined to represent what is not directly supported by the specific formalism.

2.134 *Additional semantic models*

Besides the semantic data models introduced in the previous sections, several other models have been presented in the literature. Here we present a short overview of some of them.

TAXIS [Borg84] has been designed to provide a programming language that offers data management facilities through the use of a semantic data model. It is a language for the design of interactive database systems that emphasizes classification and generalization abstraction mechanisms. It permits multiple inheritance and uses abstractions to model exception handling and transactions.

SAM* [SuSY83] has been designed mainly for scientific-statistical databases. A SAM* model is a network of atomic and non-atomic concepts (or objects). Non-atomic objects are designed by using a recursive nesting approach. At the lowest level, they are represented as abstract data types. A graph-based representation for SAM* schemas is proposed in [SuSY83]. In the same paper, an approach for implementing SAM* by using data structures called *G-relations* is also proposed. G-relations resemble non-first normal form relations. The basis for SAM* schema is provided by atomic objects (strings, integers, structured programming language data types). Abstract objects are then represented by using non-atomic objects, obtained from the atomic ones by applying the association abstraction. To this purpose, the model supports seven types of associations, among them the membership association, the aggregation association, the generalization association, and the cross-product association. The semantics of these associations may overlap but they are distinguished by their associated update semantics and constraints.

IFO [Abit87a] has been defined in order to provide a theoretical framework for studying structural aspects of semantic models. The basic element of an IFO schema is a *fragment*. Fragments, used as abstraction mechanisms for representing the object structure, are quite similar to frames [BracR85a] and provide a natural way for representing nested or context-dependent attributes.

All the models cited above try to support a large set of modelling structures in order to help the user in modelling the application domain. A different approach has been taken in defining *binary models*. The aim of binary models is to supply a small set of modelling structures that can then be combined to build more powerful constructs. Among the proposed binary models are those presented in [Abri74], [BracG76]. In particular, in the semantic binary data model [Abri74], data is represented by using only two constructs: entity sets and binary relations. A schema for this model consists of a labelled graph. A data definition language for such a model is presented in [Abri74].

Among semantic models there are also those that have been defined as direct extensions of the relational model. Among them is the structural model [Wied80], using relations for simulating an object-oriented approach, that incorporates aggregation, single- and multi-valued attributes; RM/T [Codd79], using various types of relations for modelling different semantic constructs; and GEM [Tsur84], [Zani83], that has been defined as an experiment in supporting a semantic data language by extending a relational query language.

2.14 Hyper-semantic data models

Hyper-semantic data models extend the set of modelling constructs supported by semantic data models in order to capture the application meaning in a better way. More precisely, hyper-semantic data models focus on capturing the objects, the operations, the relationships and the knowledge associated with an application ([Pott88], [Pott89], [Pott93]). Objects and operations support the representation of a given knowledge domain by using several abstraction mechanisms, extending those supported by semantic data models. On the other hand, knowledge represents all the implicit and explicit restrictions placed upon objects, operations, and relationships, together with specific heuristics and inference procedures. In summary, hyper-semantic data models combine concepts coming from semantics data models with concepts coming from artificial intelligence, such as heuristics, uncertainty, inference, and constraints, typical of knowledge-based systems. Since they support inference, some relationships can be stated between the area of hyper-semantic models and deductive databases (*see* Section 3.2).

The modelling constructs characterizing hyper-semantic data models can be summarized as follows:

- *generalization*, *classification*, and *aggregation*, deriving from semantic data models;
- *membership*, by which several object-types are considered as a higher-level set object-type via the 'is-a-member-of' relationship;
- *constraint*, by which a restriction is placed upon some aspect of an object, an operation, or a relationship via the 'is-a-constraint-on' relationship;
- *heuristic*, by which inference mechanisms are modelled;
- *temporal*, by which specific object-types are related to synchronous or asynchronous characteristics and considered as a higher-level object-type.

Membership, constraints, heuristics, and temporal constructs make the difference between hyper-semantic data models and semantic models. In particular, the temporal relationship provides the representation of synchronous and asynchronous events. Synchronous objects are related to other synchronous objects by either a predecessor or a successor relationship.

Thus they can be linked to form a single high-level object. On the other hand, asynchronous objects are related to other asynchronous objects by a concurrent or parallel notion. They are characterised by a precondition, a procedure to be performed, and a postcondition that may trigger some other object. In this respect, temporal aspects in hyper-semantic models have several similarities with active rules that will be introduced in Section 2.3.

Hyper-semantic models provide a homogeneous way to access data (i.e. values of attributes), metadata (i.e. the schema), knowledge (i.e. constraints and heuristics), and meta-knowledge (i.e. constraints and heuristics applied to constraint or heuristic objects). As with all the other objects, constraints, heuristics, and temporal constructs can be aggregated, generalized, and classified.

In order to show an example of the capabilities of hyper-semantic data models, we consider an example taken from [Pott89] – *see* Figure 2.2. It refers to an academic knowledge/data-based system. In this example, we consider three main object-types (classes): COURSE_OFFERED, STUDENT, and FACULTY. For the sake of simplicity, not all the attributes of all classes are shown. Besides classification relationships, also present in the entity relationship model for example, we note the presence of computed and inferred values. For example, CORE_COURSE and ADVANCED_COURSE are inferred information, whose values are computed by using heuristics starting from the values of other attributes. A core course is a course without prerequisites whereas an advanced course has prerequisite courses that have prerequisites. As an example of heuristic definition, consider the object-type COURSE_OFFERED in Figure 2.3. In this definition we can see that, besides traditional attributes, we have some attributes defined through heuristics. The set of object instances is also specified.

From the previous example it follows that hyper-semantic models introduce several concepts in semantic data models that will later also be proposed by deductive and active databases. They therefore represent an important development in the context of conceptual data models.

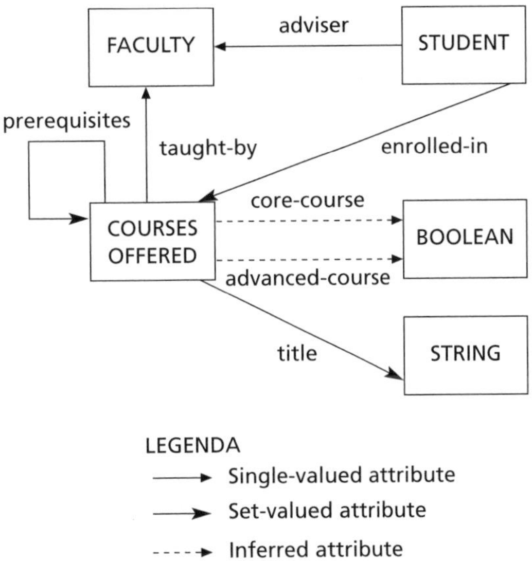

Figure 2.2 A hyper-semantic schema

OBJECT-TYPE: course-offered HAS
ATTRIBUTES:
Taught-by: faculty;
Title: STRING;
Prerequisites: SET OF course-offered;
Core-course: BOOLEAN
    WITH HEURISTICS
    IF prerequisite(C) IS EMPTY

```
                THEN core-course(C):= TRUE;
Advanced-course: BOOLEAN
        WITH HEURISTICS
        FOR ALL X IN prerequisite(C):
                IF PREREQUISITE(X) IS EMPTY
                        THEN advanced-course(C):= FALSE;
...
INSTANCES:
        co06, co07, co08, co09, co10
END-OBJECT-TYPE
```

Figure 2.3 An example of object-type definition in a hyper-semantic model

2.15 Object-oriented approaches to semantic data modelling

As we have already remarked, semantic data models have been introduced with the aim of overcoming the semantic limitations of the relational model, especially in the conceptual design phase. With the diffusion of the object-oriented model (*see* Section 2.2), a similar need arose for conceptually designing object-oriented databases or for designing a relational database by using an object-oriented approach. To this purpose, some object-oriented models tailored to the conceptual modelling have been defined.

In traditional semantic data models, such as the one we have introduced above, entities and relationships among entities play a central role. However, operations that have to be executed on these entities are not taken into account. This means that they provide a good way to represent just the static aspects of a database. On the other hand, in traditional methodologies for the design of software systems, the emphasis is on the functionality that the system has to implement. Thus only dynamic aspects are taken into account. The two approaches can be combined by using an object-oriented approach in the design phase. Indeed, in the object-oriented terminology, an object is characterized both by a state and its behaviours and so it represents the right concept for a mixed static-dynamic database modelling. Section 2.2. is devoted to the presentation of the object-oriented model. Here, we want to introduce object-oriented methodologies that have been proposed for analysis and design of software systems and that can be successfully applied in the database context as well.

Two main methodologies have been defined: the object modelling technique (OMT) [Rumb91] and the unified modelling language (UML) [Booc98]. In both cases an overall design methodology has been provided, together with some models for representing the result of the design. Here we are simply interested in the proposed models. In the following, both the models underlying OMT and UML are introduced briefly. We refer the interested reader to [Booc98], [Rumb91] for additional details about models and methodologies.

2.151 *The object modelling technique (OMT)*

In OMT, database description is provided by the use of three distinct models that represent three different ways of using the database: the object model, the dynamic model and the functional model [Rumb91].

Object model

This describes the object structure and the relationships among objects, represented by using an *object diagram*. Objects are organised in classes that are described using a class diagram. For each class, information about identity, relationships with other classes, attributes and operations is supplied. In this framework, relationship cardinality can also be specified in a clear way. Classes are organised in aggregation and inheritance hierarchies. Moreover, to improve design, it is possible to break down a class diagram into more interconnected subdiagrams; which is useful when designing very complex application domains.

In order to show the basic notation used in a class diagram, Figure 2.4 represents a portion of the class diagram for the school database. The diagram contains two classes, STUDENT and COURSE. For each class, the name of the class, the attributes and the operations to be executed against the objects of that class are specified. In this example, we have considered only three operations: one for inserting a new object, one for deleting an object, and one for changing the student address. The classes are connected by a relationship. Note that, 1+ means 'one or more'.

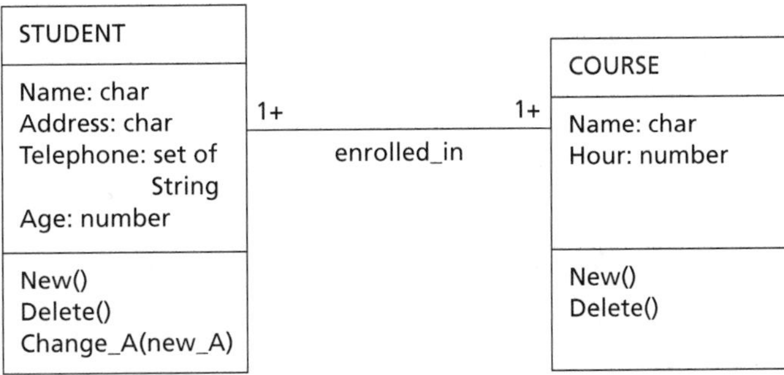

Figure 2.4 An OMT class diagram for a portion of the school database

Dynamic model (or event model)

This describes the dynamic aspects of the application domain. The dynamic model specifies the sequences of operations that may be executed without specifying the semantics of such operations or their implementation. It is represented by using a *state diagram* for each class represented in the class diagram. In particular, each state diagram specifies states and events that may arise for a considered class. Events represent requests to which the database objects should reply. A typical event for the school database is: 'Change the John Ross address.' States represent the values of object attributes and the set of relationships in which each object is involved between two different events. Thus, the state diagram specifies how the state of the objects, instances of a given class, is changed according to specific events and which additional actions are executed by the objects (for example, some messages can be sent to other objects). *See* Section 2.152 for additional information on state diagrams.

Functional model

This describes all aspects concerning object transformations, without specifying when such transformations take place. Such description is represented by using *dataflow diagrams* that for each operation introduced in the object model provide a clear representation of the input/output flow and of the internal modifications.

Each model describes a specific aspect of the database. However, the models are strongly interrelated. For example, operations pointed out in the object model correspond to events in the dynamic model and to functions in the functional model. In summary, for a given application domain the functional model specifies 'how', the dynamic model specifies 'when', and the object model specifies 'what'. It is important to note that in a database context, the class diagram is certainly the most relevant one.

It can be shown that the models supported by OMT permit the representation of all the typical semantic constructs presented in Section 2.13. However, the dynamic and the functional models can also be used to specify system dynamicity, i.e. changes in the database.

Finally, it is important to point out that OMT is a technique and not just a model. Thus it provides methodologies for analyzing and designing complex (not necessarily database) applications.

2.152 The unified modelling language (UML)

The *Unified Modelling Language* was defined following a request from the Object Management Group (OMG) to provide a standard language for specifying, constructing, visualizing and documenting a software system [Booc98]. So again the model has not been specifically proposed for the database context but, like OMT, it can be used successfully for this purpose.

The main thing that led to the definition of UML was the existence of several object-oriented methodologies and languages for modelling software applications, each with specific characteristics. For example, OMT, defined by Rumbaugh [Rumb91], was recognized to be very good for analysis purposes, especially for data-intensive information systems; the object-oriented analysis and design (OOAD), defined by Booch [Booc92], performed very well for what concerned design; and the object-oriented software engineering (OOSE) approach, proposed by Jacobson [Jaco92], was appropriate for business engineering and requirement analysis purposes.

Starting from these considerations, it was necessary to unify all these methodologies and languages to provide a standard to be used in all the phases of software development and for communication and storage.

The definition of UML started in 1995 and is ongoing. Version 1.0 was submitted to OMG in January 1997 and Version 1.1 was accepted by OMG in September 1997. The basic idea in defining UML was not to define a new model (overall, several models already existed) but to take the best from any existing model in order to define a common and widely usable approach, overcoming the limitations of all the composing approaches.

UML takes part of its definition from the three main approaches cited above: OMT, OOAD and the OOSE approach. UML is an evolution of all three methods, providing more semantics, more flexibility and covering a large number of applications, thus providing more generality. At the same time, it is more expressive, simpler, and more formal than all three methods. By integrating these methods, UML introduces new aspects, most of them taken from additional existing models and methods. Thus it can be seen as a rational synthesis of all object-oriented methods existing in the literature and in the market.

By using UML we can model both static and dynamic aspects of a system through the use of a set of diagrams. The functional model is no longer part of the model.

Static modelling

Static aspects can be modelled by means of object and class diagrams, similar to those proposed in OMT and OOAD, with some extensions. Class diagrams provide the specification of classes, their type, the behavioral specification of the class, and interfaces, the externally visible behaviour of the class. As in OOAD, it is possible to model parametric classes (templates). Among the proposed extensions is the introduction of constraints. UML provides a formal constraint language (called object constraint language – OCL) by which constraints can be formally specified during the analysis and design phases of an application. Another important aspect concerns *stereotypes*, i.e mechanisms that allow the user to define a new class of elements starting from existing classes. Classes connected by some application or functional logic can be grouped in a *package*, representing a portion of the diagram. As with OMT, classes and packages can be generalized and refined, introducing more information concerning a given element, thus providing several abstraction levels.

Example 3. In Figure 2.5 we present an example of a class diagram dealing with the organization of work inside a company, adapted from [Alhi99]. The efforts inside the company can be classified as projects, activities and tasks, and they inherit the characteristics from the effort class. Generalization is represented by using a white triangle pointing to the more general class. A project is composed of one or more activities, and an activity is part of a single project. Given a project, we can access its associated activities, and given an activity, we can access its associated project. The composition association, represented by a black diamond, indicates that an activity is deleted when the project it belongs to is deleted. An activity is composed of one or more tasks, and a task is part of a single activity. Given an activity, we can access its associated tasks, but given a task, we cannot access its associated activity (this navigation constraint is represented by the arrow). When an activity is deleted, all the composing tasks are deleted too (represented by the black diamond). An activity contains one or more products (documents, etc.) and a product may be a part of one or more activities. Products are not deleted when the activity they belong to is deleted (white diamond). Finally, a task is associated with one resource (person) and a single resource may be associated with up to six tasks.

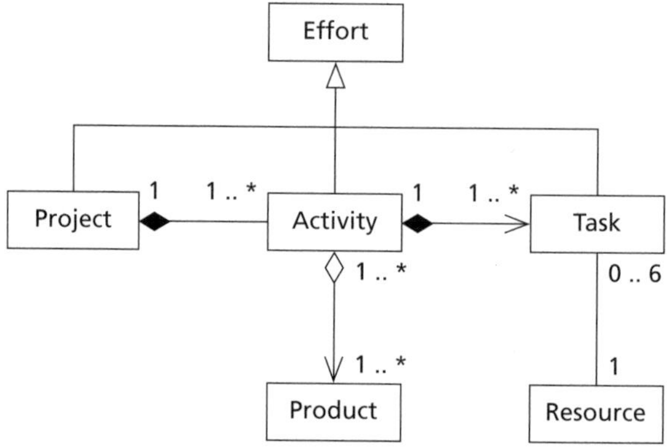

Figure 2.5 An example of a class diagram in UML

Dynamic modelling

For dynamicity, UML supports the following diagrams:

- *use case diagrams*, taken from OOSE, specifying what the system should execute as an answer to an external event, generated by some actor;
- *behavioural diagrams*, specifying the dynamic behaviour of the static structures defined in class and object diagrams. The supported diagrams are the following:
  - *sequence diagrams*, depicting an interaction among the elements of a system organised in time sequence. Sequence diagrams have already been used in OMT. In UML they are extended to deal with time information, constraints, synchronous and asynchronous events, and conditional instructions;
  - *collaboration diagrams*, depicting an interaction among elements of a system and their relationships organised in time and space. Each collaboration diagram can be associated with a class, a method, or a use case. It can be seen as a graph-based representation of a sequence diagram;

– *statechart diagrams*, taken from OMT and OOAD, specifying how the state of the objects – instances of a given class – is changed according to specific events and which additional actions are executed by the objects. A graph-based notation is used for their representation. Each node (represented as a rectangle) corresponds to a given state of a class or object whereas each edge corresponds to a transition from one state to another due to a given event;
– *activity diagrams*, a special case of statechart diagrams, specifying the internal execution flow of a given class, operation, or use case. They are used when most of the events concerning a given class, operation, or use case represent the end of the execution of some action generated inside the considered element. On the other hand, statechart diagrams are used for modelling asynchronous events.

All the previous diagrams are used in the dynamic analysis of a given application domain. More precisely, use case diagrams are first used to specify the interaction of the system with the external environment. Then, for each use case, a sequence and/or a collaboration diagram have to be provided to better specify each interaction. After this step we have a clear representation of the interactions arising between objects and/or classes. Statechart and activity diagrams are then used to specify the dynamic behaviour of each class, starting from the information contained inside sequence and collaboration diagrams. Often, each sequence diagram corresponds to a path in the statechart diagram.

Example 4. Consider the application domain introduced in Example 3. Figure 2.6 presents an example of use case for this example (adapted from [Alhi99]) pointing out that a project manager (the actor) interacts with the project management system through the following functionalities: add project, remove project, assign resource, and unassign resource.

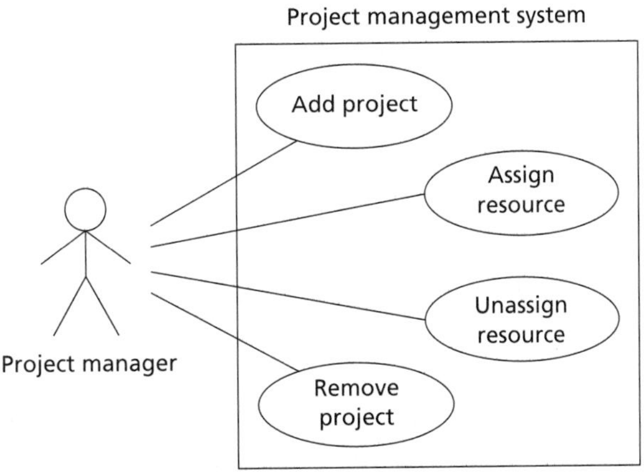

Figure 2.6 An example of use case in UML

For each use case a sequence diagram has to be provided, describing in detail the interactions among objects. Figure 2.7 presents an example (adapted from [Alhi99]) of a sequence diagram for the 'Add project' use case. A line is provided for all the objects involved in the use case: the project manager, the user interface, and the project. The project manager specifies the project name and the start date, and saves the project. The large 'X' at the end of the project object lifeline indicates that no further operation is performed on that object. Rectangles over a lifeline groups operations together. For example, the insertion of the name and the start date corresponds to two different operations for the project object but to just one operation for the user interface.

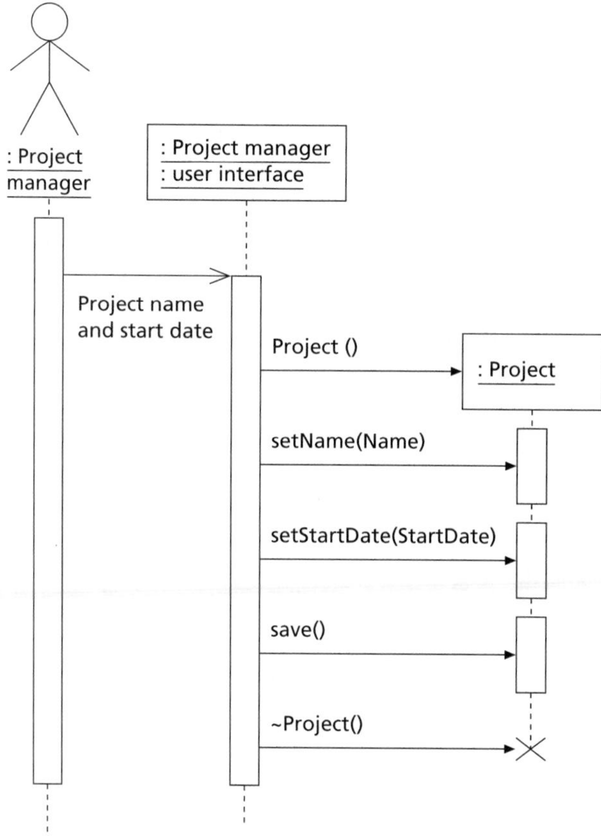

Figure 2.7 An example of a sequence diagram in UML

Figure 2.8 shows an example (adapted from [Alhi99]) of a statechart diagram, presenting two states from the life cycle of a resource object. Initially, an object is in the unassigned state, as indicated by the small black circle. Edges represent transitions and are labelled with the list of events, separated by a slash, that cause the object to change state.

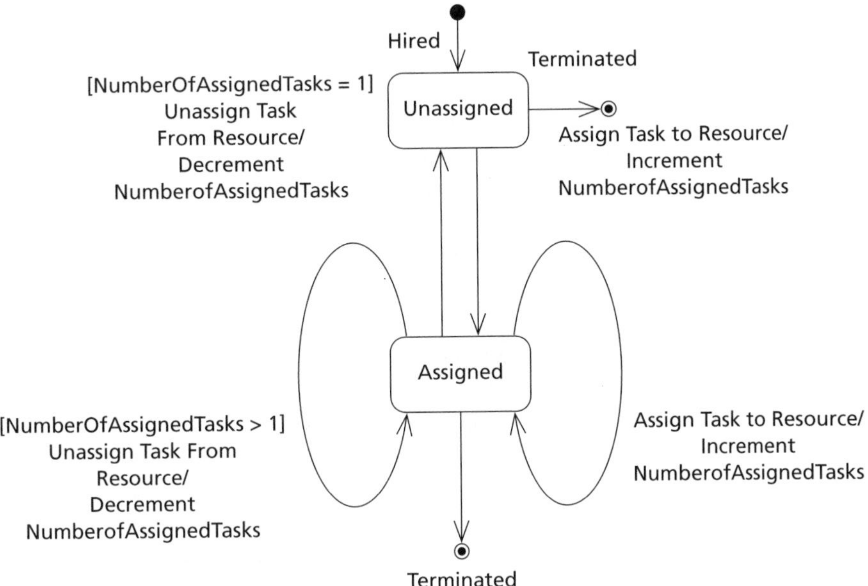

Figure 2.8 An example of a statechart diagram in UML

UML also supports implementation diagrams, deriving from OOAD, for designing software components. In particular, these support the design of the code structure by using *component diagrams*, and the system structure at run-time by using *allocation diagrams*.

From the previous discussion it follows that UML does not introduce new formalisms; rather, it can be seen as a summa of the methods previously defined, removing from them any inconsistency and extending their capabilities in order to support a larger class of applications. Among the proposed extensions is the ability to specify the following concepts:

- extension mechanisms, such as constraints and stereotypes;
- threads and processes;
- distribution and concurrency;
- collaboration;
- activity diagrams;
- refinements between various abstraction levels;
- interfaces and components.

All the previous concepts can be used in any phase of the software development, providing at the same time documentation of each step.

Unlike most other proposals, a formal semantics is supplied for UML. All information about such language, as well as any information about the standardization process, can be found at *www.rational.com*.

2.16 Conclusions

The need to provide more expressive power in data representation and querying has led to the definition of several data models, or rather, several classes of data models. In this section we have looked at some of them: the nested relational model – introducing sets and tuples inside the relational model – semantic data models – overcoming the semantic limitations of the relational model in modelling real-world applications by supporting more abstraction mechanisms – hyper-semantic models – extending semantic data models to deal with inference and temporal concepts – and object-oriented models for software design.

Most of the previous models are relevant as theoretical background for more recent data models. For example, the nested relational model had some impact in the definition of object-relational models (*see* Section 2.2.), while some aspects of hyper-semantic data models have been developed in the context of deductive databases (*see* Section 3.2). Moreover, the entity-relationship model and UML represent the most used approaches to conceptually modelling information systems, thanks to their independence from the underlying platform.

2.2 Object-oriented database systems

Object-oriented database management systems (OODBMSs) derive from the integration of database technology with object-oriented programming languages. This integration is very promising, in that the object-oriented paradigm has been recognized as the most valid approach to software development [DeutP91]. The use of OODBMS allows the benefits of the object-oriented approach to be transposed to the area of data management applications.

Many of the underlying concepts of object-oriented programming languages derive from the Simula language [Dahl66]. However, this programming approach began to be widely used only after the introduction of Smalltalk [GoldA83]. Following Smalltalk, other languages were developed, such as C++ [Stro86], CLOS [Moon89] and Eiffel [Maye88]. The basic principle of object-oriented programming is to view a program as consisting of a number of independent objects, collected in classes, which interact by means of messages; classes can be defined by specialization from other classes, thus increasing software reusability.

Despite the fact that the object-oriented approach is now widely used and is characterized by large industrial efforts, there is no consolidated standard definition of an object model. Therefore, a large number of variations can be found when comparing the different object-oriented programming languages. Even though an object data model standard, known as the ODMG standard [Catt97], has been developed recently, OODBMSs also have a lot of variations and therefore there is no consensus about the specific features of an object-oriented data model. It is possible, however, to identify some basic concepts, collectively referred to as the *core model*. The core model is powerful enough to satisfy many of the requirements of advanced applications, and moreover can be used as the basis for discussing the main differences in conventional data models, such as the relational model. It also serves as a basis for discussing the data models of the various OODBMSs.

The core model is presented in Section 2.21. Section 2.23 discusses object-oriented query languages and the associated query processing techniques, and Section 2.24 discusses some operational aspects, such as versioning and authorization. In particular, the discussion in Section 2.24 shows the impact of an object-oriented data model on database system architectures. Section 2.25 presents an overview of selected OODBMS. To complete the discussion, Section 2.26 presents a short survey of the ODMG object data model, while Section 2.27 describes the recent object-relational data models, resulting from the extension of SQL with object modelling primitives. Finally, Section 2.28 briefly discusses solutions that aim at providing persistence for Java, and Section 2.29 outlines some conclusions.

2.21 Basic concepts of a core object-oriented data model

The core model is based on five fundamental concepts.

- Each real-world entity is modelled by an *object*. Each object is associated with a unique identifier.
- Each object has a set of instance attributes (instance variables) and methods; the value of an attribute can be an object or a set of objects. This characteristic allows arbitrarily complex objects to be defined as an *aggregation* of other objects. The set of attributes of an object and the set of methods represent, respectively, the object *structure and behaviour*.
- The attribute values represent the object's state. The state of an object is accessed or modified by sending messages to the object to invoke the corresponding methods.
- Objects sharing the same structure and behaviour are grouped into *classes*. A class represents a template for a set of similar objects. Each object is an instance of some class.
- A class can be defined as a *specialization* of one or more classes. A class defined as a specialization is called a *subclass* and *inherits* attributes and methods from its *superclass*(*es*).

There are, however, many variations on these five concepts, as we will see in the remainder of this section. In fact, we use them mainly as a way to organize the discussion, rather than as a definition of the object-oriented paradigm. It is also important to note that similar concepts have been proposed in models developed in the context of knowledge-based systems. This is the case, for example, in the model of the Back language, based on terminological logics. Those models are discussed in detail in Sections 3.1 and 3.3. A short discussion on the main differences between object models of OODBMS and object models of knowledge-based systems is presented at the end of this section.

An OODBMS can be defined as a DBMS that directly supports a model based on the object-oriented paradigm. As with any DBMS, it must provide persistent storage for objects and their descriptors (schema). The system must also provide a language for schema definition, and for manipulation of objects and their schema. In addition to these basic characteristics, an OODBMS usually includes a query language, and the necessary database mechanisms for access optimization, such as indexing and clustering, concurrency control and authorization mechanisms for multi-user accesses and recovery. In the remainder of this section, we elaborate on the basic concepts of an object-oriented data model.

2.211 Objects and object identifiers

In object-oriented systems, each real-world entity is uniformly represented by an object. Each object is uniquely identified by an object identifier (OID). The identity of an object has an existence which is independent of its value. The use of OIDs allows objects to share sub-objects and makes it possible to construct general object networks. The notion of an object identifier is different from the concept of a key in the relational data model.

A key is defined by the value of one or more attributes and therefore can undergo modifications. By contrast, two objects are different if they have different object identifiers, even if all their attributes have the same values. Note that object sharing in models where identity is based on values leaves the applications with the problem of managing key values and the associated normalization problems.

The notion of object identity introduces at least two different notions of equality among objects. The first, denoted here by '=', is the *identity equality*: two objects are identity-equal, or *identical*, if they have the same OID. The second, denoted here by '= =', is the *value equality*: two objects are value-equal if all their attributes that are values are equal, and all their attributes that are objects are recursively value-equal, i.e. the two objects have the same 'information content' even if they have two different identifiers. Two identical objects are also value-equal, but two value-equal objects are not necessarily identical. Figure 2.9 shows an example of different objects that are equal. The figure also introduces a graphical notation for objects. Each object is represented as a box, with two regions: the upper region contains the object's OID; the second region contains the object's attributes. In the graphical representation we use logical OIDs, consisting of the name of the object's class and a numeric identifier unique within the class. For example, Window[i] denotes the i-th instance of the class Window. For each attribute, the box contains the name and the value. When the value is a reference to another object, the attribute contains the OID of the referenced object. For example, attribute 'title' of object Window[i] contains as the value the OID Title[j] to denote that Window[i] references object Title[j]. Note that both Window[i] and Window[k] are equal; indeed, they have the same values for attributes 'x', 'y', 'width', 'height'. Moreover, these objects reference – through the attribute 'title' – two distinct objects, Title[j] and Title[h], which are in turn equal.

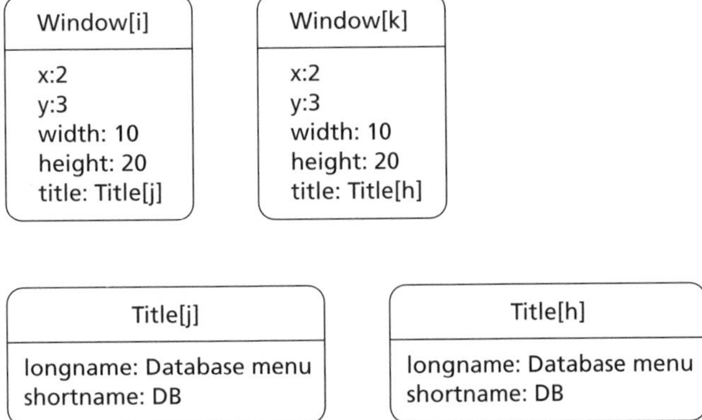

Figure 2.9 An example of equal objects with different identifiers

We note, however, that there are models in which both objects and values are allowed; in these models not all entities are objects. Informally, a value is self-identifying, and has no OID associated with it. In some models, all the primitive entities, such as integers or characters, are values, while all other entities are objects. Other models, notably O_2 [Deux90] and AVANCE [Bjor89], provide the possibility of defining complex (or structured) values. Complex values cannot be shared among objects. They are built using the same constructors used for objects. In general, complex values are useful in situations where aggregates (or sets) must be defined to be used as components of other objects but will never be used alone. If complex values are not allowed, these aggregates must be defined by using a class and must have an OID associated with them. Therefore, some performance penalty is incurred. An example is represented by dates. Suppose that a date is defined as a tuple of three components, representing respectively month, day and year. Dates are likely to be used as components of other objects. However, it is unlikely that a user will issue a query on the class of all dates. Therefore, it appears more convenient to define dates as complex values rather than as objects.

To illustrate the difference between the use of complex values and the use of objects, consider the objects illustrated in Figure 2.10, representing two journal papers. Each object contains the following attributes: the title, the status, the authors, the journal name where the paper will appear, and the publication date. Note that the attribute 'authors' is a multi-valued attribute; this is denoted graphically by enclosing the set of attribute values in curly brackets ({}). In the objects in Figure 2.10, the publication date is represented as a value. Suppose now that the publication date of Paper[i] is changed to 'April 1990'. After this update, the state of the two objects can be seen in (b). Suppose that the two papers must be published in the same issue of the journal. Enforcing this constraint on the objects represented in Figure 2.10a means ensuring that an update performed on the attribute 'date' of one of the two objects is propagated to the other object. A more adequate approach is to model the date as an object, as illustrated in Figure 2.11a.

The constraint that the two objects must be published in the same issue is simply modelled by having the two objects referencing the same 'date' object. The sharing of a reference is emphasized in Figure 2.11 by an arrow connecting object Paper[i] (Paper[j]) to object Date[i]. Any change to the object Date[i] will be visible by both the other objects. Figure 2.11b shows the state of the objects after the change of the date from 'March 1990' to 'April 1990'. Note that, because an object does not change its identity even if its state changes, no updates are required to objects Paper[i] and Paper[j] upon the update to object Date[i].

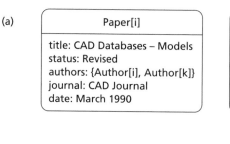

(a)

Paper[i]	Paper[j]
title: CAD Databases – Models status: Revised authors: {Author[i], Author[k]} journal: CAD Journal date: March 1990	title: CAD Databases – Tools status: Revised authors: {Author[i], Author[k]} journal: CAD Journal date: March 1990

(b)

Paper[i]	Paper[j]
title: CAD Databases – Models status: Revised authors: {Author[i], Author[k]} journal: CAD Journal date: April 1990	title: CAD Databases – Tools status: Revised authors: {Author[i], Author[k]} journal: CAD Journal date: March 1990

Figure 2.10 (a) object state before and (b) after the update to attribute 'date' of object Paper[i]

Different approaches for building OIDs can be devised. For example, in the approach used in the Orion system [KimW89a], an OID consists of the pair <class identifier, instance identifier>, where the first element is the identifier of the class to which the object belongs, and the second identifies the object within the class. The complete definition of attributes and methods for all instances of a class is factorized and kept in an object representing the class itself (called *class-object*). When a message is sent to an object, the system extracts the class identifier from the object identifier and accesses the class-object to determine the message validity and fetch the corresponding method. This approach has the major disadvantage of making object migration from one class to another very difficult (for example in cases of object re-classification) or even impossible, since this would require the modification of all object identifiers and all references to migrated objects would be invalidated. In another approach, used for example in the GemStone system, the OID does not contain the class identifier. The identifier of the class to which an object belongs is in general kept as control information stored in the object itself. To determine whether a message is valid for a given object, the system must first fetch the object and then retrieve from it the class identifier. Therefore, non-valid messages cause useless object accesses and type checking is rather expensive.

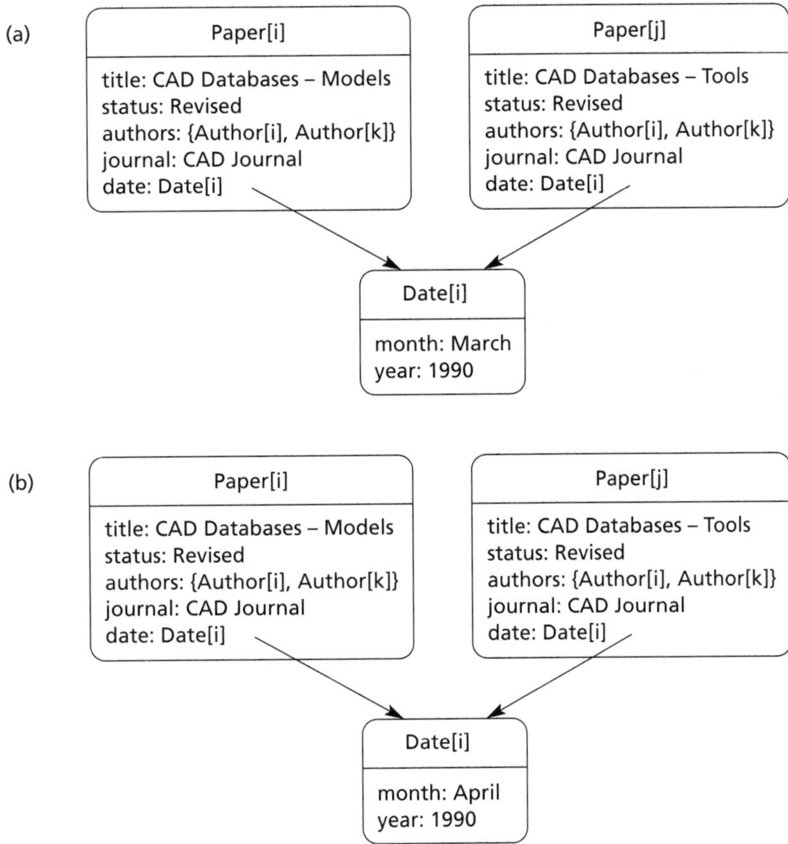

Figure 2.11 Modelling publication date as an object: object state (a) before and (b) after the update to attribute 'month' of object Date[i]

Note that in both previous approaches, the OID is *logical*, i.e. it does not contain any information about the object location on secondary storage. Therefore a correspondence table exists mapping OIDs on to physical addresses. A different approach, based on *physical identifiers*, is used in O_2 [Deux90], where each object is stored in a WiSS[1] record and the OID is the record identifier (RID). The RID does not change even if the record is moved to a new page, for example when the record grows too big for the page it resides in. A forward marking technique (as in

1 O_2 uses the Wisconsin Storage Subsystem (WiSS) as a storage subsystem.

the relational systems System R and Ingres) is used to handle cases of records that are moved to different pages. The approach used in O_2 has the main advantage that persistent OIDs are provided supporting fast access to objects since there is need to map the OID on the physical location. The major disadvantage is that a temporary OID must be assigned to an object created on a site different from the object store site (for example on a workstation). In order to avoid exchanging a large number of messages, the permanent OID is assigned only when the object is stored in the corresponding WiSS record, at transaction commit time. This implies that all references to newly created objects generated during the transaction must be updated at transaction commit time.

The OID may also contain object location for distributed databases. For example, in the distributed version of the Orion system [KimW89a], the OID contains the identifier of the site where the object was created. When an object migrates to a different site, its OID does not change. The object-creation site keeps information concerning the new storage site of the object so that messages can be appropriately forwarded to the object.

2.212 *Aggregation*

The values of an object's attributes can be other objects, both primitive and non-primitive. When the value of an attribute of an object *O* is a non-primitive object *O'*, the system stores the OID of *O'* in *O*. When complex values are supported by the model, the system usually stores the entire complex value in the object attribute.

In defining complex objects and values, different constructors may be used. A minimal set of constructors that should be provided by a model includes set, list and tuple [Atki89]. In particular, the set constructor allows multi-valued attributes and set objects to be defined. The list is similar to the set, but it imposes an order on the elements. Finally, the tuple constructor is important because it provides a natural way of modelling properties of an object. As discussed in [Atki89], the object constructors should be orthogonal, i.e. any constructor should be applicable to any object, including of course objects constructed using any constructor. We note that some models impose the constraint that the tuple must be the first-level constructor. This implies that when defining a set object, for example, the object must be defined as a tuple of a single attribute, which is in turn defined as a set.

The notion of *composite* objects is found in some data models. As we have already stated, a complex object may recursively reference any number of other objects. The references, however, do not imply any special semantics that may be of interest to different classes of applications. One important relationship that could be superimposed on the complex object is the *part-of* relationship, i.e. the concept that an object is part of another object. A set of component objects forming a single entity is a composite object. A similar concept is found in [Atki89], where two different types of references are defined: 'general' and 'is-part-of'. The part-of relationship among objects has some consequences on object operations. For example, if the root of a composite object is removed, all component objects are deleted. Moreover, in some models of composite objects an object can be part of only one object, that is, the 'part-of' relationship imposes an exclusivity constraint. In some systems, a lock on the root of a composite object is propagated to all the components. Some extended relational models and object-oriented programming languages (for example, the Loops language) also provide the notion of composite objects. Note, however, that in some models and papers the term complex object is used with the meaning of composite object.

2.213 *Methods*

Objects in an object-oriented database are manipulated using methods. In general, a method definition consists of two components. The first is the method *signature*, specifying the method name, the names and classes of the arguments, and the class of the result, if there is one. Some systems, such as Orion [KimW89a] for example, do not require the class of the arguments and the results to be declared. This happens when type checking is executed at run-time and therefore there is no need to have this information in advance. The second component is the method *implementation*, consisting of code written in some programming language. Different OODBMSs use different languages for method implementation. For example, both Vbase and O_2 use the C language, while Orion uses Lisp. GemStone uses OPAL, which is nearly identical to Smalltalk. ObjectStore uses C++. In addition to the method signature and implementation, other components may be present in a method definition. For example, in Vbase a method definition may specify, in addition to the base method, some trigger methods and exceptions that can be raised by the method execution. Trigger methods are often used to augment the semantics of inherited methods and of system-defined methods, for example the creation and deletion methods. The language used to write methods is also often used to write applications. In addition, some systems provide access to the database from conventional languages, such as GemStone supporting access from C and Pascal.

Very often in object-oriented programming languages, object attributes cannot be directly accessed. Instead the only access is by invoking the methods available at the object interface (*strict encapsulation*). In databases, a lot of applications simply read or write attribute values. Queries are very often expressed as a Boolean combination of predicates on attribute values. Therefore, most OODBMSs provide direct access to attributes by means of system-defined methods. Examples of these methods are *get* and *set* of Vbase [AndrT87], used to respectively read and write a given attribute. These methods, being provided as part of the system, have very efficient implementation and save the users from writing a large amount of trivial code. The major drawback of providing these system-defined methods is that sometimes the manipulation of an object attribute must be performed only through some user-defined methods. If, however, these system-defined methods are available, nothing prevents a user from using the system-defined rather than the user-defined method (unless authorization is established or the users are very disciplined). Therefore, some systems (for example Vbase [AndrT87] and the system described in [Bert89]) allow the users to redefine the implementation of these methods for a given attribute. Each time the attribute is accessed, the user-defined method implementation is invoked instead of the system-defined implementation. This allows the correct semantics to be imposed, when needed, on the system-defined methods. Moreover, this capability is useful when importing data from external databases. In O_2 [Deux90] direct access to attributes is provided only on user demand. In O_2, two special tags, *public read* and *public write*, allow the declaration of public attributes in read or write mode. If the read (or write) tag is associated with an attribute appearing in the definition of a class *C*, the system automatically allows direct read (write) operations on this attribute.

In OODBMSs characterized by distributed or client-server architectures, an important architectural issue concerns the site where an invoked method is executed. In Gemstone [Brei89], for example, the application designer has the option of moving an object, on which a method has been invoked to the client, and then executing the method locally, or executing the method remotely on the server. A similar option is provided in the O_2 system. In general the choice concerning the method execution site may be rather complex, since different factors must be taken into account, such as the complexity of the manipulations executed on the object, the references made to other objects during method execution, the network bandwidth, and the competition for the network and the server.

2.214 Classes and instantiation mechanisms

The instantiation is a first reusability mechanism (the second is inheritance) in that it makes it possible to reuse the same definition to generate objects with the same behaviour and structure. Object-oriented data models provide the concept of class as the instantiation basis. A class is an object that acts as a template. As such, a class specifies the intended use of its instances by defining:

- a structure, i.e. a set of instance attributes (or instance variables);
- a set of messages that define the external interface;
- a set of methods that are invoked by messages.

In this sense, the class can be viewed as a specification (*intension*) for its instances. Since the class factorizes the definitions of a set of objects, it is also an abstraction mechanism.

Given a class, it is possible to generate through the instantiation mechanism objects that 'answer' all messages defined in the class. The O_2 system keeps the attribute values for each object separately. It is not necessary to replicate the message and method definitions as these are kept in the class object since they are the same for all the class instances. All instances of a given class have the same structure and behave similarly. The system, however, allows exceptions to be defined at instance level. In O_2, an instance may have additional attributes and methods. Additional methods are used to characterize the exceptional behavior of an instance. If an additional method has the same name as a method defined at class level, the instance method definition overrides the method definition provided at class level.

An alternative approach to instantiation is to use *prototypical objects*. This approach consists of generating a new object starting from another existing object by modifying its attributes and/or its behaviour. Therefore, a prototype is an individual object containing its own description that can also be used as a model for creating other objects. This approach is useful when objects evolve (i.e. modify their structure and behaviour) quickly and are characterized more by their differences than their similarities and also when there are few instances for each class. In this way, the proliferation of a lot of classes, each with very few instances, is avoided. In general, the approach based on the instantiation mechanism is more appropriate for mature application environments, in which the object properties and behaviours are consolidated. In fact, the approach based on instantiation makes it more complicated to experiment with alternative object structures and behaviours.

The prototype-based approach appears more appropriate in the initial phase of application design or in application environments that evolve quickly with less consolidated objects, and in applications in which classes have very few instances. OODBMSs have usually adopted the instantiation approach since in most cases database applications have a lot of instances of each class for which an efficient storage organization must be provided. However, it is to be expected that as the scope of database applications broadens, it will result in the use of prototypical objects or similar mechanisms.

So far we have implicitly assumed that an object is an instance of only one class. However, in some models the instances of a class *C* are also *members* of the superclasses of *C*. Note that, as in [Moon89], we distinguish between the notions of 'instance of a class' and 'member of a class'. An object is instance of a class *C* if *C* is the most specialized class associated with the object in a given inheritance hierarchy. An object is a member of a class *C* if it is an instance of some subclass of *C*. Most object-oriented data models restrict each object to be an instance of only one class, even though they allow an object to be a member of several classes through inheritance. However, object-oriented data models [Zdon90] can be found allowing an object to be an instance of several classes. Consider as an example a class Person with subclasses Student and Pilot, and the case of a person *P* being a student and a pilot. This situation can be modelled easily by associating both classes with *P*. Therefore *P* will be an instance of both Student and Pilot and will also be a member of Person through the inheritance hierarchy. These models provide name qualification mechanisms to solve any conflicts deriving from attributes and methods with the same name being used in the classes of which an object is an instance. Note, however, that even if the data model imposes the restriction that each object is an instance of only one class, multiple inheritance (which we discuss later on) can be used to handle situations like the above one. For example, we could define a subclass Student-Pilot, having as superclasses both Student and Pilot, and make *P* an instance of this subclass.

In all object-oriented database models, each attribute has associated with it a domain specifying the class of the possible objects that can be assigned to it as values. This differs from certain programming languages, such as Smalltalk, where instance variables do not have an associated type. It is obvious that for data management applications requiring efficient management of persistent data, the system must know the types of the possible values taken by attributes in order to be able to allocate the appropriate storage and access structures. Thus, even the GemStone system, derived from Smalltalk, requires the declaration of the instance variable domains.

The fact that an attribute of a class C has a class C' as a domain implies that each instance of C takes an instance of class C', or of any subclass of C' as value of the attribute. This establishes an *aggregation relationship* between the two classes. An aggregation relationship from class C to class C' specifies that C is defined in terms of C'. Since C' is in turn defined in terms of other classes, the definition of a class C results in an *aggregation graph*. An aggregation graph may contain cycles, since classes can be recursively defined.

An important question concerning instances and classes is whether an object can change class. The ability to change the class of objects provides support for object evolution. It allows an object to change its structure and behaviour and still retain its identity. The GemStone [Brei89] and the ENCORE [Zdon90] systems provide this capability, while most of the other OODBMSs do not.

A domain constraint problem arises when objects are allowed to change class. As we discussed earlier, the value of an attribute A of an object O can be another object O'. If O' changes class, and its new class is not compatible with the class domain of A, O will contain an incorrect object as value of A. A possible solution is illustrated in [Zdon90] and consists of placing a 'tombstone' in O' to indicate that the object has changed class. This solution has a major disadvantage in that the applications must contain code to handle the exception of the referenced object being an instance of a class different from the expected one.

In addition to acting as a template, in some systems the class denotes the collection of all its instances, that is, its *extension*. This is important because the class becomes the base on which queries are formulated. The concept of query has a meaning only if applied to sets of objects. In systems where the class does not have this extensional function, the model provides set constructors for object grouping. Queries are then issued on the sets defined by these constructors. In this respect, there are differences among the various systems.

- In some systems, for example GemStone, the class has only an intensional meaning. A collection constructor is used to group objects of the same class. It is also possible to define several collections all containing instances of the same class. Queries are issued on object collections. Moreover, indexes are defined on collections and not on classes.
- In other systems, for example ORION, the class has both an intensional and an extensional meaning.
- Finally, other systems, for example O_2, provide the notion of *type* and the notion of class. In O_2, instances of types are values and therefore do not have OIDs (i.e. types are used to generate complex values), while instances of classes are objects. Moreover, in O_2 a class does not have its extension associated and therefore extensions must be explicitly managed by users.

In general, the decoupling of the intensional notion from the extensional notion is correct and provides increased flexibility. The major drawback is that the data model becomes more complex compared with a simpler model in which the class acts as both object template and object extent.

2.215 Metaclasses

If each object is an instance of a class, and a class is an object, the model should provide the notion of *metaclass*. A metaclass is the class of a class. Metaclasses are crucial to support expert systems and AI applications. However, most OODBMSs do not provide metaclasses. Finally, some data models provide the possibility of defining attributes and methods that characterize the classes as objects. Such attributes and methods, called here *class-attributes* and *class-methods*, are used to specify the properties and behaviour of the class and not of its instances. As such they are not inherited by the instances of a class. An example of a class-attribute would be an attribute containing the average of an attribute value, evaluated on all instances of a class.

2.216 Inheritance

The concept of inheritance is a second reusability mechanism. It allows a class, called *subclass*, to be defined starting from the definition of another class, called *superclass*. The subclass inherits the superclass attributes, methods, and messages. In addition, a subclass may have specific attributes, methods, and messages that are not inherited. Moreover, the subclass may override the definition of the superclass attributes and methods. Therefore, the inheritance mechanism allows a class to specialize another class by *additions* and *substitutions*. Inheritance represents an important form of abstraction, since the detailed differences of several class descriptions are abstracted away and the commonalities factored out as a more general superclass.

A class may have several subclasses. Some systems allow a class to have several superclasses (*multiple inheritance*), while others impose the restriction of a single superclass (*single inheritance*). Based on inheritance, the set of classes in the schema can be organized in an *inheritance graph* (orthogonal to the aggregation graph). The inheritance graph is a tree when the model does not provide multiple inheritance. An inheritance graph may not have cycles, unlike the aggregation graph.

The possibility of defining a class from other classes simplifies the task of class definition. However, it may cause conflicts, especially in the case of multiple inheritance. If the name of an attribute (or method) explicitly defined in a class is the same as an attribute of a superclass, the attribute from the superclass is not inherited – the definition in the subclass overrides the superclass definition.

If the model provides multiple inheritance, other types of conflict may arise. For example, two or more superclasses may have an attribute with the same name but different domains. Usually, rules are defined for solving conflicts. If the domains in the superclasses are related by inheritance relationships, the most specific domain is chosen for the subclass. If the domains are not related by inheritance, the user can specify from which superclass the attribute must be inherited. For example, in O_2, the attribute name in a subclass may be followed by the *from* clause containing the superclass from which the attribute definition must be inherited. If the user does not specify the inheritance paths, the solution used in most models is to inherit the attributes (or methods) based on an order of precedence among superclasses.

However, in the last two cases problems may arise over the validity of inherited methods. An inherited method may contain in its implementation a reference to an attribute *A*, which however has not been inherited in a given subclass *C*, since an attribute with the same name but different domain has been inherited in the subclass from a different superclass. When the inherited method is invoked on an instance of the subclass, inconsistencies may arise when the semantics and properties of A are not those expected in the method.

As we mentioned earlier, the inheritance mechanism allows the implementation of an inherited method to be overridden in the subclass. This is accomplished by simply defining in the subclass a method with the same name and a different implementation. Each time a message is sent to an instance of the subclass, the implementation local to the subclass will be used to execute the method. This results in a single name denoting different method implementations (*overloading*). This unit of change (i.e. the entire method) may be too coarse, however, since in some situations it may be desirable to *refine* the object behaviour rather than change it completely. Mechanisms to accomplish this have been proposed in the framework of object-oriented programming languages and adopted in several OODBMSs. For example, GemStone supports procedural combination of new and inherited behaviour through the pseudo-variable 'send super' (denoted as ←*Super*). When send super is used during the execution of a method invoked by a message *m*, the superclass method answering message *m* is invoked. The CLOS language [Moon89] provides mechanisms supporting declarative method combinations, based on the notions of *before method*, *primary method*, and *after method*. All before methods are invoked before the primary method, whereas all after methods are invoked after the primary method. Before and after methods are subject to some limitations in that they cannot modify the control structure or the results of the primary method. In addition, CLOS provides *around methods* supporting procedural method combinations. An around method, if applicable, takes precedence over all other methods and controls whether and when all other methods are called. Moreover, an around method can modify the input parameters and results of the methods it invokes.

An OODBMS providing procedural method combination is Vbase [AndrT87], which provides a pseudo-variable '$$' for this purpose. As we discussed earlier, in this system a method definition may contain a base method and an arbitrary number of trigger methods. When a method is invoked, the first trigger method is actually invoked. From this trigger method the control is then transferred to the next method by using the '$$' syntax. The next invoked method is the next trigger method, or the base method if there are no more trigger methods. Once the base method is executed, the superclass method is invoked. Therefore, in Vbase there is a fixed invocation order: first all trigger methods, on the basis of their declaration order in the method definition, then the base method, and finally the superclass method. When there are no trigger methods, the '$$' pseudo-variable behaves like the ←*Super* of Smalltalk. Note that this method combination is procedural, since the control to the next method must be explicitly passed by using the '$$' syntax. Therefore, the first invoked method may decide, on the basis of certain conditions, to return from the execution without invoking the other methods.

Very often the notion of subtyping is also found in OODBMSs. It is important, however, not to confuse inheritance with subtyping, even if there is often a unique mechanism providing both functions. For the purpose of the present discussion, we briefly characterize the difference between these two concepts as follows.

Inheritance is a reusability mechanism allowing a class to be defined from another class, by possibly extending and/or modifying the superclass definition. Instead, a type *T* is a subtype of a type *T'* if an instance of *T* can be used wherever an instance of *T'* is used. Therefore, subtyping is characterized by a set of rules ensuring that no type violations occur when the instance of a subtype *T* is used in the place of an instance of a supertype of *T*. Note that the fact that a class *C* is a subclass of a class *C'* does not necessarily imply that *C* is also a subtype of *C'*. However, subtyping, influences inheritance since it may restrict overriding and may impose conditions on multiple inheritance so that the subtyping rules are not violated. An example of restriction on overriding is to require that when the domain of an attribute is redefined in a subclass, this domain must be a subclass of the domain associated with the attribute in the superclass. A discussion of inheritance and subtyping is presented in [Wegn87].

For the purpose of the present discussion, we distinguish between *behavioural* and *structural* (or *inclusion*) subclassing. In behavioural subclassing, a class *C* is a subclass of *C'* if *C* provides methods with the same name and the same (or compatible) arguments as *C'* (and possibly additional ones). Criteria for behavioural subclassing are often based on the notion of conformity [Blac87]. Conformity can be used only when the method signatures include the types of the arguments and of the result. In structural subclassing, a class *C* is a subclass of *C'* if *C* provides the same attributes as *C'* or attributes compatible with those of *C'* (and possibly additional ones).

Usually, most OODBMSs only enforce structural subclassing, even if subclasses inherit both attributes and methods from the superclasses. For example, the O_2 system [Deux90] uses structural subclassing, while a condition different to conformity is used for methods. This condition leads to a less restrictive type system that does not guarantee that an instance of a subclass may always be safely used in the place of an instance of a superclass. Instead, the Vbase system [AndrT87] enforces both structural and behavioural subclassing, using the notion of conformity.

2.217 An example

An object-oriented database schema may be represented as a graph. In this representation, a node (denoted by a box) represents a class. A class node contains the names of all instance attributes and methods. The latter are underlined. Finally, the class-attributes (and methods) are distinguished by the instance attributes (and methods) by enclosing them in an ellipse. Nodes can be connected by three types of arc. An arc from class C to C' denotes different relationships between the two classes depending on the arc type. A normal arc (i.e. non-bold and non-hatched) indicates that C' is the domain of an attribute A of C, or that C' is the domain of the result of a method M of C. A bold arc indicates that C is the superclass of C'. A hatched arc indicates that C is the class of an input parameter for some method M of C'.

Consider the example in Figure 2.12. We assume that in the Team class there is a method, 'project-budget'. This method is applied to a team and receives as input parameter a project; the method output is an integer that represents the amount of budget allocated by the team on the project. Moreover, we assume that a class attribute, called 'maximum-salary', is defined for class Permanent. This attribute defines the maximum amount of monthly wage that can be assigned to a permanent employee without requiring special authorizations and checkings. The class attribute 'maximum-wage' of class Consultant has a similar meaning.

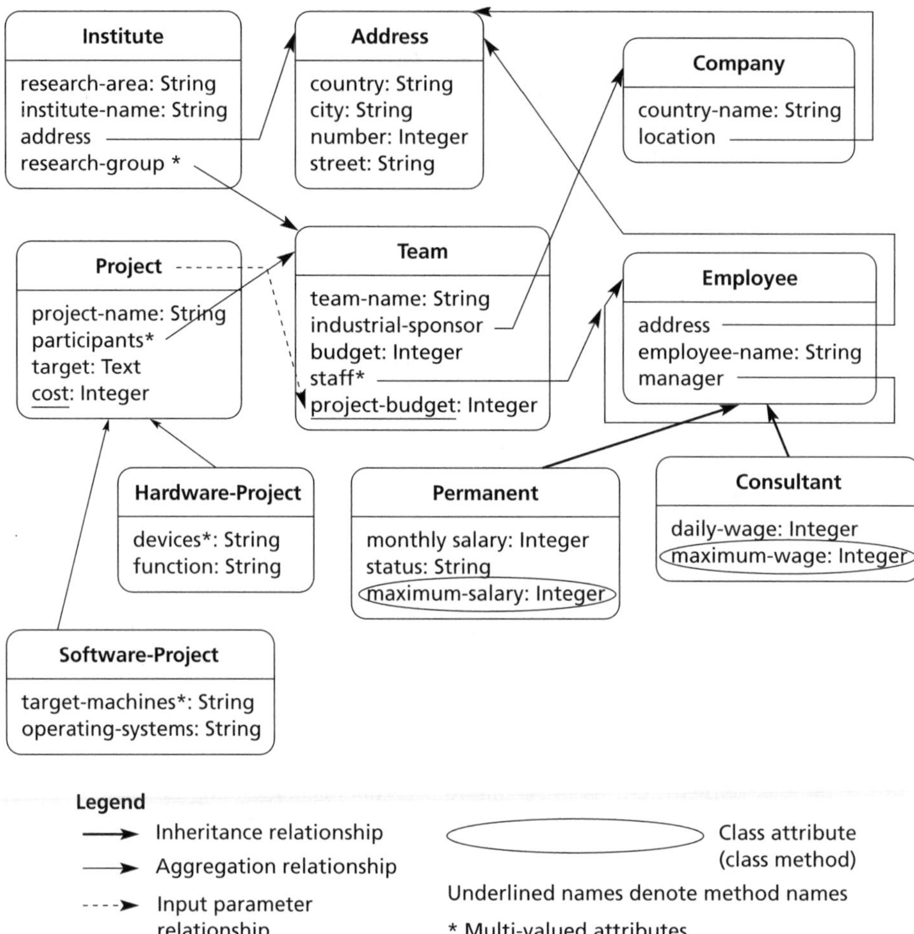

Figure 2.12 A database schema example

2.22 Comparison with other data models

2.221 *Comparison with semantic data models*

In the database systems area, semantic data models have been a relevant research topic [Hull87]. These models are characterized by a greater expressive power than the relational, hierarchical, and network data models. Usually, a semantic data model has mechanisms such as aggregation, specialization, and generalization, and it can therefore be considered similar to an object-oriented data model. A brief discussion that characterizes the differences between the two types of model is presented in [Hull87].

In general, the main difference is that the goal of semantic models is to provide mechanisms for structural abstraction. From this viewpoint, semantic models are close to knowledge representation models (such as KL-ONE). The major goal of object-oriented data models is to provide mechanisms for behavioral abstraction, and therefore they are similar to programming languages. However, this distinction is not sharp and advanced object-oriented database models are characterized by having powerful mechanisms to support both types of abstraction adequately.

2.222 Comparison with object models of knowledge-based systems

Object models developed in the framework of knowledge-based systems, such as the BACK language (*see also* Section 3.132), are definitely richer in terms of declarative modelling capabilities than object models of OODBMS. These two categories of models have several concepts in common, namely the notion of class (called concept in BACK), the notion of instance, and the notion of reference (somehow similar to the notion of role filler in BACK). Both categories of models also have the notion of intensional database schema (*see* as an example the notion of TBOX in BACK) and extensional database, representing the set of instances present in the database. However, they also have several differences. In BACK, objects are automatically classified into concepts depending on the values of their attributes. Therefore, predicates are associated with concepts and whenever a new object is created, a classification process (which is sometimes computationally very expensive) takes place to determine the concept that should be associated with the instance. As a consequence updates are not well supported by such an object model.

By contrast, object models developed in the context of OODBMS have the notion of methods, derived from the object paradigm as developed in the object-oriented programming area. Such a notion is usually not present in object models of knowledge-based systems. It is important to remark that OODBMS and object-based knowledge representation systems have been developed with different goals. The latter have as their main goals the representation of knowledge and the support of various forms of reasoning. Other features, such as data maintenance, transaction management, and access controls, are not among their priorities. OODBMS, on the other hand, must provide all database features and such a requirement has forced developers to limit the richness of the models.

2.223 Comparison with relational and CODASYL data models

The differences between an object-oriented data model and traditional database models should already be clear from the previous discussion. We will summarize them briefly here. The relational model differs from the object-oriented data model in that it does not provide the possibility of directly modelling complex objects (since attribute domains can only be primitive domains) and of defining inheritance relationships among sets of entities. Furthermore, there are no mechanisms to associate object behaviors with object definitions at schema level. The semantics of object behaviors are dispersed among the application programs. Finally, object identity, independent of object status, is not supported. Nested-relational models overcome only the first of these limitations in that they allow the definition of complex objects but they lack inheritance, object identity and computational completeness.

The CODASYL data model allows complex objects to be defined and supports some form of object identity. However, as pointed out in [Atki89], in CODASYL the object constructors are not orthogonal. Moreover, relationships are restricted to 1:N and therefore object identity is not treated uniformly. In addition, the CODASYL model does not provide concepts such as methods and class hierarchies. In conclusion, the most significant difference between traditional database models and the object-oriented model is that in the latter the model is used to describe not only object structures but also their behaviours.

2.224 Comparison with object-oriented programming languages

The object-oriented paradigm was introduced primarily in the field of programming languages and several object-oriented programming languages (OOPLs) can be found, such as Smalltalk, CLOS and C++ (defined as an extension of C). The latest OODBMSs share many characteristics with OOPLs and infact some OODBMSs were defined from existing OOPLs (as GemStone defined from Smalltalk for example). An OODBMS, however, differs from an OOPLs in that its focus is to efficiently manage large amounts of persistent, reliable and shared data and to provide declarative primitives for data access and manipulation (i.e. a query language).

2.23 Query languages and query processing

Query languages are a fundamental aspect of DBMSs. A query language allows users to retrieve data by simply specifying conditions on the data contents. The major advantages of a query language are that it is high level, declarative, efficient, and application independent [Atki89]. In relational DBMSs, the query language is the only way to access data. OODBMSs usually provide two ways to do this. The first is navigational and is based on OIDs. Given an OID, the system can directly access the referenced object, allowing the application to navigate through objects by following object references. The second access type is based on a query language, as in relational DBMSs. The two access types are often used in a complementary way. A query is used to select a set of objects. The retrieved objects and their components are then accessed using navigational capabilities.

In general, object-oriented query languages are similar to relational ones; very often the former are defined as an evolution of the latter. Moreover, nested relational languages have many similarities with object-oriented query languages. However, there are also some differences. We will go on to discuss some characteristics of object-oriented query languages.

A first characteristic concerns the notion of equality. As we have mentioned, different types of equality among objects may be defined. The type of equality used is important. It determines how operations such as union, difference, intersection, and duplicate elimination are performed. Most object-oriented query languages include identity equality. Therefore, when complex objects are compared, their OIDs are compared. Other languages, *see* [Bert92], provide both types of equality.

A second characteristic concerns aggregation hierarchy. An important requirement is to easily navigate through object structures in order to impose conditions on objects' nested attributes. Consider the query:

> *Retrieve all teams with a budget greater than $50,000 and supported by a company located in Turin.*

In relational calculus-like language, this query could be expressed as follows:

```
{v | ( w) (∃ g) (∃ i)
(Team(w) AND Company(g) AND Address(i)
AND w=v AND w.budget > 50,000 AND w.industrial-sponsor=g
AND g.location=i AND i.city='Turin')}.
```

The previous query requires the introduction of two variables, g and i, and two join predicates to impose a restriction on a nested attribute of the target class. To simplify the formulation of conditions on nested attributes, query languages often include some form of path-expression. A path-expression specifies an implicit join between an object and a component object. Therefore, in object-oriented languages, it is useful to distinguish between the implicit join, deriving from the hierarchical nesting of objects, and the explicit join, which is similar to the relational join where two objects are explicitly compared by using either the value or the identity equality. The previous query can now be expressed more concisely as follows:

```
{v | (∃ w)
(Team(w) AND w=v AND w.budget > 50,000 AND
w.industrial-sponsor.location.city = 'Turin')}.
```

A predicate on a nested attribute of an object is called a *nested predicate*. Note that path-expressions do not add expressive power to the language since it is possible to express their semantics by using additional variables and explicit joins. However, they are very useful in increasing the *conceptual conciseness* of the query language. A language is conceptually concise if it does not require the introduction of artificial elements – variables in our case – when specifying a query. These path-expressions, or similar syntactical notations, are provided by most object-oriented query languages. Conversely, not all object-oriented query languages provide explicit joins. The motivation for this is based on the argument that in relational systems joins are mostly used to recompose entities that were decomposed for normalization [Brei89]. Since the same function of those joins is provided by path-expressions, it appears that in OODBMSs there is no strong need for explicit joins.

Other relevant issues are related to inheritance hierarchies. A query on a class may actually apply to the class only, or to the class and all its subclasses. Most languages provide both possibilities. For example, in Orion [KimW90b], when the name of a class is specified alone, the query applies only to that class. If the name of the class is followed by *, the query applies to all classes in the inheritance hierarchy rooted at the class specified in the query. For example, the query

Retrieve all instances of the class Project and all its subclasses having as participant a team supported by a company located in 'Turin'

is expressed as follows:

```
{ v | ( ∃w)(∃ u) (Project*(w) AND Team(u) AND
w=v AND u ISIN w.participants AND
u.industrial-sponsor.location.city = 'Turin')}.
```

The * operator applied to the class Project denotes that the query is applied to all classes in the inheritance hierarchy rooted at Project. In the query, the set-membership operator ISIN has been used.

Since subclasses may have their own attributes in addition to those inherited from the superclasses, it may be useful to express queries with *alternative predicates*. Very often, two attributes in two subclasses are semantically similar. For example, the attribute 'monthly_salary' of the class Permanent can be considered equivalent to the attribute 'daily_wage' of the class Consultant, once the latter is multiplied by a given factor. An alternative predicate applied to classes $C_1, C_2, \ldots, C_n$ has the form (an actual syntax is specified in [Bert92]):

```
if class(x)=C1 then pred1
if class(x)=C2 then pred2
.................
if class(x)=Cn then predn.
```

In the previous expression, x is a variable denoting an object; 'class(x)' is a special message that when applied to an object returns the object class. An alternative predicate is useful when queries contain other predicates on the common attributes in the inheritance hierarchy. For example, the query

Retrieve all employees living in Rome, such that if they are permanent staff their salary is higher than 4,000, if they are consultants their daily wage is higher than 500

is expressed as follows (using the syntax defined in [Bert92]):

```
{ v | (∃w) (Employee*(w) AND v=w AND w.address.city = 'Rome 'AND
CLASS_OF(w)= [       (Permanent: w.monthly-salary >4,000)
                     (Consultant: w.daily-wage > 500)])}.
```

Other issues concern the use of methods in queries. Methods can be used in queries as *derived attribute methods* and *predicate methods*. A derived attribute method has a function comparable to that of an attribute. An attribute stores a value while a derived attribute method is a procedure computing a value from the attribute values of an object or the attribute values of other objects in the database. In the latter case, the execution of the method causes the invocation of methods on other objects. An example of a query invoking a derived attribute method is the following:

Retrieve all projects whose target is database and whose cost is greater than 50,000.

Predicate methods return the logical constants True or False, while derived attribute methods return objects (i.e. primitive values or OIDs). The value returned by a predicate method can then participate in the evaluation of the Boolean expression that determines the objects satisfying the query.

A relevant property of the relational model is that the results of queries are relations. Therefore queries can be composed, i.e. the results of a query can be provided as input to another query. In general applying the same principle to object-oriented queries may be rather expensive. In particular, if the data model does not support complex values, the result of a query is an object, or set of objects, of a class that usually is not already defined in the database schema. In other words, a query may define a new class. Since queries apply to sets of objects (classes or collections depending on the data model), they can be composed. This approach is conceptually correct. However, it imposes some performance penalties since the creation of a new class may be rather expensive. Therefore, some query languages impose restrictions on project operations in queries. A common restriction is that either all attributes or only a single attribute are retrieved. Under this restriction, a query result is a set of objects whose class already exists in the database schema.

In data models where complex values are supported, a common solution is to define the results of a query as a set of tuples. An attribute of a tuple contains either a value or the OID of an object in the database. That is, the tuple results have pointers to the database objects satisfying the query. Note that these tuples are not objects, they are simply complex values. Another solution is to consider the results as a set of object instances of a general class which accepts all objects and whose methods permit only objects to be displayed and printed. This solution, however, makes it difficult to reuse the results of a query and to invoke other methods on the retrieved objects.

The characteristics of object-oriented query languages make query processing in such systems different, under certain aspects, from the case of relational systems. Join operations in relational systems are always executed by comparing values; this is not always the case in OODBMSs, where joins are very often implicit joins along aggregation hierarchies and based on identity. Thus it is possible to define some specific indexing techniques (*see* [Brei89] for a discussion). In addition, a query can have not only a class but also an inheritance hierarchy as its scope. Finally, the employment of methods extends the complexity of query processing and the efficient execution of queries containing method invocations is still an open problem.

In order to discuss query strategies, the concept of a *query graph* is useful. A node in a query graph represents a class involved in a query. The root of the graph is the class target of the query. The target is the class whose instances must be returned as the query result. A query graph may have several roots if the query language allows the explicit join of several classes to be returned as a query result. Other classes are included in the query if they must be traversed to evaluate nested predicates or if they are subclasses of other classes in the graph. An example of a query graph is presented in Figure 2.13 for a query that retrieves all computer science institutes located in Rome with teams whose budget is greater than $50 000. In the remainder of this section, we limit the discussion to the case of single-target queries.

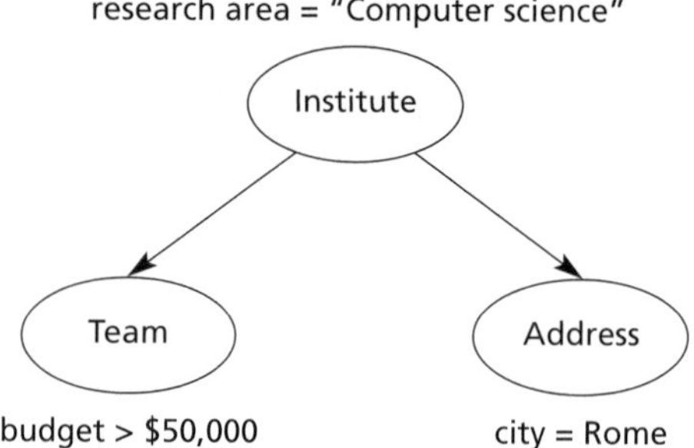

Figure 2.13 An example of a query graph

To evaluate a query, all nodes in the query graph must be visited. Different visiting strategies have been proposed [KimW90a]. Note that even if the discussion is in the framework of the ORION system [KimW90a], it applies to the processing of several other query languages since these share many characteristics (such as implicit joins) with the ORION query language.

- *Forward.* The first node visited is the root of the graph. The other nodes are visited in any depth-first order. Two possible strategies of this type for the example query are
  (Institute Team Address)
  (Institute Address Team).
- *Reverse.* The first node visited is one of the leaf nodes. The search then continues upward in the graph. The root is the last node visited. Two possible strategies of this type for the example query are
  (Team Address Institute)
  (Address Team Institute).
- *Mixed.* This strategy is a combination of the previous two. Two possible strategies of this type for the example query are
  (Team Institute Address)
  (Address Institute Team).

A second dimension in query strategies is the technique used to retrieve data from the classes that are visited for the evaluation of nested predicates. In [KimW90a] two methods are considered for retrieving data from a visited class. The first is called *nested-loop* and consists of instantiating separately each qualified instance of a class. The instance attributes are examined for qualification if there are simple predicates on the instance attributes. If the instance qualifies, it is passed to its parent node (in the case of the reverse strategy) or to its child node (in the case of the forward strategy). The second method is called *sort-domain* and consists of instantiating all qualified instances of a class at once. All the qualifying instances are then passed to their parent or child node (depending on the strategy used).

By combining visiting strategies with techniques for retrieving instances, different query-execution strategies are obtained. They are discussed in detail in [KimW90a] and other related papers. The spectrum of possible strategies is extended when indexing techniques are also considered.

We mentioned earlier that the usage of methods in queries has several implications on query processing. In the remainder of this section, we will briefly discuss some of these issues. First, the optimization of queries containing method invocation is difficult. A method is a program and therefore the estimate of a method cost and selectivity may be difficult, if indeed possible. A common strategy used in most systems is to restrict the set of objects as far as possible before applying the method. Therefore, predicate methods or predicates on attribute methods are evaluated as late as possible in the query execution. This strategy may be inefficient in several cases however. In other approaches, the user provides such information on the method's cost and selectivity as input to the system. With this type of approach the main disadvantage is that it may be difficult for the user to determine this information. In addition, methods with side effects may make the result of the query dependent on the evaluation order of the various predicates. Therefore some systems do not allow methods with side effects to be used in queries. Others do not take any measures and leave the responsibility to the user. It should be noted that forbidding the invocation of methods with side effects in queries may be too restrictive. An open issue is to determine under which conditions these methods can be invoked without making the query results dependent on the query evaluation strategy.

2.24 Operational aspects

Effective support of an object-oriented data model requires techniques and algorithms traditionally used for data management to be extended and/or modified. Moreover, applications that are expected to use an OODBMS require additional functionalities, such as version mechanisms and long transactions, that are not usually provided by traditional DBMSs. In this section we illustrate this point by discussing operational aspects of data management in OODBMSs.

2.241 Versions

Usually, in traditional DBMSs, once transaction updates have been committed and permanently installed, the previous values of data are discarded. However, advanced applications, and especially design applications, require facilities to maintain object versions, i.e. to keep different states of the same object. This requirement is inherent in applications that are exploratory and evolutionary.

Versions are a useful mechanism to maintain object histories, i.e. to keep track of object evolutions over time. Moreover, versions can be used to provide alternatives for the same object. This is particularly useful in design applications, where different designers may need to explore in parallel different design choices. OODBMSs providing versions include AVANCE [Bjor89], and ORION [KimW90a].

In an OODBMS, a *versioned* object O is a collection of objects that are derived directly or indirectly from O. The fact that a version V_i is derived from a version V_j establishes a *derivation relationship* between the two version objects. The set of all versions related by derivation relationships is a *version hierarchy* [KimW90a]. Note that V_i and V_j are first-class objects. Therefore, they have their own OIDs, and can be directly accessed and modified. Each version is a snapshot of an object state. The version management mechanism maintains all the information necessary to connect all versions of an object. A common way to represent the version hierarchy is to store it in a special object, called here the *generic object*. This object has its own OID, like any other objects. All version mechanisms provide operations for the management and inspection of version hierarchies, such as determining the predecessors or successors of a given version. A taxonomy of operations is presented in [Bjor89].

A versioned object O can be referenced by another object by either a *specific* reference (called also *static* [KimW90a]), or a *generic* reference (*dynamic* in [KimW90a]). In the first case, the reference is to a specific version of O, while in the second it is to the generic object of O. When a generic reference is used, the system has the task of determining the version to be returned. This version is the *default* version and is usually the last version generated. Figure 2.14 illustrates an example of a version hierarchy. Object Memo[i] is the generic object of the version hierarchy. Therefore it contains the version derivation relationships for all the objects in this version hierarchy and the default version.

Versions are very often classified in:

- *stable* versions: considered consolidated enough to be used as a basis for branching alternatives, or important enough to be saved as a reference point in object histories. In general, some restrictions are placed on modifications that can be executed on a stable version. For example, it is possible to delete but not modify a version if other versions have been derived from it. Updating a stable version would require update propagation algorithms to ensure that versions derived from it are properly updated. As noted in [Kim, 1990a], if a stable version needs modification, a version may be derived from it containing the desired changes;
- *non-stable* versions: not consolidated yet and therefore can undergo modifications. A non-stable version can change into a stable version upon explicit user request (through operations such as *freeze* [Bjor89] or *promote* [KimW90a]) or automatically. For example, in ORION [KimW90a], a non-stable version is automatically promoted by the system if a version is derived from it.

In general, most version mechanisms do not support version merging, i.e. a new version is constrained to have only one direct predecessor. The AVANCE [Bjor89] system provides some limited support for version merging. Whenever a new version must be derived by merging several existing versions, the user has to indicate among these one *main* version. Only the main version is copied into the new version, while it is left to the user to access the other versions to be merged and extract relevant information from them. The system connects the new version as a direct successor to the merged versions. Therefore the version hierarchy becomes a general graph.

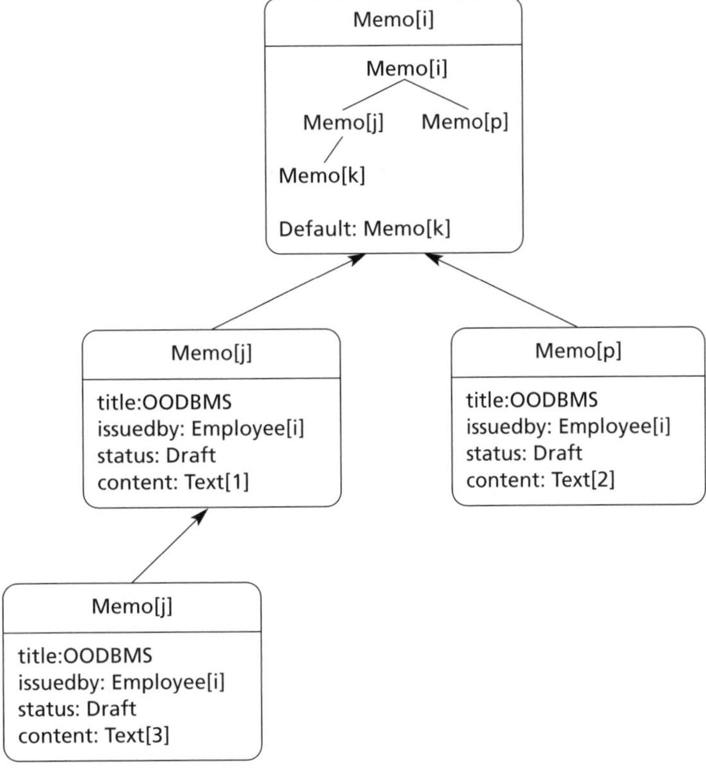

Figure 2.14 An example of a version hierarchy

Some version mechanisms support versions of classes. A major application of this is in the support of schema evolution, since it is possible to first define a class and then modify it without losing the previous class definition and the instances generated from it. We will look briefly at versions of classes together with schema evolution.

2.242 *Concurrency control and transactions*

Transactions in advanced application environments differ from those in traditional environments in the following ways:

- their length can be in days or weeks, rather than a few seconds;
- in some cases, it is not acceptable to lock an object through the entire transaction, since the concurrency degree would be drastically reduced;
- while in a traditional environment, at a given point in time, there is a unique 'valid' object state, in advanced environments several valid states of a given object may exist;
- advanced applications are characterized by group of users working together. Therefore support for co-operative transactions must be provided.

The support of transactions with these characteristics requires specific concurrency control and recovery mechanisms. One approach is to have a public, shared database and a number of private databases (*user databases*). Each user database is a single-user system with a traditional transaction mechanism. Note that a single-user system still needs a transaction mechanism for recovery. Moreover, concurrency control mechanisms may be needed if the user is allowed to execute several tasks in parallel. When a user needs to work on an object, the object is extracted from the public database and transferred (only logically in some cases) through a *check-out* operation into the user private database. The modified objects are copied back into the public database with a *check-in* operation. A large time interval may elapse between a check-out operation and the corresponding check-in operation. Therefore, objects in the public database are locked with *long duration locks*. These locks are stored on secondary storage so that they may survive system crashes or shutdowns.

This approach, however, does not allow a user to share objects that are stable, but not yet completed, with other authorized users. A situation in which this would be desirable could occur for example in the case of two users co-operating on a task. For a user to pass such objects to other users in the above system, a check-in operation must be executed. A model solving this problem was presented in [KimW84]. In the proposed approach, a third type of database, called a *semi-public database*, is introduced in addition to the public and private databases. A semi-public database is associated with each long transaction and contains all objects that are not yet ready to be copied back into the public database but that are sufficiently consolidated to be passed to other authorized users. A transaction can check an object into the semi-public database by using the *downward commit* primitive. The objects in the semi-public database can then be accessed from other transactions. When a transaction T_i checks out object O from the semi-public database associated with a transaction T_j, T_i becames a descendant of T_j. When T_i terminates the manipulations on object O, T_i can return O to T_j by using the *upward commit* primitive. When a transaction with no ancestors executes an *upward commit*, the object is copied back to the public database. Transaction T_i, in turn, may have other descendant transactions. Therefore a transaction hierarchy is generated. This approach is very useful in situations where groups of users co-operate in complex tasks, since it allows the users to exchange incomplete objects in a controlled way. In general, most OODBMSs support or plan to support mechanisms for long-duration transactions.

Another important concept is that of a *hypothetical transaction*. A hypothetical transaction allows a user to experiment with complex changes without permanently installing them at transaction commit. It should be noted that a conventional transaction with the abort command available at application interface level may provide the same functionality. However, a conventional transaction would have a non-negligible impact on the performance because of log management. In this regard, hypothetical transactions are more efficient.

A mechanism for hypothetical transactions has been designed and implemented within the framework of the ORION system [KimW89a]. Each time an object is modified during a hypothetical transaction, the system creates a copy (called *current copy*) of the object. The original object (called *shadow copy*) is not modified. Further accesses and updates to the same object from the transaction are executed on the current copy. The current copy is simply deleted when the transaction terminates, whatever the transaction outcome (abort or commit). If there are several hypothetical transactions working on the same objects, each transaction receives a different current copy of the object. Therefore several hypothetical transactions can concurrently access and modify the same set of objects. The only restriction imposed is that the shadow copy be locked in shared mode. This prevents a normal transaction from modifying an object accessed by hypothetical transactions and thereby causing these transactions to read inconsistent data.

Most OODBMSs use locking mechanisms for concurrency control. In ORION, the locking mechanism has been extended to account for some requirements deriving from the object-oriented data model. For example, one extension concerns inheritance hierarchies, since a class inherits attributes and methods from the superclasses. Therefore, when a user accesses a class or the instances of a class, the system locks the definitions of all superclasses to avoid schema changes that would propagate to the accessed class. A second extension concerns composite objects considered as locking units. A special protocol allows the system to lock a composite object and all its components, without explicitly locking all the components.

The GemStone system supports an *optimistic* concurrency control mechanism in addition to the locking used for *pessimistic* concurrency control. It is possible for a transaction to access data in both pessimistic and optimistic modes. When a transaction *T* accesses an object using the optimistic protocol, *T* may be aborted at commit time. This happens if *T* has read or modified data that have been modified by another transaction that has executed the commit before *T*. This does not happen if *T* uses the pessimistic protocol because locking is used. The optimistic protocol can be easily supported in GemStone, since the recovery mechanism used by the system is based on the *shadow pages* mechanism. This mechanism is based on maintaining two page tables during the life of a transaction, called respectively *current* page table and *shadow* page table. When the transaction starts, both page tables are identical. The shadow page table never changes during the execution of the transaction. The current page table is used to locate the page addresses on disks. The first time a page must be modified by the transaction, a copy of the page is made and the updates are made on the copy. The current page table is modified to contain the address of the copy. All further updates are performed on the copy. If the transaction commits, the shadow page table is discarded and the current table becomes the new page table. If the transaction aborts, the current page table is simply discarded. In general, the optimistic protocol is used for read-only transactions. The transaction receives a consistent copy of the data, executes the read operations and, since it does not execute modifications, does not conflict with other transactions. The integration of the two mechanisms is described in [Brei89].

Finally, for recovery purposes, some systems use the log mechanism while others, such as GemStone, use the shadow pages. In general, the log-based approach is considered more efficient and preserves the physical contiguity of data. However, this mechanism is inefficient for multimedia data such as image and voice. Log mechanisms require before and after data images to be saved. In the case of multimedia data a large amount of information must be stored. Therefore, a common solution is to integrate the log mechanism used for normal data with the shadow pages mechanism used for multimedia data. This approach is used in the ORION system.

2.243 Authorization

The authorization subsystem is a basic component of any DBMS. The authorization model, in particular, must be consistent with the data model provided by the system. Current authorization models have been defined mainly in the framework of the relational model. These models usually assume that the relation, or the attribute, is the authorization unit. In some cases, a view mechanism is used to support authorization on subsets of a relation's tuples. In OODBMS, the minimum granularity level that must be supported is the object. The object represents the logical access unit since the user may directly access a single object. In addition, an object-oriented data model must account for additional aspects such as inheritance hierarchies, versions and composite objects.

The definition of an authorization model satisfying the previous requirements is rather complex and its implementation is crucial because of the impact that authorization checkings can have on the performance. An object-oriented authorization model has been defined in the framework of the ORION system [KimW89a]. Other systems implement less sophisticated models or have no authorization mechanisms at all. For example, in GemStone, the unit of authorization is the *segment*. Each user owns at least one segment. All objects created by a user are stored into the segment owned by the user. A user may grant read or write authorization on his own segments to other users. An authorization on a segment implies the same authorization on all objects contained in the segment. Therefore, the authorization granularity provided is rather coarse.

In the model defined for ORION [KimW89a], objects are organised with respect to the authorization in a *granularity hierarchy*. This hierarchy defines how objects are organised in terms of other objects. Given an object *O*, the hierarchy defines the composition of *O* in terms of objects at a lower level than *O*. Figure 2.15 illustrates an example of granularity hierarchy. The example refers to a database, named CNR, containing the classes illustrated in the schema in Figure 2.12. It is possible to grant an authorization right for any object at any hierarchy level. For example, it is possible to grant an authorization on the entire database or on a single instance. A fundamental concept in the authorization model is represented by *implicit authorization*: given an access right A to an object O for a user U, U implicitly receives authorization A for all objects which compose O. For example, if a user has received the Read access right for the class Project, the user implicitly receives the same access right for all instances of this class. However, if a user has the Read access right for a single instance of a class, this authorization does not imply that the user can read other instances of the same class. The concept of implicit authorization avoids the explicit granting and storage of all those authorizations that can be derived from others. In addition, it provides a certain degree of efficiency in some situations. If, for example, a user accesses an instance of a class and the system determines that the user is authorised to access the entire class, further accesses to other instances of the same class within the same transaction do not require authorization checks.

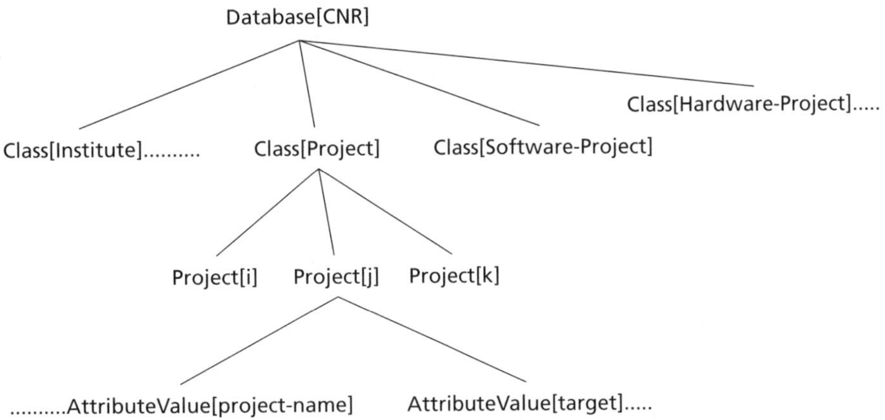

Figure 2.15 An example of granularity hierarchy

The concept of implicit authorization had already been introduced in previous authorization models. In the model developed for the ORION system [KimW89a], this concept has been extended with the notion of *weak/strong* authorization, and *positive/negative* authorization. A strong authorization does not admit exceptions on the implicit authorizations derived from it, while a weak authorization can be overridden, i.e. it can have exceptions that are specified by using positive or negative authorizations. For example, if a user receives a weak read authorization for the class Project and later on a negative read authorization for the i-th instance of class Project (the instance is denoted as Project[i] in Figure 2.15), the user can read all instances of Project except this instance. Note that, since an exception can be a weak authorization, it is possible to define exceptions of exceptions.

Another contribution of this authorization model is that it directly supports the object-oriented paradigm and, in addition, takes into account aspects such as versions and composite objects. For example, an issue regarding inheritance hierarchies is whether a user holding an authorization for a class implicitly receives the same authorizations for all the subclasses of this class or not. The second solution has been chosen for the model, i.e. the user does not implicitly receive authorizations for the subclasses. This choice encourages the re-use of existing classes without diminishing privacy. In fact, if a user were not sure about his own data privacy, he would probably not define his class starting from another class. Of course, the model has a special authorization right that allows a user to derive a subclass from a given class. Therefore, in order to create a subclass of a given class *C*, a user *U* must have the authorization to generate subclasses from *C*. The creator of *C*, however, will not implicitly receive any authorization of the subclasses created by *U* from class *C*.

The authorization model allows the user to treat composite objects as an authorization unit. For example, an authorization for the root of a composite object implies the same authorization for the component objects. If an object is a component of several composite objects, as in the extended model defined for the ORION system [KimW89a], a user may receive several implicit authorizations for this object. Note that because of negative authorizations, conflicts may arise on implicit authorizations on a component object. Algorithms for conflicts detection have been defined for the ORION authorization model. Similarly, versioned objects can be treated as an authorization unit. For example, an authorization on the generic object of a versioned object *O* implies the same authorization on all versions of *O*. The user, however, can adopt a finer granularity because it is possible to grant an access right to a specific version. Such an authorization implies no authorization on other versions of the same object. We also note that there is a specific access right that allows a user to derive a new version from a given versioned object.

2.244 *Schema evolution*

Schema evolution is not inherent in the object-oriented paradigm. However, the application environments that are expected to use an OODBMS require mechanisms to support complex schema changes. These applications are characterised by the fact that schema modifications are a rule rather than an exception. For example, it is common that during a design application, the ways of classifying objects and their interrelationships evolve. The modification primitives provided by relational systems are rather limited. Moreover, the modifications on a relation do not affect other relations. The situation is more complex in object-oriented systems as the spectrum of possible modifications is larger, due to the increased complexity of the model. Moreover, modifications to a class may affect other classes. For example, if an attribute is removed from a class definition, the attribute must be removed from all subclasses of the modified class.

A taxonomy of *basic schema changes* is presented in [Bane87]. Possible modifications include:

- changes to the definition of a class, such as adding, renaming, and dropping an attribute or a method, and changing the inheritance of an attribute or a method;
- changes to the inheritance hierarchy, such as adding or removing a superclass of a class.

Basic modifications also include operations for creating, renaming, and removing a class. Schema change operations must keep the database schema *consistent*. Therefore, rules ensuring schema invariance have been defined (*see*, for example, [Bane87] and [Brei89]). In addition to these, some *complex changes* can be devised. They are complex because they can be implemented by using the basic modification primitives. Complex changes include:

- merging two or more classes into their superclass – this is possible if the merged classes have the same attributes and methods as their superclasses;
- generalization of two or more classes – this modification consists of creating a superclass of the given classes. The superclass contains the common attributes and methods of all subclasses;
- modifications to the aggregation hierarchy – in particular, one modification consists of promoting an attribute (or set of attributes) of a class *C* to a class. As an example, consider the class HWProject in Figure 2.15 and its attribute 'function'. The domain of 'function' is a string. Suppose that more information must be provided about the function of a hardware project. A possibility is to create a class called HWProjectFunction containing all the attributes needed. Then, the domain of attribute 'function' in the class HWProject is changed to the newly created class HWProjectFunction.

  Another modification consists of the inclusion of a class *C* in a class *C*', where *C* is a domain of some attribute of *C*'. An an example, consider the classes Address, Employee, Company, and Institute in Figure 2.15; the inclusion of Address into Employee, Company, and Institute consists of adding the attributes 'country', 'city', 'number, and 'street' to these classes, and then removing the attribute 'address' from Employee and Institute, and the attribute 'location' from Company, and finally discarding the class Address.

Note that not all the complex changes can be supported by any system. In particular, changes that involve migrating instances from one class to another (as the merge operation) may not be supported by systems where the OIDs contain the class identifier. In this case, migrating an object would invalidate all references to it.

An important issue in supporting schema changes is how to propagate them to the instances of affected classes. This issue concerns only some types of schema changes, such as the deletion of an instance attribute from a class, for example. Other modifications, such as the deletion of a method, do not impact instances. Some approaches have been defined for the case of basic schema changes. A first approach, called *deferred*, delays the application of changes to instances, even indefinitely. A proposal based on this approach is described in [Zdon90]. It is based on the use of versions of classes. Each time a class *C* is modified, a new version of *C* is generated. Each instance of *C* is connected to the version under which it has been generated. In addition, an *exception handler* is defined for each new class version. If an application tries to access or modify an instance created under a version different from that used by the application, an exception arises. This event activates the appropriate exception handler that in most cases propagates the schema change to the instance. An approach based on class version is also used in the AVANCE system [Bjor89]. A second deferred approach has been defined and implemented as part of the ORION system. In this case, affected instances are never modified for schema changes. For example, when an instance attribute is removed from a class, no actions are taken on the class instances. Simply, the deleted attribute is screened out when the instances are retrieved and presented to the user. A second approach, called *immediate*, consists of modifying the instances right after the change is issued. This approach is used in the GemStone system [Brei89].

The deferred approach has the advantage that schema change operations are not expensive. However, the screening may make instance accesses more expensive. Conversely, the schema change operations are very expensive under the immediate approach, while instance accesses have no additional cost. Since schema changes are very frequent in applications supported by OODBMSs, an open problem is how to combine these two approaches to obtain a more flexible mechanism. Furthermore, efficient implementation schema for complex changes should be investigated.

An important consideration is whether existing methods have to be recompiled when schema changes are executed. For example, a method may invoke another method that has been deleted. This issue arises in systems where type checking and binding are executed at compile-time. In these systems, dynamic schema changes may not be supported. An interesting approach is provided by the O_2 system [Deux90], which supports two different application running modes: the development mode and the execution mode. The first mode is used during the development phase of applications. The application designer may interactively modify the schema, without having to perform extensive recompilations since features such as late binding are used under this mode. Therefore an increased flexibility is achieved, which is important during the database schema and application prototyping. Under this mode, however, the performance may be rather low and errors may arise due to possible schema mismatches. The execution mode is used by the end-users to run applications which are stable. To generate the execution mode for a given application, the system provides a compile command that produces an optimized executable code. This command has the effect of disallowing some modification operations (such as classes, attributes, and methods deletions) on the portion of the schema used by the compiled application. However, increased performance and safety are achieved.

2.25 Systems

In this subsection, we briefly describe the models of four systems: GemStone [Brei89], O_2 [Deux90], Orion [KimW89a], and ObjectStore [Andr87]. Such systems have been chosen mainly because they differ in several aspects of the data model and the query and access languages. This allows us to illustrate several variations to the core model. Note, however, that to date there are more than 20 OODBMSs available as products. The reader is referred to [Jeff91] for an overview of most of the available systems.

2.251 GemStone

The GemStone system has been one of the first OODBMSs to appear on the market. The data model and the access/manipulation language (Opal) has been defined as an extension of the Smalltalk language. On closer analysis, Opal shows the features that must be added to a programming language to make it suitable as a database language. GemStone is based on a client/server architecture and is available on several hardware/sofwtare platforms, such as DEC (Vax and Dec-station), Sun, and IBM (RS6000). Moreover, it supports clients on IBM PCs and Apple Macintoshes. Applications can be written in a number of languages, including Smalltalk, C++, C, and Pascal. The system also provides a number of tools, such as an advanced 4GL, an interface generator, and a schema browser.

In order to illustrate the features of the Opal data model, we show how the class Institute of the example database schema in Figure 15 is defined:

```
Object subclass 'Institute'
        instVarNames: #('research-area', 'institute-name',
                         'address', 'research-group')
        classVars: #()
        poolDictionary: #()
        inDictionary: UserGlobals
        constraints: #[#[#research-area, String],
                       #[#institute-name, String],
                       #[#address, Address],
                       #[#research-group, Teams]]
        instanceInvariant: false
        isModifiable: false.
```

In Opal, the definition of a class is always performed by sending to the proper superclass the message 'subclass' for which there exists a system-defined method in each class in the database. Messages in Opal have the format <receiver> <selector> where <receiver> is the object to which the message is being sent, and <selector> consists, usually, of a list of pairs of the form <argument-name> <argument-value>. The selector is used by the system to choose the proper method to execute for answering the message. In the above example, the class Institute is not a subclass of any other user-defined class. Therefore it is created as a subclass of the system-class Object. A limitation of the GemStone data model is that no multiple inheritance is supported. In addition to the name of the new class, a class definition message contains other arguments describing relevant characteristics of the new class. In particular:

- the clause **instVarNames** has a list of strings denoting the names of the instance variables (i.e. attributes) of the class. Note that no domains are specified for the attributes. Domains are specified in the clause **constraints** (see below);
- the clause **classVars** has as arguments a list of class instance variables (i.e. class-attributes). These instance variables are not inherited by the instances of the class; however, methods of instances may access them during their execution. In the above example, since the class Institute has no class-attributes, the clause **classVars** is followed by an empty list;
- the clause **poolDictionary** has as argument a list of *pool variables* that are shared by several classes and their instances. The pool variables enable several objects, instances of a different class, to share common information;
- the clause **inDictionary** specifies the name of a dictionary which has already been defined, where the name of the class is inserted on its creation. In the above example, class Institute is inserted in a dictionary named UserGlobals. This is a standard dictionary defined for each user. Users, however, may define additional dictionaries;
- the clause **constraints** is an important one in that it specifies the domain's attributes. The clause has as argument a list of domain specifications, where a domain specification is a pair where the first element is the name of an attribute, and the second element is the name of the domain of this attribute. For example, the pair [#research-group, Teams] specifies that the domain of attribute 'research-group' is the class Teams. Note that in GemStone domains need not always be specified. This specification is mandatory if an index must be allocated on the attribute, or queries will be issued against instances of the class;
- the clause **instanceInvariant** specifies whether the instances of the class can be modified or not. This clause has as argument the Boolean value True in the first case, and the value False in the second case. When the **instanceInvariant** flag is True, an instance of the class can be modified only during the transaction that created it. Once the transaction commits, the instance can no longer be modified;
- the clause **isModifiable** specifies whether the class itself can be modified or not. This clause has as argument the Boolean value True in the first case, and the value False in the second case. When this flag is True, the class definition may be modified by adding/removing instance variables and constraints. The only restriction is that a class which is modifiable cannot be instantiated. A class that is initially declared as modifiable can, however, be made non-modifiable later on and therefore can be instantiated. By contrast, a class which is non-modifiable cannot become modifiable.

Methods in GemStone are defined by means of the message 'method'. This message has as argument the name of the class to which the method belongs and the method specification, which consists of a message pattern and a body. The message pattern is, in essence, the specification of the method interface. Two example methods, defined for the class Institute, are as follows. The first method, when invoked on an instance of class Institute, returns the value of attribute 'research-area' of the instance, whereas the second method modifies the value of attribute 'research-area':

```
method:        Institute
     research-area          'message pattern'
     ^research-area         'return statement'
%

method:        Institute
     research-area: anArea 'message pattern'
     research-area:= anArea
     ^self                         'return statement'
%
```

Note that the two methods have different message patterns. Indeed, the first method has no input parameter, whereas the second method has one (i.e. the new value of attribute 'research-area'). GemStone supports full encapsulation; therefore, a pair of methods like the ones above must be defined by the users for each attribute that must be directly accessed and modified.

A characteristic of the GemStone model is that the class does not have an extensional function. Indeed, queries and indexing are possible only on sets of instances and not of classes. Suppose that queries must be issued against the instances of the class Institute defined above. An approach is to define a class as follows:

```
Set subclass 'Institute-Set'
      instVarNames: #()
      classVars: #()
      poolDictionaries: #()
      inDictionary: UserGlobals
      constraints: Institute
      instancesInvariant: false
      isModifiable: false.
```

The above class is defined as a subclass of the system-class Set. Therefore, the instances of the class Institute-Set are sets. In Opal, a class defined as subclass (direct or indirect) of the system-class Set cannot have instance variables. Therefore, the **instVarNames** clause must necessarily have as argument an empty list. The **constraints** clause is followed by the name of the class Institute. Therefore, this constraint specifies that all members of the sets, instances of class Institute-Set, must be instances of the class Institute. In summary, the instances of the above class are sets of institutes. It is then possible to define multiple extensions for the class Institute, in that every instance of class Institute-Set represents a partial or complete extension of class Institute. Different extensions may have common instances, since an object may belong to multiple sets. Note that adding/removing instances of class Institute to/from the various extensions is, however, left to the applications, since in GemStone there is no automatic management of class extensions by the system.

In addition to navigation capabilities commonly provided by all OODBMSs, Opal provides a query language supporting set-oriented queries. Queries can only be issued against set objects, and not against classes. As an example, suppose that an instance of the class Institute-Set has been defined having the name 'an-Institute-Set' and that instances of class Institute have been added to this set. A query retrieving from the set 'an-Institute-Set' all institutes doing research on databases is formulated in Opal as follows:

```
DB-Institutes := an-Institute-Set select: {aSet | aSet.research-
area = 'Databases'}
```

The result of the query is a set which is assigned to variable 'DB-Institute'. Then the elements of the results can be extracted by using the usual operations on the sets. Queries may contain a Boolean combination of predicates as well as path-expression. The following query retrieves all institutes doing research on databases and located in Italy:

```
Italian-DB-Institutes := an-Institute-Set select:
      {aSet | aSet.research-area = 'Databases' &
aSet.address.country='Italy'}.
```

The **select** message requires all instance variables on which conditions are issued in the query to be constrained, i.e. a domain must have been specified for these instance variables. Opal provides additional messages, such as **detect** which returns only one of the instances satisfying the query (whereas the **select** message returns all instances satisfying the query), and **reject** which returns all the instances that do not satisfy a given query. We refer the reader to [Bert93b] for additional details on the Opal language and on the architecture of GemStone.

2.252 O_2

Unlike GemStone, the data model of the O_2 OODBMS [Deux90] has not been defined from an existing object-oriented programming language. Rather, the data model has been designed from scratch, whereas the language for defining method implementation, called CO_2, is an extension of the C programming language with constructs for objects and sets manipulation. The discussion on O_2 in this section is based on the Version 1.0 of the system [Alta89]. O_2 is based on a client/server architecture and is available on the Unix platform. The system provides a number of tools, such as a visual schema definition interface and browser, and an object-oriented programming environment.

The data model of O_2 provides the notions of classes, encapsulating data and behaviour, and types, which are not encapsulated. Therefore, types can be seen as concrete types whose purpose is the definition of arbitrarily complex data structures. In particular, the instances of classes are objects, whereas the instances of types are (complex) values. The main differences between objects and values in O_2 can be summarized as follows [Deux90]:

- an object is a pair (identifier, value), an object can only be manipulated through methods, an object can be shared by other objects;
- a (complex) value does not have an identifier and cannot be shared by objects, a (complex) value can be directly manipulated through system-defined operators (i.e. no encapsulation is provided for values).

In order to illustrate the features of the O_2 data model, we show how the class Institute of the example database schema in Figure 15 is defined:

```
class Institute
        type tuple: (research-area: string,
                     institute-name: string,
                     address: Address, research-group: set(Team))
        public read institute-name, write research-area
        method init(string, string, Address, set(Team)):
        Institute is public;
```

The above definition illustrates three of the main components of the class definition. In particular:

- The clause **type tuple** specifies the structure of the objects, instances of the class. In the above example, the structure consists of a tuple of four elements; the last element of the tuple, in turn, is defined as a set. In addition to the **tuple** and **set** constructors shown in the above example, the **list** constructor is provided by the O_2 data model. These constructors may be arbitrarily nested, thus allowing the definition of complex object structures. Note that two of the tuple components have as domains other classes, namely 'address' and 'research-group'; therefore, objects may reference other objects.
- The clause **public** specifies which attributes of an instance of this class can be directly accessed in read or in write mode. In the above example, the attribute 'institute-name' can be directly read (i.e. no method is required for reading the value of this attribute). The attribute 'research-area' can be directly modified and thus can also be directly read. Indeed, a public write implies a public read. By contrast, all the other attributes can be accessed or manipulated only through methods encapsulating the object.
- The clause **method** specifies the signature of a method. Note that several **method** clauses can be specified in the definition of a class, one for each method that is defined for the class. Such a clause has as argument the name of the method, the list of argument types, and the type of the result. Moreover, a method can be declared as private or public. Private methods can be invoked

only by other methods of the same object. They cannot be invoked from outside the object. Private methods are usually methods that are used in the implementation of other methods.

A limitation of the O_2 data model is that class-attributes and class-methods are not supported.

Method implementations are defined by means of the **body** command. The following example shows the implementation of the method 'init' defined in the previous example. This method simply initializes an object by assigning to the object's attributes the values of the arguments.

```
body init (r-area: string, i-name: string, i-address: Address,
      i-teams: set(Team)): Institute
in class Institute co2{
        self -> research-area = r-area;
        self -> institute-name = i-name;
        self -> address = i-address;
        self -> research-group = i-teams;
        return(self)
}$
```

The O_2 data model supports multiple inheritance. Moreover, the special qualifier **from** allows implementations of methods from classes that are not direct superclasses to be inherited. As an example consider the following class definitions. In the definition the clause **inherits** specifies the direct superclasses of the class being defined.

```
class  Employee
        type tuple (name: string, address: Address, salary:
        integer)
        method init (string, string, integer): Employee;

class Temporary-Employee inherits Employee
        method init (string, string, integer) : Temporary-
        Employee;

class Student-Employee inherits Temporary-Student
        method init (string, string, integer) :
        Student-Employee from Employee;
```

In the above example, the class Student-Employee inherits the implementation of method 'init' from its indirect superclass Employee, and not from its direct superclass Temporary-Employee.

With respect to class extensions, O_2 has a similar approach to GemStone in that objects must be grouped into sets, and these sets must be managed by the applications since the system does not automatically maintain the extents of classes. In O_2, the definition of those sets can be handled in two different ways. The first is the same as that illustrated for GemStone. It involves defining a class whose instances are sets. The members of these sets are in turn constrained to be instances of the class whose extents must be maintained. An example of such a class definition is:

```
class Institute-set type set(Institute);
```

An alternative approach, which is useful mainly when a single extent must be provided for a class, is based on the use of complex values. Under this approach a complex value, having the set structure, is defined. An example of such a value definition is:

```
name an-Institute-set: set(Institute);
```

The **name** command has the effect of creating a value, having a set structure, and assigning to it the name 'Institute-set'. Once a value receives a name, the value becomes persistent and global, i.e. it can be referenced globally across the entire system. The following example presents a fragment of CO_2 code which shows how such a set is initialized and how an instance of the class Institute is added to it. In particular, the example shows how sets are manipulated in CO_2.

```
execute co2{ o2 Institute tmp;         /* declare a variable of type
                                          Institute */
        an-Institute-set = set();      /* initialize the set of
                                          institute to an empty set */
        tmp = new(Institute); /* create a new instance of class
                                          Institute */
        an-Institute-set = set(tmp);   /* add the new institute to
                                          the set */
}$
```

The O_2 query language has been defined as an extension of the SQL language. Queries, as in GemStone, can only be issued against sets and not against classes. The query that retrieves from the set 'an-Institute-Set' all institutes doing research on databases is formulated as follows:

```
Select x from x in an-Institute-Set where
       x.research-area = 'Databases'
```

The result of a query in O_2 is in general a complex value. In the above query, the result is a complex value defined as a set of instances of the class Institute. Both projections and joins can be formulated in the O_2 query language. Indeed, because the result of a query is a complex value and not an object or a class, projection and join operations do not generate new objects. Rather, these operations simply generate new values. It should be noted that query languages of other OODBMSs do not allow joins and allow only very restricted projection operations to avoid the problem of queries generating new objects. In general, this problem is overcome when the data model provides complex values, as in O_2. Queries may contain a Boolean combination of predicates as well as path-expressions. The following query retrieves all institutes doing research on databases and located in Italy:

```
Select x from x in an-Institute-Set where
x.research-area = 'Databases' and x.address.country='Italy'.
```

In addition, the query language provides a large number of features, including aggregate functions, subqueries, nesting and unnesting of complex objects, and result restructuring functionality. We refer the reader to [Clue89] for details on the O_2 query language.

2.253 Orion

The Orion system, initially developed at Microelectronics and Computer Corporation (MCC), is now a product marketed by Itasca. The data model of Orion has been developed as an extension of Common Lisp. The model is based on the notion of class, and unlike GemStone and O_2, also has an extensional notion. The Orion system has a number of advanced features, such as composite objects [KimW89a], object version and schema version, dynamic schema changes, and a sophisticated authorization mechanism. Moreover, three different architectures have been developed for this system. The first is completely centralized, whereas the second is based on a client/server architecture. Finally, the third architecture, in addition to the client/server approach, supports the distribution of the server itself, thus allowing the data to be distributed across several nodes in a network.

In order to illustrate the features of the Orion data model, we show how the class Institute of the example database schema in Figure 15 is defined:

```
make-class 'Institute'
              superclasses: nil
              attributes    '((research-area: domain string)
                              (institute-name: domain string)
                              (address: domain Address)
                              (research-group: domain (set-of
                               Team)))
```

The first clause in the above definition is the **superclasses** clause specifying the list of superclasses of the newly defined class. The second clause contains a list of attribute specifications. Each of these consists of an attribute name and an attribute domain. An attribute may be specified as multi-valued by using the key word **set-of** in the domain specification. In the above class definition, for example, the attribute 'research-group' is defined as having sets of instances of the class Team as values. Default values may be specified for attributes. This feature is not provided by either GemStone or O_2. The Orion data model supports multiple inheritance, and provides the possibility of defining class-attributes and class-methods. Orion does not support full encapsulation, since all attributes of an object can always be directly accessed for reading and writing.

Methods in Orion are written in Common Lisp and are defined through the command **def-method**. The following example shows the implementation of the method 'init' which initializes an object by assigning to the the object's attributes the values of the arguments.

```
(def-method init (self Institute) (r-area) (i-name) (i-address)
(i-teams)
        (setf research-area r-area)
        (setf institute-name i-name)
        (setf address i-address)
        (setf research-group i-teams))
```

In Orion, the system automatically inserts all instances upon creation into the extent of their classes. Therefore, the approach of Orion to class extents is much simpler than the approaches of GemStone and O_2. Indeed, in Orion, once an object is created, the application does not have to explicitly insert it into some set or collection. Note, however, that in Orion objects can be explicitly deleted by the applications, whereas in both GemStone and O_2 there is no delete command available to the applications. Therefore, in GemStone and O_2 referential integrity is maintained, since these systems remove objects only when they are no longer referenced. By contrast, in Orion an object may be removed even if there are references to it, and so dangling references may arise. In Orion nothing is done to prevent dangling references; simply, the system returns an exception when a reference to a deleted object is made. In Orion, therefore, OIDs are never re-used.

Orion provides a query language which allows content-based access to objects. The query language has some limitation in that no join operations may be performed and, moreover, projection operations have some limitations. Specifically, a projection operation must either be on a single attribute or retrieve all the attributes of the selected objects. This approach has been chosen because it ensures that the results of a query are always objects of some existing class. Thus no creation of objects arises as a result of queries. The query retrieving from the class 'Institute' all institutes doing research on databases is formulated in Orion as follows:

```
(Institute select :I (:I research-area = 'Databases'))
```

The query retrieving all institutes doing research on databases and located in Italy is formulated as follows:

```
(Institute select :I ((:I research-area = 'Databases') and
                      (:I address country = 'Italy'))).
```

Note that, unlike GemStone and O_2, queries are issued against classes. We refer the reader to [KimW90b] for an extensive discussion of the Orion system.

2.254 ObjectStore

The ObjectStore system has been developed starting from the C++ language as a system to provide persistency to C++ objects according to the persistent programming language approach. In particular, ObjectStore exploits the C++ class definition language as data definition language. Actually, an extended version of the C++ language is used that includes specific constructs for data management. Objects in a class can be transient – they can be deleted at the end of the program that created them – or persistent – permanently stored in the database. However, objects are manipulated by the applications independently from their persistency status. Persistence is thus an orthogonal property with respect to object use. However, persistent objects can be shared among several programs whereas transient objects cannot.

The type system and the data definition language in ObjectStore are based on the type system and the class definition mechanism of C++. In particular, C++ distinguishes between objects and values, and so does ObjectStore. More specifically, instances of base types such as character (char), integer (int), real (float), and string (char*) are values. Moreover, the struct constructor allows one to specify structured values, whereas an asterisk (*) is used to specify a reference (pointer). ObjectStore extends C++ with a set constructor. Set types can be specified by declarations of the form **os_Set** <*Argument Type*>, where *Argument Type* is the type of objects that can be members of the set being defined. For example, the type os_Set <Project *> is a set of references to objects of type Project. ObjectStore also extends C++ with multiset (bag) and list constructors; these constructors are **os_Bag** and **os_List** respectively.

In order to illustrate the features of the ObjectStore data model, we show how the class Institute of the example database schema in Figure 15 is defined:

```
class Institute {
        public:
        char* research-area;
        char* name;
        Address*    address;
        os_set<Team*> research-group;
}
```

In the above example, the **public** clause introduces the list of declarations of public features (attributes and methods) of the class. Such features can be directly accessed from outside the objects. In the above example, all features are public. The **private** clause, by contrast, introduces features that can only be accessed by methods of the class.

A further important extension of ObjectStore with respect to C++ is related to the notion of *relationship*. This extension allows one to specify inverse attributes, representing binary relationships. This functionality is requested through the keyword **inverse_member** associated with an attribute and followed by the inverse attribute name. ObjectStore automatically ensures relationship consistency. As an example, consider the schema in Figure 15 and suppose that a company can be a sponsor for at most a team and that an additional attribute sponsor-of, having class Team as the domain, is included in the class Company. The relationship between a team and a company corresponding to the fact that a team has a sponsor and vice versa can be modelled by the inverse attributes 'industrial-sponsor' in Team and 'sponsor-of' in Company. The relevant fragments of the definitions for classes Team and Company are expressed in ObjectStore as follows:

```
class Team {
        ...........
        Company*    industrial-sponsor
              inverse_member Company::sponsor-of;
        ............
}

class Company {
        ...........
        Team* sponsor-of
              inverse_member Company::industrial-sponsor;
        ............
}
```

Through the **os_Set** constructor, one-to-many and many-to-many relationships can be represented as well.

In ObjectStore, method implementation is specified through the C++ language extended with methods defined for the collection types built through the constructors **os_Set**, **os_Bag**, and **os_List**. Those methods include **insert(e)**, **remove(e)**, and **create** which, respectively, insert and delete an object from a collection and create a new collection. A **foreach(e,c)** statement for iterating over the elements of a collection c is also provided.

As an example suppose that the following methods are defined for the class Project (for simplicity they are not reported in the database schema in Figure 15):

```
void change-target (char* new-target);
void delete-part (Team* part);
void add-part (Team* part);
int total-budget ();
```

These operations change the project target, delete and add a participant to the project, and compute the total of all the budgets of all the teams participating to the project. The following are possible implementations for these operations:

```
void Project::change-target (char* new-target)
        {strcy(target,new-target); }

void Project::delete-part (Team* part)
        {participants -> remove(part); }

void Project::add-part (Team* part)
        {participants -> insert(part); }

int Project:: total-budget ()
        {int sum = 0; Team* t;
         foreach (t, participants) { sum += t -> budget; }
         return sum;
        }
```

Another C++ feature inherited by ObjectStore is related to class *constructors*. A class can have a method whose name is the same as the class name; this method is executed each time a new object of the class is created. Constructors can have arguments; several constructors can be associated with the same class (of course, the number of arguments must be different). In ObjectStore, as in many other OODBMSs, inherited methods can be redefined.

In ObjectStore, as in GemStone, persistence is not an automatic property of objects. To create an object or a persistent collection of objects the application must assign it a *name*, which is also referred to as the *persistent variable*. This name can be seen as a persistent reference, stored by the system, to the object. An object member of a persistent collection of objects is automatically made persistent. The statement for assigning a name to an object at object creation time has the following format:

```
Type&Name = Type :: create(DB_Name);
```

The following ObjectStore statements illustrate the specification of a collection, called 'Employees', and the creation of an object instance of class Employee which is made persistent by inserting it into the collection:

```
os_Set<Employee*>&Employees = os_Set<Employee*>:: create(my_db);

Employee* e = new(my_db) Employee;

Employees.insert(e);
```

Like C++, ObjectStore supports explicit object deletion through the **delete** operation. Referential integrity is ensured for relationships but not for attributes. For what concerns relationships, upon the deletion of a participating object, the relationship is also deleted. Thus, no dangling references can arise. It can also be specified that the object participating in the relationship with the deleted object must in turn be deleted.

ObjectStore also provides a query language, which can be used to select a set of objects from a collection by specifying a selection condition. The query result is a set of pointers to objects satisfying the condition. The query language statements can be embedded in C++ programs.

2.26 The ODMG standard

ODMG-93 [Catt97] is an OODBMS standard, consisting of a data model and data definition and manipulation languages. Its development was initiated in 1993 by a consortium including all the major companies producing OODBMSs (such companies cover 90 per cent of the market). This consortium includes as voting members Object Design, Objectivity, O2 Technology and Versant Technology, with several other companies as non-voting members. The ODMG-93 standard consists of the following components:

- a data model (ODMG object model)
- a data definition language (ODL)
- a query language (OQL)
- interfaces for the object-oriented programming languages C++, Smalltalk and Java, and data manipulation commands for embedding into these languages.

2.261 ODMG object model

The ODMG model supports both the notions of object and value – literal in the ODMG terminology. Literals can belong to: i) atomic types, such as long, short, float, double, Boolean, char, and string; ii) types defined through the set, bag, list, and array constructors; iii) enumeration types, defined by the **enum** constructor; iv) the predefined, structured types date, interval, time, and timestamp. Objects have a state and a behaviour. The object state consists of a number of properties, which can be either attributes or relationships. An attribute is related to a class, whereas a relationship is defined between two classes. Only binary relationships are supported by the ODMG model. However, such relationships can have different degrees: one-to-one, one-to-many, and many-to-many. A relationship is defined through the specification of a pair of traversal paths, enabling applications to traverse the logical connection between the objects participating in the relationship. Traversal paths are declared in pairs, one for each traversal direction of the relationship, very much like in ObjectStore. The **inverse** clause of the traversal path definition specifies that two traversal paths refer to the same relationship. The DBMS is in charge of ensuring referential integrity for relationships. Therefore, if an object participating in a relationship is deleted, any traversal path leading to this object is also deleted.

The ODMG class definition statement has the following format:

```
interface ClassName: SuperClassList
  [ (extent ExtentName
     key[s] AttributeList ]
  { persistent | transient }
  {       AttributeList
          RelationshipList
          MethodList
  }
```

where:

- the **extent** clause specifies that the extent of the class must be handled by the OODBMS; when no extent clause is specified, the extent must be handled by the applications;
- the **key**[**s**] clause can appear only if the **extent** clause is included in the class definition statement; it specifies that the attributes in the *AttributeList* are a key for all instances belonging to the extent and therefore no two different instances can have the same values for all these attributes;
- each attribute in *AttributeList* is specified as **attribute** *Domain Name*;

- each relationship in *RelationshipList* is specified as
  relationship *Domain Name*
  [**inverse** *Class*:: *InverseName*]
  where *Domain* can be either *Class* or a collection of *Class* elements, and *InverseName* is the name of the inversal traversal path, whose specification is optional;
- each method in *MethodList* is specified as
  Type *Name*(*ParameterList* [**raises** *ExceptionList*]
  where *ParameterList* is a list of parameters specified as
  in | **out** | **inout** *ParameterName*
  and the **raises** clause specifies the exceptions that the method execution can raise. No specific method definition language is defined in the ODMG standard, since the idea is that any object-oriented programming language, such as C++, Smalltalk and Java, should be used to such purpose.

The definition of class Institute from the example database schema in Figure 4 is specified in ODL as follows:

```
interface Institute
(       extent Institutes
        key name) persistent
{       attribute   string name;
        attribute   string research-area;
        attribute   Address address;
        attribute   set<Team> research-group; }
```

2.262 *Object manipulation and query language in ODMG*

ODMG does not support a single object manipulation language (OML for short); instead two different OMLs are provided, one related to C++ and the other one related to Smalltalk. These OMLs are based on different persistence policies, corresponding to different object management approaches in the two languages. For example, the OML for C++ supports an explicit delete operation (**delete_object**), whereas the OML for Smalltalk uses a garbage collection mechanism.

ODMG does, however, provide an SQL-like query language (OQL), based on queries of the form 'select-from-where'. For example, the query retrieving all institutes doing research on databases and located in Italy is expressed as follows:

```
Select distinct x from Institutes x where
x.research-area = 'Databases' and x.address.country='Italy'.
```

OQL is a functional language in which operators can be freely composed as a consequence of the fact that query results have a type that belongs to the ODMG type system. Thus queries can be nested and results of queries can be assigned to program variables. As a stand-alone language, OQL allows the user to query objects denoted by their names. A name can denote an object of any type (atomic, collection, structure, literal). The query result is an object whose type is inferred from the operators in the query expression.

OQL is a rich query language. OQL queries can return structured values having objects as components, as they can combine attributes of different objects. Path expressions and method invocations can be used in queries, as well as explicit joins and projections on object attributes. Finally, OQL supports aggregate functions, such as min, max, avg, sum, count, and subqueries.

2.27 The object-relational data model

Because of the relevance of object-oriented modelling capabilities, many vendors of relational DBMSs have started to extend their products with these capabilities. The main goal of such extensions is to maintain upward compatibility with existing relational applications and to provide customers with object-oriented extensions of SQL. Such extended systems are often called object-relational DBMSs to emphasize the fact that they support object-oriented extensions to the relational data model and SQL language. Object-relational DBMs include DB2 [Cham96], UniSQL [KimW94], Illustra/Informix [Illu], Oracle, and Sybase. In all these DBMSs the type system has been extended in some way with object-oriented modelling capabilities, and the possibility of defining methods to model user-defined operations on types has been introduced. In what follows, we discuss the most relevant type system extensions. Note, however, that to date no standard object-relational data model has been developed, even though some standardization efforts for the object-oriented extensions of SQL are under way as part of the new SQL standard, known as SQL-3 [Melt93]. Therefore, the extensions we discuss may not be present in all systems and substantial differences may exist among the various systems.

2.271 Primitive type extensions

Relational DBMSs usually support only predefined data types such as integers, floating points, strings and dates; such types are usually referred to as predefined primitive types. Object-relational DBMSs support both the definition of new primitive types, called user-defined primitive types, starting from the predefined primitive types, and the definition of user-defined operations for these new primitive types. Operations on predefined primitive types are inherited by the user-defined primitive types, unless they are explicitly redefined. Consider as an example the 'yen' type, corresponding to the Japanese currency. In a relational DBMS, this type can be represented as a numeric type with a certain scale and precision – for example, decimal (8,2). The predefined operations of the decimal type can be used on values of this type, but no other operations are available. Thus, any additional semantics – for example, converting yen to Italian liras – must be handled by the applications, and presented to the users according to a specific format.

In an object-relational DBMS, by contrast, a type 'yen' can be defined and proper functions can be associated with it, as illustrated by the following statements:

```
create distinct type yen as decimal (8,2)
        member function add(yen,yen) return yen,
        display function display(yen) return char(11).
```

2.272 Complex types

A complex, or structured, type includes one or more attributes. This notion corresponds to the notion of struct of the C language or to the notion of record of the Pascal language. Complex types are called *named row types* in SQL-3. As an example, consider the type 't_Address' defined as follows:

```
create type t_Address (country     char(20),
                        city        char(20),
                        number      integer,
                        street varchar (50));
```

Relations can contain attributes whose domain is a complex type. These relations are called *object tables* or *named row type tables* in SQL-3. For example, given the 't_Address' type defined above, the following is a definition of a named row table (in the definition we use the domain constructor **table of ref** that we introduce later on):

```
create table Institutes (research-area  char(20),
                         institute-name char(20),
                         address        t_Address,
                         research-group table of ref t_Team);
```

In the above relation, two attributes, namely 'address' and 'research-group', have as their domain a named row type. The above relation can be equivalently specified as:

```
 create type t_Institute (research-area   char(20),
                          institute-name  char(20),
                          address         t_Address,
                          research-group  table of ref t_Team);

create table Institutes of t_Institute.
```

In the first definition, the table and the type of its tuples are defined by a single statement, very much like in the traditional SQL. In the second definition, the table and the type of its tuples are defined separately. Therefore, the same type can be re-used in the definition of multiple tables.

Components of attributes, whose domain is a complex type, are accessed by means of the dot notation. For example, the cities where institutes are located can be denoted by the expression Institutes.address.city. Methods can be defined on complex types, as part of the type definition. With each complex type a constructor type is associated, having the same name of the type. As an example, the invocation

t_Address('Italy', 'Milano', 35, 'Via Comelico')

creates a value of type 't_Address'. The application must, moreover, provide methods for comparing and ordering values of complex types.

2.273 *Encapsulated types*

These types model objects or complex values whose components can only be accessed through methods. For example, had 't_Address' been defined as an encapsulated type, its structure could only have been accessed through methods, called *accessors* and *mutators*. Thus, an accessor method should be defined for accessing the 'country' attribute, another one for the attribute 'city', and so on. These types are also called *abstract data types* (adts) in SQL-3. The statement for defining an encapsulated type is **create value type** instead of **create type**.

2.274 *Reference types*

These types model relationships among type instances. They allow a column in a relation to refer to a tuple in another relation. A tuple in a relation is identified through its OID. For example, consider the following definition of a type 't_Team' and of a relation storing tuples of such type (in the definitions, we assume that a type 't_Company' modelling companies and 't_Employee' modelling employees are defined):

```
create type t_Team    (team-name           char(20),
                       industrial-sponsor  ref t_Company,
                       budget              integer,
                       staff               table of ref t_Employee);

create table Teams of t_Team.
```

Given the above definition of table 'Teams', the 'industrial-sponsor' attribute of a tuple in such table refers to a tuple whose type is 't_Company', corresponding to the company sponsoring the team represented by the tuple. The attributes of the referred tuple can be accessed by means of the dot notation. For example, the countries of the companies sponsoring the teams stored in the Teams relation are denoted by the following expression:

```
Teams.industrial-sponsor.location.country.
```

2.275 *Collection types*

Object-relational DBMSs support constructors for grouping several instances of a given type. Those constructors model collections of type instances and include the **set**, **multiset**, **list**, **array** and **table** (multiset of tuples) constructors. Referring to the above definition of the 'Institute' table, the domain of the 'research-group' attribute is defined through the '**table**' constructor. Specifically, the domain definition specifies that values for such attributes are tables (e.g. multisets) of references to instances of type 't_Team'.

Collection elements are accessed differently depending on the constructor used to define the collection. For instance, in the case of arrays, collection elements are denoted by indexes. As an example, given the attribute definition 'a_emp **array of** t_Employee', the expression 'a_emp [5]' denotes the fifth employee in the array.

Multisets and tables can be iterated over through an SQL query as any other table. As an example, the SQL statement

```
select t.team-name, (select e.employee-name
                     from t.staff e)
from Teams t where budget >'50,000;
```

returns the team name and the names of all employees in the staff of the team for all the teams whose budget is higher than $50 000.

2.276 Inheritance

Inheritance specifies subtype/supertype relationships among types. Subtypes inherit attributes and methods from their supertypes. Object-relational DBMSs allow one to specify inheritance relationships among types and among relations. The following definitions specify types 't_Permanent' and 't_Consultant' as subtypes of the 't_Employee' type:

```
create type t_Employee     (address          t_Address,
                            employee-name    Varchar(50));

create type t_Permanent    (monthly-salary   decimal (8,2),
                            status           Varchar(50))
  under t_Employee;

create type t_Consultant   (daily-wage       decimal (8,2))
  under t_Employee;
```

The following definitions, by contrast, specify inheritance relationships among relations:

```
create table Employees of t_Employee;
create table Permanents of t_Permanent under Employees;
create table Consultants of t_Permanent under Employees;
```

At the data level, these definitions imply that instances of 'Permanents' and 'Consultants' relations are also instances of the 'Employees' relation and these instances inherit all attributes defined for the 'Employees' relation. Inheritance among types and relations also implies method inheritance and overloading. Overriding and late binding are supported. Multiple inheritance is also supported.

2.277 LOBs

Object-relational DBMSs provide LOB (large object) types to support the storage of multimedia objects, such as documents, images, and audio. LOBs are semantically stored as columns of relations. Physically, however, they are stored outside the relations, typically in external files. Usually, for efficiency reasons, such external files are not manipulated under transactional control (or at least, logging for such long data is disabled). LOBs can be either CLOBs (character LOBs) or BLOBs (binary LOBs). Ad hoc indexing mechanisms are exploited for efficiently supporting storage and retrieval operations for LOBs. The following relation definition illustrates the specification of an attribute containing textual information and an attribute containing an image:

```
create table Patients (name              char(20),
                       ssn               integer,
                       age               integer,
                       clinical-register CLOB
                       x-ray             LOB);
```

2.28 Java and databases

Java has quickly established itself as the programming language for Web applications. The increasingly wider use of Web-related technologies, together with the fact that Java can be considered as the last evolution of other object-oriented languages, combining the advantages of previous languages such as C++ and Smalltalk, has made Java the most commonly used object-oriented programming language.

Different alternatives have been proposed to enhance Java with persistence capabilities. The simplest is based on the serialization facility of the language. Such facility allows one to flatten objects into a stream of bytes that, when read later, can recreate objects equivalent to those that were written into the stream. This approach, however, is viable for a small amount of data for which reliability and other typical DBMS features are not required. A second solution is based on the use of relational DBMSs (RDBMSs) to store Java data, connecting Java applications to an RDBMS through a set of Java database connectivity (JDBC™) classes. These classes, introduced by JavaSoft, represent a standard SQL database interface. Storing Java data in a relational database actually requires much more work than enabling just access to an RDBMS; Java objects must be mapped to the relational schema. Such mapping can be performed with the help of commercial tools that provide support for obtaining a relational database to store a set of objects, relying on mapping mechanisms between the object and the relational data model.

A third solution is that of Orthogonally Persistent Java (OPJ). This is the goal of the Forest project at Sun Microsystems Laboratories. Persistent object systems, which rely on the notion of orthogonal persistence, automate data management tasks and provide a single model for both short-term and long-term data. This means, for instance, that there is no visible or separate database from the perspective of the programmer. In the OPJ approach, the Java Virtual Machine (JVM) is responsible for managing the entire storage hierarchy, thus the programmer simply views the Java platform as a database. Note that in this approach persistence is provided, but many database features (such as querying, data sharing, durability, etc.) are missing.

Finally, Java objects can be stored in an OODBMS. The impact of Java on the OODBMS world has been considerable and most commercial OODBMSs have been extended to offer native support for storing Java objects. OODBMSs such as

POET and ObjectStore, initially developed to store persistent C++ objects, now provide versions to store persistent Java objects. This can be achieved by minimal modifications of the Java code in applications. Such extensions are based on the use of a pre-processor that automatically prepares objects for storage in an object database. The development effort when one uses an OODBMS with native support for Java is significantly lower than the effort required when one uses a RDBMS, since the modifications required to Java applications in order to add persistence-related operations are very small. As a consequence of the development and increasing popularity of Java, the second version of the ODMG standard has added a Java programming language binding to the C++ and Smalltalk bindings defined in the first version. Moreover, the influence of Java is also reflected in many changes to the object model, such as the notion of interface and the introduction of two different inheritance hierarchies.

2.29 Conclusions

OODBMSs appeared on the market more than a decade ago as revolutionary systems with respect to existing (mainly relational) DBMSs. They offer several advantages over RDBMSs, such as direct storage of complex data and representation not only of data but also of behaviour. Another important advantage of OODBMSs, related to the increasing usage of object technology, is represented by the fact that a single paradigm (the object-oriented one) is used in all phases of software development, from analysis to coding, and at all levels. Thus there is no need to separately design the database structure, and there are no communication problems between the DBMS and the programming language. The object paradigm, and thus OODBMSs, also offers great potential for heterogeneous systems integration.

Since the early years, OODBMSs have certainly improved as products and today represent a mature technology, which has been able to evolve and adapt itself to the constant technological innovations. At the same time, some competitor systems have emerged, such as persistent object systems and object-relational DBMSs. However, the application requirements met by these kinds of systems are different from those of OODBMSs. Thus, it seems that these technologies can coexist. For example, OODBMSs offer a number of advantages over object-relational DBMSs for applications that require seamless integration with a specific object-oriented programming language and use a navigational approach to data access.

To overcome the difficulties due to the presence of several different systems, each one with some distinctive characteristics, a standard for OODBMSs has been defined. However, although a consortium comprising almost all OODBMS vendors has defined the standard, much work still needs to be done in making existing systems compliant. For example, the standard defines a declarative query language (OQL), but only a few OODBMSs claim to support it. This gives the impression that the companies participating in ODMG are not actively supporting the standard, and it seems to have gained more attention from academia than from industry.

OODBMSs, far from having reached a level of usage similar to that of RDBMSs after a comparable period from their birth, are enjoying success in only a number of vertical markets, such as telecommunications and finance. However, they seem to be a promising technology for handling Web-related semi-structured data and several OODBMS vendors are already offering tools and facilities for storing and querying XML data. The last chapter of this book will discuss this topic in more detail.

2.3 Active database systems

Traditional DBMSs are *passive*, i.e. queries, updates, and transactions are executed only when explicitly requested. Many applications, such as inventory control, co-operative processing, and factory automation, are not well supported by passive DBMS. Those applications require automatic monitoring of conditions defined over the database state and the ability to take actions (possibly subject to timing constraints) when the state of the underlying database changes. A database system augmented with such capabilities is an *active database system*, i.e. it is able to react to events. Therefore an active database system monitors the conditions triggered by events, representing database updates or occurrences external to the database, and if some specified conditions are evaluated to true, then some actions are executed.

Conventional solutions to the task of monitoring event occurrences and reacting to them are based on encoding into application programs specific code to perform such tasks, or on building some special application software that periodically polls the database to determine relevant events. The first solution has several drawbacks, including the fact that the specifications of the events and the corresponding conditions and actions are spread into possibly several application programs, thus making their maintenance very difficult. Moreover, these specifications are coded in terms of the application language, and thus are very difficult to understand, being expressed as program code fragments. Under the second solution, the specification of events, conditions, and actions is centralized in a single application; however, events, conditions, and actions are still expressed in a low-level language. The right polling frequency is a critical issue in such a solution. If polling is occasional, the system may miss the right time to react; if, by contrast, polling is very frequent, the performance of the system may be adversely affected.

Because of the drawbacks of the above solutions, many systems have been extended with a built-in generalized subsystem providing active capabilities. All approaches are centred on the notion of *active rule*, also called *trigger*; an active rule specifies in a high-level declarative language the action to be executed upon the occurrence of a given event; this event is called the *triggering event* of the rule. A rule may contain a condition which is tested when the event occurs to determine if the action is actually executed.

The integration of active capabilities into DBMSs started in the framework of relational DBMS and has been pursued according to two basic strategies: i) extending current relational DBMSs in order to include active rule facilities; ii) using database technology to efficiently implement OPS5-like production rule languages. Examples of the first category are the Starburst rule system [Wido96a] and the Postgres Rule System [Pota96]. Examples of the second category are the Relational Production Language [Delc88], developed from production rule systems typical of AI, and RDL1 [Kier90], developed in the context of deductive database systems. Lately, however, efforts have been reported to extend object-oriented DBMS with trigger facilities [Bert00a], (Gatz92], [Lieu96]. However, despite several differences in the various developments, there exists a common understanding of what an active rule is and its various dimensions. A basic model for active rules is presented in Section 2.31, while Sections 2.32 and 2.33 discuss issues for active rule modes and the architectural approaches to implement active rules. Section 2.34 presents a short overview of the Starburst active rule model, while active rule languages of commercial DBMSs are discussed in Section 2.35. A basic model, such as the one we describe in Section 2.31, is quite independent from any specific data model. However, additional issues arise when introducing an active rule model developed in the framework of a relational data model into an object-oriented data model. These issues are discussed in Section 2.36. Finally Section 2.37 discusses active rule languages developed in the AI area.

2.31 Basic concepts

A common specification paradigm for active rules is based on the notion of event-condition-action-rule (*ECA-rule*). An ECA-rule has the form

```
ON Event IF Condition DO Action
```

where the first two components – the event and the condition – specify a 'situation' and the third component – the action – specifies a 'reaction'. The semantics of such a rule can be characterized as 'when **E**vent occurs, check **C**ondition and if it holds, execute **A**ction'. An informal example of the ECA-rule is the following. Let Employee be a relation and Salary an attribute of this relation.

```
ON Update of Employee's Salary
IF the new salary is greater than $10,000
DO Rollback the update.
```

This monitors updates to the attribute Salary and, whenever an update increases a salary over $10,000, undoes the update.

There have been proposals for several variations to the above simple rule format to increase the expressive power of ECA-rules which we will discuss in the remainder of this section. We will say that:

- a rule is *activated* if the event in the rule has happened and has been detected by the system;
- a rule is *evaluated* if the condition in the rule has been evaluated (by possibly a query against the database);
- a rule is *executed* if the action in the rule has been actually performed.

The common processing model is that a rule must be first activated, then evaluted, and finally executed, although these three steps may actually be performed at quite different times. We discuss rule processing models in Section 2.32.

2.311 *Events*

The notion of event is a basic one in the ECA paradigm for rules. An event is something which happens within the database or outside the database and which is of interest for a given application domain. The possible event types which can be referred to in rules can be categorized as follows:

- **Database updates and events**: in a relational database, update operations include insertions into tables, deletions from tables, and updates to columns of tables. Events may refer to the beginning of these operations or to the end. In the former case, the rule where the event is referred to is activated (and possibly executed) before the update is executed, in the latter the rule is activated (and possibly executed) after the update has been executed. Events may also refer to queries performed against the database, or to other database operations, such as user login, begin-transaction, abort-transaction, commit-transaction, authorization grant and revoke.
- **Temporal events**: a temporal event may be specified by giving the time at which the rule must be activated. The time specification may be given as absolute time (for example, 3 March 1996 at 10:00am) or as a periodic expression (for example, each 15 minutes; each week, on Monday, at 8:00).
- **Application-defined events**: an event can be external to the database (for example, a temperature increase reported by a sensor). In such cases, the event cannot be directly detected by the DBMS. Rather, it is detected by the application programs that notify the DBMS of the event occurrence. Usually, the event is given a name, which is referred to in the rule(s) associated with the event. To support application-defined events, the DBMS must make available some special operation, such as the raise operation, which is invoked by the application program to signal the occurrence of an event to the DBMS.

These simple events may be combined into *composite events* through the use of composition operators. Possible composition operators include:

- **logical operators**: the events are combined using operators such as AND, OR, NOT;
- **sequence**: a rule may be activated whenever two or more events arise according to a particular ordering in time;
- **temporal composition**: a rule may be activated by a specific combination of temporal and non-temporal events arising (for example, five seconds after the occurrence of event E1).

In general, there is a trade-off between the minimality of the operator set, the ease of use, and efficiency. Ensuring efficiency for composite event detection is quite difficult and thus, most DBMS do not support composite events.

In rule languages, developed in the AI context, the event component is often not present. Rules have the simpler format: Condition **DO** Action. In such languages, a rule is activated whenever the condition becomes true; the rule is thus considered to be always activated. Therefore rule designers do not have to worry about identifying the events that may activate a given rule. The reason for including the event component is to improve efficiency. In database systems, where efficiency is crucial, the specification of the event activating a given rule allows the system to evaluate the condition part of the rule only when the event actually happens as opposed to evaluating the condition for any possible event. Because the evaluation of a condition may be very expensive (see below), such an approach makes rule processing more efficient.

2.312 *Conditions*

The condition component of a rule specifies an additional check which is performed once a rule is activated and before it is executed. An activated rule is executed only if the condition is evaluated to the Boolean value True. In general, conditions are expressed very much in the same way as queries are expressed. Because most systems use SQL as the query language [Melt93], conditions in rules are expressed in SQL as well. However, depending on the specific rule language, different condition formats may be allowed, such as:

- **search predicates**: this type of condition uses a restricted version of the query language. In most cases, conditions are expressed very much like the WHERE clause of the SELECT statement of SQL;
- **database queries**: this type of condition uses the complete query language. A query is issued as part of the condition evaluation, and if the query returns a non-empty result, the condition is evaluated to true;
- **application procedures**: this type of condition uses a procedure written in some host programming language, with possibly embedded database queries. The procedure is executed as part of the condition evaluation and if the procedure returns a proper result (e.g. True), the condition is evaluated to True.

Predicates in a condition may also refer to special system variables (such as the CURRENT USER) or to the old and new database state. The latter capability, often supported by the *delta tables mechanism*, is particularly important in that it supports conditions based on database state transitions.

2.313 *Actions*

Several actions may be executed by a rule. These may include:

- **data updates**: very often the goal of rules is to automatically execute updates on data based on other updates performed on the same or other data. In general, all possible data modification statements, such as the INSERT, DELETE, and UPDATE statements of SQL, can be invoked;

- **queries and other database operations**: both simple and complex queries can be used, such as all queries that can be expressed by the SELECT command of SQL. Among the database operations that can be invoked, we recall operations for transaction management, such as commit and abort;
- **calls to application procedures**: a rule may contain a call to an application procedure that may perform any general computation, including other updates to the database.

A rule may invoke a single action or a sequence of actions. For example, consider the SQL data manipulation commands, such as Insert, Delete or Update. A rule may contain in its action component an Insert, followed by an Update. It is important to note that most of the above action types may activate, as side effects of their executions, other rules. If rules are not carefully programmed, cyclic activations, leading to non-termination, may arise.

2.32 Issues

Developing a rule processing system entails solving several issues. Two important issues concern the rule processing model and the interaction of the rule processing activity with the usual query and transaction processing that we discuss in the remainder of this section.

A simple execution model is reported in Table 2.3.

Table 2.3 A simple rule processing model

```
Activity 1
    while true do
        {detect events;
        trigger appropriate rules}
Activity 2
    while there are triggered rules do
        { 1. select a triggered rule R;
          2. evaluate R's condition C;
          3. if C then execute R's action}
```

According to the model, rule processing is organised into two activities: the first deals with detecting events and triggering the corresponding rules; the second deals with actually evaluating the triggered rule and possibly executing the rule actions. Because in general several rules may have been triggered, the second activity is organised as a loop selecting a rule at the time for evaluation and execution. The two activities are usually executed concurrently. A rule as part of the execution of its action may in turn generate events which must be detected to determine the triggered rules. However, a given rule may not be necessarily processed as soon as it has been triggered. For example, a rule may be triggered at the beginning of a transaction execution and processed by Activity 2 at the end of the transaction. In this respect, there is a large number of variations among the various rule systems.

An important question is how often Activity 2 must be invoked. There are various options:

1 always, whenever Activity 1 generates triggered rules;

2 whenever an atomic manipulation operation is performed, such as insertion, deletion or update of a single tuple;

3 whenever a data manipulation command, such as an SQL Delete, Insert or Update, has been executed;

4 at the end of the transaction;

5 upon user demand.

Note that data manipulation commands, such as the SQL ones, are set-oriented and therefore consist of several atomic operations – one for each tuple in the set manipulated by the operation. Therefore, if option (2) above were chosen, a single data manipulation command manipulating a set of tuples would result in invoking Activity 2 a number of times equal to the number of elements in the set, whereas under option (3) Activity 2 would be invoked only once at the end of the command.

An important distinction among rule processing models is between *iterative* and *recursive* processing, related to the fact that a rule may trigger during Step 3 of Activity 2 of its processing other rules. The difference in processing arises, for example, when a rule executes a sequence of actions. The processing is recursive if it is invoked after each action within the sequence; it is iterative if it is invoked only when all the actions in the sequence have been completed.

A relevant issue related to rule processing is how to select a rule at Step 1 in Activity 2 whenever several rules have been triggered. The presence of several triggered rules, called *conflicting rules*, is a common situation in most systems. Rules may be triggered simultaneously for many reasons, including the fact that a given event may have several rules associated with it, or that a rule is not selected at Step 1 and thus is still triggered when Step 1 is executed again. To solve such a problem, different approaches are possible including random selection, use of priorities, and use of rule static properties (such as activation time of the rule). These approaches may also be combined. For example, several systems allow users to state the priority of a rule against other rules. However, the ordering obtained by such priorities is often a partial ordering. Therefore, whenever two conflicting rules are not comparable under the partial ordering, derived from the priorities, a random selection is performed. The selection criteria are quite important because selecting different rules for evaluation and execution may lead to different final database states. An alternative approach consists of *concurrently executing* all rules that are triggered rather than selecting just one at Step 1. Thus all rules are concurrently evaluated and their actions are also concurrently executed. Such an approach requires the use of a concurrency control mechanism for synchronizing the actions of the various rules as well as the condition evaluation activity.

Another important issue is related to the *coupling mode* between the transaction during which a rule (or set of rules) has been triggered and the evaluation and execution of the rule (the set of rules). A basic question concerns when during the execution of the transaction the condition of a triggered rule is actually evaluated and when the action is executed once the condition has been evaluated. The coupling modes can therefore refer to the coupling between the event detection and the condition evaluation (EC mode), and between the condition evaluation and the action execution (CA mode). For example, consider a rule that has been triggered by an update performed by the transaction. The condition of the rule may be evaluated as soon as possible after the event detection and the action executed immediately afterwards; or the action can be deferred at the end of the transaction. Yet another possibility is evaluating the condition at the end of the transaction, thus also deferring the action at the end of the transaction. The condition (action) of a rule may also be evaluated (executed) outside the scope of the transaction that triggered the rule. The following coupling modes can thus be devised: immediate, deferred, and decoupled. Under the immediate mode the rule is processed as soon as possible; under the deferred mode the rule is processed at the end of the transaction; under the decoupled mode the rule is processed outside the transaction as part of a separate transaction. The last mode actually has two variations, referred to as d*ependent coupling* and *independent coupling*. Under dependent coupling, the separated transaction is activated only if the original transaction commits. The independent coupling does not impose such a restriction. Because a transaction usually makes several changes to the database state, different choices for the time of the rule condition evaluation and the rule action execution may result in a different behaviour. In general, the choice of when processing a rule depends on the data semantics and, thus, most rule systems allow users to specify when rules are to be processed within transactions.

A final issue concerns the *termination* of the rule processing activity. Because a rule may activate other rules as a side effect of its execution, there is a risk of non-terminating executions. When a large number of rules must be programmed, it is difficult for programmers to ensure that rule execution will always terminate, whatever the state of the database. This is still an open problem and no satisfactory solutions have yet been devised. In particular, deciding the termination of a set of rules is possible only under a number of very restrictive conditions. Current systems either accept the possibility of non-terminating executions (thus leaving the responsibility to the rule designers) or impose a limit on the number of rules that can be handled during rule processing. Another possibility is imposing some syntactic restrictions on rules – however, those restrictions are in general too strict for most real applications. The difficulty in predicting the combined behaviour of large sets of rules has hindered the widespread use of active rules in real applications which can easily require hundreds or thousands of rules.

It is important to note that the choices among the various dimensions concerning rule languages and rule processing models are not completely orthogonal. We refer the reader to [Wido96b] for an extensive discussion on the above topics.

2.33 Architectures

In order to support a rule language, a DBMS must include in its archictecture a number of specialized components for (i) rule definition and management; (ii) event detection; (iii) rule execution. There are three main approaches to extending a DBMS architecture for rule support:

- The layered approach consists of adding a specialized layer on top of a passive (non-active) DBMS. This approach can be implemented easily and moreover allows one to add the same functions for rule support to different DBMSs, making such an approach particularly suitable when integrating heterogeneous DBMSs. It has, however, two main drawbacks. The performance may not be good because of the communication overhead between the various levels and the possible duplication of certain activities. Moreover, it may be difficult or impossible to support typical DBMS functions for rules, such as authorization and coupling modes.
- The integrated approach consists of completely revisiting the DBMS architecture by modifying existing components and adding new components for rule support. This approach has good performance and it allows one to fully support the rule language. It is, however, much more difficult to implement because it may require extensive modifications to the existing, passive DBMS. In some cases, the entire active DBMS must be built from scratch.
- The compilation approach consists of compiling all functions for rule support into application procedures and database operations. This approach has the advantage that no special activity is required at run-time. The complexity in the DBMS implementation is reduced and the performance improves.  However, this approach has a number of serious drawbacks. First, it can only be applied to limited classes of rule languages. Second, all events must be detected by the compiler. Therefore, the only events that can be detected are the database events; no temporal or external events can be detected. Third, under this approach it is not possible (or it is very difficult) to support rules that recursively trigger themselves or other rules. Such limitation is too restrictive for most applications.

There are a number of interesting implementation issues concerning efficiency of rule processing. In general, the most critical aspects are related to the condition evaluation which may introduce significant overhead; the rule retrieval when dealing with large rule sets; the event detection especially when composite events are supported. Several approaches based on finite state automata and Petri nets have been proposed to efficiently detect composite events.

2.34 Research relational prototypes – the Starburst rule system

Because of the interesting issues involved, active database systems have been intensively investigated from both a theoretical and an architectural point of view. Among the research efforts, the Starburst rule system is the most notable in that a number of important concepts in rule processing were established by this system. Moreover, the Starburst rule processing has been fully implemented and integrated within the Starburst extensible DBMS [Haas90]. Therefore the impact of rule processing on all the other aspects of a DBMS, such as query processing, authorization, concurrency control and recovery, has been fully investigated. In the remainder of this section, we discuss such a rule system to show in detail a concrete example of a rule language. Other research prototypes, similar to the Starburst rule system, include the RPL system developed in an AI context and discussed in Section 2.37 [Delc88], the Ariel rule system, also based on the AI production rules paradigm [Hans92], and the Postgres rule system [Pota96]. Other research efforts include the Alert project [SchrU91], whose goal is to investigate how to support active rules on top of a passive DBMS with minimal extensions, and the Heraclitus project [Ghan93], whose goal is to extend persistent programming languages with active capabilities.

The general format of the rule definition statement is as follows. In the syntax, clauses between square brackets denote the optional clauses of the statement:

```
create rule name on table
when triggering operations
[if condition]
then list of actions
[precedes list of rules]
[follows list of rules]
```

In the above statement, name is the name to be assigned to the rule for future reference to the rule as part of other rule management statements. The **when** clause lists the events upon which the rule is activated. In Starburst, the possible events are: **inserted**, **deleted**, **updated**, **updated(c1, c2,..., cn)**. These events correspond to the insert, delete and update operations on a table. In particular, the **updated** event arises whenever any column of table is updated, whereas the **updated(c1, c2,..., cn)** arises whenever one of the columns c1,c2,....,cn is modified. Note that a rule in Starburst can be activated by several events. Therefore, whenever one of the operations listed in the **when** clause is executed on the table specified in the **on** clause, the rule is activated. The **if** clause specifies a SQL query statement representing the condition to be evaluated for actually executing the rule. Any SQL query can be used; the condition is evaluated to the Boolean value True if the query has a non-empty result. When the **if** condition is missing, the condition of the rule is considered to be always True.

The **then** clause specifies a sequence of actions to be executed by the rule. Actions are executed according to the order in which they are listed in this clause. The actions that can be executed include SQL data manipulation operations (insert, delete, update, select) on the same table specified in the **on** clause of the rule, or on other tables; data definition operations (create/drop table, create/drop view, drop rule); and the rollback transaction management operation.

Finally, the **precedes** and **follows** clauses are used to specify the priority of the rule being defined with respect to other rules. Such priority is used by the rule processing system for choosing a rule in the event that several rules have been activated simultaneously. In particular, the rule being defined has a higher priority than the rules listed in the **precedes** clause and has a lower priority than the rules in the **follows** clause.

The following example shows an active rule that performs a rollback whenever the salary of an employee in a department is greater than the salary of the manager of the department. In the example, we consider a relation Employee, whose schema contains the attributes emp#, salary, and dno# representing the number, salary and department of an employee, and a relation Department, whose schema contains the attributes dno#, and mgr#, representing the number and manager of a department. The rule is to be activated whenever the salary of an employee changes or whenever the department of an employee changes, whenever a new employee is inserted.

```
create rule high-salary on employee
when inserted, updated(salary), updated(dno)
if SELECT * FROM Employee E, Employee M, Department D
       WHERE E.salary > M.salary AND E.dno# = D.dno# AND
       D.mgr# = E.emp#
then rollback;
```

Note that the above rule actually implements the integrity constraint stating that an employee cannot have a salary higher than the salary of the manager of his/her department. Because updates on the table Department may lead to a violation of such an integrity constraint, a similar active rule should be defined on the relation Department.

In many cases, rules may need to refer to the set of tuples that are actually deleted, inserted or updated. It is important to be able to refer exactly to such tuples in order to limit the evaluation of the rule condition to only those tuples. For this purpose, the Starburst rule system provides the notion of *transition tables*. These are **inserted**, **deleted**, **new-updated**, **old-updated**, which correspond to the basic SQL data manipulation statements. The **inserted (deleted)** table contains all the tuples inserted into (deleted from) a table by an Insert (Delete) SQL operation. The **new-updated** and **old-updated** transition tables are related to the Update SQL operation; they contain, respectively, the modified tuples after the update and before the update. The transition tables can be referred to in both the condition and action components of rules. The following examples, from [Wido96a], illustrate the use of the transition tables.

```
create rule big-raise on employee
when updated(salary)
if EXISTS (SELECT * FROM old-updated ou, new-updated nu
       WHERE nu.salary - ou.salary > 10 AND nu.emp#=ou.emp#)
then rollback;

create rule ins-to-hp on employee
when inserted
then insert into high-paid
       SELECT * FROM inserted WHERE salary > 100
follows big-raise;
```

The first of the above rules enforces the constraint that a salary cannot increase by more than $10. To determine whether an updated tuple satisfies the constraint, the value of the attribute salary of the tuple before the update is compared with the value of the attribute salary of the tuple after the update. The second rule inserts into the high-paid table all newly inserted employees whose salary exceeds the amount of $100. Note that in the first rule the transition tables are referred to in the condition component of the rule, whereas in the second rule the transition table is referred to in the action component. Moreover, note that the rule ins-to-hp has lower priority with respect to the big-raise rule. Therefore, whenever both rules are activated – for example, a new employee is inserted and then his salary is increased in the same transaction – rule big-raise is executed before rule ins-to-hp.

In addition to the create rule command, the Starburst rule language includes a number of other commands for rule manipulation, such as drop for removing a rule, alter for modifying a rule, deactivate for enabling a rule, and activate for disabling a rule.

In Starburst, rules are executed by default at the end of transactions. Other *rule processing points* during transaction execution can be explicitly requested in application programs by means of the *process rules* command. This command may, optionally, receive as argument a rule or set of rules; the specified rule(s), if activated when the process rules command is invoked, is (are) then executed. If no rule is given as input, all activated rules are executed. We refer the reader to [Wido96a] for a discussion on Starburst rule semantics and architectural issues related to rule processing.

2.35 Commercial relational approaches

Triggers are supported by most of the current commercial relational DBMSs. There are, however, several variations among the models supported by the various DBMSs. Here we will discuss briefly the models of the most well-known systems. We also include a short discussion on triggers for SQL3 – the new SQL standard.

2.351 Oracle

The statement for creating a trigger in Oracle has the following format (in the syntax used for the statement, the clauses enclosed in {} denote multiple choices, not always exclusive):

```
create trigger name
{before | after} {insert | delete | update [of list-of-column-
names]}
on table-name
[referencing references]
[for each row]
[when condition]
PL/SQL block;
```

A first aspect to note in the above statement is that in Oracle triggers can be executed before or after the triggering event arises. Such an option is specified by the clause **before** or the clause **after** which follow the name of the table on which the trigger is defined; of course, the two options are mutually exclusive. The only events that can be specified in Oracle are those related to the SQL manipulation operations – it is not possible to include application-specified events or queries among the events of a trigger. The operations specified as events in a trigger are called *triggering statements*. Note that several events (among the supported ones) can be specified in a single trigger. However, the same event for a given table can appear in only one trigger. The **for each row** clause is used to specify that the trigger must be executed for each tuple involved in the execution of the SQL statement, referenced as event in the trigger. Therefore the trigger may be executed multiple times according to the number of tuples modified by the SQL statement. When such a clause is omitted, the trigger is executed only once after or before the execution of the entire SQL statement, referenced as event in the trigger. Therefore, by combining the before and after options with the options concerning when to execute a trigger, four different possibilities are obtained, as summarized here by Table 2.4 reported from [Orac92].

Table 2.4 Options resulting from the before/after option with the statement/row options

		FOR EACH ROW option
BEFORE option	**BEFORE statement trigger:** the trigger is fired once before executing the triggering statement	**BEFORE row trigger:** the trigger is fired before modifying each row affected by the triggering statement
AFTER option	**AFTER statement trigger:** the trigger is fired once after executing the triggering statement	**AFTER row trigger:** the trigger is fired after modifying each row affected by the triggering statement

The **when** clause, specifying the condition component of the trigger, can be specified only when the trigger is executed for each tuple. The condition is restricted to a very simple format – it can only be a simple predicate involving just the attributes of the modified tuple, therefore no subqueries or joins are allowed. The **referencing** clause supports the declaration of names for denoting the old and/or values of the updated tuples. The references contained in such a clause are specified according to the following formats:

```
old as old-value-tuple-name    /* indicates the name to be used
                                  for the old value */
new as new-value-tuple-name    /* indicates the name to be used
                                  for the new value */
```

If such variable names are not provided in the trigger specification, some system names are provided that are OLD and NEW respectively.

Finally, the PL/SQL block represents the action component of the trigger. PL/SQL is a programming language used among other things for coding stored procedures. It provides all constructs of general programming languages, such as variable declarations and control statements. A PL/SQL block may contain both queries and updates.

The following example, from [Orac92], illustrates the statement for creating triggering. The trigger in this example checks that whenever a new employee is inserted or the salary or job of an employee is modified, the salary falls within a specified range. The range for each job is specified in a table sal_guide. This constraint, however, must not be enforced for the president of the company.

```
create trigger salary_check
before insert OR update of salary, job
on employee
for each row
when (new.job <> 'PRESIDENT')
declare          /* start of PL/SQL block */
    minsal      number;
    maxsal      number;
begin
    select minsal, maxsal from sal_guide
    where job =:new.job;
    if (:new.sal < minsal OR :new.sal > maxsal)
    then raise_application_error (-20601, 'salary' | | :new.sal | |
    'out of range for job' | | :new.job | | 'for employee' | |
    :new.name);
    end if;
end;             /* end of PL/SQL block */
```

Oracle provides a number of other commands for trigger management, including **alter trigger** with the options **enable** and **disable** to activate and deactivate triggers, and **drop trigger** to remove a trigger.

2.352 *Sybase*

Sybase provides two variants for the trigger definition statement. One does not allow updates on specific columns to be included among the triggering events, whereas the other does not have such restrictions. The formats of the two variants are presented below:

```
create trigger name on table-name
for {insert | delete | update}
as SQL-statements;
```

```
create trigger name on table-name
for {insert | update}
as [if update (column-name)]
[{and | or} update (column-name)]...]
as SQL-statements;
```

Note that the second format does not include the delete among the triggering events. Moreover, it is possible to specify composite update events as the conjunction or disjunction of two update events through the connectives **and** and **or**. Examples of composite update events are:

```
update (salary) or update (job)
update (salary) and update (job).
```

Whereas the first event fires the trigger when one of the columns salary and job is modified, the second event fires the trigger only when both columns are modified. Note that the composite update events of Sybase obtained by disjunction can also be supported by Oracle, because Oracle supports the specification of multiple update events in the same trigger. By contrast, the composite update events obtained by conjunction cannot be modelled in Oracle.

Sybase, as most DBMSs, provides a way to reference the old/new states of modified tables. However, whereas in Oracle users can choose their own names, in Sybase there are only two table names, predefined by the system: **deleted** and **inserted**. These tables contain, respectively, all tuples that were deleted or inserted by the triggering operations. Updates are handled as deletions followed by insertions. Therefore, whenever a tuple is modified, the old value of the tuple is in the **deleted** table, whereas the new one is in the **inserted** table. Finally, note that a trigger may contain a list of SQL statements, including calls to stored procedures as an action component. Moreover, the **rollback transaction** and **rollback trigger** commands may be included in the action component of a trigger. Their effect is to roll back the entire transaction and the effects of the triggering operations respectively.

The following example illustrates the statement for creating triggers. It considers three relations: an employee relation, a project relation, and a temp relation. Each employee is assigned to a project. Whenever a project is deleted, all the employees in the project are removed from the relation employee and stored in the temp relation.

```
create trigger project-del on project
for delete
as     insert into temp
               select employee.* from employee
               employee.proj# = deleted.proj#;
       delete employee from employee, deleted
               where employee.proj# = deleted.proj#;
```

Note that the **deleted** table contains the tuples which have been deleted from the project relation.

2.353 DB2

The statement for creating a trigger in DB2 has the following format (in the syntax used for the statement, the clauses enclosed in {} denote multiple choices, not always exclusive):

```
create trigger name
{no cascade before | after}
{insert | delete | update [of list-of-column-names]}
on table-name
[referencing {old as transition-variable | new as transition-
variable |
       old_table as transition-variable | new_table as
transition-variable}
[{for each statement | for each row} mode DB2SQL]
[when condition]
begin atomic sequence of SQL statements
end!
```

As shown by the above statement, the triggering events in DB2 include only the database modification operations. In DB2, triggers can be activated before or after the triggering operation is performed. A trigger that is activated before the operation is called *before trigger*, whereas a trigger activated after is called *after trigger*. Moreover, triggers can be row triggers or statement triggers. The difference between a row trigger and a statement trigger is the same as that for Oracle. The main difference between Oracle and DB2 is that in DB2 there is the limitation that a before trigger must necessarily be a row trigger, so before statement triggers are not currently supported by DB2 whereas they are supported by Oracle.

The trigger definition language of DB2 supports the declaration of *transition variables* in the **referencing** clause for referring the old and new database states. Transition variables can refer to a table or to a row, thus resulting in the following four types of transition variables [Cham96]:

- *old row variable*: this represents the value of the modified tuple before the execution of the triggering operations;
- *new row variable*: this represents the value of the modified tuple after the execution of the triggering operations;
- *old table variable*: this represents a transition table (*see* Section 2.34 on Starburst) containing all the modified tuples as they are before the triggering operation is executed;
- *new table variable*: this represents a transition table containing all the modified tuples as they are after the triggering operation has been executed.

All these variables can be used in both the condition and action components of a trigger. There is the (obvious) restriction that a **referencing** clause in a trigger definition can contain at most a variable of each type.

The **when** clause specifies the condition component of the trigger. Unlike Oracle, the condition in DB2 can be a complex query, including subqueries and joins. The following example from [Cham96] illustrates the transition variable declaration and its use in the condition component. The example refers to a table named employee having among its attributes salary and jobcode.

```
referencing new as newrow          /* declare a new row variable */
referencing old as oldrow          /* declare an old row variable */
referencing old_table as oldtable  /* declare an old table variable */
when (newrow.salary < oldrow.salary)
when (newrow.salary > (select max(salary) from employee
                       where jobcode = newrow.jobcode))
when (select count(*) from oldtable) > 100)
```

The first of the above **when** clauses specifies a condition which is true when the new salary of the modified tuple is lower than the salary before the update. The second of the above **when** clauses specifies a condition which is true when the new salary is greater than the maximum salary of all the employees having the same job of the employee whose salary has been modified. Finally, the third **when** clause specifies a condition which is true when the number of modified tuples is greater than 100. Note, however, that not all variable types can be used with all the possible types of triggers. For example, a variable whose type is oldrow cannot be used in a before trigger whose triggering operation is insert. In this case, the inserted tuples do not have an 'old' state. By contrast, such a variable can be used in a before trigger whose triggering operation is update. We refer the reader to [Cham96] for a detailed specification of the correct use of transition variables according to the specific format of the trigger.

The last component of the trigger definition statement is the list of SQL statements representing the action component of the trigger. All the statements that appear in such a list are executed according to an atomic execution, which includes in its scope the triggering operation of the trigger. Therefore, if one of the statements in the action component of the trigger fails, the triggering operation and all the statements in the action component are rolled back. Note, however, that a transaction which has issued a triggering operation failing because of errors in the execution of some triggers is not rolled back.

Two final remarks concern the clauses **no cascade**, used in the specification of a before trigger, and **mode DB2SQL**, used in the clause referring to whether the trigger must be executed for each row or for each statement. The **no cascade** is simply a reminder that a before trigger never activates another before trigger. The clause **mode DB2SQL** refers to the trigger processing model implemented by version V2 of DB2. It is used to ensure backward application compatibility if new processing modes are added to the system in the future. The use of such a clause ensures that existing applications will not be affected by possible extensions to the trigger processing mode.

The following example from [Cham96] illustrates the trigger definition language in DB2. The example refers to the employee table; we make the assumption that such a table includes the manager of the employee (column manager) for each employee and for an employee who is a manager the number of managed employees (column span). Note that the span column keeps track of the employees managed directly or indirectly by an employee. The value of the span column must be automatically updated whenever a new employee is added or an employee removed or transferred under another manager.

```
create trigger emp_hire
after insert on employee
referencing new as newrow
for each row mode DB2SQL
update employee
  set span = span + 1
  where emp# = newrow.manager!
```

```
create trigger emp_quit
after delete on employee
referencing old as oldrow
for each row mode DB2SQL
update employee
 set span = span -1
 where emp# = oldrow.manager!
```

```
create trigger emp_transfer
after update of manager on employee
referencing old as oldrow new as newrow
for each row mode DB2SQL
begin atomic
update employee
  set span = span - 1 where emp# = oldrow.manager;
update employee
  set span = span + 1 where emp# = newrow.manager;
end!
```

```
create trigger emp_propagate
after update of span on employee
referencing old as oldrow new as newrow
for each row mode DB2SQL
update employee
  set span = span + newrow.span - oldrow.span
where emp# = newrow.manager!
```

The first (second) trigger above simply increments (decrements) one of the attribute spans of the manager of the employee who has been hired (fired). The third trigger takes care of an employee transfer from one manager to another. The span of the old manager must thus be decremented, whereas the span of the new manager must be incremented. Finally, the fourth trigger implements the recursive calculation of the span attribute. Whenever the span of a manager is incremented, the span of the manager of this manager must be incremented, and so on. This effect is achieved by defining a trigger emp_propagate that is activated by the updates performed by any of the other three triggers and by the updates performed by trigger emp_propagate itself. Therefore, whenever the span attribute is updated (as an effect of the other triggers) for a certain employee, the difference between the old value and the new value is computed for this employee. This difference is then added to the span value of the manager of this employee. The above example illustrates the power of recursive trigger invocation.

As with other DBMS statements, DB2 provides for dropping and changing triggers. We refer the reader to [Cham96] for an extensive discussion on triggers in DB2.

2.354 SQL3 proposal

Because triggers represent an important functionality, SQL3, the new SQL standard [Melt93], will incorporate a trigger definition language. The SQL3 statement for trigger definition has the following format:

```
create trigger name
{before | after}
{insert | delete | update [of list-of-column-names]}
on table-name
[referencing old [as] old-correlation name
             new [as] new-correlation name
[when condition]
list-of-statements [for each {row | statement}]
```

As we can see, the SQL3 proposal for triggers shares many aspects with trigger languages of current RDBMSs. It is important to remark that the proposal only includes database modification operations as events. The **referencing** clause specifies names for referring to the old and new states of the table referenced in the **on** clause of the trigger definition. According to [Melt93], correlation names can be used only when the triggering event is the **update**. The statements that can be executed as the action part of the trigger include only the SQL modification commands – **delete**, **update**, and **insert**. The first two can also include search conditions. Finally, the processing granularity of the trigger can be the row or the statement. If the row granularity is specified, the trigger is executed for every row that is inserted, deleted, or updated by the statement. By contrast, if the statement granularity is specified, the trigger is executed only once.

2.36 Research object-oriented prototypes

Most research and development efforts in active databases have been in the framework of RDBMSs. Most current OODBMSs do not provide active rules, except for research prototypes. One possible reason is that OODBMSs incorporate methods as well as data, and therefore it is less obvious why active rules are still useful in object databases. In relational databases, the actions to be taken upon certain events can be specified either by rules or by applications. In object-oriented databases, those actions can be specified by rules, by application programs, or by methods. However, specifying the actions to be taken through rules has three important advantages over coding them into methods [Bert00a]. First, the actions coded into methods are executed only when the methods are explicitly invoked by the applications; by contrast, active rules are automatically activated, independently from the applications. Second, the semantics represented by a single active rule often need to be replicated into several methods. Finally, a specialized trigger subsystem, internal to the database system, supports a more efficient active behaviour processing than an approach by which active behaviour is coded into methods.

The extension of an OODBMS to support active rules requires revisiting the functions as well as the mechanisms by which active capabilities are incorporated into DBMS. The object-oriented data model, in particular, has a number of features that complicate the extension of object-oriented database systems with active rules. First, in an object-oriented data model, in contrast to a fixed number of primitive events of the relational model, every method/message is a potential event. Very often, triggers in OODBMSs are used to check the correctness of method arguments before method executions or to verify postconditions after method executions. Second, encapsulation introduces issues related to scope, accessibility and visibility of object states with respect to rules. However, the most relevant issue is related to rule inheritance and overriding. The approach taken by the majority of the systems for rule inheritance is to simply apply all the rules, defined in a class, to the entire extent of the class, i.e. to all instances of the class and of all its subclasses. No rule overriding is supported by those systems; therefore a rule defined in a class cannot be modified, in any of its components, in the subclasses inheriting this rule. Only a few systems (Gehani and Jagadish, 1996, Kappel *et al*, 1994) support overriding, although in a completely uncontrolled way. It is important to note that there are many cases in which rule overriding is useful. However, overriding should be controlled to ensure that i) the redefined rule is triggered each time the overridden one would be triggered; ii) the redefined rule does at least what the overridden would do. The last condition is important in that it ensures that the behaviour of subclasses is actually a refinement of the behaviour of the superclasses. We refer the reader to [Bert00a] for an extensive discussion on these issues.

In the past few years, an increasing interest in developing active OODBMSs has resulted in a number of research prototypes. One of the earliest object-oriented active database projects is HiPAC [Daya96]. HiPAC supports a rich rule language with flexible execution semantics, providing a full range of coupling modes through a nested transaction model. There are some projects on active OODBMSs that are a follow-on of HiPAC, including Sentinel [Anwa93] and REACH [Bran93]. One of the best-known active OODBMSs is Ode [Geha96], which extends the O++ database programming language with facilities for expressing triggers. Other relevant projects include Adam [Diaz91], NAOS [Coll94], SAMOS [Gatz92], TriGS [Kapp94], and Chimera [Bert00a], [Ceri96].

Table 2.5 from [Bert00a] compares the above systems in a number of aspects. NAOS and TriGS are extensions of commercial OODBMSs. All the systems support the ECA paradigm for active rules; however, in some systems, such as Ode, conditions are part of the event specification as a mask that qualifies the event and can refer to parameters of the method call defining the event. Triggering events, supported by most systems, include database operations, temporal events, external (that is, raised by the application) and user-defined events. Database operations are object accesses, attribute value updates, object creations and deletions, method executions and calls to transaction primitives (e.g. commit). In Chimera, object migration between classes is included among events. Triggering events may also be composite, i.e. combinations of other events. Some systems allow events to be parameterized – when a parameterized event occurs, values related to the event are bound to the event parameters and these parameter values can be referenced in rule conditions or actions. Some systems only consider as an implicit parameter the identifier of the object receiver of the event, i.e. the object on which the rule is executed. The considered systems differ not only with respect to the supported rule language but also for the rule execution semantics.

The main differences in execution semantics are with respect to the coupling mode and whether rule evaluation is instance-oriented or set-oriented. By instance-oriented evaluation we mean that a rule is executed once for each object triggering the rule and satisfying the rule condition. By contrast, rule execution is set-oriented if the triggered rule is executed once for all database instances triggering the rule and satisfying the rule condition. Another difference among existing systems is whether rule definitions are attached to classes. Attaching rule definitions to classes enhances modularization and allows an efficient detection of relevant events whereas there are sometimes useful rules triggered by events spanning sets of objects possibly from different classes. Rules defined in the context of a single class are called *targeted triggers*, while rules over multiple classes are called *untargeted triggers*. Finally, among the considered systems, only TriGS and Ode – though with some restrictions – support rule overriding.

Table 2.5 Comparison of active object-oriented data models

	HiPAC	**Ode**	**Adam**	**NAOS**	**TriGS**	**SAMOS**	**Chimera**
Reference	[Daya96]	[Geha96]	[Diaz91]	[Coll94]	[Kapp94]	[Gatz92)	[Ceri96]
o-o data model	oodaplex	new	new	O_2	GemStone	new	new
primitive events	messages db ops temporal external	messages db ops temporal	messages	messages db ops user-def	messages	messages db ops temporal user-def	messages db ops migrations
event composition	YES	YES	NO	NO	NO	YES	YES (1)
conditions on past states	NO	NO	NO	NO	NO	NO	YES
evaluation mode	immediate deferred decoupled	immediate deferred decoupled	immediate	immediate deferred	user-specified	immediate deferred decoupled	immediate deferred
untargeted/ targeted rules	untargeted	targeted	untargeted	untargeted	both	both	both
overriding	NO	YES	NO	NO	YES	NO	NO

(1) In [Ceri96] only disjunction of events is considered; an extension of Chimera with other kinds of event composition is presented in [MeoR96]

2.37 AI production rule languages

Because forward-chaining production rule languages, such as OPS5 (*see* Section 3.122), share many similarities with triggers, the integration of production rule languages with database technology resulted in systems providing very much the same functions of active DBMSs. One of the best-known systems, developed as an extension of an AI production rule language, is RPL (Relational Production Language). RPL uses the relational data model as the basic framework for implementing a full production system (i.e. an expert system 'shell') which, in turn, allows for the construction of 'ordinary' expert systems. In this way:

- ESs written in RPL have direct access to conventional databases because RPL relies on a relational query language in order to express rules;
- ES inferencing power immediately enriches conventional DB systems.

RPL's architecture is based on a two-level database hierarchy in which the system's outer level corresponds well to the Fact DataBase, FDB, of our initial definition of an IDBS, and the inner level to the Rule Base, RLB. The outer level comprises conventional DB; the inner level, in the core memory, contains an RPL interpreter employing a memory-resident relational DB to replace the 'working memory' proper to production systems. The system uses RPL rules to express and control data exchange between levels; once a situation that requires inferencing has been identified, an RPL rule can load data necessary for inferencing from the outer level into the 'working' relational DB.

Given that RPL views the working memory as a relational database, the fundamental functions of the production system interpreter can be realized with DBMS assistance. In particular, an RPL program contains a production rule set in which each rule's LHS ('left hand side') is a relational query, profiting from the fact that the LHS of a production rule in the OPS5 style is essentially a limited form of database query. The RHS ('right hand side') comprises normal actions supported by OPS5, the only difference being that INSERT, UPDATE and DELETE operations replace OPS5 'make', 'modify' and 'remove' actions respectively, in order to conform to SQL syntax. The following is an example of an RPL rule that determines which employees have had declining sales by comparing the sales of the current and previous months for each employee. For such employees, the rule records the difference in sales between the two months.

```
declining-sales:
for all
        select E.number, E.negative-rating
        from employee E1, employee E2, evaluation E
        where E1.number = E2.number and E.number = E1.number
              and E1.month = current and E2.month = previous and
              E1.sales < E2.sales
do
        update evaluation
              set E.negative-rating = (E2.sales - E1.sales) ;
end
```

Notice that, unlike rule languages developed for database systems, RPL rules do not include any event specification clauses. Therefore RPL rules are always activated and their actions are executed whenever the conditions, expressed in the SQL query, are true. More precisely, the actions are executed for the tuples selected by the query.

A language very similar to RPL is A-RDL, developed at INRIA (France) in a context of 'deductive DBs' research [Simo92]. A-RDL extends a deductive database system with active rules. In A-RDL, rules are encapsulated into *rule modules*. A module contains the declaration of the base relations corresponding to relations that are physically stored in the DB, and a set of rules that applies to those relations. The following is an example of an A-RDL rule which removes an employee if this employee's department does not exist.

```
module ref_constraint_emp_dept;
base  EMP (name string, emp_no integer, dept_no integer, salary
      integer);
      DEPT (mgr_no integer, dept_no integer);
rules
r is deferred
if EMP (x) and not exists y in DEPT (x_dept_no = y.dept_no)
then - EMP (x);
end module
```

The keyword **deferred** indicates that the rule is executed at the end of the transaction. Intuitively, this module defines a rule that is activated whenever the EMP or DEPT relations are modified. Thus, if for example an employee with no department is inserted, it will be rejected (i.e. deleted from the set of employees to be inserted). Note that even though the syntax is quite different, the rules are similar to DATALOG rules, extended with updates.

Other systems which reconstruct an OPS5-like environment by making use of the relational mechanisms include DIPS [Sell88] and DATEX [Bran93].

2.38 Conclusions

Active rules are a simple yet powerful mechanism able to represent knowledge on events of interest and to code actions to be taken upon occurrence of these events. Active rules are supported by all DBMSs. By contrast, knowledge-based systems seldom support this type of rule. Even though research on active rules is quite consolidated, there are still a lot of issues to be investigated. A relevant issue is represented by design methodologies for developing rule bases. In particular, rules should be designed so that termination is always ensured. This is, however, quite a difficult task when dealing with hundreds, or thousands, of rules as in several database applications. Other issues are related to the development of active rules for Java-based databases, and comparison, and possible integration, of active rule mechanisms with exception handling mechanisms.

3 Efforts originated in a prevailing AI context

3.1 Characteristics and classification of the knowledge-based systems

3.11 Introduction

Knowledge-based systems (KBSs) differ considerably from conventional DBs. The most outstanding difference – at least partially blurred in the case of the active database systems (*see* Section 2.3) – is that KBSs typically contain explicitly represented rules (as well as simple facts) and components which can make inferences over the global 'knowledge base' (rule base, RLB, + fact database, FDB), thereby providing some form of deductive retrieval facility. The consequence of this is that the information dealt with by the KBSs consists not only of the explicitly stored facts and rules but also of what can be derived from the KB by suitably applying (some set of) rules on (some set of) facts.

Even if a formal approach to the KBSs domain cannot do justice to all its proper characteristics (*see* Sections 3.3 and 3.4), it may be useful to adopt a (very softened) version of it in order to introduce some useful classifications of the domain. We can then affirm that all the KBSs range between two possible basic forms:

- pure rule-based representations supporting inference by resolution; inside this first category it is at least pragmatically useful to distinguish between the systems developed in a logic programming context and the simplest expert systems shells based on the production rules paradigm;
- pure frame- or object-based representations supporting inference by inheritance, and also admitting defaults and procedural attachment. A particular class of inheritance-based systems that are fashionable today are the so-called description logics (terminological logics) systems.

In reality, the commercial realizations of frame- and object-based systems are normally configured as independent but sufficient software environments for application development, therefore, they are usually endowed with the possibility of giving the user alternative inference methods and representation schemes, such as rule-based inference components. We shall refer to this class of powerful 'hybrid' systems as the knowledge engineering software environments (KESEs).

We will present, in Section 3.12, the resolution principle. Subsection 3.121 will deal with logic programming, and subsection 3.122 with the (production) rule paradigm. Section 3.13 will discuss inference by inheritance: after having recalled in subsection 3.131 the main principles of frame systems (and, more in general, of KESEs), we will devote subsection 3.132 to a discussion of description logics. Section 3.14 will be the conclusion of this section. Note that we will not deal explicitly here with a KBS paradigm that was once very popular, i.e. semantic networks (*see,* however [Lehm92]) given that the modern realizations of this paradigm coincides practically with the frame-based systems. For advanced types of representation which derive in some sort from semantic networks such as conceptual graphs and NKRL (Narrative Knowledge Representation Language), *see* Section 3.4.

Before entering into details about the above topics, we can note that the four representation techniques – logic programming, production rules, frame systems and description logics – all concern, from an artificial intelligence point of view, the so-called 'symbolic paradigm' of the knowledge representation domain. We recall here that AI classifies the knowledge representation techniques into two main classes (all sorts of mixed approaches are obviously possible):

- techniques that follow the 'symbolic' approach. They are characterised by i) the existence of a well-defined, one-to-one correspondence between *all* the entities of the domain to be modelled (and their relationships), and the symbols used in the knowledge representation language, and ii) the fact that the knowledge manipulation algorithms (inferences) take explicitly into account this correspondence;
- techniques that we can define as 'biologically inspired', such as genetic algorithms or neural nets. In these techniques, only the input and output values have an explicit, one-to-one correspondence with the entities of a given problem to be modelled. For the other elements and factors of the problem, i) it is often impossible to establish a *local*, one-to-one correspondence between the symbols of the knowledge representation system and such elements and factors, and ii) the resolution processes are not grounded on any explicit notion of correspondence, and iii) statistical and probabilistic methods play an important part in these resolution processes.

When fuzzy logic techniques are added to genetic algorithms and neural nets, we are in the domain of knowledge representation and inference techniques that is often referred to as 'soft logic' or the 'soft programming' domain. Obviously the soft programming paradigm can be used to build up fully fledged KBSs systems; however, the generality of these systems is lower compared with that of KBSs based on the symbolic approach and in the main their relationships with the DB domain are less evident and less compelling. The soft programming techniques will not be examined, then, in this book – for an introduction to these techniques *see*, for example, [Zarr99a].

3.12 The resolution principle

The resolution principle originates in the area of automatic theorem-proving, an artificial intelligence discipline where computers are used to try to prove that a 'theorem' – a clause (*see* below) whose truth value is yet unknown – can be derived from a set of 'axioms' – clauses that are assumed to be true. The resolution principle was introduced by J.A. Robinson in a famous paper, [Robi65] (*see also* [Robi82]).

In its most simple formulation ('chain rule'), the resolution principle can be reduced to an inference rule expressed as:

```
From (A ∨ B) and (¬ A ∨ C), deduce that (B ∨ C).    (a)
```

In (a), we follow the usual conventions of the predicate calculus of logic (*see*, for example, [Nils80: 131–159]). A, B and C are then 'atomic formulas' or 'literals', i.e. in their most general form they are expressions of the type $P(t_1 \ldots t_n)$ where P is a 'predicate' and $t_1 \ldots t_n$ are 'terms'. Predicates represent statements about individuals, both by themselves and in relation to other individuals, and from a 'semantic' point of view, they can assume the value of either TRUE or FALSE – note that TRUE and FALSE are 'truth values' having a very precise and limited meaning in a predicate calculus context and, on the contrary, very remote relationships with the usual, natural language meaning of the adjectives 'true' and 'false'. Terms may be constant symbols, such as 'Peter' – constant symbols are the simplest form of term, and they are used to represent the 'interesting' entities (physical objects, people, concepts, etc.) in a given domain of discourse. A simple atomic formula can then be 'love(Peter, Mary)', where 'love' is the predicate, and 'Peter' and 'Mary' are the terms. But terms may also be variables, or expressions of the form $f(t_1 \ldots t_n)$, where f is a n-place function and $t_1 \ldots t_n$ are again terms. It is important to recall here that functions, unlike predicates, do not return TRUE or FALSE, but that they behave like operators returning objects that are related to their arguments. For example, the function 'father-of', applied to the argument (a term represented by a constant symbol) 'Peter' would supply the value 'John'. The symbols ∨ and ¬ (logical connectives) represent the inclusive or and the negation respectively.

The 'disjunctions' (A ∨ B), (¬ A ∨ C) and (B ∨ C) that appear in the expression (a) above are particularly important types of well-formed formulas (wff) of the first-order predicate calculus that take the name of 'clauses'. It can be shown (*see also* below) that each standard expression of predicate logic can be reduced to a set of disjunctive clauses, where the variables possibly included in the clauses are (implicitly) universally quantified. However, the intuitive meaning (the direct translation into an English statement) of the original logic expression is often completely lost after the 'translation' into clausal form, *see*, for example, [Kowa79: 426–427].

From (a), it is then evident that the resolution process, when it is applicable, can take a pair of parent wffs in the form of clauses to produce a new, derived clause (the 'resolvent'), on condition that one of these clauses contains a literal (atomic formula), ¬ A, which is the exact negation of one of the literals, A, in the other clause. The literals A and ¬ A appear as 'cancelled'. The resolution method for automatic theorem-proving is then a form of proof by contradiction. In its more general formulation, this method consists of assuming that if a theorem follows from its axioms, the axioms and the negation of the theorem cannot be simultaneously true. The proof of a theorem using the resolution principle takes the following steps:

1 Negate the theorem to be proved, and add the negated theorem to the list of axioms.
2 Put the new list of axioms in clausal form, thus obtaining a global set of clauses.
3 Simplify the clauses and produce the corresponding resolvents through the application of the chain rule (a) to the clauses of the global set.
4 Add these resolvents to the global set, and produce recursively new resolvents through the systematic application of (a).
5 Halt the procedure when a contradiction can be found, i.e. when an 'empty clause' is produced; in this case, report that the theorem is TRUE. If the empty clause, denoted as □, cannot be produced, report that the theorem is FALSE.

Resolution is a particularly powerful procedure, given that it can be shown that resolution is 'complete' for first-order predicate logic (i.e. it can prove all the theorems in this particular useful form of logic); moreover, it is 'sound', i.e. it will not affirm that particular non-theorems are true. Note, however, that, if the theorem is FALSE (i.e. the empty clause □ cannot be produced), the process is, in general, unable to terminate.

To give a first, very simple example, let us consider the case of the well-known 'modus ponens' in logic, which affirms that, from p and $p \supset q$ (i.e. p and $p \supset q$, the axioms, have both a truth value = TRUE), we can deduce the theorem q. Using the well-known logical equivalence, $\neg x_1 \vee x_2$ eq. $x_1 \supset x_2$, we can reduce the two axioms to the clauses (i) p and (ii) $\neg p \vee q$ which are congruent with (a); according to the resolution principle, we add to these two clauses a third clause given by the negation of the theorem, i.e. (iii) ¬ q. Resolving now the three clauses against each other leads immediately to the reciprocal cancellation of p and ¬ p in (i) and (ii), leaving us with the final contradiction q and ¬ q. The theorem then has the truth value TRUE.

We can now consider a slightly more complex example, trying to prove by resolution that $(C_3 \vee C_4)$ follows from $(C_1 \supset C_2 \vee C_3) \wedge (C_1 \vee C_3 \vee C_4) \wedge (C_1 \supset \neg C_2)$. The connective ∧ is the logical and for simplicity's sake, we assume here that the above wffs are 'ground formulas', i.e. that their literals are reduced to constants, C_n, or that the included terms do not contain variables.

To be able to apply rule (a), we use once again the logical equivalence $\neg x_1 \vee x_2$ eq. $x_1 \supset x_2$. As a consequence, we must now prove that $(C_3 \vee C_4)$ follows from $(\neg C_1 \vee C_2 \vee C_3) \wedge (C_1 \vee C_3 \vee C_4) \wedge (\neg C_1 \vee \neg C_2)$. The negated theorem is $(\neg (C_3 \vee$

C_4)). Before adding this last clause to the set of axioms, we transform it into $(\neg C_3 \wedge \neg C_4)$ using one of de Morgan's laws, $\neg (x_1 \vee x_2)$ eq. $(\neg x_1 \wedge \neg x_2)$; suppressing now all the $\wedge$ symbols (*see* below), we finally obtain the global set of clauses:

1 $(\neg C_1 \vee C_2 \vee C_3)$;

2 $(C_1 \vee C_3 \vee C_4)$;

3 $(\neg C_1 \vee \neg C_2)$;

4 $(\neg C_3)$;

5 $(\neg C_4)$.

According to the resolution principle, if the theorem follows from the axiom, a contradiction must be implicitly hidden in the five clauses above, which cannot be simultaneously true. Resolving the clauses using the chain rule (a) above, we obtain:

$$\begin{array}{lll} \text{Resolution } \alpha: & 1) & (\neg C_1 \vee C_2 \vee C_3) \\ & 2) & \underline{(C_1 \vee C_3 \vee C_4)} \\ & & (C_2 \vee C_3 \vee C_4) \end{array}$$

$$\begin{array}{lll} \text{Resolution } \beta: & 2) & (C_1 \vee C_3 \vee C_4) \\ & 3) & \underline{(\neg C_1 \vee \neg C_2)} \\ & & (C_3 \vee C_4 \vee \neg C_2) \end{array}$$

$$\begin{array}{lll} \text{Resolution } \gamma: & \text{Resolution } \alpha & (C_2 \vee C_3 \vee C_4) \\ & \text{Resolution } \beta & \underline{(C_3 \vee C_4 \vee \neg C_2)} \\ & & (C_3 \vee C_4) \end{array}$$

$$\begin{array}{lll} \text{Resolution } \delta: & \text{Resolution } \gamma & (C_3 \vee C_4) \\ & 4) & \underline{(\neg C_3)} \\ & & (C_4) \end{array}$$

$$\begin{array}{ll} \text{Resolution } \delta & (C_4) \\ 5) & \underline{(\neg C_4)} \\ & \square = \textit{contradiction} \end{array}$$

The theorem is then proved (□ symbolizes the 'empty clause').

We can now give some further, technical details. From what we have said, a first phase in the resolution process consists in converting the (negation of the) theorem and the axioms into a set of disjointive clauses; even if, as already stated, it can be proven that this conversion is feasible for any possible wff, the real implementation can be relatively complex, especially in the presence of functions, variables and quantifiers. The details of this conversion process can be found in [Nils80: 145–49]. It consists of a series of transformations that make use of well-known properties of the predicate calculus, and which result in the elimination of the symbols different from $\vee$ and $\neg$ and of the quantifiers $\forall$ (for all) and $\exists$ (there exists), and in a progressive simplification of the original formulas.

For example, the first step of the transformation process consists of getting rid of the implication symbol, $\supset$: this is eliminated by using the property: $x_1 \vee x_2$ eq. to $\neg x_1 \supset x_2$ already mentioned. The two de Morgan's laws, $\neg (x_1 \wedge x_2)$ eq. to $\neg x_1 \vee \neg x_2$, and $\neg (x_1 \vee x_2)$ eq. to $\neg x_1 \wedge \neg x_2$, are used to reduce the scope of the negation symbols, i.e. to constrain the negation symbols to apply to at most a single literal ('moving inward'). Existential quantifiers $\exists$ are, in general, simply eliminated by introducing a constant c; e.g. $\exists x$ P(x) is replaced by P(c). We represent the claim that an x exists by selecting a particular constant to replace x.

Existential quantifiers $\exists$ that occur within the scope of a universal quantifier $\forall$ present additional problems. They are eliminated by replacing their variables with a function ('Skolem function') of the universally quantified variable. Let us consider, for example, $\forall y \exists x$ P(x, y), to be read as 'for all y, there exists an x such that P(x, y)'. Given that the existential quantifier is within the scope of the universal quantifier, we can suppose that the x 'that exists' depends on the value of y, i.e. that it is always possible to find a function that takes argument y and systematically returns a proper x. A function like this is called a Skolem function, Skolem(y), which maps each value of y into x. Using this Skolem function in place of the x 'that exists', we can eliminate the existential quantifier and rewrite the original formula as $\forall y$ P(Skolem(y), y) (*see* [Nils80: 146–47]).

The explicit occurrences of the symbol $\wedge$ (and) are eliminated in the transformed formula, resulting in this formula 'breaking' into a set of disjointed clauses as required by the resolution principle (*see* the previous examples); this makes sense because each part of a conjunction must be TRUE so that the whole conjunction can be TRUE. Further steps consist of renaming, if necessary, all the (universally quantified) variables so that no two variables are the same in different disjunctive clauses; eliminating the universal quantifiers (in reality, this elimination is only a formal step given that, as already stated, all the variables are assumed as implicitly universally quantified within the resulting clauses); etc.

We must now mention a very important point about the resolution principle. As we have seen in the previous examples, a fundamental step in the procedure consists in the identification of two literals, A and $\neg$ A, where the second is the exact negation of the first: this allows us to eliminate the two. If, as in the previous example, the literals are reduced to atomic constants, 'green' and '$\neg$ green', or when the terms they include do not imply the presence of variables, their identification is immediate. This is not true when variables and Skolem functions are present: to give a simple example, to cancel the literals P(a) and $\neg$ P(x), where a is a constant and x a variable, it is necessary to recognize that i) the literal $\neg$ P(x) asserts that there exists no x for which P(x) is true (x is universally quantified), while ii) P(a) asserts that there is an object a for which P(a) is true. Then in general, to be authorized to cancel two literals, it is necessary to first execute their 'unification' – unification can be informally defined as the process of finding a common 'substitution instance' for the arguments of the predicates making up two literals that can render these literals identical (*see*, for example, [Knig89]). In our case, the substitution instance is obviously the constant a.

We can now develop this point briefly by using a very simple example only slightly adapted from [Knig89: 100–101]. Let us suppose we are dealing with the two statements:

1 *Teachers get angry when pupils do not accept their suggestions.*

2 *When someone is angry, he does not accept suggestions.*

We want to use the resolution principle to infer from the above a third statement:

3 *If a pupil is angry, then also his teacher is angry.*

To reduce the three statements to clausal form, we must first express them in logical form:

1a $\forall z : \text{pupil}(z) \supset (\neg\, \text{acceptsuggestion}(z, \text{teacher}(z)) \supset \text{angry}(\text{teacher}(z))$

2a $\forall x, y : \text{angry}(x) \supset \neg\, \text{acceptsuggestion}(x, y)$

3a $\forall w : \text{pupil}(w) \supset (\text{angry}(w) \supset \text{furious}(\text{teacher}(w)))$,

where 'pupil', 'acceptsuggestion' and 'angry' are predicates, and 'teacher' is a function.

According to the conversion process expounded before, we can now drop the universal quantifier and, making use of the property $x_1 \vee x_2$ eq. to $\neg\, x_1 \supset x_2$, remove the implication symbol. We then obtain the clauses:

1b $\neg\, \text{pupil}(z) \vee \text{acceptsuggestion}(z, \text{teacher}(z)) \vee \text{angry}(\text{teacher}(z))$

2b $\neg\, \text{angry}(x) \vee \neg\, \text{acceptsuggestion}(x, y)$

3b $\neg\, \text{pupil}(w) \vee \neg\, \text{angry}(w) \vee \text{angry}(\text{teacher}(w)))$.

As in the previous examples, we must now try to deduce a resolvent from 1b) and 2b) making use of the chain rule (a). To show that the two literals, l_1 = acceptsuggestion(z, teacher(z)) and $l_2 = \neg$ acceptsuggestion(x, y), play the role of the literals A and $\neg$ A in the chain rule, we must now use one of the several unification algorithms ([Knig89]) to find a substitution σ that makes l_1 and $\neg\, l_2$ identical. In this case, as it is easy to verify, $\sigma = \{x \leftarrow z, y \leftarrow \text{teacher}(z)\}$; according to the resolution principle, removing l_1 and l_2 from 1b) and 2b), and applying σ to the term $\neg$ angry(x) in 2b), we obtain the resolvent:

4 $\neg\, \text{pupil}(z) \vee \text{angry}(\text{teacher}(z)) \vee \neg\, \text{angry}(z)$.

If we now reorder the disjuncts and rename the unbound variables, we can affirm that 3b and 4 are identical. Negating then the theorem 3b, as requested by the resolution principle before adding its clauses to the set of axioms, will lead us to the empty clause, □, and then to a contradiction: the theorem is proved, i.e. the resolution principle has made the desired inference.

We will conclude by mentioning an important technical point. To make use of the resolution principle in practice, we also need a 'search strategy' that should be complete – it should be able to derive □ from the negation of any theorem. In this context, we can introduce informally the distinction between top-down and bottom-up strategies. Top-down strategies start from the clauses that represent the negation of the theorem to be proved; bottom-up strategies (used implicitly in the previous examples) first apply the resolution principle to the clauses that arise from the axioms. In expert systems terms – see Section 3.122 – the top-down style of search is normally called 'backward chaining': it starts from the 'theorem' to be proved and works backwards from this to show that this theorem can be derived from the given axioms. Bottom-up search corresponds to the 'forward chaining' because it works forward from the hypotheses (i.e. the given set of axioms) to derive the theorem.

3.121 *Logic programming*

Logic programming refers to a programming style based on writing programs as sets of assertions in predicate logic (clauses): these clauses have both i) a declarative meaning as descriptive statements about entities and relations proper to a given domain and ii) a procedural meaning by being executable by an interpreter. The procedural meaning is based mainly on the resolution principle, and its central operation is represented by unification involving the use of a pattern-matching algorithm. We will see that restriction to a resolution theorem prover for the 'Horn clauses' subset of logic – *see* [Kowa82], [Lloy87] – provides the logical basis for the well-known programming language PROLOG (PROgramming in LOGic), and supplies PROLOG and its derivatives with a relative tractability of deductions.

As we have just seen, a clause in general is a particular form of logical formula that consists of a disjunction of literals, i.e. a disjunction of atomic formulas and of negations of atomic formulas. We can then write a clause as:

$$A_1 \lor A_2 \ldots \lor A_m \lor \neg B_1 \lor \neg B_2 \ldots \lor \neg B_n \quad m, n \geq 0 \qquad \text{(b)}$$

The clause (b) can now be written as $A_1 \lor A_2 \ldots \lor A_m \lor \neg (B_1 \land B_2 \ldots \land B_n)$ making use of one of the two de Morgan's law (*see* the previous section) and then $\neg (A_1 \lor A_2 \ldots \lor A_m) \supset \neg (B_1 \land B_2 \ldots \land B_n)$ using the equivalence $a \lor b$ eq. to $\neg a \supset b$. We can now use the so-called 'contrapositive law', $a \supset b$ eq. to $\neg b \supset \neg a$ (*see* [Nils80: 138]) to write (b) as:

$$(B_1 \land B_2 \ldots \land B_n) \supset (A_1 \lor A_2 \ldots \lor A_m) . \qquad \text{(c)}$$

The result obtained is particularly interesting, given that it states that any clause is equivalent to an 'implication', where $(B_1 \land B_2 \ldots \land B_n)$ is the 'antecedent' or the 'conditions' of the implication, and $(A_1 \lor A_2 \ldots \lor A_m)$ is the 'consequent' or the 'conclusion' of the implication. Stated in different terms, (c) says that, if the different conditions $B_1, B_2, \ldots, B_n$ are all verified (TRUE), they imply a set of alternative conclusions which are expressed by $A_1, A_2, \ldots, A_m$. The standard conventions for expressing implications (*see*, for example, [Kowa79: 425–427]) avoid the use of the usual logical connectives such as $\land$, $\supset$ and $\lor$; we will write then (c) as:

$$A_1, A_2, \ldots, A_m \leftarrow B_1, B_2, \ldots, B_n \quad m, n \geq 0, \qquad \text{(d)}$$

keeping in mind that the arrow ← is the connective 'if' representing the implication, $B_1, \ldots, B_n$ are the *joint* conditions and $A_1, \ldots, A_m$ the *alternative* conclusions. $B_1, \ldots, B_n$ and $A_1, \ldots, A_m$ are 'literals' (atomic formulas) as defined in the previous section. We recall here that a literal is an expression in the form $P(t_1, \ldots, t_n)$, where P is an n-place predicate symbol and $t_1, \ldots, t_n$ are terms. A term, in turn, may be a variable, a constant symbol, or an expression in the form $f(t_1, \ldots, t_n)$, where f is an n-place function and $t_1, \ldots, t_n$ are again terms. All variables $x_1, \ldots, x_k$ that appear in a clause C are implicitly governed by the universal quantifier ∀, so that a clause C like the clause represented by (d) is, in reality, an abbreviation for $\forall x_1, \ldots, \forall x_k$ C. Examples of clauses written according to the (d) format are: Grandparent(*x*, *y*) ← Parent(*x*, *z*), Parent (*z*, *y*), (m = 1), which expresses the implication that '*x* is grandparent of *y* if *x* is parent of *z* **and** *z* is parent of *y*', and Male(*x*), Female(*x*) ← Parent(*x*, *y*), (n=1), saying that '*x* is male **or** *x* is female if *x* is parent of *y*'.

Horn clauses

We can now introduce the 'Horn clauses' (named after Alfred Horn, who first investigated their properties). Horn clauses are characterised by the fact of having at most one positive literal. The expression (b) above can then be written as:

$$A \vee \neg B_1 \vee \neg B_2 \ldots \vee \neg B_n \qquad n \geq 0; \qquad \text{(e)}$$

executing on (e) the same transformations we have applied to (b), and expressing the result according to the standard convention for implications, we will obtain then:

$$A \leftarrow B_1, B_2, \ldots, B_n \qquad n \geq 0; \qquad \text{(f)}$$

(f) translates the fact that Horn clauses represent a particular sort of implication which contain at most *one* conclusion; restriction to Horn clauses is conceptually equivalent to disallowing the presence of disjunctions (∨) in the 'conclusion' part of the clause. Note that in (f) we can now give to the comma, ',', the usual meaning of logical and, ∧. When n = 0, the implication becomes an 'assertion' and the symbol ← can be dropped; an example is Grandparent(John, Lucy), asserting the fact that John is a grandparent of Lucy. The interest of using Horn clauses – which are less expressive, from a knowledge representation point of view, than the general clauses considered until now – is linked with a well-known principle emphasized mainly by Ronald Brachmann and his colleagues (*see* [BracR85a] and Section 3.132). This suggests reducing the power of the knowledge representation languages so that the formalization of interesting applications is still possible but at the same time the corresponding computation tasks are computationally feasible, i.e. polynomially tractable or at least decidable. We recall that, very informally, 'decidable' means it is possible to automatically assign a truth value, TRUE or FALSE, to the assertion that a given procedure *p* can produce a result within a limited time span when applied to some data *d*. Linear algorithms exist for dealing with propositional logic in Horn clauses form (*see*, for example, [Dowl84]).

Until now, we have implicitly associated a 'declarative' meaning with (Horn) clauses, which represent static chunks of knowledge such as '*x* is grandparent of *y* if *x* is parent of *z* and *z* is parent of *y*' (whatever the values of the variables *x* and *y* may be), or 'John is a grandparent of Lucy'. But we can also associate a 'procedural' meaning with a clause like (f). In this case, and assuming a top-down resolution strategy, (f) may be viewed as a procedure declaration that reduces the problem of the form A to subproblems B_1, B_2, ..., B_n, and where each subproblem is interpreted in turn as a procedure call to other implications. The conclusion A of the implication is the 'head' or the 'name' of the procedure, and it identifies the form of the problems that the procedure can solve. The 'procedure calls' B_i, or 'goals', form the 'body' of the procedure. Looked at in this way, the first example given at the beginning of this paragraph (an implication) can be interpreted as 'to find an *x* that is a grandparent of *y*, try to find a *z* who has *x* as a parent and who is, in turn, a parent of *y*', and the second example (an assertion) can be interpreted as 'when looking for grandparent of Lucy, return the solution John'.

To complete the procedural interpretation of Horn clauses, and to show how this interpretation is perfectly coherent with the mechanisms of the resolution principle introduced in the previous section, we must now introduce – after the 'implications' and the 'assertions' – a third form of Horn clauses, the 'denials'. In this case, the literal A of (f) disappears, and a denial is represented then as: $\leftarrow B_1, B_2, \ldots, B_n$, with $n > 0$. The name 'denial' comes from the fact that, if we drop the only positive literal A from the original expression of a Horn clause, (e), and we apply one of the two de Morgan's law, (e) is transformed into $(\neg B_1 \vee \neg B_2 \ldots \vee \neg B_n)$ eq. $\neg (B_1 \wedge B_2 \ldots \wedge B_n)$. Then, a denial like ← Male(*x*), Grandparent(*x*, Lucy) means literally – in a declarative meaning – that, for no *x*, *x* is male and is the grandparent of Lucy. Denials are used, in a logic programming context, to express the problems to be solved. To be congruent with the resolution principle process, we will assume that a particular denial, which complies with the clause format, is the negation of the 'theorem' to be proved and, as usual, we will add this denial to the existing assertions and implications (clauses), the 'axioms', to try to refute it and prove the theorem. Returning to the previous example, Male(*x*), Grandparent(*x*, Lucy) is now the theorem to be proved; in the procedural interpretation, we will assume this as 'query' that – according to the top-down strategy chosen for the procedural interpretation – represents the starting point of the normal resolution process. Unification must, of course, be used in order to derive the empty clause, □, that according to the procedural interpretation can then be considered as a STOP instruction.

Following [Kowa79: 428], we can now describe the general format of a logic program in a (slightly) more formal way. Let us assume a set of axioms represented by a set of Horn clauses represented in the form (f):

$$A \leftarrow B_1, B_2, \ldots, B_n \qquad n \geq 0. \qquad \text{(f)}$$

According to the procedural interpretation, A is the 'name' or the 'head' of the procedure, which denotes the problems the procedure can solve; B_1, B_2, ..., B_n is the 'body' of the procedure, consisting then of a set of 'procedure calls'. As already stated, an 'assertion' is a clause (f) consisting only of the head A. The conclusions to be derived from the above set of axioms must, according to the resolution principle, be negated (i.e. represented as a denial) and added to the set. According to what has already been expounded, they (the 'query') are then expressed as a clause of the form (g), consisting solely of procedure calls C_i which behave as goal statements:

$$\leftarrow C_1, C_2, \ldots, C_m \qquad m > 0; \qquad (g)$$

The proof consists now in trying to obtain the empty clause □ through a resolution process where a procedure call C_i in the goal statement (g) invokes a procedure like (f) according to the following modalities:

- by unifying the call C_i in (g) with the head (the name) of (f);
- by replacing in (g) the call C_i with the body of (f), obtaining the new goal statement:
  $$\leftarrow C_1, \ldots, C_{i-1}, B_1, \ldots, B_n, C_{i+1}, \ldots, C_m$$
- by applying to (g) the substitution instance σ,
  $$\leftarrow (C_1, \ldots, C_{i-1}, B_1, \ldots, B_n, C_{i+1}, \ldots, C_m)\sigma,$$
  where σ replaces variables by terms in order to render the head A and the call C_i identical, $A\sigma = C_i\sigma$.

We give now a very simple, self-evident example. Let us suppose we have the following set of Horn clauses, which includes both implications and assertions:

1 Grandparent(*x*, *y*) ← Parent(*x*, *z*), Parent (*z*, *y*)

2 Parent(*x*, *y*) ← Mother(*x*, *y*)

3 Parent(*x*, *y*) ← Father(*x*, *y*)

4 Father(John, Bill)

5 Father(Bill, Lucy).

We can remark here that 2) and 3) are the Horn equivalents of a general implication which could be expressed as 'Father(*x*, *y*), Mother(*x*, *y*) ← Parent(*x*, *y*)', i.e. '*x* is the father of *y* **or** *x* is the mother of *y* if *x* is parent of *y*'. We will use now a goal statement like

6 ← Grandparent(John, Lucy)

i.e. we want to prove that John is really a grandparent of Lucy. According to the above algorithm, we must find i) a clause head which can unify the (unique) procedure call represented by (6). This clause head is, of course, the head of (1), and the unification produces the bindings *x* = John, *y* = Lucy. Taking these bindings into account, and applying the second step of the algorithm, we obtain, from the body of (1), a new goal statement:

7 ← Parent(John, *z*), Parent (*z*, Lucy).

We apply again the algorithm using the first procedure call, C_1, of (7), i.e. Parent(John, *z*); this unifies both the heads of (2) and (3), producing, with the bindings *x* = John, *y* = *z*, two new goal statements, (8) and (9):

8 ← Mother(John, z), Parent (z, Lucy)

9 ← Father(John, z), Parent (z, Lucy).

The procedure call C_1 of (8), Mother(John, z), fails to unify the set of Horn clauses; the procedure call C_1 of (9), Father(John, z), unifies on the contrary with (4) linking z with Bill. Given that (4) does not have a body, the second and third steps of the algorithm simply reduce the goal statement (9) to Parent(Bill, Lucy) that, through (3), becomes Father(Bill, Lucy) producing finally the empty clause □ through the unification with (5).

A 'modern' application of logic programming that is particularly popular is 'constraint logic programming' (CLP) – *see*, for example, [Jaff94], [DayW97]. This combination of constraint satisfaction techniques with the principle of logic programming is a natural extension of the traditional logic programming approach, given that the unification procedures which are of prime importance in logic programming can be seen as a special case of constraint satisfaction. This means that, for example, the unification of f(x, A) with f(B, y), where x and y are variables, is equivalent to solving, in a constraint satisfaction framework, the Boolean comparison f(x, A) = f(B, y).

PROLOG and DATALOG

If now, in (f), we substitute the symbol ← with :-, with the same meaning, we obtain the usual representation of a PROLOG clause:

$$A \text{ :- } B_1, B_2, \ldots, B_n \qquad n \geq 0, \qquad \text{(h)}$$

where A (the head) and B_i (the body) have the same interpretation of above and the symbol :- stands for the logical implication 'from right to left', i.e. it means that to solve the goal expressed in the head, one must solve all subgoals expressed in the body. A 'fact' is represented in PROLOG by a headed clause with an empty body and constant terms as the head's arguments: father(Bill, Lucy). A 'rule' is represented by a headed clause with a non-null body, *see* the 'classical' PROLOG example:

```
ancestor(X, Y) :- father(Z, Y), ancestor(X, Z)
```

meaning that, for all the PROLOG variables X, Y, and Z, if Z is the father of Y, and X an ancestor of Z, then X is an ancestor of Y. A 'query' is represented by a headless clause with a non-empty body, *see* :- father(Lucy), 'who is the father of Lucy?'. A query without variable arguments produces a 'yes' or 'no' answer, see :- father(Bill, Lucy), 'is it true that Bill is the father of Lucy?'. PROLOG (PROgramming in LOGic) was originally a strongly constrained resolution theorem prover. Around 1972, it was turned into a 'normal' programming language – for the purpose of implementing a natural language question-answering system – by a team led by Alain Colmerauer in Marseilles (*see* [Colm73], [Rous75]). Van Emden and Kowalski [vanE76] then provided an elegant formal model of the language based on Horn clauses.

To fulfil its functions of 'normal' programming language, PROLOG introduces several important modifications (some 'extra-logical features') with respect to the pure logic programming paradigm. First of all, it must obviously introduce some built-in predicates for input and output, i.e. to allow clauses to be read and written to and from terminals (and databases). Secondly, PROLOG adopts a very strict discipline for control. When executing a program – i.e. when trying to match a literal in the goal statement (query) against the head of some clause, to substitute then the goals (if any) in the body of that clause for the original literal in the query (*see* the logic programming example in the previous section) – PROLOG follows these two rules:

- the clauses that together make up the 'program' are tested strictly in the order in which they appear in the text of the program; in the current goal statement, the leftmost literal (procedure call) is systematically chosen;
- when a success or a failure is attained, the system 'backtracks' – the last extensions (substitutions) in the goal statement are undone, the previous configuration of the statement is restored (chronological backtracking), and the system looks for alternative solutions starting from the next matching clause for the leftmost literal of the reinstated statement.

This means in practice, among other things, that PROLOG's goals are executed in the very order in which they are specified, therefore, PROLOG programmers arrange their goals so that the more selective ones are declared first. For the optimization of this search mechanism (i.e. depth-first search with backtracking), PROLOG makes use of other extra-logical features, such as the built-in predicates 'fail' (which automatically triggers a failure) and 'cut', which is represented as '/' or '!' and is used to limit too expensive choices-tree searches due to the systematic use of backtracking (*see* below). Moreover, PROLOG provides some limited data structures (e.g. lists, trees), means for dealing with variables (e.g. isvar, rreal, integer), and arithmetic. Finally, some utilities for debugging and tracing programs are also provided. Some of these features could also be expressed in first order logic; others (read/write, cut) have no logical equivalent.

We will not explore the technicalities of PROLOG programming in depth here as they are outside the scope of this book, and we will mention only two particularities of this language that have generated a large debate from a theoretical point of view – the absence of the 'occur test' in the standard implementations of PROLOG, and the 'cut'.

According to its logic programming derivation, PROLOG makes extensive use of unification. The first modern algorithm for unification proposed by Robinson [Robi65] already contained what is now known as the 'occur check': very informally, it says that, when one of the two terms t_1 and t_2 be unified is a variable x, and when the same variable occurs anywhere in the second term t – i.e. if occur(x, t) is true – then the unification fails (*see* [Knig89] for more details). The check was introduced with the aim of avoiding any infinite loop due to the fact that, when trying to unify x and f(x), the substitution σ that renders the two terms identical is $\{x \leftarrow f(f(f(\ldots)))\}$. In the original implementation of PROLOG, Colmerauer left out the occur check for efficiency's sake – for example, it can be shown (*see* [Colm82]) that the concatenation of two lists, a linear-time operation in the absence of the occur check, becomes an $O(n^2)$ time operation in the presence of this check.

PROLOG implementations that follow Colmeraurer are then based, more than on unification, on 'infinite unification', which can lead, in particular cases, to wrong conclusions (*see also* [Plai84]). In [Colm82], Colmeraurer proposes a new theoretical model, based on 'infinite trees', for PROLOG interpreters that do not implement the occur check. In this model, the usual unification of two terms is replaced by the problem of verifying that a system of 'equations' (ordered pairs of terms (s, t)) has at least one 'tree-solution' where the variables are associated with (possibly infinite) trees.

The 'cut' mechanism allows a programmer to tell PROLOG that some choices made during the examination of the goal chain need not be considered again when the system backtracks through the chain of the goals already satisfied. The main reason for using this mechanism is linked with the fact that the system will not waste time attempting to satisfy goals that the programmer knows will never contribute to a solution. From a syntactical point of view, a cut is equivalent to a goal that is represented by the predicate '!' (or an equivalent symbol) without any argument. It can then be inserted in the subgoals chain that makes up the right-hand side of a PROLOG clause. As a goal, it is immediately satisfied, and the program continues exploring the chain of goals at its right; as a side effect, it 'freezes' all the decisions made since the clause considered was entered. This means, in practice, that all the alternatives still opened between the invocation of the rule by the parent goal and the goal represented by the cut are discarded.

If we transform now the clause (h) given before into (i) by adding a cut goal:

$$\text{A :- } B_1,\ B_2,\ B_3,\ !,\ B_4,\ B_5,\ \ldots,\ B_n \qquad n \geq 0, \qquad \text{(i)}$$

the result we obtain is that the system backtracks regularly among the three subgoals B_1, B_2, B_3 and, when B_3 succeeds, it crosses the 'fence' (the 'one-way door') represented by the cut goal to reach B_4 and continues in the usual way, backtracking included, until B_n (*see*, for example, [Cloc81: 66–67]). But if backtracking occurs, and if B_4 fails – causing the 'fence' to be crossed to the left – given that the alternatives still opened have been discarded, no attempt can be made to satisfy the goal B_3 again. The final effect is that the entire conjunction of subgoals fails, and the goal A will also fail.

Apart from its appearance as a 'patch' from a strictly logical point of view, the use of the cut introduces some very practical problems, all linked, fundamentally, with the necessity of knowing perfectly well the behaviour of the rules (PROLOG clauses) where the cut must be inserted. Given in fact that its use precludes, in practice, the production of some possible solutions, the use of the cut in a not perfectly controlled environment can lead to the impossibility of producing a perfectly legal solution (*see* again [Cloc81: 76–78]). To control expensive tree search, several researchers have suggested using tools 'external' (metalevel control) to the specific clause processing mechanism of PROLOG – *see*, among many others, the work described in [Gall83].

In the context of a discussion about the relationships between logic programming and databases, the DATALOG language must of course be mentioned. It has been, in fact, designed specifically for interacting with large (traditional)

DBs, thanks to the possibility of immediately translating DATALOG programs in terms of (positive) relational algebra expressions. DATALOG and deductive DBs will be dealt with in more detail in Section 3.2.

From a syntactical point of view, DATALOG can be considered as a very restricted subset of general logic programming. In its formalism, both facts and rules are represented as Horn clauses, having the general form reproduced in (j):

$$A \text{ :- } B_1,\ B_2,\ \ldots,\ B_n \qquad n \geq 0; \qquad (j)$$

According to the procedural interpretation of Horn clauses, (j) also represents a DATALOG rule, reduced to an 'assertion' or a 'fact' when (j) consists only of the head A. Each A or B_i is then a literal of the form $P(t_1 \ldots t_n)$ where P is a predicate and t_i are the terms; the basic DATALOG restricts the type of terms, however, which can be only *constants or variables*, to the exclusion of, for example, the *function symbols*. Extensions to the basic DATALOG language intended to deal with functions, with the negation of predicates P_i etc., have been proposed – *see also* Section 3.2. A literal, clause, rule or fact that does not contain any variable is called 'ground'. In particular, in order to have a *finite set* of all the facts that can be derived from a DATALOG program P, the following two conditions must be satisfied:

- each fact associated with P must be ground;
- each variable that appears in the head of a rule of P must also appear in the body of the same rule.

A DATALOG program is a finite set of clauses that are divided into two disjoint subsets: a set of ground facts, called the 'extensional database' (EDB), and a set of DATALOG rules, called the 'intensional database' (IDB). The important point here is that, given the restriction to constants c_i of the terms included in a DATALOG ground fact, the EDB can 'physically' coincide with a normal relational database. If we call now EDB-predicates all those occurring in the EDB, and IDB-predicates those that occur in IDB without also occurring in EDB, we require as additional conditions that i) the head predicates of each clause (rule) in IDB (the 'core' of the DATALOG program) be only IDB-predicates (sometimes IDB-predicates are therefore called 'intensional predicates') and ii) EDB-predicates may occur in the IDB rules, but only in the B_i (clause bodies). The correspondence between EDB (ground facts) and the relational database is implemented in such a way that each EDB-predicate G_i corresponds to one and only one relation R_j of the base: each ground fact $G_i(c_1 \ldots c_n)$ of EDB is then stored as a tuple $< c_1 \ldots c_m >$ of R_j. Also the IDB-predicates can be identified with relations, called IDB-relations, which in this case are not stored explicitly in the DB: they are therefore sometimes named derived or intensional relations, and correspond to the 'views' of the relational DB theory. The main task of a DATALOG compiler or interpreter is precisely that of calculating efficiently these views: the output of a successful DATALOG program is a relation for each IDB-predicate.

To define the semantics of a DATALOG program P (i.e. the 'meaning' of what is really computed by P) it is possible to have recourse to the usual interpretation in terms of the resolution method. Normally, however, this definition is given in terms of model theory – more precisely, of the 'least' or 'smallest' model. Very informally, a model (Herbrand model) of a DATALOG program P is a set of predicate instances (predicate extensions) that contains all the input relations (EDB) and all the tuples that can be derived from EDB and the intensional database IDB. Starting from a model, it is always possible to generate a different model, for example by associating the literals of the original model making use of the operators $\wedge$ and $\vee$. An interesting property of DATALOG concerns the fact that the intersection of two non-empty models of P is still a (Herbrand) model of P. As a consequence, there is necessarily a 'smallest' or 'least' model that is the intersection of all the models of P and that corresponds to the canonical interpretation of a DATALOG program, in that it contains exactly all the facts (predicate instances) I that it is possible to deduce from P.

The least model of a program P can be calculated making use of the operator T_p (T = Transformation) of Van Emden [vanE76], [AptK82], which is used in a recursive way to build up I progressively. Very simply, T_p can be defined as:

> T_p(I) = {instanced literal A, assuming that: 1) A_1 :- B_1, B_2, …, B_n is a clause of P ; 2) for a given instantiation Θ of the variables in the body of the clause, Θ(B_1, B_2, …, B_n) is true in I ; 3) A = ΘA_1}.

This means that, for a given step in the construction of I, if there exists a clause of P that can be instantiated making use of the facts of I – i.e. if there exists an instantiation Θ of the variables that transforms the literals of the body of the clause into facts of I – then we can add to I the fact that corresponds to an instantiation of the head of the clause through the use of the instantiation Θ. The recursive procedure begins with an empty set I, I = ∅; the first application of T_p gives all the facts of the DATALOG program. If we now consider this simple program P:

1 Ancestor(*x*, *y*) :- Parent(*x*, *y*)

2 Parent(*x*, *y*) :- Mother(*x*, *y*)

3 Parent(*x*, *y*) :- Father(*x*, *y*)

4 Father(John, Bill)

5 Mother(Lucy, Bill) ,

we will have: $T_p(\emptyset)$ = { Father(John, Bill); Mother(Lucy, Bill) }; $T_p^2(\emptyset)$ = { Father(John, Bill); Mother(Lucy, Bill); Parent(Lucy, Bill); Parent(John, Bill) }; $T_p^3(\emptyset)$ = { Father(John, Bill); Mother(Lucy, Bill); Parent(Lucy, Bill); Parent(John, Bill); Ancestor(Lucy, Bill); Ancestor(John, Bill) }. Any new application of T_p does not give rise to any new fact, i.e. $T_p^4(\emptyset) = T_p^3(\emptyset)$; $T_p^3(\emptyset)$ is, therefore, the least model of our program P. Without entering into any further technical details, we can say that:

- a DATALOG program P can be considered as a 'query' against the extensional database EDB of the ground facts; the definition of the correct answer to P can then be reduced to the derivation of the least model of P (*see* [Lloy87]);

- we have already mentioned before that a relationship exists between DATALOG and relational databases (*see*, for example, [Ceri89]). We can add now that DATALOG can deal with recursivity, which is not allowed in relational algebra – on the contrary, relational queries that make use of the 'difference' operator cannot be expressed in pure DATALOG. To do this, it is necessary to enrich pure DATALOG with the use of logical negation ($\neg$) (*see* Section 3.2).

We can conclude by saying that DATALOG, as a restricted subset of general logic programming, is also a subset of PROLOG; hence, each set of DATALOG clauses could be parsed and executed by a PROLOG interpreter. However, DATALOG and PROLOG differ in their semantics. As we have seen, DATALOG has a purely declarative semantics with a strong flavour of set theory; therefore, the result of a DATALOG program is independent from the order of the clauses in the program. On the contrary, the meaning of PROLOG programs is defined by an operational semantics, i.e. by the specification of how the programs must be executed. A PROLOG program is executed according to a depth-first search strategy with backtracking; moreover, PROLOG makes use of several special predicates, such as the 'cut', that accentuate its procedural character. This strategy does not guarantee the termination of recursive PROLOG programs.

Notwithstanding its nice formal properties linked with its clean declarative style, DATALOG has been severely criticized on occasion from a strictly 'programming' point of view. As a programming language, DATALOG can be considered in fact little more than a toy language, a 'pure' computational paradigm that does not support many ordinary, useful programming tools like those, extra-logic, added to PROLOG to avoid the same sort of criticism. Moreover, from an AI point of view, we can add that a very strict declarative style may be dangerous when it is necessary to take control of inference processing by stating the order and method of the execution of rules, as happens in many ES shells.

3.122 *Rule programming and ESs' inference engines*

Returning to the formula (c) given at the beginning of Section 3.121,

$$(B_1 \wedge B_2 \ldots \wedge B_n) \supset (A_1 \vee A_2 \ldots \vee A_m), \qquad \text{(c)}$$

we have already said that it establishes a very important result, namely that any clause of first order logic is equivalent to an 'implication', where $(B_1 \wedge B_2 \ldots \wedge B_n)$ is the 'antecedent', or the 'conditions' of the implication, and $(A_1 \vee A_2 \ldots \vee A_m)$ is the 'consequent' or the 'conclusion' of the implication. Formula (c) states that, if the different conditions $B_1, B_2, \ldots, B_n$ are all verified (TRUE), they imply a set of alternative conclusions which are expressed by $A_1, A_2, \ldots, A_m$. Expressing (c) succinctly as:

If B *Then* A, (k)

where we retain for B and A the meaning of a conjunction and a disjunction of terms respectively, we obtain the well-known notation used for the 'production rules' – production rules constitute the basic knowledge representation tool used in a majority of expert systems. Production rules were first introduced in symbolic logic by Emil Post [Post43] as a general symbol manipulation system which used grammar-like rules to specify string replacement operations. An example of such a rule could be $C_1 X C_2 \rightarrow C_1 Y C_2$, meaning that any occurrence of string X in the contest of C_1 and C_2 would be replaced by the string Y. Production rules were then used in mathematics under the form of Markov normal algorithms [Mark54], and by Chomsky as rewrite rules in the context of natural language processing [ChomN57]. They became very popular in the artificial intelligence milieus in the mid-1960s, thanks to the development of the first expert systems like DENDRAL and MYCIN.

Thanks to the equivalence between (c) and (k) – i.e. between production rules and logical implication statements – it is now evident that production rules can be interpreted as logical expressions and then submitted to the usual processing techniques of first order logic. Even the 'procedural' interpretation that is characteristic of the use of production rules – *see* Post's productions mentioned above – is not really contradictory with the basic 'declarative' nature of logic – *see* the procedural interpretation of Horn clauses in Section 3.121; at the end of the same section we also see that an interpretation of logic formulas in terms of the resolution principle is not strictly necessary (*see* the definition of the DATALOG semantics in terms of model theory). This explains why, whenever it is necessary to establish some theoretical sound results about some particular application of production rules, the usual strategy consists of converting the set of production rules into a set of logic formulas in the form (c) and operating on this using the customary logic tools. As an example, we mention here a paper by Vermesan [Verm98] where, in the first part of the paper, the author explains how a knowledge base of production rules of the form: $B_1 \wedge B_2 \ldots \wedge B_n \rightarrow A$ ('$\rightarrow$' is the implication symbol, B_i and A are first-order literals) can be converted into a set of first order formulas which are then used to set up a theoretical framework for the verification of the consistency and completeness of the original knowledge base.

Basic principles about rule programming

A typical 'expert system' making use of production rules works as follows:

- The system includes a 'rule base' – an unordered collection of production rules. In this base, rules r can assume in general the form: $c_1 \wedge c_2 \ldots \wedge c_n \rightarrow a_1 \wedge a_2 \ldots \wedge a_m$; this form is not contradictory with (c), as can be seen if we split (c) into as many rules as the terms of this consequent, and assume that each single term in the consequent part of each new rule is expressed by the necessary conjunction, $\wedge$, of several low order terms. We give now to the c_i the meaning of 'conditions' (facts) that must be satisfied, and to a_i the meaning of 'actions' that must be performed if the conditions are satisfied. The c_i represent the 'left-hand side' of r, a_i the 'right-hand side'.
- The system includes a 'working memory' (WM) which stores the facts submitted as input to the system or automatically inferred during its functioning.
- During its functioning, the system repeatedly performs a 'recognize-act' cycle, which can be characterized as follows in the case of 'conventional' expert systems (condition-driven ESs, *see* below):

- in the 'selection phase', for each rule *r* of the rule base, the system i) determines whether LHS(*r*) is satisfied by the current WM contents, i.e. whether LHS(*r*) matches the facts stored in the WM ('match subphase') and, if so, ii) it adds the rule *r* to a particular rule subset called the 'conflict set' (CS) ('addition subphase'). When all the LHS are false, the system halts;
- in the 'conflict resolution phase', a rule of the CS is selected for execution. If it is impossible to select a rule, the system halts;
- in the 'act phase', the actions included in RHS(*r*) are executed by the interpreter – this is often called 'firing a rule'. Firing a rule will normally change the content of WM and, possibly, the CS. To avoid cycling, the set of facts ('instantiation') that has instantiated the LHS variables of the fired rule becomes ineligible to provoke the firing of the same rule again – which, of course, can fire again if instantiated with different facts.

A possible way of schematizing the recognize-act cycle is represented in Figure 3.1. The name 'conflict set' is due to the fact that, among all the competing selected rules that are in agreement with the current state of WM, it is necessary to choose the only rule to be executed by the interpreter in the current cycle – choosing and executing multiple rules is possible, but more complex. The specific procedures to be implemented for performing the resolution of the conflicts depend on the application, and can be very complicated, given that the execution of a rule may lead other rules to 'fire', or on the contrary prevent their firing, etc. It is then possible to make use of user-defined priorities: the user is allowed to choose a particular strategy, such as giving preference to rules that operate on the most recent information added to WM, or that match the highest number of items, or the most specific rule, i.e. the one with the most detailed LHS that matches the current state of WM. It is also possible to make use of pre-defined criteria for ordering the rules that may be static (i.e. a priority ordering is assigned to the rules when they are created) or dynamic. In a database environment, it is also possible to try to execute all the selected rules in parallel under the control of a concurrency control manager in the DBMS – *see* [Sell88] for the technical details.

The architecture expounded in Figure 3.1 is at the origin of a very important property of production systems: the independence of *knowledge* from the *control* on how the knowledge is applied. Each set of rules making up a particular knowledge base is created totally independently from the control structure; each rule in the set must express a relationship between LHS and RHS that must hold *a priori*, in a static way. In other words, the validity, the 'truth' of the rule, must subsist independently of when the rule is applied. Making a comparison with conventional programming techniques, we can also say that, in a production (or, more generally, rule-based) system, a change in the knowledge base is not propagated throughout the program as can happen in a procedural program. This also means that the LHS must express, at least in principle, all the necessary and sufficient conditions that will allow the RHS to be applied.

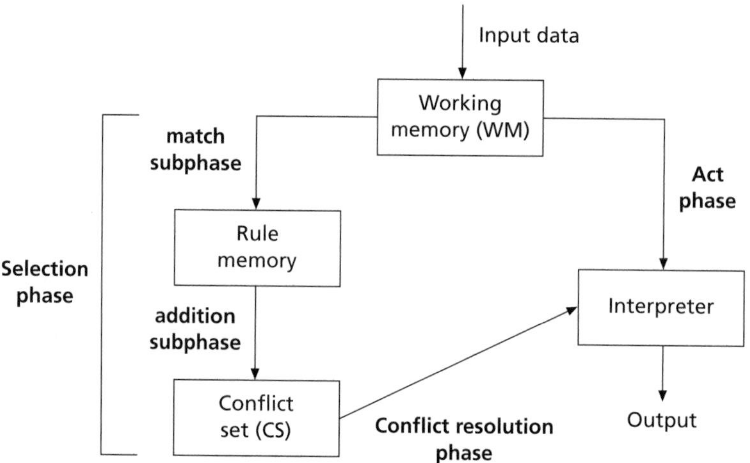

Figure 3.1 The 'recognize-act' cycle

In reality, production systems can be classified into two categories according to the way rules are compared with data of WM. In the 'conventional' production systems, the comparison is between LHS(r) and WM as illustrated in Figure 3.1 ('condition-driven' or 'forward-chaining' systems). But it is also possible to compare RHS(s) with WM ('action-driven' or 'backward-chaining' systems). Here, the formula (l) that we have taken as representative in general of the production rules

$$c_1 \wedge c_2 \dots \wedge c_n \rightarrow a_1 \wedge a_2 \dots \wedge a_m \qquad (1)$$

is used in a way that coincides particularly well with the interpretation of logical clauses as implications, with the a_i, i.e. acting as the subgoals to be satisfied to prove the condition. We can then say that logic programming, and PROLOG and DATALOG in particular, work by backward-chaining from a goal.

In general, the condition-driven, forward-chaining production systems are useful to deal with large rule sets, where the number of possible goal states is very high and it is impossible to select some best goals *a priori*. It is then better to deal with the data opportunistically, as they arrive in the environment of the system, and to be driven by the data towards a suitable goal. The action-driven, backward-chaining production systems allow more efficient and more focused strategies to be implemented. In these systems, in fact, a goal G is chosen – in its initial state, WM is reduced to G – and the system selects all the rules that may lead to G, i.e. all the rules where G appears (match) among the a_i of the RHS. If several rules are selected, we have again a CS non-empty, and a conflict resolution problem. In the act phase, the c_i in the LHS of the fired rule are chosen as the new subgoals, they are added to WM, and a new recognize-act cycle begins; the process continues until all the inferred subgoals are satisfied. The efficiency is linked with the fact that the rules are selected in a sequence that proceeds towards the desired goal.

To give an example of an actual rule, we propose in Table 3.1 the natural language version of a production rule, 'rule 88', which is part of about 500 rules used in one of the best known and historically important expert system, the MYCIN system [Shor76]. MYCIN – built up in the mid-1970s – was designed to perform medical diagnosis (prescribe antibiotic therapy) in the field of bacterial infections, thanks to a medical knowledge of approximately 100 causes of infection buried into its rules. The MYCIN system was a backward-chaining system, i.e. the logical functioning of Rule 88 was to deduce, from the assertion 'there is evidence that the organism is bacteroides', the simultaneous existence of the facts 'the infection type is primary-bacteremia', 'the suspected entry point is ...', etc.

Table 3.1 A MYCIN's rule

Rule 88 **IF:**

1. the infection type is primary-bacteremia, *and*
2. the site of the culture is one of the sterile sites, *and*
3. the suspected portal of entry of the organism is the gastro-intestinal tract

THEN:

there is suggestive evidence (0.7) that the identity of the organism is bacteroides.

Additional technical details

The numeric value that appears in the RHS of the rule of Table 3.1 is a 'certainty factor' (CF), a way of estimating belief in the conclusions of a rule-based system that has been popularized by MYCIN. We can say that the presence of CFs or similar tools constitutes the main difference between a simple production system and a 'real' expert system – and, *a fortiori*, between a logic programming system and an expert system. Through the CFs, and other more sophisticated mechanisms (*see* below), ESs are able in fact to express, even in a very rough way, the *uncertainty* that is linked with a given assertion, instead of, as in PROLOG and DATALOG, affirming that all the assertions are simply true or false. Another important difference of an ES with respect to a simple rule system concerns the possibility to provide a sort of explication of its behaviour. This can be obtained in a very simple way by printing the 'chain' of rules that have led to a given conclusion, and making use of the fact that each rule directly states the information on which its particular deduction was based, and the reason why this deduction holds.

A CF can be considered as the composition, according to the expression CF = MB – MD, of a 'measure of belief' (MB) and a 'measure of disbelief' (MD), where MB and MD can take a value between 0 and 1. CF can then vary in value between –1 and +1. If the value is = 0, this means there is no evidence for the hypothesis that is being examined. When the value of CF is > 0 and is moving towards +1, this means that 'evidence' is increasingly supporting the hypothesis; when CF <0 and is moving towards –1, the hypothesis is increasingly unsupported by the evidence. An important point here is that CFs are *not* probabilities – they do not deal with the dependence/independence problems typical of probabilities and, moreover, are defined and combined through a very *ad hoc* system of rules.

The CFs associated *a priori* (off-line) with the rules of a production system can be modified when the rules are 'chained' together during the functioning of the system: as the rules fire according to the recognize-act cycle of Figure 3.1, there is a sort of 'propagation' of the CFs down the inference chain that results in an increase, decrease or stabilization of the different CFs encountered along the chain. The modifications are executed according to the *ad hoc* rules proper to the certainty factor theory; among them, three sorts of rules are particularly important, the 'parallel combination rule', the 'propagate changes rule', and the 'Boolean combination rule'.

The first is used when we have several rules (at least two) characterized by the presence of *sure* (but distinct) LHSs – i.e. the LHSs are *facts* that, as in the LHS of the Rule 88 above, are not affected by any sort of uncertainty – and asserting the *same* RHS that is, however, characterised by *different* CFs according to the different rules. Indicating with u and v the CFs associated with the RHS of two rules r_1 and r_2 respectively, we will have a situation like: $r_1 \equiv \text{LHS}_1 \rightarrow \text{RHS},u$; $r_2 \equiv \text{LHS}_2 \rightarrow \text{RHS},v$. In order to be able to reuse the (identical) RHS in the chain of deductions, it must be associated with a new CF, w: this will depend on the sign of u and v according with the following expressions:

$$u,\ v > 0 \Rightarrow w = u + v - uv;$$
$$u < 0 \vee v < 0 \Rightarrow w = (u + v)/(1 - \min(|u|,\ |v|));$$
$$u,\ v < 0 \Rightarrow w = u + v + uv.$$

The 'propagate changes rule' modifies the CF associated with RHS(r) when the rule r itself is uncertain, i.e. as the result, for example, of a chain of inferences, the corresponding LHS(r) is associated in turn with a CF. If the rule r is now LHS(r),u → RHS(r),v , the new CF w associated with RHS(r) will be:

$$w = v\ \max(0,\ u).$$

Finally, the 'Boolean combination rule' must be used when LHS(r) is, as usual (*see* 'Rule 88' above), a Boolean combination of literals. The CF w resulting from the 'and' and 'or' combinations of two LHS literals l_1 and l_1, characterized respectively by the CFs u and v, will be:

$$l_1,u \wedge l_2,v \Rightarrow w = \min(u,\ v);$$
$$l_1,u \vee l_2,v \Rightarrow w = \max(u,\ v).$$

This means that, if the literals (predicates) are ANDed, it is the lowest value CF that is propagated in the LHS; if they are ORed, it is on the contrary the maximum value CF to be propagated.

The CFs approach has several advantages, the main being that they are considerably less difficult to evaluate than probabilities, and that they are independent so that we can consider their modifications a rule at a time. Independence also means that adding or deleting rules does not imply any remodelling of the entire system of CFs. On the other hand, they can also lead to very strange results, as happens when the number of parallel rules supporting the same hypothesis is high: in this case, for example, the application of the parallel combination rule produces CFs that approach systematically 1 even in the presence of small values for the original CFs (*see*, for example, [Norv92: 562]). Moreover, the result of the application of the above rules are *monotonic*, i.e. the CFs cannot be adjusted if some facts that have been used in the processing are later retracted.

The Dempster-Shafer theory (DST) – *see* [Demp67], [Shaf76], [Krus91] and also [Baue95], [Baue97] – has more reliable mathematical foundations than the CF approach, even if it is neatly more complex from a computational point of view. DS includes both the classical statistical model and the CF proposals as special cases.

In the classical (Bayesian) statistical model, it is assumed that phenomena are of a Boolean nature, i.e. either they exist or they do not exist. As a result, if a certain 'degree of belief' – 'beliefs' (belief functions) intend to model and to quantify the subjective convictions induced by some 'evidences' – is assigned to the hypothesis (proposition) A assessing that a given phenomenon exists, has existed or will exist, the remaining belief is automatically assigned to the negation $\neg A$ of this hypothesis. In other terms, if there were a limited belief in the existence of a phenomenon, this would imply, under the 'classical' formulation, a very strong belief in its non-existence. DST considers, on the contrary, only the evidence that is specifically in favour of a proposition A; there is no longer a causal relationship between A and its negation, so that the lack of belief does not automatically indicate disbelief. DST dismisses then one of the main axioms of the Bayesian theory: $P(A) + P(\neg A) = 1$ *for any proposition* A. On the contrary, if there is no evidence at all, for or against A, DST assumes that the degrees of belief for both A and $\neg A$ are $= 0$: in 'classical' terms, this should mean that $P(A) + P(\neg A) = 0$. To model this sort of intuition, DST needs to find a way of describing explicitly the degrees of belief and disbelief in A.

To do this, DST makes use of a sort of combination calculus where, given a set of hypotheses (e.g. ES rules), all the possible combinations in the hypothesis set are considered. This is coherent with the observation that often the experts find evidence that is associated with a subset of hypotheses rather than with just one. The set Θ including *all the mutually exclusive and exhaustive hypotheses* about a problem domain – in Θ, the hypotheses are then considered as 'singletons' – is called the 'frame of discernment'. 2^Θ is the powerset that includes *all the possible subsets* (all the possible combinations) of Θ; each of these subsets – which may be atomic, consisting then of a singleton, or compound, consisting of a conjunction of singletons – may be interpreted as a general proposition in the problem domain. The main element of DST is now an 'amount of belief function' or 'mass function' or 'probability density function' or 'basic probability assignment (bpa) function':

$$m : 2^\Theta \rightarrow [0,1]$$

that allows assigning an evidential weight (bpa) in the range between 0 and 1 to each element of 2^Θ (not only to the singletons).

Note that, in contrast with probability theory, a value of 0 does not say that a given alternative is impossible, but only that there is no evidence that supports directly the truth of this alternative. If a non-singleton alternative A receives a non-null bpa, while all the single alternatives that constitute the subset A have a 0 bpa, this attests that evidence is sufficient to assert that one of the elements of A is enough to describe the state of the world, but this evidence is not specific enough to assert the likelihood of the specific subsets of A. This is the situation corresponding to the evidence that a given crime has been perpetrated by a blond-haired person given that a blond lock of hair has been found in the hands of the victim. In this case, a high bpa is associated with the element A of 2^{Θ} formed by the union of all the possible blond-haired people potentially involved in the crime, the different singletons of A having, on the contrary, bpa = 0.

The function m satisfies the following properties:

$$m(\varnothing) = 0 \ ; \ \Sigma_{A \subseteq \Theta} m(A) = 1,$$

where $\varnothing$ is the empty set; the subsets $A \subseteq \Theta$ with non-zero bpa values are called the 'focal elements' of m. They represent alternatives being directly supported by the evidence encoded by m.

To give a simple, concrete example, see [Baue95], let us suppose that a dice is thrown, and an observer tells us that an odd number was thrown. If the observer's report is considered reliable, this leads to a bpa $m(\{1, 3, 5\}) = 1$ and $m(A) = 0$ for all the other hypotheses $A \subseteq \Theta = \{1, \ldots, 6\}$. If the reliability of the report is subject to caution, $m(\{1, 3, 5\}) < 1$ and the remaining belief is assigned to the largest hypothesis set, the global frame of discernment $\Theta = \{1, \ldots, 6\}$ – for example, if it is known that the observer is usually wrong 1/10 of the time, then $m(\{1, 3, 5\}) = 0.9$ and $m(\{1, \ldots, 6\}) = 0.1$. If the report is considered to be totally unreliable, then $m(\{1, \ldots, 6\}) = 1$, corresponding to a situation of total ignorance.

As the above discussion should have made clear, $m(A)$ measures the amount of belief that can be attributed *exactly* to A given the state of the evidence – because of our lack of knowledge – without saying anything about its subsets. The total 'degree of belief' that can be assigned to A *and* to its components (B) is quantified by the 'belief function', $Bel : 2^{\Theta} \rightarrow [0,1]$, defined as:

$$Bel(\varnothing) = 0 \ ; \ Bel(\Theta) = 1 \ ; \ Bel(A) = \Sigma_{B \subseteq A} m(B). \qquad \text{(m)}$$

If, for example, $A = \{B_1, B_2\}$, $Bel(A) = m(\{B_1, B_2\}) + m(\{B_1\}) + m(\{B_2\})$; $m(\{B_1, B_2\}) = m(A)$. The 'disbelief' in A is now simply the belief in the complement of that set, $Bel(\neg A)$. The 'plausibility' of an alternative A, $Pl : 2^{\Theta} \rightarrow [0,1]$, is now defined as the sum of the bpas that are allocated to all the alternatives B that do not contradict A, i.e. that are not implying $\neg A$. We have then:

$$Pl(A) = \Sigma_{B \cap A \neq \varnothing} m(B),$$

where Bel and Pl are related through the following expression:

$$Pl(A) = Bel(\Theta) - Bel(\neg A) = 1 - m(\varnothing) - Bel(\neg A).$$

Plausibility measures the extent to which evidence in favour of $\neg A$ 'leaves space' for belief in A: in particular, having firm evidence in favour of $\neg A$ implies that $Bel(\neg A) = 1$ and then $Pl(A) = 0$. It can be shown that $Bel(A)$ and $Pl(A)$ give, respectively, the lower and the upper bounds for the 'usual' (but unknown) probability of A; as already stated, the DST approach includes as a special case the classical Bayesian approach. The interval $[Bel(A), Pl(A)]$ is called the 'belief interval' for a given A; its size represents the 'degree of ignorance' with respect to a given A. DST can also be seen, therefore, as an extension of probability theory that allows 'intervals of probability' to be dealt with.

To be able to make use of the concepts introduced before in the context, for example, of a concrete ES, it is also necessary to have a means of combining the belief functions that, in DST, have the same function as the CFs examined previously. The so-called 'Dempster's rule' (*see* [Demp67]) supplies a means of combining two independent pieces of evidence, encoded in the bpas m_1 and m_2, into a new bpa $m_1 \oplus m_2$, defined as:

$$(m_1 \oplus m_2)(A) = \frac{\sum_{B_1 \cap B_2 = A} m_1(B_1)\ m_2(B_2)}{1 - \sum_{B_1 \cap B_2 = \varnothing} m_1(B_1)\ m_2(B_2)}$$

for non-empty A and with $(m_1 \oplus m_2)(\varnothing) = 0$, where B_1 and B_2 range over all the non-empty subset of Θ. Having determined the new, combined amount of belief $m_1 \oplus m_2$ that can be attributed exactly to A, the definition (m) can then be applied again to determine the total degree of belief that can be assigned to A giving its components – i.e. the combined 'belief function' for A, $Bel_1 \oplus Bel_2(A)$ – using the new bpas calculated for A and for all its components according to the Dempster's rule above. As already stated, using DST brings about very complex computational problems linked with the use of the bpas m: several methods have been proposed in order to reduce the number of focal elements of Θ (*see*, for example, [Baue97]).

However, the prevailing tendency in the domain of the uncertain reasoning techniques seems to be to ground these techniques on probabilistic 'graphical' models like the very popular Bayesian networks (also known as 'belief networks' and 'causal probabilistic networks'). A probabilistic graphical model is a graph where the nodes represent variables and the arcs, directed or undirected, represent dependencies among the variables. They can be used to represent the joint (conditional) probability distribution of the variables. Besides Bayesian networks, these models can represent influence diagrams in decision processes, hidden Markov models, connectionist feed-forward networks, etc. (*see* [Bunt94]).

Bayesian networks – *see* [Pear88] and [Char91] for an introduction – are very general tools that can be used to represent extremely different situations such as the probability of failure of a given component in a digital system, the probability of a certain page in a computer's cache memory, to be asked for in the short term, the probability for a given document to be relevant with respect to a given query, etc. In formal terms, a Bayesian network B for a set of variables $\mathbf{X} = \{X_1, \ldots, X_n\}$ is a pair (S, P). The random variables X_i represent important parameters in a domain of interest; some variables can also be 'hidden', and correspond to some unknown parameters that influence the observable variables. S is a DAG, i.e. a directed graph without directed cycles; the nodes of the DAG represent the variables of $\mathbf{X}$ and the arcs $\{X_i, X_j\}$, $X_i \neq X_j$, represent *conditional dependencies* among the variables, i.e. an arc from X_i to X_j means that the probability value associated with X_i has a direct effect on the probability of X_j. P is a set of local, conditional probability distributions, $p(x_i | \mathbf{pa}_i)$, associated with each variable X_i given the set of its parents $\mathbf{Pa}_i$, where we indicate with x_i the state (i.e. the value) proper to the variable X_i and with $\mathbf{pa}_i$ the state of the parents $\mathbf{Pa}_i$ of X_i. The multivariate joint probability distribution for $\mathbf{X}$ is given by the product, over all the nodes, of the conditional probability of the node given its parents; for all the possible instantiations $\mathbf{x}$ of all the n variables, we will have:

$$p(\mathbf{x}) = p(x_1, \ldots, x_n) = \prod_{i=1}^{n} p(x_i | \mathbf{pa}_i) .$$

A proof of the above expression can be found in [Char91: 55–56]. Figure 3.2, adapted from [Bunt94], shows a simple Bayesian network for a reduced medical problem.

For this situation, $\mathbf{X}$ = {*Age, Occ, Clim, Dis, Symp*}; $p(\mathbf{x})$ = $p(age)p(occ)p(clim)p(dis/age,occ,clim)p(symp/dis)$; the root nodes *Age, Occ, Clim* have associated prior probabilities, $p(x_i)$; the non-root nodes *Dis* and *Symp* – an interior and a leaf node – have associated, according to the Bayesian model, conditional probabilities given their parents, $p(x_i/\mathbf{pa}_i)$. Bayesian networks allow the conditional probabilities associated with the nodes of the network to be calculated under the condition that the prior probabilities of some of the nodes have been assigned. In practice, each non-root node is characterized by an associated conditional probability table (CPT). In this, the first positions of each row represent a possible combination of states of the parent nodes of the node considered – for example, for the node *Dis* of Figure 3.2, the first three positions of each row represent possible combinations of values for the variables *Age, Occ* and *Clim* – and the last position of the row corresponds to the conditional probability (Bayesian probability, belief) that the node considered is correspondingly in a certain state. We can note that, in general, the complexity of the problem concerning the calculation of the multivariate joint probability distribution for $\mathbf{X}$ is NP-hard (*see* [Coop87]); solutions can be obtained in polynomial time if the network is 'singly connected' (is a 'polytree'), i.e. the underlying DAG, as in Figure 3.2, has no more than one path between any two nodes. For a discussion about the 'exact' and 'approximate' solutions for Bayesian networks, *see* again [Char91: 56–59].

Bayesian networks can be 'learned', which means learning the network structure and the parameters of the conditional probabilities. A well established technique for this sort of learning consists of the definition of a scoring metric that measures the 'fitness' of a network structure with respect to the experimental data, and of the search for network structures characterized by a high scoring in terms of the defined scoring metric (*see*, for example, [Coop92], [Heck95]).

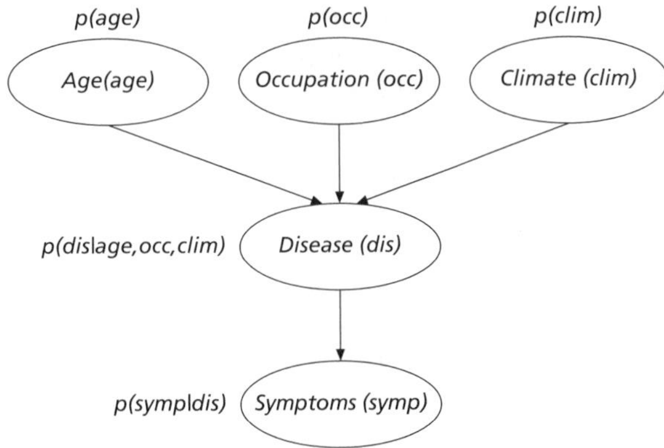

Figure 3.2 A very simple example of a Bayesian network

We will conclude this description of rule programming and production systems with a brief account of the RETE algorithm. Returning to the differentiation between backward-chaining and forward-chaining introduced in the previous section, forward-chaining often involves dealing with a large quantity of data and a large set of rules. Unlike backward-chaining systems, in fact, where the goal-directed reasoning guides the execution of the rules, in a forward-chaining system every fact entered into WM must be compared with every LHS of every rule, leading to a number of combinations that can prove unmanageable without the aid of some mechanism to improve efficiency. The RETE algorithm, developed by Charles L. Forgy in the mid-1970s, [Forg82] and inserted in the OPS5 production rules language, enables this heavy matching process to be speeded up. OPS5 is one of the most popular tools for developing ESs according to the production rule paradigm; its latest version, OPS/R2, supports both forward and backward-chaining, and objects with inheritance. A detailed study on the response time of the OPS5-like languages is given in [ChenA00]; *see* [Forg95] for an historical overview of the development of OPS.

To understand more precisely the need for such a speed-up mechanism, it is necessary to understand the modalities of construction of the conflict set. Suppose that a fact of WM is used in the instantiation of a rule r_1, and that the firing of another rule r_2 produces the deleting of this fact. This modifies the conditions under which the LHS of r_1 has been instantiated, and the rule r_1 must be suppressed from the conflict set. That is to say, the conflict set must be recreated for every cycle, by examining all the rules and producing for each of them a list of all the possible instantiations according to the contents of the working memory. This process is particularly inefficient given that, in most production systems, WM changes slowly from cycle to cycle (less than 10 per cent of the facts are changed in a cycle). This means that a neat majority of the production rules are not affected by changes with respect to their instantiations, and that a program that reiterates the construction of the conflict set on each cycle will probably repeat the same, large amount of operations, again and again. The main idea of the RETE algorithm is to save the state of CS at the end of a given cycle and, in the next cycle, generating only a list of the changes to be incorporated to CS as a function of the changes that have affected WM. The pattern matcher can then be viewed as a 'black box' where the input is labelled as 'Changes to WM' and the output 'Changes to CS' [Forg82: 22]; in practice, the black box is implemented as a data-flow graph (the RETE network).

The descriptions of the WM changes are called 'tokens' – a token is an ordered pair composed of a tag and a list of data elements. In principle, only two tags are needed, + and –, where + indicates that something has been added to WM and – indicates that something has been deleted. When a data element of WM is modified, two tokens are sent as inputs to the RETE network, the first to say that the previous form of the element has been deleted from WM, and the other to say that a new form has been added. The network is compiled from the LHSs of all the productions contained in the rule base, and contains two kinds of nodes, called 'alpha' (or 'intra-elements' features) and 'beta' (or 'inter-elements' features). Both act as filters that execute tests on some features of the tokens and send the tokens that pass the test to their successors in the network. Alpha nodes perform tests on individual facts, beta nodes perform tests that look at more than one fact at a time. Let us consider an example from the very popular 'block world'. Adopting the terminology of [Forg82], we will call 'patterns' the different literals that appear in the LHS of a production rule; we will assume, moreover, that the patterns that refer to the objects of the block world have the following format in some sort of simplified OPS5:

```
(object <o_i> name <n_i> type <t_i> colour <c_i>),
```

i.e. these patterns are lists of pairs attribute-value, where the symbols within angle brackets are 'pattern variables'. A pattern variable will match any value in a WM element, but if a variable occurs more than once in the LHS of a particular production, all the occurrences of the variable must match the same value. This mechanism of OPS5 simulates a 'join' of the traditional relational DB algebra through the use of common variable names. A possible rule $\mathbf{r}_1$ to express that 'if we have a brick and a pyramid of the same colour, and if the pyramid is on the brick, assert that the two blocks form a tower of that particular colour' will thus be (*see also* [Grah90]):

```
(r_1
      (block <n_1> brick <c_1>)
      (block <n_2> pyramid <c_1>)
      (on <n_2> <n_1>)
→
   (assert <n_1> and <n_2> tower <c_1>).
```

The third pattern of LHS is an instance of the general pattern for relations: (**relation** $<r_i>$ **first-arg** $<n_i>$ **second-arg** $<n_j>$); in rule $\mathbf{r}_1$, for simplicity's sake, we have indicated only the values, constant or variables of the attributes associated with the block world objects.

When the compiler that builds up the network processes the LHS of a particular rule, it begins with the intra-elements (alpha) 'features', i.e. it determines the constant values (features) that characterize each LHS pattern of the rule considered *in isolation* and build up a linear sequence of nodes for the pattern, where each node tests for the presence of a feature. For the LHS of $\mathbf{r}_1$ then, the compiler will insert four alpha nodes: i) the root nodes α_1 and α_2 that will test the presence of, respectively, 'block' as the first feature of the first and second pattern, and 'on' as the first feature of the third pattern, and ii) two nodes derived from α_1 which express the alternative 'brick' (α_3) or 'pyramid' (α_4) as the third element of the first and second pattern – *see* the first part of Figure 3.3, adapted from [Grah90]. After the compiler has finished with the alpha features, it builds the nodes that allow testing for the inter-elements (beta) features. Each of the beta nodes has two inputs in order to be able to perform tests on two sets of facts simultaneously, and they then can join two paths of the network into one. The first beta node joins the linear sequences of alpha type that stem from the two first patterns, the second joins the output of the first beta node with the sequence alpha for the third pattern, and so on. We need only two beta nodes for $\mathbf{r}_1$ – *see* Figure 3.3 – node β_1 will pass only the pairs of WM elements that have an identical fourth value; node β_2 will pass those triples of WM elements, $\{w_k, w_l, w_m\}$, where the second value of w_m, corresponding to $<n_2>$ in $\mathbf{r}_1$, is the same as the second element of w_l, and the third value of w_m, corresponding to $<n_1>$ in $\mathbf{r}_1$, is the same as the second value of w_k. An additional, important feature of the beta nodes is that each of them contains two lists called its left and right memories – 'lm' and 'rm' in Figure 3.3. The left memory holds copies of the tokens that arrive at its left input, the right memory holds copies of the tokens that arrive at its right input. This feature allows the beta nodes to compare new facts with facts that have already traversed their inputs.

Let us suppose now that the WM of the production system is empty, and that we assert the following three facts:

```
(block b-1 brick red)
(block b-2 pyramid red)
(on b-2 b-1).
```

Three tokens, $T_1 \equiv$ (+(block b–1 brick red)), $T_2 \equiv$ (+(block b–2 pyramid red)), $T_3 \equiv$ (+(on b–2 b–1)), where the tag + indicates an addition to WM, are then created and inserted *successively* in the network.

T_1 and T_2 pass the test in α_1 and are sent to α_3 and α_4; T_3 passes α_2 and is stored in the right memory (rm) of β_2. T_1 passes the test α_3 and is stored in lm of β_1; T_2 fails on α_3 but passes the test α_4, and is stored in rm of β_1. The particularity of the beta nodes, with respect to the alpha, is that if they receive only one input they save it until the second input comes along; this means that if, sometime later in the ES functioning, the second element enters WM, the pattern matcher does not have to process the first element all over again. β_1 can now check whether the new token T_2 is in agreement with the token T_1 which was already stored in its lm; the test succeeds, and the new combined token

```
T1,2 ≡ (+(block b-1 brick red)
          (block b-2 pyramid red)),
```

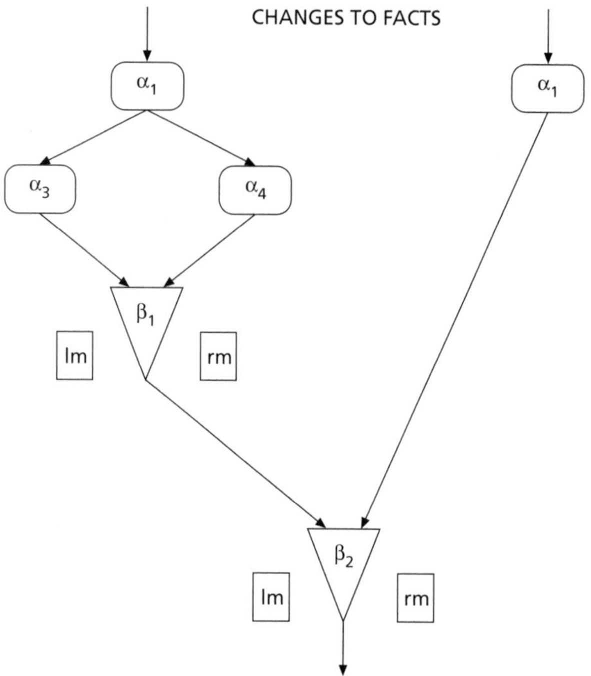

Figure 3.3 An example of a RETE network

is stored in lm of β_2. This new token is congruent with the token T_3 that was stored in the rm of β_2; the new token

```
T1,2,3 ≡ (+ (block b-1 brick red)
            (block b-2 pyramid red)
            (on b-2 b-1))
```

is then created and, given that no further node exists, $T_{1,2,3}$ is the output of the RETE network and, at the same time, *it represents a new instantiation*. The presence of additional rules in the rule base corresponds to the addition of more nodes in the graph. An important contribution to the efficiency of the RETE approach is given by the possibility of sharing the alpha node, as we have shown in our example. Note that this sharing is also possible for patterns that pertain to different rules.

The mechanism for adding or deleting instantiations making use of the RETE network is based on the following principles [Forg82: 26]:

- The terminal nodes on the network, β_2 in Figure 3.3, make use of the tag associated with the instantiations (complex tokens) they receive to understand whether this instantiation must be added to the conflict set, or deleted from the set.
- The construction of a 'negative' instantiation (a final complex token characterised by the tag '–') follows the same general philosophy used for the 'positive' instantiations. The tokens representing deletions are processed in

the usual way by the alpha nodes. The beta nodes behave in a slightly different way: when a negated token reaches one of the inputs, it is not stored in the corresponding memory but, on the contrary, any corresponding positive token stored there is removed by that memory. This ensures the elimination of any untrue fact that is still stored in the network. The negated token is then matched, as usual, against the tokens in the other input; the tag of the compound token is now, however, '–' (more in general, the tag of the compound token is always equal to the tag of the incoming token).

The RETE algorithm is particularly clever and elegant, but it is not exempt from drawbacks. The main one is linked with the (normally reasonable) assumption that WM changes slightly from one cycle to another. When a large proportion of WM changes on each cycle, the RETE mechanisms could as well reconstruct the conflict set each time. Another problem is linked with the fact that, given that a deletion is processed (almost) as an assertion, dealing with assertions in RETE is computationally expensive. The TREAT algorithm [Mira87], a variant of RETE, tries to fix this last problem.

In the context of this book, it may be interesting to remark here that RETE-like mechanisms have also been used in the DB field to set up efficient tools in an active databases and rule-based systems context – *see*, for example, [HansM89], [Delc89], etc., and Section 2.3. DBRete, *see* [Sell88], [Sell93], is a proposal for implementing the RETE algorithm in a relational DB environment. In this proposal, DBRete makes use of the possibility of matching OPS5 patterns into relations thanks to the representation of the patterns according to an attribute-value format; secondary storage is used to store the WM elements.

3.1 3 Inference by inheritance

Inheritance is one of the most popular and powerful concepts used in the artificial intelligence domain. It has, at the same time, a very high value *at least* as:

- a *static*, structuring principle that allows similar notions to be grouped together in classes, and to economize on the description of some attributes of the entities of the low-level classes because these descriptions can be inherited from the entities of the high-level classes;
- a *dynamic*, inferencing principle that allows deductions to be made about the properties (attributes) of the low-level entities that are *a priori* unknown because these properties can be deduced from those that characterize the high-level entities – with the well-known problems linked with the fact that, for example, 'penguins' and 'ostriches' pertain to the class 'birds', but they cannot inherit from the description of this general class the property 'can_fly';
- a *generative* principle that allows new classes to be defined as variants of the existing ones: the new class inherits, in fact, the general properties and behaviours of the parent class, and the system builder must only specify how the new class is different.

Inheritance is often conceived as a typical, fundamental principle proper to the artificial intelligence field, and it will be dealt with in this way in this section. However, its significance goes well beyond the strict AI domain, and its importance for the DB domain is continually increasing. We have already seen that inheritance constitutes a key element of all the object-oriented systems. We can add now that a data model such as OEM (object exchange model, *see* [PapaM95]) – OEM is structured as a labelled directed graph that coincides practically with inheritance hierarchy – is gaining popularity for dealing with 'semi-structured data' such as those stored on the World Wide Web.

In the AI domain, the inheritance principle is normally used to set up hierarchies of 'concepts' or 'ontologies', to use an up-to-date and very fashionable term, *see* [Frid97], [Gome98] and Chapter 4. The intuitive idea of concept is not easy to define in a very precise way. As a useful approximation, we can think of concepts in the context of a practical application as the important notions that it is necessary to represent to obtain a correct modelling of the particular domain examined; moreover, the most general among them, such as *human_being* or *physical_object*, are common to a majority of domains. Concepts in AI correspond then to 'classes' in object-oriented representations, and to 'types' in the standard, procedural programming languages. In this section, we will deal mainly with the general, 'architectural' issues related to the construction of well-formed hierarchies of concepts; we will examine in the next two subsections the specific issues concerning the modelling of the internal structure of a concept, i.e. how the 'attributes' (proprieties, roles, slots, etc.) that characterize a given concept are represented.

The main conceptual tool for building up inheritance hierarchies is the well-known IsA link – called also AKindOf (Ako), SuperC, etc. – see Figure 3.4. We will attribute to IsA, at least for the moment, the less controversial and plain interpretation (*see* [BracR83a]), saying that this link stands for the assertion that *concept_b* (or simply *B*) is a specialization, IsA, of the more general *concept_a* (*A*). This sort of relation is sometimes expressed in logical form as:

$$\forall x (B(x) \supset A(x)); \qquad \text{(n)}$$

(n) says that, if any *elephant_* (*B*) IsA *mammal_* (*A*), and if clyde_ is an *elephant_*, then clyde_ is also a *mammal_* – see also the notion of 'subsumption' in section 3.132. We adopt here the convention of writing down the *concepts_* in italics, and their instances_ (e.g. clyde_, an 'individual') in roman characters. When (n) is interpreted strictly, it also implies that the *instances* of a given concept *B must* inherit *all* the features (properties) of *all* the more general concepts in the hierarchy that have *B* as a specialization; we speak in this case of 'strict inheritance'. In reality, using both the notions of 'concept' and 'instance' in the definition of inheritance instead of sticking to the simple notion of concept introduces some difficulties in terms of logic and semantic interpretation of the inheritance hierarchies, as we will see later.

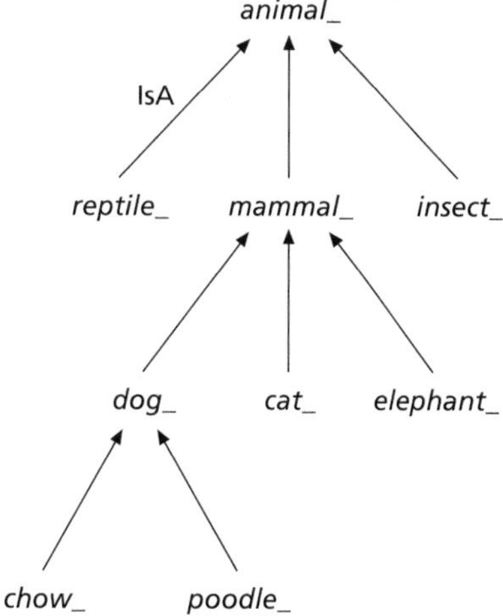

Figure 3.4 A simple inheritance hierarchy

The ordering relation supporting the algebraic structure of these hierarchies is the 'property inclusion' or 'entailment'. Also the 'property exclusion' gets involved in the definition of the semantics of the well-formed hierarchies by assuming that the siblings' immediate descendants of the same parent node are mutually exclusive. This means that, if we consider that *dog_*, *cat_* and *elephant_* are all siblings deriving directly from *mammal_*, the properties (not inherited from *mammal_*) that characterize them as separate concepts must all be mutually exclusive.

The necessary complement of IsA for the construction of well-formed hierarchies is therefore some form of InstanceOf link. Note that the awareness of this necessity is relatively recent in the knowledge representation domain – in the 1980s, several running systems (commercial and not) based on inheritance mechanisms were still unable to make any distinction between concepts, and instances of the concepts. A well-known example in this domain is that of KEE (knowledge engineering environment) [Fike85], one of the early and most powerful commercial environments for the development of complex KBSs (*see also* Section 3.131). Followers of a uniform approach in which all the 'units', to adopt the KEE terminology, have the same status, claim that, for many applications, this distinction is not very useful and only adds some important logical and semantic difficulties.

The difference between *B* IsA *A* and *C* InstanceOf *B* is normally explained in terms of the difference between the two options of i) considering *B* as a subclass of *A* in the first case, operator '$\subset$', and ii) considering C as a member of the class *B* in the second, operator '$\in$'. Unfortunately, this is not sufficient to eliminate any ambiguity about the notion of instance, that is, eventually, much more controversial than the notion of concept. The main problems concern i) the possibility of considering as instances in themselves all the nodes of a hierarchy like that of

Figure 3.4 to the exclusion of the root, instead of admitting that the instances can only be some 'leaves' strictly dependent on these 'basic' nodes; ii) even limiting the notion of instance to this last interpretation, the possibility of having several levels of instances, i.e. instances of an instance.

If a very liberal interpretation of the notion of instance is admitted, clyde_ is an instance of *elephant_* but *elephant_* can also be considered, to a certain extent, as an instance of *mammal_*: this is accepted in some object-oriented systems, *see* Section 2.2. In this case, the logical and semantic properties of the instances are likely to become strongly dependent on the particular choice of primary concepts selected to set up a given inheritance hierarchy. For example, in front of a figure like Figure 3.4, and according to the definition given in (n), it could be easy to infer that the InstanceOf relationship is, like IsA, always transitive: if fido_ InstanceOf *poodle_*, fido_ is also, evidently, InstanceOf *animal_*. But if, in this same figure, we substitute the root *animal_* with the root *species_*, we can still consider that *poodle_* InstanceOf *species_*, but it becomes very difficult to assert fido_ InstanceOf *species_* (*see also* [Lena90b: 332–339]). A solution to this problem, that we favour, consists of adding to the set-oriented definition of an instance a sort of 'extensional' definition in the Woods style [Wood75]. According to this principle, we consider that all the nodes of a well-formed inheritance hierarchy like that of Figure 3.4 must be considered only as 'concepts', i.e. general descriptions/definitions of generic intensional notions, like that of 'poodle'; when necessary, an InstanceOf link can be added to each of these nodes having the meaning of a specific existence predicate: for example, we can declare that a specific, extensional incarnation of the 'concept' *poodle_* is represented by the 'individual' fido_. In this way, the introduction of instances becomes strictly a local operation, to be executed explicitly, when needed, for each node (concept) of the hierarchy – *see also* the 'overriding' phenomenon below. Another consequence is represented by the fact that, in this way, concepts participate in the inheritance hierarchy directly; instances participate indirectly in the hierarchy through their parent concepts.

Making local the introduction of instances clarifies considerably the meaning and the practical modalities of use of this notion, but it is not yet sufficient to eliminate any ambiguity. In fact, it remains to be decided whether the instances are to be systematically considered as terminal symbols or whether it can be admitted that an instance can be characterized in turn by the presence of more specific instances. The classical example – *see*, [Zarr97a] – is given by paris_, an individual that is an instance of the concept *city_*, but which could be further specialized through the addition of proper instances (i.e. viewpoints) such as 'Paris of the tourists', 'Paris as a railway node', 'Paris in the *Belle Epoque*', etc. If, for clarity's sake, instances are always considered as terminal symbols, viewpoints can be realized according to a solution which goes back to the seminal paper by Minsky about frames [Mins75]. This solution consists of introducing into the inheritance hierarchy specialized concepts such as *tourist_city*, *railway_node*, *historical_city* that all admit the individual paris_ as an instance; paris_ inherits then from each of them particular, 'bundled' sets of attributes (slots) such as, for example {UndergroundStations, TaxisBaseFare, EconomyHotels'...} from *tourist_city*, {TypesOfMerchandise, DailyCommutersRate...} from *railway_node*, etc.

The precise definition of the meaning of InstanceOf is not the only problem that affects the construction and use of inheritance hierarchy, especially when the inheritance considered is more a 'behavioural' than a 'structural' one, i.e. it is more interested in the actual behaviour and meaning of the properties inherited than in the pure mechanical aspects of the propagation. From this point of view, we have to face two main problems: 'overriding' (or 'defeasible inheritance', or 'inheritance with exceptions') and 'multiple inheritance', *see* Section 2.3.

Overriding consists of the possibility of admitting exceptions to the 'strict inheritance' interpretation of (n) introduced above. Let us consider this group of assertions:

1 Elephants are grey, except for royal elephants.

2 Royal elephants are white.

3 All the royal elephants are elephants.

Assertion 3 introduces a new concept, *royal_elephant*, as a specialization of *elephant_* of Figure 3.4. If now clyde_ InstanceOf *royal_elephant*, the strict inheritance law would lead us to conclude that the property (slot) ColourOf of clyde_ is filled with the value *gray_*, but from 1 and 2 we know that the correct filler is instead *white_*. This means that *royal_elephant* has an 'overriding property', ColourOf or, in other terms, that the property ColourOf of *elephant_* must not be considered as a systematically inheritable property. An at least implicit differentiation between 'overriding properties' and 'non-overriding properties' is then introduced in the set of properties (attributes, slots, etc.) that characterize a given concept: for *elephant_* and all its instances and specific terms we can say, for example, that FormOfTheTrunk is a non-overriding property given that its associated value will always be *cylinder_*; ColourOf will be, on the contrary, overriding. Figure 3.5 visualizes the situation described in the three assertions above. The crossed line ('cancel link') indicates that the value associated with the overriding property ColourOf has been actually changed passing from *elephant_* to *royal_elephant*. Note that in most of the implemented KBSs, the cancel link is not explicitly implemented, and the overriding can be systematically executed.

In a well-known paper [BracR85b], R.J. Brachman warns about the logical inconveniences linked with the introduction of an unlimited possibility of overriding. Under the complete overriding hypothesis, the values associated with the different properties of the concepts, and the properties themselves, must be interpreted simply as 'defaults' that are always possible to modify. Brachman gives in particular an extreme example, linked with the possibility that the properties can be overridden leaving, on the contrary, the values unchanged: a *giraffe_* is then considered as an *elephant_*, where the value *cylinder_* associated with the property TrunkOf of *elephant_* is unchanged, but the property itself has been overridden, and it is now called NeckOf for *giraffe_* [BracR85b: 85–86]. It is evident that it now becomes infeasible to make use of inheritance as a 'definitional' principle, i.e. to make use of the internal structure of the different concepts – linked with the presence of particular properties and values – to determine whether, for example, a given concept *A* is more general or more specific than *B* (i.e. to determine if it is a 'generalization' or 'specialization' of concept *B*). This leads, *inter alia*, to the impossibility of determining automatically the position of a new concept in the inheritance network. With the loss of all the definitional properties associated with the hierarchies of concepts, these last cannot, in principle, express even very simple composite descriptions stating universal truths such 'every rhombus is a quadrilateral'. Given, moreover, that all the properties of the concepts are now purely local, any concept acts as a 'primitive' whose properties must be explicitly asserted each time; this leads once again to the impossibility of concluding that a hypothetical *elephant_with_three_legs*, or a *yellow_elephant* (this last is an unfortunate elephant suffering from hepatitis) is still an *elephant_*. The benefits associated with the use of the inheritance hierarchies are on the verge of vanishing; without endorsing such catastrophic conclusions, it appears clear that an uncontrolled amount of overriding can introduce some serious coherence problems.

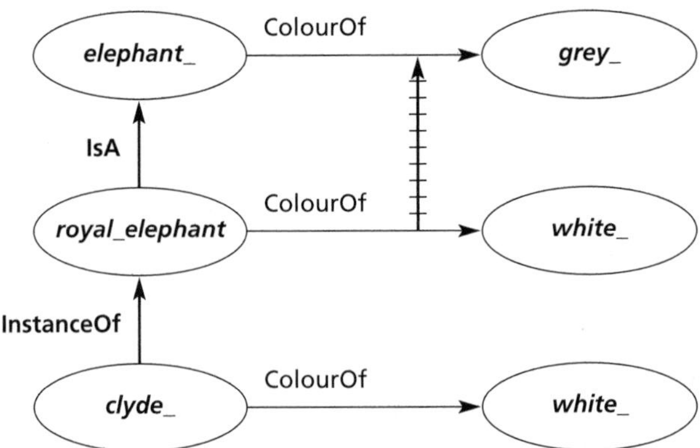

Figure 3.5 Overriding (defeasible inheritance)

Given, however, that dealing with exceptions is an evident necessity in the knowledge representation domain, AI researchers have tried to avoid the danger of an uncontrolled use of overriding techniques by using some form of non-classical logic to provide a formal semantics for inheritance hierarchies with defaults. For example, both Etherington (*see* [Ethe87], [Ethe88]), and Nado and Fikes (*see* [Nado92]) make use of Reiter's Default Logic [Reit80], [Reit83]. Very briefly, a 'default theory' is a pair (D, W) where D is a set of 'default rules' (seen as a sort of inference rules) normally concerning the properties of the concepts, such as 'Typically, elephants have four legs', and W is a set of 'hard facts' such as 'All elephants are mammals' (or 'Margaret Mitchell wrote *Gone With the Wind*'). Formally, W is a set of first order formulae, while a typical default rule of D can be denoted as:

$$\frac{\alpha(x_1, \ldots, x_n) \ : \ \beta(x_1, \ldots, x_n)}{\gamma\ (x_1, \ldots, x_n)} \qquad (0)$$

where α, β and γ are again first order formulae whose free variables are among x_1, ..., x_n. The notation $\omega(x_i)$ used for the first order formulae of (o) is here an abridged logical-like notation representing in general both x_i IsA ω, x_i InstanceOf ω, and x_i HasProperty ω. Informally, a rule like (o) means then: for any individuals x_1, ..., x_n, if $\alpha(x_1, ..., x_n)$ is inferable, and if $\beta(x_1, ..., x_n)$ can be consistently assumed, then infer γ $(x_1, ..., x_n)$. For the previous example concerning royal elephants, (o) becomes:

$$\frac{elephant\_(x) : gray\_(x) \ \wedge \neg \ royal\_elephant(x)}{gray\_ \ (x)}.$$

From the informal definition above, it can be seen that, if we assume simply that clyde_ InstanceOf *elephant_*, we can affirm that clyde_ ColourOf *gray_* and ¬ clyde_ InstanceOf *royal_elephant* are consistent with this assumption; hence, clyde_ ColourOf *gray_* can be inferred – in logical notation, from the initial assumption *elephant_*(clyde_), and having verified that *gray_*(clyde_) and ¬ *royal_elephant*(clyde_) are consistent with the assumption, we can infer *gray_*(clyde_). On the other hand, if the initial assumption is now *royal_elephant*(clyde_), using the hard fact *royal_elephant* IsA *elephant_* (*see* Figure 3.5), we can be reduced again to the situation of the previous example, i.e. *elephant_*(clyde_); in this case, however, the consistency condition $\beta(x_1, ..., xn) = gray\_(x) \wedge \neg royal\_elephant(x)$ is violated given the initial assumption *royal_elephant*(clyde_) that 'blocks' the default rule, preventing the derivation of *gray_* (clyde_). A formalization of inheritance with exceptions in terms of modal logic instead of default logic is given in [Haut92].

The inheritance hierarchy of Figure 3.4 is a 'tree', i.e. each node (concept) has only one node immediately above it (its 'parent node') from which it can inherit the properties. In this case, the mode of transmission of the properties is called 'single inheritance'. Normally, however, in the inheritance hierarchies used in the real world, a concept can have multiple parents and can inherit properties along multiple paths; for example, the *dog_* of Figure 3.4 can also be seen as a *pet_*, inheriting all the properties of the ancestors of *pet_*, pertaining maybe to a branch *private_property* of the global inheritance hierarchy. This phenomenon is called 'multiple inheritance'; the inheritance hierarchy now becomes a 'tangled hierarchy' as opposed to a tree – a partially ordered set (poset) from a mathematical point of view. We can note here that the inheritance hierarchies admitting multiple inheritance can be assimilated with the 'standard' form of the well-known semantic networks – *see* again the extensive collection prepared by F. Lehmann [Lehm92] on this last subject.

Multiple inheritance contributes strongly to the simplification of the inheritance hierarchies by eliminating the need for the duplication of the concepts and of the corresponding instances that would be required to reduce the hierarchy to a simple tree – possible example of duplicated concepts could be *dog_as_valuable_object* and *dog_as_carnivore_mammal*. The use of the multiple inheritance approach can, however, give rise to conflicts about the inheritance of the values associated with particular properties.

To illustrate this problem, we will use an example that relates to one of the most intricate issues in the construction of well-formed ontologies, the classification of the 'substances' – *see* [Guha90a], [Lena90a], [Zarr97a], and Section 3.4. According to a majority of researchers, concepts such as *substance_* and *colour_* must be regarded as examples of 'non-sortal concepts'. The 'sortal concepts' correspond to notions that can be directly materialized into enumerable specimens (i.e. instances), *see* concepts like *chair_* or *lump_* (which are *physical_objects*); the non-sortal concepts cannot be directly instantiated into enumerable specimens – note that a non-sortal concept like *white_gold* is then a specialization of *gold_*, not an instance. Let us look at Figure 3.6 that can be considered as a first, rough solution to the problem of classifying correctly a notion such as 'nuggets of gold' – the entire situation is, of course, highly schematized. This notion corresponds certainly to a (sortal) *physical_object* – and, thanks to this fact, it admits the existence of direct instances, gold_nugget_1, gold_nugget_*n*, etc. On the other hand, it can also be considered, to a certain extent, as a specialization of *gold_*, given that it inherits from this concept at least some 'intrinsic properties', such as ColourOf, MeltingPoint, etc., and the corresponding values. Adopting, however, a solution like that of Figure 3.6, an evident inheritance conflict appears, given that, according to the organisation adopted in this figure, *gold_nugget* may inherit both the values 'yes' and 'no' for the property HasInstances.

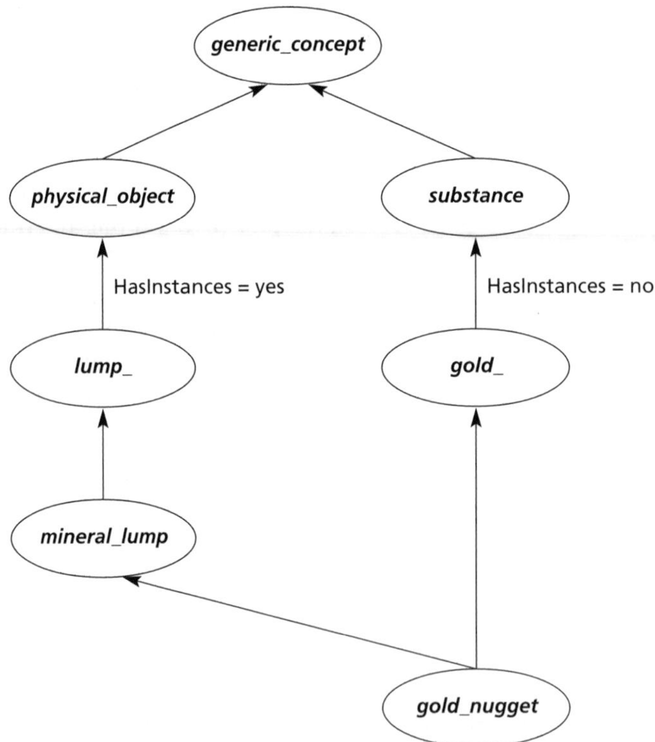

Figure 3.6 A (very schematized) example of conflict concerning the inheritance of properties

A multiple inheritance conflict can be resolved thanks to two basic techniques. In the first, 'mechanical' technique, a precedence list is computed in a mechanical way by starting with the first leftmost concept that represents a generalization (superconcept) of the concept where the conflict has been observed – in the case of Figure 3.6, the leftmost immediate superconcept of *gold_nugget* is *mineral_lump*. The construction of the precedence list proceeds by visiting depth-first the nodes in the left branch, then those of the right branch, then the join, and up from there. In our example, this list corresponds to (*mineral_lump, lump_, physical_object, gold_, substance_, generic_concept*); *gold_nugget* inherits then the properties of *mineral_lump*, including HasInstances = yes, as required. This technique is, obviously, strictly dependent on the particular arrangement adopted in the construction of the inheritance hierarchy, and can help in inserting a number of 'dummy concepts' (analogous to the 'mixins' of object-oriented programming) in order to establish a correct precedence list.

The second technique is an 'explicit' technique that attributes to the user the responsibility of specifying from which superconcept a given conflicting property must be inherited. Environments (knowledge engineering software environments, or KESEs, *see* Section 3.131) for the set-up of large KBSs, such as Knowledge Craft or ROCK by the Carnegie Group Inc., allow for a particularly neat implementation of this principle. In fact, they supply the user with tools for specifying exactly the 'inheritance semantics' for the properties of a given concept, i.e. the information-passing characteristics that indicate which slots and values must be 'included', 'excluded', 'introduced' further, or transformed during inheritance ('mapped'). In this way, it becomes easy to impose, when defining the properties of *gold_nugget*, that this last concept is a specialization of *mineral_lump* (and, therefore, of *physical_object*), and that it only inherits the set of intrinsic properties from *gold_*. The new arrangement can be depicted as in Figure 3.7, which gives a more precise representation of the relationships between the concepts involved in this (very stereotyped) situation.

When defeasible inheritance (materialized by the presence of cancel links) and multiple inheritance combine, we can be confronted with very tricky situations, such as the notorious 'Nixon Diamond' (*see* Figure 3.8). In this version of the Diamond, which is the most frequently used, we admit that it is possible to have an individual, nixon_, as a common instance of two different concepts, *republican_* and *quaker_*. Several inheritance-based systems do not allow this possibility: postulating, however, the presence of an intermediate concept such *republican_having_quaker_convictions*, which specializes both *republican_* and *quaker_* and to which we could attach the nixon_ instance, would not change the essence of the problem. If we ask now: 'Is Nixon a pacifist or not ?', we are in trouble given that, as a Quaker, Nixon is (typically) a pacifist but, as a Republican, Nixon is (typically) not a pacifist. A reasoner dealing with this situation must then choose between two possible attitudes. According to a 'sceptical' attitude, it will refuse to draw conclusions in ambiguous situations and, therefore, it will emit no opinion as to whether Nixon is or is not a pacifist. According to a 'credulous' attitude, the reasoner will try to deduce as much as possible, generating all the possible 'extensions' of the ambiguous situation. In the Nixon Diamond case, it will generate both the solutions pacifist_ and ¬ pacifist_.

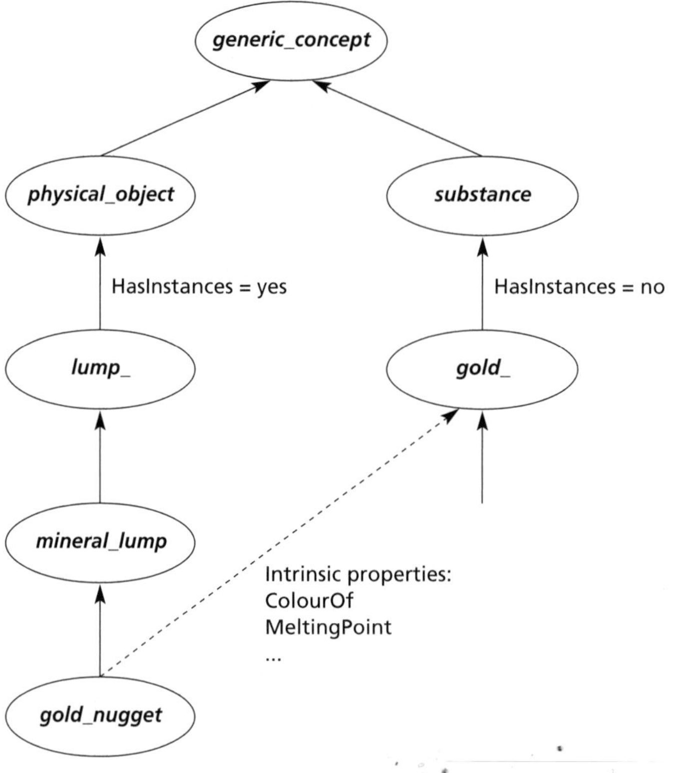

Figure 3.7 Use of the inheritance specifications to better outline the relationships among concepts

This problem (and similar ones) has given rise to a flood of theoretical work; among the 'classics', we will mention here [Fahl79], [Tour86] and [Sand86]. Even if, as also noted by [Brew87], the topology and properties of the inheritance hierarchies appear as particularly simplified in these sorts of studies, and the researchers in this field seem to have great fun in proposing ever new, sophisticated solutions, the problem is nevertheless a real and a very important one.

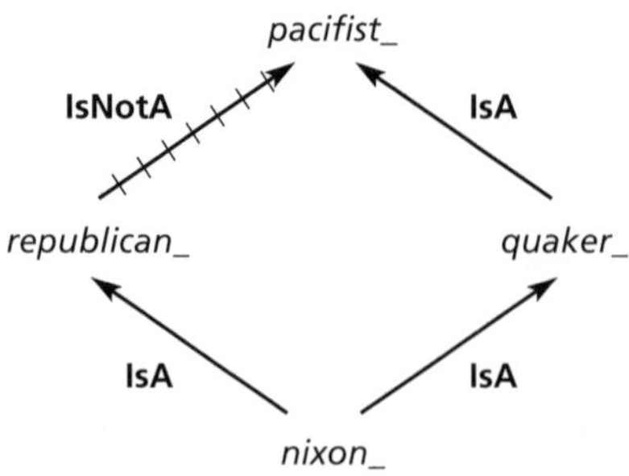

Figure 3.8 The Nixon Diamond

Fahlman's solution to the problem of inheritance with exceptions (non-monotonicity of inheritance) is summarized by the so-called 'shortest-path principle'. Let us assume that the individual tweety_ normally inherits the properties of *flying_thing* through the node *bird_* (the 'normal' path from tweety_ to *flying_thing* has length 2). If now a *direct* cancel link exists between tweety_ and *flying_thing*, inhibiting the inheritance from this last concept (Tweety is maybe a penguin, or maybe dead ...), Fahlman asserts that this cancel link must be preferred to the normal one because its length is only 1 which, in this case, is in agreement with our intuition. Touretzky demonstrated that, in general, the shortest-path principle is not valid – and, incidentally, it is certainly not valid for the Nixon Diamond example. If we redraw the inheritance network of Figure 3.5 as in Figure 3.9 – i.e. by introducing an explicit concept *grey_thing* and a 'redundant link' that associates directly the instance clyde_ with the concept *elephant_* – it appears clear that a shortest path leading from clyde_ to *grey_thing* (through *elephant_*, positive path, or through *royal_elephant*, negative path) does not exist and this allows us to deduce automatically that Clyde is or is not a grey thing.

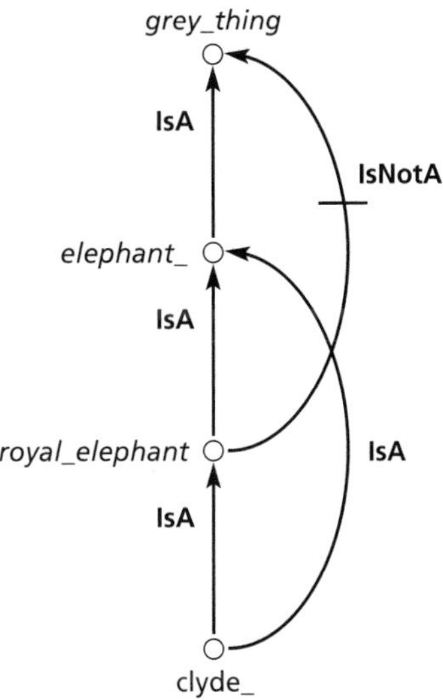

Figure 3.9 An apparently simple, but puzzling in fact, inheritance problem

The essence of Touretzky's formal proposal ('on-path pre-emption') for going beyond an impasse like that of Figure 3.9 consists of taking into account the 'specificity' (= specialization) of the nodes when choosing the paths for traversing the inheritance hierarchy. In the example of Figure 3.9, *royal_elephant* is a specialization of *elephant_*: it is more specific than *elephant_*, and it is able to prevent inheritance from this last node. A path like clyde_ —> *royal_elephant* —> ¬ *grey_thing* 'pre-empts' a path like clyde_ —> *elephant_* —> *grey_thing* on the condition that the pre-empted path contains a redundant link that would short-circuit part of the pre-emptor (*see* Figure 3.9). This principle is, obviously, still inoperative in the Nixon Diamond case.

Sandewall claims that the on-path pre-emption principle is too restrictive and, in particular, it does not work in cases where the redundant link (between clyde_ and *elephant_* in Figure 3.9) is itself interrupted by the insertion of another node, for example *african_elephant* in Figure 3.10; we can note that the situation depicted in Figure 3.10 is very similar to that illustrated by the Nixon Diamond. Sandewall proposes then a more liberal rule, the 'off-path pre-emption' principle. In the example in Figure 3.10, the node *african_elephant* does not offer any specific information about greyness at the difference of the node *royal_elephant*. In cases of conflict, the path passing by this last node should be preferred in order to infer the correct answer, given that *royal_elephant* overrides the greyness property inherited from the *elephant_* node with more specific information. The off-path pre-emption principle – which, once again, is inoperative in the case of the simple Nixon Diamond – is considered more liberal than the Touretsky principle given that it is less dependent on the specific structure of the inheritance network.

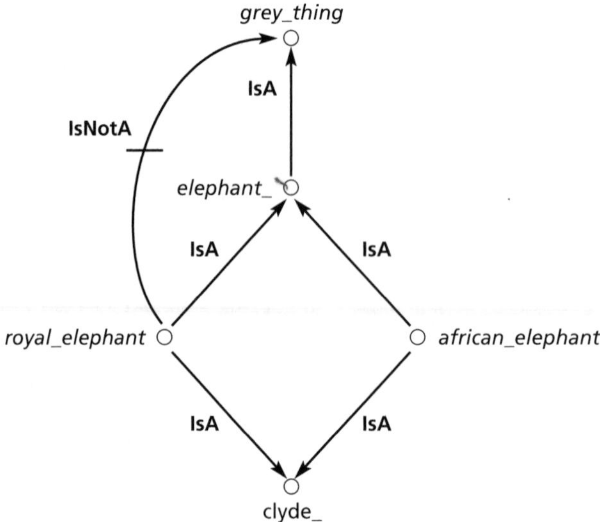

Figure 3.10 Touretzky's example revisted

The introduction of the off-path pre-emption principle is only an additional step in the discussion. In [Tour87], Touretzky and his colleagues consider examples where, when changing the names of the concepts in Figure 3.10 while conserving the same topological structure of the figure, the application of the Sandewall's principle can lead to conclusions that are not intuitively supported (*see*, in [Tour87], the 'George the chaplain/marine' example); they conclude by stating that, especially in the case of a credulous reasoner, the more cautious approach of on-path pre-emption may be recommended. Al-Asady and Narayanan [AlAs93] try to reconcile the on-path and off-path approaches by introducing the so-called 'exceptional inheritance logic', based on the idea of inserting in the hierarchy, whenever a contradiction is detected, an 'exceptional class' (exceptional concept) Ψ that contains the 'exceptional' (and nevertheless inheritable) information that has given rise to the contradiction, such as the information about the non-greyness of Clyde. Padgham [Padg92] proposes some solutions to the Nixon Diamond quandary by introducing specific assumptions about the concepts to be considered, for example by stating that only *typical* Quakers are pacifists or, on the contrary, that Quakers are *always* pacifists. These approaches, and the second in particular, confirm once again a well-known principle: to obtain sound solutions to the most complex knowledge representation problems, the possibility of disposing of large amounts of domain knowledge is at least as important as the conception of clever formal solutions.

The existence of a non-monotonic form of inheritance (*see* the second part of this section) makes it clear that a formal theory of inheritance based simply on FOL or clausal logic – in the style of Deliyanni's and Kowalski's proposals for the formalization of extended semantic networks, [Deli79], or Hayes' 'Logic of Frames' [Haye79] – can be only of a limited interest. We have already mentioned the utilization of Reiter's default logic for formalizing the properties of inheritance hierarchies with defaults. Brewka [Brew87: 483] remarks that default logic – like Touretzky's and Sandewall's proposals – does not formalize explicitly the principle that is at the base of non-monotonic inheritance: the concepts that are specializations of higher-order concepts can always inherently override the latter. All the theories we have examined in this section require in fact that exceptions be explicitly indicated as cancel links (*see also* Figures 3.5, 3.8, 3.9 and 3.10).

Brewka defines firstly a 'normal' frame language (*see* next subsection) where the usual frame features, such as slots, values, specialization, multiple inheritance, etc., are all present. He introduces a predicate EXCEPTIONAL as a three-place variant of the ABnormal predicate defined in McCarthy's circumscription technique [McCaJ80] – we are then already beyond standard logic, even if circumscription is relatively close to this last one. Intuitively, EXCEPTIONAL(x, $Slot_1$, $Frame_1$) can be read as 'x (a frame) does not inherit information about property $Slot_1$ from $Frame_1$'.

3.131 Frame systems and KESEs

In the previous paragraphs, we have considered the concepts as they were characterised solely by i) a conceptual label (a symbolic name) and ii) the hierarchical relationships with other concepts that are symbolized by the IsA links. In reality, the main reason for the persistent popularity of frame-based systems in industry and research is linked with the fact that these systems allow the association with any concept of a 'structure' reflecting, often in a very natural way, the knowledge human beings have about i) the intrinsic properties of these concepts and ii) the network of relationships, other than the hierarchical one, the concepts have with each other. The current interpretation of frames corresponds to a sort of 'assertional interpretation' that views frames as knowledge representation systems able to represent a collection of statements about the important notions of a given application domain. Note that this interpretation only partly coincides with the original motivations that were behind the introduction of frames by Minsky (*see* [Mins75]). These can be summarized roughly by saying that, for Minsky, the utility of this knowledge representation tool was mainly in the possibility of semantically controlling the inference activities of scene-analysis systems by instantiating the descriptions of stereotypical situations under the form of frames. For the well-known debate initiated by Hayes about the possibility of fully reducing frames to a simple notational variant of first-order logic, see the Hayes paper [Haye79] already mentioned, and also [Ring88].

A frame is basically a named data structure – very similar to the 'objects' we examined in Section 2.2 – that includes a flexible collection of named 'slots' (or fields, roles, etc.) that can be associated with 'values'. Usually, the slots are distinguished from their fillers (values) – *see*, however, [Skuc95]. Usually, again, there is no fixed number of slots, nor a particular order imposed on these slots; they may be accessed by their name. The slots represent in general the important 'properties' that it is necessary to introduce to characterize a given concept in a complete way.

Unfortunately, a 'definition' like this is too vague and imprecise to constitute a valid direction for creating the 'correct' set of slots. The arbitrariness linked with the subjective choice of the slots in the frame systems is denounced, for example, in [Wile87] – in some knowledge representation tools conceived to facilitate the construction of KESEs (knowledge engineering software environments), such as CRL (Carnegie Representation Language) by the Carnegie Group, Inc., this arbitrariness is (very partially) obviated by making use of metastructures that describe in a precise way the computational behaviour of a given slot. For example, in CRL, a 'slot-control schema' – a particular structured object containing information about the properties of a specific slot, for example the restrictions concerning the domain, the range and the cardinality, the inheritance specifications, etc. – can be added to each slot as a sort of formal definition. In other frame-oriented tools, such as KEE (knowledge engineering environment), this function is assigned to the 'facets' that represent annotations on the slots. Like the slots, facets can have values; facets are normally used to specify a slot constraint, or a method for computing the value of a slot, or simply to introduce some documentation string about the slot itself (DOCUMENTATION facet). The most commonly used facets are those used to specify a type restriction on the values of the slot (VALUE-TYPE facet) and to specify the exact number of possible values that a slot may take on (CARDINALITY facet). Some facets on the **PREMISE** and Procedure1 slots are shown in Table 3.2 on p. 153.

A relatively clear understanding of the operational behaviour of a set of slots can be obtained through a sort of 'functional' definition. For example, in the (quite standard) frame component of NKRL – *see* [Zarr97a] and Section 3.3 for a more complete description – the slots are grouped in three different classes: 'relations', 'attributes', and 'procedures'. A general schema of a frame representing an NKRL concept or individual is represented in Figure 3.11. OID stands for the symbolic name of the particular concept or individual.

```
{OID
        [Relation       (IsA | InstanceOf :
                         HasSpecialization | HasInstance :
                         MemberOf | HasMember :
                         PartOf | HasPart :)
                         (UserDefined_1 :
                        ...
                        UserDefined_n : )
         Attribute      (Attribute1 :
                        ...
                         Attributen : )
         Procedure      (Procedure1 :
                        ...
                         Proceduren : ) ] }
```

Figure 3.11 A general schema for NKRL concepts and individuals

The slots of the 'relation' type are used to represent the relationships of an NKRL frame, concept or individual, to other frames – these slots represent the privileged tools to set up complex systems of frames. NKRL provides for eight general, system-defined relationships. They are: IsA, and the inverse HasSpecialization, InstanceOf, and the inverse HasInstance, MemberOf (HasMember) and PartOf (HasPart) – IsA and InstanceOf have been discussed at length in the previous section; we can note that MemberOf and PartOf correspond, respectively, to the 'Aggregation' and 'Grouping' relationships that, with 'Generalization' (IsA), characterize the semantic models in the database domain. Some of the formal properties of the direct relationships are shown in Figure 3.12.

$(A \text{ IsA } B) \wedge (B \text{ IsA } A) \leftrightarrow A \equiv B$
$(A \text{ IsA } B) \wedge (B \text{ IsA } C) \rightarrow (A \text{ IsA } C)$ (IsA is a partial order relationship)
$(A \text{ IsA } B) \wedge (A \text{ IsA } C) \rightarrow \exists \text{ D } (B \text{ IsA D}) \wedge (C \text{ IsA D})$
$(A \text{ PartOf } B) \rightarrow \neg (B \text{ PartOf } A)$
$(A \text{ PartOf } B) \wedge (B \text{ PartOf } C) \rightarrow (A \text{ PartOf } C)$
$(A \text{ IsA } B) \wedge (B \text{ PartOf } C) \rightarrow (A \text{ PartOf } C)$
$(A \text{ IsA } B) \wedge (A \text{ PartOf } C) \rightarrow (B \text{ PartOf } C)$
$(B \text{ IsA } C) \wedge (A \text{ IsA } C) \rightarrow (A \text{ PartOf } B)$
$(A \text{ IsA } B) \wedge (B \text{ MemberOf } C) \rightarrow (A \text{ MemberOf } C)$
$(\text{C InstanceOf } A) \wedge (A \text{ IsA } B) \rightarrow (\text{C InstanceOf } B)$
$(\text{C PartOf D}) \wedge (\text{C InstanceOf } A) \wedge (\text{D InstanceOf } B) \rightarrow (A \text{ PartOf } B)$
$(A \text{ PartOf } B) \wedge (\text{D InstanceOf } B) \rightarrow \exists \text{ C (C InstanceOf } A) \wedge (\text{C PartOf D})$

Figure 3.12 Some properties of IsA, InstanceOf, PartOf, MemberOf

An important point concerns the fact that, because of the definitions of 'concept' and 'instance' given in the previous section, and of the properties of IsA, InstanceOf, PartOf and MemberOf illustrated in Figure 3.12, a concept or an individual (instance) cannot make use of the totality of the eight relations. More exactly:

- the relation IsA, and the inverse HasSpecialization, are reserved for concepts;
- HasInstance can only be associated with a concept, InstanceOf with an individual (i.e. the concepts and their instances, the individuals, are linked by the InstanceOf and HasInstance relations);
- moreover, MemberOf (HasMember) and PartOf (HasPart) can only be used to link concepts with concepts or instances with instances, but not concepts with instances.

Note also that in NKRL as in many other 'semantic network' systems (in the widest meaning of these words), *see* [SchiU89], only two 'meronymic' relations, MemberOf and PartOf (and their inverses), are included among the system-defined relationships. The basic criterion for differentiating between the two is the homogeneity (HasMember) or not (HasPart) of the component parts; moreover, PartOf is characterized by a sort of 'functional' quality – *see*, for example, 'a handle is part of a cup' – that is absent in MemberOf. As is well known, six different meronymic relations are defined in [Wins87]: component/integral object (corresponding to PartOf in NKRL), member/collection (corresponding to MemberOf), portion/mass, stuff/object, feature/activity, place/area. Note that [Wins87] is still the reference paper for people interested mainly in the pragmatic use of meronymic concepts; for an overview of more theoretical (and description logics-oriented) approaches, *see* [Arta96]. The justification of the simplified approach followed by NKRL (and similar systems) is twofold:

- A first point concerns the wish to keep the knowledge representation language as simple as possible. In this context, the only 'relations' which are absolutely necessary to introduce (in addition, of course, to IsA, InstanceOf and their inverses) are MemberOf and HasMember: in NKRL, for example, they are used regularly to represent plural situations, *see* again [Zarr97a].
- On the other hand, dealing systematically with the examples of 'non-NKRL' relations given by Winston and his colleagues by using only the existing NKRL tools leads to results which are not totally absurd, even if, sometimes, some aspects of the original meaning are lost. For example, 'this hunk is part of my clay' (portion/mass) can also be interpreted as a MemberOf relation, such as 'this tree is part of the forest', given that we can interpret an individual like generic_portion_of_clay_1 as formed by several hunks, hunk_1 ... hunk_*n* which, like the trees in a forest, are all homogeneous and play no particular functional role (as in the PartOf examples) with respect to the whole, i.e. generic_portion_of_clay_1. 'A martini is partly alcohol' (stuff/object) can be easily rendered using, for example, the 'attribute' slots – *see* below. 'An oasis is a part of a desert' (place/area) can be regarded as PartOf, etc.

We can conclude about the 'relation' slots by saying that NKRL allows the use of specific 'user-defined' relations to enhance the system-defined relations – *see*, for example, in [Zarr97a], the utilization of a user-defined GetIntrinsicProperties relation to solve the problem of the intrinsic properties inheritance evoked previously. In these cases, of course, the properties of the new relation (*see* Figure 3.12) and the inheritance semantics (i.e. the information-passing characteristics indicating which slots and values can be inherited over that relation) must be explicitly specified.

The slots of the 'attribute' type are used to represent the characteristic properties of an object. For example, for a concept like tax_, possible attributes are TypeOfFiscalSystem, CategoryOfTax, Territoriality, TypeOfTaxPayer, TaxationModalities, etc. – the arbitrariness in the choice of the properties to be selected for a given frame is particularly evident here. Fillers of the attribute slots can be both:

i 'real' fillers (instances): this is often the case for the slot fillers of individuals. For example, we can assume that the slot filler of the Owner slot of the individual rose_27 (a particular instance of the concept *rose_*, the flower) is the individual mary_. Note, however, that the slot filler of the ColourOf slot of the same rose_27 could be, for example, *velvety_crimson*, a concept: in NKRL, in fact, *colour_* and all its specializations, such as *red_* and *velvety_crimson*, are examples of *non_sortal_concept* that do not admit the existence of direct instances (individuals) – *see* Section 3.452 and, [Zarr97a];

ii 'potential' slot fillers represented by concepts that, acting like implicit variables, define the set of legal, real fillers (specialized concepts or individuals): this is normally the case for the slots fillers of the concepts. For example, the slot filler of the Owner slot in the concept *rose_* (the flower) could be *human_being* indicating that, in the individuals which represent the instances of *rose_*, like rose_27, this particular slot can be filled only by instances of *human_being*, for example mary_. Analogously, the ColourOf slot in the concept *rose_* will be simply the concept *colour_* (a superconcept of both *red_* and *velvety_crimson*). Note that, in general, the restrictions about the sets of legal fillers can also be expressed by particular combinations of concepts: for example, in the KEE formalism, an expression such as '(INTERSECTION *human_being* (UNION *doctor_ lawyer_*) (NOT.ONE.OF fred_))' designates a class of fillers that are men, can be doctors or lawyers, but cannot be Fred, *see* [Fike85: 909–910].

Figure 3.13 reproduces a fragment of Figure 3.4 where the concepts are now associated with their (highly schematized) defining frames – note that the two fillers (non-sortal concepts) *male_ / female_* could also have been replaced by their subsuming concept *sex_*. This figure makes the meaning of 'inheritance of the properties' (inheritance of 'attributes', in NKRL's terms) explicit: supposing that the frame for *mammal_* is already defined, and supposing we now tell the system that the concept *dog_* is characterized by the two specific properties Progeny and SoundEmission, what the frame *dog_* really includes is represented in the lower part of Figure 3.13.

The convenience of being equipped with slots of the 'procedure' type is linked with a remark made in the introduction to this chapter. As frame-based systems are very popular tools for the set-up of commercial KBSs, they tend to be configured as independent but sufficient knowledge engineering software environments for applications development: they must normally provide alternative inference and representation schemes in addition to the inheritance-based methods and representations. This is the function that is assigned to the slots of the 'procedure' type which, in general, provide various ways of attaching 'procedural' information to frames, normally expressed using ordinary programming languages such as LISP or C.

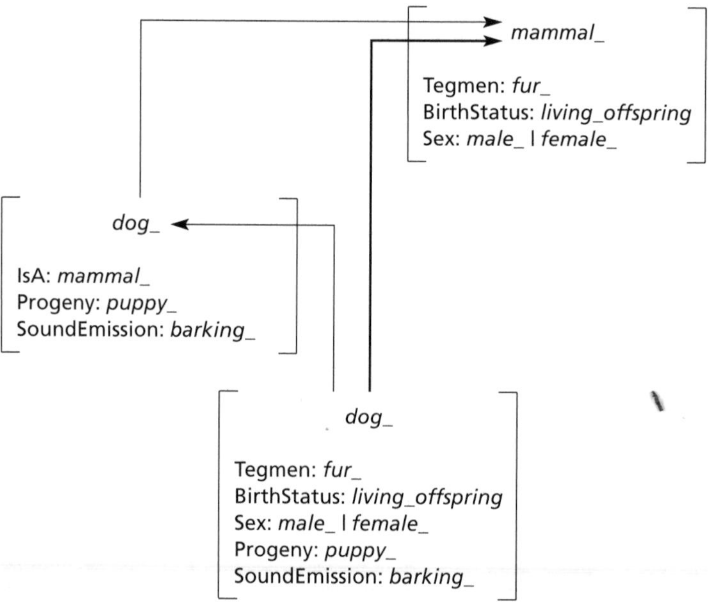

Figure 3.13 A simple example explaining the 'inheritance of properties'

This way of making use of the procedure slots in order to transform the (relatively static) frame systems into real KESEs can be generalized, by specializing some of these slots so that they can represent, for example, the CONDITION, CONCLUSION and ACTION parts of a production rule – *see* Section 3.122. In this way, production rule systems can be implemented as frame systems, with the following advantages:

- recalling that frames ≡ concepts ≡ classes or types, the fact that each single production rule is realized like a frame means that all these rules can be smoothly grouped into classes, and it is then easy to realize powerful indexing schemata to superpose to the simple, sequential list of rules;
- the reasoning mechanisms proper to the frame systems (mainly inheritance) may be used to obtain the values necessary to instantiate the different parts of the rules, thus facilitating the task of the production rules inference engines.

As an example, Table 3.2 gives two (fragmentary) examples that show the use of frame-like structures to implement rule-like structures. The first part of the table displays an example adapted from [Fike85: 913]. It concerns the use of a frame ('unit' in the KEE jargon) BIG.NON.RED.TRUCKS.RULE – which is a specific term ('member') of the class TRUCK.CLASSIFICATION.RULES – to implement a rule for identifying 'big non-red trucks'. Only the slot PREMISE is shown; note that the 'wff' (well-formed formulas) that constitute this premise are automatically 'parsed' by the KEE system starting from a more readable formulation expressed by the system-builder in a first-order logic language. The second part of the figure concerns an example adapted from [Zarr92a], and showing the NKRL representation of the beginning (the 'topic' part of a complex rule) of a normative text (the 'rule') that corresponds to article number 57 of the French 'General Taxation Law'. See Section 3.452 for details about the 'descriptive' formalism proper to NKRL. This beginning says, according to a rough English translation: 'In order to determine the income tax payable by companies which are under the authority of, or which exercise a control over, companies domiciled abroad ...'. As it appears from Table 3.2, art._57 (the global NKRL representation of the normative rule) is interpreted as an individual, instance of the general concept *norms_for_indirect_transfer_of_revenues_abroad*. In this case also, a 'translation' from an understandable formulation (here, plain natural language) into formal language can be executed (at least partly) automatically – *see* [Zarr92a], [Zarr95a].

3.132 Terminological (description) logics and the 'fundamental trade-off'

Terminological languages (also called 'concept' or 'description logics' languages) – such as KANDOR [Pate84], KRYPTON [BracR85c], NIKL [Kacz86], LOOM [MacG87], CLASSIC [BracR91], KRIS [Baad91], BACK [Hopp93] – find their origin in Brachman's KL-ONE [BracR85d], a highly influential knowledge representation system founded on a formalization and generalization of the basic principles of frames and semantic networks, and intended to permit the construction of complex and structured conceptual descriptions.

Table 3.2 Using frames to represent rules

```
Unit: BIG.NON.RED.TRUCKS.RULE
  Member: TRUCKS.CLASSIFICATION.RULES
  ...

  OwnSlot: PREMISE
      Inheritance: UNION
      ActiveValues: WFFINDEX
      Values:       /Wff: (?X IS IN CLASS TRUCKS)
                    /Wff: (THE WEIGHT OF ?X IS ?VAR29)
                    /Wff: (GREATERP ?VAR29 10000)
                    /Wff: (?X HAS AT LEAST 10 WHEELS)
                    /Wff: (NOT (THE COLOR OF ?X IS RED))
```

...

art._57

InstanceOf : *norms_for_indirect_transfer_of_revenues_abroad*
...

SubjectOfTheImposition : *transnational_company*
TerritorialValidity : france_
ValidityStart :
ValidityEnd :
DocumentationSource : french_general_taxation_law
...

Procedure1 :
topic : bloc–1
premise : bloc–2
norm : bloc–3
exceptions :
commentaries :
...

BLOC–1 : (ALTERN (COORD t1 t2 t3) (COORD t1 t4 t5))

```
t1) PRODUCE   SUBJ x1
              OBJ (SPECIF calculation_ income_tax )
              DEST x2 : france_

    x1 = human_being_or_social_body ; x2 = company_

t2) OWN       SUBJ x2 : france_
              OBJ (SPECIF control_power x3 )

    x3 = company_ ; x2 ≠ x3

t3) EXIST     SUBJ x3 : foreign_country

t4) OWN       SUBJ x3 : foreign_country
              OBJ (SPECIF authority_ x2 )

t5) EXIST     SUBJ x2 : france_
```

'determination of the income tax payable by companies under the authority of companies domiciled abroad, or which control such companies'
...

A sketchy description of KL-ONE

Figure 3.14 – slightly modified from [BracR85d: 183] and reproducing the definition of the 'primitive concept' *message_* – shows some of the main structures of KL-ONE. KL-ONE admits several sorts of concepts: the most important are the 'generic concepts' such as *animal_*, *mammal_*, *human_* etc., each of which is a description that represents many individuals (instances) in the world. Generic concepts – from this point on, simply 'concepts' – can be 'primitive' or 'defined'. They are primitive when they have no internal structure or when they cannot be defined in terms of necessary and sufficient properties; they are defined when they are built up from primitive concepts and other defined concepts and have all their necessary and sufficient properties defined.

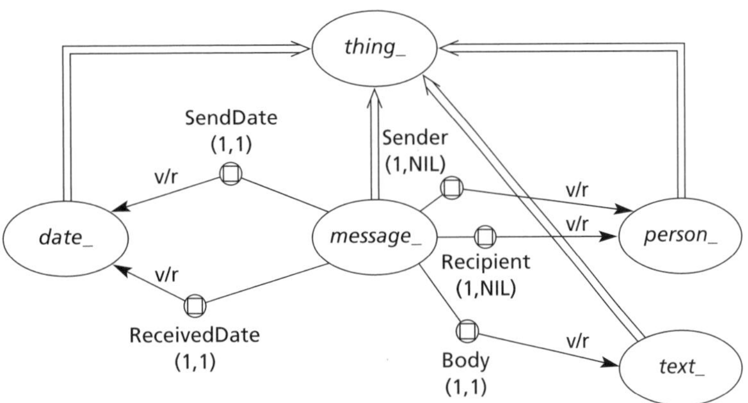

Figure 3.14 Pictorial representation of the definition of the KL-ONE concept *message_*

For example, we can assume *point_* and *line_segment* as primitive concepts without internal structure; for *polygon_* we can decide to include in its description only the property that a polygon has three or more sides that are line segments. In this case, given that we have not attempted to specify all the necessary and sufficient conditions for *polygon_* – i.e. the definition of *polygon_* is incomplete – *polygon_* still represents in KL-ONE a primitive concept. If we define now a *triangle_* as a 'polygon with exactly three sides', this definition supplies both the necessary and sufficient conditions for being a triangle; *triangle_* is then a defined concept.

The fact that the defined concepts are made up from the primitive ones and other defined concepts implies that concepts in KL-ONE are inserted in a basic taxonomy where some concepts 'subsume' or are subsumed by other concepts – one of the most important contributions of KL-ONE to the theory of knowledge representation is the precise characterisation of the notion of 'subsumption'. By subsumption, in KL-ONE and in all its derivatives, it is meant informally that, given a concept *D* and a 'SuperConcept' *C* (higher than *D* in the hierarchy) that 'subsumes' *D* (i.e. *D* is a specialization of *C*), an instance of *D* will always be, by definition, also an instance of *C*. In a more concise way, *C* subsumes *D* if the extension of *D* is a subset of the extension of *C*. KL-ONE includes a 'classifier' that, on the basis of the subsumption relationships, can automatically insert new concepts into their correct place in the hierarchy. The subsumption relationships are denoted in KL-ONE by 'SuperC(oncept)' links, which are depicted as wide arrows ('cables'): *see* in Figure 3.14, the SuperC links that define *thing_* as the common subsuming concept of *date_*, *message_*, *person_* and *text_*. As usual, a KL-ONE concept can have multiple SuperConcepts – for example, *woman_* is subsumed by both *female_animal* and *human_*. Then KL-ONE taxonomies are actually lattices.

In KL-ONE, the defining components of a concept are:

- its subsuming concepts (i.e. its SuperConcepts);
- its local internal structure, expressed in turn in terms of:
  - 'roles', that describe the potential relationships between the instances of the given concept and those of other closely associated concepts that contribute to its characterization;
  - 'structural descriptions', which express the mutual relationships between the roles, i.e. which represent a set of relationships between the role fillers that must hold when the concept, and hence the roles, are instantiated.

Roles in KL-ONE – like the slots in the frame systems – can be thought of as the 'attributes' associated with the concepts. Roles i) supply information about the function of the attribute, i.e. the 'intension' of the attribute (for example, sender of a message, upright of an arch, officer of a company, etc.) and, moreover, ii) carry the description of the potential fillers, i.e. the 'extension' (the instances) of the attribute by denoting a specific set of individual role players (for example, all the officers of a given company). In Figure 3.14, each of the encircled squares represents a generic role; we can see that *message_* (an e-mail message perhaps) is characterized by the five roles SendDate, ReceivedDate, Sender, Recipient, and Body. Roles have 'value' and 'number' restrictions. Value restrictions (v/r, *see* Figure 3.14) are interpreted as necessary restrictions on the type of role fillers: in this way, the Sender and the Recipient of an instance of *message_* are necessarily instances of *person_*. No cancellation of the value restrictions is allowed. More generally, given that the roles are considered as necessary attributes of a concept, they are not cancellable: this avoids at least some of the 'overriding' problems examined in Section 3.13. If more than one v/r is applicable to a given role, the restrictions are taken conjunctively. Number restrictions carry cardinality restrictions: they are expressed as pairs of numbers, which represent a lower and upper bound for the cardinality of the sets of fillers – *see* Figure 3.14 again. NIL is used to represent infinity in cases where there is no finite upper bound: for example, any *message_* has at least one Sender and one Recipient. The pictorial representation of Figure 3.14 can be paraphrased as: 'A *message_* is, among other things, a *thing_* with at least one Sender, all of which must pertain to the type *person_*, at least one Recipient, all of which must also be of the type *person_*, a Body, which must be of the *text_* type, and a SendDate and a ReceivedDate, which are both instances of the *date_* type' – *see* [BracR85d: 183].

As for frames, the description of a concept in KL-ONE includes not only the local idiosyncrasies of this concept – the specific new roles that characterise it, for example – but also the components it inherits from its ancestors. To give an example, we can define *private_message* as a specific term of *message_* of Figure 3.14. If we now query the system about the components of *private_message*, the reply will be that *private_message* is characterized by the five roles Sender, Recipient, Body, SendDate and ReceivedDate it has inherited from *message_*. There is, however, a difference that concerns the number restriction for Recipient, which is now (1,1), to emphasize the fact that a private message cannot have more than an addressee. This last modification has been introduced locally in the description of *private_message*, making use of a particular link labelled 'restrict' that carries the indication (1, 1) and goes from *private_message* to the encircled square individuating Recipient in the description of *message_*. The definition of the restrict link is: 'If concept *A* with role Ra subsumes concept *B*, and if role Rb of *B* restricts Ra, then every set of fillers of Rb satisfies all the restrictions on both Ra and Rb. Moreover, roles Ra and Rb specify the same type of two-place relation' – *see* [BracR85d: 183].

As already stated, structural description is used to specify the relationships that must exist between the role fillers. It may be used, for example, to express the fact that the instance of *date_* that fills SendDate represents a temporal value that must precede the temporal value that fills ReceivedDate, or that the Recipent of a *private_message* should be the Sender's supervisor. Structural descriptions often give rise to complex syntactic constructions, especially when the relationship between the role fillers is expressed through the use of particular concepts. An example is given in [BracR85d: 195–197]: having defined *reply_requested_message* as a new specialization of *message_* characterized by the presence of the role ReplyByDate, we have now that '… an *urgent_message* is a *reply_requested_message* whose [roles] ReceivedDate and ReplyByDate satisfy a [specific KL-ONE concept] *less_than* whose Lesser [role] is the ReceivedDate, whose Greater [role] is the ReplyByDate, and whose Difference [role] is 1_hour [instance of the concept *time_period*]' [BracR85d: 196]. The complexity in the management of the structural description is one of the most common criticisms of KL-ONE.

Description logics

Terminological languages (or 'description logics', DLs) generalize KL-ONE's ideas; among other things, they enforce the distinction between 'terminological' (TBox) and 'assertional' (ABox) knowledge.

Terminological knowledge captures the intensional aspects of a domain; the domain representation is expressed, as in KL-ONE, in terms of concepts and roles. In DLs, knowledge is declaratively represented in a concept-centred way. Concepts correspond to unary predicates in first-order predicate logic (FOPL) and stand for classes of objects and notions, while the associated roles denote (classes of) binary relations among concepts. To define complex concepts (defined concepts) in term of existing concepts and restrictions on the roles, each DL makes use of a finite set of specific operators whose semantics is very precisely determined. Assertional knowledge describes the extensional aspects of a domain, and concerns the individuals constituting factual entities that are instances of the concepts and notions proper to the terminological component. Individuals correspond to constants in FOPL.

If we assimilate an implemented DL application to a knowledge base (KB), the TBox is the general schema of the KB that concerns the classes of individuals to be represented, their general properties and mutual relationships; the ABox is a partial instantiation of this schema, that contains assertions linking individuals with classes, or individuals with each other. As MacGregor, however, has remarked ([MacG91: 393–394]), the distinction between terminological and assertional knowledge is not always easy to make in the context of concrete applications.

As a first, simple example, the 'description' of the individual mary (assertional knowledge, ABox) in the BACK DL is expressed as in Table 3.3, (*see* [Hopp93]). In DLs, 'descriptions' (more precisely, concept descriptions, role descriptions, individual descriptions) is the term used to indicate the complex 'objects' recursively formed using the basic coding elements, concepts, roles and individuals, proper to such languages – the term 'description logics' originates from these 'descriptions'. The meaning of the different codes used in Table 3.3 is as follows (we make use here, for the concepts, individuals and roles = slots, of the usual typographical conventions we have used until now):

Table 3.3 An example of individual entity (assertional knowledge, ABox) in BACK

mary_ :: *person_* **and**
  atmost (1, Child) **and**
  all(Child, *female_*) **and**
  all(Daughter, **all**(Age, **gt**(10))) **and**
  Child: louise_.

- mary_ is the symbolic name which characterises a unique individual in the knowledge base. mary_ is an instance of the concept *person_*.
- There is at most one different individual in the Child relation (role) with mary_. All the individuals in the Child relation (all the fillers of the role Child of mary_) must be instances of the concept *female_*.
- The Age of all the individuals in the Daughter relation (role) with mary_ has a value greater than 10, and there is an individual named louise_ in the Child relation with mary_.
- *person_* and *female_* are concepts which must be defined by the user. Child, Daughter, and Age are roles that must also be defined by the user.
- **and**, **atmost**, **all**, **gt** and : are built-in, description-forming operators proper to BACK used for building complex conceptual objects – *see also* Table 3.4. The description-forming operators introduce the roles associated with the concepts or individuals, and the constraints linked with these roles. The constraints concern in general i) the 'co-domain' of the role (**all**) – i.e. the concept which is the target of the relation established by the role, *see* the 'value restrictions', v/r, in KL-ONE – and ii) the 'cardinality' of the role (**atmost**, **gt**) – i.e. the minimum and maximum number of elementary values that can be associated with the role, *see* the 'number restrictions' in KL-ONE. :: is the built-in operator used in BACK for associating individuals with their descriptions.

The definitions of the concepts and roles used in Table 3.3 (and of some related concepts and roles) are given in Table 3.4. Note that:

- Concepts, in BACK and in the DLs in general, can be 'primitive concepts' or 'defined concepts', where the meaning of 'primitive' and 'defined' is the same as in KL-ONE (the features, if any, associated with a primitive concept are 'necessary'; those associated with a defined concept are 'necessary and sufficient'). The former are used in the description of the latter: in particular, if a concept is 'defined', this means that it is always associated with a complex, structured description. Analogously, roles can be primitive or defined. In Table 3.4, :< and := are the operators for introducing first the primitive concepts and roles and second the defined concepts and roles. The insertion of a 'defined' concept in the concept hierarchy is achieved under the control of a 'classifier' à la KL-ONE, which makes use of the fact that the features of its structured description are 'sufficient' to characterize the concept – *see* below.
- *anything_* is the built-in universal concept, which is true for any individual; *nothing_* is the dual empty concept.
- The built-in operator **and** indicates in general that a concept (role) is defined as a conjunction of concepts (roles), which are then the immediate ancestors of the new concept (role) in the hierarchy – the roles are then inserted in a hierarchical organisation, *see* in Table 3.4 the role Daughter which is subsumed by Child. **atleast** is a new built-in operator used to specify the cardinality of a role. **domain** and **range** are built-in operators for building role descriptions: **domain** specifies the sort of concept with which the role can be associated, **range** the sort of concept that can fill the role.

Table 3.4 Definition of concepts and roles (TBox) in BACK

*person_*	:< *anything_*.
*female_*	:< *person_* **and not**(*male_*).
Child	:< **domain**(*person_*) **and range**(*person_*).
Daughter	:= Child **and range**(*female_*).
*parent_*	:= **atleast**(1, Child).
*mother_*	:= *parent_* **and** *female_*.
*grandmother_*	:= *female_* **and atleast**(1, Child **and range**(*parent_*)).

We can note that the syntax used in the two tables above is very easy to understand and is not very different from the usual FOPL notation; in the majority of the theoretical papers about description logics, however, another syntax is used, sometimes called 'German syntax'. For example, if we consider a 'minimal' terminological language, $\mathcal{AL}$ – i.e. a terminological language endowed with a minimal set of operators, where the set can be progressively enlarged to give rise to more powerful families of languages – the corresponding grammar is supplied in Figure 3.15, both in a (prefixed) logic notation not very different from that used in BACK and in German notation – *see also* [Napo97].

C, *D* →	*A* |		
	*top_* |	⊤	universal concept
	*bottom_* |	⊥	empty concept
	(and *C D*) |	*C* ⊓ *D*	concept conjunction
	(not *A*) |	¬ *A*	concept negation
	(all R *C*) |	∀ R.*C*	value restriction
	(some R)	∃ R	exists restriction

Figure 3.15 Prefixed logic notation (left) and German notation (centre) for the minimal language $\mathcal{AL}$

In Figure 3.15, *C* and *D* represent generic concepts, *A* is a primitive concept, and R a primitive role. *top_* (⊤) and *bottom_* (⊥) correspond respectively to *anything_* and *nothing_* in BACK. **and** (⊓), **all** (∀) and **not** (¬) have the same meaning they have in BACK; note that in $\mathcal{AL}$, as Figure 3.15 clearly shows, the negation is applied only to primitive concepts. The existential quantification **some** (∃) corresponds, in practice, to the introduction of a role R, and it affirms the existence of at least a pair of individuals which are connected by means of R – a stronger, 'typed' existential quantification requires that the second individual Y of the pair (X, Y) related by the role R should be an instance of a given concept *C* – *see* KL-ONE and the **range** operator in BACK. Here are some examples that show how $\mathcal{AL} \equiv \{\top, \bot, C \sqcap D, \neg A, \forall R.C, \exists R\}$ can be enriched with additional operators (*see* again [Napo97]):

- We can introduce the negation of both primitive and definite concepts, noted as (not *C*) or ¬ *C*. This extension is denoted as $\mathcal{ALC} = \mathcal{AL} \cup \{\neg C\}$.
- We can introduce the disjunction of concepts, noted (**or** *C D*) or $C \sqcup D$. The extension is denoted as $\mathcal{ALU} = \mathcal{AL} \cup \{C \sqcup D\}$. We can remark that $\bot \equiv C \sqcup \neg C$ and $C \sqcup D \equiv \neg(\neg C \sqcap \neg D)$.
- We can introduce, as in KL-ONE and BACK, a cardinality restriction on the roles R, denoted as (**atleast** n R) or ≥n R, and (**atmost** n R) or ≤n R. The extension is denoted as $\mathcal{ALN} = \mathcal{AL} \cup \{\geq n\ R, \leq n\ R\}$. We can remark that $\exists R \equiv \geq 1\ R$.
- We can introduce the conjunction of the roles, denoted as (**and** R_1 R_2) or $R_1 \sqcap R_2$, where R_1 and R_2 are primitive. The extension is denoted as $\mathcal{ALR} = \mathcal{AL} \cup \{R_1 \sqcap R_2\}$. If $R = R_1 \sqcap R_2$, then R is a subrole (specific role) of R_1 and R_2.

If we take now the union of $\mathcal{AL}$ and all these extensions, and if we include in the resulting language the typed existential quantification mentioned before, $\exists R.C \equiv \neg(\forall R.\neg C)$ – the corresponding extension is denoted as $\mathcal{ALE}$ – we obtain the language $\mathcal{ALCNR} \equiv \{\top, \bot, \neg C, C \sqcap D, C \sqcup D, \forall R.C, \exists R.C, \geq n\ R, \leq n\ R, R_1 \sqcap R_2\}$ (the letters $\mathcal{UE}$ are usually replaced by $\mathcal{C}$ because of the equivalences introduced above). To define the semantics of a language such as $\mathcal{ALCNR}$, the 'classical' way consists of using an 'interpretation', $\mathcal{I}$: concepts are 'interpreted' as subsets of some domain of interest, and roles as binary relations over the domain. Formally, [Buch93], an interpretation $\mathcal{I}$ consists of a non-empty set $\mathcal{O}^{\mathcal{I}}$, called the domain of the interpretation, and of an interpretation function $\cdot^{\mathcal{I}}$. The interpretation function associates with each concept name C a subset $C^{\mathcal{I}}$ of $\mathcal{O}^{\mathcal{I}}$, and with each role name R a binary relation $R^{\mathcal{I}}$ on $\mathcal{O}^{\mathcal{I}}$, namely a subset of $\mathcal{O}^{\mathcal{I}} \times \mathcal{O}^{\mathcal{I}}$. Other methods exist (*see* [Borg92], for example) where a natural deduction system is used.

Reasoning, in BACK as well as in all the other DLs, includes at least the following operations: 'consistency checking', 'completion of partial descriptions' and 'classification' (subsumption) – *see also* [Buch93]. Consistency checking concerns the coherence control in both the definitions of the concepts and the description of the individuals. For example, the following constraint expression for a role (expressed in BACK notation), **atmost**(0, R) **and atleast**(1, R), is not admissible for any possible R, given that this role should be filled simultaneously by at least a value and at most zero values. Another example could concern the definition of a concept where the role Child would be filled by individuals which are instances, at the same time, of *male_* and *mother_*: a definition like this is not contradictory *per se*, but it is in contrast with the definition of *mother_* in Table 3.4, where *mother_* is defined as *female_*. Completion means being able to derive all the consequences from the definition of the concepts, the descriptions of the individuals, and the application of all the possible rules (normally, forward-chaining rules) defined for a given DL application. For example, querying a knowledge base that contains the description of Table 3.4 for all the individuals older than 10 after the introduction of the rule: **atleast**(1, Child) ⇒ **all**(Age, **gt**(13)) – which states that the restriction of having at least one child implies that age must be greater than 13 – allows the retrieval of both mary_ and louise_. The first value is retrieved because of the firing of the rule, and the second because the constraint for Daughter in the description of mary_ is propagated to the filler of Child given that Daughter, according to Table 3.4, must be a Child.

The last modality of reasoning is characteristic of the terminological languages, and concerns the process ('subsumption') of automatically finding the correct position of a concept in the hierarchy of all the concepts (*see also* the discussion about KL-ONE in the previous subsection) – note that subsumption concerns also the possibility of organising the role into hierarchies. In particular, for each concept it is possible to find the most general concepts, the most specific ones, and the disjoint ones: formally, if we note with $D \sqsubseteq C$ the fact that a concept D is subsumed by C, two concepts G and F are disjoint if $F \sqcap G \sqsubseteq \bot$, *see*, for example, *man_* $\sqcap$ *woman_* $\sqsubseteq \bot$, where $\bot$, *bottom_*, is the empty concept. *top_* ($\top$) and *bottom_* ($\bot$) are, respectively, the concept that subsumes all the others and the (empty) concept which is subsumed by all the others. The subsumption relationship is a 'reflexive' one (a concept is subsumed by the concept itself); it is 'transitive' given that, as already stated, if $D \sqsubseteq C$ and $C \sqsubseteq A$, then $D \sqsubseteq A$. Subsumption is also 'antisymmetric' because if $D \sqsubseteq C$, and $C \sqsubseteq D$, then $C \equiv D$. The subsumption relationship is a partial order relation organising the concepts into a lattice where each concept is formed of a proper 'description', *see* above, and of a description which is in common with its subsuming concepts.

Subsumption is particularly important for DLs because most of the inference procedures that can be executed in the framework of those languages can be reduced to determining subsumption relationships. For example, determining whether a concept can have instances – a form of completion inference, *see* above – can be equated to determining whether this concept can be subsumed by a concept that is known not to have any instances. Consistence checking (incoherence checking) can be reduced to subsumption by checking whether a known incoherent concept subsumes the given concept, which must then be incoherent as well [Nebe88a: 373]. In particular, because we can define a concept description as 'coherent' if and only if it is not the case that the description denotes the empty set in any world, the coherency check of a concept description can be reduced to subsumption by checking whether $\bot$ subsumes this description, etc. There are fundamentally two different approaches to the computation of subsumption relationships: the use of the so-called 'normalization-comparison algorithms', or NC-algorithms, and a method derived from the semantic tableaux method in classical logics.

In the first case, subsumption is determined by way of syntactic comparisons between the descriptions of the defined concepts *C* and *D*. To do this, there is first a 'normalization' phase in which all the components of the local descriptions of *C* and *D* are developed and rearranged, the descriptions in common with their subsuming concepts are made explicit and copied in the descriptions of *C* and *D*, etc. The final aim of the normalization phase is that of expressing the descriptions in conjunctive form: the defined concepts *C* and *D* are then replaced by their normalized descriptions (in this way, all the symbols denote primitive role and concepts), $C = (C_1$ **and** $C_2, \dots$ **and** $C_n)$, $D = (D_1$ **and** $D_2, \dots$ **and** $D_n)$. As a result, in the 'comparison' phase, it is possible to unify two normalized descriptions by using (relatively simple) 'comparison' rules that execute few syntactic operations, usually comparing pairs of subterms built with the same operators (*see* [Roye93], for example).

Let us suppose that we have a defined concept *C* whose defining description (in BACK notation) is *game_* **and atleast**(2, Participant). Suppose now we introduce a concept *D* defined as *game_* **and atleast**(4, Participant) **and all**(Participant, (*person_* **and all**(Gender, *female_*))) – i.e. a game with at least four participants where the fillers of the Participant role must be instances of the concept *person_*, which have themselves the Gender role filled with instances of the concept *female_*. We recall here that **atleast**(n, R) means that the number of fillers of role R is restricted (cardinality restriction) to n. A 'comparison rule' concerning **atleast** – *see* Table 3.5 – states that, to accept $D \sqsubseteq C$, $n_C \leq n_D$ and $R_D \sqsubseteq R_C$ must both be verified; moreover, another comparison rule (expressed in a very synthetic way) says that the subsumption relation (*C* **and** *D*) $\sqsubseteq$ *C* is always satisfied whatever the description *D* (this explains why the normalization phase aims to put descriptions in conjunctive form). In this case, very simple syntactic comparisons will indeed determine that concept *D* is subsumed by *C*. This technique has been used in the implementation of BACK, and of other DLs such as KANDOR, CLASSIC and LOOM.

The 'soundness' of the NC-algorithms – an inference algorithm is 'sound' when any conclusion (here, the existence of a subsumption relationship) that can be derived by a KB of (DL) expressions using this algorithm is logically implied by the KB – is relatively easy to prove. On the contrary, the 'completeness' – an inference algorithm is 'complete' when any conclusion (here, subsumption relationships) logically implied by a (DL) KB can be derived using this algorithm – is much more difficult to assert. Using counter-examples, it is possible to prove that the majority of the NC-algorithms are incomplete, with the exception of those proper to the simplest terminological languages, such as the language $\mathcal{FL}$ which includes only this very reduced set of operators: $\{C \sqcap D, \forall$ R.$C, \exists$ R$\}$ (*see also* [Napo97: 18–21]). We will return to the historical importance of the $\mathcal{FL}$ language later.

The second technique for computing subsumption ('tableaux calculus'), used in KRIS, for example, *see* [Baad91], is based on a theorem-proving approach, i.e. it makes use of the same type of 'proof by contradiction' we encountered in Section 3.12. The main principle consists of transforming a subsumption question of the type 'Is it the case that $D \sqsubseteq C$' into a contradiction-checking question such as 'Is $D \sqcap \neg C$ inconsistent?', which can then be answered using the usual problem-solving techniques. In practice, this contradiction-checking problem is reduced to the problem of verifying the 'satisfiability' of a terminological knowledge base (i.e. a set of Tbox axioms like those in Table 3.4 and of Abox assertions like those in Table 3.3) because of the importance that the KB-satisfiability problems have in general in a DL context (*see* [Buch93]). Given a knowledge base $\Sigma = \langle \mathcal{T} \Leftrightarrow \mathcal{A} \rangle$, $\mathcal{T}$ = Tbox, $\mathcal{A}$ = Abox, and an individual 'a' not appearing in Σ, $D \sqsubseteq C$ iff $\langle \mathcal{T} \Leftrightarrow \mathcal{A} \cup \{(D \sqcap \neg C)(a)\} \rangle \leftarrow$ is not satisfiable. The notation C (a) states in general that the individual a is an instance of the concept C; a generic KB Σ is satisfiable whether there is at least one complete 'model' of Σ.

Very sketchily – *see* [Buch93], [Bres95], [Napo97] etc. for more details – to find a model of Σ, Σ is firstly 'normalized' by eliminating in the descriptions all the negations except those of the form $\neg A$, where A is a primitive concept. To do this, 'normalization rules' in the style of $\neg (C \sqcap D) \rightarrow \neg C \sqcap \neg D$; $\neg (\forall$ R.C) $\rightarrow \exists$ R.C; etc. are used. All the Abox assertions of Σ are then translated into 'constraints' thanks to a new system of rules, the 'propagation rules', *see* again [Buch93], [Bres95], etc. To be able to denote the constraints, a system of variables is needed; constraints are then expressions that can assume three basic forms, namely x: C (instantiation), xRy (relationship via a role), $x \neq y$ (conflicting interpretations), where C is a concept, R is a role, x and y are either individuals that have been introduced via the ABox or variables pertaining to a predefinite set of variable symbols. For example, an Abox assertion such as C(a), where a is here an individual, is transformed into the constraint a: C; an assertion like R(a, b) – the two individuals a and b are linked through the role R – is transformed into the constraint aRb if the role is an atomic one, into $\{aR_1b, aR_2b\}$ if $R = R_1 \sqcap R_2$; etc. The propagation rules are first applied to the initial Abox assertions, and then recursively applied to the produced constraints until a model of Σ (a complete and non-contradictory constraint system) is explicitly obtained or, according to the 'proof by contradiction' paradigm, a contradiction (named a 'clash' in the DL jargon) is generated; the propagation rules maintain satisfiability. A clash is an unsatisfiable constraint system, where the constraints assume forms of the type $\{x : \bot\}$, $\{x : A, x : \neg A\}$, where A is a primitive concept, $\{x \neq x\}$, $\{x$Ra, xRb$\}$, etc. Completeness and soundness of the algorithms based on the semantic tableaux method are, in general, easier to prove than in the case of the NC-algorithms.

Subsumption is a hard problem, very difficult to deal with in an algorithmic way even when the solution is intuitively evident. Let us consider the simple example described in Table 3.5 and derived from [Napo97: 27]; we make use here of a BACK syntax compatible with an $\mathcal{ALNR}$ syntax ($\mathcal{ALNR} \equiv \{\top, \bot, C \sqcap D, \neg A, \forall R.C, \exists R, \geq n\ R, \leq n\ R, R_1 \sqcap R_2\}$. In this table, concept C describes a 'person having at least two children', and concept D a 'person having at least a child and a daughter': it is clear that, intuitively, any instantiation of concept D must also be an instance of concept C. An NC-algorithm of polynomial complexity for the class of the $\mathcal{ALNR}$ languages, derived from [Nebe90a], is now described in a detailed way in the appendix of [Napo97]. The subsumption rule specified in the bottom part of Table 3.5 is included in this algorithm: $D \sqsubseteq C$ is accepted if the role of C subsumes that of D (in the table, Daughter and Son are effectively specific terms of Child), and if the cardinality of the C-role $\leq$ the cardinality of the D-role. This last condition is not verified in this example; with respect to an $\mathcal{ALNR}$ language, the algorithm is, therefore, 'incomplete'.

Table 3.5 A rule for comparing two ALNR–like descriptions

C :=	person_ **and atleast**(2, Child)
D :=	person_ **and**
	atleast(1, Daughter) and
	atleast(1, Son).

[atleast] : if C = **atleast**(n_C,R_C) and D = **atleast**(n_D,R_D), then test n_C n_D ≤ and $R_D \sqsubseteq R_C$.

The 'fundamental trade-off'

Several well-known papers written mainly in the 1980s – *see* [BracR84], [Nebe88a], [Nebe90b], for example – have shown that the mechanized procedures for the computation of subsumption are sound, complete and 'tractable' only for the simplest terminological languages such as $\mathcal{FL}$ mentioned above or $\mathcal{FLN} \equiv \{C \sqcap D, \forall R.C, \geq n\ R, \leq n\ R\}$. 'Tractable' means solvable in polynomial time in the worst case: 'tractability' is, with soundness and completeness, another important propriety studied in the complexity theory of algorithms – *see* [Gare79]. When even very slight extensions of these languages are proposed, especially when these extensions concern the introduction of operators affecting the roles (for example, when adding an operator such as **restrict** in order to avoid the use of cumbersome combinations of **or**, **and**, and **not**, *see* below), the polynomial time algorithms become incomplete, and it is possible to prove that a really complete algorithm for the evaluation of the subsumption relationships would be computationally 'intractable' – according to the definition given in [Gare79], a problem is 'intractable' if it is so hard that no polynomial time algorithm can possibly solve it.

A first demonstration of this fact has been given by Brachman and Levesque in [BracR84], when they examined the effect on the subsumption problem of the use of the **restrict** operator. **restrict** is included in the definition of the language

$\mathcal{FL} \equiv \{C \sqcap D, \forall R.C, \exists R, R|C\}$, where it is noted as $R|C$ in German notation; $\mathcal{FL}$ is then an extension of $\mathcal{FL}$ or, better, $\mathcal{FL}$ is a simplification of $\mathcal{FL}$ where the use of **restrict** is not admitted in order to assure the tractability of subsumption. **restrict** applies to the roles; it allows the definition of a new role from R by requiring its values to be of the type defined by the concept C (**restrict** R C). It imposes a constraint on the co-domain of R. The differences between **restrict** and the typed existential quantification $\exists$ R.C, (**some** R C), which appears for example in $\mathcal{ALCNR}$, concern the fact that:

i restrict applies to the roles and not, like $\exists$ R.C, to the definitions of the concepts;

ii restrict, at the difference of the typed existential quantification, only imposes a constraint on the co-domain of R, without also associating an existence constraint with this role.

An example of the use of **restrict** could be the following: C := *person_* **and some**(Child) **and all**(**restrict**(Child, *male_*), *doctor_*), which defines a person with at least one child, whose male children, if any, are doctors. The justification for the introduction of **restrict** derives, in this case, from the possibility of avoiding the use of complex descriptions where we should introduce an alternative (OR) about the possibility that i) the children are both (AND) male and doctors, otherwise ii) they are NOT male.

Returning now to [BracR84], after having shown that subsumption in $\mathcal{FL}$ can be computed using an O(n^2) algorithm where n is the sum of the lengths of the two descriptions being compared, Brachman and Levesque prove that subsumption in $\mathcal{FL}$ is co-NP hard. The proof is not a direct one, but it proceeds by showing equivalence with the problem of deciding the unsatisfiability of Boolean formulas in conjunctive normal form, which is an co-NP-complete problem, a complementary form of a NP-complete problem. The NP-complete and co-NP-complete problems are strongly believed not to be solvable in time polynomially proportional to the size of the problem description, i.e. they are strongly believed to be 'intractable'. A more detailed proof is given in [Leve87]. Note that this result, as the majority of those mentioned in the following, has been obtained in a 'pure subsumption' context, i.e. when analyzing the complexity of subsumption only for simple concepts, and i) without considering the necessity of expanding the definitions associated with these concepts when other concepts appear within them, and ii) without taking into account the specific ABox subsumption problems.

As clearly expressed by the title of [Nebe90b], 'Terminological Reasoning is Inherently Intractable', the situation evoked for $\mathcal{FL}$ is quite general and, apart from the simplest cases, terminological reasoning is really characterized by an exponential complexity which, according to the different cases, may be NP-hard, co-NP-hard, NP-complete, PSPACE-complete. Some of the results for the DL languages we have mentioned in this section are presented in Table 3.6 where, for simplicity's sake, we have assumed that top ($\top$) and bottom ($\bot$) are implicitly included in all the definitions.

Table 3.6 Some complexity results for terminological languages

name	concept operators	role operators	complexity
$\mathcal{FL}^-$	$\{C \sqcap D, \forall R.C, \exists R\}$	–	polynomial
$\mathcal{FL}$	$\{C \sqcap D, \forall R.C, \exists R\}$	$R \mid C$	co-NP-hard
$\mathcal{FLN}$	$\{C \sqcap D, \forall R.C, \geq n\ R, \leq n\ R\}$	–	polynomial
$\mathcal{AL}$	$\{C \sqcap D, \neg A, \forall R.C, \exists R\}$	–	linear
$\mathcal{ALU}$	$\{C \sqcap D, \neg A, \forall R.C, \exists R, C \sqcup D\}$	–	co-NP-hard
$\mathcal{ALCNR}$	$\{C \sqcap D, \neg C, \forall R.C, \exists R.C, C \sqcup D, \geq n\ R, \leq n\ R\}$	$R_1 \sqcap R_2$	PSPACE-complete

More precisely, we can note that [Doni91] defines two 'maximum' sets of constructors, collected into the two $\mathcal{PL}_1 \equiv \{C \sqcap D, \neg A, \forall R.C, \geq n\ R, \leq n\ R, R^{-1}\}$ and $\mathcal{PL}_2 \equiv \{C \sqcap D, \forall R.C, \exists R., R_1 \sqcap R_2, R^{-1}, R_1 \circ R_2\}$ languages that represent a sort of 'border' that cannot be overstepped, by adding new constructors, without immediately abandoning the polynomial algorithms area. R^{-1} denotes the inverse relation for a role, and $R_1 \circ R_2$ the role composition. $\mathcal{PL}_1$ tries to refine the definition of concepts, whereas $\mathcal{PL}_2$ is more interested in the possibilities linked with the use of roles.

The most popular terminological languages we mentioned at the beginning of this section have followed very different approaches to dealing with the complexity problems (*see* [Spee95]). Some of these languages, such as KRYPTON and CLASSIC, make use of a limited set of operators and are then characterized by inference procedures that are correct, complete and tractable (i.e. of polynomial worst-case behaviour). These formalisms have a restricted expressive power, but they avoid the possibility that some 'legal' inference is missing because of the incompleteness problems. Others, such as BACK, are more expressive but in general intractable, i.e. characterized by subsumption procedures that are worst-case NP-hard. Moreover, subsumption, in this second class of terminological systems (KRIS being an exception) is also often incomplete. As shown in [Pate89], NIKL and LOOM – and KL-ONE, *see* [SchmS89] – are undecidable, i.e. it is impossible to identify clearly the semantic characteristic of the missing inferences and then establish whether complete procedures, even if intractable, can ever exist.

We can note here that these sorts of problems – even if they have been particularly studied in a terminological logics context, see again [Buch93] – are absolutely general, and they concern all the types of symbolic knowledge representation (KR) we have examined until now. For example, FOL has a well-defined semantics, and very strong deductive capabilities but, when its expressive power is extended to cope exactly with all the relevant facts and entities of a given application domain, it quickly becomes 'computationally impracticable', where impracticability ranges from undecidability (in this case, the impossibility of determining whether a logical sentence follows from another) to NP-completeness (i.e. the general impossibility of solving a problem in time polynomially proportional to the size of the problem description). As stated in [Nebe88a: 381], '...we know that almost all representation formalisms used in artificial intelligence are intractable or even undecidable'. Faced with this problem of the 'practicability of reasoning', all the proposed approaches to symbolic KR lay between two extreme positions:

- The first considers only KR languages that, like KRYPTON and CLASSIC, have a limited expressive power (accepting the risk that they could be of limited practical interest for describing a certain number of domains) but that show inference capabilities that are both tractable and complete. Filling the gap between what can be expressed in the language and what is needed by a specific application is left to the user, who will normally resort to programs written in a procedural language. This approach has been severely criticized in [Doyl91], where the authors argue that logical soundness, completeness and worst-case complexity are inadequate measures for evaluating the utility of a representation system, and that this evaluation should make use of a broader notion of utility and rationality. Note that developers of CLASSIC have recently increased the expressiveness of their language by allowing, for example, intractability in those (concrete) cases where it is unlikely that worst-case constructions that can be responsible for intractability will occur (*see* [Spee95: 60]).
- The second accepts on the contrary the fact that general-purpose symbolic KR languages are intractable, or even undecidable, and favour expressiveness with respect to the computational practicability – note again that, from a pragmatic point of view, problems about practicability concern, normally, only the 'worst cases'. In the specific domain of DLs, this second attitude is realized in practice according to two different modalities:
  - some designers favour the implementation of expressive terminological reasoners characterized by the fact of still being 'sound' and 'complete', even if, according to what has been expounded before, they are certainly intractable in the worst case – this is the approach followed in KRIS, for example. It must be noted that these reasoners are usually *particularly slow*, and that optimization techniques must be used in order to improve their performance in concrete (average) cases. However, the main problem here concerns the 'unpredictability' of such systems, i.e. the difficulty of determining the circumstances under which the system will require an exorbitant amount of time;
  - some designers favour, on the contrary, the implementation of *relatively fast* terminological reasoners that are 'sound' but 'incomplete'. This means that, given their incompleteness, if they fail to determine a subsumption relation, no conclusion about the existence or not of this relation can be derived, i.e. their results are only partially in accordance with what their semantics should normally imply. This is the approach followed by BACK, NIKL and LOOM – LOOM in particular is explicitly described as supporting a very expressive DL in an incomplete manner, see [MacG87]. For the two last systems, as already stated, this incompleteness state is even indecidable. The main problem here concerns the difficulty of providing the user of systems like these with a sufficiently comprehensive picture of their computational behaviour.

To sum up, 'There is a trade-off between the expressiveness of a representational language and its computational tractability ... We do believe, however, that the trade-off discussed here is fundamental. As long as we are dealing with computational systems that reason automatically (without any special intervention or advice) and correctly (once we define what *that* means), we will be able to locate where they stand on the trade-off: they will either be limited in what knowledge they can represent or unlimited in the reasoning effort they may require' [Leve85: 42–43].

The 'concrete' systems

We will conclude the discussion on DLs with some short remarks about the 'practical', 'concrete' systems. Four of them – BACK, CLASSIC, KRIS and LOOM – have been examined in depth in the framework of a detailed study concerning the performances of the terminological representation systems [HeinJ94], *see also* [Spee95]. A first finding of this work concerns the astonishing differences that exist in the syntax – and therefore the semantics – of these languages. This is particularly evident when examining their 'expressiveness', i.e. the concept and role-forming operators that are (sometimes only implicitly) present in the different languages. For example, $C \sqcup D$ (disjunction of concepts) is present in KRIS and LOOM but absent in BACK and CLASSIC; $\neg C$ (negation of concepts) is present only in KRIS; $R_1 \sqcap R_2$ (conjunction of roles) is present in BACK, KRIS and LOOM, but not in CLASSIC, etc. Of the 20 or so concept-forming operators and more than 15 role and attribute-forming operators (an attribute is a single-valued role) that can be defined for a 'common terminological language', *see* [HeinJ94: 371–375], only the following operators, $C \sqcap D$, $\forall$ R.C, $\geq$n R, $\leq$n R (and the possibility of introducing defined and primitive concepts), are effectively present in all the languages examined in the study. An important consequence of this is that the sharing of knowledge bases between the different systems becomes extremely difficult. Moreover, the authors note that each system presents at least one deviation from the corresponding documentation. For example, with respect to the possible TBox inferences that the different languages are able to implement, some unexpected failures are noticed for systems that, like CLASSIC and KRIS, are supposed to be complete. These two systems were in fact unsuccessful when dealing with some test cases concerning reasoning over chains of attributes, a situation which in principle is easy to deal with in a terminological framework.

3.14 Conclusion

Comparing the different knowledge representation paradigms we have expounded in this chapter in order to find the 'best' one is, of course, pure nonsense without a precise description of the class of applications they are supposed to be used for. For example, FOL is acclaimed for presenting a formalism that is really not ambiguous, is perfectly controlled and well understood at the theoretical level, and for being endowed with a very powerful deductive formalism. However, its style of knowledge representation is inappropriate for using in domains not very easy to formalize (many sectors of the human and social sciences, for example); moreover, the type of reasoning we commonly use in the real-world problems is not necessarily a deductive one. But for problems sufficiently well-defined and circumscribed, and not necessarily as trivial as the simple examples of kinship processing like those examined in Section 3.12, FOL and its derivatives can represent the 'right' solution. Analogously, production systems have been criticized, *inter alia*, because of their poor knowledge representation power. This did not hinder the production paradigm from being used in a vast majority of the expert systems in use today and from producing some well-known 'success stories' such as that of R_1/XCON, the VAX configuration system [McDeJ81].

We can only say that, if the problem under consideration is a complex one, dealing with knowledge about structured domains (implying the presence of many parameters) and requiring therefore the use of structured data implying properties and attributes, the representation systems based on the inheritance principle seem to present some definite advantages – also taking into consideration the fact that, as we have seen above, the rule paradigm can be easily implemented in an inheritance context, giving rise to the KESE systems, for example. In the previous section we examined two possible implementations of the inheritance principle, frame systems and DLs. The latter were widely publicized in the academic milieus during the 1980s when they were sometimes presented as a sort of 'final' answer to all the knowledge representation problems, given that they unify the 'traditional' formalisms such as frames, semantic networks, semantic data models and object-oriented representations within a rigorous formal framework. However, after a peak of interest at the beginning of the 1990s, they seem to have attained a more relaxed cruising speed. The perplexities about the real import of this type of solution, especially from a practical point of view, are not really linked with problems like incompleteness, undecidability, etc. We have already mentioned Nebel's assertion – a very reasonable one – stating that almost all the representation formalisms used in artificial intelligence are intractable or even undecidable in a worst-case situation, and we must be, on the contrary, grateful to the DL scholars for having settled the 'practicability of reasoning' problem on a rigorous and rational basis.

These perplexities relate, on the contrary, to some 'structural' problems of DLs, linked mainly with fundamental choices inherited from KL-ONE. One of these problems concerns the decision of operating a neat differentiation between 'primitive' and 'defined' concepts. The former have an *a priori* 'descriptive' semantics, similar to that which characterizes the concepts of the usual ontologies (hierarchies of concepts); the latter have, on the contrary, an *a posteriori* 'definitional' semantics, implying the necessity of 'unfolding' the definitions and of devolving to the (automatic) process of classification the insertion of a new concept in the hierarchy. As we have seen, it is the presence of this classification process, unnecessary in a traditional ontological context, that is at the origin of all the computational problems of DLs, especially when complex inheritance operations on the roles are involved. Another important difference between ontologies and DLs concerns the systematic use, in the latter, of the operator **and** for defining the concepts; this implies a (probably unnecessary) degree of freedom in the construction of concepts, that can lead sometimes to the construction of really odd defined concepts such as the well-known 'people whose friends are all male redheaded athletes' [Will88]. Other criticisms that can be found in the literature concern i) the expressiveness of the terminological reasoning component (TBox), too restricted for the purposes of many applications given that the terminological reasoning is based only on the relatively inexpressive classification mechanism (subsumption), *see* [Doyl91]; ii) the inadequacy of the assertional reasoning component (ABox) for dealing with the volumes of data proper to realistic applications – note that the ABox reasoning mechanism is usually incomplete; iii) the lack of a description logics standard; etc.

From a 'practical use' point of view, the main interest of subsumption lies in the possibility of executing some sort of online, generalized question-answering on the concept hierarchies. By expressing the query as a concept description, it becomes in fact possible, using the usual DLs classification techniques, to insert such description in the concept taxonomy: this gives direct access to the set of instances that satisfy the query, *see* [Dami90], [Deva91], [Bagn91], [Wrig93], [DiEu94], etc. This approach can be useful for solving configuration problems, for example. It must be noted, however, that the practical problems we can deal with using subsumption can also be solved using more conventional techniques – as Guha and Lenat say in a CYC context (*see* Section 3.4), '... CyCL has the ability to do subsumption ... However, in practice we have found – somewhat to our surprise – that very few real-world problems naturally fall in this category, so this is one of the less heavily used inference mechanisms' [Guha91a]. This perhaps explains why the development of industrial products based on the terminological logics principles seems to be so difficult.

With the caveat stated in the first paragraph of this section, we can conclude that the most recent versions of the frames systems – especially when they can be integrated with object-oriented representations, *see* [Kife95] – are still probably the best support, at least in principle, for the development of the most complex and structured KBSs.

See, in this context, the Open Knowledge Base Connectivity Protocol, OKBC [Chau98] and the Protégé-2000 system [Frid00], an OKBC-compatible KB-editing environment. The Protégé-2000 knowledge model is endowed with some interesting characteristics. For example, in the Protégée-2000 frames, as in OKBC, a slot itself is a frame; in particular, slots are first-class objects that are defined independently of any class (frame). For example, it is possible to define *a priori* a slot like Name and attach it both to the class (frame) *newspaper_* and to the class *author_* to denote, respectively, the name of a newspaper and the name of an author. Even if a system like this can prove difficult to use in concrete, complex situations, it represents, however, another sort of reply to the 'arbitrariness' problem evoked above in Section 3.131.

3.2 Deductive database systems

One of the most fundamental tasks of a computer system is to store and manage data from which users can extract information relevant to them. This task is particularly difficult with the presence of large amounts of complex data. Data management techniques today are very sophisticated when it comes to issues such as access techniques, query optimization, failure recovery and transaction management. However, the problem of understanding and interpreting large amounts of data with the goal of actually extracting information has not been fully addressed to date. The problem is even more complex when information must be derived according to some inference rules which could be complicated.

An approach to this problem would be to encode such rules into application programs. However, this has a number of drawbacks. First, from the application programs it is very difficult to understand the inference rules. Second, programming such rules is an expensive task since it entails developing quite complex application programs which are in turn very difficult to maintain, in case extensions or modifications to the inference rules are required. Deductive database systems make a step towards solving this problem by storing not only *explicit data* but also *deductive rules* that enable inferences to be made from the stored data. Data obtained from the stored data through deductive rules are often referred to as *derived data*. Deductive databases are a result of the integration between the area of logic programming (*see* Section 3.1) – based on the use of mathematical logic for directly modelling computational concepts – and the database area. Therefore, a deductive database system is characterized by the capability of handling large amounts of data as well as performing reasoning based on that information. In particular, the term deductive database emphasizes the ability to use a logic programming approach for representing deductions concerning the contents of a database.

The use of a logical approach in database systems has a number of relevant advantages [DasS92]. Logic has a well-defined semantics and can be used as a uniform formalism for representing data, derivation rules, integrity constraints and queries. The use of derivation rules allows one to replace a possibly large collection of explicit data with a single rule. The notion of relational database can be seen as a specific case of deductive database. In particular, several relevant issues concerning relational databases, such as null values and undefined data, have solutions in the logic context.

This chapter is organized as follows. The basic concepts underlying a deductive database are introduced in Section 3.21, whereas the DATALOG language, resulting from the integration of the Prolog language with database technology, is discussed in Section 3.22. When discussing the DATALOG language, we also discuss DATALOG queries, extensions proposed to DATALOG, and relevant properties of DATALOG databases. Even though DATALOG has been derived from Prolog, substantial differences exist between these two languages that are discussed in Section 3.23. Sections 3.24 and 3.25 complete the introduction to deductive databases by presenting architectural approaches for implementing deductive database systems, and relevant research prototypes. The subsequent sections of this chapter discuss more advanced topics. In particular, Section 3.26 discusses the problem of updates in deductive databases. This is a difficult issue since the introduction of update functions in deductive languages may lead to non-declarative languages. Then, Section 3.27 discusses the introduction of object-oriented modelling primitives into deductive languages, yielding models known as deductive object-oriented models. Finally, Section 3.28 introduces constraint database languages, resulting from the introduction of the constraint programming paradigm into database languages.

3.21 Basic concepts

A deductive database consists of two well-distinguished components:

- a set of data, also called **facts**, representing information explicitly given by the user; these data are collectively referred to as an **extensional database**;
- a set of inference rules, also called rules, encoding knowledge according to which other data can be derived from the facts; these rules are collectively referred to as an **intensional database**.

From a logical perspective, each fact is a ground atom and all predicates defined by ground atoms are called **extensional predicates**, whereas all predicates that appear in the heads of the inference rules are called **intensional predicates**. We denote the set of extensional predicates and intensional predicates of a database by $Pred^e$ and $Pred^i$ respectively. Very often, the assumption is made that the two sets are disjoint. The reason is that the techniques used for the management of the extensional database are different from those used for the intensional database. Different techniques are crucial in order to ensure satisfactory performance. The schema of a deductive database thus consists of the schema of the extensional predicates, very much like in relational databases, and of the inference rules.

3.22 DATALOG language

Most of the research activity in the area of deductive database systems has focused on the development of the DATALOG language (*see also* Section 3.121). DATALOG extends relational languages without negation with recursion. Such language has attracted mainly the interest of the academic community rather than the industrial community; however, it is worth mentioning that some optimization techniques developed for DATALOG have recently been applied to optimization of SQL queries. Moreover, recent extensions of SQL support some limited form of recursive queries, such as a recent version of DB2 [Lind95].

3.221 Syntax

A DATALOG rule is a Horn clause satisfying a number of properties, among which is the absence of function symbols. The terms that can appear in clauses are therefore only constant symbols and variable symbols. A DATALOG rule has the form

$$H(v) \leftarrow B_1(u_1), \ldots, B_n(u_n)$$

where: $n \geq 1$, H, $B_1, \ldots, B_n$ are predicates, and v, $u_1, \ldots, u_n$ are tuples of terms (that is, tuples of constants and/or variables) of the proper arity. Note that H must be an intensional predicate, whereas $B_1, \ldots, B_n$ can be either intensional or extensional predicates. DATALOG rules must be *range restricted*, that is, each variable in v must appear among the variables contained in $u_1, \ldots, u_n$. This fact, together with the requirement that each fact belonging to a DATALOG database must be a ground fact, ensures that only a finite number of facts can be deduced from a DATALOG database.

The following example shows the schema of a DATALOG database. The database, called Company database, contains three extensional predicates, storing facts about employees and departments of a given company. In the example, we assume that the manager of a department may also be a member of another department, though not a manager of the latter department. Moreover, it includes two rules to determine all supervisors, direct or indirect, to whom a given employee reports.

```
Extensional database
    Employee(Emp#,Name,Job,Salary,Bonus)
    Department(Dept#,Name,Division,Mgr#)
    Empd(Emp#, Dept#)
Intensional database
    Supervisor(Emp#,Mgr#) ←  Employee(Emp#,Name,Job,Salary,Bonus),
                             Empd(Emp#, Dept#),
                             Department(Dept#,Name,Division,Mgr#).
    Supervisor(Emp#,Mgr1#) ← Employee(Emp#,Name,Job,Salary,Bonus),
                             Empd(Emp#, Dept#),
                             Department(Dept#,Name,Division,Mgr#),
                             Supervisor(Mgr#,Mgr1#).
```

3.222 *Semantics*

The semantics of a DATALOG database can be defined very much like the semantics of a logic program, with some slight differences. As we have mentioned, a deductive database consists of two distinct components, an extensional database and an intensional one. Whereas the intensional database does not change and we can assume it to be fixed, the extensional database undergoes modifications. The semantics of a deductive database takes into account such a feature and it is thus defined differently with respect to the semantics of logic programs. In particular, let DDB be a deductive database; the semantics of DDB is defined as a function from sets of facts defined over Pred^e to sets of facts defined over $\text{Pred}^e \cup \text{Pred}^i$. Such semantics is in accord with the fact that the information obtained from a deductive database consists of all the facts explicitly stored in the database plus all the facts that can be derived through the derivation rules. Because IDB is assumed to be fixed, the semantics of a deductive database DDB = IDB $\cup$ EDB is often denoted as $\mathbf{S}_{\text{IDB}}(\text{EDB})$.

The absence of function symbols from DATALOG also has the important consequence on the semantics that the Herbrand universe of a DATALOG database coincides with the set of the constant symbols of the language. Because such a set is finite, the Herbrand universe, and consequently the Herbrand base, are finite sets. Therefore, the semantics of a DATALOG database is always a finite set.

We will discuss briefly the three possible approaches to modelling the semantics of logic programs in the framework of DATALOG databases.

Model-theoretic semantics

The formal definition of *consequence* of a DATALOG database is given in terms of interpretations and Herbrand models, very much like in the case of logic programs. Therefore, for DATALOG the minimal Herbrand model represents the model-theoretic semantics of a database. Note that such a model is always finite due to the absence of function symbols.

Operational top-down semantics

The SLD resolution method, developed for logic programs, can also be used for DATALOG databases, but note that unification techniques are simpler for DATALOG than for logic programs because of the absence of function symbols in DATALOG. This method, however, suffers from some problems. It is prone to recursive loops, it may perform repeated computations of some subgoals, and it is often hard to detect when all solutions to the query have been found.

Operational bottom-up semantics

According to such an approach, the rules of a DATALOG database are used to deduce new facts starting from a given set of facts. Such semantics is based on a *least fixpoint iteration* that at each iteration step computes a new set of facts that can be deduced from the set of facts derived at the previous iteration step and the derivation rules in the IDB. At the first step, the set of facts used is the set of facts stored in the EDB. The operator used at each step is called the *immediate consequence operator*; the model of a DATALOG database is represented by the least fixpoint of such an operator. Because the semantics of a DATALOG database is always a finite set, the bottom-up semantics allows the model of a DATALOG database to be computed in a finite time. Therefore, the bottom-up semantics represents a constructive semantics for DATALOG databases. The bottom-up evaluation is desirable in a database context because it avoids the problem of looping, which is inherent in the top-down approach. Moreover, the bottom-up evaluation directly supports set-at-a-time operations, such as relational joins, which are very efficient in the context of disk-resident data, whereas the top-down evaluation uses tuple-at-a-time operations.

3.223 Queries

As for logic programs, a query against a deductive database is represented as a goal of the form $\leftarrow A_1,\ldots,A_n$, where $A_1,\ldots,A_n$ are atoms, not necessarily ground. The following are examples of queries against the Company database:

- determine the supervisors of employees whose job is programmer;
  the corresponding goal is
  ← Supervisor(Emp#,Mgr#), Employee(Emp#,Name,programmer,Salary,Bonus)

- determine the supervisor of the employee named Rossi;
  the corresponding goal is
  ← Supervisor(Emp#,Mgr#), Employee(Emp#,Rossi,Job,Salary,Bonus)

An important difference between Prolog and DATALOG is with respect to queries. Let ← A be a goal. In DATALOG, we want not only to determine whether *at least* one solution exists, as in Prolog, but to determine *all* solutions. Such semantics for goals is consistent with the set-oriented meaning of queries in databases, where all answers to a query must be determined. Because of such query semantics, the bottom-up database semantics, being set-oriented, is preferred with respect to the top-down semantics. By contrast, goals in logic programs are tuple-oriented, i.e. they are based on returning only one answer at a time, among the set of possible answers. The bottom-up semantics, even though it is set-oriented and therefore more suitable for supporting database queries, has the major disadvantage that it does not take into account early on the constants appearing in the goal. Therefore, the goal evaluation process may generate a much larger set of facts with respect to those required to answer the queries. Several optimization techniques have been developed for the bottom-up semantics, most of which are based on rewriting the original DATALOG database (or a portion of it) into a new DATALOG database whose bottom-up evaluation generates far fewer facts than a bottom-up evaluation of the original DATALOG database. We refer the reader to [Cata95], [Cata96] for an extensive survey of such techniques.

3.224 Extensions of pure DATALOG

DATALOG in its basic form is not fully suited to data applications since it does not include many features that are required to support these applications. In order to overcome such drawbacks, a number of extensions to DATALOG have been proposed, some of which have also been incorporated into research prototypes. Here we will discuss two of those extensions: *negation*, and *built-in predicates*. Other extensions dealing with updates and complex objects are discussed in greater detail in Sections 3.26 and 3.27.

The possibility of deriving information when other information or facts do not hold is an important functionality for many applications. In particular, DATALOG is a monotonic language and therefore it is unable to express simple queries, such as the difference between two relations. Thus the introduction of negation in DATALOG is crucial in order to make such language expressive enough for many relevant queries. The extension of DATALOG with negation, however, raises several issues related to both the semantics and computational models of DATALOG. The most common approach to support negation in DATALOG is to allow negative literals of the form $\neg A_i$, where A_i is an atom, to appear in the bodies of rules. The resulting language is known as DATALOG¬. Semantics and computational problems are addressed by either imposing syntactic restrictions, as that program is stratified, or by adopting a different semantics. Stratification imposes that no predicate be negatively dependent on itself. Simple algorithms exist to determine whether a DATALOG¬ database is stratified. However, not all DATALOG¬ databases are stratified. In particular, stratification prohibits recursive application of negation and therefore severely reduces the expressive power of DATALOG¬. So alternative semantics for DATALOG¬ have been investigated. Among those, we recall the well-founded semantics based on the idea that a given database may not necessarily provide information on the truth or falsehood of every fact. Rather, for some facts the database may simply reply that the truth value of a given fact is unknown. We refer the reader to [Ceri90] and [Abit95] for extensive discussion on such topics.

Most database applications require the ability to formulate comparison predicates when selectively accessing data from a database. Comparison predicates between variables or constants occurring in the body of a DATALOG rule or goal are formulated in terms of comparison relationships, such as those denoted by the symbols ≥, <, ≤, >, and so on. To make practical selective data accesses, it is important that such comparison relationships be directly embedded into DATALOG. The idea is to consider them 'built-in' predicate symbols, whose semantics is implicitly known by the system. The use of such comparison predicates, however, may lead to infinite sets of answers to queries unless some specific safety conditions are observed in their use (*see* [Ceri90]).

3.225 Properties of DATALOG databases

A number of important properties for DATALOG databases have been devised. A major issue is to determine whether they are decidable by a static analysis of the intensional database. Static analysis for declarative languages in general concerns the detection, at compile time, of program properties that can be used to better understand the program semantics and to improve the efficiency of the program evaluation. For example, suppose that a predicate is proved to be unsatisfiable. This means that the predicate cannot generate any solution for any extensional database. From an optimization point of view, this allows us to remove the rules defining the predicate from the intensional database. However, this information can also be interpreted as the detection of an error arising in the IDB. Among relevant properties we recall:

1 *equivalence/containment* [Shmu93]: an intensional database IDB_1 is contained in an intensional database IDB_2 (denoted as $IDB_2 \subseteq IDB_1$) if for any possible extensional database EDB and for any intensional predicate p, defined in IDB_1, the answers to p in $IDB_1 \cup EDB$ are contained in the answers to p in $IDB_2 \cup$ EDB. Two intensional databases IDB_1 and IDB_2 are equivalent, denoted as $IDB_1 \approx IDB_2$, if $IDB_2 \subseteq IDB_1$ and $IDB_1 \subseteq IDB_2$;

2 *satisfiability* [Levy93]: an intensional predicate p defined in an intensional database IDB is satisfiable if there exists some extensional database EDB such that the evaluation of p in IDB ∪ EDB generates a non-empty set of answers;

3 *boundness* [HillG91]: a recursive intensional database IDB_1 is bound if there exists a non-recursive intensional database IDB_2 such that $IDB_1 \approx IDB_2$.

The above properties have been investigated for pure DATALOG and for some of its extensions, such as DATALOG with negation and with mathematical constraints. The properties may or may not be decidable depending on specific restrictions or extensions to the DATALOG language. Table 3.7 summarizes decidability results for DATALOG and some of its restrictions or extensions.

Table 3.7 Decidability results for DATALOG and some of its restrictions or extensions

Language	Decidability
Equivalence/Containment	
DATALOG	indecidable
DATALOG with intensional predicates of arity 2	indecidable
DATALOG with intensional predicates of arity 1, negation on non-recursive predicates and ≠	indecidable
DATALOG with stratified negation [(a)] and extensional predicates of arity 1	decidable
Satisfiability	
DATALOG	decidable
DATALOG with constraints over a dense ordering [(b)]	decidable
DATALOG with constraints over a dense ordering and stratified negation applied only to extensional atoms	decidable
DATALOG with stratified negation and extensional predicates of arity 1	decidable
Boundness	
DATALOG	indecidable
Linear DATALOG databases [(c)]	indecidable
DATALOG with intensional predicates of arity 1	decidable

(a) A DATALOG database with stratified negation admits the use of negation with the restriction that no predicate in the database negatively depends on itself.

(b) Constraints over a dense order are constraints of the form $X \theta Y$ or $X \theta c$, where $\theta \in \{\leq, \geq, =, <, >, \neq\}$, c is constant, X and Y are variables interpreted over a domain D for which a dense order is defined.

(c) A linear DATALOG database is a recursive DATALOG database such that the body of each rule includes at most one predicate which is mutually recursive with the predicate in the head of the rule.

3.23 Deductive database systems and logic programming systems – differences

Even though deductive database and logic programming technologies are based on a common paradigm, there are several relevant differences between the two types of systems [DasS92]. These are basically due to the fact that a deductive database system must store large amounts of facts from which useful information needs to be extracted through the use of queries, whereas a logic programming system must only support programming and is not required to have special features for data modelling and managing. Some relevant differences between the two types of systems are as follows [DasS92]:

1. A deductive database system typically stores a number of facts which is much larger than the number of rules. There is no such difference in a logic program.
2. As mentioned in Section 3.21, the set of predicates in a deductive database is partitioned into two disjoint predicate sets: the set of extensional predicates and the set of intensional predicates. There is not such partition in a logic program.
3. Typical languages for deductive databases, such as DATALOG, are in general function-free or at most include some specific functions, such as arithmetic ones, and are range-restricted. Logic programming languages, by contrast, fully support general functions and do not impose any range restriction.
4. Deductive database systems have support for integrity constraint definition and enforcement. Constraints are an important functionality of database systems, whereas there is no such concept in logic programming.
5. A typical database query seeks all solutions satisfying the predicates stated in the query, whereas a goal in a logic program needs to determine only one solution among the possible solutions. This is a major difference that motivates why techniques for query execution in deductive databases differ from those used for the refutation process in logic programs.

Other important differences are discussed in [DasS92], which also presents a detailed comparison between deductive database and logic programming terminology.

3.24 Architectural approaches

The various architectural approaches to deductive databases can be categorized based on how the co-operation between IDB and EDB is activated. Two basic approaches can be devised [Leun88]:

- a *homogeneous approach*, in which a single, integrated system is used to manipulate both EDB and IDB, and to perform deductive reasoning over them;
- a heterogeneous approach, in which a relational DB is used to manage the extensional database, and a logic-programming system is used to perform deductive reasoning based on the intensional database.

In the homogeneous approach, the same programming system (i.e. the same formalism, for example, Prolog) is used to represent both rules and facts. In a 'pure logic system', facts and rules reside on secondary storage; they are loaded into the main memory by the operating system prior to system execution and must remain there until the execution has been completed. When a query must be answered, unification is performed on the clauses stored in the main memory; little or no access to secondary storage is made. The drawbacks are:

- representing facts and rules in exactly the same way may be misleading. Facts and rules differ in size as well as in the ways they are utilized and managed; thus, representing and accessing them separately with different access methods may result in better performance;
- storing all rules and many facts in the main memory severely limits the size of the knowledge base the system can handle, even if this problem can be partially addressed by the use of virtual-memory techniques.

Normally, the homogeneous approach is implemented by using 'enhanced logic systems': in these systems, some typical data management functions (indexing techniques, buffer management, query optimization) are directly 'reconstructed' (using Prolog, for example) inside the logic system (IDB). These functions can manage, in particular, data residing on external storage (EDB), so that facts in the external database can be accessed from the logic system when needed.

The heterogeneous approach uses two separate subsystems, a logic system (LS) and an ordinary (relational) DBMS. The LS (in Prolog style) can be considered as a front end where the rules (logic formulae) are stored and the inference performed; it corresponds well, therefore, to the rule base of an intelligent database system. The DBMS can be viewed as a back end to the LS, which returns results to the LS in response to LS requests; it represents the fact database of an IDBS.

Heterogeneous systems can be categorized as compiled or interpreted (with some variations on the theme, for example partial compilation approaches) depending on the granularity of the interaction between the two subsystems. The compiled approach includes two distinct phases, compilation and execution. In the compilation phase, the LS compiles the user query and the rules into an (iterative or recursive) autonomous database program that references only base (stored) relations. In the execution phase, the DBMS executes the program as a single entity, generates all answers to the query using the 'extensional' database only, and finally returns the answers to the LS. Interaction between the LS and the DBMS is at a large granularity (i.e. the two systems are 'loosely coupled'). When a query references base relations only, it can be evaluated directly by the relational DBMS. When the query references both base and virtual relations, it must be transformed according to the rules defining the virtual relations, so that only base relations are referenced. Problems arise in the case of virtual relations defined recursively because a potentially infinite sequence of subqueries may result.

In the interpreted approach, facts are retrieved from the DBMS whenever the LS needs them in order to continue execution (this approach can, therefore, be defined as 'tight'). The interaction is frequent and of a small granularity, as most requests are for single facts. The main benefit of this approach is, of course, its flexibility in controlling the search process; however, it requires a large number of interactions between the two subsystems and causes communication overhead, thereby slowing the global operations. Furthermore, since single requests rather than sets of subqueries (as in the compiled approach) are sent to the DBMS, global optimization within the DBMS becomes less effective.

The architectural schemas of the various approaches are summarized in Figure 3.16 while Figure 3.17 presents a taxonomy of the various approaches.

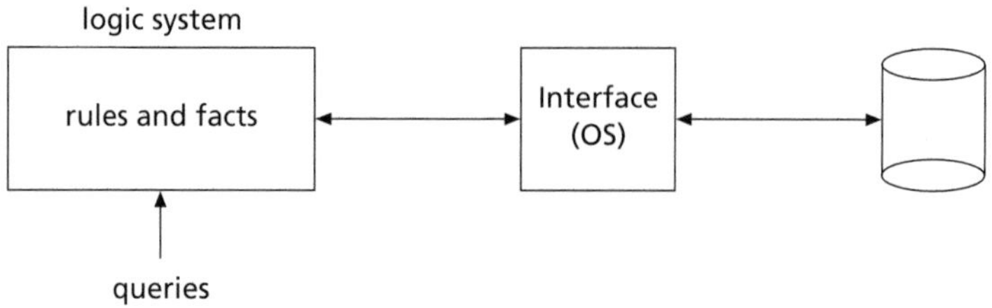

Homogenous approach: a *pure logic system*

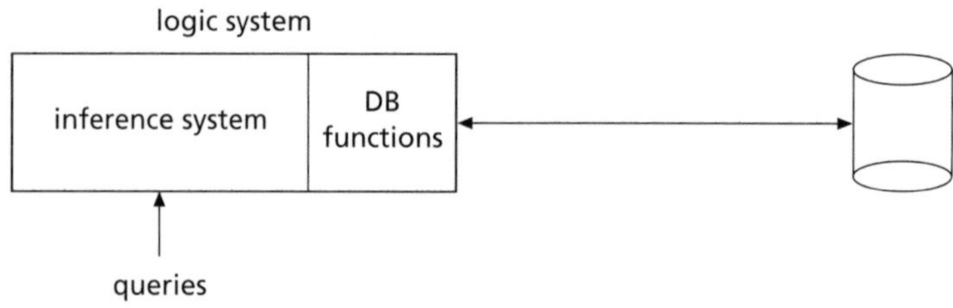

Homogenous approach: an *enhanced system*

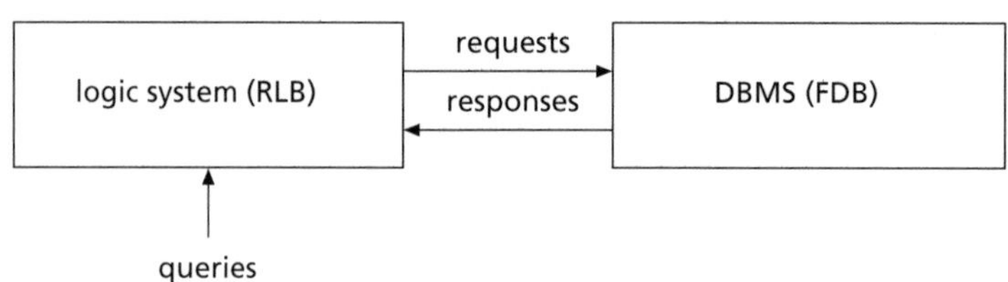

Heterogeneous approach

Figure 3.16 Deductive database architectures

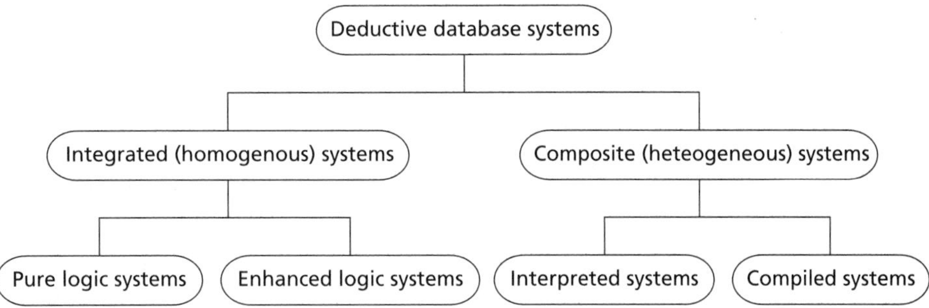

Figure 3.17 A taxonomy of architectual approaches to deductive database

3.25 Research prototypes

An early example of a deductive database system based on the heterogeneous approach is PROSQL (IBM San Jose Research Laboratory), which associates Prolog as a front end with a SQL/Data System relational back end. Basically, a PROSQL program is a Prolog program that uses the special predicate 'SQL' to create tables and views and to insert and delete tuples to and from the DB system; the SQL predicate contains as its argument a legal SQL statement that is passed to SQL/DS for execution. A PROSQL program can operate in either compiled or interpreted mode.

NAIL! (Not Another Implementation in Logic!) is a compiled system developed at Stanford University: it links DATALOG to a conventional SQLDB system and can handle non-linear recursive rules (i.e. rules with more than one recursively defined predicate on the right-hand side). A successor of NAIL! is Glue-Nail, again developed at Stanford University. A notable feature of this system is the support of two languages: Nail, providing declarative statements based on Horn clauses, and Glue, which is procedural and used for I/O, updates, and control constructs. The system is single-user and memory resident.

The aim of the LDL (logic data language) project at MCC (Micro-Electronic and Computer Corporation) has been to correct some limitations of the 'normal' heterogeneous approach – for example, the clause-at-a-time computation model of Prolog (see PROSQL) is substantially different from the set-at-a-time model of relational DBs, and difficult to integrate with it. In order to provide a better interface between the logic system and the DB (and produce a real 'tightly coupled system', *see* Section 3.3), LDL, a (declarative) DATALOG extension, is enriched with many features not found in languages of the Prolog class. A significant improvement concerns the way LDL handles sets and negation. Unlike Prolog, which emulates sets with lists, LDL allows the use of sets as data primitive objects in specifying rules and facts. Negation is based on set difference computed on the underlying domains; this formulation replaces the notion of 'negation by failure' employed in Prolog and the relational data model. LDL makes use of bottom-up techniques for compiling the queries, coupled with several optimization techniques, such as magic sets ([Cata95], [Cata96]). A later version of LDL, called LDL++, provides interfaces to procedures in C and in C++, as well as abstract data types. Moreover, the system can be interfaced to traditional relational systems.

MegaLog was developed at ECRC (the European Computer Research Center). It supports the manipulation of large amounts of data, while also providing Prolog features. Because the behaviour is dictated by Prolog, it does not guarantee termination even for DATALOG programs. It is an efficient system even for large databases. One of its most well-known contributions is the development of a multi-dimensional grid file system called Balanced and Nested Grid File (BANG) used as support for efficient query execution. EKS has been developed at ECRC on top of MegaLog. The language of EKS is DATALOG (thus, no function symbols). It supports a large number of features: general integrity constraints (with references to recursive predicates and aggregate operations), rules with recursion through aggregates, materialized views, hypothetical query facilities, negation. For query evaluation, it uses a set-oriented top-down evaluation scheme with memoing.

Lola was developed at the Technical University of Munich. The system is implemented by compiling Horn clauses, which may contain lists, into a Relational Lisp program with embedded SQL statements. The deductive part of this system is memory-resident and therefore the system does not scale well to large databases when intermediate relations are large.

Coral was developed at the University of Wisconsin at Madison. Coral uses bottom-up query evaluation extended with a large number of optimization techniques. The system is single-user and memory-resident. It is interfaced with the Exodus storage manager for access to permanent relations. It is not clear whether this integration scales up to large databases in performance terms.

Aditi was developed at the University of Melbourne. It uses a bottom-up query evaluation strategy. However, top-down query evaluation is also possible, upon user demand. Both permanent and temporary relations can be disk-based and therefore the system scales well to large databases. The language supports function symbols, negation, and aggregate functions.

3.26 Updates in deductive databases

An important requirement for any database system is the ability to support dynamic changes to the data. Therefore, even though logical languages were conceived as query languages, the problem of updating deductive databases is relevant. The introduction of update primitives in a logical database language, such as DATALOG, raises several issues, however, which are in particular related to set-orientedness and determinism. Set-orientedness makes it possible to simultaneously apply an update operation to several data items, selected by queries. We can therefore consider a *set-oriented update execution* as consisting of a query component – selecting the data to be modified – and an update component – performing the changes. Note that SQL commands, such as Update and Delete, are based on this approach: the tuples to be modified (deleted) are determined by evaluating a predicate; then the updates (deletions) are atomically applied to all the selected tuples. Determinism guarantees that the evaluation of a goal generates a single result, independently from the chosen evaluation strategy. The relevance of a set-oriented deterministic update execution has also been recognized as an important requirement for update commands in SQL, when features such as check and referential constraint processing are present [Lind95].

Two main problems arise when trying to achieve this sort of goal in a deductive language such as DATALOG. The first one is related to possible interferences between the query and update components of the same update execution. If updates are performed as soon as they are generated, as a side effect of the query evaluation (thus, by applying an *immediate semantics*), the query may return different results, depending on the evaluation order of rules and atoms used in answering the query. In this case, the determinism of the query part, as well as the determinism of the update part, may not be achieved. The second problem is related to the fact that multiple inconsistent updates (for example, inserting and removing the same fact) may result from the same set-oriented update execution. This leads to a non-deterministic update of the database, unless specific solutions are taken.

Because of the difficulty in overcoming these problems, most solutions to obtain set-oriented and deterministic logical update languages are based on separating the update language from the query language, as in Glue-Nail [Derr93], or on relying on some syntactic ordering of rules and update atoms, or imposing strong syntactic conditions. For example, in LDL [Kris89], no multiple rules defining the same predicate are allowed when the rules perform updates. The first class of solutions does not achieve the integration between the query language and the update language. The second class of solutions allows special update atoms to appear in rules, with special syntactical notations for distinguishing between deletions and insertions. However, it leads to languages that are not truly declarative and for which not all computational models defined for DATALOG are valid. Languages adopting solutions in such a class include many well-known languages, such as Dynamic Logic Programming (DLP) Declarative Language (DL) [Abit88], and RDL1 [deMa88]. In particular, languages in the second class can be categorized according to whether update atoms appear in the heads or in the bodies of rules. In general, the position of update atoms determines the evaluation model defined for the language; in most cases, languages with update atoms in the heads admit only the bottom-up evaluation model, whereas languages with update atoms in the bodies admit only the top-down evaluation model. Finally, the third class of solutions limits the expressive power of the language.

The following example illustrates the second class of solutions by considering first DLP – a language for which only the top-down evaluation is defined – and then DL – a language for which only the bottom-up evaluation is defined.

Consider the following DLP rule and the extensional database Company. The rule makes use of arithmetic constraints and of special predicates for computing aggregate function which are DATALOG extensions supported by DLP. The parentheses emphasize the order of evaluation.

```
Hire(Emp#, Ename, Salary, Bonus,Dept#)
                    ← <+Employee(Emp#,Name,Job,Salary,Bonus)>
                      (<+Empd(Emp#, Dept#)>
                      (avgsal(Dept#,avg), avg≤50k)).
```

When called by the query ?Hire(1024,Smith,Engineer,60k,0,10) the above rule will add the facts (1024,Smith,Engineer,60k,0) and (1024,10) to the extensional predicates Employee and Empd respectively. The average salary of the sales department is then computed and the updated extensional database is returned if this average is less than or equal to 50k. If the average is greater than 50k, the rule will fail and no update is performed. It is important to note that the updates +(1024,Smith,Engineer,60k,0) and +(1024,10) are not executed together but +(1024,Smith,60k,0) is executed before +(1024,10). The execution order is based on the order according to which the update atoms appear in the body of the rule.

Consider now the following DLP query:

```
?Employee(1035,Black,Secretary,30k,0),<+Empd(1035,10)>
(Supervisor(1035,X))
```

The query checks whether the fact Employee(1035,Black,Secretary,30k,0) is true in the current extensional database. If this fact is true, the query adds the fact Empd(1035,10) to the extensional databases and then determines the supervisor of employee 1035. Note that the atoms Employee(1035,Black,Secretary,30k,0) and Supervisor(1035,X) are not evaluated together, rather they are evaluated in a specific sequence. Moreover, if the evaluation order of these two atoms were changed, the results of the query could be different. This example illustrates how DLP is not fully declarative; the order in which atoms appear in rules determines the evaluation order of the atoms. It is also important to note that a bottom-up evaluation for DLP databases has no meaning.

Consider now the following DL rules [Abit91]. In the rules s is an extensional predicate, and r and t are intensional ones.

```
r(X) ← s(X), -t(X)
t(X) ← s(X), -r(X).
```

Suppose that those rules are applied to the extensional database {s(1), s(2),s(3)}. According to the deterministic bottom-up evaluation model, defined for DL, all applicable intensional predicates are fired simultaneously. This evaluation returns the unique result {s(1), s(2), s(3), r(1), r(2), r(3), t(1), t(2), t(3)} in a single step. Note that such a result could not be obtained if a top-down evaluation model were used. It is also worth noting that DL does not have a model-theoretic semantics; rather, as illustrated by this example, it has an operational semantics based on the bottom-up evaluation model.

Different, more satisfactory solutions may be devised to the above two problems however. The problem of interference between the query and update components can be solved by adopting a *deferred update semantics*. Under such semantics, the updates are not applied as soon as they are generated during the query evaluation; rather, they are executed only after the query evaluation has been completed. The second problem can be solved by allowing inconsistent updates to be generated and providing a conflict resolution policy. Possible policies are i) considering inconsistent updates as a logical error and thus aborting the execution [MontD97]; ii) defining priorities among updates, for example by executing insertions before deletions (or vice versa) [Abit87]; (iii) not executing inconsistent updates, thus removing the causes of non-determinism [MontD97], [ChenW91].

Based on the previous discussion, we can classify the various approaches proposed for the inclusion of update capabilities in declarative languages under a number of aspects.

1 *Queries/updates*: as we discussed above, languages modelling updates do not always model queries and vice versa. Modelling both queries and updates is important for the development of logical languages.

2 *Semantics*: it is important that the semantics of update languages be declarative. A semantics is declarative if it is model-theoretic.

3 *Evaluation*: evaluation must be correct and complete with respect to the formal semantics. As we have seen, computational models for deductive database languages may be top-down or bottom-up. Not all logical update languages provide both evaluation techniques. This restriction implies, in those cases, that limited optimization techniques can be used.

4 *Update position*: in logical languages, updates can be inserted in the bodies or in the heads of the rules. Often, updates in the bodies correspond to a top-down evaluation whereas updates in the heads correspond to a bottom-up evaluation. Special cases are U-DATALOG [MontD97] and Transaction Logic [Bonn94], as they insert updates in the bodies of rules but provide both bottom-up and top-down computational models.

5 *Update execution*: in logical languages, updates can be interpreted as operators changing the theory on which a query is evaluated. We can distinguish between languages changing the theory during the computation – in this case we say the language has an immediate semantics – and languages changing the theory only after the logical computation is terminated – in this case we say the language has a deferred semantics. The last class of languages is powerful enough only if it is coupled with some control operators, external to the logical language, as in U-DATALOG.

6 *Non-determinism*: update languages can model non-determinism, even if no general agreement exists that this is a useful feature. However, almost all languages have some non-deterministic construct.

7 *Set-oriented updates*: set oriented updates are obtained by applying an update operation on a set of data objects, obtained as result of a query execution.

8 *Parallelism*: parallel updates are applied simultaneously to the same current database. It is different from concurrent transactions, that may be executed in parallel but are semantically serialized.

9 *Conflict resolution policy*: multiple inconsistent updates – for example, inserting and removing the same fact – may result from the same update execution. This leads to non-deterministic executions unless specific solutions are taken.

Table 3.8 outlines a comparison of several languages with respect to the above dimensions.

Table 3.8 Update languages properties

Language	Query/updates	Semantics	Evaluation	Update position	Update execution	Non determin.	Set-oriented updates	Parallelism	Conflict resolution policy
LDL [Kris89]	integrated	Model theoretic (propositional dynamic logic)	top-down	in the body of extended DATALOG rules	immediate	no	yes	not always	Syntactic conditions and priorites among atoms
TL [Abit87]	only updates	operational		in procedural constructs	immediate	yes (in a distinct version of the language)	yes (in the deterministic version)	yes (in the deterministic version)	Priorites to insertions (in the deterministic version)
DL [Abit88]	the same lang. can be seen either as a query or an update language	operational (inflationary fixpoint)	bottom-up	head of DATALOG rules with negated subgoals	immediate	yes (in a distinct version of the language)	yes (in the deterministic version)	yes (in the deterministic version)	No explicit deletion is allowed (thus no incosistency arises)
DLP [MancS89]	both, modelled by distinct rules	model-theoretic (dynamic logic)	top-down (incomplete with respect to model theory)	in the body of extended DATALOG rules	immediate	yes	no	no	Explicit ordering among updates
Update/calculus [ChenW91]	integrated	model-theoretic	a sound and complete method is given	inside first-order formulas	deferred	yes	yes	yes	Inconsistent updates are not executed
U-DATALOG [MontD97]	integrated	2 phases: the first is model-theoretic	top-down and bottom-up	in the body of DATALOG rules	deferred	no	yes	yes	Either inconsistent updates are not executed or the transaction is aborted
Transaction logic [Bonn94]	integrated	path model semantics	top-down and bottom-up	inside extended first-order formulas	immediate	yes	yes	yes	Non-determinism is allowed

3.27 Integration of deductive database and object database technologies

A relevant class of extensions to the deductive database technology is represented by the integration of such a paradigm with object-oriented modelling capabilities. Such extensions have been motivated by the fact that an important requirement, not addressed by current OODBMSs, is to store into the database not only data but also knowledge. Moreover, current OODBMSs are based mainly on the usage of imperative programming languages, thus not supporting a declarative style of programming. Logic-based data management systems overcome the previous drawbacks. Such systems, however, while being characterized by sound theoretical basis, declarative style, and powerful inference capabilities, lack modularity and structuring capabilities typical of object-oriented data models and languages. The integration of the two approaches is thus quite interesting and has motivated a number of research efforts in this direction.

There are several orthogonal dimensions along which the approaches to the integration of the deductive and object paradigms may be classified. A first dimension is whether the logical equivalent of the notion of object is that of term or theory (i.e. a set of logical clauses). Other dimensions could be whether state evolution and behavioral components of objects are considered, and whether a schema level is present.

We classify the considered approaches into two main groups:

1. *Extensions to logic programming towards modularity and object-orientation.* Under this approach, objects (modules) are often seen as theories. Moreover, no notion of schema or any kind of object evolution are provided. A complete survey of these approaches can be found in [Bugl94].
2. *Deductive object databases.* Under this approach, objects are often seen as terms. Moreover, this approach in general accounts for the distinction between the schema and instance levels, and provides the notion of object state.

The above classification is not strict of course. For example, the language LOGIN [AitK91] is an object-oriented extension of Prolog, which considers as object granularity that of term. Since LOGIN has greatly influenced other proposals on logics for objects developed in the database field, we discuss it in Section 3.272.

3.271 From logic programming to modular and object-oriented Logic programming

The research in the field of modularity in logic programming has evolved in two different directions. One is based on instrumenting modular systems with compositional operators for incrementally building programs by combining separate and independent components. The other extends logic programming with abstraction and scoping mechanisms, thus extending classical logic languages, like those based on Horn clauses.

Modular programming as algebraic program composition

This approach derives from the software engineering view that programs should be incrementally developed by defining multiple units and their interfaces and then by composing them. Thus, this approach to modularity is based on the notion of program composition. Logic programs are interpreted as elements of an algebra and their composition is modelled in terms of the operators of the algebra. Logic programming is extended with modularization constructs without any need to extend the language of Horn clauses. Module composition is indeed an inherently meta-linguistic mechanism.

The compositional frameworks proposed in [MancS88], [Brog90], as well as open logic programs [Boss94] and differential logic programming [Boss93], can be seen as different formulations of this idea. Mechanisms for information hiding and encapsulation, based on this notion of module composition, have been adopted by prototypical implementations, such as the Godel system [HillP94].

Viewing modularity as algebraic program composition offers several advantages. First, composition is a powerful tool for structuring programs without any need to extend the theory of Horn clauses. Second, it naturally supports the reuse of the same program within different composite programs and the replacement of equivalent components. Finally, when coupled with mechanisms for specifying the interfaces among components, it provides powerful forms of encapsulation and information hiding.

We will discuss briefly some of the proposals in this approach.

Open logic programs. The form of program composition which is considered is $\approx_{\Omega}$, which is a generalization of program union where the set of predicates Ω specifies which predicates can be shared by different programs. The definition of any predicate symbol $p \in \Omega$ in a Ω-open program can always be extended. Therefore, a deduction dealing with a predicate symbol of a Ω-open program can be either complete (when it takes place completely in the program) or partial. A partial deduction can be completed by the addition of new clauses, i.e. by the composition with a program in which more clauses for the predicate are specified.

The composition of programs through the union operator implements a form of dynamic scoping rule, since each reference to a predicate in a program refers to a different definition depending on the composition the program is part of. The composition by union has been shown to be well suited for implementing forms of knowledge assimilation, where knowledge is dynamically updated as new information becomes available. Each program can, in fact, be thought as open with respect to (composition with) other programs. This corresponds to thinking of an open program as an incomplete description of some knowledge domain. The composition of open programs may increase the degree of completeness of the description. Indeed, something which does not hold in one program can hold in another one, and the former can exploit the latter, or vice versa, to derive new knowledge.

An important property which does not hold in the traditional standard semantics for logic programs is compositionality. Compositionality is related with a (syntactic) program composition *op*, and holds when the semantics of the compound program *P op Q* is defined by semantically composing the semantics of the constituents. In the case of logic programs, the union of clauses raises a compositionality problem. The related property is something called OR-compositionality. In [Boss94] a compositional semantics for open programs is defined. In order for the semantics to be compositional it must contain information in the form of a mapping from sets of atoms to sets of atoms. This mapping is nothing other than the usual concept of clause.

Differential logic programming. In [Boss93], a semantics compositional with respect to other composition operators is considered. A general inheritance operator is proposed which captures the semantics of several specialized mechanisms such as static and dynamic inheritance and composition by union of clauses. Inheritance is viewed as a mechanism for differential programming, i.e. for building new program components by specifying how they differ from existing ones. Differential programming is achieved by using filters to modify the external behavior of existing components. Accordingly, a modified version of a component is obtained by defining a new component that performs some special operations and possibly calls to the original one.

Differential programs are program components, i.e. logic programs annotated by three sets of predicate symbols: statically inherited predicates, dynamically inherited predicates, and extensible predicates. These predicates are the external interface of the object. The remaining predicates are internal to the program. Similarly to classes in the object-oriented paradigm, differential programs can be organized in ISA hierarchies and can use inherited definitions according to their external interfaces. Statically and dynamically inherited predicates are evaluated according to the overriding semantics. Extensible predicates model an orthogonal mechanism defined with an extension semantics, whereby local definitions are extended with inherited ones, not overriding them.

The operational semantics for hierarchies is given by defining suitable inference rules obtained by modifying the SLD-resolution to take into account the inheritance mechanism expressed by the ISA construct. A syntactic composition operator provides an alternative and equivalent characterization of the operational semantics of ISA hierarchies, by transforming a ISA hierarchy into an equivalent program, without hierarchy, which can be evaluated by standard SLD-derivation.

Modular programming based on extensions of Horn clauses

The composition operators among programs, seen as elements of an algebra, as outlined above, allow one only to specify the collection of modules that must be used for evaluating a top-level goal. Once the modular configuration of the program has been set, there is no way to dynamically modify its structure and enforce the evaluation of a (sub-)goal to occur in a collection of modules different from the one associated with the top-level goal. To obtain a richer notion of composition, the operators for building and composing modules must act as built-in mechanisms that directly affect the language evaluation procedure. Thus approaches aiming at instrumenting logic programs with linguistic mechanisms richer than those offered by Horn clauses have been proposed. The idea is to model the operators for building and composing modules directly in terms of the logical connectives of a logic language defined as an extension of Horn clauses. This was introduced by Miller with implicational goals [MillD86]. Unfortunately, this technique is not appropriate for databases since it only extends temporarily the program with modules defined in the goal – after the goal evaluation such modules are discarded. Along the approach of Miller, we find contextual logic programming [MontL90] and messages used as a way to achieve a logical reinterpretation for some of the distinguishing features of the object-oriented paradigm ([Bugl92], [McCa92]). A prototypical system supporting knowledge partitioned in theories and in which goal refutation can move from one theory to another through context switches, which are message calls, is KBMS1 [Manl90].

Contextual logic programming. This is an extension of logic programming based on the ideas of context-dependent predicate definitions and variable context of proof. The two basic notions are those of unit, a naming mechanism to denote a set of clauses, and of extension goal. A program is a set of units, where each unit is a named set of clauses; a clause may contain extension goals in its body. The evaluation of an extension goal of the form $u > g$ in a context causes the context to be extended (with overriding) with the denotation of the unit u. Thus the set of clauses available for reduction (the context) may change during the derivation. To derive a goal in a context, the idea is to derive the goal in the unit most recently added to the context, using the other units if the predicate symbol of the goal is not defined in the most recent one. Thus, in the evaluation of an extension goal the new definition in the nested scope overrides the corresponding definition in the outer scope. The nested scope depends on the outer one only for those definitions that are not local to the nested one.

Different levels of nesting are allowed. Thus a reference to a predicate cannot be statically bound to the definitions occurring in the outer scope. The early proposal adopts a lexical (static) policy of scope. Further extensions capturing a notion of dynamic scoping while retaining the overriding semantics have been proposed.

Message passing and inheritance. Message passing and inheritance are embodied in logic programming in the SelfLog language [Bugl92] which has been greatly influenced from the class template language proposed in [McCa92]. Such language is an extended Horn clauses language which has an embedded form of modularity whereby a set of clauses can be collected into a named theory (an object or unit) and different objects can communicate by requesting the evaluation of a goal from one another. The object co-operation mechanism of message passing is thus modelled. Clauses may contain message-goals of the form $o{:}g$, requesting g to be evaluated in object o. The ':' symbol causes a change of context from the current object to object o. This mechanism for interobject invocation captures the idea of message passing. The notion of inheritance is added to such language, resulting in the SelfLog language, which extends the former by allowing the hierarchical relationship between two objects to be explicitly declared. In SelfLog, the meaning of the goal $o{:}g$ is to enforce the evaluation of the goal g not in the object o, but in the composition of o with all its ancestors. Both static and dynamic inheritance are considered. The ideas of inheritance and interobject goal invocation are combined into a single framework. The semantics of a program is considered as a function over Herbrand sets rather than a simple Herbrand set.

3.272 *Deductive object-oriented databases*

Several research proposals have attempted to combine object-orientation, databases and logical languages. A first research direction uses logic to formalize the notions underlying object-oriented data models, resulting in the so-called logics for objects. The approaches in this area consider (complex) objects as terms, take into account a notion of schema, and put a great emphasis on formal semantics. No update and evolution aspects are considered. Another research direction is that of employing logical languages as query languages for object-oriented databases, leading to the definition of object-oriented logical languages primarily used for querying object-oriented databases. The most significant example of such language is IQL [Abit89]. The last direction to consider is that of extending DATALOG to specify object-oriented databases. In this type of extension, the logical component is used to specify the schema of the databases, and a distinction is made between base relations and derived relations. Examples of systems based on such an approach are LOGRES [Caca89], COMPLEX [Grec90], and DATALOG^{Meth} [Abit93].

Logics for objects

The approaches we classify in this category consider objects as terms and do not take into account state evolution of objects. These proposals originate from Maier's O-logic [Maie86], and evolve in C-logic [ChenW89] and the revised O-logic [Kife89]. These proposals are also strictly related to the LOGIN language [AitK86]. The final effort in this direction, which extends the previous ones, is Frame Logic (F-logic) [Kife90]. In particular, F-logic extends the previous proposals with higher-order features to accommodate methods with complex terms. The motivation underlying these approaches is the development of a logical framework for representing complex objects. It thus overcomes the absence of formal foundations for object-oriented data models. These approaches attempt to define model-theoretic semantics for object-oriented logics. C-logic and O-logic deal with complex objects and object identity, taking into account an inheritance hierarchy on classes, whereas F-logic extends them by also considering methods and schema.

In LOGIN, classes and objects are represented as compound terms whose arguments designate the object attributes. A labelling schema over terms is employed to logically link objects into inheritance hierarchies. In LOGIN, first-order terms are extended in ψ-terms which incorporate taxonomic information as record-like structures. They exploit variable typing with the notion of inheritance. Attribute inheritance is then achieved by overloading unification to take into account term hierarchy when attempting to match two terms. An efficient type unification algorithm is supported. LOGIN may be seen as a typed extension of Prolog, with type inheritance as in semantic networks, where taxonomic information is provided by complex objects and a set-at-a-time model of computing is supported. However, no notion of object identity is present, nor methods considered. LOGIN incorporates inheritance into logic programming by means of a unification algorithm, whose semantics can be specified using equational logic. LIFE [AitK91] is an extension of LOGIN combining logic and functional programming, with a type system designed to accommodate multiple inheritance.

Both C-logic and O-logic model complex objects as extended terms. An extended term consists of an object identifier, a type and a structured value. A structured value is a record with a number of labels, where each label is assigned a value. Properties of an object are thus represented by labelled values. Both approaches consider sets in that they support non-functional set-oriented labels. Inheritance is taken into account by having the set of classes as a partially ordered set. A dynamic notion of type (i.e. its extent instead of its structure) is considered.

F-logic extends the previous logics by incorporating the notions of methods and schema. However, in F-logic the schema level and the instance level are not distinguished. Thus a unique ISA hierarchy represents both the subtype and instance-of relationships. In F-logic the distinction among objects, classes and relationships is abolished. Thus inheritance, methods and schema can be reasoned about in the formalism. In F-logic, both classes and individual objects are taken from the same domain and are organized in a lattice. In F-logic, inheritance is built into the semantics, i.e. whenever an element p precedes an element v in the ordering associated with the lattice, the properties of p also hold for v. They support a monotonic overriding (not a complete one) – the most specific information for an object is added to more general ones without nullifying it. When inheritance contradicts the other information, a local inconsistency arises.

Although F-logic formally has a first-order semantics, it is able to model some higher order features such as sets, class-subclass hierarchies and schema. Schema can be reasoned about because labels – attribute names – are virtually indistinguishable from objects. F-logic also supports declarative method specification, through rules. Declarative definitions of methods are possible since methods are labels with parameters.

Logic as a query language for object-oriented databases

The first approach in this direction has been a DATALOG extension to deal with structured objects, defining query languages whose corresponding data model is not a first normal form (1NF) relational model but an extended relational model. COL (Complex Object Language) [Abit90] is an example of a deductive language for value-based models supporting structured objects. Even though COL is not an object-based language, it is a DATALOG extension allowing the manipulation of structured values obtained using tuple and set constructors. Besides relations, base and derived ones, the language supports data functions. Data functions are multi-valued functions defined either extensionally (base ones) or intensionally (derived ones). A data function is a relation satisfying a functional dependency. Those functions support the manipulation of structured values. In COL, besides types obtained by applying tuple and set constructors, union types are considered since they support the manipulation of heterogeneous sets. The language does not consider object identity or inheritance.

IQL. IQL (Identity Query Language) [Abit89] is an extension of COL with the notions of object identity and inheritance. It is centred on the concept of object identifier as a powerful primitive for database query languages. Informally, OIDs in IQL are typed pointers. OIDs are used for three main purposes: i) representing structures with sharing and cycles; ii) set manipulation; iii) enriching the expressive power of the query language. The IQL data model is an object-based model, with a clear distinction between schema and instances. The model supports both relations and classes. The IQL language is rule-based, statically typecheckable and complete. It is obtained by extending DATALOG to generate an object-based language with sufficient expressive power to invent OIDs. Besides tuple and set types, IQL supports a weak mechanism of OID assignment. OID invention is performed through variables appearing in rule heads but not in rule bodies. OID invention is used to store query results in objects, for set manipulation, and to ensure language completeness. All algebraic transformations on complex objects may be expressed in IQL. IQL also supports inheritance, which is, however, not handled directly but using the notion of union types.

The semantics of the language is defined in terms of an inflationary fixpoint operator, extended by the mechanism of OID invention. It is important to note that the language supports object creation, but neither object deletion nor state update are available.

LLO. LLO (Logic Language for Objects) [LouY91] is a declarative query language for an object-oriented data model, also including methods. A method is defined as a clause, whose head is the method interface and whose body is the method implementation. A query is seen as a message and the unification algorithm takes care of message handling. Metavariables (i.e. variables which assume types as values) are introduced in the data model and are used for data abstraction, information hiding and inheritance. Inheritance hierarchies are obtained by instantiating metavariables. In LLO, each object has a state and a behavior. The structure of an object is described by its type. A predicate name is seen as an object identifier whose extension is the object value. The structural part of an object consists of an OID and a complex state. The object state may be directly accessed if the object is not encapsulated, otherwise interface methods must be defined. An LLO rule is a method. Methods are used to access object attributes and for deriving new information from object states. Both method overloading and method overriding are supported. Method inheritance is handled following class/type hierarchies. Behavior inheritance is thus supported.

DTL. DTL (Data Type Log) [BalR93] has been designed as a query language for a database specified in the TM language. TM [Bals93] is a high-level specification language for object-oriented database schemas, incorporating predicative sets as first-class objects and static constraints in the context of multiple inheritance and full static typechecking. In TM, objects have an object identifier used for sharing and referential integrity. Unlike F-logic and LIFE, a distinction is made between types and instantiations of types. DTL incorporates general set constructions, combining predicates and (multiple) inheritance. It offers the possibility of freely navigating through the terms by successive projections on attribute components. DTL is a typed extension of DATALOG supporting complex terms (with record and set constructors), attribute projections, and using strict typing rules for equality predicates. An ISA predicate, that allows a more liberal comparison of specialized expressions with generalized ones, is provided. Predicate inheritance is also considered in DTL. It specifies a simple but powerful way of combining multiple inheritance with predicates in logic programming.

Object-oriented extensions of DATALOG

This category of proposals includes systems which do not use logic only as a query language but in which logic is used also in the specification of the data model.

LOGRES. The LOGRES language [Caca89] integrates an object-oriented data model with a rule-based approach for expressing queries and updates. The data model supports object sharing and inheritance hierarchies, whereas the query language is a DATALOG extension with general type constructors. The static structure of the database is specified through type equations and integrity constraints. The LOGRES data model supports both classes and relations, whose schema is defined through type equations. The main features of the model are static typecheckability, separation of schema and instance levels, associations and complex type constructors, data functions. The LOGRES rule language is a typed extension of DATALOG characterized by a deterministic semantics, data functions, complex typed variables, object creation through OID generation, negation in rule bodies and rule heads. Negated literals in rule heads are interpreted as tuple deletions, thus LOGRES supports an explicit deletion mechanism.

LOGRES also provides a modularization functionality, in that it is possible to define modules encapsulating queries and updates. A module is a collection of type equations and rules. Moreover, update modules may be defined to provide state evolution. When specifying the application of a module to a database, the application mode must be specified, thus different rule semantics are supported. Modules partition rules into various components, with different semantics corresponding to different module application modes. The declarative semantics of rules is preserved, whereas the control strategy is inserted into modules. The most remarkable feature of LOGRES is its approach for introducing updates in a declarative language by keeping separated logic in rules and control in modules, whose application mode determines the effect on the database. Intensional updates are also supported. Explicit deletions in rule heads and OID invention are introduced in a deterministic framework with inflationary semantics. Note, however, that LOGRES provides a modularization unit, but this notion is orthogonal to the notion of object, which – also in this approach – is that of a term.

COMPLEX. COMPLEX [Grec90] is a system whose language (C-DATALOG) is an extension of DATALOG with constructs for handling complex objects, object identity and (multiple) inheritance. Such language supports completely declarative programming; query evaluation may be performed either top-down or bottom-up. In C-DATALOG, there are two kinds of entities: classes, whose instances are base facts stored in the database, and derived relations, which describe relationships among class instances. Class instances (objects) have identifiers and are organized into a hierarchy. By contrast, an instance of a derived relation, called object association, is a tuple of objects describing relationships among objects that are not stable but are derived by using deductive rules. The separation between schema and instance levels is maintained. With each class name, a set of ground facts, called the class definition, is associated representing the class proper instances. The definitions of classes must satisfy a number of constraints, namely OID uniqueness and referential and type integrity. The definition of a derived relation is a set of rules used for inferring the instances in its extension. Given a schema, the corresponding C-DATALOG program is a set of definitions, one for each entity of the schema.

Class atoms may appear in rule bodies and support a form of functional composition that allows navigating through objects using their connections. C-DATALOG allows complex objects and aggregation links to be modelled. However, no constructors of set and tuple for structured types of such objects are provided. In COMPLEX, an object is modelled as a tuple of a relation.

DATALOG^{Meth}. This is an extension of DATALOG with methods, inheritance, overloading, and late binding [Abit93]. The main issue addressed by such a proposal is inheritance with overriding. Classes are structured in a class hierarchy, and each class has an extension, the set of OIDs of the objects assigned to the class, and a behavior, which is the set of its methods. Methods and predicates are used to express properties of objects. Methods are functions, whereas predicates are not. Methods are specified at class level, i.e. the rules which define methods are attached to classes. By contrast, facts for each predicate are specified for each object through object attribute values. A resolution mechanism for DATALOG^{Meth} is specified, taking into account overriding. Such a resolution mechanism can be seen as an application of metaprogramming.

3.273 A comparison

Table 3.9 summarizes some of the differences between the different approaches to the integration of the object and deductive paradigms. It points out that most of the approaches do not consider state evolution of deductive objects. More precisely, the characterization of objects as logic theories does not account for any notion of state. McCabe suggests that the state change for an instance can be simulated by creating instances [McCa92]. Other proposals simulate state changes by using assert and retract, but this approach lacks any logical foundation. In [ChenW88] intensional variables are introduced to keep track of state changes without side effects. In other proposals, multi-headed clauses are used for similar purposes. However, the notion of updates to object states does not fit well in the object-oriented extensions of logic programming. In addition, the approaches developed in the database area, like COMPLEX [Grec90] and LLO [LouY91], do not support state evolution.

Another drawback of the approaches deriving from the logic programming area is that they do not consider a schema level, i.e. the notion of class. Moreover, even though inheritance is supported in some cases [Boss94], [Bugl92], the form of inheritance considered is among objects, i.e. a sort of delegation. Other approaches consider state evolution [Andr90], [Caca89] but objects have the granularity of terms. In addition, many of the approaches do not consider the behavioral components of objects, i.e. the methods.

3.28 Constraint databases

Constraint database systems represent one of the latest evolutions in the database field, originating partially from the deductive database system area. Constraint database systems are defined as the integration of (deductive) database technology with the constraint programming paradigm.

Such a paradigm is not recent. In artificial intelligence, constraints have been used for a long time and several issues related to constraint resolution have been addressed. The main idea of constraint languages is to state a set of relations, called *constraints*, among a set of objects in a given domain. It is a task of the *constraint satisfaction system* to determine a solution satisfying these relations. An example of a constraint is $F= 1.8 *C +32$, where C and F are the Celsius and Fahrenheit temperature. Constraints have been successfully integrated with logic programming. One reason for this success is that the operation of first-order term unification is a form of efficient constraint solver. Additional constraint-solving techniques increase the effectiveness of the approach. The constraint paradigm is fully declarative, in that it specifies computations by detailing how these computations are constrained.

Even though the constraint programming paradigm has been used in several fields, it has been used in databases only recently. Traditionally, constraints have been used in databases to express conditions on the semantic correctness of data. Such constraints are usually referred to as *semantic integrity constraints*. However, the use of constraints intended as in constraint programming languages is recent in the database area.

Constraint systems can be included in a database system at different levels. At data level, constraints can finitely represent infinite sets of data. For example, in the context of a constraint relational model, the constraint $X < 2 \wedge Y > 3$ represents the infinite set of tuples having the X attribute lower than 2 and the Y attribute greater than 3. Constraints are thus a powerful mechanism to model spatial and temporal concepts, where often infinite information should be represented. Spatial objects, for example, can be seen as composed by an infinite set of points, corresponding to the solutions of particular arithmetic constraints. For example the constraint $X^2 + Y^2 \leq 9$ represents a circle with center in the point (0,0) and with radius equal to 3. From a temporal perspective, constraints are very useful in representing situations that are infinitely repeated in time – for example, we may think of a train, leaving every day at the same time.

At query language level, constraints increase the expressive power of query languages by allowing arithmetic computations. This integration raises several issues. Constraint query languages should preserve all the nice properties typical of query languages, such as the relational ones. For example, they should be closed and bottom-up evaluable. Moreover, advanced features, such as aggregate functions and indefinite values, should be supported. Another interesting topic is related to the definition of update languages for modifying constraint databases. Related to this topic, there is the need to define integrity constraints, extending functional and multivalued dependencies to constraint databases.

Table 3.9 Comparison between different approaches to the integration of deductive and object-orientation paradigms

Language	Granularity	Updates	Methods	Schema	Inheritance	Message passing	OID invention
Open Logic Programs [Boss94]	theory	no	yes [(a)]	no	no	no	no [(b)]
Differential L.P. [Boss93]	theory	no	yes [(a)]	no	yes	no	no [(b)]
CxLP [Mont90]	theory	no	yes [(a)]	no	no [(c)]	no [(c)]	no
SelfLog [Bugl92]	theory	no	yes [(a)]	no	yes	yes	no
DATALOG^{Meth} [Abit93]	Theory [(g)]	no	yes [(a)]	yes	yes	yes	no
LOGIN-LIFE [AitK86]	term	no	no	yes [(d)]	yes	no	no
F-Logic [Kife89]	term	no	yes	yes [(d)]	yes	no	no
COL [Abit90]	term	no	no	yes	no	no	no [(b)]
IQL [Abit89]	term	yes [(e)]	no	yes	yes	no	yes
COMPLEX [Grec90]	term	no	no	yes	yes	no	no
LOGRES [Caca89]	term	yes	no	yes	yes	no	yes
LLO [LouY91]	term	no	yes	yes	yes	no	no
DTL [BalR93]	term	no	no [(f)]	yes	yes	no	no

(a) For those approaches that do not differentiate between the structural and behavioural components of objects, this item does not apply.
(b) The approach does not support the notion of OID.
(c) Inheritance and message passing can, however, be easily expressed in contextual logic programming through extension goals.
(d) A schema level is present, but the language does not distinguish between types and instantiations of types, collapsing the subtype and instance-of hierarchies in a single relationship. In approaches that do not differentiate between the structural and behavioural components of objects, this item does not apply.
(e) Only creation of objects is supported, whereas object deletion and state evolution are not considered.
(f) The TM data model considers methods, but they are not declaratively expressed by the DTL query language.
(g) In DATALOG^{Meth} an object is identified by an identifier and associated with a class. Object behaviour is associated with classes, whereas the state is represented as a set of predicates relating properties of object identifiers.

As pointed out by Kanellakis, Kuper and Revesz [Kane90], the integration of constraints in traditional database systems must not compromise the efficiency of the system. This means that optimization techniques developed for traditional database systems should be extended to deal with constraints. To this purpose, specific indexing techniques should be developed to retrieve constraint tuples; moreover, logical and cost-based optimization techniques should be extended to benefit from the use of constraints to further reduce the query execution costs.

Even if several approaches have been proposed in order to integrate constraint programming and database systems, the research in this field is still in the early stages. However, it is recognized that several applications, such as spatial and temporal ones, can benefit from constraint database systems.

Here, we discuss some of the above aspects by identifying several database contexts in which the constraint programming paradigm can be used. First, we survey the use of constraints at the data modelling level, introducing the so-called *constraint data models*. Then, we analyze the impact of constraints on query languages. We cast our discussion in the framework of relational and deductive databases because most proposals for constraint data models have been proposed for these data models. A brief discussion concerning the integration of the constraint programming paradigm in the object-oriented data model is, however, included at the end of this section. We conclude this section by discussing some constraint database prototypes.

3.281 Preliminaries

The constraint languages we consider here are obtained by adding a logical theory either to relational languages or to DATALOG. In the latter case, they can be modelled by using the *CLP(X)* scheme of constraint logic programming [HeinN87]. The most important aspect of constraint logic programming is that it establishes a clean interaction between the underlying logic programming framework and the way constraints are used. Each instance of the schema is a programming language, obtained by specifying a computation structure *X*, i.e. the domain of discourse, the functions and relations on this domain characterize the language. A key aspect of the *CLP(X)* scheme is that all its instance languages are soundly based on a single formal semantic framework.

A *CLP(X)* rule has the form $H \leftarrow c_1,....,c_n, B_1,....,B_m$ where $c_1,....,c_n$ are constraints on domain X , and $B_1,....,B_m$ are atoms, in the usual sense. For example, the rule

```
p(X) ← X < 2, Y > 5, h(X), f(Y)
```

is a CLP rule, where $X < 2$, $Y > 5$ are constraints, and h(X), f(Y) are atoms.

Semantically, the domain is a structure, in the usual first-order logic meaning. A constraint c is solvable in a structure R if there exists a mapping θ from the set of variables to the structure domain R such that $c\theta$ is true. In this case, θ is a R-solution for c.

The logical programming computational model can be extended to the CLP case by using the notion of solvability and introducing the notion of *constrained* atoms. The operational and fixpoint semantics for logic programs are modified by allowing a derivation step only if the new constructed constraints are satisfiable. The *constraint solver* has the task of determining constraint satisfaction and monotonically adding new constraints to the existing ones during the computation. The following is an example of a CLP program:

```
h(X) ← X ≤ 7, f(X)
f(X) ← X ≥ 4, k(X).
```

Assume that k(3) and k(5) hold. Consider the goal h(X). Under a top-down evaluation, the goal is rewritten into $X \leq 7$, f(X). Then, by expanding f(X), it is rewritten into $X \leq 7$, $X \geq 4$, k(X). The only solution to the query h(X) is X=5.

3.282 *Constraints and data representation*

The introduction of constraints to model data is based on the consideration that a relational tuple is a particular kind of constraint [Kane90]. For example, the relational tuple (3,4) for a relation R with attributes X and Y can be interpreted as the constraint $X=3 \wedge Y=4$. Thus, constraints can be interpreted as *generalized tuples*. Similarly, ($X < 2$, $Y > 5$) is another generalized tuple for the relation R. Under this meaning, constraints support a finite representation of infinite tuples. The constraint $X < 2 \wedge Y > 5$ corresponds to the infinite set of relational tuples with two attributes, X and Y, having X lower than 2 and Y greater than 5. A set of generalized tuples defines a *generalized relation*, and a set of generalized relations defines a *generalized database*.

In general, a constraint identifies a formula of a decidable logical theory. Several classes of constraints have been proposed. For example:

- *Real polynomial inequality constraints*: all the formulas (and their negation) of the form $p(X_1,\ldots,X_n)\ \theta\ 0$, where p is a polynomial with real coefficients in variables $X_1,\ldots,X_n$ and $\theta \in \{\leq, \geq, =, <, >, \neq\}$. The domain D is the set of real numbers and function symbols +, *, predicate symbols θ and constants are interpreted in the standard way over D.
- *Dense linear order inequality constraints*: all the formulas (and their negation) of the form XθY and Xθc, where X, Y are variables, c is a constant, and $\theta \in \{\leq, \geq, =, <, >, \neq\}$. We assume D to be a countably infinite set (e.g. the set of rational numbers) with a binary relation that is a dense linear order. Constants and predicate symbols are interpreted in the standard way over D.
- *Equality constraints over an infinite domain*: all the formulas (and their negation) of the form XθY and Xθc, where X, Y are variables, c is a constant, and $\theta \in \{=, \neq\}$. We assume D to be a countably infinite set (e.g. the set of integer numbers) but without ordering relation. Constants and predicate symbols are interpreted in the standard way over D.

When polynomials are linear, the corresponding class of constraints is of particular interest. A large range of applications use linear polynomials. Moreover, linear polynomials have been investigated in various fields (linear programming and computational geometry) and therefore several techniques have been developed to handle them [LassJ90].

The following definition formalizes some of the above concepts: Let ϕ be a class of constraints (a decidable logical theory).

- A generalized k-tuple over variables $x_1,\ldots,x_k$ in the logical theory ϕ is a finite conjunction $\varphi_1\wedge\ldots\wedge\varphi_N$, where each φ_i, $1\leq i\leq N$, is a contraint in ϕ. The variables in each φ_i are all free and among $x_1,\ldots,x_k$.
- A generalized relation of arity k in is a finite set $r = \{\psi_1,\ldots,\psi_M\}$, where each ψ_i, $1\leq i\leq M$, is a generalised k-tuple over the same variables $x_1,\ldots,x_k$ and in ϕ.
- The formula corresponding to a generalized relation $r = \{\psi_1,\ldots,\psi_M\}$ is the disjunction $\psi_1 \vee\ldots\vee \psi_M$.
- A generalized database is a finite set of generalized relations.

The following example illustrates some of the concepts introduced by the previous definition. Consider a spatial database consisting of a set of rectangles in the plane. In the relational model such a database can be represented by means of a relation R, containing a tuple of the form (n,a,b,c,d) for each rectangle. In such a tuple, n is the name of the rectangle with corners (a,b), (a,d), (c,b), and (c,d). In the generalized relational model, rectangles can be represented by means of generalized tuples of the form $(Z=n) \wedge (a \leq X \leq c) \wedge (b \leq Y\leq d)$. The latter representation is more suited to a larger class of operations. The advantages in using a constraint representation will be better illustrated in the following section, where we discuss constraint query languages. Figure 3.18 shows the rectangles corresponding to the generalized tuples contained in relation r_1 (white) and relation r_2 (shadow). r_1 contains the following generalized tuples:

$r_{1,1}$: $1 \leq X \leq 4 \wedge 1 \leq Y \leq 2$
$r_{1,2}$: $2 \leq X \leq 7 \wedge 2 \leq Y \leq 3$
$r_{1,3}$: $3 \leq X \leq 6 \wedge -1 \leq Y \leq 1.5$.

r_2 contains the following generalized tuples:

$r_{2,1}$: $-3 \leq X \leq -1 \wedge 1 \leq Y \leq 3$
$r_{2,2}$: $5 \leq X \leq 6 \wedge -3 \leq Y \leq 0$.

As we can see from the previous example, constraints model spatial data very well. Indeed, a constraint finitely represents an (infinite) set of points, representing its solutions. However, the previous generalized relational model supports only the representation of *definite* data. Therefore, there is no uncertainty in the values contained in generalized relations. Thus, a constraint represents the set of *all* its solutions. An extension of this model to deal with indefinite data is proposed by Koubarakis [Koub94]. Such an extension is based on the consideration that a constraint can be seen as a set of *possible* values for a certain variable used in the tuple. For example, the constraint $X < 2 \wedge Y > 5$, associated with a relational tuple t with attribute X and Y, means that values for X and Y in t should belong to the set of solutions for this constraint. In this case, the constraint is interpreted in an existential way and, for example, 1 and 6 are some safe values for variables X and Y.

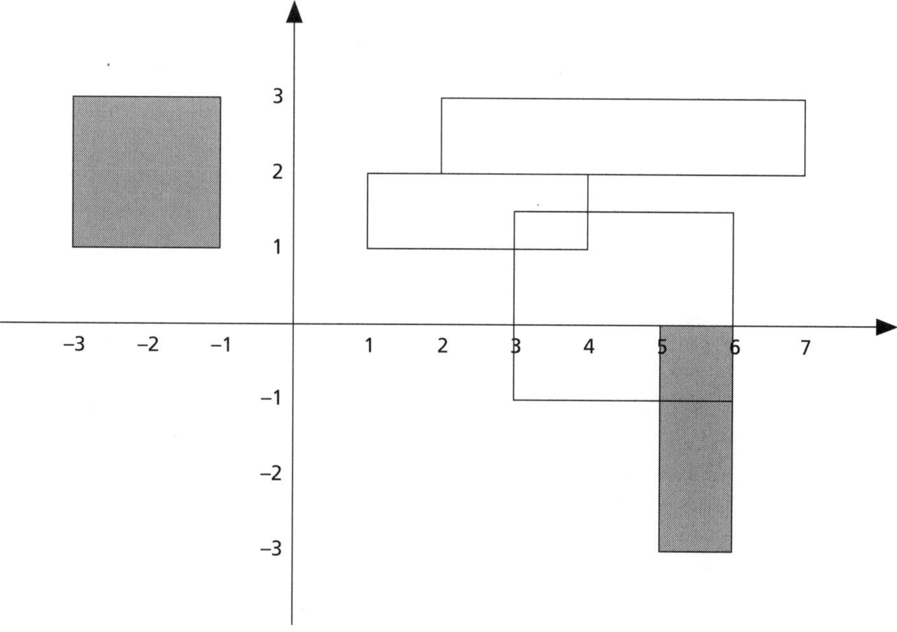

Figure 3.18 Relations r_1 (white) and r_2 (shadow)

Another important aspect of the relational model that has been inherited by constraint data models is the existence of a formal logical basis. Grumbach and Su [Grum94] have shown that constraint databases have a formal representation in terms of *finitely representable models.* As for finite model theory, it can be proved that most of the well-known properties holding in model theory (compactness, completeness, *see* [ChanC73]) do not hold for finitely representable models.

From a representation point of view, constraints are usually modelled by using *canonical forms.* A canonical form is a standard form for constraints which is usually computed by simplification and removal of redundancy from the constraints. In most cases, canonical forms are expensive to compute, also for a simple theory, as the linear polynomial constraint theory [BrodA93]. For example, removing redundant generalized tuples from a generalized relation is a co-NP complete problem [Sriv97]. In general, only partial simplifications are performed. An interesting canonical form for linear polynomial constraints, based on tableaux, has been proposed by Kanellakis and Goldin [Kane94].

3.283 Constraints and queries

From the language point of view, it is important to develop declarative, powerful and, at the same time, efficient and bottom-up evaluable constraint database languages. One of the first approaches in this direction has been proposed by Hansen *et al* [HansM89]. In their proposal, constraints modelling infinite relations are used to increase the expressive power of relational languages. However, the first general principle underlying the design of constraint database languages has been developed by Kanellakis, Kuper and Revesz [Kane90]. In their paper, the syntax of a constraint query language is defined as the union of an existing query language and a decidable logical theory. For example: relational calculus + the theory of real polynomial constraints, DATALOG + Boolean equations. The following example illustrates a constraint language query.

Let ϕ be the class of dense linear constraints and let R be a predicate symbol of arity 2. Then, the following is a query:

$$q(x_1,x_2) = R(x_1,x_2) \wedge \exists y(R(x_1,y) \wedge (x_1 \leq y) \wedge (x_2 \leq y)).$$

In order to formally define the meaning of the above query, we need interpretations for the predicate symbols and for the symbols in the constraints. The meaning of predicate symbols depends on the input of generalized relations, whereas the meaning of constraint symbols depends on the particular constraint theory. Thus, the semantics of the language is based on the semantics of the chosen decidable logical theory, by interpreting database atoms as shorthand for formulas of the theory.

For example, consider query $q(x_1,x_2)$, and suppose predicate R is shorthand for a generalised relation r with two attributes, X and Y, given as input to the query. Suppose that r contains the generalized tuples $X \geq 2 \wedge Y \leq 1$, and $X = 3 \wedge Y \geq 4$, the query on relation r can be represented as $a\{(a_1,a_2) \mid q[R/r]$ is true$\}$ where $q[R/r]$ means that we replace $R(x_1,x_2)$ in q with the constraint $(X \geq 2 \wedge Y \leq 1) \vee (X = 3 \wedge Y \geq 4)$.

An important advantage of using constraint query languages is that they support more compact and clear query representation, as illustrated by the following example. Consider the query retrieving all the pairs of intersecting rectangles from a relation r containing a set of given rectangles. Assume that in such relation, each rectangle is represented by a tuple containing the rectangle identifier and the coordinates of the topmost left corner and of the lowermost right corner. In relational calculus, the query is formulated as follows (in the query, R is a predicate of arity 5 denoting relation r):

$$\begin{aligned}\{(n_1,n_2) \mid n_1 \neq n_2 \wedge (\exists\ & a_1,a_2,b_1,b_2,c_1,c_2,d_1,d_2)\\ & (R(n_1,a_1,b_1,c_1,d_1) \wedge (R(n_2,a_2,b_2,c_2,d_2)\\ & \wedge(\exists\ x,y\ E\{a1,a2,b1,b2,c1,c2,d1,d2\})\\ & (a_1 \leq x \leq c_1 \wedge b_1 \leq y \leq d_1 \wedge a_2 \leq x \leq c_2 \wedge b_2 \leq y \leq d_2))\}\end{aligned}$$

By contrast, in a constraint relational database, rectangles can be simply represented by a generalized relation over three variables and the above query can be modelled more simply as follows:

$$\{(n_1,n_2) \mid n_1 \neq n_2 \wedge (\exists\ x,y)\ (R(n_1,x,y) \wedge R(n_2,x,y))\}.$$

The above example shows how constraint query languages support a more compact and clear query representation.

An important requirement for constraint database languages is, however, that the results of queries have closed form. Closed form means that the output of a query applied to any input generalized relation on theory Φ is a generalized relation on Φ. It is not always possible to obtain closed query languages, as the following example shows. Consider the theory of real polynomial equalities. These are constraints of the form $p(x_1,...,x_k)\ \theta\ 0$, where $\theta \in \{=, \neq\}$. Let R(x,y) be a binary predicate symbol for the input generalized relation $\{y = x^2\}$. The result of ∃x.R(x,y) is the set $\{y \mid y \geq 0\}$, which cannot be represented by polynomial equality constraints.

Constraint query languages can, however, be used in practice only if the *data complexity* of the obtained queries is low. A query Q has data complexity in the complexity class C if there exists a Turing machine that, given an input generalized relation d, produces a generalized relation representing the output Q(d) and uses time in class C, assuming a standard encoding of generalized relations. The constraint query language framework is interesting because many combinations of database query languages and decidable theories have PTIME data complexity [Afra94]. The complexity of some constraint query languages is reported in Table 3.10. DATALOG¬ corresponds to DATALOG with inflationary negation [Kola88]. It is important to note that the integration of DATALOG¬ with real polynomial constraints is not closed. Several approaches have therefore been proposed, defining subsets of DATALOG¬ for which closure can be guaranteed. We refer the reader to [Kupe00] for more on this topic.

Table 3.10 Complexity of some constraint query languages

Language	Polynomial	Dense order	Equality
Relational Calculus	NC	LOGSPACE	LOGSPACE
DATALOG¬	Not closed	PTIME	PTIME

In order to be practically usable, constraint query languages should model as much as possible relational features. Kanellakis and Goldin proposed a relational algebra for the theory of linear polynomial constraints, equivalent to the calculus proposed by Kanellakis, Kuper and Revesz, but more suitable for optimization [Kane94].

Another interesting issue is related to the integration of aggregate functions inside constraint query languages [ChomJ95]. In such a context, the useful functions represent operations on the spatial objects represented by constraints, such as length, area, and volume. The negative result is that those functions may make the language not closed. In particular, the closure property does not hold for any of the interesting classes of constraints, i.e. dense order, linear or polynomial. Aggregate functions have also been investigated by Ross, Srivastava, Stuckey and Sudarshan [Ross94]. They propose a class of constraints defined by aggregate functions, such as $\min(X) \leq 5$, and prove that checking for solvability of a conjunction of aggregate constraints is in general undecidable. Then, they develop an algorithm to test satisfiability in some particular cases.

Finally, in order to query indefinite data, Koubarakis has proposed an extension of the relational calculus and algebra to deal with uncertainty [Koub94]. The two languages are based on modal logic and are proved to be equivalent.

Other relevant issues that to date have not been much investigated include query optimization and indexing techniques. Few preliminary results for query optimization have been developed by Brodsky, Jaffar and Maher [BrodA93], whereas an overview of the few indexing techniques proposed for constraint databases can be found in [Bert97].

3.284 *Applications*

In the previous sections we have discussed the integration of constraint technology and database technology. Due to their ability to finitely represent infinite information, constraints have been used to support spatial and temporal applications. Moreover, they represent an interesting means to extend the object-oriented model for dealing with spatial/temporal objects. In the following, we briefly survey the use of constraints in such contexts.

Temporal databases

The management of temporal information has been an important topic in database research. Most models extend the well-known relational model to include temporal features and define extensions to relational query languages to handle the temporal dimension of data. Unfortunately, most of these models do not take into account the infinite nature of time. This means that there is an *a priori* limit to the temporal extension of the predicates represented by the relations in the database. Even if those limits are known, the representation can involve a large number of tuples.

Due to their ability to finitely model infinite sets of points, generalized databases have been successfully used to represent infinite temporal information, *see* [Baud91], [Kaba90]. The used constraints are known as linear repeating points. They correspond to sets of the form {x(n)}, where each x(n) is an expression of the form c+kn. Constants c and k are integer numbers and the variable n takes values from the set of all integer numbers. Thus, each linear repeating point represents an infinite sequence of time points. A generalized tuple, therefore, consists of a set of linear repeating points and a set of non-temporal data values. Additional constraints on temporal attributes can be added to each tuple. An extension of this model to deal with repetition schedules (calendars) has been proposed by Niezette and Stevenne [Niez92].

Spatial databases

Spatial applications require relational query features, arithmetic calculations, and extensibility to define new spatial data. Both the relational and the object-oriented data models have failed to model spatial data. There are several reasons for such inadequacy. Relational models for spatial data have often been developed as *ad hoc* models and thus are not logically extensible. Moreover, relational and spatial data are often implemented by separated subsystems, leading to non-homogeneous systems. The extension of indexing techniques to those integrated systems has to bridge the gap between a declarative access to large volumes of spatial data (through a relational language) and the execution of computational geometry tasks. Even though object-oriented databases provide a rich, flexible and extensible type system, they do not directly support the geometry of point sets as part of their data models. Queries containing spatial operations are therefore difficult to optimize [Gaed95].

These drawbacks are overcome by contraints database systems. Such systems support a homogeneous description of spatial data together with simple relational data, through the use of multiple constraint theories. The geometry of point sets is implicit in the concept of constraint. Constraints describe point sets such that all their points are in the database. These point sets are accurate representations of spatial objects. Even if not all-useful spatial operations can be directly represented in the chosen logical theory, and therefore external functions are required, the constraint theory often supports a direct representation of several spatial operations. Thus, such operations are directly optimized in the query optimization process. Kanellakis [Kane95] claims that by generalizing relational formalisms to contraint formalisms it is in principle possible to generalize all key features of the relational data model to spatial data models. A first step in this direction is represented by the constraint relational algebra proposed for spatial databases by Paredaens *et al* [Pare94].

Object-oriented databases

The model proposed by Kanellakis, Kuper and Revesz is based on the relational data model. Thus it inherits all its limitations. For example, it cannot directly model complex objects, or support relevant modelling abstractions such as aggregation, specialization and generalization. The object-oriented data model overcomes these limitations with respect to new emerging applications. An interesting problem is how the constraint data model can be merged with an object-oriented data model. Several applications could benefit from a constraint object-oriented data model, such as:

- *Multidimensional space design.* In this context, objects are characterized by attributes without extension, such as colour and name, and attributes representing the spatial extension of objects. Constraints can be used to represent extensions. Several relationships exist among objects and the database system should be able to answer queries concerning the relative position of an object with respect to the other objects. In modelling problems of this kind, the object-oriented model supports a direct representation of objects and subobjects, whereas constraints support a direct representation of extensions, as well as the possibility of easily expressing queries about object positions.
- *Resource allocation.* This is a typical operations research problem. In this case, the use of the constraint paradigm allows the user to obtain infinite answers to queries, finitely represented as constraints.

- *Data fusion and sensor control.* This is a problem arising in several applications, such as environmental analysis, command and control, and military surveillance. In such applications, sensors are periodically assigned to areas of responsibility. Sensor outputs are collected, correlated, fused and analyzed to form a representation of the environment. The fused data is then used to discover patterns of behavior, assessing threats, taking appropriate actions. The use of a combined object-oriented/constraint technology supports not only a convenient representation of spatial objects but also object monitoring in both space and time.

The use of constraints thus supports the modelling of complex objects, maintaining both spatial and temporal information about these objects. Some preliminary approaches have been proposed in order to extend object-oriented models and languages with constraints. In particular, Srivastava, Ramakrishnan and Revesz add constraints to an object-oriented data model in order to support partially known attributes [Sriv94]. They also propose several semantics reflecting different understandings of incomplete information. Brodsky and Kornatzky extend the object-oriented data model by introducing constraints as first-class objects [BrodA95]. Constraints are thus seen as objects, whose identifiers are their canonical forms. Thus, equivalent constraints with different normal forms are considered different. Constraint objects are organized in classes. The class *CST*(*k*) identifies all constraints with *k* variables. Methods are in this case represented by the usual operations on constraints, such as union and intersection. Inheritance relations are defined among classes. In particular, *CST*(*k+1*) is a subclass of *CST*(*k*).

3.285 Prototypes

Three main prototypal constraint database systems have been developed. CCUBE [BrodA99] is a constraint object-oriented database system. It has been implemented on top of a commercial object-oriented database system and therefore supports standard database features. *LyriC* is the available query language. The database supports extensible constraint families, aggregation, optimization and indexing.

Another implementation effort is the DISCO system [Byon95]. DISCO (DATALOG with Integer and Set Order COnstraints) has good expressive power due to the considered class of set constraints and the underlying query language. However, its data complexity is exponential in the size of the database and it does not support relevant database features such as persistent storage.

Finally, DEDALE [Grum98] is a recently developed prototype of recent definition, introducing linear constraints inside the generalised relational calculus. As with CCUBE, DEDALE has been implemented on the top of an object-oriented database system. One of the main goals in developing such a system was the comparison of two different database technologies: constraint databases and spatial databases. For this reason, several optimization aspects have also been addressed in its development.

3.29 Conclusions

Deductive database technology represents an important step towards the development of highly declarative database programming languages. An important difference that sets apart a deductive database system with respect to a relational one is that the former stores not only data but also rules that allow additional information to be derived from the data stored into the database. Moreover, a deductive database system offers a uniform, declarative paradigm, based on formal logic, for defining data, rules, integrity constraints, and more powerful languages for expressing queries and updates.

Deductive capabilities have also been integrated in other database paradigms. Besides the integration of deductive and object-oriented databases that we have looked at in this chapter, we recall the integration of deductive and active databases. The main aim in this context is to provide a uniform logical formalism for representing both deductive and active rules. We refer the reader to [Frey98] for additional information.

Even if a lot of work has been done from a theoretical point of view and several deductive database prototypes have been defined differently from object-oriented and active database technology, deductive databases have not had a great impact on the market. However, they have been successfully used in scientific and (as a special case) medical information systems (*see* Chapter 4).

Constraint databases represent one of the latest evolutions in the database field, originating partially from deductive databases. Their ability to finitely represent infinite sets of tuples makes them quite useful in modelling temporal and spatial applications. They are also useful for representing behavioural patterns, similar to those generated from data mining and data warehousing tasks, and for modelling interoperability and data integration. These topics will be described in Chapter 4.

Coupling knowledge-based systems (KBSs) with 'standard' database management systems (DBMSs)

3.31 Introduction

In this section, we will examine the solutions proposed for marrying KBS and DBMS technologies, including in KBSs both KESEs and ES shells. We will consider only the solutions where it is possible – even when considering examples of a 'very tight coupling' approach – to isolate in the global system two co-operating but separated subsystems, i) a KBS, and ii) a general-purpose DBMS.

We can note here that these types of intelligent database systems had their moment of glory in the mid-1980s when the excitement about expert systems was at its height. Recently, interest in this topic seems to have abated somewhat, at least as a theme of research. With respect to its specific artificial intelligence aspects, more glamorous topics are now in the limelight, such as the advanced solutions examined in the next section or some of the topics expounded in Chapter 4. With respect to its database aspects, we can note that the prevalent approach to add 'intelligence' to a DBMS is now that of building condition-action rules directly inside the DBMS – *see* Section 2.3 and [Bara94]. In this last paper, the authors introduce the term of 'expert database systems' that they define as conventional DB systems directly extended with a facility for creating and automatically executing condition-action rules. However, a book about IDBSs cannot completely elude the topic of coupling KBSs and DBMSs, for at least two reasons:

- historically, the IDBS domain has its origins in research about this theme (and about the deductive database systems examined in the previous section);
- the architectural solutions to the coupling problem we will examine in this section are of interest, in general, for the *entire* IDBS domain – and not only for the deductive solutions.

Normally (although it is not mandatory, *see* next section), in the KBS/DBMS association the KBS will act as a front end to be used as a repository for the domain-specific knowledge as well as for the implementation of the reasoning mechanisms required by the user's tasks. The DBMS is used as a back end that stores the facts required for front-end reasoning – *see also* the heterogeneous approach to the construction of deductive database systems, Figure 3.16. In this section, we assume that the DBMS is a 'standard' one – for different presuppositions *see* Section 3.4: all the solutions examined here present the advantage of including an essential component consisting in an already available online database. In this way, there is no obligation to restructure and recode the database information, or to execute any unreasonable amount of change in existing applications. This advantage has sometimes been defined as the '80-20' rule [SohC92]: making use of this type of approach to the construction of IDBSs it could be possible, at least in principle, to achieve 80 per cent of the benefits of integration at only 20 per cent of the costs. Therefore, it is not surprising that practically all the existing commercial KBSs provide some – albeit often rudimentary – facilities to implement the coupling with an existing DBMS (*see also* Section 3.34).

An important point to emphasize is that, unlike what we have seen in deductive databases, no theoretical framework exists for the type of expert database systems we want to examine here. The description of these systems will be tackled here from a strict 'engineering' point of view: it will come down, practically, to the description of five general architectures that have been proposed to realize the KBS/DBMS link, and to the description of a series of concrete examples implementing these architectures.

Moreover, it is not only a unified theory of this IDBS sub-domain that seems to be lacking, but the principle itself of coupling a KBS and a DBMS while preserving their independence has been severely criticized in the past from a 'theoretical' point of view – *see* [Tsur88], [Zarr90], [Khos91]. In particular:

- Several authors say that there is a fundamental mismatch between the two types of subsystems; this mismatch takes, at least, three different forms.
  - The first concerns the knowledge representation aspects ('semantic mismatch'). 'Pure' relational algebra and 'flat' relations characteristic of 'standard', relational DBMSs are not really compatible with the frames and semantic networks typical of KESEs, to say nothing of the *ad hoc* ways of structuring the Fact Database (FDB) that are current in many ES shells. In this last case, the FDB is often realized according only to the constraints imposed by the characteristics of a particular inference engine and by the properties of the problem at hand. Severe performance problems arise from this mismatch, often requiring, *inter alia*, the use of redundant data descriptions to make data exchange possible.
  - The second type of mismatch concerns the operational aspects of the global system ('impedance mismatch'). The inferential knowledge of an AI system – i.e. the knowledge taking charge of the operational aspects of this system – is basically static, given that it is represented mainly by the declarative knowledge stored in the rule base (RLB). On the contrary, the operational component of a database system is dynamic, and represented by the knowledge embedded, in a procedural way, inside an application program: in complex applications, the data is retrieved from a DBMS using a DB query language such as SQL, and then manipulated through routines written in a conventional programming language such as C or PL/1. Co-operation between the two systems will therefore imply, at least in principle, continuously translating static inference processes into dynamic queries, and vice versa. Another aspect of this mismatch concerns optimization. While optimization of the KBS programs is left largely to the programmer, optimization of the relational DB is left to the system: an overall global optimization of computations is, at least in principle, precluded.

  - The third type of mismatch concerns the granularity of the data to be handled ('granularity mismatch'). An AI reasoning mechanism makes use of data to instantiate its variables; therefore, it requires some data during each inference, and under an atomic form (individual tuples of data values). On the contrary, a relational DBMS answers a query by returning results as sets of tuples. Accordingly, when the KBS breaks down a query into a sequence of queries on tuples, each of them incurs a heavy DBMS performance overhead: we lose, therefore, the benefits of the set-oriented optimization which is characteristic of DBMSs. Moreover, unlike what happens with traditional algorithmic programming, it is impossible to completely anticipate the data access needs of a KBS given that, in these systems, control knowledge is separated from the (domain-specific) problem-solving knowledge, resulting in a reasoning process which is highly problem-dependent.

- A second class of criticisms, of a more fundamental nature, concerns the loss of information linked to the limited modelling capabilities of the relational paradigm used to implement the DBMS, i.e. the use of formatted alphanumeric data in the form of files of records to represent an original information which is often extremely rich and structured. Note, however, that the coupled systems examined in this section share this criticism with several other 'intelligent' solutions examined in this book, for example, deductive databases and rule-based systems. Many authors advocate, therefore, the use of advanced 'semantic' models to describe information in the fact database and, possibly, a uniform, high-level type of representation in both the KBS and the DBMS subsystems (*see also* some of the 'advanced solutions' expounded in Section 3.4).

As noted above, the development of commercial solutions in this style seems to have been unaffected by the aforementioned criticisms: these systems reply, indubitably, to a real need of a majority of ES users. However, they cannot supply an ultimate answer to the general problem of constructing intelligent DBMSs; it is likely that this technology will be confined, in the future, to provide the support for some standard functions that will be present in the everyday ES and KESE tools.

3.32 Architectural solutions

A first approach to the classification of the architectural solutions which have been suggested for coupling KBSs with existing DBMSs has been, traditionally, to separate them into 'loose coupling' and 'tight coupling' solutions (*see* [Jark84a]).

Loose coupling refers to the presence of a communication channel between the two subsystems that allows the extraction of a 'snapshot' of the required data from the existing DB, and the subsequent storage of this snapshot in the internal database of the KBS. Data extraction occurs *statically*, before the KBS's inference engine can be activated, which means that DB actions are performed independently of the actual rule execution. The main drawback of this solution obviously concerns its impracticability whenever the choice of the snapshot to load is a function of the decisions taken by the KBS, and the snapshot is not known until the inference procedures are already well under way – during the same session, many different portions of external DBs may be required at different times. Moreover, if the DBs are frequently updated, the snapshots can rapidly become obsolete.

In tight coupling, the communication channel between the two subsystems must be implemented in such a way that the external DB appears to the KBS as an extension of its own database – data extraction occurs *dynamically*. Coupling actions are performed within the context of the execution of each rule: whenever the inference system needs some data, the interface between the two components is activated. Obviously, the generality of this second approach is particularly high; however, the technical problems are also particularly difficult, given that the KBS must know *when* and *how* to consult the DBMS, and must be able to understand the answers. Moreover, the impedance and granularity mismatch evoked above come into play here.

We can note that the technical problems proper to the two approaches, and the solutions adopted, have some evident analogies with those concerning the 'compiled' and 'interpreted' approaches in a deductive database framework. The main difference concerns the fact that, here, the inference operations are those typical of the KESEs' or ESs' ordinary 'inference engines', instead of the 'logic deductions' in a Prolog or DATALOG style.

This approach to classification is, of course, perfectly correct, and we will refer constantly to it in the following; however, it does not take into account all the 'topological' differences among the different architectures and, moreover, it applies equally to many other sorts of 'intelligent' systems examined in this book, for example, deductive databases and rule-based systems. Therefore, several proposals concerning the classification of the functionalities required for coupling KBSs with existing DBMSs – *see* [AlZo87], [Rupa91], [SohC92], etc. – suggest the five 'prototypical' architectures illustrated in Figure 3.18.

Before discussing the five architectures, we would like to specify exactly which type of systems will be examined here. They concern only 'well-structured' solutions that imply a real interaction between the two components, i.e. we do not consider all the approaches to integration consisting simply of storing, for example, AI objects in DB systems according to a 'quasi off-line' modality. We can note that simple solutions in this style have normally been implemented according to two principles (*see* [BrodM88]):

- In a first solution, the AI objects are systematically translated into and out of DB objects, which are generally fixed-length record structures formed from fields based on a small set of data types (for example, character string, integer, and real). This obviously generates heavy overheads.
- An alternative solution is that of storing AI objects in their native format directly in DBs, as long characters or bit strings for example. This technique brings about new sorts of difficulties given that, even if relatively efficient methods for database access can be developed, most of the usual DBMS functionalities (query optimization, search for subobjects, integrity constraints, security, views, etc.) are not available.

Coming back to the five architectures, (a) of Figure 3.19 corresponds to what we may call the 'full bridge' solution: coupling KBSs with existing DBMSs is realized here by explicitly building up a third component, an independent subsystem acting as a communication channel between the first two. No system dominates, at least in principle: in all the systems examined in Section 3.33, the KBS component is clearly the predominant one. However, this architecture allows the DBMS to operate as a totally separate system, with its own set of DB users. The appeal of this general solution is balanced by the difficulty of implementing efficient systems: all the 'mismatch' drawbacks described in the previous section intervene fully here. Solution (a) entails at least two variants, depending on whether the control of the interactions between the two subsystems is located on the central bridge or distributed, with the processing, between the two original components, *see* [AlZo87] and Section 3.332.

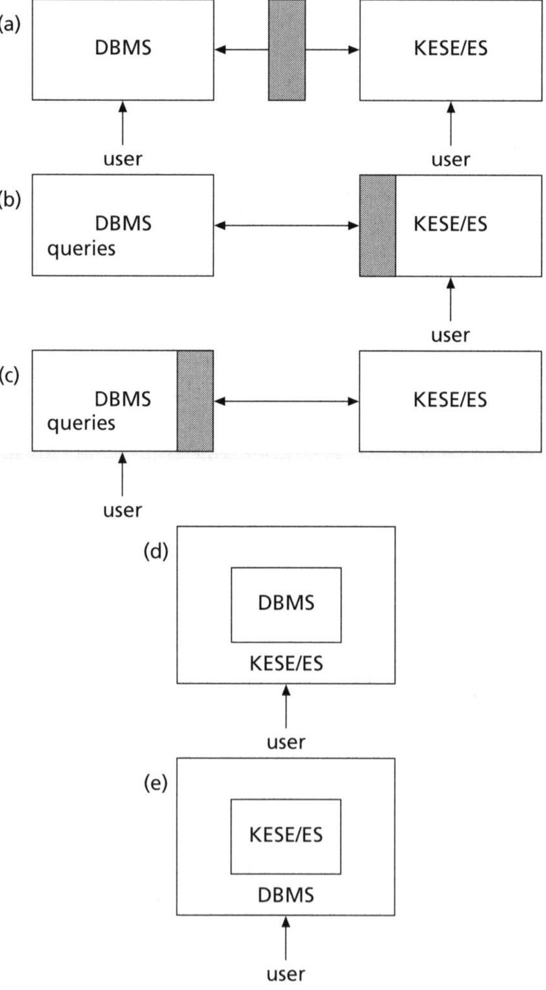

Figure 3.19 Architectural solutions for KBS/DBMS integration

A simple solution that can be associated with this category, and which was used intensively in the early times of the KBS/DBMS integration era, consists of using a flat file as the intermediary medium. To transfer information from the KBS to the database, the former writes the information into the file, possibly using determiners to mark certain syntactic forms. The flat file is transferred to the DBMS, which reads it and stores it as rows. The DBMS transfers information to the KBS with the converse procedure. Of course, this straightforward approach – which can be considered as the prototype of any 'loose coupling' approach – is suitable only for knowledge-based applications that reason over a well-specified data set, and in which the interaction between the DBMS and the KBS is kept to a minimum. The main limitation concerning this particular interpretation of the approach of Figure 3.19(a) is, of course, the creation of systems that do not scale up well.

The architectural solution of (b) in Figure 3.19 consists of extending a KBS with components proper to a DBMS. A first approach to be considered could be that of extending the AI language proper to the KBS with database functionalities. Concretely, this technique has been used only for KBSs written in Prolog or DATALOG, *see* Section 3.2. This approach pertains mainly, therefore, to the deductive databases domain. In the context of this section, we will therefore examine only those systems where there is no direct modification of the knowledge representation language and where, on the contrary, the inference engine of the KBS is provided with data management functions giving direct access to a generalized DBMS – *see also* the 'enhanced deductive databases systems' introduced in the previous section. The database functionalities can be realized according to a loose or tight coupling approach.

It must be noted that, especially when a tight coupling is chosen and in spite of the use of a general-purpose DBMS, the DB itself is completely devoted to the KBS application. This fact is symbolized in Figure 3.19(b) by indicating that the user gains access to the global system through the KBS subsystem alone. Solution (b) is, therefore, less general (but easier to implement) than solution (a). Moreover, the *concrete* realizations of *all* the architectures displayed in Figure 3.19 have a feature in common, i.e. as we will see in the following sections, the KBS subsystem can normally access the associated DB(s) only if the logical schema of this last component has been explicitly enclosed in the interface's structure, for example, by making use of a data dictionary (*see* the next section). This fact is particularly evident in the systems implementing the architecture of Figure 3.19(b) where, until very recently, each KBS/DB link provided access to a specific version of a DBMS product running under a specific operating system on a specific machine. In this context, we note here that one of the first realizations in this domain has been IntelliCorp's KEEConnection product. This product allowed KEE (knowledge engineering environment, a powerful KESE) to access DB information as if it were part of the KEE knowledge base, by automatically formulating SQL queries to move data between the DB (fact database) and the KB (rule base). KEEConnection could connect to a fixed number of DBMSs using different network protocols, but only if these systems were anticipated in the design of the product. Even if the basic implementing techniques of the solutions of Figure 3.19(b) have not changed substantially, the most modern realizations of this architecture try to be as general as possible (see, for example, Section 3.341).

The approach described in Figure 3.19(c) is symmetric to the previous one, and consists of extending a DBMS with components proper to a KBS. When the database application must access the inference engine and the knowledge base of the KBS subsystem, two strategies are usually employed, resulting in an 'explicit' or 'implicit' access procedure, *see* [CoheB89]. In the first case, which makes use of a procedure call interface, an explicit call to the KBS must be inserted in the application program: this is the strategy followed in many of the commercial solutions to the integration problem. In the second case, the application itself does not explicitly call the KBS, and all access to the inference engine is through the same query interface used to access data; queries look like ordinary SQL queries, without any explicit mention of a possible intervention from the KBS side. When some of the attributes mentioned in the query must be derived (i.e. their values are not explicitly stored in the DB), their values are obtained by inference from the KBS. Information about how to deal with such attributes is transparent to the user and stored in an active repository. For example, in a query such as 'select amount, recommendation from credit approval where ...', which refers to a credit authorization application [CoheB89: 28], the repository knows that 'amount' and 'recommendation' are derived attributes, and triggers the corresponding rules in the rule base of the KBS. We can note here that all the solutions proposed for extending the possibilities of the existing DBMSs that we have examined in Section 2.3 can be considered as particular applications of the architecture of Figure 3.19(c). Therefore, we will not dwell on this particular approach to integration.

In the approaches described in Figure 3.19(d) and (e), the functionalities of the DB and KBS systems are strongly integrated, and the designer is concerned with only one environment. This means, for example, that the 'data model' used in the DB component and the 'knowledge representation language' of the KBS component are now unified. As a consequence, any threat of a 'semantic mismatch' disappears. However, systems like these represent an (at least partial) departure from the traditional approaches to integration: in the literature, the descriptions of systems based on the solutions (d) and (e) that are not simply general suggestions or, at best, experimental prototypes are, therefore, still relatively rare. We can add that, according to the DB community, commercial systems based on the architecture (d) should constitute an exception in the future. They affirm, in fact, that the main disadvantage of this solution is that it requires the construction *ex nihilo* of a DB system after (or during) the set-up of the KBS. In many cases, this implies the need for long sessions of sequential dialogue with the user to collect the input data while, making use of the solution (e), the DB already contains the data needed to feed the KBS. Moreover, DBMS technology is more stable and mature than KBS technology, and the installed base of DBs is definitely larger than the KBSs base; a number of conventional applications already use the DBMS technology, etc. Therefore, they conclude that DBs are probably a better place for incorporating ES functionalities than vice versa, at least in a context of strong integration. Without endorsing fully this position, we will not dwell further here on the solutions of the type (d): note, however, that all the 'advanced solutions' described in Section 3.4 can be considered as applications of the architecture (d).

In the following sections, we will examine some examples of the architectures (a), (b) and (e) of Figure 3.19.

3.33 The 'general bridge' solution

3.331 The DBCL (and HYWIBAS) approach

DBCL is a relatively simple example of the general bridge approach that can be considered in between a deductive database system and a ES/DBMS system, confirming the important architectural similarities between these two classes of IDBSs. It concerns the 'tight coupling' between a Prolog-based expert system and a relational DBMS accessible through SQL, (*see* [Jark84b]). In this case, the bridge between the two components is realized through an intermediate language, called DBCL (data base call language), which is a variable-free subset of Prolog. The general architecture of the system is presented in Figure 3.20.

The problem addressed here is mainly that of the 'granularity mismatch', i.e. the translation of a series of tuple-oriented data requests, addressing parameterized and possibly recursive views in Prolog, into (sequences of) set-oriented queries to base relations. The task of DBCL is twofold:

- it must collect tuple-oriented requests to form set-oriented queries; and
- it must optimize the processing of parameterized queries.

The procedures indicated in Figure 3.20 denote respectively:

- the predicate 'metaevaluate' translates Prolog statements into DBCL statements. More exactly, the function of metaevaluate is to delay the execution of database-related clauses in Prolog, and to collect the related DB calls for set-oriented processing. If the original predicate involves recursion, a sequence of DBCL statements is generated;
- 'translate' is an algorithm that generates a set of queries in SQL from a DBCL predicate: the translation process can be described as a mapping from the DBCL syntax tree to an SQL syntax tree;
- 'local optimize' removes redundancy from a DBCL predicate to eliminate the execution of unnecessary operations;
- 'global optimize' has two functions. First, it determines which parts of a DBCL expression can be evaluated using the internal Prolog database, and for which parts external DB queries must be, on the contrary, generated. Second, it decides whether query results must be stored for future references: this is particularly important for the processing of recursive database calls.

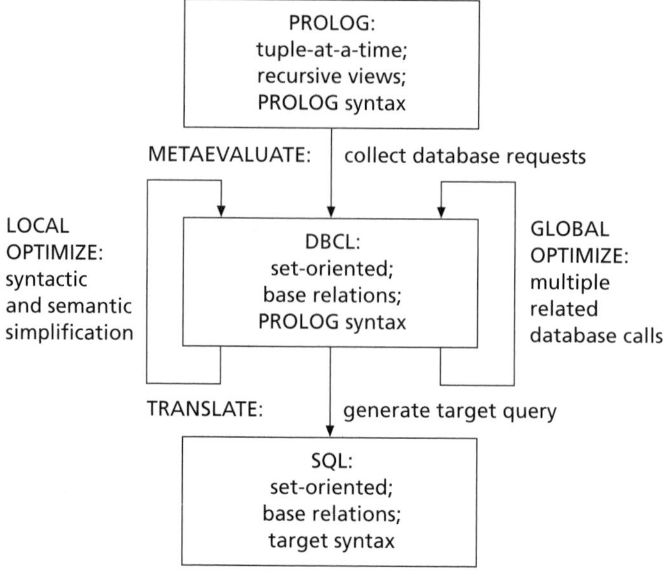

Figure 3.20 Architecture of the DBCL approach

Further technical details, and a complete example of resolution of a Prolog-like query, are given in [Jark84b]. Note, of course, that the approach presented in this subsection is undoubtedly interesting but limited given the confinement of this approach to a strict Prolog context.

A recent system adopting an architectural approach similar to that illustrated in Figure 3.20 is HYWIBAS [Norr94]. It concerns the mapping between a frame-based knowledge representation model, strongly influenced by the terminological logics paradigm, and a relational DB system (INGRES). In this case, the central 'bridge' is not a subset of Prolog as in Figure 3.20 but an object data model, COCOON [Scho92].

COCOON has two basic representation structures, the 'class' and the 'type'. Very classically, the 'class' represents a group of objects sharing the same semantic properties, and pertaining to a given 'type'. The 'type' declares which functions are applicable to an object of this particular type. Frames representing concepts in the KBS level are mapped to specific combinations of types and classes in COCOON. For example, a frame-level concept such as *Computer_Delivery* is translated firstly into a COOCON type *computer_delivery* in such a way that, for every slot such as Supplier and Price, we have a function with the same name. Second, a class *Computer_Delivery* of the *computer_delivery* type is generated, with an associated class predicate such as **where** covering all the remaining features of the original concept, such as the fact that the Recipient is a *Company_ or* a *Person_*. The strategy for the conversion from the object-oriented level to the relational level is only sketchily outlined in [Norr94]. The authors say they employ an extensive replication strategy. For example, all the COCOON classes are represented explicitly, and since a COCOON object may belong to many classes, an object representation may be replicated in several DB relations. The penalty associated with this approach concerns the cost of the update operations: an update on a single object can require updates on a large number of DB relations involved in the representation of the object.

3.332 The DIFEAD system

DIFEAD (dictionary interface for expert systems and databases) was implemented at Trinity College, Dublin, in the mid-1980s, *see* [AlZo87]. A more general solution than the previous ones, DIFEAD is particularly interesting for at least two reasons: i) it is one of the first systems to explicitly present an architecture where an independent subsystem acts as a communication channel between a DBMS and some KBSs (ESs in this case); ii) it is among the first realizations to base the interface's functionalities on the 'data dictionary' concept – this approach constitutes one of the most popular answers to the connection problems.

Generally speaking, a data dictionary collects all the information known about the data managed by a DBMS. It then stores, in compiled format:

- information independent from the physical storage, for example, meaning and source of data, relationships to other data (conceptual schemata etc. that define the database), relationship to the DB functions and rules assuring the correspondence among the different levels. This type of information is used mainly by the end-user that has to evaluate the data. It consists mainly of unformatted explanatory text;
- information related to data storage, for example, storage device, file structure, coding. Since this type of information is needed by the DBMS for processes such as selecting the proper functions for data access or conversion, it consists mainly of strongly formatted data.

The dictionary itself may be conceived as a database; in this case, it fulfils the role of a meta-base, i.e. of a DB which describes the other DBs.

More precisely, DIFEAD makes use of a 'data dictionary directory system' (DD/DS), *see* [AlleF82]. The heart of a DD/DS is a specialized, independent database called the data dictionary directory, which is associated with the DBMS of the global database system. If the data managed by the DBMS are defined by {attribute, value} pairs, then the data dictionary directory stores all the data attributes (metadata) that describe entities such as information, processes, users, and hardware. For example, for the entity 'number of dependants', the directory can inform the user that the attributes are 'length', 'type' and 'value range': however, it will not contain the actual number of dependants. According to [AlleF82: 247], adding a DD/DS to the 'normal' DBMS enables three main objectives to be attained:

- DD/DS helps to control the data resources by providing an inventory of such resources, including data names, definitions, locations, storage formats, sizes, and other characteristics;

- DD/DS helps to control the costs of developing and maintaining applications by providing accurate and complete data definitions for use both in application programs and in program generators such as report writers and query processors;
- DD/DS provides for independence of metadata across computing environments, improving resilience to the effects of hardware and software changes.

DIFEAD implements the independent, central bridge module that characterises the 'general bridge' solution under the form of a DD/DS. In DIFEAD's terminology, this central bridge is called 'metalevel component' (MLC). MLC makes use of two types of data, 'dictionary data' and 'control data'. The dictionary data concern generic documentary information about the application domain, the access privileges, and the size of both the ES and the DB. Control data supply more strategic information, in particular, the information about the ES and the DB enabling DIFEAD to control the interaction between the two, for example:

- the availability of data in the DB for each rule (or set of rules) in the ES;
- the location of such data in the DB;
- the need for and the timing of translation between internal DB format and user formats;
- the need for and the timing of direct interaction with the user, in case an answer to an ES query is not available in the DB.

In DIFEAD, the DD/DS implementing the MLC bridge is realized, for flexibility's and generality's sake, as a component that is totally autonomous from the global DBMS and that performs its own data management functions. This approach allows, *inter alia*, the storage of metadata concerning many different classes of information (flat files, text, image data, etc.), not simply the data in the DB. It is particularly useful, therefore, in a heterogeneous environment, and can automatically interface one or more ESs or DBMSs. The data dictionary directory for the MLC is built using a process similar to that of building a 'normal' DB: it stores the data in the same way as a DB; analogously, it answers the queries – for example, a query concerning the use of a particular ES rule – using the usual DB modalities.

The organisation of MLC – the DIFEAD bridge element, *see* Figure 3.21 (adapted from [AlZo87]) – includes three main modules:

- The USER interface module (UIM) is responsible for interfacing with the user, for input validation, and for displaying any ES request/answer in a format acceptable to the user. Its main function is, however, that of decoding a user request and sending it to the ES involved via the second module, the metadata query module (MQM).
- The MQM is responsible for all communication between the ES and the DB. In particular, it can decide whether an ES request can be answered automatically from the application DB or whether it is necessary to require input from the user. This involes checking first the DD/DS by issuing a query to its proper DBMS (i.e. to the DBMS proper to the DIFEAD system) and then, depending

upon the response, querying either the application DB or the user. For example, to answer a simple question posed by a medical diagnostic ES like 'How old are you ?', DIFEAD will consult its metadata to see whether an attribute 'date of birth' is present in the patient record stored in the application DB; it will be able to calculate the value from the corresponding field, and to supply it to the ES.

- The third module is the Data Update Module (DUM): this is responsible for updating the data dictionary directory and/or the application DB. Updating can be triggered either by the user, or by the DIFEAD system itself. When triggered by the user, updating is purely a DB activity. On the other hand, the MQM can decide to update the data dictionary directory and/or the application DB automatically, for example, after the ES has inferred a new fact, or to store a conclusion of the expert system in the application DB. The decision to perform the update will be taken on the basis of the control data stored in the MLC (i.e. in the DD/DS). For example, a patient record in a clinical DB (i.e. the application DB) may be updated by using the disease that has been diagnosed by a medical diagnosis ES.

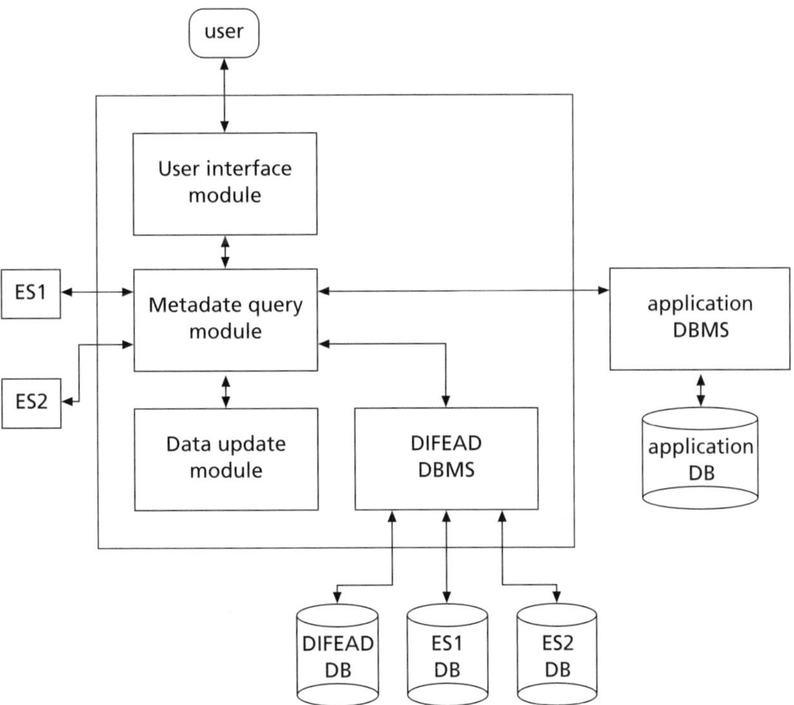

Figure 3.21 The DIFEAD architecture

Note that access to the application DB can be achieved either through DIFEAD or through the standard DBMS query language, whereas the ES can be accessed only via DIFEAD – this approach removes the need to provide a good user interface from the ES.

Prototype versions of DIFEAD have been implemented on Unix machines, and used to interface a simple medical diagnosis system (like MDS) with a clinical DB.

3.333 KADBASE

As already stated in Section 3.32, a variant of the architecture schematized in Figure 3.19(a) implies that the general control functions of the overall system – which, in the DIFEAD system, are located in the central 'bridge' – are distributed over the different subcomponents. We will examine briefly in this context the KADBASE prototype – *see* [Howa87], [Howa89] – implemented at the Carnegie Mellon University (Pittsburgh) on VAX machines. A general overview of the KADBASE distributed architecture is given in Figure 3.22 – Figures 3.22 and 3.23 have been adapted from [Howa89].

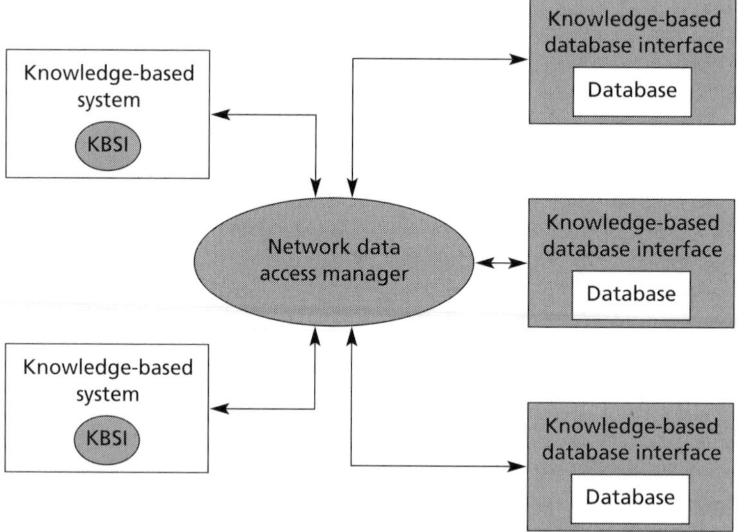

Figure 3.22 General overview of the KADBASE architecture

The conceptual basis for KADBASE's organisation corresponds to integrating information contained in the schemata of the individual engineering databases into a single global schema based on a semantic model – a frame data model, *see* below. A request for data issued by a KBS is translated from the data manipulation language (syntax) and data structure (semantics) of the requesting component into a global syntactic expression referencing the global schema. The mapping process is divided into two separate processes:

- first, a syntactic translation from the KBS's data manipulation language to the global data manipulation language;
- second, a semantic translation from the KBS's data structure to the global data structure.

After the request has been mapped, the interface identifies the target DBs that contain information required to answer the query, and generates subqueries to those DBs to gather that information. Each subquery to a target DB is translated to the syntax and semantics of the specific database, and the corresponding DBMS is invoked to process resultant subqueries. Inverse mapping returns results to the requesting component. The three basic components of KADBASE *see* (Figure 3.22) are the following:

- The knowledge-based system interface (KBSI), which is part of each KBS linked with the global system. KBSI formulates queries and updates sent to the central network data access manager and processes replies from this last element. The KBSI has at its disposal knowledge about the KBS data space schema, and uses that knowledge to perform semantic and syntactic translations for queries, updates, and replies.
- The knowledge-based database interface (KBDBI), which acts as an intelligent front end for each DBMS: KBDBI accepts queries and updates from the network data access manager and returns appropriate replies. Like the KBSI, the KBDBI has at its disposal knowledge about the local DB schema and the local language for data manipulation requests. It uses that knowledge to perform semantic and syntactic translations for queries, updates, and replies.
- The network data access manager (NDAM) provides the central interface between the different components. It receives requests (queries and updates) from the KBSs (through their KBSIs) expressed in terms of the global schema. Using information associated with this global schema, the NDAM locates sources for data referenced in the requests and decomposes each request for subqueries or updates to individual target DBs. These subrequests are sent to the corresponding KBDBIs for processing. Replies from KBDBIs are combined to form a single reply to the original query and sent to the requesting application through its KBSI.

The different components of KADBASE are structured as KBSs: for each of them, knowledge is grouped into 'knowledge modules', which process knowledge about particular subproblems, and 'knowledge sources', which are passive, descriptive information about the components. Typically, knowledge modules perform control and translation tasks, while knowledge sources represent schema descriptions. Throughout KADBASE, a frame data model represents schema definitions, syntactic translation procedures, queries, and answers. In this model, frames are used to describe entities; slots may be attributes (which contain simple descriptive values) or relationships (which link the entity to another entity type).

KADBASE's 'syntactic' translation transforms requests (queries and updates) between external data manipulation languages (such as QUEL and SQL) and the internal KADBASE request representation. Syntactic translation is performed by KADBASE's local system (KBSI or KBDBI), given that it depends only on the local data manipulation language; the same syntactic processor can be used for multiple applications of the same DBMS or ES shell. Each syntactic processor maps requests between two fixed languages: the component data manipulation language and KADBASE's internal representation. The syntactic processor can be a special-purpose algorithmic program, since translation does not vary with applications. Internally, KADBASE uses frame networks to represent requests; the organisation of the request frame representation serves as the global data manipulation language, paralleling the global schema.

With respect now to the knowledge used for the 'schema description and mapping', KADBASE integrates the data spaces of the different components through a global schema – equivalent to the data dictionary approach used in DIFEAD – based on the frame data model. Schema description knowledge required by the interface is partitioned into three levels: the component's local data representation, expressed in the component's own data model (hierarchical, network, relational, frame-based, or object-oriented); the component's local data representation, expressed in terms of the global frame model; and the global schema, expressed in terms of the global frame model. KADBASE's knowledge-based components represent this information as knowledge sources.

Figure 3.23 describes relationships in KADBASE between schema decriptions and mapping knowledge sources.

- The 'local schema' describes how the component's local data structure is organised in terms of the local data model. The character of the local schema is highly dependent on the type of DBMS or KBS being described. In relational DBMSs, the local schema contains definitions of relations and their attributes in the DB. In a KESE or object-oriented ES, the local schema contains definitions of the hierarchy of object classes.
- The 'local frame-based schema' (LFBS) represents the local schema in the semantics of the frame data model. The LFBS should be a fully updatable view of the underlying data structure, expressed in local terminology (the names for entities and attributes). The LFBS organization may differ from that of the local schema, given that the LFBS may group slots from several underlying data structures (such as relations and frames) into a single entity if those data structures have the same primary or candidate keys. The LFBS should also contain or be able to reference all information in the local schema with respect to constraints, key attributes, and domain properties (including data types, ranges, and dimensions). The LFBS may contain information regarding relationships not found in underlying data models; therefore, the LFBS can provide an enhanced semantic data model when the local model cannot express relationships between entities.

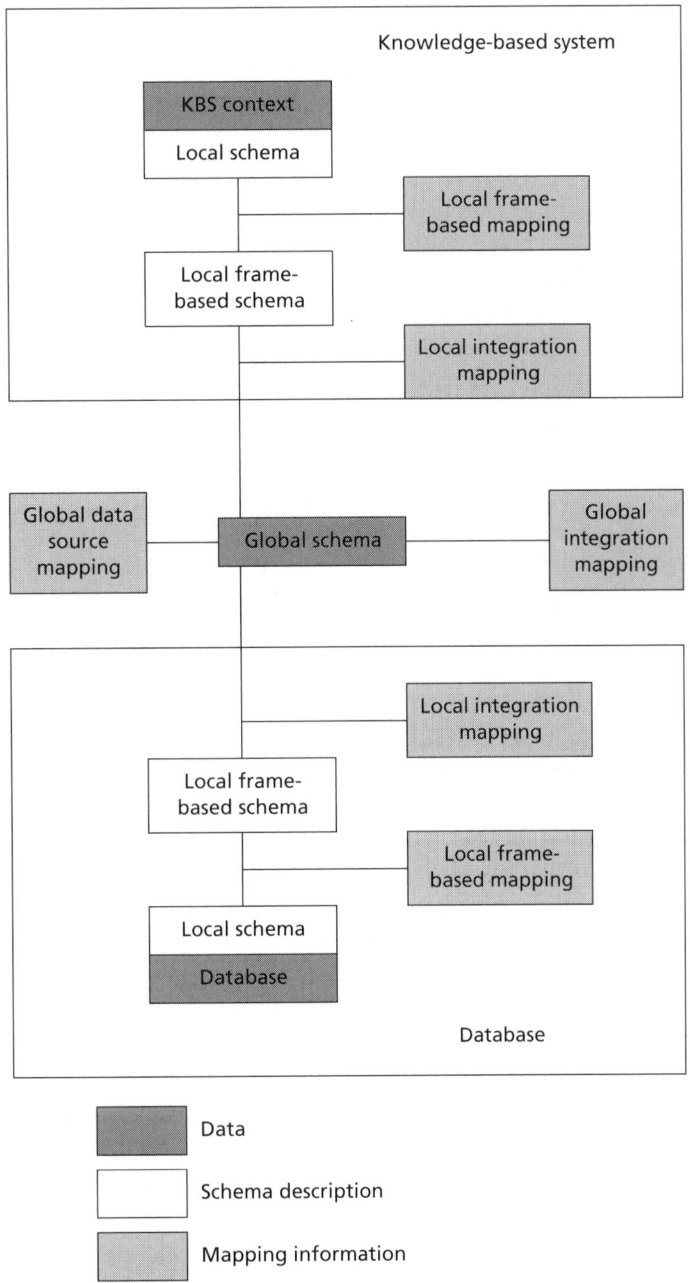

Figure 3.23 KADBASE schema ingration mappings

- The 'global schema' represents the common data space shared by all the components of the integrated global system. In effect, the global schema combines all frames and slots from the LFBSs. Since LFBSs may differ with respect to terminology (the names for common frames and slots) and slot domains (data types and dimensions), establishing the global schema involves selecting a single set of global names and domains. The selection is performed by the global schema administrator, which is responsible for the global schema's consistency and completeness.

Each of the three schema description knowledge sources represents a specific data structure in terms of a specific data model. Schema description knowledge sources do not contain knowledge about how to relate that data structure to other schema representations, i.e. how to map between schemata (local schema to LFBS and LFBS to global schema, for example). Two additional knowledge sources contain that schema-mapping knowledge, as follows:

- The 'local frame-based mapping' (LFBM) describes organizational mapping between the local schema and the LFBS. The LFBM is necessary because the LFBS may group slots from several underlying local schema data structures (including relations and frames) into a single entity if those data structures have the same primary or candidate keys. The LFBM contains information relating each slot in the LFBs with its counterparts in the local schema.
- The 'local integration mapping' (LIM) contains mapping information necessary to integrate the LFBM into the global schema. The LIM is necessary because the LFBS can differ from the global schema in entity and slot names, and in attribute value domains. The LIM represents the former with terminology (name) mappings for entity and slots names, and the latter with domain mappings for attribute values (tables or functions that map local values into corresponding global values when domain attributes differ). Domain mappings are required whenever the local component represents an attribute value in terms different to those used by the global schema.

The global level requires two additional mapping-knowledge sources (*see* Figure 3.23):

- The 'global data source mapping' (GDSM) relates each slot (data item) in the global schema to the list of DB and KBS contexts containing that slot.
- The 'global integration mapping' (GIM) contains constraints and functions relating slots in the global schema. These mappings represent mathematical and logical interrelationships between attributes found in different DB and KBS contexts.

The KADBASE prototype [Howa89] integrates LFBSs into global schemata 'by hand'; it requires a global 'expert database' administrator to standardize terminology for global entities and slots, select global slot domain properties (data types and units), and define global relationships and constraints.

With respect to the 'semantic' mapping, the semantic translation of requests (queries and updates) and answers (data) in KADBASE is independent of the types of KBS and DBMS involved. Semantic processing is based on information provided in the schema description and mapping-knowledge sources described above. Therefore, an application-independent knowledge module performs semantic translations.

The semantic translation process involves two steps: from local schema to LFBS, and from LFBS to global schema. The first step translates only local information (local schema, LFBM, and LFBS) and, using the application-independent semantic translation module, should be performed with the KBS's interface or KBDBI. The second step involves both local and global information (LFBS, LIM, and global schema) and can be implemented locally (as in the prototype) or globally. In addition, KADBASE divides semantic translation into two types (requests and replies) and two directions (local to global, and global to local). Details about the semantic translation processes, and the KBSI interface, can be found in [Howa89].

In the same paper, some details are given about two experiments concerning the use of the KADBASE prototype in a structural-engineering context. In the first, SPEX (an ES for the design of structural components) searches, using KADBASE, a DB of standard structural steel shapes that satisfy certain given requirements. This experiment tests the syntactic translation and flexible query formulation properties of KADBASE. In the second experiment, HICOST (a KBS cost estimator for detailed building design) accesses, through KADBASE, three DBs, a building design database, a project management database, and a unit cost database. This experiment illustrates the semantic translation process and the possibilities of multidatabase requests proper to KADBASE.

To conclude this subsection, we mention another architecture for distributed IDBSs, MOBY [Bein87], where the KBS component is an expert system. In MOBY, both the rules of the ES (in OPS5 format) and data are distributed among a set of processing elements (PEs). These last are connected through a control unit that is responsible for the control of the recognize-act cycle (realized here under the form of a RETE algorithm, *see* Section 3.122) that characterizes the functioning of the ES.

3.334 The Europe-Brücke approach

The KBS components included in the systems examined in the previous subsections were, essentially, relatively simple rule systems (ESs). If the KBS component can be brought back to an expert system, the 'semantic' mismatch defined in Section 3.31 is considerably reduced: the <Attribute, Object, Value> paradigm ('associative triples') normally used for knowledge representation purposes in the simplest ES shells is, in fact, compatible with the pairs 'attribute-value' stored in a relational DB.

The system we present now, Europe-Brücke (EB, *see* [Mena93]), concerns the connection of BACK, an advanced 'terminological' language in the KL-ONE style, with external, relational DBs – as KL-ONE [BracR85d], BACK is based on a hierarchical description of 'concepts' with associated 'slots' and 'fillers'. In the Europe-Brücke case, the 'mismatch' between the KBS and the DB is particularly important, and the solutions required to build up the 'central bridge module' are very complex.

The general philosophy underlying the establishment of the KBS/DBMS connection in EB is that the BACK knowledge base contains a specific interpretation of the meaning of the general data available in the corporate relational DBs. The 'bridge' should, in this case, guarantee the automatic access to the DB according to the specific interpretation of the data associated with each particular knowledge-based application: note that, in general, this interpretation is different from the data model incorporated in the schema of the corporate DB. This implies that the approach to integration cannot be based on the assumption that a one-to-one correspondence exists between BACK 'concepts' and DB 'relations' as well as between BACK 'roles' and DB 'attributes'. A really free connection must, therefore, be allowed, for example, several relations can be mapped to a single concept, a single relation can be spread on a concepts hierarchy and instances as well as attribute values can be originated by complex queries. No constraints are imposed on the structure of the mapping or on the involved concepts and relations. The DB is accessed only for retrieval purposes – data from the DB on which some query answering or problem-solving reasoning has to be performed must, in any case, be actually loaded into BACK instances when the reasoning process takes place. No other assumption is done about the time at which the transformation takes place or about the lifetime of the transformed data in the knowledge base. The kind of transformation to be accomplished depends on the structure of the mapping and on the queries to be answered, and it is thus application dependent.

The generality of the EB approach can justify, in our opinion, the insertion of this system in the 'general bridge' category, even if other characteristics (unlike, for example, KDBASE, only relational DBs are interfaced; the DB is accessed only for retrieval purposes; etc.) could suggest an insertion in the 'extending KBS' class instead (Figure 3.19b). The construction of Europe-Brücke has been carried out in the framework of AIMS (Advanced Information Management Systems), a European ESPRIT project, *see* [Mett88], [Dami92], [Bert93a].

In Europa-Brücke, we can distinguish between three different levels in the procedures implementing the connection KB-DB.

- The first level concerns the definition of the specific language allowing the explicit description of the mapping between concepts and roles in the KB and relations and attributes in the DB. The language declaratively describes how to transform DB data into role fillers for concept instances (i.e. ABox knowledge) in the BACK knowledge base and, as already stated, it is not constrained as a one-to-one correspondence. The descriptions expressed using the mapping language are introduced into the KB as internal mapping information.
- The second level ('view generator') is constituted by a set of four operators – EBDifference, EBize, EBGenerate and EBAssoc – that support the user in managing and/or building the mapping information to be used by the 'access module' (third level). For example, 'EBDifference' builds a mapping expression (EB_expr, *see* below) as a difference between the mapping expressions associated with two different concepts. 'Difference' here means that the final expression can be used to construct a SQL query able to retrieve the set of tuples equivalent to the difference between the two sets identified by the two original mapping expressions. The EBize operator is used to build EB expressions for new concepts introduced in a BACK knowledge base in which some

'linked' concepts are already defined; a linked concept is a concept that has a mapping expression (EB_expr) associated with it. When a new concept is introduced in the KB, it is possible to use the 'classification' (subsumption) inference procedures proper to BACK to insert the new concept in the concept hierarchy: it will then have both some fathers and some children. EBize works on the set of the fathers and children to produce the final mapping expression for the new concept – more details on the characteristics of the four operators can be found in [Mena93: 15–30].

- The third level ('access module') includes some applications that are used mainly:

  a to interpret the queries addressed to the BACK knowledge base, taking into account the KB concepts and their associated internal information, and, if needed, generating SQL queries to access the requested information;

  b to load the instances for a particular concept from the DBMS using the mapping information associated with a concept that has been introduced with the mapping language;

  c to generate the answers in terms of instances that are entered into the knowledge base, using, when needed, the inferential mechanisms of the BACK language (classification etc.);

  d to implement a strategy for DBMS integration based on structural mapping (also called schema mapping), i.e. on a mapping relating the elements of the BACK data model (concepts, roles, and subsumption hierarchies) to the elements of the relational data model (relations and attributes).

We will now give some information about the 'first level', i.e. the Europa-Brücke language itself; more details, and a formal description of the grammar of the language, can be found in [Mena93]. Using this language, the mapping information associated with a single KB concept must provide a two-level description of the links among concept instances and KB relations:

- 'Concept retrieval information': such information describes i) the relations (and the eventual conditions on these relations) from which the tuples must be retrieved, and ii) the 'identity', i.e. the attributes whose values will be used to automatically build instance names. In a BACK ABox, each instance has a unique name, which can be entered by the user or automatically built up by the system. To make use of this last possibility, it is necessary, for each instance that corresponds to a DB tuple, to specify the information about the main relations involved in the tuple retrieval and the fields or the roles whose values will be used for the name of instances.
- 'Fillers retrieval information': this information is linked with the BACK roles, and it describes, for any given concept, the way in which its role fillers must be retrieved from the database. A role can be linked with one or more attributes taken from one or more relations, or it may be associated with a concept linked with the DBs. In order to ensure that the attributes retrieved from the

database can be safely realized as role fillers for instances of the proper concept, it is necessary to take into account the implicit 'closed worlds assumption' of the DB. Therefore, no modification of the database is allowed outside the KB connection.

For any concept, making use of the information above, it is possible to build up expressions called 'EB_expr' (EB stands, obviously, for Europa-Brücke) similar to SQL-like expressions: the EB language covers the main operations of relational algebra such as 'Projection', 'Selection' and 'Join'. EB_exprs make use of the EB predicate '**link**', which specifies information about the tables involved in the tuple retrieval, and describes the way in which its role fillers are retrieved from the DB. To build the EB_exprs, it is necessary to be in possession of the link information for every concept in the KB. This happens because a BACK concept can refer to another one. Therefore, when we deal with the first concept, we could need some information pertaining to the second one. As a consequence, we must introduce all the links of the concepts present in the knowledge base; a parser will be used to verify the formal correctness of the link expressions introduced in this way.

A general model of EB_expr, including both 'concept retrieval information' and 'fillers retrieval information', is given in Table 3.11. As already stated, such expressions will then be associated with the BACK concepts, and stored in the BACK KB. In the first part of Table 3.11, the 'tables' are those from which we want to retrieve the information to transform in the knowledge base; the 'conditions' are applied to every instance retrieved from the DB. In the second part, the '**slot_extract**' primitive contains all the information needed to the role filler retrieval. The 'extract_statement' can contain any combination of selection, projection and join operations; it also contains conditions that constrain the fields involved in the role filler retrieval.

Table 3.11 A general model of EB_expr

Concept retrieval information:

link (concept_name, tables_specification && **condition** (condition) &
name_from_db (field_name))

Fillers retrieval information:

link (role_name, **for_concept** (back_concept_name) &
with_range (range_type) & **slot_extract** (extract_statement)
& **group_by** (field_name) & **option** (option_name)) .

Let us now examine the EB_exprs proper to a simple example which concerns a relational database about university students (*see* Figure 3.24); first normal form is assumed as a minimal requirement for the DB representation. The relation STUDENTS, whose primary key is ID, contains information about students, while the relation SUBJECT, whose primary key is ID, contains information about subject names and teachers. The relationship between a student and its subjects is held by the relation MARKS, with primary keys STUDENT_ID and

SUBJECT_ID; STUDENT_ID is a foreign key for the relation STUDENTS, while SUBJECT_ID is a foreign key for the relation SUBJECTS. Moreover, the relation MARKS contains, for each couple student-subject, information about the scores obtained. In the BACK knowledge base, the concept '**students**' is related to the concept '**subjects**' through the role '**has_subject**' that has range '**subjects**'. The relationship between '**students**' and '**subjects**' is represented by the concept '**marks**', through the roles '**mark_to_student**' and '**mark_for_subject**'.

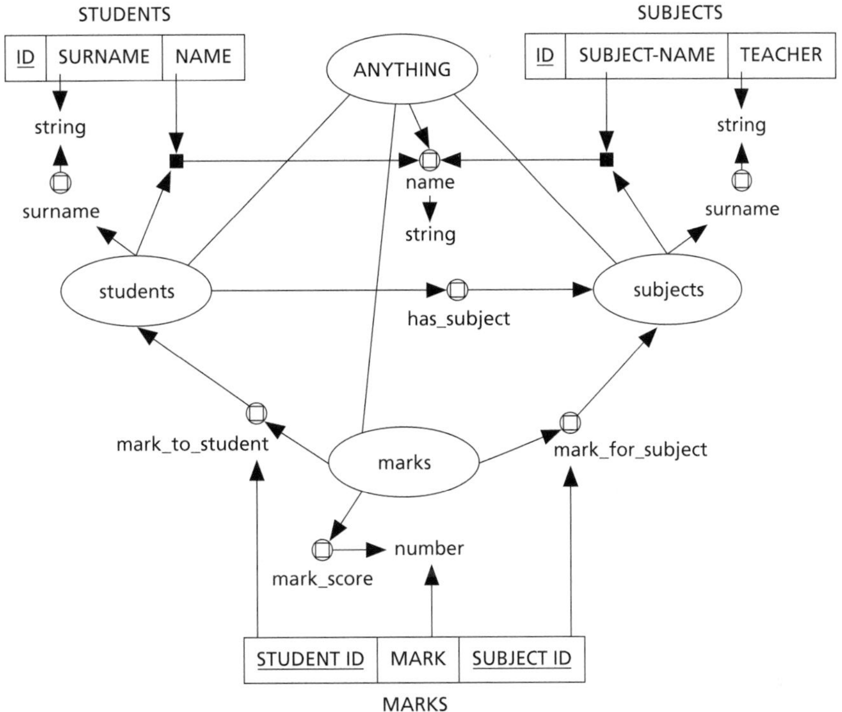

Figure 3.24 An example of BACK–relational DB correspondence

The support of the concept 'subjects' is the relation SUBJECTS in the DB; the fillers for roles '**name**' and '**teacher_name**' are obtained projecting the fields SUBJECT-NAME and TEACHER in the relation SUBJECTS – *see* the mapping expressions in Table 3.12.

Table 3.12 EB_expr for the concept '**subjects**'

link (subjects, **db**(database) & **owner**(owner) & **table**(subjects)
& **name_from_db**([id]))

link (name, **for_concept**(subjects) & **with_range**(string) &
extract(Proj(subjects,database.owner.subjects.subject_name)))

link (teacher_name, **for**_concept(subjects) & **with-range**(string) &
extract(Proj(subjects,database.owner.subjects.teacher)))

For the concept '**students**', the support is the relation STUDENTS: Table 3.13 gives the 'concept retrieval information' part of the EB_expr linked with this concept. Fillers for the roles 'name' and 'surname' in 'students' are obtained by projecting the fields NAME and SURNAME in the relation STUDENTS. Note that, in the BACK knowledge base corresponding to the example (*see* Figure 3.23), there is a unique role which is labelled '**name**', having '**anything**' as domain and '**string**' as range. The modalities for obtaining the role filler from the DB are different, however, according to the concept that inherits this role. Thus, internal information about how to obtain a '**student**' name differs from the information about how to obtain a '**subject**' name. The filler for the role '**has_subject**' of '**students**' is a set of instances of the concept '**subjects**'. In the actual query-building process, the linking information about the role range has to be examined: all the fields that must be projected in order to fill the proper instances of '**subjects**' will be collected and projected over the relations described in the join expression. Table 3.14 gives the 'fillers retrieval information' for the concept '**students**'.

Table 3.13 'Concept retrieval information' for the concept '**students**'

link (students, **db**(database) & **owner**(owner) &
table(students) & **name_from_db**([id]))

Table 3.14 'Filler retrieval information' for the concept '**students**'

```
link (has_subject, for_concept(student) & with_range(subject) &
        extract(Join (support_list
                      (students,marks,subjects),
                      condition_list
                      ((database.owner.students.id
                      =
                      database.owner.marks.subject_id)
                      AND
                      (database.owner.marks.subject_id
                      = database.owner.subjects.id )))))
```

For the concept '**marks**', the support is the relation MARKS: the corresponding 'concept retrieval information' is given in Table 3.15. The filler for the role '**mark**_score' of the concept '**marks**' is obtained by projection on MARKS support, while information enabling the connection of an instance of 'marks' to the corresponding instances of '**students**' and '**subjects**' is linked with the roles '**mark_for_subject**' and '**mark_for_student**' – *see* Table 3.16.

Table 3.15 'Concept retrieval information' for the concept '**marks**'

```
link (marks, db(database) & owner(owner) & table(marks)
      & name_from_db( [student_id, subject_id] )) .
```

In BACK, querying is expressed by using the primitive '**ask**'. An example which refers to our sample database is given in Table 3.17. This table shows how an original BACK query concerning the instances (individuals, ABox knowledge) of the concept '**marks**' is translated in the corresponding SQL query: it is now well evident how, using Europa-Brücke, a single AI concept can access several AI relations.

Table 3.16 'Filler retrieval information' for the concept '**marks**'

```
link (mark_for_subject, for_concept(marks) & with_range(subjects)
            & extract(Join (support_list
                                (marks,subjects),
                                condition_list
                                (database.owner.marks.subject_id
                                = database.owner.subjects.id )))
link (mark_to_student, for_concept(marks) & with_range(students)
            & extract(Join (support.list
                                (marks,students)
                                condition_list
                                (database.owner.marks.student_id
                                = database.owner.students.id )))
```

Table 3.17 An example of a BACK ABox query

<u>*BACK query*</u>:

```
ABoxask ( X = getall (marks))
```

<u>*SQL query*</u>:

```
SELECT db.owner.marks.student_id, db.owner.marks.subject_id,
       db.owner.marks.mark,
       db.owner.subjects.id, db.owner.subjects.subject_name,
       db.owner.subjects.teacher,
       db.owner.students.id, db.owner.students.name,
       db.owner.students.surname,
FROM db.owner.marks, db.owner.subjects, db.owner.students
WHERE db.owner.marks.student_id = db.owner.students.id
       AND
       db.owner.marks.subject_id = db.owner.subjects.id
```

3.34 Extending a KBS with components proper to a DBMS

The systems we will examine in the following subsections are relatively general, in that they can guarantee the access to a number of different DBs. Solutions supplying a KBS with some facilities in order to extract information from a unique, specific type of DB are now quite common: we will limit ourselves to two recent solutions in this style, of a different order of complexity. The first is the knowledge manager system, *see* [Bert00b], allowing the storage and retrieval of 'NKRL predicative occurrences' (complex three-fold AI structures, *see* Section 3.452) into and from a DB2 relational DB through an elaborate Web-based approach that makes use of a specific XML interface language called KMIL. The SOPHIA system [Aber99] stores elementary frames represented in an attribute-value style into the tables of a relational DB making use of a particularly simple mapping schema: a single row of the general 'Frames' table includes a single slot of a particular frame and its value. A frame is represented by a sequence of rows in Frames, and there is not a mapping from individual knowledge classes to separate tables.

Returning now to the 'quite' general solutions, we have already mentioned the KEEConnection product. We will now describe summarily, first, another well-known product in a similar vein, KBMS (Knowledge Base Management System), originally developed by one of the AI pioneer companies, AICorp. KBMS can access several SQL DBMSs, making use, once again, of procedures in the data dictionary style. The system, a real KESE, is also particularly interesting because of its natural language (NL) facilities.

Even if KBMS integrates the object-oriented paradigm as a basic component of its design, it is, fundamentally, used for the development of rule-based systems, i.e. of ESs. It may be interesting to see how 'genuine' KESEs (providing, for example, inheritance-based inference mechanisms) can deal with the integration problem within an extending KBS framework. We will, therefore, supply some information about the connection techniques used by ROCK, a KESE commercialized by the Carnegie Group Inc., and SPOKE, a KESE produced by the Alcatel-Alsthom group in France. These techniques can be considered, in fact, as 'paradigmatic' for providing very powerful KESEs with a DB access.

We will note, eventually, that the solution 'extending DBMS' is also the architectural solution adopted by the vendors of the main ES tools in order to provide their systems with some elementary possibilities of extracting information from a database. For example, the EXSYS Professional tool (EXSYS Inc., Albuquerque, NM, USA) gives access to 17 different SQL DBMSs. In this context, we can also mention the 'Gensym's G2 Connectivity Solutions'. Gensym Corporation (Cambridge, MA, USA), founded in 1986, is one of the 'historical' AI companies offering ES tools. Its leading product is G2, an object-oriented environment for building and deploying ES applications. G2 connectivity solutions are object-oriented bridge products and tool kits that allow G2 applications to interface with other systems, in particular DBMSs such as Oracle, Sybase, Informix, etc. Note that, in the industrial (as in the research) domain, no standard approach exists for realizing the access functions, even if variants of the 'data dictionary' technique are largely used.

3.341 *KBMS*

KBMS, written in C language, was initially developed for use in the IBM production environment, and then extended for use on other mainframes and personal computers. A very general presentation of this tool is given in Figure 3.25. KBMS is a complete development environment for rule-based KBSs, i.e. ESs; as such, it is endowed with an inference engine that is the heart of the system. Rules are 'if-then' rules where the left-hand side includes support for ANDs and ORs, relations, algebraic expression, parametric functions, and SQL-like dot qualification of attribute names to allow for multiple bindings of an object. The right-hand side includes commands such as CREATE, UPDATE, DELETE, CALL, PRINT, RUN, etc., and control of debugging functions. Rules can be written in English, taking advantage of the natural language features incorporated within this system.

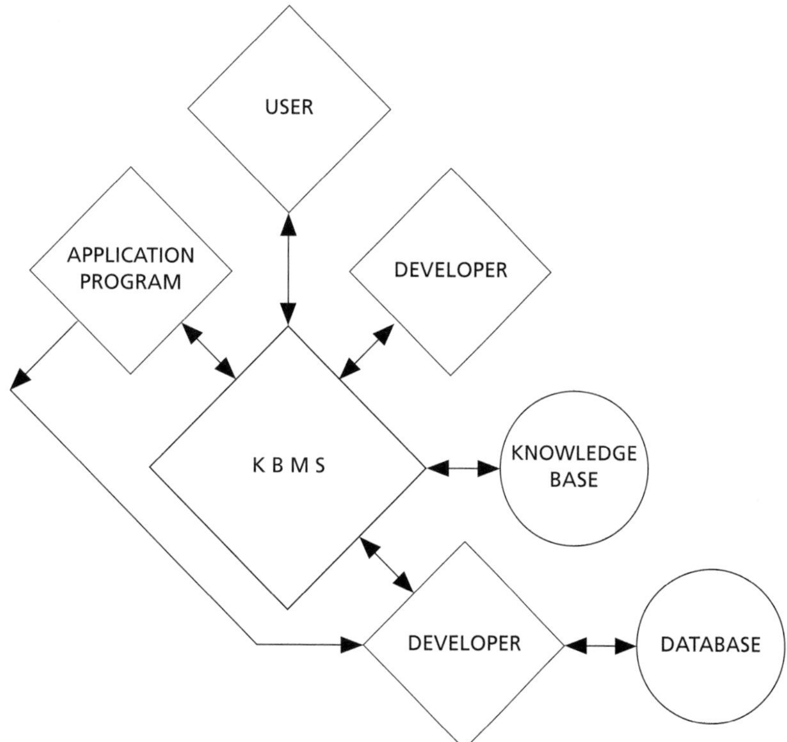

Figure 3.25 General architecture of KBMS

The reasoning strategies supported by the inference engine are the following:

- Backward-chaining (goal-directed reasoning). As we know from Section 3.122, this is a problem-solving strategy that starts from the goal and works backwards, establishing subgoals and reviewing data until it appears that one of the goals can be supported by the data. In KBMS, the backward-chaining facility automatically creates menus and prompts the user for input as needed.

- Forward-chaining (data-driven reasoning). This problem-solving strategy uses a set of facts to derive new facts until a goal is satisfied; it is used when no specific goal is defined, but any of a number of goals is acceptable, depending on changing circumstances. KBMS makes use of the RETE algorithm – *see* [Forg82] and Section 3.1 for improving the performance of the inference engine.
- Hypothetical reasoning, which allows several alternative solutions to be explored at the same time. This strategy identifies and evaluates potential alternatives to determine the sequence of steps that will be used to attain a desired result.
- A (somewhat downgraded) version of object-oriented programming – this particular version has a central role in the KBMS's organization, given that many basic features such as the database interface, the graphic interface, and the co-operative processing capabilities are supported by an object-oriented architecture. A KBMS object is a logical grouping of elementary facts, and supplies the basis for both the data and the knowledge representation paradigms. The KBMS's object-oriented facility includes multiple inheritance, message passing, rule attachment (whenever an object is used in an application, the rules associated with it are automatically executed), class and subclass distinction.

The inference engine is strictly associated with the KBMS knowledge base, used i) to store the rules implementing the reasoning strategies evoked before; ii) to store the data and the objects (with attributes and values) that are relevant to the application area. An interactive, full screen editor helps the user to develop and maintain knowledge bases, and to guarantee their integrity. If a developer changes a calculation or definition, the editor identifies all references to that item throughout the knowledge base, and automatically makes the corrections that are needed.

KBMS incorporates an NL facility derived from AICorp's INTELLECT product, one of the first and the most well-known interfaces for querying DBs in natural language, *see* [Harr84]. This facility, as mentioned before, allows application developers to write rules, or the steps needed to reach a solution or a recommendation, in English. For example, a KBMS rule in a credit authorization system could be written exactly as: 'IF the customer has an overdue balance outstanding, THEN credit risk is high.' The NL facility is also used to question the knowledge base, to activate the inferencing procedures, etc.

If we consider the ways in which the user can access the system (*see* Figure 3.25), KBMS provides three methods of interacting with the knowledge base applications:

- a graphic user interface (GUI), i.e. an object-oriented (active objects) facility allowing a developer to create icons and other graphic images as an integral part of an application, and to interact with the application through a 'point and click' strategy: information is sent back and forth between the images seen by the user and the KBMS programs running in the background;
- a natural language interface;
- a traditional menu-driven interface.

Another important component of the system from a KESE point of view is the 'developer' (*see* Figure 3.25). The developer interface includes a graphic interface, which displays a graphical representation of the objects defined in a knowledge base and the relationships defined between these objects. Graphical representations of the objects are mouse or cursor sensitive, allowing a developer to click on a particular object and see the attributes defined for it. The interface can also be used to display a graphic representation of an existing database, and to visualize sets of rules in graphical form, as well as the transaction flow from one set of rules to another. Other graphical facilities are an interactive full screen editor, a screen painting facility allowing the developer to design his own input and output screens, etc.

With respect to the connection KBS/DBMS, KBMS provides for the automatic generation of object and attribute definitions from existing data dictionaries and constitutes, therefore, a good example of the techniques used in the ES industry to ensure an access to external repositories of data. As already stated, KBMS can automatically interface with commercial DBMSs for IBM personal computers and workstations and Unix machines. This means that, at least to a limited extent, KBMS application programs are independent of the data (it is possible to use the same rules syntax for all applications) and that the KBMS application developer does not need to code data access routines. When a rule needs a data object, KBMS can retrieve it through the central pieces of its access mechanism, i.e. the 'automatic database interfaces' which generate the SQL statements needed to access or update the data. If the data are moved to a different storage facility, no changes to the application rules are needed.

KBMS provides several different 'automatic database interfaces', each specializing in the production of data access code required for a specific DBMS or file system supported by KBMS; applications and rules can access multiple databases simultaneously. The interfaces are based on the 'automatic data definition' (ADD) facility: an ADD automatically loads data definition information from a data dictionary or catalogue into KBMS (see the DIFEAD system examined in Section 3.332). ADDs are offered for the most popular DBMS and file storage systems, such as DB2, SQL/DS, IMS, Adabas, or ORACLE.

KBMS also provides a manual DB interface, relying on user-written data access procedures and allowing applications to be built that can access data not automatically accessed by KBMS, such as data stored in a proprietary or custom-developed database.

Finally, KBMS includes its own relational data storage facility (KDB, the knowledge database). This facility allows data to be stored and shared by multiple applications without requiring the overhead of an external DBMS. Moreover, KDB can be used to develop and test applications without impacting the production database. It is possible then to go into production simply by redefining the objects from KDB to the production database – KBMS will automatically generate all the data access logic. KDB data can be accessed by KBMS rules, graphical objects, the KBMS knowledge base editor, or by English language questions through KBMS's natural language facility.

3.342 The ROCK approach

ROCK is a frame- and object-oriented tool based largely on a well-known tool from the Carnegie Group's, CRL (Carnegie representation language), a fundamental component of the Knowledge Craft development environment (KESE) for developing KBSs. ROCK can be seen as the C/C++ version of CRL (which was implemented in COMMON LISP). The techniques for accessing SQL DBs developed in a ROCK context can be considered as typical of the solutions adopted by a majority of high-level KESE tools.

As CRL, ROCK offers a set of advanced knowledge representation features, such as:

- relations, including both system-defined relations (ISA and Instance) and user-defined relations;
- (multiple) inheritance, allowing user-defined inheritance and providing the 'local slot view' capability that allows inheritance characteristics to be attached to slots in a particular frame, then inherited to slots lower in the hierarchy;
- contexts (virtual snapshots of the knowledge base): users can make changes to frames in a context without affecting their original knowledge base, then can either make the changes permanent or discard them;
- metaknowledge, to support the inclusion of relevant definitional and background information;
- integration of frames and rules: once a knowledge base has been defined, the application developer is able to write rules that match specific frames, resulting in optimized inferencing performance.

In relation to the 'knowledge base' aspects of ROCK, the tool provides an 'integrated frame base' (IFB) facility, providing permanent storage of the frame knowledge base developed for a given application. This allows the knowledge base to be preserved so that updates are available to the application on subsequent executions, or so that other applications may use the same knowledge base in different ways. For example, in an ORACLE context, an IFB is initially created through the use of the utility program **create_oracle_ifb**; when an IFB is no longer needed, it is removed by **delete_oracle_ifb**; other self-explanatory commands are **backup_oracle_ifb**, **restore_oracle_ifb**, **reset_oracle_ifb**, etc. Of course, we cannot define this type of DB management as the equivalent of a real DBMS, given that several of the usual DBMS functionalities (such as query optimization, search for subobjects, integrity constraints, security, views, etc.) are not – or cannot be – available. What IFB offers is in fact pure permanent storage of ROCK class- and instance-frames. Slot declarations and slot-control frames (metaknowledge) are also saved, as are copies of frames in subcontexts. Interestingly, however, IFB also offers what ROCK people call 'transaction-like support'; this name has been chosen given that:

- An IFB 'transaction' moves from one fully consistent knowledge-base state to another fully consistent knowledge-base state, thanks mainly to the fact that a single IFB (operating in a single subspace) is open within a single application.

However, the knowledge base stored in an IFB can be accessed by any number of applications simultaneously; to preserve the integrity, a locking mechanism is used which restricts the type of access an application can have to an IFB.

- Functions are provided to save or abort a set of changes.

An important effort has been accomplished to realize an efficient access mechanism. The IFB implements keyed access to frames, which are stored in a compact form, thereby minimizing the file input/outout (I/O) required to access a frame; communication between a ROCK application and an IFB is based on a client-server model. Read or write access to an IFB is controlled by the locking mechanism evoked before. Note that IFB frames never need to be explicitly loaded by an application: a frame is implicitly loaded, or faulted-in, from the IFB, and created in memory the first time it is referenced by the application.

The relational database (RDB) interface has been designed to enable a ROCK application to retrieve data from relational databases and convert them into a frame representation; more exactly, RDB allows database records to be represented as instance frames in the knowledge base, and columns to be represented as attribute slots. Moreover, modifications made to slot values in RDB frames can be automatically reflected in the corresponding records in the database, and the RDB interface can be used to create new records in existing database tables as well as to retrieve and modify existing RDB records. Note, however, that RDB does not directly support the main administrative functions of the relational DB: no capabilities are provided for creating new tables in the DB or for modifying the definition of an existing table, such as adding a new column. The interface functions act, as usual, through the use of ROCK-generated SQL calls to the DB.

The mapping of records from an RDB table to ROCK instances is mediated by user-defined 'RDB class frames': ROCK provides the system-frames **kb_RDB_Class** and **kb_Contextless_RDB_Class** to serve as the parent classes for all the possible user-defined RDB class frames. The mapping specifies a *direct relationship* between a *database table* and a ROCK *RDB class*, where, in the simplest case, the RDB class has the same name as the table, each record in the database table is mapped to an instance of the RDB class, and each column in the table maps to an attribute slot in the class. Each instance of RDB gets the value from a column as the value of the corresponding attribute slot. As we can see, we are far from the generality and the flexibility of the mapping KB/DB provided by the Europa-Brücke system. Within this basic one-to-one-mapping framework, ROCK provides special system-slots for specifying some special options (*see* below), giving the developer more flexible control over both the table-to-class mapping and the column-to-slot mapping. The definition of **kb_RDB_Class** is given in Table 3.16. The definition of **kb_Contextless_RDB_Class** is identical except that this last class is a subclass of **kb_Contextless_Object**.

In Table 3.18, the system-defined slot **kb_getAllColumns** is used as follows. Supplying KB_TRUE as the value for this slot means that all columns of the RDB table are to be mapped into attribute slots. Attribute slots for the columns will then be created, and added to the RDB class as needed when the RDB class is compiled. Supplying KB_FALSE as the value on this slot specifies that only the attribute slots explicitly included *locally* in the RDB class are to be associated with columns in the database table; no inheritance is performed to find additional slots. The default value for the **kb_getAllColumns** slots of the user-defined RDB classes, inherited from **kb_RDB_Class**, is KB_FALSE. **kb_RDB_Lock** is a system-defined slot whose value identifies the type of locking mechanism that RDB will use to control the access to its tables: note that the data stored in RDB can be accessed by a number of applications simultaneously. This value will be used when the function **kb_StartRDBTransaction** (*see* below) begins an RDB transaction. The default is KB_DEFAULT_LOCK, which indicates that no explicit lock will be placed on the table. The message **kb_afterSelect** will be sent by the function **kb_SelectRDBRecords** (*see* below) after a record has been retrieved and an instance has been created; the message **kb_beforeCommit** is sent by the function **kb_CommitRDB** (*see* below) before an update or insert operation is performed on an RDB table for a given instance.

Table 3.18 System-defined parent class for all user-defined RDB classes

```
class_frame kb_RDB_Class
    {
            subclassOf: kb_Object;
            attributes:
                kb_RDBTableNames;
                kb_RDBKeyColumns;
                kb_getAllColumns = KB_FALSE;
                kb_RDB_Lock = KB_DEFAULT_LOCK;

            messages:
                kb_afterSelect;
                kb_beforeCommit;
    }
```

Table 3.19 represents a simple DB table for a part inventory; for each part, the part_number, description, quantity and price are stored in columns. The records in this table may be represented in a ROCK application as instances of an RDB class with the same name of the table. The columns in the table map to attribute slots declared for the class. Thus, the INVENTORY table can be represented in the knowledge base by the slot declarations and RDB class definition given in Table 3.20. Note that the 'key columns' are the set of columns in a table which together uniquely identify the row in a DB table which corresponds to an instance of the RDB class. Key columns are used to maintain a one-to-one correspondence between the records in a table and the instances of the corresponding class. Developers specify the key-column names for the DB table as values on the system-defined slot **kb_RDBKeyColumns**, *see* Table 3.18. Specification of key columns is mandatory for all DB tables to be accessed by ROCK.

Table 3.19 An RDB part inventory

PART_NUMBER	DESCRIPTION	QUANTITY	PRICE
ws12	toaster	7	39.95
px77	mixer	3	47.50
cb31	can opener	5	27.85

Table 3.20 Mapping the INVENTORY table to the KB

```
declare_attribute_slots:
    {
        single kb_STRING PART_NUMBER;
        single kb_STRING DESCRIPTION;
        single long      QUANTITY;
        single flot      PRICE;
    }
    class_frame INVENTORY
    {
        subclassOf: kb_RDB_Class;

        attributes:
          kB_RDBKeyColumns = 'PART_NUMBER';
          PART_NUMBER;
          DESCRIPTION;
          QUANTITY;
          PRICE;
    }
```

In the above example, we deal with a simple but very common style of RDB-to-ROCK mapping where the column names and types are the same as the attribute slot names and types, and all columns are mapped to attributes; therefore, the application developer can limit himself to supply only minimal information. Remembering the definition of **kb_RDB_Class** given above, he will be able to describe the entire mapping by supplying the reduced frame definition given in Table 3.19.

Table 3.21 Reduced frame definition

```
class_frame INVENTORY
    {
        subclassOf: kb_RDB_Class;

        attributes:
           kb_getAllColumns = KB_TRUE;
           kb_RDBKeyColumns = 'PART_NUMBER';
    }
```

When the RDB class is compiled by **kb_StartRDBTransaction**, ROCK assumes that the name of the RDB table is INVENTORY (which is the same as the name of the class). Since the value for the **kb_getAllColumns** slot is KB_TRUE, ROCK looks up the INVENTORY table definition in the RDB data dictionary, and then adds an attribute slot to the INVENTORY class for each column defined in the table. The names of the attribute slots are the same as the names of the corresponding RDB columns; when records are downloaded from INVENTORY, all of the table's columns are selected.

Data in the INVENTORY table can now be retrieved by a ROCK application (using the function **kb_SelectRDBRecords**) and converted into instances of the class **INVENTORY;** for example, records of Table 3.19 correspond to the instances of Table 3.22.

The **INVENTORY** class and its instances can be manipulated and reasoned about in the same manner as other frames. Modifications can be made to the values on the slots that are mapped from columns. If the application is permitted to write in the database table, the records in this table can be automatically updated to reflect the modifications to the instances.

The basic steps required to use the ROCK/RDB interface are as follows:

1. Define the RDB to ROCK mapping for each database table to be accessed; as already stated, a DB table may be mapped to only a single RDB class in the knowledge base. Minimally, this involves creating a class which is a subclass of the ROCK system-frame **kb_RDB_Class** (or **kb_Contexless_RDB_Class**), *see* Table 3.18, to be associated (with the same name) with that database table; the table name will be used to form the FROM/INTO clause that is used during SQL *SELECT*, *INSERT*, *UPDATE*, and *DELETE* commands. Some, more complex, options are:
   - the DB table name and the ROCK class name may be different;
   - the name of an attribute slot may be different from the name of the corresponding DB column;
   - the value type of an attribute slot may be different from the data type of the corresponding DB column: the application developer may supply conversion methods for translating data for a designated attribute slot;
   - a WHERE-clause in standard SQL syntax may be specified as an optional argument to the function **kb_SelectRDBRecords**: only the records in the DB table that are qualified by the WHERE-clause are downloaded to the knowledge base;
   - etc.
2. Call **kb_OpenRDB** to open the database that contains the table(s).
3. Call the function **kb_StartRDBTransaction** to begin a transaction. This function locks all necessary database tables and generates the appropriate commands to the DB to begin a transaction. The first time **kb_StartRDBTransaction** is called, the function also verifies that the RDB class definitions agree with the table definitions that are stored in the database, and

'compiles' the RDB classes (and any mapping information specified in attached slot-control classes). ROCK stores the mapping information in a quickly accessible internal format.

Table 3.22 Instances of the class (frame) INVENTORY

```
instance_frame (INVENTORY) : 0x1077ed40
    {
     instanceOf: INVENTORY

     attributes:
        PART_NUMBER = 'ws12';
        DESCRIPTION = 'toaster';
        QUANTiTY = 7;
        PRICE = 39.95;
     }

    instance_frame (INVENTORY) : 0x1077fe40
    {
     instanceOf: INVENTORY

     attributes:
        PART_NUMBER = 'px77';
        DESCRIPTION = 'mixer';
        QUANTITY = 3;
        PRICE = 47.50;
    }

    instance_frame (INVENTORY) : 0x1078ab40
    {
     instanceOf: INVENTORY

     attributes:
        PART_NUMBER = 'cb31';
        DESCRIPTION = 'can opener';
        QUANTITY = 5;
        PRICE = 27.85;
     }
```

4 Use the function **kb_SelectRDBRecords** to download records from the database table(s); the downloaded records are automatically converted into instances of their corresponding RDB classes. A default *SELECT* query is created for each RDB class when it is compiled. This default query downloads all records in a table. Only key columns and columns that correspond to attribute slots in the class, as specified in the mapping, are downloaded. For example, the default *SELECT* query, that selects all the records in the INVENTORY table of the example above, is:

```
SELECT PART_NUMBER,DESCRIPTION,QUANTITY,PRICE
FROM INVENTORY;
```

An optional WHERE clause can be supplied to the **kb_SelectRDBRecords** function to qualify the record selection. The WHERE clause is a string which satisfies the SQL syntax for WHERE clauses; column names, not slot names, must be used in the WHERE clause string. For example, for the following call to **kb_SelectRDBRecords**, only two of the records of Table 3.19 are downloaded; the 'can opener' record does not qualify.

```
kb_SelectRDBRecords (INVENTORY, 'PRICE' > 30.').
```

In response to that call, ROCK issues the following SQL query:

```
SELECT PART_NUMBER,DESCRIPTION,QUANTITY,PRICE
FROM INVENTORY WHERE PRICE > 30.;
```

5 Use the function **kb_CommitRDB** to update the records in the DB to reflect changes made to values on the slots that correspond to columns in the RDB instances. This step requires that the application is able to write to any database table(s) which are to be updated. ROCK builds and executes the necessary DB commands.

6 Repeat steps 3 to 5 as necessary.

7 Call **kb_CloseRDB** to close the database.

3.343 SPOKE

SPOKE is a KESE, written in C, which stems from the research project LORE at Alcatel Alsthom Recherche – *see* [Capo98] for a recent application of this KESE in the context of an Esprit European project. Its connection module to external databases is called SPOKE ACCESS.

The SPOKE model is based on the concepts of 'types' and 'properties'. Types are the support for classes, and properties for relationships among types. In this way, an object-oriented language is modelled by a type hierarchy (an inclusion graph) and by relational and functional properties which are defined on Cartesian products of types. Both types and properties are first-class objects, which means they are themselves objects. An abstract data type (ADT) encapsulates information that provides a representation for an object, such as a stack, and embodies operations for the manipulation of the object. The internal representation of the object represented by an ADT should be completely hidden from the user, and only the operations that implement manipulations of this representation are made available to the object user.

In SPOKE, a subtype inherits and may extend both the state representation (attributes) and the operations (methods) of its supertypes. Thus, in a first approach, a SPOKE programmer needs to specify only additional attributes or methods that characterize the new type of object. SPOKE allows multiple inheritance. Properties are SPOKE entities defining the behaviours attached to types of objects. In general, a property is characterized by i) its domain, a tuple of types on which it is defined; ii) its condition, the type of the value returned by the property; iii) its type, i.e. its behaviour (the way it is applied to its arguments, for example). The programming environment of SPOKE (SPOKE TOOLS) includes, among other things, the SPOKE interpreter, a set of user-friendly debugging tools (SPOKE DEBUG), a graphical interface (SPOKE WINDOWS+), a C/C++ interface, and SPOKE ENGINE. SPOKE ENGINE is a forward-chaining inference system with variables which, together with SPOKE, provides the user with all the power of an advanced rule-based system. SPOKE ENGINE is a SPOKE library; therefore, each SPOKE ENGINE object is a SPOKE object.

The purpose of SPOKE ACCESS is to provide an object vision of a standard relational data base, i.e. relational data can now be refined and manipulated in object terms as required by the object-oriented model of SPOKE. The SPOKE ACCESS query language allows the user to query and manipulate objects; it can perform all the operations on objects within the relational database environment by, as usual, generating and executing SQL commands addressed to the relational DBMS. Queries are performed via basic operators of relational algebra, and authorize operations on sets such as selection, projection, etc. Generation and sending of commands can be executed either i) automatically, by making use of calling procedures which are predefined by particular object classes in the SPOKE ACCESS library, *see* below; or ii) explicitly by the user.

The basic principle underlying SPOKE ACCESS is that of allowing the data from a relational diagram to be mapped to new object classes provided by the SPOKE ACCESS library. More exactly, these new object classes are the 'dbtype' classes, i.e.:

- 'dbdatabase', which allows us to establish the connection with one or more databases and to perform transactional operations;
- 'dbclass', the purpose of which is to define the data types of the particular relational (ORACLE, for example) database;
- 'dbattribute', used to define attributes whose values are stored in the DB;
- 'dbquery', which authorizes the execution of queries to manipulate large amounts of data or to store user-specific classes;
- 'dbsend', used to access the database in all the cases which are not taken into account by 'dbquery'.

The general architecture of SPOKE ACCESS is summarized in Figure 3.26. The use of SPOKE ACCESS implies the following steps:

- connection with the database;
- object-oriented definition of the database;
- beginning of the transaction;
- data manipulation by using objects;
- validation or cancellation of the modifications and end of the transaction;
- connection closed.

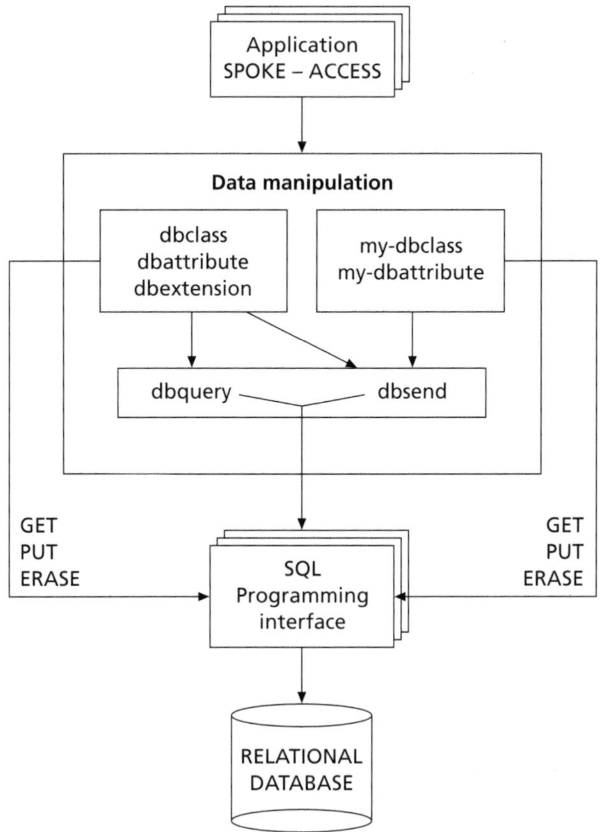

Figure 3.26 General architecture of SPOKE

3.35 The 'tight coupling' approach

This section concerns the implemented systems that are instances of the architecture of Figure 3.19(e), i.e. systems organized according to a tight coupling approach where the DBMS acts as a host to incorporate the ES functionalities, and which cannot be assimilated to some form of deductive database. As already stated, there are relatively few examples of this class of systems in the literature. We can suppose that this phenomenon is linked mainly with the difficulty of being able to make use of a common representation language, different from the predicate calculus, for both the AI and the DB components.

Of the two examples examined here, the first, ARCHES (American Red Cross Health Education System, *see* [Rupa91]), is relatively simple. It has been chosen, mainly, to show that: i) even the recent examples of implemented, really integrated systems do not seem able to deal with problems of too large size and/or complexity; ii) on the other hand, the need for some form of KBS capability can arise in the context of (apparently standard) common database problems. The second, more complex example of the 'tight coupling' approach described here is given by the KBase system, *see* [SohC89], [SohC92].

3.351 The American Red Cross Health Education System (ARCHES)

The goal of ARCHES is to automate the management of health education activities of the American Red Cross. More precisely, the Red Cross management needs to keep track of all the relevant entities in their health education system (instructors, courses, students, supplies, etc.). Therefore, they need to have easy access to instructors' and students' personal data (name, address, social security number, phone number, etc.). They also want to keep track of the instructorships held by the 'active' instructors at any time; an active instructor is someone who is currently authorized to teach one or many courses. Based on the evidence of sufficient teaching activity, the instructors are allowed to retain their instructorships ('reauthorized'), *see* below. The students are given a grade upon successfully finishing a course, and are issued certificates. Red Cross is a not-for-profit organization but charges the students a nominal fee to cover its costs. Most of the courses involve some material supplies: therefore an inventory must be maintained for these supply items, etc. Each Red Cross local chapter must submit specific information to the national chapter in Washington at the end of the year to receive 'fair money'. Fair money is the money allocated by the national chapter to the local chapters; this is proportional to their overall teaching activities. Therefore, the information supplied by the local chapters must include a breakdown of the courses taught by town number, course number, and course category number.

Based on these requirements, and on their (apparent) 'plain database' character, a first data model of the Red Cross application was established, with the aim of implementing this model by using a 'classical' DBMS approach. But this model soon proved to be inapplicable because of the reauthorization process. Reauthorization extends the expiration date for instructor's instructorships which are due to expire, based on the evidence of sufficient teaching activities; in this case, the expiration date is extended by the so-called 'reauthorization period'.

Evidence of 'sufficient teaching activity' is both time dependent and course dependent. With respect to time, for a particular instructorship the reauthorizing authority has to look as far back in time as the last date of reauthorization, which is done at the end of a calendar year. For the courses taught during this time span, it is necessary to look for the instructorship and course numbers, both of which are identified by a five-digit field: the first four characters are numbers and the fifth character is an 'I' for instructorship numbers and either a blank or an 'R' for course numbers – 'R' stands for a review course: for certain popular and relatively more important courses, the Red Cross offers review courses so that students can refresh their knowledge. For example, the 'advanced first aid' course has a course number equal to '3208'; '3208R' is the 'advanced first aid – review' course, and '3208I' is the 'advanced first aid' instructorship number. For some instructorships having a numerical root *xxxx*, teaching either a course with the same number *xxxx* or a review course with an 'R' attached to the same number can be a sufficient basis for reauthorization. In summary, for a majority of instructorships, teaching at least one course with the same numerical root or a review course within *n* number of years from the last date of reauthorization, where *n* is equal to the reauthorization period, is a sufficient basis for reauthorizing.

The above discussion leads to a general rule ('default rule'), given in Table 3.23. Once again, if this rule was applicable for all instructorships, it could have been programmed as procedural code in a conventional database-driven application without any need to consider ES techniques. However, there are a few instructorships that do not obey this rule and have additional rules for reauthorization. A further complicating factor concerning such instructorships is that the application of one of these additional rules may change the original instructorship. For example, a community basic life support instructor (instructorship = 3213I) may end up being reauthorized as an adult basic life support instructor (instructorship = 3212I) or an infant and child basic life support instructor (instructorship = 3210I) under special circumstances. Another important factor to consider is that these additional rules (called 'exception rules') themselves change over time and across the different local Red Cross chapters.

Table 3.23 Default rule for reauthorization in ARCHES

For	an instructorship *xxxx*I
If	the course(s) taught is/are *xxxx* (or *xxxx*R if applicable) within *n* years of reauthorization date
Then	reauthorize the instructor as *xxxx*I (i.e. extends the instructorship expiration date)

Table 3.24, extracted from [Rupa91: 416], lists examples of exception rules for particular instructorships. The 'default rule' has been explained before; the numbers '0.', '1.' ... on the left are 'rule priority numbers' that facilitate the ordering of exception rules. Let us consider, for example, the target instructorship 3214I in Table 3.20. If the exception rules were not applied in a prescribed order, it is possible that an instructor holding 3214I might end up being incorrectly reauthorized as 3210I. This can happen if the last exception rule is applied first instead of the first exception rule.

The above discussion demonstrated, eventually, the impossibility of developing the Red Cross application making use of database techniques only, and the necessity of performing (simple) reasoning processes making use of the particular expertise about the exception rules. Note that these rules, as shown in Table 3.20, are in the usual form of production rules.

The final ARCHES system has been developed primarily in the CLIPPER language, i.e. in a DBMS-driven environment. CLIPPER is a high-level compiled language similar to dBase; it uses the same data format as dBase and incorporates a semi-relational database manager. CLIPPER has been enhanced by using

OVERLAY, a Gambit Software product. OVERLAY allows a CLIPPER application to call practically any program from any point within the application and return to the same point.

With respect to the expert system functions needed to deal with the rules, i) the requirement proper to every integrated approach of making use of the same representation tools for both the AI and the DB components, and ii) the general DBMS context of ARCHES have led the developers to express such rules as data instead of procedures. This approach also allows the user to easily manage and manipulate (i.e. add, edit, delete, resequence, etc.) the rule knowledge, of course. The total rule set has been separated into two sets, where the first contains (implicitly) all the generic rules which could be derived as particular instances of the 'default rule' of Table 3.23. In reality, this set contains only the default rule since it is quite stable across all Red Cross chapters, and it has been hard-coded to yield the fastest possible execution time. The second set contains the 'exception rules', like those of Table 3.24: they have been stored in a ASCII (text) file, called an exception rules file, mainly to facilitate the processing and editing functions executed locally, in each chapter, by the Red Cross management personnel. The description of the inference engine operating on the two sets of rules is given in [Rupa91: 417–423].

Table 3.24 Exception rules in ARCHES

Target Instructorship is 3213I.
0. Activate the default rule first.
1. If the courses taught are 3210 and 3212 then reauthorize as 3213I.
2. If the course taught is 3212 then reauthorize as 3212I.
3. If the course taught is 3210 then reauthorize as 3110I.

Target Instructorship is 3214I.
0. Activate the default rule first.
1. If the course taught is 3213 then reauthorize as 3213I.
2. If the courses taught are 3210 and 3212 then reauthorize as 3213I.
3. If the course taught is 3212 then reauthorize as 3212I.
4. If the course taught is 3210 then reauthorize as 3210I.

Target Instructorship is 3305I.
0. Do not activate the default rule.
1. If the courses taught are 3304 or 3305 then reauthorize as 3305I.

Target Instructorship is 3430I.
0. Do not activate the default rule.
1. If the courses taught are:
   3400 or 3402 or 3403 or 3404 or 3405 or 3406 or 3411 or 3412 or
   3413 or 3414 or 3415 or 3415R

   Then reauthorize as 3430I.

3.352 KBase

The second example of the tight coupling approach examined here is KBase, which can be considered as an extension of a DBMS in the style of the popular dBase database system mentioned in the previous section; as with ARCHES, KBase has been built up using CLIPPER. The general aim of this system is to put at the user's disposal a reduced but powerful set of features for the development of KBSs, putting aside what the authors call the most 'exotic features' [SohC92: 416] of the usual AI software, but taking advantage of a total compatibility with a standard dBase environment.

KBase allows the user to build knowledge bases of objects, rules and user-defined functions; the knowledge base files are in dBase format. Each knowledge base, consisting of a collection of objects, rules and user-defined functions, corresponds to a KBase application – 'objects' are assumed as the basic representation paradigm for both 'knowledge' and 'data'. At any time during the development, a new base can be created, or an existing base can be renamed or deleted. The user can also switch to another knowledge base to be used through the rest of the session. An example of a data object – all the examples in this section are extracted from [SohC92] – is given in Table 3.25, in which '*concrete*' refers to another object with its own fields and values representing all the properties and characteristics of the concrete material.

Table 3.25 An example of a KBase data object

Editor for the PILED_FOUNDATION object	
Type	*:concrete*
Number	*:24*
Shape	*:square*
Size	*:305_mn*
Length	*:16_m*

Rules have three parts: the name, the predicate (which says when the rule should fire), and the action. Rules are separated into rule sets, each of which has a name for identification. An example of a rule is given in Table 3.26.

KBase emphasizes consistency in the user's and developer's interface. Editing a rule is similar to editing an object. This is made possible by the common way in which rules and data objects are represented in KBase using the dBase language. The user can choose 'Edit' under the 'Rules' menu. From a selected rule set, KBase will ask for the rule to edit. Editing, adding, deleting, renaming, duplicating, clearing, and flushing rules are similar to those same operations for data objects. The rules in a rule set are fired in the unspecified order as displayed in the rule set.

Table 3.26 An example of a KBase rule

Editor for rule INSTALL_PILE

RULE SET: PILED_FOUNDATION

IF:	*(GET('Type','pile') = 'concrete' .OR. GET('Type', 'pile') = 'steel') .AND. GETN('Length','pile')< = 20_m .AND. GET('Type','soil') = 'loose' .OR. GET('Type','soil') = 'medium')*
THEN:	*PROMPT('You may install the piles as a single piece.')*

As already stated, KBase uses the dBase programming language in its code: the user can, therefore, use the same commands and functions in dBase to build additional user functions. A 'function' is like an object with the following fixed set of fields: 'Parameters', 'Private', 'Body', and 'Return'. 'Parameters' contains the arguments (values) passed to the called function. 'Private' is the declaration of local variables used in the body of the function. 'Body' contains a series of dBase commands, and other functions to be executed when the function is called. The function returns the value of the expression or variable in the 'Return' field. Editing a function is like editing an object – *see* the example in Table 3.27. In this example, 'install_pile_activity' is passed 'crew_size' and 'install_pile' as arguments. Its body then computes 'activity_duration', which is declared as a local variable. If 'activity_duration' is positive, 'install_pile_activity' returns the number of piles to be installed divided by 'activity_duration'. Otherwise, it returns 0.

Table 3.27 An example of a KBase function

Editor for the INSTALL_PILE_ACTIVITY function

PARAMETERS	*: crew_size, install_pile*
PRIVATE	*: activity_duration*
BODY	*: activity_duration = GETN('crew_size,install_pile) *GETN('efficiency',crew_size)*
RETURN	*: IF(activity_duration>0, GETN('Number', 'pile')/ activity_duration, 0)*

With user-defined functions and a comprehensive function library, the user can considerably enrich the knowledge-base environment. Rules can be made more powerful because they can make use of arbitrary Boolean combinations of functions, and execute complex functions with their action sides. For example, the library function 'QUERY' can be used in a KBase application to ask the user about unknowns in the system; both menu-based and form-based interfaces can be integrated in the query.

Another example is the library function 'INFER'. This system-provided function takes two arguments: i) a rule set to consider; and ii) a logical expression that describes the goal. 'INFER' runs all the rules in the rule set until the goal is achieved or it is unachievable, i.e. no rule in the rule set applies or, if any applies, it cannot be of help. For instance, in Table 3.28 the function call runs over all the rules in the rule set named 'Piled_foundation'. The goal expression that is considered requires that the 'activities' (*see* below, the CICONSA application) of installing a piled-foundation be known, as well as the duration and precedence of each of these activities. In this example, the 'INFER' function may be called, for example, by a rule that can detect when a building should have a piled-foundation and, when fired, calls 'INFER' to find the details of installing the foundation.

Table 3.28 An example of the KBase, system-provided, INFER function in use

```
INFER('Piled_foundation',
'KNOWN('Activities','foundation').AND
KNOWN('Duration','activities').AND.KNOWN-
('Precedence','activities')')
```

While it may be generally sufficient to build customized functions in the KBase programming language, KBase has an open architecture that allows integration with user-written C and/or assembler code.

Figure 3.26 shows the general architecture of CICONSA, a KBS application developed in a database environment that has been built on top of the KBase system. CICONSA attempts to emulate the behaviour of a scheduling expert who sets up building construction schedules. CICONSA, through an end-user interface, interactively asks for all the necessary factual inputs, pre-processes this information, and then generates an output that can be utilized for scheduling. Scheduling can be of two types: 'rough scheduling' and 'detailed scheduling'. A rough schedule is intended for quick estimates of the duration of activities (during tendering, for example), while a detailed one is for more accurate models and estimates (for example, during construction). CICONSA is coupled to a commercial project management system, HORNET, by UK company Claremont Controls Ltd via the dBase III Plus DBMS.

CICONSA first generates the description of the construction activities, along with their estimated duration and precedence. The output is then passed out to HORNET for the scheduling process, taking full advantage of its established algorithms and report forms. The DBase III Plus database system provides all the necessary common interface for the transfer and storage of information between the constituent components in the integrated system. This thus provides easy access for storage and retrieval of data, such as the crew's productivity data, etc., stored in dBase files/tables. Results of consultations with the application system can also be stored in dBase files: these can be read by HORNET via its masks and instruction files.

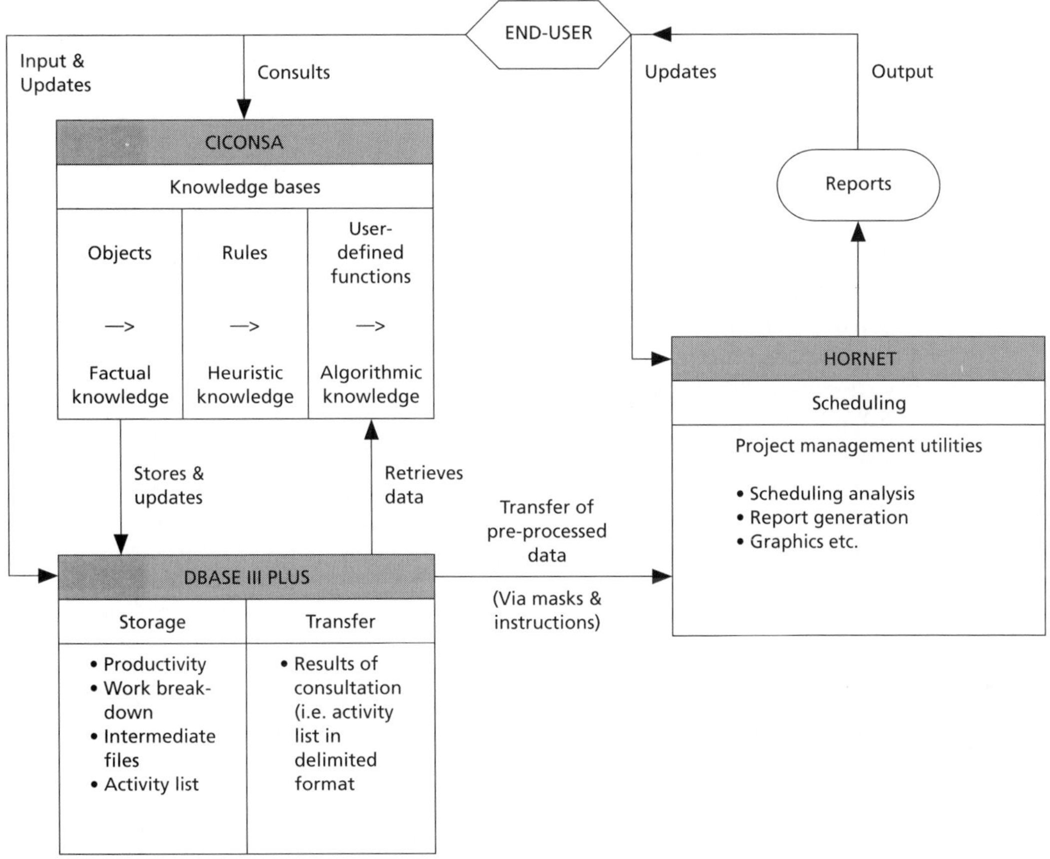

Figure 3.27 General architecture of CICONSA, a KBase application

In CICONSA, 'activities' are defined as the result of the application of an action element such as '***excavate***', '***form***', '***rebar***', '***place***' (meaning placing concrete), '***cure***', etc. to an 'object' element such as '***column_footing***', '***ground_beam***', '***ground_slab***', etc. The action elements are represented by system-defined functions – *see* Table 3.27 and Figure 3.27. For example, an activity '***<place_column_footing>***' is the action of placing concrete to the object '***<column_footing>***'. Description of all the activities leading to the completion of a component can thus be defined.

Based on the end-user's input during the interactive consultation, CICONSA's inference engine can perform activity definitions and duration estimations for all the components. Inference is achieved via manipulation of the 'static' factual knowledge stored in the object knowledge base, using the production-rules and the user-defined functions stored in the 'active' knowledge base. The 'static' knowledge refers to the information required to describe the physical system and/or the assumed states addressed in a problem, such as the physical components of a building and their dimensions and geometry. On the other hand, 'active' knowledge such as the choice of construction methods in concreting, and gang size, form the procedural knowledge that instructs the system to change the state of the problem considered.

3.36 Conclusion

In this section we have examined several architectural solutions for the problem of coupling knowledge-based systems with database management systems. We have seen that when the KBS system was an 'advanced' one – i.e. when its knowledge representation system was more complex than a simple 'if–then' rule system – the coupling always involved particularly complex solutions, not very well adapted to the development of practical, commercial products. On the contrary, all the 'usual' ES tools are now endowed with some possibilities of extracting information from a database making use, mainly, of variants of the 'data dictionary' technique and of an architecture in the Figure 3.19 (b) style ('extending a KBS with components proper to a DBMS').

3.4 Advanced solutions

3.41 Introduction

The architectural solutions examined in this section can be considered in some ways as a generalization of the 'tight coupling' approach examined in the previous section. They share, in general, the following characteristics:

- as in the tight solutions, only one environment exists: in this case, a 'pure' knowledge-based system environment. The dichotomy DB/KBS, with its sequel of mismatch problems, is now ignored;
- in this environment, the sole 'data model' to be used is some sort of (AI) knowledge representation language – this is normally employed to express both the proper data and the rules;
- the reasoning (inferencing) aspects now acquire very important status – all sorts of inference techniques are used in these systems, the ordinary 'deductive' ones, but also, for example, 'abductive' techniques (abductive reasoning

is based on inferences of the type 'If A implies B and B has been observed, hypothesize A', that are particularly useful for dealing with interpretation tasks such as diagnostics);

- moreover, the (unique) KBS environment should be able to supply the same kinds of services (i.e. persistency, efficiency, security, concurrent access, etc.) that are usually provided by the DBMS systems over large sets of information – in this respect *see*, however, Section 3.47.

Solutions in this style have sometimes been described as examples of an 'integral AI approach' to the construction of intelligent database systems (IDBSs). For simplicity's sake, we will adopt this terminology, speaking of integral (artificial intelligence) approach systems, or IASs – in short, we could define the integral approach as the attempt to use some kind of artificial intelligence system to deal *directly*, in a DBMS style, with large quantities of persistent information. The field is relatively new, and no predominant, theoretical paradigm has emerged until now; the only way to apprehend its main characteristics is, therefore, to examine in some depth some representative examples of IAS. In Section 3.42, we will introduce first some general conceptual tools that have been proposed for interacting with this sort of system; we will conclude the section by outlining the description logics version of the integral solution approach. In Section 3.43, we will illustrate TELOS, a language (and an IAS system) developed at the University of Toronto; the TELOS results are particularly important because they represent one of the (rare) implemented examples of IAS provided with a management system having the same potentialities of a DBMS. In Section 3.44, we will discuss a highly controversial issue, the system CYC by Douglas Lenat and R.V. Guha. Section 3.45 will explore some additional suggestions for setting up an integral solution which come from conceptual graphs and from a specialized language (NKRL) for dealing with 'narrative' texts. Section 3.46 will describe the so-called 'lexical' approaches to the construction of large knowledge bases – even if, in reality, these systems are not really characterized by all the properties evoked at the beginning of this section, their novelty, and the rupture they represent with respect to the traditional DBMS philosophy, can justify their presence in this section. Section 3.47 represents the conclusion.

3.42 A 'knowledge level' approach to the interaction with an IAS

In a 'traditional' DBMS, the core conceptual element is represented by the particular data model supported, which determines exactly both the data structures in which to store the information to be collected and the operations needed to work on that particular information. In a KBS, it is relatively easy to establish a correspondence between the formal and expressive properties of the particular AI knowledge representation language chosen and the 'traditional' data structure aspects. On the contrary, a well-known characteristic of KBSs is that the operational side of these systems is, very often, only loosely defined. Frequently, users have a very imprecise idea of what can logically follow from the AI representation language they use – the interpretation of links in semantic nets, or of slots in frames, is not always well defined – and, therefore, a very imprecise idea of what they are getting from the system, and how.

3.421 *Introducing the ASK and TELL operations*

A situation like this is, obviously, unacceptable if the new generations of information systems must be capable of dealing with important quantities of information with the same degree of security and accuracy that characterize the ordinary DBMSs. Levesque and Brachman (*see* [Leve86]) have therefore proposed a methodology – now adopted to some extent in the IAS field – for defining, in a precise way, all the possible interactions of a user with an IAS through a very reduced set of operations. This methodology is therefore similar in intent and approach to the formal specifications techniques.

According to this methodology, an IAS is no longer characterized according to the formal properties of the particular AI language used but functionally, in terms of what the system knows about the world in which it is embedded and, therefore, in terms of what it can be asked or told about the domain. This represents a typical 'knowledge level' approach to the interaction problem, according to the well-known differentiation introduced by Newell between knowledge and symbol level [Newe82]. More precisely, at the knowledge level, the knowledge base (KB) of an IAS 'is treated as an abstract data type that interacts with a user or system through a small set of operations' [Leve86: 14]; the complete functionality of the KB is defined only in terms of these operations. In contrast, the symbol level will concern a particular implementation of the algorithms for carrying out the operations defined at the knowledge level, in conformity with the semantics of the chosen representation language. The aim of this approach is to free the user from any need to know the details of the AI data structures to be manipulated, and to allow him to concentrate on what the IAS knows and what follows from what it knows. Moreover, the user is isolated from any decision concerning the implementation design: he cannot, therefore, rely on the data structures to encode knowledge in a way contrary to the intentions of the system designers. As Brachman and his colleagues put it, '... in other words, incidental properties of an implementation that are not part of the defined interface (such as the current number of concepts below another in a taxonomy or the current number of sentences in a theory) cannot be used as an alternate method of representing knowledge' [BracR85e: 424].

Levesque and Brachman introduce two basic operations which define functionally – i.e. specifying what the behaviour should be, but without saying how it should be implemented – the interactions with the KB of an IAS. They are:

- an 'ASK' operation, roughly analogous to the 'query' operations in a DBMS, which is used to ask the KB questions about some application domain; and
- a 'TELL' operation, analogous to the 'update' operations in a DBMS, which is used to inform the KB about that particular domain.

A first, intuitive definition of ASK and TELL is given in Table 3.29. The first expression says that we can discover answers to questions by using knowledge; the second, that knowledge can be augmented by asserting new information. Levesque and Brachman affirm that there are, presumably, a large number of ASK and TELL operations, corresponding to the multiple ways knowledge can be accessed and acquired. Moreover, many other operations of this type can also be functionally defined, including CREATE, FORGET, ASSUME, etc., *see also* the next sections. ASK and TELL describe, however, the basic modalities of the interaction.

Table 3.29 Intuitive definition of ASK and TELL

ASK: KNOWLEDGE $\times$ QUERY $\rightarrow$ ANSWER {yes, no, unknown}

TELL: KNOWLEDGE $\times$ ASSERTION $\rightarrow$ KNOWLEDGE

3.422 *A more formal account of ASK and TELL*

To give a formal definition of the two operations, it is necessary, as usual, to make a certain number of assumptions and simplifications. For example, one of the assumptions says that what a KB is told or asked by the user is always about the external world (external to the user). A very important simplification consists in taking into consideration only the 'yes/no questions'. This allows us to assume that the same (logical) language can be used for both the queries and the assertions: for the former, we ask the KB of an IAS to recognize whether the particular query is true, for the latter, we tell the KB that a particular assertion is true. Using this simplification, ASK now takes a sentence and a KB and returns 'yes' or 'no'. Analogously, TELL takes a sentence and a KB and returns a new KB that knows that the sentence is true. The simple definition of Table 3.29 can now be modified as in Table 3.30. In this figure, α is a sentence, i.e. a closed wff (well-formed formula) of the language; w is a *truth valuation*, i.e. any mapping from sentences to truth-values.

Table 3.30 Formal definition of ASK and TELL

$$\text{ASK}[\alpha,\text{KB}] = \begin{cases} \textit{yes}, \text{ if for each } w \text{ in KB, } w(\alpha) = \textit{true}, \\ \textit{no}, \text{ otherwise.} \end{cases}$$

$$\text{TELL}[\alpha,\text{KB}] = \text{KB} \cap \{w \mid w(\alpha) = \text{true}\}.$$

Given the above definition, there are a number of important properties that can be proved about the two operators. For example, as a consequence of the fact that TELL works monotonically – anything that is believed continues to be believed as new events or new definitions emerge – we can show that ASK and TELL satisfy the relationship of Table 3.31. A complete formal discussion can be found in [Leve86]. We can note that the 'declarative' type of definition of the behaviour of an interface given in Table 3.30 – nothing is said about a particular type of implementation of the KB, and there is no symbol-level description of anything like a program – has sometimes been criticized because it cannot guarantee the same range of concrete capabilities offered by its procedural counterparts, *see* [Karp95], for example.

Table 3.31 Monotonicity of TELL

ASK[α, TELL(α, KB)] = *yes*

3.423 *An example*

In [Leve86], Levesque and Brachman present two examples of how it is possible, thanks to the approach illustrated in the previous subsections, to use an AI knowledge representation language to build up an IAS having an operational behaviour as well defined as that of a 'usual' DBMS. The AI languages used here are KRYPTON ([BracR83b], [BracR85c], [BracR85e]), one of the earliest 'terminological' or 'description logics' languages (*see* Section 3.132), and a modal language (KL), which allows an interaction with the KB which is more expressive than that which could be achieved by making use of an ordinary first-order language. We will limit ourselves to a (simplified) exposition of the KRYPTON example.

In KRYPTON, the TBox language is a sort of special-purpose, frame-based language very similar to that of KL-ONE [BracR85d], *see* again Section 3.132; the ABox language is a standard first-order language, where the sentence-forming operators are the usual logic operators Not, Or, ThereExists, etc. We recall here that, in a DL language, the TBox is used to establish taxonomies of structured terms (concepts) and to answer questions about the relationships ('subsumption') among these terms; the ABox allows assertions to be made and questions to be answered about the world by using statements concerning the terms of the TBox. The connection ABox-TBox is assured in KRYPTON by the fact that the non-logic terms used in the ABox are not mere atoms but TBox terms regularly defined in the TBox component of KRYPTON. The mapping between these ABox terms and their TBox definitions is maintained by a 'symbol table', which is shared by the two components.

As usual in DLs, concepts and roles of KRYPTON are formed by combining or restricting other concepts and roles, and a set of operators is available for this purpose. For example, the language includes an operator, ConjGeneric ('conjoined generic'), that takes as arguments any number of concepts, and yields a concept corresponding to the conjunction of the arguments. In this way, a *bachelor_* can be defined by assigning it the 'description':

(**ConjGeneric** *man_ unmarried_person*)

where *man_* and *unmarried_person* are pre-existing concepts. Concepts can also be formed by restricting other concepts, making use of particular conditions imposed on their roles. For example, another KRYPTON operator is VRGeneric ('value-restricted generic'), whose arguments are two concepts *C* and *D* and a role R, and which returns a new concept corresponding to *C* where any filler of R is restricted to be an instance of *D*. Therefore, the expression

(**VRGeneric** *person_* Child *doctor_*)

defines 'a person all of whose children are doctors', Child being the role. A third operator is RoleChain. The expression

```
(RoleChain Child Child)
```

stands for the definition of the new role Grandchild. These are the three operators formally defined in [Leve86]; in other papers on KRYPTON, such as [BracR83b], [BracR85e], additional operators are defined but, apparently, only these three have been fully implemented. The TBox terms are, as usual, organized taxonomically.

The general organization of a KRYPTON-based system is shown in Figure 3.28 derived, with some slight modifications, from [BracR83b] and [BracR85e]. The usual, graphical KL-ONE conventions for 'concepts' and 'roles' are used in this figure. With respect to the interrogation of a KRYPTON KB, the user has at his disposal a fixed set of operations over the TBox and ABox languages, and all the interactions between the user and the system are mediated by these operations. These query operations include both TELL operations, used to augment the KB, and ASK operations, used to extract information; in the two cases, they can concern either the terminological (TBox) or assertional (ABox) components.

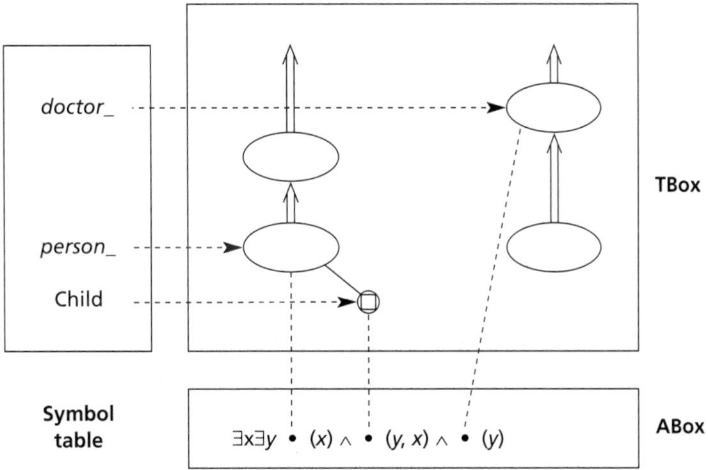

Figure 3.28 General architectural of KRYPTON

Taking into account the restriction to 'yes/no questions' introduced in the previous section, we can say that, from an assertional point of view, TELL takes a sentence written in the ABox language and asserts that it is true, i.e. it changes the knowledge base into a new one whose theory of the world implies this sentence. ASK takes an assertional sentence and asks if it is true; the result is determined on the basis of both the theory asserted by the KB and the vocabulary used in the sentence (the latter is defined in the TBox). Therefore, in an assertional context, the two operations coincide with the formal definitions given in Table 3.28; some slight modifications were introduced in [Leve86] to allow the implementation of the subsumption operations.

Some new operations are defined for the TBox. In this context, the equivalent of TELL is DEFINE, which takes a TBox symbol, like *bachelor_* or Grandchild, and a TBox expression like those mentioned before, and tells KRYPTON's KB that the symbol is defined by that particular 'description'. The result of DEFINE boils down, therefore, to transforming the TBox component of the KB into a new one whose vocabulary includes the symbol defined by a particular description. With respect to the ASK operations, we will mention here two of them which are of particular importance. The first is SUBSUMES which, as usual, takes two TBox terms (two descriptions) and returns 'yes' or 'no' according to whether the first subsumes the second. Another important operation is DISJOINT, which takes two TBox terms and returns 'yes' if one TBox term is conceptually disjoint from the second. We give, in Table 3.32, a (very schematic) definition of the three operations introduced in this paragraph, which are derived from the definitions given in [BracR83b], [BracR85e] – more details about 'subsumption' and the 'disjunction text' can be found in Section 3.132.

Table 3.32 Schematic definition of the TBox operations

DEFINE: KB × SYMBOL × TERM → KB
By symbol, *we mean now the* term: *(see the corresponding description)*

SUBSUMES: KB × TERM × TERM → {yes, no}
Does term_1 *subsume* term_2 ?

DISJOINT: KB × TERM × TERM → {yes, no}
Is term_1 *disjoint from* term_2 ?

Additional ASK operations can be introduced; in particular, operations that are not limited to a 'yes/no' answer, *see* again [Leve86]. Given the definitions of Table 3.32, there is an important number of KRYPTON's properties that can be formally proved – *see* the two examples of Table 3.33 ([Leve86: 30]) whose meaning is intuitively evident.

Table 3.33 Schematic definition of the TBox operations

SUBSUMES[p_1, (**ConjGeneric** p_1 p_2), KB)] = yes (for any KB)

ASK[$\forall x$ *man*(x) $\supset$ *person*(x),
DEFINE[*man*, (**VRGeneric** *person sex male*), KB]] = yes (for any KB)

3.424 Description logics proposals for the set-up of an IAS

Even if the TELL/ASK approach is very general, and it is not linked with a particular knowledge representation theory, its history, and the personal history of its authors, Brachman and Levesque, is strictly intermixed with that of the terminological (DL) languages. Therefore, it is reasonable to conclude the present section with some information about the DL proposals in the IAS domain.

Accessing a DBMS from a DL system

These proposals have been limited, originally, to the 'classical' problem of accessing a database from a DL system in a way transparent to the user – *see*, in Sections 3.2 and 3.3, the analogous proposals developed in a 'deductive' and in a 'coupling' framework.

In this context, we can mention here, firstly, the solutions proposed in [Borg93] and [Deva93]. In these, primitive concepts and roles in the DL system are made to correspond, respectively, to unary and binary tables in a database; a 'loose coupling' approach is then used, based, as usual, on the pre-loading of data from the DB into the DL system before these data (equivalent to TBox individuals) can be used for the reasoning operations. The novelty of the approach is that, whenever possible, the process of making inferences about the DB individuals is executed directly during the pre-loading operations, i.e. the inference process is replaced by a collection of queries directed to the relational DB that perform the inferences 'in bulk', and can then add directly the results to the DB without further processing. For example, for each class (concept) description, a query is issued that retrieves exactly in the DB the instances in that class, therefore avoiding the activation of the classification (subsumption) inferences, *see* [Borg93: 220]. The task of optimizing inference execution is left to the DBMS, and the DL system can thus deal with comparatively fewer cases where complex reasoning is needed.

Bresciani, on the contrary, makes use of a 'tight coupling' approach (implying, therefore, an 'on demand' access) to establish a connection between the DL system and the DBMS, *see* [Bres94], [Bres95]. The coupling principle adopted here consists of considering the external DB as a third DL component, called DBox (where 'D' stands for 'data'), which is then seen as an extension of the usual ABox of the DL system: given that Bresciani's implementation relies, in fact, on a DBMS with SQL, the DBox is represented in practice by a relational DB, and queries to the DBox can be expressed in SQL. The mapping between the TBox and the DBox is realized in two steps. First, a partial mapping *PM* is given, that concerns the correspondence between primitive terms (primitive concepts) of the TBox and the tables of the DBox. The TBox terms for which *PM* is defined are called $\mathcal{D}$-terms. Given this mapping, the non-primitive terms of the TBox can also then be recursively mapped into views of the DB using *PM*. Problems can arise, however, in the presence of (expanded) definitions ('descriptions') of non-primitive terms containing both $\mathcal{D}$-terms and non-$\mathcal{D}$-terms given that, in this case, the non-primitive term is mapped into a DBox view that does not contain all the instances of this term. Bresciani introduces the following constraints (*see*, by contrast, in Section 3.3, the generality of the Europe-Brücke approach):

1. Every table in the DBox must correspond to one primitively defined term in the TBox, called a '$\mathcal{D}$-term'. To avoid the necessity of extensive consistency checking, $\mathcal{D}$-terms must be 'leaf' terms in the TBox hierarchy, i.e. terms which cannot be specialized by any other TBox term.
2. The expanded definitions of non-primitively defined terms of the TBox must contain either only $\mathcal{D}$-terms, or no $\mathcal{D}$-terms at all.

Giving the above restrictions, and calling $\mathcal{T}$ (terminology) the set of all the terms (concepts) included in the TBox, Bresciani can define the partial mapping as:

$$PM: \mathcal{PT} \rightarrow \mathcal{DB}_{table}$$

where $\mathcal{PT}$ is the set of primitive terms in $\mathcal{T}$, and $\mathcal{DB}_{table}$ is the set of tables in the database. As stated above, the views corresponding to non-primitive concepts can be built via a recursive partial mapping, *RM*:

$$RM: \mathcal{T} \rightarrow \mathcal{DB}_{table} \cup \mathcal{DB}_{views}$$

where $\mathcal{DB}_{views}$ is the virtual set of views in the DB. In practice, *RM* maps DL descriptions into the corresponding SQL-expressions.

As an example, and assuming also that i) the concepts, as in Borgida and Brachman above, are mapped into unary tables with one column called `lft`, and roles into binary tables with two columns called `lft` and `rgt`, and ii) that non-primitively defined terms which contain $\mathcal{D}$-terms in their expanded definitions are constructed using only the DL operators **and** and **some** (*see* Section 3.132), a definition of the recursive mapping *RM* can be given as in Table 3.34. *see* [Bres95].

In this table, *C* and *D* stand for names of generic terms or descriptions; R is the name of an atomic role in $\mathcal{T}$; *T* is the name of an atomic (primitive) term in $\mathcal{T}$. The last part of the definition in Table 3.34 allows all the tables and views that correspond to terms subsumed by *T* to be taken into account, whatever *T* may be. Note that *M* is, in general, a function that returns the (possibly empty) set of tables/views which are necessary to retrieve all the instances of a given concept or all the pairs linked with a given role from the DB. Its definition is then:

$$M: \mathcal{T} \rightarrow 2^{DB}{}_{table} \cup DB_{views},$$

and, for a given concept *T*:

$$M(T) = \{RM(x) \mid x \in subs(T) \wedge PM(x) \text{ is defined}\}$$

where *subs*(*T*) is the set of the terms classified under *T* in $\mathcal{T}$.

The definition of *RM* given in Table 3.34 is used to generate and answer (SQL) queries to a general knowledge base including the TBox, ABox and DBox – the details can be found in ([Bres94], [Bres95]). In spite of its limitations – some of the constraints imposed above can, however, be released, *see* again Bresciani's papers – this technique allows the execution of more complex queries than the simple asking for instances of concepts as in Borgida and Brachman's case: for example, queries such as $C(x) \wedge R(x, y) \wedge D(y)$, including roles, are now possible.

Table 3.34 Definition of the recursive partial mapping *RM*

RM((**and** *C D*)) =

```
    SELECT DISTINCT   lft
    FROM              RM(C), RM(D)
    WHERE             RM(C).lft=RM(D).lft
```

if both *RM*(*C*) and *RM*(*D*) are defined ;

RM((some R *D*)) =

```
    SELECT DISTINCT   lft
    FROM              RM(R)
    WHERE             RM(R).rgt IN RM(D)
```

if both *RM*(R) and *RM*(*D*) are defined ;

RM(*T*) = *PM*(*T*)

if *PM*(*T*) is defined ;

```
RM(T) = SELECT DISTINCT   *
        FROM              T1
        UNION
        :
        .
        SELECT DISTINCT   *
        FROM              Tn
```

if *M*(*T*) = {*T*1, ...,*Tn* }, and $n > 0$.

The KRDB workshops

Going beyond the classical problem of the KBS/DB connection, the discussion about the relationships between the DL and DBMS worlds has been quickly enlarged to more ambitious targets, such as the creation of an entirely new generation of information systems. This quantum leap has been fostered by the organization of a series of international yearly workshops on the theme 'knowledge representation meets databases' that, at least in the beginning, have been largely devoted to the discussion of DL topics. However, as a confirmation of a decreasing interest in DLs in recent years, the DL theme was absent from the 1998 workshop, *see* [Borg98]. The first two workshops were held at the German Conference of Computer Science in 1994 and 1995 ([Baad94], [Baad95]). The rest were organized in conjunction with various AI conferences (KRBD'96, Budapest, Hungary, in conjunction with ECAI'96) or DB conferences (for example KRDB'97, Athens, Greece, in conjunction with VLDB'97). KRDB'99 was held in Linkoeping (Sweden) as an affiliate event of the 1999 International Conference on Artificial Intelligence (IJCAI). The KRDB proceedings can be found on the Internet at the CEUR Workshop Proceedings site, *http://sunsite.informatik.rwth-aachen.de/Publications/CEUR-WS*.

The general framework of the description logics contributions presented at the KRDB workshops was the idea that DLs could be seen as very powerful 'data models' in themselves (for example, TBox languages can be used to set up complex database schemata), and as unifying formalisms that subsume and generalise many of the more recent knowledge-based representational tools proposed in the literature, such as the object-oriented, semantic and conceptual models. From a practical point of view, however, the different approaches are relatively heterogeneous, and no unified and coherent DL methodology for the construction of a complete IAS seems to have emerged.

In [Buch94], the authors propose a clear partition of the terminological component (TBox) into two separate components corresponding to the 'schema' and 'view' mechanisms of traditional DBMSs. The first component (schema) is concerned with the frame-like structures used to introduce primitive concepts and roles, the second (view) with the mechanisms allowing the definition of new concepts in terms of primitive ones by specifying necessary and sufficient conditions for concept membership. In [SchmA94], the author suggests the introduction of a 'semantic indexing' mechanism based on DLs. Instead of using indexing keys based on the values that can be linked with particular attributes of the object to be indexed as in the DB systems, the proposed mechanism is based on the idea of indexing a set of individuals using the set of 'indexing concepts' that subsume the individuals as their instances. Reimer and colleagues [Reim95] propose, classically, a mapping of FRM – a restricted form of DL – versus the object-oriented data model COCOON; the techniques used here are similar to those analyzed in Section 3.3 and concerning the mapping between DLs and existing, external relational DBs. Another proposal in the same style is included in [Kess96], where the authors describe the implementation of a DL system (C3L++), with limited expressive power, on top of an object-oriented DB. The interesting points of this proposal concern mainly the 'tight coupling' aspects of the approach, *see* Section 3.2; the integration between the KBS (DLs) and DBMS components is completely transparent for the user, who accesses only the DLs front-end. [Kand97] discusses the combination of DLs with deductive object-oriented databases in the framework of a computational linguistics problem; the work described here shares some similarities with CARIN [Levy96], a recent and well-publicized proposal for extending restricted DLs systems with Horn clauses. Some proposals concerning the use of DLs as querying languages have also been presented in the KRDB framework, for example, Beneventano, Bergamaschi and colleagues ([Bene94], [Berg95]) suggest a theoretical framework for using subsumption for the purpose of semantic query optimization.

We can conclude this subsection by mentioning the paper given by Klaus Schild at KRDB'94 [SchiK94]. In this, the authors remind us first of the well-known intractability of DLs, at least in terms of computational worst-case complexity. There is no algorithm which can decide whether a concept in KL-ONE, the father of all the DL languages, subsumes another or not. Moreover, in general there is no polynomial time algorithm which can decide, with respect to acyclic terminologies, whether a concept subsumes another one or not, except in the case of minimal DLs that comprise no primitive operators for structuring concepts and roles apart from concept conjunction and universal quantification over role names. Schild continues by outlining the main results of his thesis [SchiK95], which show that tractability – obviously desirable in a DB or KB context – can generally be obtained simply by eliminating any *incompleteness* from a DL knowledge repository. This is equivalent to saying that the 'open world assumption' normally considered in the DL should not be accepted in a DB/KB context (the open world assumption says that there can be true facts that are not contained in the KB, or that cannot be inferred from the actual data) – *see also* Hustadt's paper [Hust94] in the proceedings of KRDB'94. But a DL's knowledge base where all the incompleteness has been eliminated is equivalent, in practice, to a relational DB. On one hand, a result like this is very important because it certifies that DLs can be used as powerful but tractable query languages for relational DBs; on the other, it can raise some doubts about the real utility of complex tools such as DLs to improve only slightly on the expressive power of the 'usual' relational DBs.

3.43 TELOS, a language for implementing very large 'integral approach' systems

In this section we will describe the TELOS approach, one of the most complete and well-known proposals for building up real IASs – in [Kram91: 77], the authors declare that '... a long-term goal of this research is to develop knowledge base management systems capable of storing on the order of 10^6 facts'. The TELOS project – from the Greek word τε'λοζ meaning, among other things, 'aim, purpose'; the word 'teleology' has τε'λοζ as one of its roots – started in 1985 as part of an Esprit research project partially funded by the European Communities. It was launched by a group of researchers including Alex Borgida, John Mylopoulos and Yannis Vassiliou, and improved successively thanks to another Esprit-funded project, DAIDA. Several prototypes of TELOS-based systems have been realized, both Prolog-based (in Europe) and (Common-)LISP-based – for more details, *see* [Topa89], [Mylo90a], [Mylo90b], [Kram91], [Mylo91].

TELOS has been strongly influenced by three directions of research: i) an object-oriented style of coding, which permeates all the knowledge representation aspects; ii) the logic-based languages, that are used in TELOS for expressing deductive rules and integrity constraints; iii) an interval-based representation of time, used for handling temporal logic. We will examine these three fundamental aspects of the system in turn and will conclude this section by examining how the problem of efficiently implementing knowledge base management techniques has been dealt with in a TELOS context.

3.431 *The object-oriented knowledge representation language*

The TELOS representation language organizes the world in terms of classes and instances. These are collectively called *individuals* – they always refer to specific entities, concrete ones such as `Peter` or abstract ones such as `Person`, i.e. individuals can be both concepts or instances according to the standard artificial intelligence terminology introduced in Section 3.1. Individuals are one of the two kinds of primitive units used by TELOS, the second being the *attributes*. Attributes represent, mainly, binary relationships between entities.

From a structural point of view, there is no difference between individuals and attributes: attributes are treated as 'first-class citizens' [Mylo94] in TELOS. Individuals and attributes are both represented as *propositions*. In its most general form, a proposition is a 4-tuple, whose four components can themselves be propositions; the names of the components are 'source': `from(p)`, 'label': `label(p)`, 'destination': `to(p)` and 'duration': `when(p)`. The first three components specify a particular relationship between propositions (between individuals, for example); the fourth component represents the 'lifetime' of this relationship. Individuals are represented by self-referencing propositions `p` such that: `from(p) = to(p) = p`. Attributes are, therefore, non-individual propositions, such as the proposition: '[`Peter` (source), `employerOf` (label of the attribute), `Mary` (destination), `1995` (`duration`)]', meaning that: 'In 1995, Mary has been Peter's employee.' The individuals `Peter`, `Mary`, and `1995` are instances; the individual `employerOf` represents a class (a concept).

Propositions (individuals or attributes) are arranged along the three well-known dimensions introduced by Smith and Smith in a database context (*see* [SmitJ77]), namely aggregation, classification and generalization. Aggregation leads to structured objects consisting of collections of attributes having a common proposition, for example, an individual, as 'source'. The individual `Peter` can then be represented by the structured object (a set of propositions) represented in Table 3.35 – for simplicity's sake, the temporal dimension has been omitted, *see* Section 3.433.

Table 3.35 Aggregation in TELOS

```
{Peter, [Peter, age, 40], [Peter, homeAddress, '96 Hacker
Street'], [Peter, businessAddress, '54 Telos Blvd']}
```

Dealing with the classification dimension allows us to clarify the meaning in TELOS of notions such as 'class' and 'instance'. According to TELOS's philosophy – clearly derived from a database and object-oriented approach, *see* the discussion in Section 3.13 – each proposition is considered as an *instance* of one or more generic propositions, which play, therefore, the role of *classes*. This means that classes are themselves propositions, which are instances of other, more abstract, classes. If we consider two propositions, an individual like `Person`, and an attribute (an abstract relationship) like `[Person, address, GeographicLocation]` – which represents the notion of address relationship between persons and geographic locations – they are both classes that can have particular instances, i.e. particular individuals and particular relationships. The classification modalities of all the TELOS notions can now be made clear. Mylopoulos and his colleagues call 'tokens' the propositions having no instances, and which represent, therefore, concrete entities in the domain of discourse; 'simple classes' are the propositions having only tokens as instances; 'metaclasses' the propositions having only simple classes as instances; 'metametaclasses', and so on. With respect now to instantiation, the classes having structured objects as instances determine, obviously, the kind of attributes the latter can have and the properties they must satisfy. For example, by the fact of being an instance of Person, Peter will have attributes that are instances of [Person, address, GeographicLocation]. These attributes can have specific labels, such as homeAddress and businessAddress (*see* Table 3.35) but their values must be instances of GeographicLocation.

The last dimension, generalization, is defined in TELOS as orthogonal to the classification dimension, and is realized through ISA hierarchies admitting multiple parents, which leads to hierarchies which are directed acyclic graphs (DAGs) more than trees. We can remark that, in TELOS, inheritance is strict rather than default – this means that, for TELOS, if birds fly, so do the penguins.

Figure 3.29 (*see* [Mylo90b]) shows the relationships between the aggregation and classification dimensions in the TELOS representation language. We can note that, thanks to the unification of the notions of 'individuals' and 'attributes' under the form of propositions, the attributes (properties) are also characterized by the same type of hierarchical organization proper to the other entities of the system. A hierarchical organization of the properties – not strictly necessary, in a frame context for example – can be considered as a characteristic feature of some advanced knowledge representation systems, *see* DLs and the recent CODE4 ([Skuc95]).

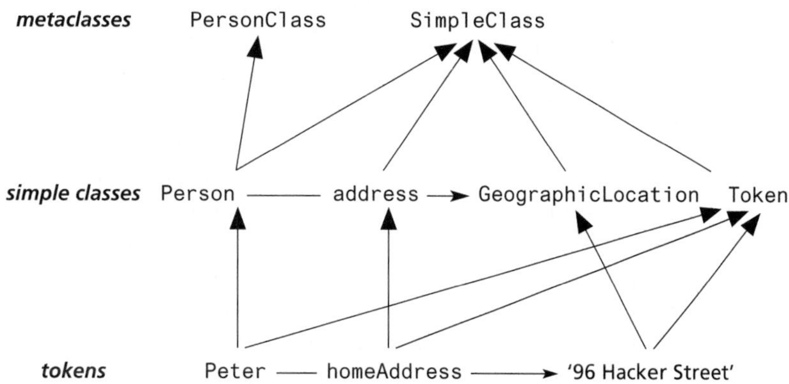

Figure 3.29 Tokens, classes and metaclasses in TELOS

Interaction with a TELOS knowledge base is accomplished through five commands. Two, **ASK** and **RETRIEVE**, pertain to the ASK category introduced in the previous sections; the other three, **TELL**, **UNTELL** and **RETELL**, pertain to the TELL category. **RETRIEVE** is a very efficient query operation that makes use only of limited built-in, predefined information, such as the structural information defined by the inheritance relationships. **ASK** utilizes, on the contrary, all the knowledge available, performing all the inferences that are admitted by the TELOS system of deductive rules. **TELL** is used, as usual, to add facts to the KB, while **UNTELL** is used to tell the knowledge base that a fact is no longer believed. The **RETELL** operations are particularly interesting because they correspond to the 'update' operations accomplished in a 'normal' DB context. They can be considered as a composition of the **UNTELL** and **TELL** operations. For example, through **RETELL**, the user can specify that Peter's address changed, instead of **UNTELL**ing explicitly the old address and then **TELL**ing the new one. The formal definition of (some of) these operations can be found in [Mylo90b: 34–35].

3.432 First-order logic tools

First-order logic tools are used in two ways in TELOS: i) to express integrity constraints, i.e. logical expressions that must be true all the time (such as a person's birth date must follow her parents' birth date by at least ten years); ii) to denote the deductions that can be made in a **TELOS** knowledge base. Integrity constraints and deductive rules are included in the descriptions of the TELOS entities as attributes, by means of two built-in attribute metaclasses labelled respectively `integrityConstraint` and `deductiveRule`.

For instance, in the framework of a possible TELOS-like information system for a hospital, we can define the class `Patient` as in Table 3.36, *see* [Mylo91]. This definition includes an integrity constraint stating that every medical record corresponds to a single patient, and a deductive rule that states that a patient's ward is the ward to which the name of the patient is attached. The special predicates **IN** and **ISA** are used to introduce, respectively, the 'instance' and 'taxonomic' relationships; please remember that, in TELOS, the 'classification' and the 'specialization/generalization' dimensions are orthogonal (*see* the previous subsection). The predicate **WITH** is used to introduce the attributes. Attribute metaclasses such as `necessary`, `single` and `association` are used to classify the attributes (`record`, `loc`, `room` ...) linked with the simple class `Patient`.

The (global) assertion sublanguage used in TELOS to express constraints and deductive rules – a typed, first-order language whose formulas are special **TELOS** propositions classified under the built-in class `AssertionClass` – comprises four special selectors. These allow the navigation through the graph structure defined by the mutual relationships among TELOS propositions, *see* Figure 3.29. The (annotated) definitions of these selectors are given in Table 3.37 – in this table, `from`, `label` and `to` refer, respectively, to the 'source', 'label' and 'destination' components of a proposition, as introduced in the previous subsection. Examples of use of the 'dot' selector appear in the constraint and the rule of Table 3.36. According to the definitions Table 3.37, `p.record` corresponds to the set of medical records linked with patient p through attributes which are instances of the attribute class `[Patient, record, MedicalRecord]` – as usual, we ignore, for the moment, the 'duration' component of propositions.

Table 3.36 Definition of the class 'Patient' in TELOS

```
TELL CLASS Patient
    IN      EntityClass
    ISA     Person
    WITH
            necessary, single
                   record: MedicalRecord
            association
                   loc: Ward
                   room: Room

                   ...
            integrityConstraint
                   $    (ForAll p, q/Patient, m/MedicalRecord)
                        [(m ∈ p.record ∧ m ∈ q.record ⇒ p = q]  $
            deductiveRule
                   $    (ForAll p/Patient
                        [x ∈ p.room.ward ⇒ x ∈ p.ward]
                   ...
                   END Patient
```

In Table 3.36 Patient is defined as an instance of EntityClass; therefore, an attribute metaclass such as single is defined as an ordinary attribute in EntityClass, with the proper constraints. Table 3.38 reproduces the integrity constraint atMostOne?, associated with single in the definition of EntityClass [Mylo91]. This constraint says that for any two instances (p and q) of an instance u of the single attribute metaclass, which is the value of the expression EntityClass!single (*see* Table 3.35), if p and q have the same source (i.e. the from component), they have the same destination (i.e. to(p) = to(q)).

Table 3.37 Selectors pertaining to the TELOS asserting sublanguage

x.p = { q | there exists an attribute v and an attribute class A such that v is an instance of A, from(v) = x, label(A) = p and to(v) = q} **(dot selector)**

x.p returns the set of all the 'destination' components of attributes that have x as source, that are instances of an attribute class having as source a class of which x is an instance, and also have label p.

x^p = { q | there exists an attribute v such that from(v) = x, label (v) = p and to(v) = q} **(hat selector)**

x^p returns the set of destinations of attributes having x as source and p as label.

x|p = { q | from(q) = x and there exists an attribute class A such that label (A) = p and x is an instance of ( ) from(A)} **(bar selector)**

x|p returns the set of attributes with source x that are instances of an attribute class where the source has x as instance and which has label p.

x!p = { q | from(q) = x and label(q) = p} **(exclamation mark selector)**

x!p returns the set of attributes with source x and label p.

3.433 *Representing temporal knowledge*

The existence of a temporal dimension allows the TELOS knowledge representation system to answer queries about its current state – i.e. about the system's current 'beliefs' – but also about the history of its states – i.e. about the past beliefs of the system.

Table 3.38 Definition of an integrity constraint for an attribute metaclass

```
TELL CLASS EntityClass
   IN      MetaClass
   WITH
                  ...
   integrityConstraint
          atMostOne? $ (ForAll u/EntityClass!single, p, q/Proposition)
          [(p in u ∧ q in u ∧ from(p) = from(q) ∧ when(p) overlaps
          when(q) ⇒ p = q] $
                  ...
END EntityClass
```

In TELOS, Mylopoulos and his colleagues make use of a model of time adapted from the well-known Allen's proposals, *see* [AlleJ83], [AlleJ84]. We can remark here that, generally speaking, the problem of building up some facilities for dealing with temporal data has received considerable attention within the database community, giving rise to a new research domain, the 'temporal databases' [Ozso95]. No commercial temporal database system seems to be actually in use, the reasons being, according to Snodgrass [Snod94a], the lack of a commonly accepted data model for temporal data and the inconsistency in the terminology. However, the temporal databases community is making a concerted effort to define some common infrastructures for dealing with temporal data [Piss94] resulting in an initial specification for a consensus temporal extension to SQL-92, which is called TSQL2 [Snod95]. For more information on this subject, *see* Section 4.2.

Returning to TELOS, Allen's representation of temporal phenomena is based on the notion of 'interval' – more exactly, of the possible relationships between two temporal intervals on the time axis. Allen identifies seven basic temporal relationships (after, before, during, end, equal, meet, start) to be used, with their inverses, to characterize the reciprocal position of two intervals, overlapping and partial overlapping included. The TELOS modifications concern, essentially, i) the possibility of also representing specific timestamps (i.e. usual dates) on the time axis, for example representing 'semi-infinite intervals' having specific dates as one endpoint (*see* Table 3.39 and also [Zarr98]); ii) restricting the power of the temporal assertions that can be told to the system.

Getting inspiration from one of the examples of [Mylo90b], we can now show how temporal information can be added to the assertions that are inserted in a TELOS knowledge base. In Table 3.39 we give the description of the token `telos` that we will consider as an instance of the class Manual during an unbounded ('semi-infinite') time interval starting October 1992. This manual has `Peter` as its first author for a period that coincides with the above interval; `Mary` was involved in the preparation of the manual from January 1993, while `Bruce` has worked on this manual for some time before May 1993, and we are now unable to supply any further detail. The attribute proposition (binary relationships) involving `telos` and `Peter` is: `[telos, firstAuthor, Peter, 1992/10..*]`; as already stated in Section 3.431, the 'duration' component of a proposition `p` can be accessed using the operator `when(p)`.

Table 3.39 Temporal data in TELOS

```
TELL TOKEN telos
   IN     Manual (at 1992/10..*)
   WITH
          author
              firstAuthor: Peter (at 1992/10..*)
                         : Mary (at 1993/1..*)
                         : Bruce (before 1993/5)
          title
              : 'The Final and Definitive Telos Report'
END telos
```

From this example, the nature of the restrictions introduced by Mylopoulos and his colleagues with respect to the Allen's model now becomes more evident. These restrictions consist essentially of allowing a *single* temporal relationship (interval) to appear in each of the temporal components of a given definition, while Allen's algebra had been conceived to represent the relationships between *two* intervals. To justify this choice – *see* again [Zarr98] for a similar approach – Mylopoulos mentions a result by Vilain and Kautz [Vila86], showing that verifying the consistency of a network of temporal relations represented according to the Allen's algebra is NP-hard.

Using this type of mechanism, TELOS is able to represent two sorts of time, the 'historical time' and the 'belief time': at least in principle, every TELOS relationship has two time intervals associated with it, the first reserved to the historical time and the second to the belief time. The time interval associated with the historical time represents the time during which these facts are true in a given application domain. The modalities of use of the belief time interval are linked with that of the commands **TELL**, **UNTELL** and **RETELL**. The belief time begins when a given fact is asserted (**TELL**) and ends at the earlier of i) the present time; ii) the time at which the knowledge base was told that the fact was no longer true (**UNTELL**, **RETELL**, 'belief revision'). All belief time intervals are assumed to be semi-infinite until the system is informed otherwise.

The differentiation between 'historical time' and 'belief time' is TELOS's answer to the well-known problem concerning the plausibility of assuming as true the 'persistence of a situation', i.e. the plausibility of inferring that 'if fact P is true now, it will remain true until noticed otherwise' (*see* [Zarr98]).

3.434 Using TELOS to set up real prototypes of 'integral approach' management systems

One of the main reasons for including a description of TELOS in this book is that the authors have always corroborated their knowledge representation suggestions with concrete proposals. These concern mainly the realization of management tools in DBMS style, in agreement with the fourth 'characteristic' of IASs listed in the introduction to this chapter.

We have already evoked the TELOS versions of the ASK and TELL operations. We can now show in Table 3.40 two simple examples of the use of TELOS's **ASK**. This operation (like the **RETRIEVE** operation) can be used according to two different deductive modalities: i) to prove that a closed formula of the TELOS assertion sublanguage follows from the knowledge base – see the first question of Table 3.40; ii) to find the propositions in the knowledge base that render a given formula true – see the second question. Please note, in this table, the use of the 'dot selector' introduced in Table 3.37, properly extended to return a set of destination components which make reference to an interval `t - 1994` in the figure – where the relation `r - before` in the figure – is valid. Moreover, the optional clause **TRUE** can be used to supply a default history time for the atomic formulae in the query. Alternatively, the queries can refer to the history time explicitly, as in the first query of Table 3.40. The **BELIEVED** clause identifies the belief times which are of interest to the user; when it is not explicitly expressed, it is assumed to be `Now`, i.e. the current beliefs are queried.

Table 3.40 Simple queries in TELOS

```
ASK : Mary ∈ telos.author [over 1994]
BELIEVED at 1995/1/1

True

ASK x/Author : $x ∈ telos.author
TRUE at 1993
BELIEVED at 1995/1/1

$x <Peter, Mary>
```

As already stated, TELOS makes use of the **UNTELL** and **RETELL** operations to update the knowledge base. Updating does not mean that a particular piece of information is explicitly removed from the knowledge base, but that the semi-infinite belief time interval associated with such information is ended. For example, using, on 14 May 1995, the **UNTELL** operation to inform the system that it was not true that Peter was associated with the redaction of the TELOS report results in the termination of the belief interval associated with the propositions asserting that Peter was an author of this report – *see also* Table 3.39. As a consequence, the answer to the second query of Table 3.40 – changing the last clause into: '**BELIEVED** at `1995/5/15`' – will now be simply '`<Mary>`'.

One of the most complete proposals for building up a powerful management system for knowledge bases represented according to the TELOS approach can be found in [Mylo94]. Mylopoulos and his colleagues propose a general architecture structured according to three layers (*see* Figure 3.30).

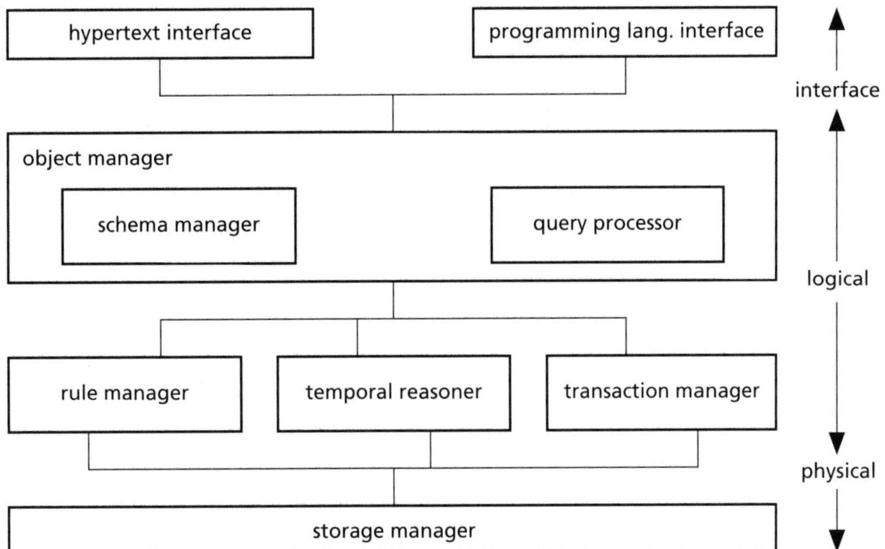

Figure 3.30 A general architecture for a TELOS-based, IAS management system

- An interface layer, which can offer different types of user interfaces. In the figure, two of them are suggested, a 'hypertext' interface, to be used to browse the knowledge base, and a 'programming language' interface, which should allow a user's behaviour similar to that of a DB user. This last interface, in fact, besides offering support for the usual operations such as accessing and updating the KB, is also intended to support a notion of 'transaction' analogous to that found in the DBMSs.
- A logical layer, which manages the descriptions of generic TELOS terms (classes), as well as the descriptions of the logical formulas that must be used as rules and constraints in the KB. Moreover, it supports syntactic and semantic query optimization.
- A physical layer, which manages the physical data structures on which the classes and the formulas are mapped, and which is responsible for disk I/O, caching, etc.

The main problems to solve in order to be able to activate an architecture like this are synthesized in this way in [Mylo94: 212–13]:

a problems concerning the design of the physical storage management and of the query processing and optimization modules, assuming the TELOS knowledge base is stored on secondary memory;

b problems concerning the design of a concurrency control system for efficient multi-user access to the knowledge base – in order to deal with the usual problem concerning an object accessed by a transaction that may be updated before the transaction is complete;

c problems concerning the formulation of efficient compilation, simplification and evaluation techniques for deductive rules and integrity constraints – note that in general, in an IAS context, 'compilation' means translating a set of **TELL** statements into storage structures.

To deal with the above problems, Mylopoulos and his colleagues have chosen, at least in a first approach, the option of trying to adapt to the new IAS context the usual database implementation techniques. Without entering into too many technical details, we can mention some points in this context.

With respect to point (a) above, physical storage management and query processing, the TELOS team suggests building up a 'storage manager' using techniques very similar to that examined in the previous chapter and concerning the problems of mapping frame-based and terminological logics objects into a relational DB. Their approach is a sort of compromise between i) the space-preserving but rigid technique asking to store a complex (TELOS) object in one relation that assigns one column to each object component or attribute, and ii) the more flexible but space-consuming technique that defines one storage relation for each object component or attribute. A 'temporal join index' (TJI, *see also* [Vald87]) is proposed to represent the temporal dependency between two classes, as in the case of two classes C_1 and C_2 where a time-dependent attribute a of C_1 takes as values some instances of C_2. Finally, query processing is optimized by using techniques similar to those used for query processing in object-oriented databases. With respect to point b), concurrency, the TELOS team proposes to use an enhanced version of the well-known 'locking-based' policy. This is a serializable, concurrency control policy that associates with each data item a particular 'lock': a transaction must get a lock on a data item before being able to get access to it and, until it releases the lock, no other transaction can access that item. The TELOS enhanced policy works also in the presence of cycles and updates of the KB. However, it does not permit concurrency *within* cycles, and this suggests that the knowledge base of a TELOS IAS must be designed, from the viewpoint of concurrency control, in such a way as to keep the number and size of cycles to a minimum [Mylo94: 216].

With respect, eventually, to point c), the evaluation of deductive rules and integrity constraints is executed by the 'rule manager', see Figure 3.30. Once again, in designing the rule manager, the TELOS team has focused on extensions to existing techniques. In this case, the management of constraint enforcement in the presence of deductive rules, and historical and belief time, is decomposed in two phases. In the first, 'compilation' phase, integrity constraints and relevant deductive rules are compiled into parameterized forms and then submitted to a 'temporal simplification' process. This sort of simplification is applied whenever this process does not introduce incomplete knowledge; an example is this conjunction of temporal relationships in the Allen's style [AlleJ83]:

```
during(t, 01/96...09/96) ∧ before(t, 05/96...12/96)
      ∧ overlaps(01/96...09/96,05/96...12/96)
```

which is simplified at compilation time into:

```
during(t,01/96...05/96).
```

In the second, 'evaluation' phase, the constraints and the rules relevant to an update, both from a logical and a temporal point of view, are selected and evaluated against the KB.

In the conclusion of the paper, Mylopoulos and his colleagues say that '... clearly, the proposed design is neither complete, nor has it seen a prototype implementation that integrates all proposed implementation techniques. Nevertheless, we believe that the results obtained so far suggest that an efficient KBMS ... *is* feasible and can be obtained by extending database techniques' [Mylo94: 219].

A particularly interesting application of the TELOS methodology concerns the construction of an experimental software repository system (software information base, SIB) providing organization, storage, management, and access facilities for reusable software components [Cons94]. This system has been developed in the context of an Esprit project, ITHACA, devoted to software engineering. We can remark here that the SIB model is based on TELOS but, characteristically enough (*see also* Section 3.47), without its temporal reasoning mechanism and its assertional sublanguage – i.e. it makes use only of the TELOS object-oriented knowledge representation language.

We can conclude this section by mentioning another recent application of TELOS (*see* [Mart98]), an Internet-oriented one that concerns the construction and the management of an application programming interface (API) for a metadata repository (MDR). The rationale for this system concerns the fact that the Internet can provide the user with an astonishing quantity and variety of information expressed as texts, sounds and images; however, this information is not maintained in 'regular' databases, but in 'passive' data sources that are deprived of appropriate tools for searching or querying the data. To deal with this problem, the MDR scholars have adopted what it is now a very popular direction of research in an Internet (WWW) environment, i.e. 'metadata' – *see* [Boll98] and Section 3.452.

Metadata (data about data) is machine-understandable knowledge that describes the properties and the relationships present in the Internet resources, and that can be used to get information about the structure and the contents of these resources. In the approach described in [Mart98], the organization of metadata is defined in a 'metadata schema'; metadata and metadata schema are represented in the TELOS formalism. More precisely, there are three basic types of TELOS objects used in the MDR project, 'Meta Meta Objects' (MMOs), 'Meta Schema Objects' (MSOs) and 'Meta

Data Objects' (MDOs). MDOs represent the real 'metadata', given that the fillers associated with their attributes describe the specific properties of a given WWW document (resource, object ...). MSOs are 'empty' MDO objects, i.e. they represent classes (types) of metadata; each MDO object is an instance of an MSO. The attributes defined at the MSO level can in turn be grouped, giving rise to MMOs; each MSO is an instance of one or more MMOs that specify the categories of its attributes. The MDR architecture is given in Figure 3.31.

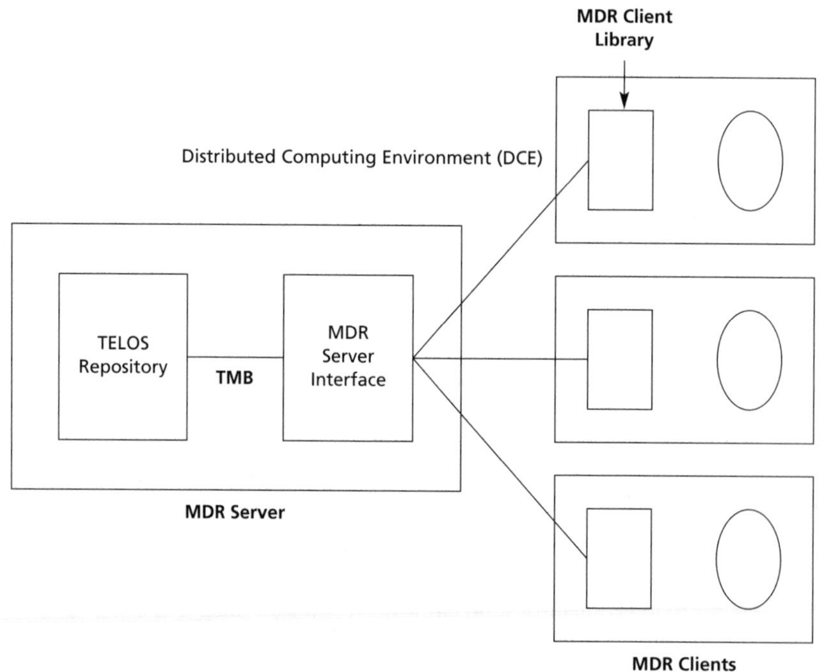

Figure 3.31 Architecture of the metadata repository (MDR)

The MDR server has two main components. The first is the TELOS repository that supplies the back-end knowledge base for the overall MDR system, and the second is the MDR server interface that accepts the requests formulated by the MDR clients and translates them into requests to the TELOS knowledge base. The MDR clients have two components as well, namely an application that requires access to the MDR, and the MDR client library that constitutes the API for accessing the MDR server. TMB is the acronym of 'TELOS message bus': requests and messages are passed along this bus in the form of strings called 's-expressions' that are parsed and interpreted by the TELOS repository. The MDR server interface supplies the user with the facility to interact with the TELOS repository that is not included in the standard TELOS interfaces. Facilities include, for example, operators for querying on the contents of the attributes of the TELOS objects as well as on the relationships among objects, and the possibility of building 'query filters' that represent conjunctions of query conditions.

3.44 The CYC project

The CYC project concerns one of the most controversial endeavours of the artificial intelligence history. Launched in late 1984 by Microelectronics and Computer Technology Corporation (MCC) in Austin, Texas, and developed by a team led initially by Douglas Lenat and later by Lenat and Ramanathan V. Guha, it ended in its MCC form in 1995. During these years, the development of CYC was supported by several organizations, including Apple, Bellcore, DEC, the US Department of Defense (DoD), Kodak and Microsoft. From 1 January 1995, a spin-off company, named Cycorp Inc. and also based in Austin, was created to further the work done at MCC. Doug Lenat is the president of Cycorp. About 30 people had worked on CYC for at least a year during its development at MCC; about 10 of them work now at Cycorp. R.V. Guha has, however, preferred not to join the new company.

The CYC project has spent its life-span of more than fifteen years in building up an extremely large knowledge base which deals with a huge amount of 'common sense knowledge' including time, space, substances, intention, causality, contradiction, uncertainty, belief, emotions, planning, etc. CYC's KB presently contains about a million hand-entered 'logical assertions', including both simple statements of facts, rules about what conclusions to draw if certain statements of facts are satisfied (i.e. they are 'true'), and rules about how to reason in the presence of certain facts and rules. These assertions associate roughly 50 000 atomic 'terms' that constitute the basic vocabulary of CYC. An inference engine derives new conclusions using deductive reasoning.

Apart from the knowledge base and the inference engine, the CYC product family includes a set of interface tools and a number of special-purpose applications modules running on Unix, Windows NT, and other platforms. The most popular interface tool is an HTML browser that allows the user to view the knowledge base as a large hypertext. This means that every occurrence of a CYC term is a link to a dynamically generated HTML page describing that term; in this way, it becomes easy to explore the KB following a network of relationships. Other interface tools include a hierarchy browser, which can display any required subtree of the CYC ontology; a parser from English to the CYC knowledge representation language (CycL), allowing the user to test the natural language facilities of the system by parsing arbitrary English strings; and a WordNet (*see* Section 3.461) interface allowing the user to examine WordNet with relation to the CYC ontology.

Even if the general philosophy and the ambitions of CYC have not changed very much since 1984, the project has evolved considerably from a technical point of view. Mainly under the influence of R.V. Guha, its approach to the knowledge representation problem moved from a quite standard, frame-based view to a system where the fundamental data objects are logical assertions, and where reasoning is based on a logic-oriented approach (microtheories). In the three following subsections, we will document this progressive shift of focus; in the two final subsections, we will try to summarize and evaluate all the arguments that have been put forward about this controversial project. Note that an 'official' and complete publication about the present state of the project is still missing (January 2000); a lot of useful information about CYC (in particular, about CycL and the ontology) can be found, however, at Cycorp Web site, http://www.cyc.com.

3.441 The first phase, 1984–1990

The starting point of the CYC project was the acknowledgement that all the knowledge-based systems, and expert systems in particular, are, as John MacCarthy calls them [McCaJ83: 129], 'brittle'. 'Brittleness' means that, because the KBSs and ESs own only a very limited and biased amount of knowledge about a specific domain, and are very difficult to expand beyond their original scope, they are unable to react in the correct way to some unanticipated situation. According to Lenat and his colleagues ([Lena86], [Lena90a], [Lena95a]), solutions to brittleness in the form of machine learning, automatic programming, and natural language understanding cannot, at least initially, represent a valid answer to this problem. They lack, in fact, common sense knowledge and, as such, they are very difficult to scale up. The CYC's approach to the brittleness problem consists, then, of trying to build up a huge knowledge base, 'one that is 10^4 to 10^5 larger than today's typical expert systems' ([Lena90a: 33]), which would contain a huge amount of common sense knowledge. This would include the factual knowledge which can be found in an encyclopaedia and, more interestingly, 'the sort of knowledge that an encyclopaedia would assume the reader knew without being told (for example, an object can't be in two places at once)' [Lenat86: 65].

[Lena86] represents the most well-known report about the first phase of development of CYC. It includes a section, 'How CYC Works' ([Lena86: 70–75]), which can be interesting to examine in brief, mainly to show how the first draft of CYC's methodology relied strongly on the choice of a representation language modelled on frame-based languages in the KRL style ([Bobr77]), RLL in particular ([Grei80], [Lena83]). RLL, the Representation Language Language, was characterized by the fact that the definitions of all the usual constructs of a knowledge representation language, such as the slots in a frame, or the inheritance mechanisms, were themselves encoded declaratively as frames. For example, the fully-fledged frames describing the semantics of a slot contain in RLL information of the type: what is its inverse? what kind of frames can include this slot? what kind of values can fill the slot? how can it be possible to find its value if this last is not currently associated with the slot? what relations of various type does it take part in with other slots? From the fact that this category of information asks for the explicit coding of the relationship of a slot to other slots, it follows that all the known slot names were recorded, in the RLL version of CYC, in the CYC 'ontology' (generalization/specialization graph of concepts) – *see also* Table 3.41. The RLL has strongly influenced the design of some high-level, commercial knowledge representation language, such as the CRL language mentioned in the previous chapter.

In this report, Lenat and his colleagues observe that there are at least two sources of brittleness in a 'normal' ES rule such as AskedInInterview, expressing the fact that, if a doctor asks a patient 'Do you have $x?' and the answer is 'yes', we can conclude that the patient has the disease x:

- The rule is an agglomeration of technical terms such as AskedInInterview, $doctor, $patient, $x, which are meaningful for a human but which, from the computer point of view, represent only generic operators (AskedInInterview) or variables ($doctor, $patient…). That is to say, these terms are only loosely related to each other through the wording of the different rules but are not 'tied up' to a global model of the real world.

- The classical way of dealing with exceptions in rules like the above is to add explicit Unless conditions, such as a condition 'unless the patient might lie about $x'. This implies that the kinds of things someone might lie about must be listed explicitly (insanity in the family, use of illegal drugs, country of birth, etc.). The risks here are of i) ignoring some very important items when creating the list; ii) being obliged to update it as a consequence of, for example, changes in the social context and social behaviour.

To overcome brittleness, we can imagine that, after the rule has been entered in an ES supported by CYC, the latter asks its author (the expert) to 'explain' all the unknown terms that appear in the rule: AskedInInterview, $doctor, $patient, and $x. If all the above terms have already been defined in the CYC ontology, to explain fully AskedInInterview, for example, the expert will only need to traverse the ontology from Anything, to Processes, to MentalProcesses, down to Communicating and Querying – *see* Table 3.41 from [Lena86: 73]).

In this table, the names of the conceptual entities, such as sets (Doctors, Symptoms) or main scripts (Communicating, Informing, Querying or Remembering), are in upper case; the names of their attributes, such as basicKindOf, actors or constraints, are in lower case. According to the RLL philosophy, all of the above symbols correspond to frames – *see* in Table 3.41 the frames (lower case) which represent attributes such as constraints or waysItFails. The required information about AskedInInterview can then be simply retrieved from the frame with this name, which is a sort of Querying, which is in turn …., etc. Analogously, the expert can access the frame Doctors to find the set over which the variable $doctor ranges, and to access the Patients to find that $patient ranges over Patients, and $x over the frame Symptoms. If, finally, when the expert arrives at the place where the frame Patient should be – as a subset of RecipientOfService – he discovers that this frame does not exist yet, he can make use of an interactive screen frame editor to build up the definition of the new frame. He can do this by editing and modifying another, already existing, RecipientOfService frame, such as Student.

An interesting remark about the ontology of Table 3.41 concerns the fact that its organization in the RLL style can be used to automatically derive the Unless conditions in the ES rules, for example the Unless condition of AskedInInterview. This particular procedure – outlined here, see [Lena86] for more details – begins asking CYC for the values of the allWaysItFails slot of AskedInInterview; calling for the value of a particular slot of a particular frame was the usual way to initiate a computation in CYC/RLL. We can suppose now of being in a situation like that of Table 3.41, where the only information known about AskedInInterview concerns the fact that this frame is an instance of Querying. The lack, in AskedInInterview, of the slot allWaysItFails tells the system to activate a procedure that goes to consult the defn slot of the frame allWaysItFails. The system finds there that it can compute the desired value by combining, see Table 3.41,

Table 3.41 A fragment of the original CYC ontology

Communicating
basicKindOf: Informing
actors: (communicator a) (recipient b) (message c)
action: (InSequence (OpeningCommunications a b)
(Telling a b c)
(RecallMatching b c)
(ClosingCommunications a b))
constraints: (CanUnderstand b a c)
(Desires a (Communicating a b c))

Remembering
basicKindOf: Informing
actors: (rememberer a) (memory b)
constraints: (Accurate (Remembering a b))
accuracy: (# ... Moderate variance High)

2WayCommunicating
basicKindOf: Communicating
action: (Repeatedly (Communicating a b c_i)
(Communicating b a d_i))

Querying
basicKindOf: 2WayCommunicating
actors: (question c_i) (declaration d_i)
constraints: (ResultOf d_i (Remembering b c_i))

AskedInInterview
basicKindOf: Querying
...
constraints

elementOf: ScriptSlots PrimitiveSlots
usedInBuilding: waysItFails
makesSenseFor: Processes

waysItFails
defn: (Lambda (u &rest) (negate (constraints u)))
elementOf: DerivedSlots UnlessFillingSlots
builtFrom: constraints
combiner: negate
usedInBuilding: allWaysItFails
makesSenseFor: Processes

allWaysItFails
defn: (Lambda (u) (MapUnion (fullAction u) 'waysItFails))
elementOf: InheritedSlots UnlessFillingSlots
builtFrom: fullAction waysItFails
combiner: MapUnion
makesSenseFor: Processes

the values of the waysItFails slots of all the specific subactions that together form the fullAction script for AskedInInterview. The frame for fullAction, not shown in Table 3.41, specifies how this script can be inherited and assembled from the frames which represent the different generalizations of the starting frame (here, AskedInInterview); basically, the action slots of all these frames are appended after having made the appropriate substitutions of variables, as specified in the actor slots along the way. In this case, starting from AskedInInterview, the system will assemble together the values of action from Querying, 2WayCommunicating, Communicating, Remembering, and other frames not shown in the table, such as Informing, MentalProcessing, Processing, Anything.

When the fullAction script for AskedInInterview has been assembled, the system realizes that none of the frames mentioned in this script have a waysItFails slot. The usual procedure is activated again, i.e. CYC consults the defn slot of the frame called waysItFails. It can find there that it can compute the desired values by negating the value of the constraints slot for each of those frames. Some of them, such as Communicating and Remembering, have indeed non-empty constraints slots; given that, in the constraints frame, there is no defn slot which could be used to compute other constraints, the session ends and the system returns as results the union of the negations of the constraints slots it has really found, *see* Table 3.42 [Lena86: 74].

Table 3.42 Automatically computing Unless condition

((NOT (CanUnderstand patient dr query))
the patient does not understand the doctor's question

(NOT (Desires dr (Communicating dr patient query)))
the doctor does not really want to ask the patient the true question

(NOT (CanUnderstand dr patient (Remembering patient query)))
the doctor misunderstands the patient's reply

(NOT (Desires patient (Communicating patient dr (Remembering patient query))))
the patient does not really want to tell the doctor the true answer

(NOT (Accurate (Remembering patient query)))
the patient mis-remembers the answer

(NOT (Accurate (Remembering dr (Remembering patient query)))))
the doctor mis-remembers the significance of the patient's answer

This result constitutes the CYC's answer to the problem of automatically computing an Unless condition for the AskedInInterview rule by linking this previously isolated term with the general knowledge base of the system. As Lenat and his colleagues remark, '... these Unless conditions are implicit in the knowledge base, specifically in the constraints slots of certain frames' [Lena86: 73]. This way of 'discovering' new information by relying heavily on the particular RLL (and LISP) semantics is typical of Lenat's work in the 1970s and early 1980s: for controversy on this point, *see* [Ritc84], [Lena84].

We can conclude this short examination of the first phase of CYC with some further details about the original aspect of CycL, the CYC's representation language. Table 3.43 reproduces a sort of 'historical' document, the frame given for Coke in [Lena86: 77–78]. This frame, which represents in CYC format a definition found in the *Concise Columbia Encyclopaedia*, was (quite arbitrarily) chosen, in fact, as a starting point for the progressive development of a first corpus of about 400 mutually distinct, coded 'articles' (frames); such corpus was intended provide a first kernel of the CYC's knowledge base. A full methodology was developed for the set-up of the kernel, an evolutionary process involving, among other things, a continuous re-examining and reformatting of the coded information already inserted in the base, *see* [Lena86: 76–82]. Manual copy&edit was then extensively used in order to quickly derive new frames from those already inserted in the KB, such as 'Irrigating' from 'Raining' or vice versa. New frames were systematically created to encode the common sense knowledge associated with the understanding of the information already stored, for example the necessity to create the 'coking' and 'smelting' frames in order to explain 'coke'. New frames were created by moving the common information found in several frames to a more general one, for example, creating a frame ReductionOfMetalOxide by abstracting several common properties found in frames of the 'smelting' type.

Table 3.43 A CYC frame for Coke

```
Coke
    basicKindOf : SolidFuelSubstances
    colour : Gray
    typeOfChemComposition : Mixture
    ingredients : (Absolute% (Carbon 98)
                       (InDecreasingAbundance
                            Metals
                            InNoParticularOrder
                                 OrganicCompounds
                                 TraceElements)))
    relativeMagnitude : (hardness High) (porosity High)
    usedAsInputTo : Smelting
    createdfAsResidueIn : Coking
    myCreator : Shepherd
    myCreationDate : '2-Feb-85 9:57:10'
    lastEditor : Lenat
    lastEditedDate : '3-Feb-85 18:22:56'
```

In Table 3.43, frames such as Absolute%, InDecreasingAbundance and InNoParticularOrder are used as 'connectives' to express concisely the fact that the coke is 98 per cent carbon, with the remaining 2 per cent being mostly metals with small amounts of organic compounds and traces of other elements.

3.442 The mid-term report, 1990

In 1990, the CYC team published a 'mid-term report' in the form of two companion papers, in the *Communications of ACM* [Lena90a] and in the *AI Magazine* [Guha90a]. This report was intended to review the team's efforts during the first five years of the project, to describe its state at that moment, and to explain the plans and expectations for the final phase of the project. The material published in the CYC book which appeared the same year [Lena90b] is useful to complement the information found in the report but is also partially misleading because it reproduces a state of the project which was already obsolete. In this subsection and in the following one we illustrate some of the main points introduced by the report. Most of the information given here is still valid in the present state of the CYC system, even if sometimes the denominations, and the implementation details, of some important functions of this system have changed – for example, the 'abnormality predicate' (*see* below) has been replaced with the two logical connectives #$ExceptFor and #$ExceptThen, without changing the general CYC's philosophy on dealing with defaults.

The first, very evident difference between the situation described in the mid-term report and that outlined in the previous subsection concerns the CYC representation language (CycL). In the *AI Magazine* paper, Guha and Lenat detail [Guha90a: 34–35] all the troubles caused by the *ad hocness* of the original version of CycL, which '... was little more than frames' [Guha90a: 34]. They say that this version was inadequate to express disjunctions, inequalities, existentially quantified statements, metaknowledge; that the associated inference mechanisms were very reduced in number and very poor (essentially, inheritance along the ISA links, rigid definitions of one slot in terms of others, and a lot of opaque LISP code under the form of demons); etc. This *ad hocness* meant the inference tools had to be continuously modified and adjusted and eventually parts of the knowledge base had to be rebuilt to assure a correspondence between this base and the way the inferences worked.

Thus a complete restructuring of CycL started in 1987, leading to the differentiation of this language into two levels – the 'epistemological level' (EL) and the 'heuristic level' (HL), *see also* [BracR79], [McCaJ87a].

The epistemological level was based on first-order predicate calculus, with a slightly different syntax and, mainly, extensions to handle equality, to represent defaults, reification (i.e. having names for propositions, and having, therefore, the possibility of making assertions about other propositions in the KB), reflection (being able to refer to the facts supporting the system's beliefs in other facts), modals (beliefs, desires, goals ...), etc. Some second-order features are included in the EL language, such as the possibility of using complete assertions as intensional components of other assertions or, in some circumstances, of using quantification over predicates. Non-monotonic constructs used in EL are the closed world assumption (CWA) and the unique name assumption described in the following subsections. When we speak today of CycL, we refer implicitly to this 'epistemological level', i.e. CycL now practically coincides EL.

The heuristic level concerned the handling of a variety of special-purpose representations and procedures to speed up inferencing, to be used whenever an inference procedure had to be activated. At the moment the heuristic level includes a set of special-purpose modules where each contains its own algorithms and data structures, and that can recognize and manage some very usual types of inferences. For example, one heuristic-level module carries out temporal reasoning by converting temporal relations into a before-and-after graph and then doing graph traversal; a truth maintenance system and an argumentation-based explanation and justification system are tightly (and permanently) integrated into the system; etc. In addition to these specialized inference engines, CYC includes numerous browsers, editors and consistency checkers. A rich interface for the system has also been defined.

The reason for defining a separate heuristic level was related to the ambition of having a clean and simple semantics for knowledge representation purposes: therefore, all the special-purpose constructs and routines intended only to improve inferencing abilities should not interfere with the necessary (and sufficient) knowledge representation tools proper to the epistemological level. In the mid-term report, it was affirmed that an external program or human user could interact with the system at either of the two levels, epistemological or heuristic. The preferred mode of communicating with CYC was, however, that of entering at the epistemological level, and there was a facility, the 'tell-ask (TA) interface', for automatically translating sentences from the epistemological level into the most appropriate representations at the heuristic level, and vice versa. In the current applications of CYC the heuristic level is, in reality, invisible to the user, and no real user, human or application program, ever writes or reads heuristic expressions. As the mid-term report affirms [Guha90a: 36], one could eliminate the entire heuristic level, and still be able to use the CYC KB with some sort of general-purpose problem solver, at the risk, of course, of slowing down the speed of the inferencing operations. Therefore, it is reasonable to see the heuristic level only as a sort of optimization level, which concerns mainly the modalities of use of the CYC inference engine and, as already stated, to consider the epistemological level as the 'real' level (CycL) that concerns the knowledge representation problems.

A plain description of the basic CycL syntax

We give here a simple description of the fundamental syntactic structures included in the CycL language. This description is based mainly on the information about CycL that can be found on the Cycorp Web site, *http://www.cyc.com* and thus can be considered as reasonably up to date.

CycL is a purely declarative language. Its basic vocabulary consists of 'terms' (constants, non-atomic terms – NATs – variables, numbers, strings, etc.); terms are linked to form meaningful CycL expressions ('formulas') that give rise, eventually, to closed CycL 'sentences' or 'assertions' without free variables. A set of sentences (original axioms provided by the KB's builder or conclusions inferred by the system) constitutes a CYC knowledge base; all the possible KBs are subsets of the 'huge common sense CYC knowledge base' mentioned at the beginning of these sections.

Among the terms, the so-called constants represent the basic 'words' that are used to create well-formed CycL sentences. CycL constants are normally referred to using the '#$' prefix, even if sometimes these two characters are left out in the CYC documentation or in particular interface tools (and in some of the following subsections). Each constant represents a *thing* or a *concept* in a given application domain. There is no differentiation at this level between 'concepts' and 'individuals' (*see* Section 3.1); therefore, a CycL constant may be #$Typewriter (the collection, i.e. the concept of all the typewriters), #$Walking (the collection of all actions in which some animate entity walks), but also 'individuals' such as #$InternalRevenueService, #$Canada, #$TonyBlair, and even #$Walking52 (a particular case of walking, possibly an ephemeral constant to be deleted after some question has been answered, or after the end of the session). Also the 'predicates', such as (using the CycL notation) #$isa, #$likesAsFriend or #$colourOfObject, are defined in CycL as constants – as we will see later, they are used in CycL to express relationships among other constants. The 'meaning' (definition) of a constant is given by the totality of the axioms pertaining to a given CycL knowledge base that include this constant.

Non-atomic terms are expressions created when constants such as #$GovernmentFn and #$FatherFn (i.e. constants that represent functions) are applied to other constants to generate new concepts. For example, the expression (#$GovernmentFn #$Canada) represents the Canadian government, and (#$FatherFn #$TonyBlair), Tony Blair's father. Each of the constituent parts of NATs, like their values, is a constant. A NAT's main function is that of avoiding a useless proliferation of terms in the CYC ontology. For example, if a constant such as #$PearTree already exists in the ontology, it is possible to make use of the NAT (#$FruitFn #$PearTree) that returns the collection of all the fruits of pear trees as a sort of 'synonymous' of the constant #$Pear, even if this term has not yet been created. Analogously, it is possible to avoid the definition of hundreds of terms like #$LiquidHydrogen ... #$LiquidLawrencium making use of the function #$LiquidFn, as in (#$LiquidFn #$Hydrogen).

Other non-constant terms are the lists, numbers, characters and strings, the latter being limited by double quotes, "". Variables, such as ?Colour, ?x or ?ARG1, are used to designate terms (constants, for example) or axioms whose identity has not been specified. Variable names must begin with a question mark; they may be of any length, and are normally expressed in upper case.

As already stated, CycL terms are combined into 'formulas'. Formulas are parenthesized expressions whose first term, which occupies the position designed conventionally as ARG0, may be i) a predicate; ii) a logical connective; iii) a quantifier. Predicates, logical connectives and quantifiers conventionally begin with a lowercase letter (a to z). The remaining arguments, in the positions ARG1, ARG2 ... ARGn, may be terms (constants, NATs, numbers, variables, etc.) or other formulas. Two examples of 'atomic formulas' – where the ARG0 position is occupied by a predicate – are:

```
(#$colourOfObject #$Car027 #$RedColour)
(#$colourOfObject ?Car ?Colour);
```

The first is a 'ground atomic formula' (GAF), since no variable occupies the argument positions; the second is not a GAF given the presence of two variables, ?Car and ?Colour.

Most predicates have a fixed arity (number of arguments); even if there is no theoretical limit to the arity of a predicate, no predicate has in reality an arity > 5 in the entire CYC KB. A few predicates, however, such as #$different, can take a changeable number of arguments. The arity of a predicate must be declared to the system; this is obtained making use of the specific 'arity' predicate, *see* (#$arity #$isa 2). Also, the 'type' of each argument of each predicate must be declared, making use of specific predicates such as #$arg1Isa, #$arg2Isa, etc. – note that in CYC specifying the type of an argument means specifying that this argument must be an 'instance' of a given 'collection' defined in the CYC ontology. We could then have, for example:

```
(#$isa #$colourOfObject #$BinaryPredicate)
(#$arg1Isa #$colourOfObject #$Object)
(#$arg2Isa #$colourOfObject #$Colour) ;
```

These definitions state that every well-formed formula having #$colourOfObject in the ARG0 position must also have an instance of #$Object in the ARG1 position and an instance of #$Colour in the ARG2 position. Predicates in the style of #$arg1Genl, #$arg2Genl ... #$argnGenl can then be used to identify the 'generalizations' (more general terms, i.e. the supersets) of the collections defining the type of the arguments.

The 'logical connectives' are special constants analogous to the operators of formal logic that are used to build up more complex formulas starting from atomic formulas or other complex formulas. Examples of CycL logical connectives are #$not, #$and, #$or and #$implies. #$not takes a single formula as argument, and it reverts its truth-value; #$and and #$or take zero or more formulas as arguments. #$implies takes exactly two formulas as arguments and, as with the 'if-then' statements in formal logic, it returns 'true' if it is not simultaneously verified that the first argument is true and the second is false – note that no strong causal interpretation can be associated with a #$implies statement. An example of the use of #$implies:

```
(#$implies
    (#$ownerOfObject #$Car027 #$John)
    (#$colourOfObject #$Car027 #$RedColour)) ;
```

This assertion says that if #$Car027 is owned by #$John, then it is a red car. Assertions built up making use of the #$implies connective are frequently used in CycL, where they are also called 'conditionals' or 'rules', with the first argument of #$implies called 'antecedent' and the second called 'consequent'.

CycL includes the universal quantifier #$forAll, and four existential quantifiers, #$thereExists, #$thereExistAtLeast, #$thereExistAtMost, and #$thereExistExactly. #$forAll takes two arguments, a variable and a formula (very often, an #$implies statement) where the variable must appear. #$thereExists takes two arguments as well, a variable and a formula. #$thereExistAtLeast etc. behave like #$thereExist, providing, however, more details from a quantitative point of view; these existential quantifiers take three arguments, a positive integer, a variable and a formula. Note that the 'unbound' variables (explicitly declared) that appear in a formula are implicitly assumed as universally quantified. The two assertions of Table 3.44 – where #$forAll is specifically expressed – state, respectively, that i) for every animal there exists at least an entity that is the mother of this animal, and ii) that all the cars must be endowed with four wheels. With respect to the latter, that may not be true in some cases, we can also note that 'common sense' truths in this style must always be interpreted as 'default truth': they are then 'true' in some very precise context.

Table 3.44 Examples of the use of quantifiers in CycL

```
(#$forAll ?A
   (#$implies
      (#$isa ?A #$Animal)
      (#$thereExists ?M
         (#$mother ?A ?M))))

(#$forAll ?C
   (#$implies
      (#$isa ?C #$Car)
      (#$thereExistExactly 4 ?WHEEL
         (#$and
            (#$isa ?WHEEL #$Wheel)
            (#$anatomicalParts ?C ?WHEEL)))))
```

Like predicates, functions normally have a fixed arity – very few CycL functions, for example mathematical functions such as #$PlusFn, can assume a variable number of arguments. The names of the functions are conventionally identified by the presence of the suffix Fn. For fixed arity functions, the types of the different arguments are introduced, as for predicates, making use of the special predicates #$arg1Isa, #$arg2Isa … #$argnIsa. At the difference of predicates, functions return a result; the type of the result is described by the predicate #$resultIsa that must appear in the definition of the function.

For example, the definition of the function #$GovernementFn is:

```
(#$arity #$GovernmentFn 1)
   (#$arg1Isa #$GovernmentFn #$GeopoliticalEntity)
   (#$resultIsa #$GovernmentFn #$RegionalGovernment).
```

This means that the unique argument of #$GovernmentFn must always be an instance of #$GeopoliticalEntity, like #$UnitedStatesOfAmerica. Note that a specific call to a function followed by one or more arguments gives rise to a NAT. An expression like:

```
(#$isa (#$GovernmentFn #$UnitedStatesOfAmerica)
#$RegionalGovernment)
```

is both well-formed and 'true', given that the NAT (#$GovernmentFn #$UnitedStatesOfAmerica) is really an instance of #$RegionalGovernment.

Note that in CycL most functions are instances of either #$IndividualDenoting Function – as #$GovernmentFn, given that a NAT like (#$GovernmentFn#$United StatesOfAmerica) indicates an individual government – or #$CollectionDenoting Function – as #$FruitFn, that returns a collection: a NAT such as (#$fruitFn#$Apple Tree) indicates the *collection* of all the apples, not a single fruit. In this last case, the definition of each instance of #$CollectionDenotingFunction must specify not only the argument types and the type of the result but also, making use of the predicate #$resultGenl, that the result must be a specific term of a given superset. For example, a formula such as (#$resultGenl #$LeftPairMemberFn #$LeftObject) is included in the definition of the function #$LeftPairMemberFn. When applied to the argument #$Shoe (the set of all shoes), this returns as its value the set of all the left shoes, which is a subset of #$LeftObject.

More advanced topics in CycL: dealing with defaults

Less than 10 per cent of the assertions in the CYC knowledge base can be considered as really monotonic, i.e. absolutely true assertions, like the axioms of mathematics that cannot be retracted because of the addition of new facts. As noted in [Lena90a: 35], 'very little that we believe about the world is certain and absolute'. Moreover, in the everyday life that CYC wants to reflect, we make use of all sorts of simplifications ('Lincoln was a good president') and approximations ('The earth goes around the sun in an ellipse'). Therefore, a correct handling of 'defaults' is particularly important in CYC, and the discussion about their implementation constitutes the core of the description of the EL component of CycL in the mid-term report. Assertions that are 'default true', in opposition to the 'monotonically true', can support exceptions. They are considered as 'true' in the majority of cases – i.e. in the most relevant cases likely to be encountered in a given application – but if necessary they can be 'overridden' without the obligation of alerting the user, at least in principle.

In dealing with default, CYC relies only minimally on the usual logical mechanisms, making use on the contrary of declarative knowledge represented as axioms in its own knowledge base. The default reasoning abilities of CYC make use of the closed world assumption and, mainly, of the notion of 'argument'. 'Argument' is taken here in its usual, intuitive meaning of an ordered set of statements in support of an 'opinion': when trying to determine whether a given sentence P is true, one builds up arguments for and against P, and comes to a conclusion after comparing these arguments. The presence of additional information can modify the pertinence of particular arguments, giving rise to non-monotonicity phenomena.

The general format of defaults in CYC is identical to that of defaults in circumscription as defined by McCarthy [McCaJ87a]; making use of the standard logic notation, the statement 'birds usually fly' is then expressed in CycL as:

$isa(x\ Bird) \wedge \neg\ ab_1\ (x) \supset flies\ (x)$,

where the isa predicate corresponds to the set-membership relation and the ab_i predicates stay for *abnormal in fashion i*, i.e. they are used to 'weaken' a monotonic statement such as 'all birds fly'. More exactly, ab_1 corresponds to being an exception in the sense of being a bird and not being able to fly: a CYC axiom says, for example, that birds with broken wings are abnormal in the sense ab_1 [Guha90a: 58]. Using this technique, defaults are reduced to CycL axioms (sentences) that can be stored in the CYC knowledge base such as the 'ordinary' axioms concerning mundane phenomena such as eating or sleeping. The difference between the two classes of axioms is that defaults are weaker than the normal ones, and they include a mechanism, the 'abnormality predicates' ab_i, used to express that they may not hold sometimes. Abnormality predicates currently implemented in CycL are #$overrides, to indicate a preference for one assertion with respect to another one, #$exceptFor, to indicate individuals that are exceptions to rules, and #$exceptWhen, that indicates, on the contrary, situations that are exceptions to rules. For example, the use of #$exceptWhen to represent the classical example stating that penguins are an exception to the rule that all birds can fly gives rise to the following default in current CycL:

```
(#$exceptWhen (#$isa ?BIRD #$Penguin)
  (#$implies
    (#$isa ?BIRD #$Bird)
    (#$skillCapableOf ?BIRD #$Flying-FlappingWings
     #$performedBy)))
```

Returning to the notion of argument, we can note that an argument for a proposition P is similar to a proof for P, but is non-monotonic, which means that later information can invalidate the argument. More precisely, in addition to the usual sentences that might appear in a proof, an argument can contain a class of sentences labelled explicitly as 'assumptions'. Assumptions (or 'abnormality literals') are sentences of the form $\neg\, ab_i$ *(...)*, where ab_i represents an abnormality predicate. $\neg\, ab_1$ *(Tweety)* is, therefore, an assumption.

If there is an argument for a P, it is reasonable to believe in the truth of P – P is then accepted as a 'theorem'. However, because arguments are a weaker notion than proof, it is possible, at a certain moment, to result in invalid arguments, i.e. arguments that try to make assumptions that are known to be false. In this case, the argument is ignored, and attention is restricted to arguments that are not yet known to be invalid. It is also possible to come out with arguments for both P and ¬ P, or to conclude that one argument is stronger than another. These notions are captured by the 'argument axiom' of CycL, which is expressed in Table 3.45 along with its formalization in standard logical terms [Lena90a]. Note that the LISP-like notation, `(*p*), refers, as usual, to the sentence *p* rather than to its truth-value.

To deal with problems such as the impossibility of proving that some arguments are not invalid, or that a better counterargument to some proposition does exist, a closed world assumption is made for the predicates #$argumentFor and #$invalidArg. Moreover, the truth-predicate #$true that is used in the argument axiom is allowed to differ from the actual truth-value of a sentence for certain sentences that are likely to be paradoxical. This means, for example, that 'true(`*p*) ∨ true(`¬ *p*)' is not a theorem in CycL.

Table 3.45 The argument axiom

```
i)     If there is an argument for a proposition P.
ii)            the argument is not known to be invalid, and
iii)           there is no preferred argument for ¬ P (except
               the arguments that are known to be invalid)
       then believe the proposition P.
```

$$(\forall (a_1, p)(\text{argumentFor}(a_1, p) \wedge \neg \text{invalidArg}(a_1) \wedge (\forall (a_2)(\text{argumentFor}(a_2, ()(\neg p)) \wedge \text{invalidArg}(a_2) \vee \text{preferred}(a_1, a_2))))) \supset \text{true}(p)$$

As we can see clearly from the formulation given in Table 3.45, a central factor of the procedures for dealing with default in CYC is the possibility of coming up with criteria for comparing arguments and deciding which to give preference to. In [Guha90b], R.V. Guha supplies a list of 'preference criteria' and shows how some of these can be axiomatized ('preference axioms'). An example of a preference criterion is 'using inferential distance': when inheriting properties from two different classes – inheriting properties is a common use of default reasoning – if we are in the presence of i) inherited properties that are contradictories, and ii) of a class that is a subset of the other, then we prefer the value inherited from the smaller set.

As already stated, an interesting aspect of this approach to default reasoning is that most of the work is accomplished by making use of axioms that are explicitly stated in the knowledge base, and not by using the properties 'wired in' the logic. This means a greater flexibility to fix problems of inadequacy, given that it is obviously preferable to add and remove axioms from the knowledge base than to change the logic, especially when a huge knowledge base founded on a certain sort of logic already exists.

The heuristic level of CycL

We recall here that the motivations of the heuristic level are strictly pragmatic: in the course of the inference procedures, its functions should find most of the desired conclusions quickly. According to the mid-term report ([Lena90a], [Guha90a]), the functionalities of the heuristic level in CycL are defined in terms of a Tell/Ask (TA) interface, which constitutes a development of the original ideas of Levesque and Brachman examined in Section 3.42. A user (human or application program) will usually communicate with CYC at the epistemological level; their (EL) utterances are then translated by the TA interface into heuristic level propositions. Following the mid-term report, TA includes six functions: **Tell** (called **Assert** in [Guha90a] and in the most recent versions of CYC), **Unassert**, **Deny**, **Justify**, **Ask**, **Bundle**. These are defined in Table 3.46. In relation to the original Levesque and Brachman's approach, Justify and Bundle are totally new. In [Dert90], the functions are reduced to four: **Ask**, split into **Ask Extensionally** and **Ask Intensionally**, **Tell** and **Justify**.

Recently the TA interface has taken the form of a standard application program interface that external programs can use to query and update a particular version of the CYC system used for a given application. This interface is called simply FI (functional interface), and includes several new functions such as **Kill**, **Rename**, **Lookup**, **Ask-status**, **Timestamp-assertion**, **Get-parameter**, **Set-parameter**, **Get-error**, etc. We will limit ourselves here to summarizing the main points of the very detailed description of **Ask** given in the mid-term report – according to the specifications for **Ask** that can be found now on the Cycorp Web site, this description is still essentially valid. The CYC team say that the way they implemented **Ask** is largely responsible for the gain in speed obtained at the heuristic level.

It must be said, as a premise, that the architecture of the heuristic level has been structured into four modules, mainly to optimize the processing of defaults.

a Argument generator: given a sentence σ, this module tries to generate an argument for it. We recall here that an argument is similar to a proof, but it can include assumptions.

Table 3.46 The functional interface of CycL

Tell: **(Σ × KB → KB)**. Given a sentence σ and a KB, after **Tell**(σ, KB) we obtain a new (modified) KB' in which σ is an axiom. σ can be any well-formed formula of the EL level of CycL.

Unassert: **(Σ × KB → KB)**. Given a sentence σ and a KB, after **Unassert**(σ, KB) we obtain a new KB' in which σ is not an axiom; nothing can be said about the truth-value of σ in KB'. **Unassert** is the direct 'undo' of **Tell**. Please note that **Tell**(¬σ, KB) is totally different from **Unassert**(σ, KB), given that, in the **Tell** case, σ is false in KB' (the explicit new axiom ¬ σ has been asserted in KB'), while σ is undefined in the **Unassert** case.

Deny: **(Σ × KB → KB)**. Given a sentence σ and a KB, after **Deny**(σ, KB) we obtain a new KB' in which σ is no longer true, i.e. in KB', all the positive 'arguments' (see the previous subsection) for σ are suppressed while the (possible) arguments for ¬ σ are not affected. Therefore, it may be the case that, after **Deny**, neither σ or ¬ σ is true in KB'. **Unassert** (σ, KB) is weaker than **Deny**(σ, KB), given that Unassert gives rise to a KB' where σ might still be true and, in turn, **Deny**(σ, KB) is weaker than **Tell**(¬ σ, KB), which gives rise to a KB' where σ is decidedly false.

Justify: **(Σ × KB → sentences)**. If sentence σ is true in the KB, then **Justify**(σ, KB) will return a minimal subset of KB from which σ can be derived, i.e. **Justify** is used to obtain the 'arguments', see the previous subsection, for a given proposition.

Ask: **(Σ × KB → truth/value/bindings)**. **Ask** is used to test the truth value of an expression σ and, if the expression contains some free variables, to find which value makes this expression true. An optional argument, 'unwanted-arguments', changes **Ask** into a generator, i.e. each new call gives rise to a new set of bindings.

Bundle: **(sequence of functional interface statements)**. Using this facility, it becomes possible to perform a series of calls to the previous five functions as one atomic macro operation.

b Argument comparator: given a set $\{A_i\}$ of arguments for and against a sentence σ, this module computes a truth value for σ, making use of the axioms of the knowledge base to verify the validity of each A_i and to decide which non-invalid A_i must be preferred over others. The sentence, with its proper truth value, is added to the knowledge base; an important point here is that a truth value is permanently attached to each assertion inserted into a CYC knowledge base. CycL allows five possible non-numeric truth values: monotonically true, default true, unknown, default false and monotonically false. Of these, only the first two are commonly used. 'True/false' sentences are those that are monotonically true (i.e. the addition of new facts cannot cause them to be retracted). 'Default true/false' are held to be true/false in most cases, but can be overridden – most rules in the CYC KB are default true. 'Unknown' is used for sentences for which unresolved conflicting arguments still exist. Deductions that require making 'assumptions' are only default true (or false), while those that do not require any assumptions are monotonically true.

c Conclusion retractor: when the truth value associated with a sentence σ changes, this module guarantees that the truth values of other sentences that depend on σ are also updated.

d Contradiction resolver: this module will detect any contradictions and will try to resolve them, for example by retracting some weak (default) assertions.

Returning now to **Ask**, and supposing that the sentence σ is a query Q, the module a) described before is called twice, to generate arguments for Q and $\neg$ Q. These arguments are then passed to module b), which checks their validity, compares them – which can lead to invoking 'preference axioms' (see the previous subsection) from the knowledge base; for efficiency's sake, many of them have been directly proceduralized at the HL level – and then decides their final truth value on the basis of this comparison. If the comparison process fails, i.e. if the arguments are incomparable, neither Q nor $\neg$ Q can be concluded.

The argument generator is responsible for most of the time spent in executing inferences; a number of techniques have been introduced in order to make this module (and the conclusion retractor module) more efficient. These inference techniques can be grouped into three categories, *see* [Lena90a], [Lena90b] for more details:

- highly specialized inference rules;
- domain-specific inference rules;
- dependency analysis of the knowledge base.

The first category of rules is based on the detection of categories of axioms that are characterized by an isomorphic syntactic structure. For example, a number of axioms in the CYC's knowledge base are instances of the scheme $(s_1\ x\ y) \wedge (s_2\ x\ z) \supset (s_1\ z\ y)$. An example of an axiom that fits this schema may be, in standard logical notation: (lastName x y) $\wedge$ (sonOf x z) $\supset$ (lastName z y). Each of these axiom schemes is managed as an inference rule and has special procedures (in modules (a), (c), and (d)) associated with it. Examples of procedures are those used for recognizing instances of a given schema (for translating from the epistemological level to the heuristic level), for applying instances of the schema to derive conclusions, and for performing bookkeeping functions such as storing justifications.

The rules of the previous paragraph are based purely on the syntactic structure of the axioms; a second category of rules ('domain-specific' inference rules) tries to make use of some special properties of a set of domain-specific axioms, or to make a domain-specific use of a set of general axioms. Examples of 'axiom clusters' that CYC is able to optimize in this way are the temporal reasoning axioms. For these, many tasks can be formulated as simple graph-search problems over graphs whose nodes are time points and whose arcs are primitive temporal relations (such as #$before, #$after, and #$simultaneousWith).

The rules of the last category ('dependency analysis rules') are based on an analysis of the structure of the axioms of the KB. For example, a dependency analysis of these axioms could lead to the detection of the circumstances according to which some circularity can occur, due to self-justifying sequences of statements, for example. It is possible to identify the only sentences that may be involved in the circular justification; being in possession of this information can greatly reduce the time necessary to search for such circularities.

CYC's ontology

As stated above, CYC's KB contains about a million hand-entered 'logical assertions' concerning concepts and individuals, predicates, functions, contexts (*see* next subsection), rules, constraints, relations, etc. The coherence of this huge KB is assured by the 'upper CYC ontology', a set of approximately 3000 terms intended to capture the most general concepts of human reality. Cycorp Inc. publicly released a beta-version of this upper ontology in 1996, which can be consulted on the World Wide Web at *http://www.cycorp.com*. It consists of 42 pages, each containing a group of concepts of the upper CYC ontology (time and dates, quantities, contexts, composition of substances, agents, professions, chemistry, general medicine, financial, geography, etc.), with concise English descriptions for each of the 3000 terms, hypertext links allowing the navigation among the terms (as CYC people say, '... there is a tremendous amount of cross-linking among them'), some examples of subclasses and instances, an alphabetical index, and facilities for searching for concepts by name.

The stabilization of the CYC's ontology seems to be relatively recent. To give a general idea of its status around 1990, we reproduce in Figure 3.32, adapted from [Guha90a: 41], a fragment of the upper level as it was conceived at that time. Note that the companion paper of [Guha90a], i.e. [Lena90a], does not supply any graphical depiction of the ontology. Moreover, the ontology presented in Figure 5–2 of [Lena90b] has several important differences to that reproduced here. One of the most evident is that the tree in Figure 3.33 is a bipartite one, while that of [Lena90b] is tripartite, with a branch 'Intangible' linked directly with the top 'Thing'. Anyway, as Guha and Lenat remark, a representation such as that of Figure 3.32 is (partially) misleading given that the arcs depicted there represent only a particular sort of relationship among all those allowed by CYC, the relation called **specs** in mid-term report terms, and corresponding to superset/subset. This predicate has disappeared in the later versions of CYC.

In the following, we will refer systematically to the WWW description of the upper CYC ontology. First of all, it must be said that each entity in the CYC KB is represented as a CYC 'constant' (or 'term', or 'unit'), and as already stated, the name of every constant begins with the symbol #$, for example, #$Leg, #$Skin, or #$StaticSituation. The fundamental properties that characterize the ontology's architecture are:

a Each constant (term), representing an entry of the global CYC ontology, is an element of one or more 'collections' that correspond, in CYC, to the usual concepts or types. For example, #$Skin is a member of the collection #$AnimalBodyPartType.

b Each constant is then endowed with an #$isa relationship, meaning 'element of a given set (collection)'.

c This relationship must not be confused with another link commonly present in the ontology's entries, #$genls, meaning 'subset of a given set (collection)'. #$genls represents then the 'subsumption' relationship.

Note that #$isa and #$genls are standard terms of the ontology and have their own entries – *see* Table 3.47 which gives descriptions of the terms and also of #$Skin, which is used as an introductory example on the WWW pages.

There is a fundamental difference between #$isa and #$genls. The latter is transitive, and if, for example, #$Person is a subset of #$Mammal, (#$genls #$Person #$Mammal), and #$Mammal is a subset of #$Animal, (#$genls #$Mammal #$Animal), it is also true that a #$genls of #$Person is #$Animal, (#$genls #$Person #$Animal). On the contrary, #$isa is not transitive: given (#$isa #$Fred #$Person) and (#$isa #$Person #$Collection), it is not true that #$Fred is an element of #$Collection, given that Fred is a person, not a collection.

Each entry in these pages includes the name of the term, an English comment about its meaning and intended use, and some hierarchical information concerning the sets (collections) of which the term is an element (this is marked as **isa** in the entries), the supersets of it (**genls**), etc. In the Cycorp WWW pages, the terms mentioned in the description of a given entry correspond normally to hyperlinks that allow the examination of their own entries. Note that, in order to reduce the complication of the descriptions, the **isa** and **genls** portions of the WWW entries contain only non-redundant terms. In this way, in the entry for #$Skin of Table 3.47 it is explicitly stated that (#$genls #$Skin #$TactileSensor); the assertion (#$genls #$Skin #$Sensor) is not, on the contrary, registered, given that #$Sensor appear in the **genls** line of the entry #$TactileSensor. Similarly, making use of the property listed in the entry #$isa of Table 3.47 – i.e. #$isa distributes over #$genls – from the assertion explicitly stated in the table for the #$Skin entry – i.e. (#$isa #$Skin #$AnimalBodyPartType) – it is possible to deduce that (#$isa #$Skin #$ExistingObjectType), (#$isa #$Skin #$TemporalStuffType) etc. given that #$ExistingObjectType, #$TemporalStuffType etc. can be reached following one or more #$genls links from #$AnimalBodyPartType.

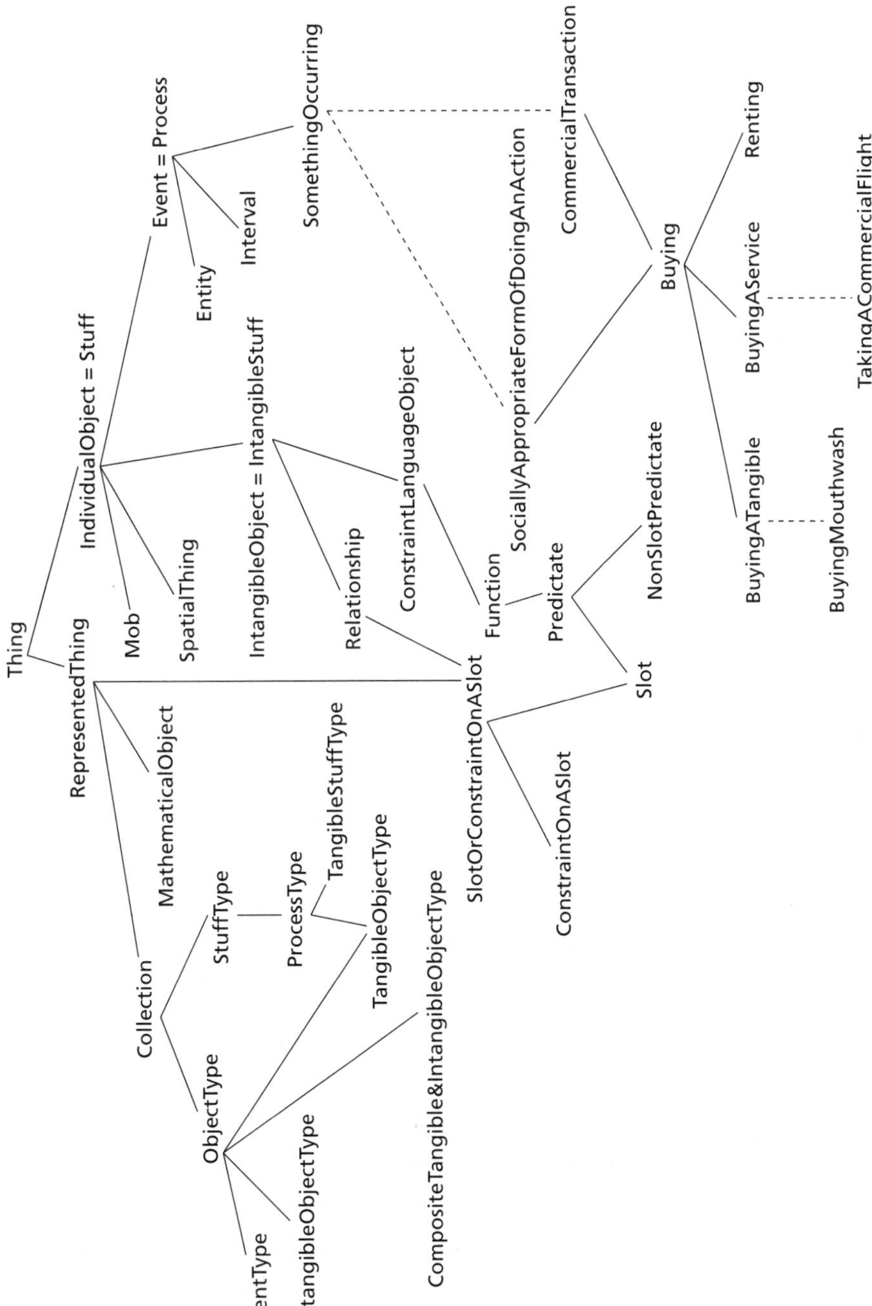

Figure 3.32 Upper level of CYC's ontology about 1990

Table 3.47 Example of entries in the WWW description of the upper CYC ontology

#$isa: **<#$ReifiableTerm> <#$Collection>**

(#$isa ?x ?y) means that ?x is an element of the collection ?y. CYC knows that #$isa distributes over #$genls; that is, if one asserts (#$isa ?x ?y) and (#$genls ?y ?z), CYC will infer that (#$isa ?x ?z). Therefore, in practice, one only manually asserts a *small fraction of the #$isa assertions – the vast majority are inferred automatically by CYC.*

isa: #$BinaryPredicate #$DefaultMonotonicPredicate #$TaxonomicSlotForAnyUnit

genlPreds: #$elementOf

some more specialized predicates: #$ethnicity #$memberOfSpecies

#$genls: **<#$Collection> <#$Collection>**

(#$genls ?X ?Y) means that ?Y is one of the supersets of ?X. Both arguments must be #$Collections. CYC knows that #$genls is transitive; that is, if one asserts (#$genls ?X ?Y) and (#$genls ?Y ?Z), CYC will infer that (#$genls ?X ?Z). Therefore, in practice, one only manually asserts a *small fraction of the #$genls assertions – the vast majority are inferred automatically by CYC.*
isa: #$TaxonomicSlotForCollections #$DefaultMonotonicPredicate #$BinaryPredicate #$ReflexiveBinaryPredicate #$TransitiveBinaryPredicate #$RuleMacroPredicate

genlPreds: #$subsetOf

some more specialized predicates: #$superTaxons

#$Skin

A (piece of) skin serves as outer protective and tactile sensory covering for (part of) an animal's body. This is the collection of all pieces of skin. Some examples include #$TheGoldenFleece (representing an entire skin of an animal) and (#$BodyPartFn #$YulBrynner #$Scalp) (representing a small portion of his skin).
isa: #$AnimalBodyPartType

genls: #$BiologicalLivingObject #$AnimalBodyPart #$SheetOfSomeStuff

#$VibrationThroughAMediumSensor #$TactileSensor

With respect to the entries #$isa and #$genls, we can also note that they are members, respectively, of the sets #$BinaryPredicate and #$TransitiveBinaryPredicate, which are in turn subsets of #$Predicate. As already noted, #$Predicate takes a number of arguments ARG0, ARG1 etc. (two for #$isa and #$genls); these must be of a particular type, for instance both must be #$Collection in the case of #$genls. When examining the entry for #$Skin of Table 3.47 we can remark that #$Skin is seen in CYC as the collection of all the possible pieces of skin, such as The Golden Fleece (the entire skin of a particular animal) or Yul Brynner's scalp (a small portion of his skin). Note that in order to reduce the number of (reified) individuals associated with the ontology (*see also* the discussion below), a solution in the form of a NAT – i.e. a call to a function with two arguments, (#$BodyPartFn #$YulBrunner #$Scalp) – has been preferred to that of introducing a specific reified term such as #$YulBrunnersScalp. Given the 'distributive' property evoked before, from the fact that #$Skin is a subset of, among other things, #$SheetOfSomeStuff and #$TactileSensor – i.e. (#$genls #$Skin #$SheetOfSomeStuff), (#$genls #$Skin #$AnimalBodyPart) – we can deduce that, if x is a piece of skin, then x is a sheet of some stuff, and x is part of the body of some animal.

The upper CYC ontology and, more generally, the CYC ontology, is a really impressive piece of software, with plenty of ingenious solutions and including an immense amount of useful knowledge. There is no doubt that every scholar interested in the construction of large knowledge bases according to the integral artificial intelligence approach should inspect this ontology as an invaluable source of useful inspiration. On the other hand, when examining this collection of terms, people are always struck by its complexity (i.e. the number of branches and interrelationships) and often wonder whether it is all really necessary.

Leaving aside, for the time being, the well-known encyclopaedic ambitions of CYC, we can discern at least a 'technical' cause giving rise to the massive proliferation of the CYC knowledge base. We can assimilate this cause to a sort of 'RLL syndrome', leading to reproduction of all the aspects of the reality according to a unique conceptual mechanism – in this case, the mechanism for defining and introducing the CYC ontology entries illustrated before. We will now illustrate the RLL syndrome with two examples.

For the first, we will limit ourselves to noting that all the 'individuals', concrete instances of some general concepts (notions), are, in CYC, integral and undivided components of the overall CYC ontology. Figure 3.33 reproduces a schema from the Cycorp Web pages that shows the top level of the present upper CYC ontology. The branch #$Individual stems directly from the root, #$Thing; #$Individual is defined as: 'The collection of all things that are NOT sets or collections. Thus, #$Individual includes (among other things) physical objects, temporal subabstractions of physical objects, numbers, relations, and groups ... Though an element of #$Individual may have parts ... that individual is NOT the same thing as the collection containing those same parts ... "Bill Clinton's immediate family" is an individual; however, the collection of persons who belong to this family is a collection. Our final example: A company belongs to #$Individual and is distinct from the collection of its employees (which #$isa #$Collection).' In the ontology's documentation we also find that: '#$Individual and #$Collection are disjoint collections: no CYC constant will be an instance of both.' From all the above we can conclude, as already stated, that #$Collection(s) correspond to the notions usually designed as 'concepts' in the 'ordinary' ontologies, *see* Section 3.1.

It becomes obvious that, given the above definitions and directions, and taking into account the very specific examples of individuals found in the CYC documentation – such as #$TheGoldenFleece or 'Yul Brunner's scalp' (or 'Bill Clinton's immediate family' or 'The US Congress on 4/1/90') – the single decision to have individuals directly inserted into the ontology leads to a considerable increase of the ontology's complexity. According to the documentation, #$Individual embraces 1400 'public' (i.e. described in the Web ontology) subsets and 13400 unpublished subsets. Some of the immediate subsets of #$Individual are #$SpatialThing, #$TemporalThing, #$Product, #$MentalObject, #$ComputationalObject, #$MathematicalObject, #$Event. With respect to the presence of this last term among the subsets of #$Individual, we can observe that, accordingly, all the events in CYC are systematically reified. Therefore – in spite of their proper temporal and relational characteristics – all the events are represented making use of the same data structures used to represent the usual, 'static' and 'atemporal' notions (concepts) that we can find normally in an ontology. *See* in Section 3.452 the opposite strategy followed in NKRL with respect to both individuals and events.

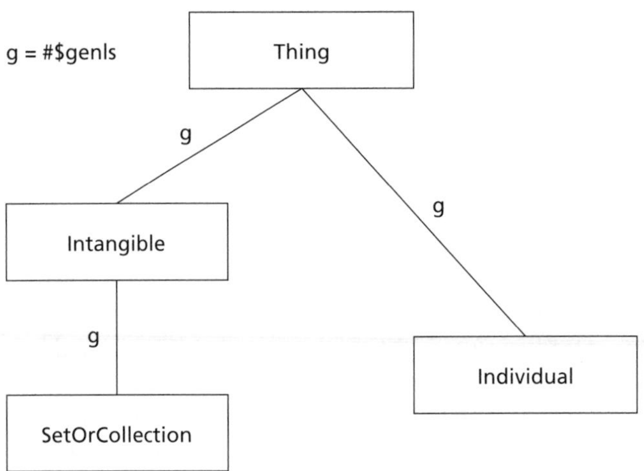

Figure 3.33 Top level of the present CYC ontology

For the second example of RLL syndrome, we will examine here the solutions adopted in CYC for the well-known problem of dealing with concepts such as 'gold', 'wood', or 'butter' that we call here generically 'substances' (corresponding, from a grammatical point of view, to the English categories of 'uncount' and 'mass' nouns). We can note that substances are characterized by the fact that they cannot instantiate *directly* into individuals. This means that individuals such as wood_1 or gold_1, derived abruptly from *wood_* or *gold_*, do not make sense: note also that notions such as *timber_* or *white_gold* are concepts, specializations of *wood_* and *gold_*, not instances of these last concepts. To produce individuals that inherit, in some way, some properties from the different substances, it is necessary to have recourse to concepts such as, for example, *physical_object*, from which – thanks to the passage through specializations of *physical_object* like, for instance, *piece_of_firewood* and *piece_of_jewellery* – we can obtain individuals as piece_of_wood_27 (or wooden_chair_42) or gold_necklace_7. These can inherit from concepts such as *wood_* or *gold_* some 'intrinsic properties' like density, flash point, etc. – *see also* Section 3.13. The CYC team has apparently missed this particular 'pseudo-sortal' nature of substances – *see also* [Guar94] on this point.

In fact, they introduce in the Web documentation the constant #$StuffType as: 'A collection of collections. Every element of #StuffType is a collection of substances that have the following logical properties: such a substance may be subdivided, spatially or temporally, and the resultant portions will also be *instances* (sic!) of the #$StuffType collection to which the original substance belonged ... Thus, if COL is some collection that is an element of #$StuffType, and ITEM is an element of COL, then if ITEM is divided into two (or more) segments, each segment is also an element of COL. Examples of #$StuffType: #$Water (the collection of all portions of water, whose spatial sub-portions are also water); #$Breathing (the collection of all events wherein someone breathes for any amount of time, whose temporal sub-events are also instances of #$Breathing).' From a concrete point of view, this means that, in CYC, a substance such as 'wood' should be interpreted as the set of all the possible pieces of wood; or, returning to a well-known example of the mid-term report, a concept such as #$PeanutButter is seen as the collection of all the possible pieces of peanut butter, *see* [Lena90a: 41], [Guha90a: 43]. Criteria in this style can, admittedly, allow us to conclude that 'wooden chair' is not a substance (an instance of #$StuffType) given that, when separating a wooden chair into its constituent elements, we do not get a collection of chairs. More precisely, for CYC, (#$isa #$WoodenChair #ExistingObjectType), where, as the documentation says: 'Each element of each element of #$ExistingObjectType is temporally stufflike yet is objectlike in other ways, e.g., spatially.' However, the strongly 'physicalist' definition given above for #$StuffType, that associates the definition of the general properties of a concept like 'wood' to the fluctuating number of pieces of wood we can find in the overall universe, is, of course, at least debatable. The quest for uniformity by the CYC's builders does not lead necessarily to the most convincing results.

Here we can note an interesting point. In the definitions reproduced in the previous paragraphs, we have always referred to the last version of the CYC upper level ontology, i.e. to the version actually existing on the Web. The present version of the 'top-level vocabulary' page of the ontology – the last update of this page goes back to 24 October 1997 – shows some subtle differences from the previous editions. In these – for example, in the 1996 versions – a specific #$Stuff constant was present, defined as: '#$Stuff is the collection of all the pieces of stuff (i.e. portions of any substance). Three kinds of #$Stuff worth mentioning here: i) Tangible Stuffs. E.g., consider any piece of wood; i.e. anything which #$isa #$Wood. #$Wood is the set of all pieces of wood. So (#$genls #$Wood #$Stuff). ii) Temporal stuffs. E.g., consider any running event; i.e. anything which #$isa #$Running. #$Running is the set of all running events. So (#$genls #$Running #$Stuff). iii) Stuffs which are neither tangible nor temporal. E.g., consider a piece of English text.' According to the definition of #$Stuff above, every instance of #$Stuff – any particular piece of wood – is also an individual thing: #$Stuff is, therefore, a subset of a constant called #$IndividualObject in the old versions of the ontology – in the recent versions, #$IndividualObject is now simply #$Individual. But again because of the #$Stuff definition, each #$IndividualObject is also a piece of some sort of stuff (a piece of some substance) and hence a member of the collection #$Stuff. Therefore, #$Stuff is also a superset of #$IndividualObject and, eventually, the two collections are co-extensional (their sets of instances coincide).

The same line of reasoning is reproduced in the mid-term report, *see* [Lena90a: 41] and [Guha90a: 43]. In mid-term report terms, it would be possible to conclude that, at the same time, #$Stuff $\subset$ #$IndividualObject and #$IndividualObject $\subset$ #$Stuff. From this, the CYC team could assert, in the 1996 version of the top-level vocabulary page, that 'this unfortunate fact forces us to define and use four collections of collections', i.e to differentiate, at the intensional (definitional) level, what seems to coincide at the extensional level (at the level of the concrete instances). The four collections of collections, as defined in the 1996 version, are: #$StuffType (see the definition of this constant, unchanged through the different versions, given in the previous paragraphs: the collections that are members of this collection refer to entities acting like a mass noun in English, as in 'wood', 'water' and 'running', i.e. substances), #$ObjectType (entities that act like count nouns in English: examples of instances of #$ObjectType are #$Automobile, the set of all cars, and #$LeapYear, the set of all leap years), #$ExistingStuffType (a subset of #$StuffType) and #$ExistingObjectType (a subset of #$ObjectType). The last two collections were necessary, according to the explications given in 1996 by CYC people, to come up, eventually, with really disjoint sets, given that an #$IndividualObject like 'my car' can also be seen generically as 'stuff' (#$StuffType) from a temporal point of view. For each of the possible time-slices that can be carved in the period during which I own the car, in fact, the car still conserves the property of being 'my car', exactly in the same way as when we take a piece of wood, water, or running, and we then take a piece of this piece, and so on, we still obtain water, wood and running. In mid-term report terms, we have: 'Anything that is spatially substance-like is also temporally substance-like, though the converse is not true' [Lena90a: 42]. This could be an interesting remark that gives us additional criteria to distinguish substances from non-substances: 'wood', a substance, is still wood when split spatially and temporally; 'car', an object, behaves like a substance from a temporal point of view, but cannot give rise to cars when split spatially.

#$Stuff has apparently been eliminated from the current version of the CYC upper ontology. This implies the elimination of this strange correspondence between the set of the instances of substance (we recall here, *inter alia*, that substances cannot support direct instances) and the set of instances of individual object. However, the four collections of collections above are still present, probably because of the remark at the end of the previous paragraph. The general aspect of the 'stuff' and 'object' section of the ontology is represented in Figure 3.34; note that #$Collection in Figure 3.34 is a subset of #$SetOrCollection of Figure 3.33. The interest of the 'interesting remark' signalled at the end of the paragraph above can now be questioned: the systematic search for a parallelism between spatial and temporal aspects leads, in fact, to the attempt to manage temporal and spatial aspects at once from both a representational and a computational point of view, and contributes, eventually, to worsening the intricacy aspects of the ontology as clearly shown in Figure 3.34. For a solution where we deal separately (but in a co-ordinated way) with the representation problems proper, on one hand, to the 'concepts' (or 'objects', 'individual notions' etc.) and, on the other hand, to the temporally characterized events, situations, etc. where these 'objects' are involved, see the NKRL subsection below.

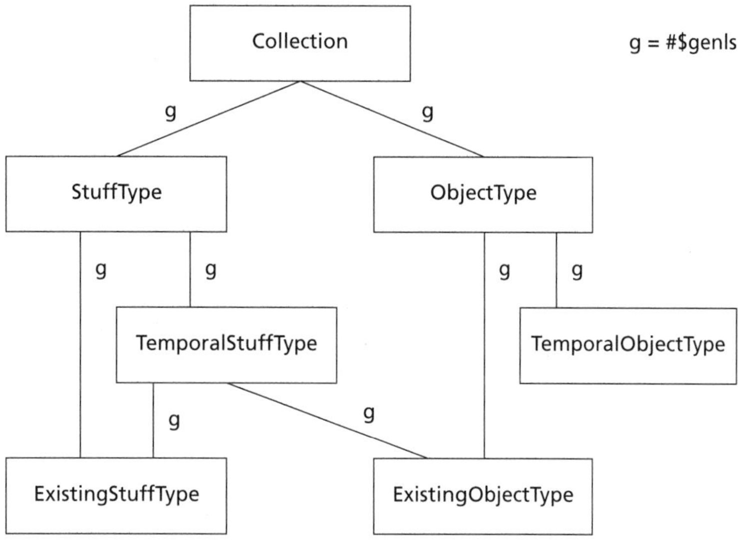

Figure 3.34 'Stuff' and 'object' segment of the upper CYC ontology

3.443 *The last developments*

The most important innovation in the second part of CYC's life cycle has been the substantial recourse to the concept of 'microtheory'. In [Lena90b: 147–48], there was only a very vague allusion to CYC's 'microworld(s)', defined as 'particular task domain(s), down to some (pre-expert) level of details'. In the mid-term report, microtheories were concisely introduced, associated with the concept of 'context', at the end of the discussion of the epistemological level [Guha90a: 38]. A quite detailed description of this new tool can be found in [Guha94] which, moreover, supplies a summary of the whole history of CYC at MCC, a 'state of the art' of the project close to the moment of its conclusion, and some indications about possible developments of CYC. A recent Lenat paper on the 'context' and 'microtheories' topics is [Lena98].

Contexts and microtheories

The introduction of 'microtheories' in CYC is an outcome of Guha's PhD thesis exploring the notion of 'context' under the supervision of John McCarthy at Stanford [Guha91b]. As affirmed in [Sowa93], probably the most important consequence of introducing this concept in CYC is the possibility of rearranging and partitioning the huge knowledge base of the project into more manageable subsets. Each microtheory – which includes the knowledge describing a very specific, restricted domain such as buying and selling – contains a (relatively) limited number of axioms (sentences or assertions) or rules that can, therefore, be carefully refined and tested. Microtheories can be assembled and integrated by importing or translating axioms from one context to another. Lenat and Guha [Guha94: 136–137] call this sort of operation 'lifting the axioms', given that some assumptions made for the axioms in a given context, or the definitions of some terms, could possibly be changed to be able to make use of these axioms in a different context; of course, 'lifting' needs to be as meaning-preserving as possible.

Going into some detail, Lenat and Guha affirm that all the assertions in CYC (axioms, statements) are not universally true, but true only with respect to a certain 'context'. For example, the sentence: '**ist**(*NTP*, $\forall x \neg supported(x) \supset falls(x)$)' asserts that, in NTP, a (particularly) Naive Theory of Physics, something that is not supported normally, falls – in CYC, a 'theory' consists of a set of CycL sentences that can be explicitly 'named' by making use of reification. A theory like NTP, which supplies the context, is also called microtheory. A sentence pertaining to a microtheory has the general form '**ist**(c, p)', which means that the proposition p is true 'in the context of' microtheory c. The context describes the assumptions made by the microtheory, what is left implicit, and so on; the addition of a fact to a microtheory always changes the theory associated with it, but this does not necessarily change the associated context. Note that, according to this particular view, the correct addition of a particular statement p to the CYC knowledge base should always be executed under the form **ist**(c, p); when a particular theory will not be explicitly associated with a particular statement, it is assumed that this statement is true in the context of the 'most expressive microtheory' (MEM). This particular approach is clearly influenced by the McCarthy's proposals [McCaJ87b] concerning the formalization of a 'context' as an abstract mathematical, first-class object; in CycL also, microtheories are (reified) first-class objects. McCarthy in turn [McCaJ93] recognizes that his notation has been influenced by that adopted in Guha's thesis.

An important point to note is that CYC's authors do not try to completely 'decontextualize' a sentence like p – for example, the sentence 'an apple costs about 30 cents'. This would require adding a lot of information, such as specifying the time period over which the statement p is true, where it is true, what exactly is meant by cost, to whom it will cost that amount of money, and so on. Saying that proposition p is true in the context of microtheory c means simply, therefore, that we are explicitly recording the fact that p has certain context dependencies, a few of which are written down. Of course, decontextualization can be expanded, but still to only a certain extent.

Table 3.38 summarizes some of the logical properties of CYC's contexts as in [Guha94: 135]. In Table 3.49 we give an example, adapted from [Guha93], of a CycL axiom where the context is explicitly mentioned. This axiom – a default, like most of the assertions in the CYC knowledge base – says that the human resources department of a company plays a central role in mediating the hiring of employees. It is one of several thousand axioms that pertain to the CYC's 'LargeCorpInternalsMt' microtheory, which deals with big late-20th-century US corporations; remember that all the CYC contexts (microtheories) are fully-fledged terms in the CYC KB.

In Table 3.49, #$LargeCorpInternalsMt is the context (*c*), where the list having the predicate #$forAll as its first term is the assertion (*p*) saying that, by default, each human resources department is assumed to mediate the hiring of the employees. In this figure, we have kept the syntax of the predicate #$forAll as given in [Guha93] – i.e. (#$forAll *?x S P*), where *P* is a proposition containing *x* as a free variable; this syntax is equivalent to $(\forall x \in S)\ P(x)$. According to the Web documentation, this syntax has been slightly modified and, mainly, #$forAll can now be omitted in the CycL formulas according to the convention that seemingly unbound variables inside formulae are assumed to be universally quantified. The quaternary predicate #$actsInCapacity, with syntax (#$actsInCapacity <#$Agent> <#$ActorSlot> <#$ScriptType> <#$CapacityAttribute>), pertains to the CYC 'occupation or position vocabulary'. This predicate is relatively frequent in the CYC knowledge base, where there exist approximately 300 assertions that relate such predicates to other predicates and to various collections. Given that the axiom of Table 3.49 pertains to the #$LargeCorpInternalsMt context, it is possible to use within it all the simplifying assumptions associated with this particular microtheory, and the meanings of the terms used in the axiom will agree with those fixed for the terms of the microtheory.

Turning to the different types of context considered in CYC, in [Guha94] Lenat and Guha say, as a premise, that contexts supply (generally) a means of referring to a group of related assertions about which something can be said. Such a group can describe:

- a general theory of some topics, such as a theory of mechanics, a theory about the weather in winter, or a theory about what to look for when buying a car. A context used in this way is what is precisely called a 'microtheory'. Microtheories are, normally, sufficiently large (i.e. they can include hundreds or thousands of axioms) and are also relatively stable; for any given topic, such as 'the weather', there can be several different microtheories, at different levels of detail and generality. An important point to raise is that, by introducing the microtheories, the management of the global consistency of the CYC knowledge base is considerably simplified, given that the problem of maintaining global consistency is transformed into a problem of maintaining local consistency, which is much simpler and faster;
- a representation of some situation that is specifically tailored for the problem it was set up to solve. Lenat and Guha give as an example that of a model of a Christmas tree as a perfect cone, which can be used for determining whether it will fit into a given space in a store window or in a car boot. Another example is

Table 3.48 Logical properties of CYC's contexts

- Within any context, it is possible to make use of all the conventional FOPC (first-order predicate calculus) tools, including its proof theory.
- Contexts are first-class objects, and the **ist** formulae are first-class formulae.
- Each context has a vocabulary associated with it. This means that a particular sentence *p* might not be asserted in a given context, or that this sentence can be stated differently in different contexts. For example, it may be possible to state *p* as '(cost Apple (Cents 30))' in context c_1, and as '($\forall x$ (apple *x*) $\Rightarrow$ (cost *x* (Cents 30) USA))' in context c_2. If the predicate 'cost' is not included in the vocabulary of context c_3, it will not be possible to assert *p* in this last context. A statement may be true in a context and false in another – e.g., a statement like 'an apple costs about 30 cents' may be false in a context about 18th-century America.
- The same symbol might denote different things in different contexts. For example, it is possible to have both **ist**(c_1, table(it)) and **ist**(c_2, chair(it)), where the same constant 'it' obviously denotes two different objects in the two different contexts.
- CYC is constantly operating within a given context. From an operational point of view, being 'in' the context *c* and then stating *p* is equivalent to being in the outer context and then stating **ist**(*c*, *p*). This means also that, when the system is in the context *c*, the only axioms available to the problem solver are those axioms *p* such that **ist**(*c*, *p*) is true in the outer context. Therefore, **ist** is normally not involved in the formulae available in a given context, and all the conventional FOPC problem solvers can then be used in that context.

Table 3.49 A CycL axiom with the context explicitly expressed

```
(#$ist #$LargeCorpInternalsMt

    (#$forAll ?x (#$HumanResourcesDepartment #$allInstances)
         (#$actsInCapacity ?x #$mediatorInProcesses
              #$EmployeeHiring #$MainFunction)))
```

that of an object reduced simply to a point mass in order to determine its trajectory. Contexts used with this aim – i.e. for a particular problem-solving task – are called problem-solving contexts (PSC). PSCs are usually created dynamically by the system, importing many axioms from several microtheories, and are forgotten and discarded after a specific answer has been produced.

- A 'slightly decontextualized' representation of the utterances made in a discourse, for instance, a representation in which an anaphoric reference like 'the person' is not systematically reduced to the specific character referred to but is represented by using a generic term such as '(The Person)'. This is possible given that, within any given context, this last term denotes a unique individual, even if the individual is obviously different in the various contexts. Such contexts are called 'utterance contexts' and, like the PSCs, are also ephemeral and relatively small.

'Microtheories' and 'contexts' have assumed an ever-growing importance for the last developments of the CYC project. Lenat and Guha insist on the positive effects linked with the possibility of having theories at different levels of granularity, i.e. of using different representations in different parts of the knowledge base, depending on the expressiveness requested. They also point out that each (explicitly reified) context can make use not only of its own knowledge base, therefore making the overall knowledge base of CYC more manageable, but also of its own, separate ontology – a separate set of collections, predicates and individuals. This means that, when a particular task requires a modified ontology, this can be created by building new contexts rather than being obliged to modify drastically the unique, 'always true' ontology [Guha93: 160–161]. This approach seems to correspond to the well-known strategy consisting of the assumption that the very specific concepts that constitute the 'lower level' of an ontology can be totally changed when moving from an application domain to a new one, *see* [Skuc95], [Zarr95a]. Finally, they point out that the microtheory mechanisms also allow making inferences to be drastically speeded up (the primary task of the heuristic level). This is possible given that most reasoning and problem solving in response to a query typically occurs almost entirely within one context. Hence, when trying to answer a question, CYC can usually ignore 99.9 per cent of the terms of the knowledge base and, therefore, all the assertions involving these terms – a way to reply to the criticism about the complexity of the CYC KB raised in the previous subsection.

In [Lena98], Doug Lenat analyzes, according to two complementary criteria, the nine years spent in modelling the CYC KB into a set of contexts or microtheories:

- a first question concerns whether the introduction of microtheories has engendered a real speeding up of the knowledge-entering;
- in the case of a positive answer to this, it is necessary to evaluate whether the reduction of time and effort can be considered as sufficient.

Lenat's answer is positive in the first case, given that i) assertions (facts, rules, etc.) tend to be more terse and simpler in form when entered in a specialized context instead of in a flat knowledge base; ii) there is also a strong probability of having to enter similar (and pertinent) assertions very close together, and this facilitates the use of copy&edit procedures. However – and this is Lenat's answer to the second question – these potential gains in productivity are strongly balanced by the difficulties encountered by the knowledge editors in selecting (or, even worse, in creating) exactly the right context each time they have to enter a new piece of domain knowledge. Therefore, the challenge becomes that of finding the good 'granularity' for the modelling of the KB, avoiding both a too coarse granularity implying rules that are huge and very difficult to debug, and a too fine granularity where it becomes hard to find the right context for a new piece of knowledge. [Lena98] suggests some answers in this context.

Natural language processing

In the long years of development of the CYC projects, Doug Lenat has on several occasions heavily criticized any pretension of building up large knowledge bases (having dimensions comparable to those of CYC) making use of some sort of knowledge acquisition techniques from natural language texts. His thesis – which, of course, cannot be challenged in principle – could be resumed saying that '... one cannot expect to shortcut the building of the large KB ... by NLU (natural language understanding) because NLU itself requires such a KB – for semantic disambiguation of word senses, resolving anaphora, inducing the meaning of ellipses, and so on' [Lena90a: 33].

In their 1994 paper – at the end of the MCC phase of the project – Lenat and Guha explain that, in their opinion, the dimensions attained by the CYC knowledge base after many years of manual development are now sufficient to hypothesize that CYC could ' ... be able to keep abreast of any reasonable fraction of the happenings in the world ... by reading texts' [Guha94: 137]. In this last paper, they give a short description of their CYC-based natural language understanding program (developed in 1993), taking care to explain that i) they do not intend, obviously, to do any 100 per cent unrestricted natural language understanding, ii) their methodology for building up CYC-NL (CYC's natural language component) has been totally empirical, and iii) they have borrowed heavily from many different approaches.

Very classically, the CYC NL subsystem consists of four main modules, according to [Guha94]: lexicon, syntax, semantics, and postsemantics (pragmatics). The main modules have been reduced to three: lexicon, syntactic parser, and semantic interpreter in the Cycorp Web documentation. The lexicon is part of the main CYC knowledge base; it contains syntactic and semantic information about English words, where the words are represented as CycL constants. For example, the constant #$Light-The Word is used to represent the English word 'light'. For each word-constant, assertions in the lexicon specify its morphological variants and the lexical properties (parts of speech); they specify also the mapping ('triggering') into the CycL constants representing the 'concepts' with which the words can be associated. For example, the constant #$Light-The Word has denotation links to the two constants #$LightEnergy and #$LightingDevice.

Looking at the syntactic module, there are some minor discrepancies between [Guha94] and the description on the Web. The paper mentions, for example, the use of sets of context-sensitive rules, whereas the documentation speaks of context-free rules organized into a phrase-structure grammar loosely based on government and binding principles. The main strategy is always, however, that of producing all the syntactic analysis compatible with the set of rules used, entrusting the semantic interpreter with the disambiguation tasks. Following the description of the CYC NL subsystem given in the paper, the context-sensitive rules do not try to produce a complete parse-tree of the whole sentence, but rather a partial analysis for the different sentence fragments. Table 3.50 reproduces an example of syntactic analysis that can be found in [Guha94] and which is relative to the sentence 'He killed the girl with a branch'; the output consists of a set of 'parselets'.

Table 3.50 The result, under the form of a set of parselets, of the partial syntactic analysis of an NL sentence in CYC-NL

```
(subjectOfVerb  [killed]  [He])
(objectOfVerb  [killed]  [girl])
(article  [girl]  [the])
(article  [branch]  [a])
(withEP  ref  [branch])
```

In this table, '[branch]' refers to a complex structure where the set of word-senses of the word 'branch' (of the CycL constant #$Branch-The Word) that are syntactically consistent with the overall sentence are registered. The other '[...]' structures have a similar meaning. 'withEP' is a predicate that points to locations in the CYC NL subsystem where the different meanings of 'with' in English (instrument, possession ...) are stored along with some information on the linguistic constraints on these meanings. 'ref', in the last parselet, is a dummy reference which, in the semantic or post-semantic phase, will be substituted with the most likely 'pp-attachment' (prepositional phrase attachment) references, i.e. 'killed' or 'girl'.

Using the results of the syntactic phase, the semantic module produces a set of CycL expressions that are 'triggered' by the words and word-types included in the original sentence and which are coherent with the syntactic results (parselets). The Web documentation makes it clear that this triggering is mainly verb-driven, in that verbs are stored in the lexicon associated with 'templates' specifying how their associated clauses must be translated into CycL. The CycL expressions are then combined according to a set of rules in Montague's style, giving rise to the overall CycL translation. During this phase, the CYC NL subsystem operates a partial disambiguation of the results of the syntactic analysis; the final semantic output still contains, however, indexicals such as 'He', 'It', 'The man' or 'Yesterday'. Table 3.51, slightly modified from Figure 4 of [Guha94: 139], illustrates the two expressions produced by the semantic module for the previous example, listed in order of decreasing preference. Note that some of the possible results, such as those relative to an interpretation of 'with' in terms of 'accompanied by', have been eliminated during this phase of semantic processing. The references corresponding to the indexicals are eliminated in the last, post-semantics phase.

Table 3.51 An example of output of the semantic module in CYC-NL

```
(#$and
      (#$allInstancesOf  ?x  #$KillingSomeone)
      (#$performedBy  ?x  He)
      (#$objectActedOn  ?x  (TheEF Girl))
      (#$toolsUsed  ?x  (AEF Branch-Tree)))

(#$and
      (#$allInstanceOf  ?x  #$KillingSomeone)
      (#$performed  ?x  He)
      (#$objectActedOn  ?x  (TheEF Girl))
      (#$holds  (TheEF Girl)  (AEF Branch-Tree)))
```

In [Guha94: 138], Lenat and Guha say that the syntactic module of the CYC NL subsystem is able to handle correctly about 75 per cent of the sentences found in the news stories of a typical issue of the newspaper *USA Today*. To be fully credible, this information should be accompanied by some statistics concerning the number of unresolved ambiguities, such as the correct attachment of the 'with a branch' prepositional phrase in the previous example. The authors also add that – in cases where the CYC NL subsystem knows all the proper names in a sentence – the semantics module is able to deal properly with 'most' of the sentences parsable by the syntactic module. 'Properly' here means that the final output must be as good as the CycL representation of the same text produced manually by one of the CYC knowledge enterers.

CYC applications

Lenat and Guha have often stated that '... the goal of the CYC project ... is *not* an experiment whose sole purpose is to test a hypothesis ... rather it is an engineering effort, aimed at constructing an artefact ... The artefact we are building is a shared information resource, which many programs can usefully draw upon' [Guha93: 150]. On the same page, they also say that: 'Of course we expect that this artefact would then be useful, once it is built'; however, experiments and applications '... are an enormous potential distraction, and should (and are being) eschewed by us' [Guha93: 153]. The reason why using CYC for some very precise task could be, at that time, a 'potential distraction' (a 'time-sink') is explained clearly later in the same paper: 'CYC itself does not contain all the knowledge required to do any of these applications. While a CYC-based application should be much more powerful and flexible than most current software, depending on the particular domain, building such applications might require a significant effort. Some of the additional knowledge will be added to CYC, and some will best just be accessed by CYC (e.g., continuing to reside as tuples in databases which are maintained by some external organisation or agency' [Guha93: 170].

In 1994, however, near the end of the MCC project, Lenat and Guha affirm they now have some good reasons to think the system has already reached a point where it could be advantageously used for concrete work. In [Guha94: 138–139], they supply a list of criteria – summarized in Table 3.52 – that, in their opinion, would characterize the practical utilizations of the CYC's knowledge base for at least the next few years. They also note that the short-term applications of CYC will probably concern some 'mundane' field such as information management or making spreadsheets smarter, rather than more 'classical' artificial intelligence problems such as that of helping expert systems to be less brittle – as Lenat and Guha recall, this was indeed one of the main motivations for starting the project in 1984.

Moreover, applications are, of course, the *raison d'être* of the new company, Cycorp; in their documentation, *see* Table 3.53, they list some tasks to which CYC was being applied in 1999 and suggest some possible future applications.

Table 3.52 Criteria for the early CYC applications

- **Low infrastructure cost**. Until CYC has completely proved its utility, it would be unwise to start CYC-based applications that could require very large retooling of the system or large investments in hardware. As an example, Lenat and Guha say that it would be great to have the possibility of using CYC in every classroom, but that this would require each classroom to have a computer running CYC.
- **Incremental use of CYC**. The applications should be of the 'fail-software' type, i.e. in case CYC was unable, for some task, to supply a valid help, the application should rely as much as possible on the existing software for this task.
- **Off-line**. Try to avoid any application for which rapid real-time response is required.
- **Moderately 'stylized' use**. This expression means that it should be possible to characterize the CYC's applications by a small number of high-frequency types of query. These query types can be optimized, if necessary, by adding more heuristics for rapid inference.
- **Need for common sense**. Even in the context of the 'mundane' applications evoked before, the use of CYC would not be justified for tasks too technical, and/or very narrow, and/or very simple, and/or very stylized, where a simple expert system (or a custom non-AI application program) could be sufficient.
- **Centralized running**. Avoid using CYC on the end-user machines – which are surely not powerful enough to run this huge type of application – and try to use instead a limited number of centralized machines (e.g., according to the example given by Guha and Lenat, one machine running CYC in each supermarket).

Table 3.53 Current and potential applications of CYC (mid-1999)

- **Applications currently available or in development**
  - Natural language processing
  - Integration of heterogeneous databases
  - Knowledge-enhanced retrieval of captioned information
  - Guided integration of structured terminology (GIST)
  - Distributed AI
  - WWW information retrieval
- **Potential applications**
  - Online brokering of goods and services
  - 'Smart' interfaces
  - Intelligent character simulation for games
  - Enhanced virtual reality
  - Improved machine translation
  - Improved speech recognition
  - Sophisticated user modelling
  - Semantic data mining

We will examine here briefly the 'integration of heterogeneous databases' task, an 'integral approach' mechanism which is probably the most popular among the CYC's applications and which constitutes one of the most convincing proofs of CYC's practical utility. This task pertains, like the knowledge-enhanced or the WWW retrieval, to a domain that CYC people call 'semantic information retrieval'. This is characterized by the fact that – to the contrary of what happens in the usual 'syntactic' approach based on the use of Boolean or SQL queries – a CYC-based system is supposed to understand exactly the meaning of the terms the user employs to communicate with it. A personnel database, for example, may know that 'John Smith' is a 'professor' working for an employer called 'Yale University' but it does not know what the three strings above 'mean', i.e. what a person, professor, or university is.

To use CYC as an intelligent front-end to several independently developed structured information sources (such as spreadsheets and databases), each of which may have a totally different format, the general principle consists of 'explaining' to CYC the idiosyncrasies of the different SISs by i) creating a new CycL context for each SIS; ii) writing for each context a number of axioms that translate into CycL the particularities of the logical schema of the SIS. The integration power stems from the fact that, if we are able to establish for each SIS the set of axioms that enable it to be mapped to CYC, CycL will be constituted like a common superset of all the logical schemes used in the different SISs, i.e. a sort of universal description language for database schemes. In [Guha94: 140], Guha and Lenat emphasize the fact that this type of approach to integration requires only *N* sets of translation axioms for *N* SISs, where a traditional approach consisting in writing translation rules for each pair of SISs would require *N*-squared sets of translation rules for *N* SISs.

To take a simple Cycorp example illustrating the core of the above strategy, let us suppose we are dealing with a simple relational DB including two tables, an 'employee' and an 'employer' table. The former has three fields – the person's name, the job title, and the name of the person's employer – and the latter two fields – the employer's name and the name of the state where the employer is situated. Querying the database with a question like 'Show me people who hold an advanced degree and live in New England' would give rise to a failure, given that the tables know nothing about what an 'advanced degree' means, and they have no information about New England. But CYC knows, on the contrary, that people such as doctors, lawyers and professors hold advanced degrees, that people generally live near their place of work, and that New England includes six states. So it can now transform this query into a query for doctors, lawyers and professors whose employer is situated in one of the six states, generating automatically the corresponding SQL code – *see* [Zarr86a]. In this way, if John Smith is stored in the tables as a professor working at Yale, he will be supplied to the user as a valid answer to the original query.

Going into some technical details, we can say that the database module of CYC deals with a user's query in three phases – an interface phase, a planner phase and an executor phase. In the first phase, the user submits his query in CycL terms, making use, in this case, of the CYC natural language module. In the case of the query examined in the previous paragraph, the CycL expression will correspond to the logical formula (a) in Table 3.54. In the planner phase, the CYC inference engine makes use of the assertions in the CYC KB to transform expression (a) into new expressions that refer to the descriptions of the database fields. One of these new descriptions will be, for example, the CycL formula labelled as (b) in Table 3.54. These expressions are now converted into an intermediate (logical level) representation format called CSQL. This then gives rise, in the execution phase, to the (physical level) SQL queries, thanks to the use of the information previously stored in CYC which concerns the characteristics of the database schema.

Table 3.54 Intelligent database querying in CYC

```
a (#$and
     (#$isa ?x #$Professor)
     (#$residesInGeographicRegion ?x #$NewEngland-USRegion))

b (#$and
     (#$is ?x #$Professor)
     (#$employees ?y ?x)
     (#$residenceOfOrganization ?y #$Connecticut-State))
```

Sowa [Sowa93: 98–99] reports on a successful application of a first version of the integration methodology of CYC concerning a car sales adviser, where the system asked questions about a customer's needs and interests and suggested car models to take into consideration. In this application, CYC was able to connect itself successfully with several different databases in order to collect useful information – with a relational DB using SQL that stored the Kelly *Blue Book* data on prices, with an object-oriented DB using ORION that stored information about options and packages, and with the *Consumer Reports* DB concerning reliability and software satisfaction. In their documentation, Cycorp people mention an integration application developed in 1995 for a major pharmaceuticals company, and used to integrate tens of gigabytes of data from more than 60 relational tables.

A second example of semantic information retrieval is offered by 'knowledge-enhanced retrieval of captioned information', an application already mentioned in [Guha94], which concerns finding images relevant to some NL query. A question like: 'find someone at risk for skin cancers' – addressed to a small repository of images where each one is described by half a dozen CycL axioms that translate their 'captions' – is able to retrieve, for instance, two photos, one describing three men in beachwear standing on a beach and holding surfboards, and the other showing a girl lying on the beach. The inferential process tries to make connections between the attributes describing the images and previously entered into CYC via the CycL axioms, and the properties indicated in the query, in this case, that risk of skin cancer is promoted by sun tanning, and that reclining on the beach implies sun tanning.

Additional evidence of the concrete utility of the CYC KB is offered by the participation of Cycorp in a recent DARPA-supported project, the High-Performance Knowledge Base (HPKB) project. This project, ended in fiscal year 1999, aimed to enable developers of military systems to build up quickly very large knowledge bases – to the order of 10^6 basic elements, rules, axioms or frames. These knowledge bases must be extensive and reusable in many applications, and they should be maintained and modified easily. An in-depth description of the first phase of the project and, more precisely, of the results of a month-long evaluation of the tools used in HPKB is given in [CoheP98].

The participants in the projects can be divided into three groups: the technology developers, the integrators, and the challenge problem developers. DARPA says that challenge problems have been a major programmatic innovation of HPKB: these problems must obviously be challenging, they 'must raise the bar for both technology and science', must have clear significance to the United States Department of Defense, should serve for the duration of the programme, becoming more challenging each year, should require little or no access to military experts of the domain, and should have unambiguous criteria for evaluating its solutions [CoheP98: 27]. Examples of challenge problems are the 'crisis-management challenge problem', devoted to carrying out tasks about international tensions that require relatively shallow knowledge (*see also* [Star98]), the 'battlespace challenge problem', designed to apply relatively specific knowledge about activities in armed conflicts, the 'movement analysis challenge problem', aimed to interpret vehicle movements detected and tracked by sensors, and the 'workaround challenge problem', which is concerned with finding military engineering solutions to traffic-destruction problems, such as destroyed bridges and blocked tunnels.

The challenge problems were managed by using integrated systems developed by two groups of HPKB partners led, respectively, by Teknowledge and SAIC (Science Applications International Corporation). Teknowledge and SAIC implemented two different strategies. Teknowledge favoured a centralized architecture based on the CYC KB (CYC ontology) and operating according to the semantic integration and semantic information retrieval strategies introduced by Cycorp and illustrated by the examples in the previous paragraphs. SAIC preferred a distributed architecture based on the sharing of specialized domain ontologies and knowledge bases, including a large upper-level ontology that contains, *inter alia*, the upper CYC ontology. The two approaches were tested in an extensive study in June 1998 – besides [CoheP98: 38–49], see also *http://www.iet.com/Projects/HPKIB/Y1Eval/*. In a very synthetic way, it is possible to affirm that the integrated systems representing the two approaches do not show major differences in performance: note also that they both include a CYC component, even if the CYC influence is, obviously, neatly more important in the Teknowledge approach. However, the Teknowledge integrated system is characterized by performances that are slightly higher than those of the SAIC system. Moreover, it is interesting to note that Teknowledge was able to translate automatically from English to a formal type of representation the questions used in evaluating the systems, whereas the SAIC teams performed very poorly at this task.

3.444 CYC facing its critics

AI literature abounds with discussions about the epistemological and implementation principles of CYC. We can mention here [Stee94] (Chapter 4 in particular: 'The Knowledge Level in Expert Systems: Conversations and Commentary') and, mainly, a special section of the *Artificial Intelligence Journal* [Stef93], which includes six reviews of the 1990 Lenat and Guha's book, and a response by Guha and Lenat. We will subdivide the criticisms addressed to CYC into two categories: those that mainly contest some technical choices made by the project, and those that challenge the global import of the CYC endeavour.

Technical remarks

In the *AI Journal* special section, Elkan and Greiner ([Elka93: 45]) raise, for example, the problem concerning the 'widespread reification' that constitutes one of the main characteristics of CycL, *see also* Section 3.442. In CYC, in fact, as already stated, all the concepts and all their instances (in CYC's terminology, all the #$Thing(s)), are referred to by making use of *explicit*, *permanent* symbolic labels (constants), and the encyclopaedic ambitions of the system leads to a proliferation of labels such as #$GeorgeBushsBody and #$GeorgeBushsMind [Lena90b: 183–185] or #$AllTheGoldInTheUniverse [Lena90b: 158]. Apart from the coherence problems that this proliferation can introduce in the CYC's knowledge base, the existence in the base of a lot of connected 'reified things' is expensive in both time and space, and can give rise to some problems in order to control inferencing. Lenat and Guha are aware of this problem, and they supply some 'common sense' criteria [Lena90b: 162] to decide when a new concept (a new 'collection') must be created. The most important suggests reifying a new collection only when there are several important properties to assert about it, in particular, a set of properties that makes sense only for the instances of that collection. Elkan and Greiner remark that, making use of a normal predicate/argument formalism, extensive reification is not necessary given that the interesting aspects of an entity can be simply represented by compound terms, for example, 'Congestion(Capital(Texas), Moderate)' can be asserted without being obliged to reify first 'Capital(Texas)'. In [Guha93: 158], Guha and Lenat do not really discuss the essence of the problem, limiting themselves to affirm that the construction of compound terms, NATs, is possible in CycL. Another of Elkan and Greiner's criticisms concerns the very *ad hoc* criteria adopted by the CYC team to validate the efficiency of the different CYC's inference mechanisms.

The organization of the CYC's ontology constitutes one of the most controversial aspects of the project. Like us, McDermott [McDeD93: 60] criticizes the '... unsatisfactory analysis of a substance as the set of all the objects made of that substance' – *see*, in Section 3.442, the definition of 'wood' as the set of all the existing pieces of wood. Skuce (an ontology's specialist) is, however, the reviewer contributing to the special section of the *AI Journal* who has produced the more detailed analysis of the principles adopted in CYC's ontology [Skuc93: 85–88].

After having paid homage to the CYC's team for their attempt to produce one of the most comprehensive ontologies ever published, he analyzes some important methodological decisions adopted by this team that are particularly questionable. He points out, firstly, the inconsistencies between the description of the ontology given in the book and that of the mid-term report, and suggests that Lenat and Guha do not seem to have a clear understanding of many of the notions they use, such as thing, set, instance, individual object, stuff, substance, etc. He then discusses in depth the way the substance-like concepts are used in CYC. In this context he criticizes the way the terms 'intrinsic properties' versus 'extrinsic properties' are used in CYC. For the CYC team, 'intrinsic properties' are those that, if owned by a particular individual, are also owned (at least as defaults) by the parts of this individual. 'Extrinsic properties' are, on the contrary, characterized by the fact that parts of individuals do not have this property even if the individual does. In the mid-term report, they state this principle: 'An object *x* typically inherits its intrinsic properties from whichever instances of **SubstanceType** (#$StuffType, according to the new CYC' terminology) it is an instance of; *x* inherits extrinsic properties from whichever instances of **ObjectType** it is an instance of' [Lena90a: 41]. This means that a particular table, #$Table001, made entirely of wood, inherits various default properties (such as density and flashPoint) from #$Wood, the kind of stuff it is an instance of: all these are 'intrinsic properties'. It inherits also some default properties (such as number of legs, cost, size) from #$Table, the kind of individual object it is an instance of: all these are 'extrinsic properties'. Skuce makes reference to assertions such as that the intrinsic properties '... can be inherited from a type of stuff to its instances' [Lena90b: 186]. According to him, in fact, i) if we equate 'type of stuff' with 'substance', as several examples in the CYC's literature authorize us to do (and as it is now official in the new CYC's terminology), it is not clear what an 'instance' of a 'substance' (water, gold, energy, peanut butter ...) can be – see our point about the 'pseudo-sortal' nature of substances in Section 3.442; ii) it is not clear at all which particular inheritance mechanism Lenat and Guha refer to in their assertions.

Lenat and Guha's answer to the above criticisms is really sweeping. After having simply referred Skuce to the mid-term report for a clarification, stating that '... we shall not provide a detailed reiteration of that material [substances, types, collections, etc.] here, because we fear that it would only further the misconception that Cyc is largely about those sorts of high-level representation issues', they assert that '... for the past several years ... our knowledge enterers have not come across statements (that they wished to enter into Cyc) touching on substances, time, types and collections, etc. that were difficult or impossible or contradictory (and which then would have been engendered changes in that part of Cyc's ontology). Almost all of their activity, and by now almost all of Cyc's knowledge base, involves much more specific ontological issues than those; e.g., buying and selling, human capabilities and preferences and desires, the weather, furniture, etc.' [Guha93: 162]. Which means in practice that, in the day-to-day reality, CYC's ontology appears to work from a very pragmatic point of view; do not worry if its theoretical foundations appear to be inconsistent and puzzling. Or, using Lenat and Guha's terms: 'Most of the knowledge in the knowledge base does not depend crucially on the exact structure of the top level' [Guha93: 164].

Another 'technical' subject of controversy concerns the global, computational efficiency of the CYC system. In the *AI Journal* section, Elkan and Greiner, McDermott, Neches, Skuce etc. had all raised some points about this specific topic. Lenat and Guha can easily respond by emphasizing the deep changes in the CYC's organization that happened in the second half of the project, from the adoption of a logic-oriented approach to the introduction of contexts. For example, they say that the context mechanism is particularly useful in helping the heuristic level to accomplish correctly its primary task, i.e. to make inference efficient. Most reasoning and problem solving in response to a query, in fact, normally occurs almost within one context, and the system can therefore focus only on a relatively tiny portion of the knowledge base in order to find an answer to the query [Guha93: 159]. With respect to the problem of efficiency, it may be interesting to report also the experience of a real user of CYC, the Computer Science Department of the Québec University in Montreal (UQAM), Canada, which acquired a copy of the CYC knowledge base, mainly to use it to support the generation of natural language, argumentative/explanatory texts [Mili95].

The UQAM's researchers remark that two difficulties stand out when trying to query efficiently the huge CYC knowledge base. The first is linked with the widespread reification used in CYC: because of the wide choice of possible terms, it becomes extremely difficult to select the right elements to construct the queries. To express, for example, a simple relationship of possession between an instance of #$Person (or #$HumanAdult) and an instance of #$Car, the CYC's user will be able to choose between several #$Predicate(s) like, at least, #$owns, #$hasOwnershipIn, #$buyer, #$actors, etc. Given the unsatisfactory state of the documentation about the system (although the situation should now change with the public release of the upper CYC ontology on the Internet), the only possible way of grasping the conceptual differences between these predicates is to pragmatically evaluate the different candidates by following the inference tracks that derive from them. This is equivalent to being obliged to execute, in reverse order, the inferences we would like to trigger starting from the terms of the question.

A second practical problem concerns the navigation within the CYC's knowledge base; this problem arises from the requirement to associate with the queries some indications, addressed to the inference engine, which concern the 'depth' of the inference operations. The use of this technique avoids a systematic activation of all the possible inferences triggered in principle by the query, which could lead to an endless exploration of the knowledge base. Each class of inferences in CYC is characterized by the association with a given 'access level': the user must, therefore, indicate the required access level when querying the system in order to trigger only the inferences proper to this particular level or those pertaining to lower levels. Moreover, the user can also specify the maximum number of answers required by specifying the 'number of bindings', and indicate the maximum time the system can spend in inferencing. The UQAM researchers emphasize that, once again, the choice of these parameters often implies knowing in advance the inferences that the system should trigger in order to supply the answer required. Moreover, the presence of these sorts of optimization tools makes it difficult, ironically, to make use of CYC for executing all possible kinds of deep knowledge exploration.

Theoretical remarks

The 'theoretical' objections are linked mainly with the radical opposition between the CYC team and its critics about the meaning of terms such as knowledge, representation and understanding. The controversy concerning 'the owl and the electric encyclopaedia' is an exemplar of this type of misunderstanding. Its origin lies in a review of Brian Cantwell Smith [SmitB91], entitled 'The Owl and the Electric Encyclopaedia', of a paper by Lenat and Feigenbaum, 'On the Threshold of Knowledge' which has been published in several versions (*see*, for example, [Lena91a]). In this paper, Lenat and Feigenbaum enunciate and discuss at length three theoretical principles which support their conception of artificial intelligence and which, in their opinion, can justify the start of a project such as CYC: i) the knowledge principle (to perform a complex task, an AI program must know a great deal about the world in which it operates); ii) the breadth hypothesis (to behave intelligently in unexpected situations, an intelligent agent must be able to fall back on increasingly general knowledge and to analogize); iii) AI as empirical enquiry (premature mathematization, or focusing on toy problems, washes out details from reality that later may turn out to be significant) [Lena91a: 185].

It is, of course, out of the question to give a detailed account of Smith's criticisms here. We will say only that, very schematically, Smith challenges energetically [SmitB91: 270] the fact that a language like CycL '...with a single structural grammar and interpretation scheme – will prove sufficient for all the different kinds of representation an intelligent agent will need' (for taking into consideration all those real-life representational phenomena such as the dependency on context and on use, experience, communication conventions, belief revision, perception, introspection, relationships and physical constraints, etc.). More precisely, he talks about the 'conceptual tunnelling', where he denotes with this term the fact that the CYC team leaps abruptly from the enunciation of very generic, common sense considerations about the nature of human knowledge – *see* the three principles above – to the description of the technical intricacies of a particular, low-level knowledge representation scheme. This means that Lenat and his colleagues have never stopped to take into serious consideration that 'hidden middle realm' that lies in between their general insights about human knowledge and their detailed implementation proposals, and that must concern an in-depth conceptual analysis of all those 'real-life representational phenomena' mentioned before. If we try to condense in a sentence the essence of Smith's arguments, we could be tempted to say that the 'knowledge' stored into CYC is only a hypersimplified, schematic image of some tiny portions of the real, everyday knowledge, or, putting it in a different way, that the existence of a biunivocal relationship between the CYC's 'knowledge' and the real, everyday knowledge is highly disputable.

Of course, this last statement can be asserted about all the existing AI knowledge representation schemes. But, apart from Lenat and his friends, it would be difficult to find today AI researchers ready to affirm that the 'knowledge' they are able to represent is really 'predictive', in the sense that, having hand-coded into a system a large amount of this stuff, this will be sufficient to bring the system to a point where it will be able to autonomously generate and assimilate new knowledge on its own ('... when enough knowledge is present, it should be faster to acquire more from texts, databases, etc.' [Lena91a: 188]). We assume here, of course, that the meaning of the term 'knowledge' is not too different from the common sense interpretation of this term that is implicit in Smith's criticisms. This charge against Lenat, which concerns a too 'mechanistic' conception of 'knowledge' and of the associated concepts, such as 'reasoning' or 'learning', is not really new. It will suffice to recall here the polemic already mentioned about another well-known Lenat system, AM, which was supposed to automatically 'discover' concepts and conjectures in elementary mathematics, *see* [Ritc84]. As Lenat himself was willing to admit (*see* [Lena84: 291]), what was presented in the AM literature as 'exploring in the space of math concepts' was in reality nothing more than 'syntactically mutating small LISP programs' by exploiting the natural tie between LISP and mathematics. The mechanistic inclinations of Lenat are, moreover, clearly evident in Lenat and Feigenbaum's reply to Smith [Lena91b]. For example, where Smith spoke about the difficulties of fully understanding an expression like 'See you tomorrow' simply by using some 'abstract species of disconnected symbol manipulation' and without taking into consideration any form of 'participatory connections with the world' [SmitB91: 279], Lenat and Feigenbaum's reply is in terms of ' ... creating a "frame" E_1 in CYC to represent that uttering event (E_1 is an instance of the set of all events). Each event is grounded in time (whether or not the absolute time is known), and the meaning of "tomorrow" is clearly the day after this event E_1 takes place. A CYC "frame" E_2 would be created, representing a second event. E_2's temporal grounding would be "the day following the day E_1 takes place", and E_2 would be a seeing or meeting type of event' [Lena91b: 247–248].

It is really difficult not to share such doubts about the 'predictive' nature of the knowledge stored into CYC. This scepticism is corroborated by another characteristic proper to the CYC's knowledge, which has been evidentiated by several researchers and which concerns the rather haphazard and chaotic way chosen by the CYC's team to select this knowledge. For example, Skuce [Skuc93: 83–84] asks: '... What are the sources of knowledge that CYC's engineers are using, how do they decide upon them, and how do they actually extract the knowledge and enter it into CYC? ... How is the knowledge validated once entered? ... Are there "knowledge reviews", and if so, does CYC assist in this process? ...' An interesting, pragmatic answer to this type of question is contained in a report, once available on the Internet, relating the visit to the CYC team on 15 April 1994 by Vaughan Pratt of Stanford University to see a demonstration of the system. After having been familiarized by Guha with the standard CYC's demos, Pratt asked Guha to pose some simple common sense questions to the system in order to check what CYC 'knows'. The first questions concerned i) whether CYC knows that bread is food, ii) whether it knows that food is not drink, iii) that people need food, etc. It may be interesting to show here the formal aspects of these questions – *see* Table 3.55 – where the forms a) and b) both translate question i), and forms c) and d) try to translate question ii), the predicate #$genls meaning, as we already know, 'subset'. a) and b) both succeeded, returning 'true'; c) and d) both failed, but this bug has since been fixed. Question iii) was dealt with asking CYC to show all the axioms having #$Dying as a consequence, but CYC was unable to find anything like 'starvation' or other causes related to (lack of) food – Guha explained that a definition of 'starvation' was, in fact, missing. Other examples were that CYC knew that #$PlanetEarth is bigger than #$PlanetVenus, but it did not know (more correctly, it did not know in April 1994) the exact size of the earth; it knew that the earth has sky, but it did not know what colour the sky is; it contained axioms indicating that the typical cost of a car was $6000 to $80 000, but it knew nothing about the number of wheels in a car, range in miles, maximum velocity etc – once again, in April 1994. We must recognize that, as Guha remarked on that occasion, at least some of the above notions can be obtained from external databases, according to the procedures evoked in Section 3.443.

Table 3.55 Questions about bread

a	`(evaluate-term '(#$genls #$Bread #$Food))`
b	`(evaluate-term '(#$genls #$Bread #$EdibleStuff))`
c	`(evaluate-term '(#$genls #$Bread #$Drink))`
d	`(#$disjointWith #$Bread #$Drink)`

Pratt's conclusions can be summarized by saying that i) even using at their best the querying techniques such those exemplified in Table 3.55, or those consisting of an associative search of CYC's half-million axioms, it seems to be extremely difficult to come out with a suite of questions that CYC is able to answer according to a reasonable percentage (at least 20 per cent); ii) with respect to the claim of the CYC team that the system is well along the path of (having the possibility of) acquiring comprehensive, general knowledge, what is lacking here is a quantitative measure of how far along – saying that CYC owns one million axioms gives no real information about the actual nature and the 'predictivity' of this knowledge.

Should the CYC endeavour be abandoned? Certainly not. Cycorp's successes (*see* Section 3.443) are a pragmatic but very convincing proof of the utility of CYC for applications in the style of those listed in Table 3.51. Cantwell Smith suggests the use of the system as an 'electric encyclopaedia'. This means that the original NL material (articles, digests, etc.) used to prepare the CycL formal structures should be retained instead of being discarded as usually happens, using the corresponding CycL data structures and the CYC's inference engines '... *as an active indexing scheme*. Forget intelligence completely, in other words; take the project as one of constructing the world's largest hypertext system ... such a system might facilitate what numerous projects are struggling to implement: reliable, content-based searching and indexing schemes for massive textual databases. CYC's inference schemes would facilitate the retrieval of articles on related topics, or on the target subject matter using different vocabulary ...' [SmitB91: 282]. And probably Lenat himself will concede that the above suggestion is not too far from the CYC applications in the semantic information retrieval style that Cycorp is now developing as a priority.

3.45 Other projects based on a 'conceptual representation' approach

In this section, we will examine two additional proposals for the definition of new, rich 'data models' according to the integral artificial intelligence approach. The first concerns a general tool, Sowa's conceptual graphs, the second a more focused tool, NKRL (narrative knowledge representation language).

3.451 *Conceptual graphs*

Conceptual graphs (CGs) are a representation system which makes use of a graph-based notation for describing knowledge and, in particular, natural language semantics. CGs were developed by John Sowa, originally for incrementing the expressive power of the database languages, and were made known to the general public in 1984, *see* [Sowa84]. Sowa has freshly published a new CGs book, [Sowa99], and a proposed ANSI standard for CGs has been recently developed.

Given that CGs can be considered, at least partly, as a generalization and formalization of previous, well-known work in the artificial intelligence field – in particular semantic networks and the work of Schank on conceptual dependency, *see also* [Smol87] – they have engendered some interest within the AI community. Several groups of CG scholars are now active across the planet, developing all sorts of theoretical and practical CGs applications; the interested reader can consult the proceedings of the annual international CGs conference – *see* [Mine93], [Elli95b], [Mugn98] – for more information.

Basic notions

In the 1984 book, Sowa utilized a (quite naive) psychological model of perception in order to introduce conceptual graphs. For a theoretical foundation of CGs he now prefers (*see* [Sowa91], [Sowa99]) to stick strictly to the graph notation for logic (existential graphs) developed by the philosopher and logician Charles Sanders Peirce in the last decades of the 19th century. Anyway, we can consider that the basic, representational primitives used in CGs are i) the types of concepts (**concept-types**, organized into a type hierarchy), ii) the **concepts** and the corresponding **referents**, and iii) the **conceptual relations**.

Concept-types represent general classes of entities, attributes, states and events; in natural language terms, they correspond not only to nouns but also to other categories of 'lexical words' such as verbs, qualitative adjectives and adverbs. We can, therefore, meet CG concept-types such as CAT, SIT, DANCE, GRACEFUL (corresponding to both the adjective and the adverb 'gracefully'), TIME, PERSON, SITUATION, PROPOSITION, etc. It is assumed that, for any conceptual graphs system, there exists a pre-defined set of such types, which is different according to the domain to formalize. As already stated, concept-types are inserted into a type hierarchy (an 'ontology' in more current terms), which is, in reality, a lattice defined by a partial ordering relation, <, which means that some concepts are totally subsumed in others. Therefore, if ANIMAL, CAT, MAMMAL and PHYSICAL-OBJECT are concept-types, they are linked, within the type hierarchy, by the relationship: CAT < MAMMAL < ANIMAL < PHYSICAL-OBJECT, i.e. MAMMAL is, at the same time, a 'supertype' of CAT and a 'subtype' of ANIMAL. Like the set inclusion, the relation < is transitive and anti-symmetric. The type hierarchy has the appearance of a lattice given that a concept like ELEPHANT may be, at the same type, a subtype of both MAMMAL and WILD-ANIMAL. In technical terms, a lattice of types is characterized by the fact that every two types must have at most one maximal common subtype and one minimal common supertype. This condition is not always easy to respect without being obliged to introduce artificial types in the lattice, in the style of a possible WILD-MAMMAL.

It may be of some interest to reproduce in Figure 3.35 the lattice of top-level concept-types as proposed firstly by Sowa in [Sowa95] and then revised in [Sowa99]. This is a very sophisticated and hyper-symmetrical construction that Sowa justifies, making reference to, among others, Peirce, Aristotle, Leibniz, Heraclitus, Quine, Kant, Plato and Husserl.

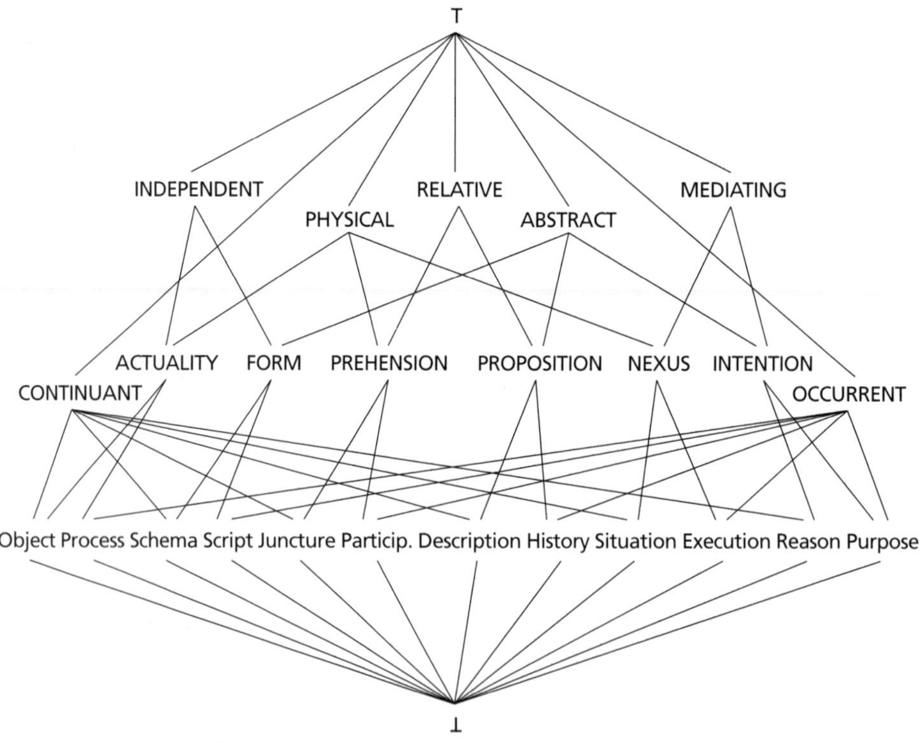

Figure 3.35 Lattice of top-level concept types

In this figure, ⊤ and ⊥ represent, respectively, the 'universal type' and the 'absurd type'. The alternative name for ⊤ is 'entity'; all the other concept-types are specializations of entity. The intuitive meaning for ⊥ can be captured if we consider that the greatest common subtype of CAT and DOG, written as CAT ∩ DOG, is the absurd type ⊥. More formally, ⊥ is a primitive that satisfies the following axioms:

- nothing is an instance of $\bot$: $\neg(\exists x)\ \bot(x)$;
- every type is a supertype of $\bot$: ($\forall t$:TYPE) $\bot \leq t$.

As for $\bot$, also $\top$, INDEPENDENT, RELATIVE, MEDIATING, PHYSICAL, ABSTRACT, CONTINUANT and OCCURRENT (*see* Figure 3.35) are characterized by sets of associated axioms. All the other types present in this figure are defined as the greatest common subtype, $\cap$, of two supertypes from which the type considered inherits the axioms, *see* [Sowa99: 497–498]. In this way, FORM is defined as ABSTRACT $\cap$ INDEPENDENT, and represents intuitively an abstract information independent from any embodiment. INTENTION = ABSTRACT $\cap$ MEDIATING is an abstraction considered as mediating other entities. PROCESS = ACTUALITY $\cap$ OCCURRENT concerns an ACTUALITY – i.e. a physical entity whose existence is independent from any other entity – considered as an OCCURRENT during the interval of interest. Here we can note that, depending on the time scale and level of detail, the same entity may be viewed as a stable object or a dynamic process. For example, a diamond may also be considered as a process on a long time period; on a scale of minutes, a glacier is a 'permanent' object, but on a scale of centuries, it is also a process. A SCHEMA = FORM $\cap$ CONTINUANT is an abstract FORM whose structure does not imply time relationships, such as geometrical forms or the syntactic structures of sentences in a given natural language. SCRIPT = FORM $\cap$ OCCURRENT is an abstract FORM that represents time sequences, such as computer programs, a recipe for baking a cake, or a sheet of music to be played. HISTORY = PROPOSITION $\cap$ OCCURRENT is a PROPOSITION or a sequence of propositions that relates some SCRIPTS to the stages of some OCCURRENT. It describes the time sequence of a PROCESS; then, if COMPUTER-PROGRAM is a SCRIPT, a computer executing the program is a PROCESS, and the information encoded in a trace of the instructions executed is a HISTORY, etc.

Returning to the basic primitives of CGs, a **concept** is an incarnation of a concept-type: a concept like [CAT] represents an (unnamed) entity of type CAT (with the meaning 'there exists a cat'), and can be considered as the simplest form of conceptual graph (singleton). Adding a 'referent field' to a concept allows us to designate specific individuals. If we know that the current cat is named 'Yojo', this situation is represented as: [CAT: `Yojo`], with the meaning 'the entity Yojo is a cat'. Therefore, a concept 'box' is normally divided into two parts: the 'type field' on the left side of the colon, and the 'referent field' on the right side.

More precisely, the referent of a concept is identified by a 'quantifier' – such as an existential quantifier like $\exists$ – and a 'designator'. The designator can be one of the following three types, *see* [Sowa99: 483–84]:

- *literals* – a literal gives a syntactic representation of the form of the referent: it can be a number, a character string as in the concept [String: 'bcdefg'], or an 'encoded literal' consisting of a pair formed by an identifier and a string;
- *locators* – a locator is a symbol that specifies how a given referent can be found. It can be simply a name like Boston. When the referent is identified with one of the entities already known to the system, the locator becomes an implementation-dependent representation where the serial number of this

entity is appended to the symbol '#'. In this way, [CAT: #123] means 'the entity #123 is a cat'. The symbol # represents in general an 'indexical referent', i.e. a definite reference to an entity that is known contextually, but that is not precisely named, as when we make use of the definite article 'the'. In this way, 'the cat' is represented as [CAT: #];

- *descriptors* – a descriptor is a full conceptual graph that is used to 'describe' the referent.

Moreover, 'qualifiers' can be used to better specify the referent. For example, plural situations require the use of a specific symbol, '*', to indicate a plural referent. The expression 'three cats' is then represented as [CAT: {*}@3]. The plural referent {*} indicates here some unspecified entities of the type CAT, and the 'qualifier' @3 indicates that there are three of them. The same type of solution is adopted in the presence of 'quantifiers', as 'many' or ∀ ('all'); the symbolism [CAT: {*}@many] corresponds to 'many cats', etc.

Finally, **conceptual relations** indicate the 'roles' that concepts play with respect to each other. They are related to the 'cases' used in the different artificial intelligence interpretations of the (linguistic) case-grammar theory – *see* [Bruc75] or [Spar87] – and to Jackendoff's 'thematic roles' [Jack90].

A first, unstructured list of these relations in a CG context was given in [Sowa84: Appendix A]. In [Sowa99], the conceptual relation topic is re-examined in depth. Very shortly, the different 'types' of conceptual relations are seen as specializations of a type ROLE that, as with PHENOMENON (an actual entity considered by itself) and SIGN (an actual entity considered as representing something to some agent), is an offspring of the ACTUALITY concept type of Figure 3.35. As already stated, an ACTUALITY is a physical entity whose existence is independent of any other entity. ROLE is, in particular, an actual entity considered in relation to something else. From ROLE, Sowa derives two lists of relation types. The first, which includes the relation types that we could identify with some sort of 'deep' or 'conceptual' roles and that share some similarities with the NKRL roles described in Section 3.452, are reproduced in Table 3.56. Sowa says [Sowa99: 89] they have a strong correlation with the syntactic categories of natural language, and seems then to adhere to Jackendoff's thesis about the need for an optimal form of correspondence between conceptual entities and the surface forms these entities can assume in a particular NL – see, for example, Jackendoff's 'θ-Criterion' [Jack90]. A second list of roles, called by Sowa 'thematic roles', is reproduced in Table 3.57. According to Sowa, these last roles – which derive in turn from ROLE (and then from ACTUALITY of Figure 3.35) through the PARTICIPANT relation type – express in particular the conceptual relations that link the concept of a verb to the concepts of the participants in the occurrent expressed by the verb. In [Sowa99], they are listed separately because of their importance in representing natural language semantics.

Note that, in the conceptual graph community, some doubts still exist about the precise list of 'legal' conceptual relations, and about the exact meaning of many of them, *see* [Luko95]. Moreover, some ambiguities are evident with respect to the exact criteria for discriminating between two or more relations, for example

Table 3.56 Conceptual relations

Conceptual relation	Definition
ACCM (Accompaniment)	An object that participates in a process with another object (e.g. John left with (ACCM) Mary).
AMT (Amount)	A quantity used as a measure of a 'characteristic' normally expressed by a noun, such as 'length', 'weight', 'age', 'temperature', etc. (e.g. the desk has a length of 150 cm).
ARG (Argument)	A relation that is used primarily for expressing mathematical relations, more precisely, the relationship between a function and its argument. If the function takes more than an input, ARG can be specialized as ARG1, ARG2, etc. (e.g. SQRT(36) = 6; in conceptual graphs terms: [NUMBER: 36] ← (ARG) ← [SQRT]).
ATTR (Attribute)	A property of some object; in English, attributes are normally expressed by using adjectives (e.g. the rose is red).
BASE (Base)	A BASE role indicates how an attribute is related to an object (e.g. 'John is a good teacher', which can be paraphrased as: 'John has
the	attribute (ATTR) good as (BASE) teacher').
BCAS (Because)	The relationship between two situations, a cause and an effect (e.g. he retired last month because of illness).
CHLD (Child)	A relationship between two human beings, a child and a parent (e.g. John is Tom's father).
COMP (Comparand)	A relationship, in the form of a comparison, between an object and the attribute of another object (e.g. John is (ATTR) taller than (COMP) Mary).
CHRC (Characteristic)	A relationship between a conceptual type (shape, colour, length, weight, etc.) whose instances are the properties of some entities, and these last entities (e.g. the rose's (CHRC) colour is red).
ROLE (Has)	'Has' is a general relation type that is used to define all roles. All the relation types listed in Tables 3.56 and 3.57 are subtypes of Has.
MANR (Manner)	A property of some process: in English, manners are usually expressed by adverbs (e.g. he returned to his office in time (MANR) for the meeting).
MEAS (Measure)	A quantity used as a measure of some attribute that constitutes the first argument of the MEAS relationship. With respect to the AMT relationship above, MEAS links an attribute with a measure, and AMT links the corresponding characteristic to the same measure (e.g. the desk is 150 cm long).
PART (Part)	An object that is a component of another object; at the difference of an attribute, a part can exist in an independent manner (e.g. a finger is part of a hand).
POSS (Possession)	The relationship between an entity owned by some animate being and its possessor (e.g. John's (POSS) flat has been totally renewed).
SUCC (Successor)	An occurrent (see the ontology of Figure 3.34) that occurs after some occurrent (e.g. after John ate the gherkin, (SUCC) he drank some vodka).

Table 3.57 Thematic roles

Thematic role	Definition
AGNT (Agent)	An active animate entity that voluntarily initiates an action (e.g. an old lady is dancing).
BENF (Beneficiary)	A recipient that obtains an advantage from the successful fulfilment of an event (e.g. money was given to John).
CMPL (Completion)	A goal of a temporal process.
DEST (Destination)	A goal of a spatial process (e.g. John (AGNT) is going to (DEST) Boston).
DUR (Duration)	A resource of a temporal process (e.g. the truck was serviced for four hours).
EFCT (Effector)	An active source, animate or inanimate, that initiates an action without voluntary intention (e.g. the tree has produced new leaves).
EXPR (Experiencer)	An active and animate goal of an experiencer (e.g. the cat (EXPR) has seen the fish).
INST (Instrument)	A resource that is not changed by an event (e.g. the key (INST) opened the door).
LOC (Location)	An essential participant of a spatial NEXUS, where a NEXUS – *see* the ontology of Figure 3.34 – is a physical entity mediating two or more other entities (e.g. the car arrived at a station).
MATR (Matter)	A resource that is changed by an event (e.g. the statue was carved out of marble).
MED (Medium)	A resource for transmitting information as the sound of speech or the electromagnetic signals.
ORGN (Origin)	A passive determinant that is the source of a spatial or ambient NEXUS (e.g. the chapter begins on page 20).
PATH (Path)	A resource of a spatial NEXUS (e.g. the parcel was shipped via Paris and Geneva).
PTNT (Patient)	An essential participant that suffers some structural changes as a result of an event (e.g. the cat swallowed Tweety the canary).
PTIM (PointInTime)	An essential participant of a temporal NEXUS (e.g. at 4:20pm (PTIM), Carla left).
RCPT (Recipient)	An animate goal of an act.
RSLT (Result)	An inanimate goal of an act (e.g. John (AGNT) built a house (RSLT)).
STRT (Start)	A determinant source of a temporal NEXUS.
THME (Theme)	An essential participant that can be moved, said, or experienced, but that is not structurally changed (e.g. John (EXPR) likes pizza (THME)).

between ATTR and CHRC, or AGNT and EXPR. As with concepts, there will be a predefined set of relation types in any particular CG system. Any conceptual relation is constrained with respect to the concepts it can connect to. For example, an AGNT – which is a conceptual relation linking the instigator or agent of an action with the action itself – will associate two concepts, one of which is a subtype of ANIMATE and the other a subtype of ACT.

Conceptual graphs and first-order logic

From a formal point of view, we can define a **conceptual graph** as a finite, connected, bipartite graph which makes use of two kinds of **nodes**, i.e. 'concepts' and 'conceptual relations'. Every arc of a graph must link a conceptual relation to a concept; it is then said to 'belong' to the relation and to be 'attached' to the concept. 'Bipartite' means that every arc of a conceptual graph associates necessarily one concept with one conceptual relation: it is not possible to have arcs that link concepts with concepts or relations with relations. A single concept – such as [CAT] seen in the previous subsection – can be considered as a conceptual graph in itself ('singleton'); a 'star' is a graph that consists of a single relation and of the concepts that are attached to it. A detailed, formal definition of CGs can be found in [Chei92].

From a semantic point of view, a conceptual graph corresponds to an assertion about some individuals that exist in the particular application domain to be considered. Accordingly, the graphical representation of Figure 3.36 corresponds to the assertion: 'A pretty lady is dancing gracefully.' The arrows on the arcs are used to distinguish the first and the second argument of the predicate ('dancing'). Very

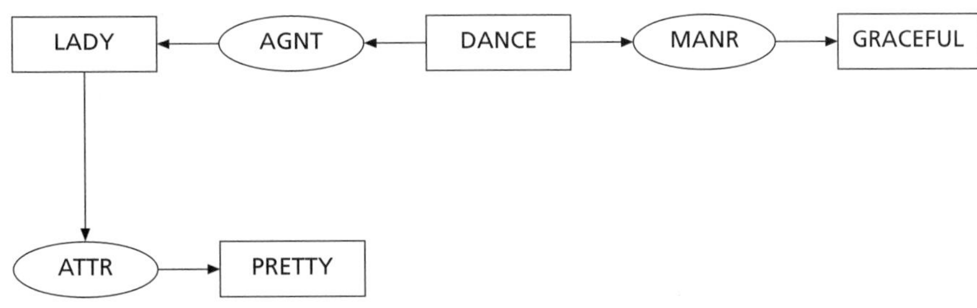

Figure 3.36 A simple example of a conceptual graph

[PRETTY] ← (ATTR) ← [LADY: #1520] ← (AGNT) ← [DANCE] → (MANR) → [GRACEFUL]

Figure 3.37 A conceptual graph in linear form

often, however, CGs are expressed in a sort of 'linear' representation; the picture in linear form of the assertion: 'The pretty lady identified as the entity #1520 of the system is dancing gracefully' is given in Figure 3.37.

An important formal property of conceptual graphs concerns the possibility of their exact mapping into formulas of the first-order predicate calculus thanks to the operator ϕ. The mapping produces a conjunction of predicates, one corresponding to each node of the graph; generic concepts map to variables, individual concepts map to constants. Therefore, if u is the graph represented in Figure 3.37, its translation in predicate calculus gives:

$$\phi u = \exists x\ \exists y\ \exists z\ (\mathtt{Lady}(\#1520) \wedge \mathtt{Attr}(\#1520,\ x) \wedge \mathtt{Pretty}(x) \wedge \mathtt{Agent}(y,\ \#1520) \wedge \mathtt{Dance}(y) \wedge \mathtt{Manner}(y,\ z) \wedge \mathtt{Graceful}(z)).$$

To give conceptual graphs the full power of predicate logic, however, it is necessary to introduce some 'second-order' extensions of the notions above.

One of the most important extensions is linked with the introduction of 'contexts': a context is a particular concept, such as PROPOSITION or SITUATION, that has a referent of the 'descriptor' type, i.e. its referent is represented by one or more nested conceptual graphs. If more than a conceptual graph appears in the referent, the latter asserts the conjunction of these particular conceptual graphs. In the graphical notation, a concept of the type context is denoted by a box including all the graphs that make up the referent.

A very simple utilization of a context such as PROPOSITION concerns the graphical notation used to express negation, where a NOT operator, regarded as a unary conceptual relation, is applied to the global context defined by PROPOSITION. In Figure 3.38, the graph inside the box (the referent of PROPOSITION) asserts that 'there exists a farmer which owns a donkey'; the application of the NOT relation allows this assertion (proposition) to be denied: 'It is not true that there exists ...'. Normally, however, boxes marked with the symbol ¬ are used directly to represent negative contexts. Note that, since the 'standard' way of passing from natural

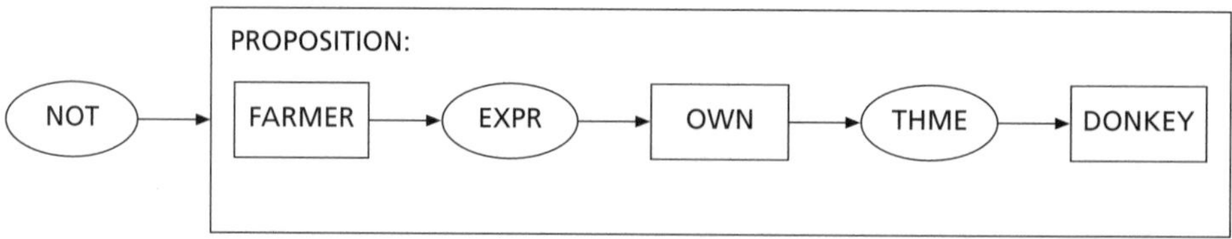

Figure 3.38 Negation of conceptual graphs

language to conceptual graphs – *see* [Farg86], [Vela88], etc. – implies that verbs are represented by concepts and not by relations, the conceptual relation EXPR (*see* Table 3.57) has been added to the conceptual graph of Figure 3.38.

A direct utilization of the above mechanism is given by the representation of implication in conceptual graphs. This is based on the well-known logical relationship stating that $(p \supset q)$ is equivalent to $\neg\ (p \wedge \neg q)$, and is given by a nest of two negative contexts. Figure 3.39 gives the graphical representation of the assertion: 'If a farmer owns a donkey, then he beats it' [Sowa91: 162–167], where the symbol ¬ is used instead of NOT to represent negative contexts. The concepts [FARMER] and [DONKEY] appear only in the *if*-context. To denote the references to these concepts in the *then*-context, two concepts of type ⊤, the top of the concept-

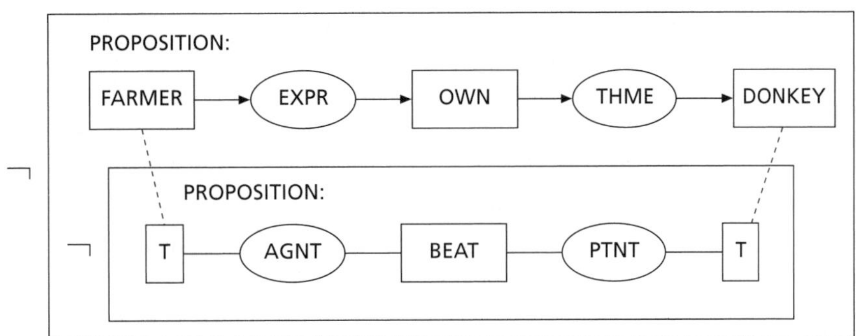

Figure 3.39 Implication in conceptual graphs

types lattice (*see* Figure 3.35) is added in this last context, and linked by dotted lines, called 'coreference links', to the concepts [FARMER] and [DONKEY] of the *if*-context. Concepts of the type ⊤ correspond to pronouns in natural language.

In the linear form, coreference links are represented by variables such as *x and *y. The concept [⊤] becomes [⊤: *x], which can be abridged as [*x], and the previous implication can be represented in linear form as in Figure 3.40. If, in this

¬ [[FARMER: *x] → (STAT) → [OWN] ← (PTNT) → [DONKEY: *y]
¬ [[*x] ← (AGNT) ← [BEAT] → (PTNT) → [*y]]]

Figure 3.40 Implication in linear form

last formula and for readability's sake, the first ¬ symbol is replaced by IF, and the second by THEN, we obtain a form which can be read directly as the English sentence: 'If a farmer x owns a donkey y, then x beats y.'

Returning to the lattice of top-level concept-types of Figure 3.35, we find SITUATION among the concept-types situated at a lower (more specific) level than PROPOSITION. The difference between the two is explained in this way by Sowa [Sowa91: 166]: 'When a conceptual graph is the referent of a concept of type PROPOSITION, it represents the proposition stated by the graph. When it is the referent of a concept of the type SITUATION, it represents the situation described by the proposition stated by the graph.' Combinations of the two are used to represent second-order structures like those corresponding to the 'subordinate' or 'completive' constructions of natural language: *see*, however, [Naza92] and [Naza93] on the difficulties and the limitations of the current conceptual graph solutions for the representation of these second-order constructions.

Figure 3.41 is a reproduction of the graphical solution proposed by Sowa ([Sowa91: 166–167]; [Sowa99: 485–486]) for the representation of the sentence 'Tom believes that Mary wants to marry a sailor'. In this figure, Tom believes a proposition: Mary, on the contrary, wants a situation; we can note that the 'subjects' of the 'states' represented by BELIEVE and WANT are represented by 'experiencers' (EXPR) rather than 'agents' (AGNT). As Sowa says, in general, negation, modalities, and the 'patients' or 'themes' of verbs like 'think' and 'know' are linked with contexts of the type PROPOSITION; times, locations, and the patients and themes of verbs like 'want' and 'fear' are linked with contexts of type SITUATION. The way contexts are nested determines the scope of the quantifiers. In Figure 3.41, SAILOR is existentially quantified inside the situation that Mary wants, which

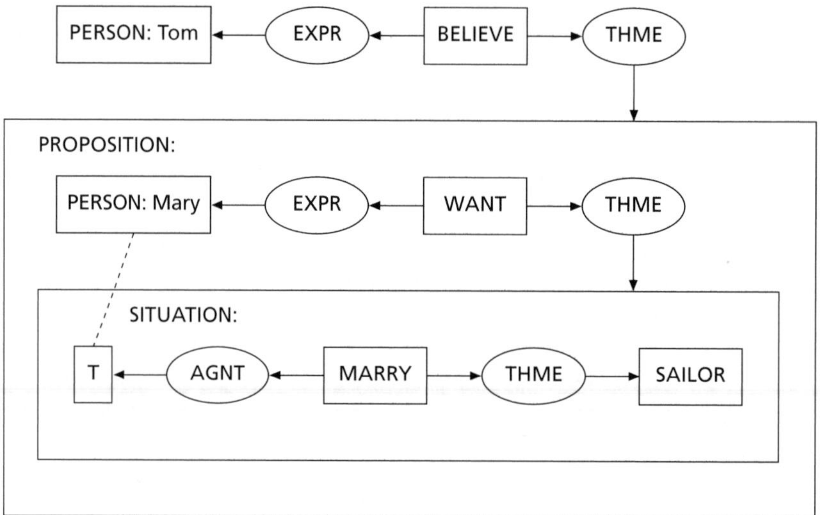

Figure 3.41 Graphical representation of second-order constructions

```
[PERSON: Tom] ← (EXPR) ← [BELIEVE] → (THME) → [PROPOSITION:
   [PERSON: Mary*x] ← (EXPR) ← [WANT] → (THME) → [SITUATION:
                  [*x] ← (AGNT) ← [MARRY] → (THME) → [SAILOR]]]
```

Figure 3.42 Linear representation of second-order constructions

is in turn existentially quantified inside Tom's belief. The linear form that corresponds to Figure 3.41 is given in Figure 3.42; as we can see, the graphical form is more legible in order to show the nesting of contexts.

We conclude with some information about an important CGs construction, the 'lambda expression'. λ-expression can be defined as a conceptual graph with one or more generic concepts identified as formal parameters (variables); the relationship with the analogous LISP construction is evident. As in LISP, the main function of λ-expression is that of allowing new definitions: monadic λ-expressions are used to define 'concept' types, *n*-adic λ-expressions are used to define *n*-adic 'relation' types. Moreover, an important, specific function of λ-expressions is that of allowing the definition of 'single-use' types: instead of inserting in the type field of a concept a label corresponding to a concept-type defined in a permanent way, this type field can contain a λ-expression that is expressly created for a single use. This possibility is typically used to represent restrictive relative clauses, *see* below. In [Sowa86: 63], the authors mention other possible utilizations of λ-expressions: for defining schemata that are used to represent defaults and expectations, for defining new individuals as aggregations of parts, or for defining typical individuals as prototypes. In Figure 3.43 we give a simple example of use of λ-abstraction to define PET-CAT as a type of CAT which is owned by some person – CAT is a supertype of the newly defined concept PET-CAT. The equals sign which appears in the definition means that the type label (PET-CAT) is a synonym for the λ-expression that defines the type, i.e. any occurrence of the type label PET-CAT could be replaced by the λ-expression.

PET-CAT = (λx) [CAT: *x] ← (THME) ← [OWN] ← (EXPR) ← [PERSON]

Figure 3.43 Defining a new concept using a λ-expression

As a second example of use of λ-expressions, we give in Figure 3.44 the representation of the sentence 'some elephants that perform in a circus earn money.' A λ-expression is used here to define the 'single-use' concept 'elephants that perform in a circus'; the BENF relation indicates that the elephants are the beneficiaries of the earning. In this conceptual graph, the (global) single-use concept has a 'generic plural referent' represented by the symbol '{*}' which in this case indicates some unspecified elements of the type 'elephants that perform in a circus.' In CGs' theory, plurals are regarded as generalized quantifiers and represented in the same way as other quantifiers. For example, the representation of the sentences 'every elephant that performs in a circus earns money' and 'many elephants that perform in a circus earn money' is still that of Figure 3.44, with the symbols '∀' and '{*}@many' in place of the generic plural referent '{*}'; '@' is a 'qualifier' (*see* Section 3.451) and the expression '@many' indicates 'many of them'. A detailed description of the CGs theory of generalized quantifiers can be found in [Sowa91].

```
[(λx) [ELEPHANT: *x] ← (AGNT) ← [PERFORM] → (IN) → [CIRCUS]: {*}] –
        (BENF) ← [EARN] → (THME) → [MONEY].
```

Figure 3.44 A λ-expression used to define a 'single-use' concept

Canonical graphs, canonical derivation rules and CGs knowledge bases

In concrete situations, when the CGs must be used to describe some real or possible state of affairs in an application domain, the problem arises of being able to differentiate the meaningful graphs from the others. This problem is tackled by constructing, for a given application, the set of graphs that can be considered as 'canonical graphs' for this particular application. To do this, a first operation is to construct *a priori* a finite set of conceptual graphs, called the 'canonical basis' (CB). The graphs included in the CB can be seen as elementary 'templates' (*see also* Section 3.452) that represent the default ways in which concepts and relations can be linked to represent well-formed CG sentences. A fragment of a possible canonical basis – derived from [Elli95a] – can be found in Figure 3.45.

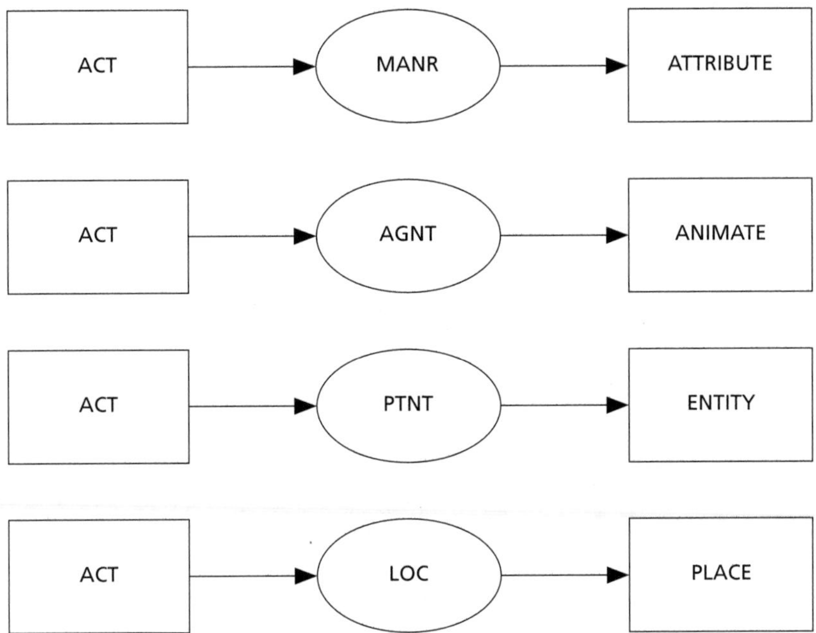

Figure 3.45 A fragment of canonical basis (CB)

Five 'canonical derivation rules' are used to obtain, from the CB graphs and the canonical graphs already derived, all the possible 'canonical graphs' for the given application; these are, therefore, the 'closure' of the CB under the canonical formation rules. We can note that the canonical graphs obtained in this way are all well formed, but not necessarily meaningful. The definitions of the five canonical rules that allow us to derive a canonical graph *w* from the (CB and canonical) graphs *u* (and *v*) are summarized in Table 3.58.

Table 3.58 Canonical formation rules for conceptual graphs

- *copy(u)*. The new canonical graph *w* is an exact copy of *u*.
- *restrict(u,c)*. In *w*, any concept-node *c* which appears in *u* can be replaced by a subtype *t*. We can also specialize *c* by adding a referent where there was none before, under the condition that *referent(c)* conforms to *type(c)*. In this way, ANIMAL can be restricted to CAT, which can be restricted in turn to [CAT: Yojo].
- *simplify(u, r, s)*. If the conceptual relations *r* and *s* between two concepts are duplicates then, to produce *w*, one of them can be removed from *u* together with all its arcs.
- *join(u, c, d)*. If, in *u*, a concept *c* is identical to concept *d* then *join(u, c, d)* is the graph *w* obtained by deleting *d* and by linking to c all the arcs corresponding to the conceptual relations that were linked to *d*.
- *fuse(u, v, c, d)*. We suppose, in this case, that *u* and *v* are two disjoint conceptual graphs. If a concept *c* in *u* is identical to a concept *d* in *v*, then *fuse(u, v, c, d)* produces as a result the unique graph *w* obtained by suppressing *d* and by linking to *c* all edges in *v* that had be linked with *d*. Note that: i) a *fuse* (as a *join*) can give rise to duplicate relations between two concepts, that can be removed using *simplify*; ii) *join* and *fuse* are sometimes conceived as the same operation (*join*), with the '*join*' defined above considered as a particular case that concerns joining a graph to itself, i.e. merging two concepts within the same graph.

Figure 3.46 illustrates the use of the canonical formation rules. We can conceive the two graphs G1 and G2 as two canonical graphs that have been derived from the CB graphs of Figure 3.45 through a first series of application of the canonical rules. The graph G3 is obtained by restricting the concept [GIRL] in G1 to [GIRL: SUSAN]; G4 is obtained by restricting the type PERSON in G2 to the subtype GIRL. The identical concepts [GIRL: SUSAN] in G3 and G4 can be fused to give rise to the single graph G5; in this last graph, the identical concepts [EAT] can be joined to produce G6. Finally, this last graph can be simplified to produce the final canonical graph G7.

A sequence of operations in this style gives rise to what is known as a 'maximal join', i.e. the result that is obtained when as much matching and merging of the original graphs as possible is performed. The maximal join is not necessarily unique because it may happen that several maximal overlaps exist between the two graphs. In more formal terms, we can say that a graph like G7 in Figure 3.46 can be qualified as 'maximal join' with respect to the original graphs G1 and G2 when i) it contains a maximal number of edges obtained by restriction from the two original graphs, and when ii) its concepts are the greater common specializations of the concepts coming from the original graphs.

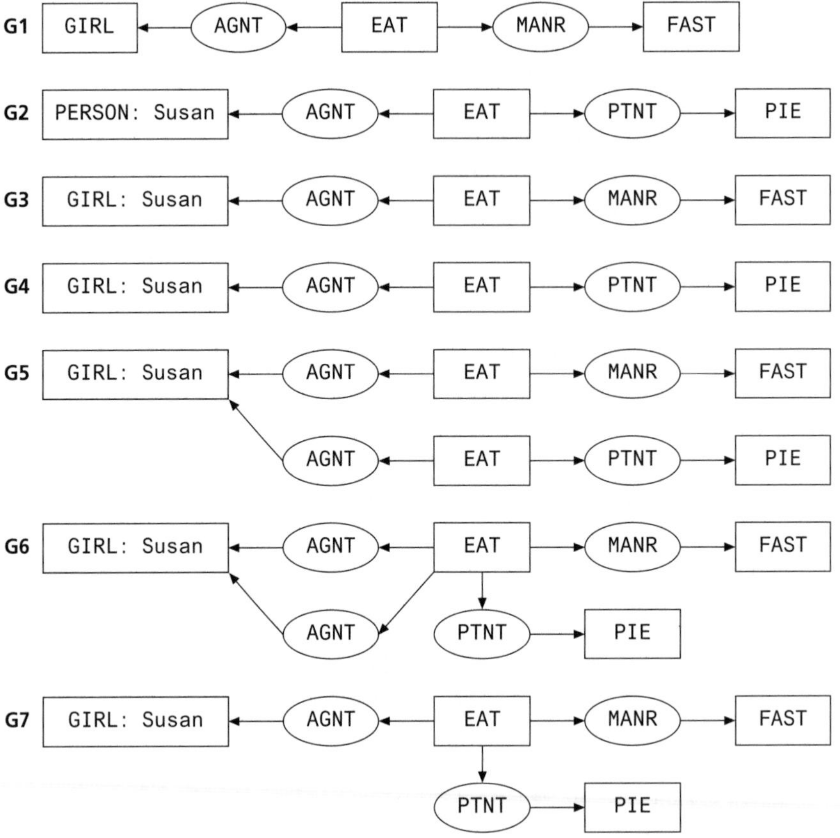

Figure 3.46 An example illustrating the use of the canonical formation rules

From an IAS and intelligent DBs point of view, it is now evident that the fact of storing the conceptual graphs that represent particular information about a specific domain into some sort of permanent storage can give rise to a 'CGs knowledge base' of the domain. In this context, one of the main problems to be solved is, as usual, that of indexing the knowledge base in order to facilitate the retrieval of the stored information. An interesting work in this domain has been accomplished, for example, by Ellis ([Elli95a]) – we will give, in the following, a very quick survey of his work.

The starting point is the definition of the operations of generalization and specialization for canonical graphs. If a conceptual graph u is canonically derivable, through the rules of Table 3.58, from a conceptual graph v (possibly including the join of other conceptual graphs $w_1 \dots w_n$), then u is called a 'specialization' of v, written $u \leq v$, and v is called a 'generalization' of u. Such operations define a partial ordering of conceptual graphs called the 'generalization hierarchy' (remember here the partial order of the type hierarchy). For any conceptual graphs u and v the properties listed in Table 3.59 are valid (*see* [Elli95a: 71]); these properties relate the existence of the two graphs to the concept of generalization hierarchy.

Table 3.59 Properties of the generalization hierachy

- *Subgraphs*. If v is a subgraph of u (i.e. u is canonically derivable from v), then $u \leq v$.
- *Subtypes*. If u is identical to v except that one or more type labels of v are restricted to subtypes in u, then $u \leq v$.
- *Individuals*. If u is identical to v except that one or more generic concepts of v are restricted to individuals of the same type (e.g. [GIRL] is restricted to [GIRL: susan]), then $u \leq v$.
- *Top*. A top graph, [⊤], is defined as the generalization of all the other canonical graphs.

Returning to Figure 3.46, we can see, intuitively, that the graphs G1, G2, G3, G4, G5 and G6 are all generalizations of the graph G7. The definition of the hierarchy is now completed by introducing a 'subsumption' test, i.e. a test allowing us to decide unambiguously whether, for two canonical graphs u and v, $u \leq v$. To do this, it is necessary to introduce the 'projection operator' π; projection is often used, in a CGs context, for querying operations on the conceptual graphs. For any conceptual graphs u and v where $u \leq v$, there must exist a mapping $\pi : v \rightarrow u$, where πv is a subgraph of u that represents the projection of v in u; π is endowed with the following properties:

- for any concept c in v, πc is a concept in πv where $type(\pi c) \leq type(c)$: e.g. GIRL < PERSON, or CAT < MAMMAL. If c is an individual, then $referent(c) = referent(\pi c)$;
- for each conceptual relation r in v, πr is a conceptual relation in πv where $type(\pi r) = type(r)$: this means, in practice, that AGNT must correspond to AGNT, PTNT to PTNT, etc. If the ith arc of r is linked with a concept c in v, the ith arc of πr must be linked with πc in πv.

For example, the projection of the graph G2 in Figure 3.46 into the graph G7 of the same figure gives rise to a graph identical to G7 except for the suppression of the branch '→ (MANR) → [FAST]'. We can now define the subsumption test as follows, *see* [Elli95a: 71–72]. Any conceptual graph v can be represented by the set of instances of the canonical formation rules that have been used to construct the graph v from the graphs $w_1 \ldots w_n$. To test whether the graph v subsumes a graph u, the same rule instances can be applied to the projections of u in $w_1 \ldots w_n$: these rule instances will succeed if v subsumes u. In this way, it is possible, for example, to construct a generalization hierarchy which includes the first three graphs of the canonical basis (CB) of Figure 3.45 and the graphs G1, GT2, G3, G4 and G7 of Figure 3.46 – *see* Figure 3.47 adapted from [Elli95a].

To be complete, we must notice that the canonical CGs considered in this subsection are only a subclass of all the possible (canonical) conceptual graphs, given that they do not contain logical connectives, nor quantification other than the default existential quantification: they are called 'atomic conceptual graphs'. Moreover, the generalization hierarchy as considered until now is not, strictly, a partial order over conceptual graphs, but rather a partial order over equivalence classes of conceptual graphs. It is, in fact, possible that, confronted with two graphs 'semantically' identical but differentiated by the presence of redundant branches, we obtain at once $u \le v$ and $v \le u$: the two graphs are then equivalent, $u = v$, and they can be intermixed from the point of view of the generalization hierarchy. In practice, graphs with redundant branches can always be simplified to derive the smallest ones in each equivalent class, and we can assume the generalization hierarchy as composed of graphs which represent the minimal elements within their own equivalence class.

We can now use the generalization hierarchy to index a knowledge base of conceptual graphs, and use this hierarchy as a content-addressable memory. To give a glimpse of the methodology, let us consider a very simple example, and suppose that we are searching, in a hypothetical CGs knowledge base that is reduced to the hierarchy of Figure 3.47, for the information: 'Is the girl Susan eating fast?' This query is represented by the graph q of Figure 3.48. We can now adopt a classical top-down, depth-first search of the hierarchy of Figure 3.47. We look then for a direct match between q and the graphs located on the nodes of the tree, and we use as a criterion for continuing the traversal of the tree the condition that the graph under examination be a generalization of q (i.e. q must be canonically derivable from this graph). In our example, we will follow the path *g1*, *g2*, *g5*, *g7* (depth-first). *g7* is still a generalization of q (in fact, *g7* is isomorphic to q); moreover, *g7* and q will match, so the search will stop successfully. The solution space contains all the specializations of the given query in the examined generalization hierarchy: in our example, we will have two answers to the query 'Is the girl Susan eating fast?' – the first, corresponding to the graph *g7*, is 'yes', the second, corresponding to the graph *g9*, is 'yes, Susan is eating pie fast'.

It is now evident that the main interest of this approach to the practical utilization of a CGs knowledge base cannot reside only in the simple, depth-first strategy of search illustrated by the example above. In reality, by developing some ideas already exposed by Woods [Wood91] and Levinson [Levi92] for example, Ellis suggests a set of algorithms for i) minimizing the number of database graphs compared with the query graph by pruning the search space using the information gathered when searching, and ii) minimizing the cost of each of these comparisons. This latter result is obtained by 'compiling' the conceptual graphs associated with a generalization hierarchy into instructions that represent specialized cases of the canonical formation rules examined at the beginning of this subsection. This means that the specific graphs are given as differences between the adjacent graphs in the hierarchy, where the differences represent the rules used in deriving a given graph from the adjacent ones.

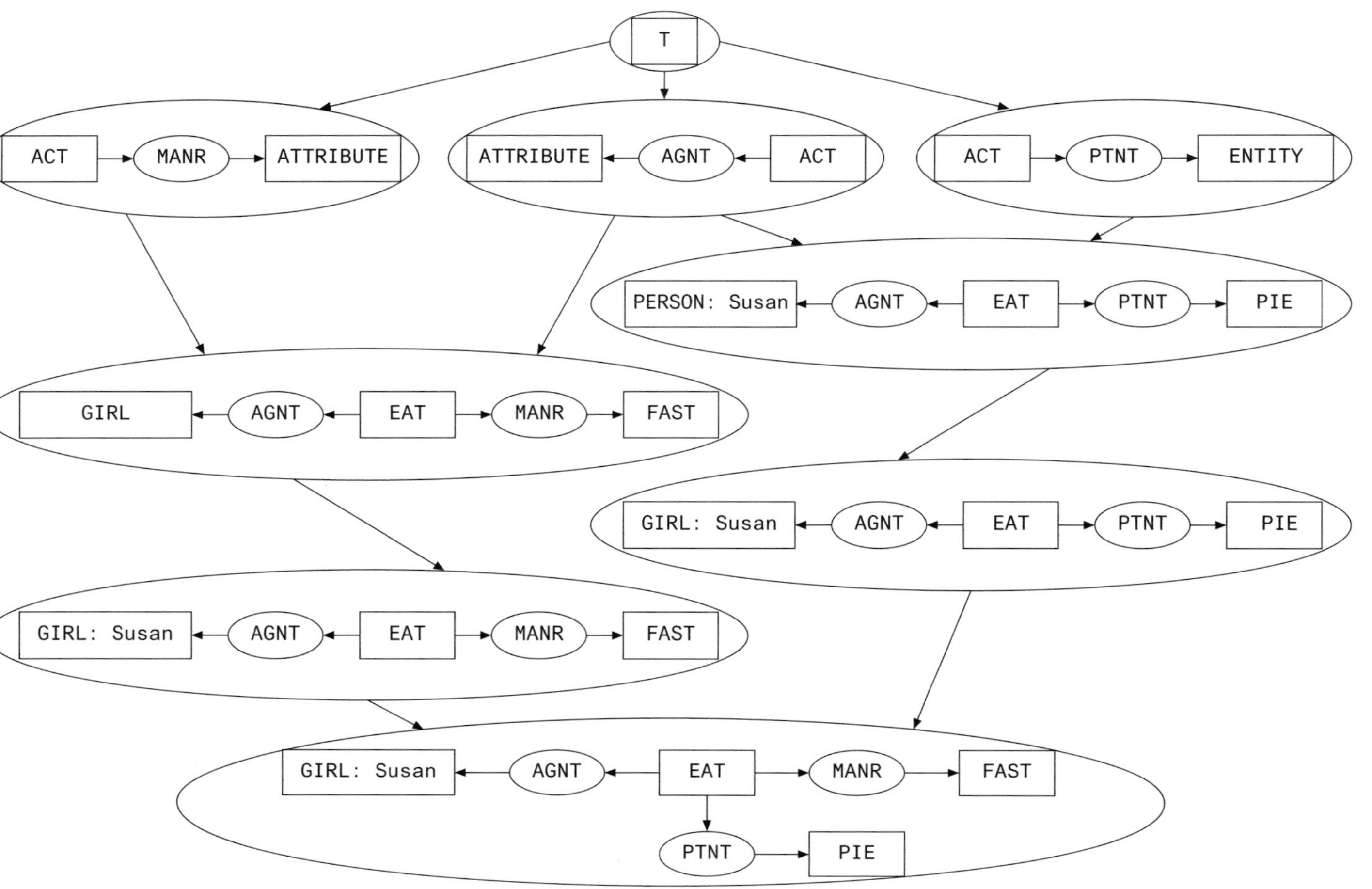

Figure 3.47 An example of a generalization hierarchy

```
[GIRL: Susan] ← (AGNT) ← [EAT] → (MANR) → [FAST]
```

Figure 3.48 The query 'Is the girl Susan eating fast?'

3.452 The NKRL technology

NKRL, short for 'narrative knowledge representation language', is a 'conceptual' language sharing some similarities with the conceptual graphs examined in the previous subsections. Unlike CGs, however – which tend to present themselves as a sorts of universal tool able to deal with all sorts of possible phenomena – NKRL has been mainly used to produce standard, language-independent descriptions of the semantic content (the 'meaning') of non-trivial, 'narrative' documents, and to supply a set of tools to exploit practically these sorts of descriptions.

We can note, in this respect, that a considerable amount of important, 'economically relevant' information is buried into natural language documents. This is true for most of the corporate knowledge documents (memos, policy statements, reports, minutes, etc.), as well as for the vast majority of information stored on the Web. A fundamental (and quantitatively relevant) subset of this useful NL information is formed by documents that relate some form of 'narratives' of an economic import. In these 'narrative' documents, the main part of the information content consists of the description of 'facts' or 'events' that relate the real or intended behaviour of some 'actors' (characters, personages, etc.). These try to attain a specific result, experience particular situations, manipulate some (concrete or abstract) materials, send or receive messages, buy, sell, deliver, etc. Note that in this sort of document the actors or personages are not necessarily human beings; we can have narrative documents concerning the vicissitudes in the journey of a nuclear submarine (the 'actor', 'subject' or 'character') or the various avatars in the life of a commercial product. Moreover, 'narrative' information is not necessarily associated with the 'material' existence of NL documents. We can make use of narratives to describe (to 'annotate', *see* below) the situations reproduced by a set of images on the Web, or those described in a video or a digital audio document.

Being able to represent the semantic content of narrative information – i.e. its key 'meaning' – in a general, accurate and effective way is both conceptually relevant and economically important. We can remark, in this respect, that the representation of narratives cannot be realized making use only of the traditional 'ontologies' (hierarchies of concepts, *see* Chapter 4). Even in the most sophisticated implementations of the ontology principles (such as the description logics models, *see* Section 3.132) the representation of the concepts is still based, in substance, on the traditional 'binary' model built up in a 'property-value' style. For the narratives, the simple description of concepts represented according to this model is not enough, and must be integrated by the description of the mutual relationships between concepts – or, in other terms, by the description of the 'role' the different concepts and their instances have in the framework of the global actions, facts, events, etc. If, making use of a very simple example, we want to represent a narrative fragment such as 'Company X will develop a new computer system...', asserting that company_x is an instance of the concept *company_* and that we must introduce an instance of a concept like *computer_system* is not sufficient at all. We must, in reality, create a sort of complex, ternary relationship (*see* the description of NKRL below). This will include a 'predicate', such as DEVELOP or PRODUCE, the two instances, and a third element, the 'roles', such as SUBJECT or AGENT for Company X and OBJECT or PATIENT for the new computer system. The roles allow us to specify the exact function of these two instances within the formal description of the event. Note that some approximate counterpart of these higher arity relations among concepts can also be simulated making use of the traditional description logics ontologies. But, given their intrinsic 'taxonomic' nature, the introduction of higher arity links among concepts is, in a way, a sort of unnatural operation, and the relationships used are always particularly simple, in the style of: 'the e-mail address of *X* is *Y*' (Ontobrocker, [Fens98]), or 'the infected species *V* has symptoms *W*' (SHOE, [Hefl99a, Hefl99b]).

NKRL has already been used as an advanced tool to model (and exploit) the semantic content of narratives in European projects such as Nomos (Esprit P5330), Cobalt (LRE P61011) and WebLearning (GALILEO Actions). In summer 2000 it was being employed in the CONCERTO project (Esprit P29159) to encode the 'conceptual annotations' (formal description of the main semantic content of a document) to be added to digital documents to facilitate their 'intelligent' retrieval, processing, displaying, etc., *see* [Zarr99b]. It will be used for describing and filtering Internet information in the new EUFORBIA European project (IAP P2104). Note that a permanent interest of NKRL's designers – see, for example, [Zarr86b] – has been that of using the NKRL high-level conceptual coding to populate large 'integral approach' knowledge bases (large knowledge repositories) able to support, thereafter, all sorts of advanced applications such as expert systems, case-based reasoning, intelligent information retrieval, temporal and causal reasoners, 'interlingua' support for mechanical translation, etc. This particular attention given to the 'intelligent database' problem makes the NKRL approach – with respect to other systems dealing with the problem of the conceptual representation of narrative documents, such as LILOG (*see* [Herz91], [Beie93]) or EL (Episodic Logic, *see* [Schu89], [Hwan93]) – particularly relevant in the context of this book.

Metadocuments and knowledge repositories

When an original digital document is 'translated' or 'descripted' into NKRL format, we obtain a 'metadocument', i.e. a conceptual representation of its informational content. Such metadocuments can then be stored into a knowledge repository and, given their role of advanced 'document models', all the traditional functions of information retrieval, such as searching, retrieving and producing an answer (and other functions like the intelligent navigation inside the repository), can be directly executed on them. Figure 3.49 illustrates a typical example of a prototypical system designed to set up and exploit a knowledge repository of NKRL metadocuments – see [Zarr97b] for additional technical details.

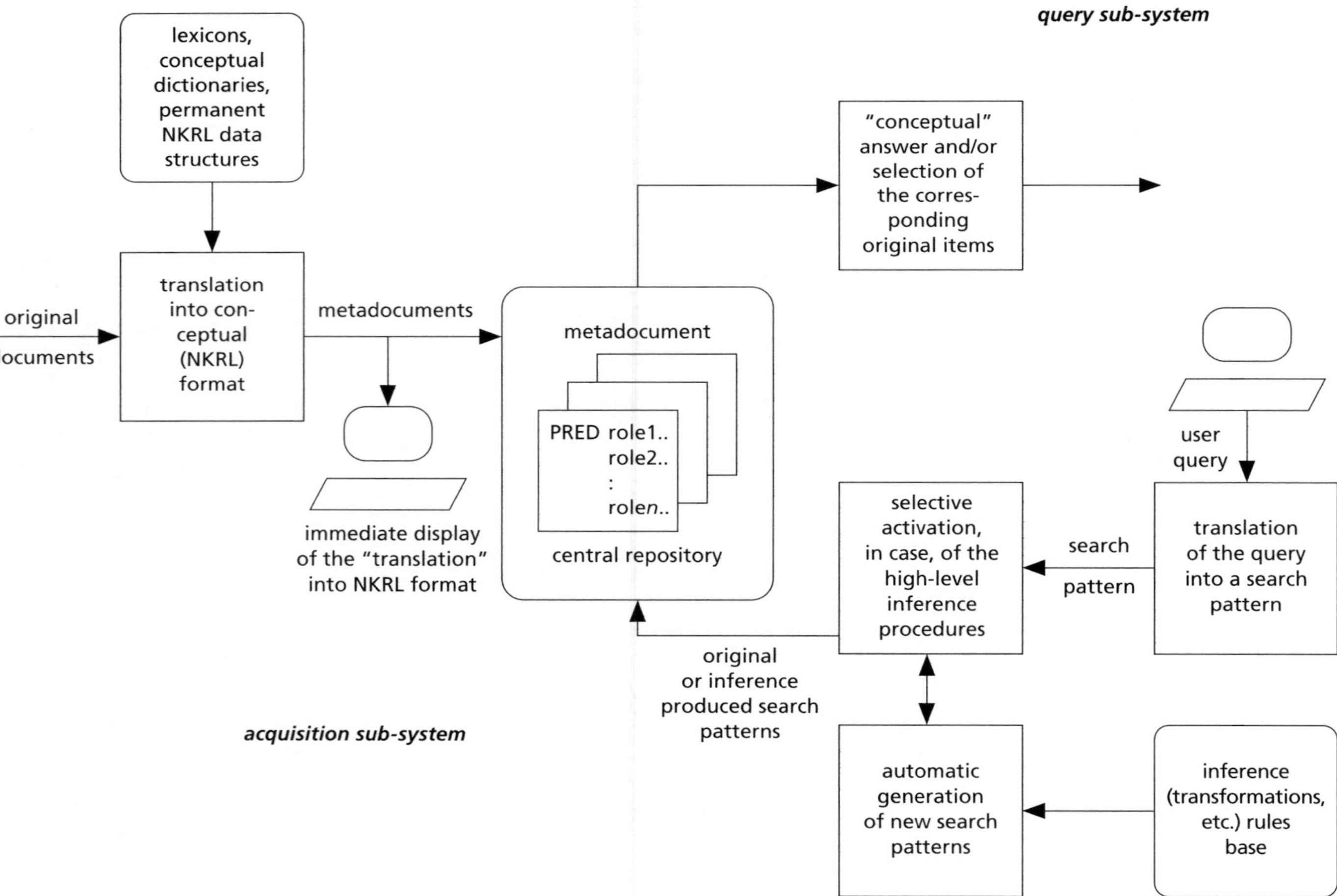

Figure 3.49 Architecture of an NKRL 'metadocument' prototype

The original documents, on the left, pass through the natural language processing modules that constitute the core of the acquisition subsystem. This subsystem executes, essentially, a conversion of the 'meaning' of the original documents into NKRL format. The results of this translation activity are stored into the central knowledge repository (metadocument knowledge repository); it is evident that, in a large environment, solutions in the form of distributed communicating repositories can be conceived. Some functions, not shown in Figure 3.48 for simplicity's sake, allow browsing and maintenance operations on the contents of the repository. Moreover, in order to i) check the correctness of the translation and ii) supply the user with a means of being informed in real time of the main characteristics of the analyzed documents, it is normal to add some possibilities of immediate display of the resulting NKRL code.

The boxes on the right-hand side of Figure 3.49 represent the query subsystem of the prototype. The user's queries are, firstly, translated into search patterns or sequences of search patterns – search patterns are NKRL data structures that represent the general framework of information to be searched for, by filtering or unification, within the metadocument repository. The metadocuments can i) directly unify the original query (search pattern) and ii) unify some new search patterns obtained by inference from the original one, *see* below. After the (possible) unification of the patterns with one or more metadocuments, these are presented to the user. The output can be shown, for example, in three different formats, which can also coexist: i) in a concise, tabular format (immediate display); ii) as an NL text generated from the selected metadocuments; iii) as the original documents if they have been stored along with the corresponding metadocuments.

The acquisition part of the system performs a set of TELL operations that modify the contents of the central KB, and the query subsystem ASKs about the contents of this base.

In the following, after a quick glimpse of the NKRL language, we will focus on the query subsystem, the more interesting one from a database point of view. With respect to the NL/NKRL 'translation' procedures, we will say here only that they are based on the well-known principle of locating, within the original NL texts, the syntactic and semantic indexes which can evoke the conceptual structures used to represent these texts. The NKRL contribution has consisted of the set-up of a rigorous algorithmic procedure, centred around two main principles:

- The use of rules – evoked by particular lexical items in the text examined and stored in proper conceptual dictionaries – which take the form of 'generalized production rules'. Their left-hand side (antecedent part) is always a syntactic condition, expressed as a tree-like structure, which must be unified with the results of the general parse tree produced by the syntactic specialist of the translation system. If the unification succeeds, the right-hand sides (consequent parts) are used, for example, to generate well-formed NKRL structures ('triggering rules').
- The use, within the rules, of sophisticated mechanisms to deal with the variables. For example, in the specific, 'triggering' family of NKRL rules, the 'antecedent variables' (*a*-variables) are first declared in the syntactic (antecedent)

part of the rules, and then 'echoed' in the consequent parts, where they appear under the form of arguments and constraints associated with the roles of the activated conceptual structures (templates). Their function is that of 'capturing' – during the match between the antecedents and the results of the syntactic specialist – NL or NKRL elements to be used as specialization terms for filling up the activated templates, and building the final NKRL structures.

A detailed description of these principles and of the corresponding tools can be found in [Zarr95b]; *see also* [Azza95]. Their generality and their detailed semantic description make possible, for example, the quick production of useful sets of new rules by simply duplicating and editing the existing ones.

The main principles of the NKRL architecture

NKRL is a two-layer language. The lower layer – which, besides conceptual graphs, also bears some resemblance to terminological languages such as KL-ONE or CLASSIC [BracR91] – supplies a set of general tools, *see* [Zarr94], [Zarr95a], [Zarr97a]. It consists of four integrated components, characterized by different data structures created to fit exactly the different sorts of phenomena they intend to model. We can thus avoid, in this way, the 'RLL syndrome' evoked with respect to CYC.

The descriptive component tools are used to set up the formal NKRL expressions (*templates*) describing general classes of narrative events. In a 'descriptive component' context, the events taken into consideration must be structured events, i.e. they must be characterized by the explicit mention of an actor, an object, a beneficiary, a location, etc. Examples of templates can be the NKRL representation of generic events such as 'moving a generic object', 'formulate a need', 'be present somewhere', 'transmitting an information', etc. Templates are structured into a hierarchy, H_TEMP(lates), which can be equated to a taxonomy (ontology) of events – one of the most important characteristics of the NKRL formalism, *see* [Zarr95a]; an (extremely simplified) example of a real H_TEMP hierarchy is given in Figure 3.50.

Templates' instances (called predicative occurrences), i.e. the NKRL representations of single, specific events such as 'Tomorrow, I will move the wardrobe', 'Lucy was looking for a taxi', 'Peter lives in Paris', are in the domain of a second component, the factual one.

In NKRL terms, templates and predicative occurrences are characterized by a complex ternary (threefold) format connecting the *symbolic name* of the template/occurrence, a *predicate* and its *arguments*. The arguments are, in turn, linked with the predicate by a set of named relations, the *roles*; roles are abstract labels that characterize the semantic relations between a predicate and its arguments. In other words, each argument of a predicate is marked with a 'role' that denotes, in a very general way, the 'semantic' function played by the argument with respect to the predicate. If we indicate with L_i the generic symbolic label identifying a given template or occurrence, with P_j the predicate used in the template (occurrence), with R_k the generic role, and with a_k the corresponding argument, the NKRL data structures for templates/occurrences will have the following general format:

$(L_i(P_j(R_1\ a_1)(R_2\ a_2)\ \ldots\ (R_n\ a_n)))$,

see the examples below. At present, the predicates pertain to the set {BEHAVE, EXIST, EXPERIENCE, MOVE, OWN, PRODUCE, RECEIVE}, and the roles to the set {SUBJ(ect), OBJ(ect), SOURCE, BEN(e)F(iciary), MODAL(ity), TOPIC, CONTEXT}.

Within the NKRL framework, a metadocument consists of the association of several predicative occurrences (more rarely, of templates). They are tied up by particular 'binding occurrences' – *see* [Zarr94], [Zarr97a] and the example of Table 3.62 – that represent the logico-semantic links (the co-ordination and subordination links, using a metaphor from the domain of natural language) that can exist between the predicative ones.

The definitional component supplies the formal representation of all the specific notions, such as *physical_entity*, *taxi_*, *location_*, which can be used as arguments of the predicates in the two components (descriptive and factual) above. The representations in NKRL terms of these notions are called concepts (basically, the corresponding data structures can be equated to frames) and are grouped into a hierarchy, H_CLASS(es) – H_CLASS corresponds well, therefore, to the usual 'ontologies' of concepts, *see* [Zarr95a].

A fundamental assumption about the organization of H_CLASS concerns the differentiation between 'notions which can be instantiated directly into enumerable specimens', like 'chair' (a physical object) and 'notions which cannot be instantiated directly into specimens', like 'gold' (a substance). The two high-level branches of H_CLASS stem, therefore, from two concepts labelled as *sortal_concepts* and *non_sortal_concepts* (*see* [Guar94] and Figure 3.50). The specializations of the former, such as *chair_*, *city_* or *european_city*, can have direct instances (*chair_27*, *paris_*), whereas the specializations of the latter, such as *gold_*, or *colour_*, can admit further specializations, *see white_gold* or *red_*, but do not have direct instances.

The instances of concepts – i.e. concrete, countable examples of the notions represented by the concepts, like *lucy_*, *wardrobe_1*, *taxi_53*, *paris_* etc. – are called individuals, and pertain to the enumerative component. For more details about other important tools of NKRL, such as those allowing the representation of modal or temporal information, *see* [Zarr92b], [Zarr98]. The reasons for distributing the threefold data structures of NKRL into two separate components, descriptive and factual, and the frame-like data structures into the definitional and factual ones, are detailed in [Zarr97a].

The upper layer of NKRL consists of two parts. The first is a *catalogue*, where we can find a complete description of the formal characteristics, the modalities of use and the mutual relationships (H_TEMP links) of the well-formed, 'basic' templates (such as 'moving a generic object' mentioned above) associated with the language. Presently, basic templates are more than 200, pertaining mainly to a (very general) socio-economico-political context where the main characters are human beings or social bodies. By means of proper specialization operations, it is possible to obtain from these basic templates – that, from a formal point of view, can be considered as the 'axioms' of the NKRL language – the (specific) 'derived' templates which could be needed in the context of a particular, practical application, and the corresponding occurrences (instances). For example, from the basic 'moving a generic object' we can obtain the derived template 'move an industrial process'; an occurrence of this last template could be: 'move, in a well-defined spatio-temporal framework, this particular industrial production from one country to another.' In NKRL, the set of legal, basic templates included in the catalogue can be considered as fixed, at least in a first approach. This means that: i) a system-builder does not have to create the knowledge needed to describe the events proper to a (sufficiently) large class of narrative documents; ii) it becomes easier to secure the reproduction and the sharing of previous results.

The second part of the layer is given by the general concepts (general notions) that belong to the upper level of H_CLASS, such as *sortal_concepts*, *non_sortal_concepts*, *physical_entity*, *modality_*, *event_*, etc. They are, like the basic templates, invariable.

Some examples of NKRL data structures

Table 3.60 gives a very simple example of NKRL 'external' code (a metadocument consisting only of predicative occurrences). It translates a small fragment of news in COBALT's style: 'Milan, October 15, 1993. The financial daily Il Sole 24 Ore reported Mediobanca had called a special board meeting concerning plans for capital increase.'

Table 3.60 An example of NKRL coding

```
c1) MOVE     SUBJ     (SPECIF sole_24_ore financial_daily): (milan_)
             OBJ      #c2
             date-1:  15_october_93
             date-2:

c2) PRODUCE     SUBJ     mediobanca_
                OBJ      (SPECIF summoning_ (SPECIF board_meeting_1
                                  mediobanca_ special_))
                TOPIC    (SPECIF plan_1 (SPECIF cardinality_ several_)
                                capital_increase_1)
                date-1: circa_15_october_93
                date-2:
```

In Table 3.60, c1 and c2 are the symbolic names of two predicative occurrences, instances of basic NKRL templates. MOVE and PRODUCE are predicates; SUBJ, OBJ, TOPIC (the theme, '*à propos* of ...', of the event(s) or situation(s) represented in the occurrence) are roles. With respect to the arguments, sole_24_ore, milan_, mediobanca_ (an Italian merchant bank), board_meeting_1, are individuals (enumerative component); *financial_daily*, *summoning_*, *special_*, *cardinality_* (which pertains to the *quantifying_property_* subtree of H_CLASS), *several_* (belonging, like *some_*, *all_* etc., to the *logical_quantifier* subtree of H_CLASS) and *capital_increase* are concepts. H_CLASS (definitional component) is the NKRL hierarchy of concepts.

In Table 3.60, we have supposed that an information element such as 'summoning' was not sufficiently important *per se* to justify its explicit representation as a specific individual, such as summoning_1. Note that, if not expressly required by the characteristics of the application, a basic NKRL principle suggests that we should try to avoid any unnecessary proliferation of individuals (and of the associated frames).

The attributive operator, SPECIF(ication), is one of the NKRL operators used to build up structured arguments (or 'expansions'); the SPECIF lists, with syntax (SPECIF e_1 p_1 ... p_n), are used to represent the properties which can be asserted about the first element e_1, concept or individual, of the list, for example, sole_24_ore in occurrence c1, *summoning_* and plan_1 in c2. *several_* is used within a *cardinality_* SPECIF list, *see* occurrence c2, to provide a standard way of representing the plural number mark – *see* [Zarr97a] for a description of the NKRL theory of the representation of plural situations. The arguments, and the templates/occurrences as a whole, may be characterized by the addition of determiners (attributes). In particular, the location attributes (lists) are associated with the arguments by using the colon, ':', operator, *see* occurance c1. For a paper on the NKRL representation of the temporal determiners, date-1 and date-2, *see* [Zarr98].

For clarity's sake, we reproduce in Table 3.61 the MOVE basic template at the origin of occurrence c1 as it appears in the 'upper level' catalogue already mentioned. Optional elements are in square brackets. In the corresponding occurrences, such as c1, the variables (*var1* etc.) are replaced by concepts (definitional component) or individuals (enumerative component) according to the associated constraints; constraints are expressed mainly under the form of associations of high-level concepts of H_CLASS. Note that this template is necessarily used to translate any event concerning the transmission of a 'structured' information ('The financial daily Il Sole 24 Ore reported...'). It makes use of what is called a 'completive construction'. Accordingly, the filler of the OBJ(ect) slot in the occurrence (here, c1) that instantiates this 'transmission' template is always a symbolic label (here, #c2); this symbolic label refers to another occurrence that bears the informational content to be spread out ('Mediobanca had called a meeting...'). For other structures (binding occurrences) that allow us to build up complex, second-order objects from first-order templates and occurrences, *see* Table 3.62 and [Zarr97a].

Figure 3.49 aims to give a very general insight about a concrete H_TEMP hierarchy, in this case the H_TEMP hierarchy used in the CONCERTO project. For clarity's sake, and in view of the space constraints, this representation has been severely abridged. Several branches (the BEHAVE, EXIST etc. branches pertaining to the first level of H_TEMP, the 'Receive:IntellectualResource' (7.2) branch in the RECEIVE subtree, the 'Move:AnimateDisplacement' (4.31) branch in the MOVE subtree, etc.) have been suppressed, and a lot of intermediate nodes (such as 5.11, 5.12, 4.31, etc.) are missing. Each node corresponds to a descriptive structure (template) in the style of the threefold structure represented in Table 3.61. Note that the great majority of the templates mentioned in Figure 3.50 are 'basic' templates. A 'derived' template introduced in the H_TEMP hierarchy for the specific needs of

Table 3.61 An example of an NKRL template

```
name : Move:StructuredInformation
father : Move:TransmitInformation
position : 4. 42
NL description : 'Transmit a Structured Information'

MOVE  SUBJ          var1: [(var2)]
      OBJ           var3
      [SOURCE       var4: [(var5)]]
      [BENF         var6: [(var7)]]
      [MODAL        var8]
      [TOPIC        var9]
      [CONTEXT      var10]
      { [ modulators ], ≠abs }

var1  =  <human_being_or_social_body>
var3  =  <symbolic_label>
var4  =  <human_being_or_social_body>
var6  =  <human_being_or_social_body>
var8  =  <action_name> | <information_support>
var9  ≠  <property_> ;
var10 =  <event_> | <action_name>
var2, var5, var7 =  <physical_location>
```

the CONCERTO project is the 'Move:Version/PartOfService' (4.2311) template, for instance. An example of its utilization concerns the creation of a predicative occurrence to represent the information: 'British Telecom will offer its customers *a trial of this service* ....'

Figure 3.51 gives a simplified representation of the upper level of H_CLASS (hierarchy of concepts, definitional component). From this figure, we can note that `substance_` and `colour_` are regarded in NKRL as examples of non-sortal concepts. For their generic terms, `pseudo_sortal_concepts` and `characterizing_concepts`, we have adopted the terminology of [Guar94]. For a discussion about `substance_`, *see* [Zarr97a]. Data structures used for concepts and individuals – i.e. for the entities included in (concepts) or associated with (individuals) the H_CLASS hierarchy – are essentially, as already stated, frame-based structures. For more details, *see* the discussion in Section 3.131 and [Zarr97a].

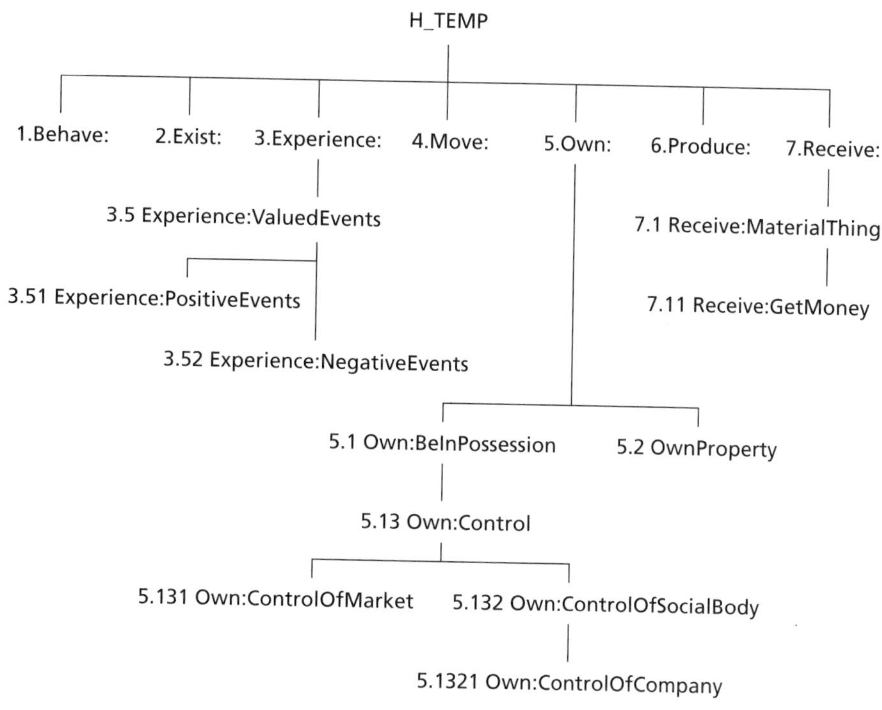

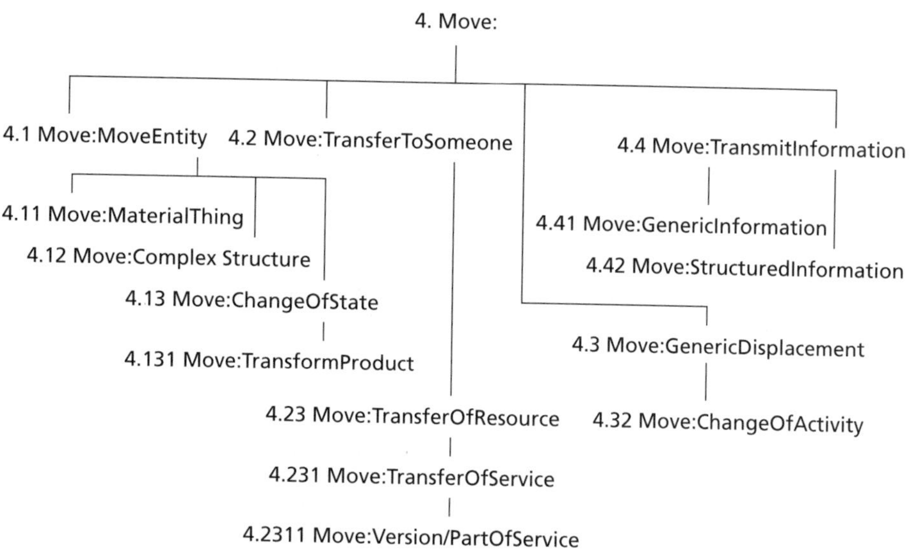

Figure 3.50 Schematic view of the H_TEMP hierachy (ontology of events)

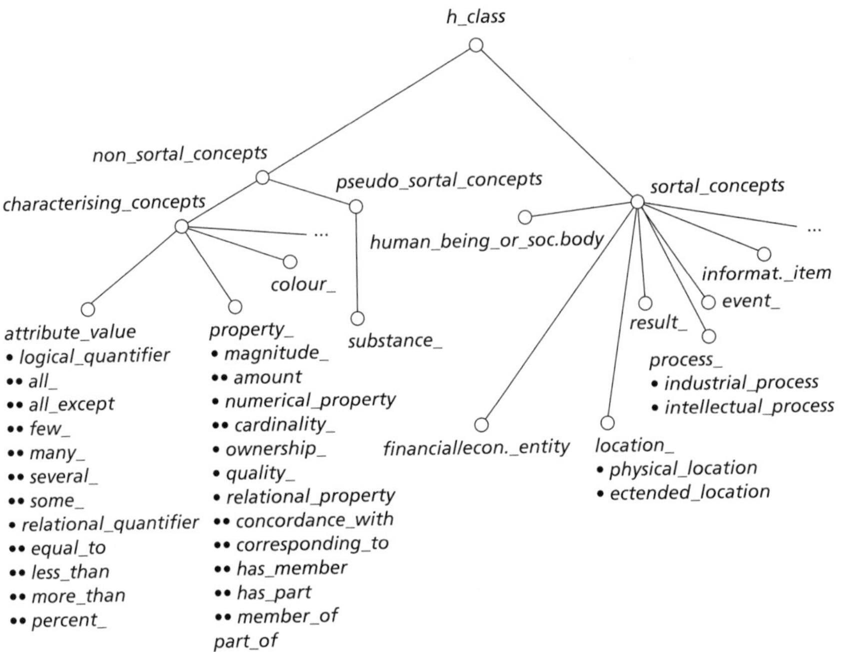

Figure 3.51 An abridged view of the upper level of H_CLASS

To give greater insight into the expressive power of the NKRL formalism, we give, in Table 3.62, an NKRL interpretation of the sentence: 'We have to make orange juice' which, according to Hwang and Schubert [Hwan93], exemplifies several interesting semantic phenomena.

Table 3.62 Representation in NKRL of 'wishes and intentions'

```
c3) BEHAVE SUBJ    (SPECIF human_being (SPECIF cardinality_ several_))
            [oblig, ment]
            date1: observed date
            date2:

c4) *PRODUCE SUBJ  (SPECIF human_being (SPECIF cardinality_ several_))
             OBJ (SPECIF orange_juice (SPECIF amount_))
             date1: observed date + i
             date2:

c5) (GOAL c3 c4)
```

To translate the general idea of 'acting to obtain a given result', we use:

- A predicative occurrence (c3 in Table 3.62), an instance of a basic template pertaining to the BEHAVE branch of the template hierarchy (H_TEMP), and corresponding to the general meaning of 'focus on a result'. This occurrence is used to express the 'acting' component, i.e. it allows us to identify the SUBJ of the action, the temporal co-ordinates, possibly the MODAL(ity) or the instigator (SOURCE), etc.

- A second predicative occurrence, `c4` in Table 3.60, characterized by a different NKRL predicate, which is used to express the 'intended result' component. This second occurrence, which happens 'in the future', is marked as hypothetical, i.e. it is necessarily characterized by the presence of an 'uncertainty validity attribute', code '*'.
- A 'binding occurrence', `c5`, linking the previous predicative occurrences and labelled with GOAL, an operator pertaining to the 'taxonomy of causality' of NKRL. Binding structures – i.e. lists where the elements are symbolic labels of well-formed NKRL expressions, `c3` and `c4` in Table 3.62 – are second-order structures used to represent the logico-semantic links that can exist between (predicative) templates or occurrences.

The general schema for representing the 'focusing on an intended result' domain in NKRL is then:

```
cα)   BEHAVE SUBJ <human_being_or_social_body>
cβ)   *<predicative_occurrence>, with any syntax
cγ)   (GOAL cα cβ)
```

In Table 3.62, `oblig` and `ment` are modulators. `ment(al)` pertains to the 'modality' modulators. `oblig(atory)` suggests that 'someone is obliged to do or to endure something, for example, by authority', and pertains to the 'deontic modulators' series, *see* [Zarr97a]. Other modulators are the 'temporal modulators', `begin`, `end`, `obs(erve)`, *see* [Zarr98]. In the constructions for expressing 'focus on...', the absence of the `ment(al)` modulator in the BEHAVE occurrence means that the SUBJ(ect) of BEHAVE takes some concrete initiative (acts explicitly) in order to fulfil the result; if `ment(al)` is present, as in Table 3.62, no concrete action is taken and the 'result' reflects only the wishes and desires of the SUBJ(ect).

Using the metadocuments for interrogation purposes

Generalities about the basic querying and inferencing building blocks. Each of the four components of the NKRL language is characterized by the association with a class of proper inference procedures. For example, the specialized query language for dealing with the definitional and enumerative component data structures fulfils the following minimal requirements:

- it must be possible to specify a query to match a specific concept/individual;
- it must be possible to specify a query to match a set of individuals characterized by being offsprings of a (set of) specific H_CLASS concepts (for example, all the financial companies, or all financial companies excepting the French ones), and, if necessary, characterized by a set of attribute-slots with specific values (for example, all companies whose 'capital' slot holds a value $\geq$ 2,000,000);

- it must be possible to introduce variables to be bound to specific parts of the matched concept/individuals.

From the above, it is now evident that the main inference mechanism associated with the definitional (H_CLASS) and enumerative components must be the usual taxonomic inheritance mechanism that proceeds over IsA and InstanceOf relations. Often the basic building blocks for this mechanism are offered for free by the knowledge representation tools that support the different implementations of NKRL: this has been the case for both CRL (Carnegie Representation Language, used in the NOMOS project mentioned above) and QSL (Quinary Semantic Language, used in the COBALT project). Note that in NKRL the subtyping relations to be used for the inheritance operations are directly encoded in the H_CLASS hierarchy supporting the definitional component.

As regards the factual component, the key inference mechanism for this component (and the basic inference tool of NKRL) is the filtering and unification module (FUM). The primary data structures handled by FUM are the search patterns that, as already stated, represent (in NKRL terms) the general properties of an information to be searched for, by filtering or unification, within a metadocument knowledge repository. A search pattern can be considered an NKRL equivalent of a simple natural language query (*see* Figure 3.49). For clarity's sake, we reproduce in Table 3.63 the search pattern corresponding to the question: 'Which was the theme of the recent board meeting called by Mediobanca?' that, obviously, unifies with occurrence c2 in Table 3.60. In Table 3.63 we have voluntarily enlarged the scope of the question by adding more constraints on the OBJ(ect) variable (*x*). The two dates of this last figure constitute the 'search interval' associated with the search pattern: this is used to limit the search for unification to the slice of time that it is considered appropriate to explore, *see* [Zarr98].

Table 3.63 A simple search pattern

```
((?w  IS-OCCURRENCE
      :predicate  PRODUCE
      :SUBJ      mediobanca_
      :OBJ       (SPECIF ?x (SPECIF ?y mediobanca_))
      :TOPIC     ?z)
      (1_october_93, 20_october_93)
      ((?x        IS-A    (:OR assembly_ adjournment_ dissolution_))
      (?y         IS-A    board_meeting)
      (?z         IS-A    planning_activity)))
```

Note that the most interesting component of the FUM module is represented by the matching algorithm that unifies the complex structures – such as '(SPECIF summoning_1 (SPECIF board_meeting_1 mediobanca_ *special_*))' in occurrence c2 of Table 3.60 – which, in the NKRL terminology, are called structured arguments, *see* the following subsections and [Zarr96] for more details.

A generalization of the FUM module is used for matching the templates of the descriptive component. A specific inference mechanism, based on FUM and proper to this last component, is a sort of join procedure ([Sowa84]) allowing for the merge of (two or more) basic or derived templates. Information on these merge procedures can be found in [Zarr95b].

The AECS sub-language. In Tables 3.60, 3.62 and 3.63, the arguments made up of a SPECIF(ication) list are examples of NKRL structured arguments (or 'expansions').

In NKRL, structured arguments of templates and occurrences are built up in a principled way by making use of a specialized sublanguage, AECS. This includes four binding operators: the disjunctive operator (ALTERNative = A), the distributive operator (ENUMeration = E), the collective operator (COORDination = C), and the attributive operator (SPECIFication = S), *see* [Zarr97a]. Their intuitive meaning is given in Table 3.64. Accordingly, structured arguments in NKRL are lists of undefined length, which may include both concepts and individuals and which are labelled by making use of the AECS operators.

Table 3.64 NKRL operators for structured arguments

Operator	Mnemonic description
ALTERN	The 'disjunctive operator'. It introduces a set of elements, i.e. concepts, individuals, or lists labelled with other expansion operators. Only one element of the set takes part in the particular relationship with the predicate defined by the role-slot to be filled with the expansion; however, this element is not known.
COORD	The 'collective operator': all the elements of the set take part (necessarily together) in the relationship with the predicate defined by the role-slot.
ENUM	The 'distributive operator': each element of the set satisfies the relationship, but they do so separately.
SPECIF	The 'attributive operator'. It is used to link a series of attributes (properties) with the concept or individual that constitutes the first element of the SPECIF list, in order to better characterize this first element. Each attribute appearing inside a SPECIF list can be recursively associated with another SPECIF list.

From a formal point of view, we can note, for example, that:

a) $(\mathtt{SPECIF}\ e_1\ a\ b) = (\mathtt{SPECIF}\ e_1\ b\ a)$;
b) $(\mathtt{ENUM}\ e_1\ e_2) = (e_1\ \mathtt{AND}\ e_2\ \mathtt{AND}\ \neg\ (\mathtt{COORD}\ e_1\ e_2))$.

The first formula says that the order of the properties a, b, ... associated with an entity e_1, concept or individual, is not significant. The second formula enunciates formally what was already stated in Table 3.64: the main characteristics of the ENUM lists are linked with the fact that the entities e_1, e_2, ... take part obligatorily in the particular relationship between the structured argument and the predicate expressed by the role which introduces the arguments, but they satisfy this relationship separately.

Because of their recursive nature, the AECS operators could give rise to very complex expressions, which are difficult to interpret and disentangle (unify). Therefore, to build up well-formed NKRL expansions, the definitions in Table 3.64 are used in association with the so-called 'priority rule', which can be visualized by using the following expression:

```
(ALTERN (ENUM (COORD (SPECIF)))).
```

This is to be interpreted as follows: it is forbidden to use, inside the scope of a list introduced by the binding operator *B*, a list labelled in terms of one of the binding operators appearing on the left of *B* in the priority expression above – for example, it is impossible to use a list ALTERN inside the scope of a list COORD. Examples of this rule being used can be found in [Zarr97a].

A query language for structured arguments. Returning to the FUM module, we have seen that the AECS language allows us to describe complex relations among concepts and individuals. While sometimes a query about an AECS structure must be able to exploit completely the information carried by this structure, the situation in which only part of this information is really useful is relatively frequent. We can take as an example the (very simple) AECS expression '(COORD john_ paul_)', that expresses the fact that both John and Paul take part in a particular event in a co-ordinated manner. Sometimes this is exactly the information looked for with a query (i.e. whether they are involved 'necessarily together' in the event, according to the definition of COORD). It is often the case, however, that the information we want to obtain is simply whether John (or Paul) takes part in the event (*see also* Table 3.66).

Therefore, a query language operating on the AECS structures must be able to express a wide range of query modalities (including the two evoked before), and to obtain constantly the correct results. Keeping in mind that it is always possible to express the AECS structures (the AECS lists) in term of trees, we can state here the following basic requirements for the AECS-query language which is part of the FUM module:

1 It must be possible to specify a 'perfect match', defined as a match that succeeds if and only if the query, and the target (matched) AECS expression, have the same identical formal structure (apart from variables), i.e. if the tree representations of the query and of the target expression are strictly identical. As an example, we can say that the query (ENUM *?x ?y*) succeeds against the target AECS expression (ENUM credit_lyonnais mediobanca_), but fails against (COORD credit_lyonnais (SPECIF mediobanca_ merchant_bank)) or against (ENUM credit_lyonnais mediobanca_ chase_manhattan).

2 It must be possible to specify a perfect match apart from 'cardinality', i.e. a match that succeeds if and only if the query, and the target AECS expression, have the same identical structure – apart from variables and, chiefly, without taking into account the cardinality of the AECS lists. In this case, (ENUM *?x ?y*) succeeds against (ENUM credit_lyonnais mediobanca_) and against (ENUM credit_lyonnais

mediobanca_ chase_manhattan), but fails, obviously, against (COORD credit_lyonnais mediobanca_).

3 It must be possible to specify a 'subsumed' match, i.e. a match that succeeds if and only if the query, and the target AECS expression, carries information which can be considered as globally congruent from a semantic point of view. For example, we admit here the presence, in the target (matched) expression, of additional SPECIF lists (additional lists of attributes). According to this paradigm, (COORD *?x ?y*) succeeds against (COORD credit_lyonnais mediobanca_), against (COORD credit_lyonnais (SPECIF mediobanca_ merchant_bank)), and against (COORD credit_lyonnais mediobanca_ chase_manhattan).

4 It must obviously be possible to mix the above kinds of queries in such a way that, for example, *perfect match is required for the top level structure of the query and target trees but not for the underlying parts, see also* the examples of Table 3.65 below. In this way, for example, (ALTERN *?x ?y*) can match against (ALTERN chase_manhattan (COORD credit_lyonnais mediobanca_)).

We can remark that:

- The first requirement is necessary to guarantee that all the information included in the target templates and occurrences can be used effectively and in a correct way. If this requirement did not exist, the AECS language would be richer than we could actually use. For example, if we need to ask if credit_lyonnais (alone) is the protagonist of some event, we must not match something as (ENUM credit_lyonnais someone_else).
- The second and third requirements are necessary to simplify queries, for example, allowing the user simply to ask for credit_lyonnais and to match both credit_lyonnais, (COORD credit_lyonnais ...), (ENUM credit_lyonnais ...), etc. This possibility entrusts to the query interpreter the burden of executing some quite basic inferences that would be left, if these requirements did not exist, to the user of the query language, with the consequence of making queries complex, less readable and, eventually, more error prone. For the previous example, the user would be asked to write something like: (OR credit_lyonnais (COORD credit_lyonnais *?x*) (ENUM credit_lyonnais *?x*) (ENUM *?x* (COORD credit_lyonnais ?y)) ...)).
- The last requirement is only a consequence of having accepted the previous ones.

We can now define a query language for AECS structures. For clarity's sake, the query language is based on the logical structures of the original AECS sublanguage, augmented to allow i) the use of variables, and ii) the correct specification of the kind of match required by the query. The AECS query language is therefore defined in the following way. Take the AECS descriptive language as the basis, but allow:

- the use of variables (?*x*), possibly with constraints, instead of concepts or individuals;

- the use of the special construct STRICT-SUBSUMPTION, taking as argument an NKRL entity (variable, concept or individual) or a complex AECS structure. Bearing in mind the priority rule introduced in the previous subsection, these complex AECS structures, expressed as trees, may consist of: a simple list COORD (coord-list); a coord-tree, subsuming as 'branches' at least two coord-lists; an enum-tree, subsuming one or more coord-trees (or coord-lists); an altern-tree, subsuming any of the previous tree-structures;
- the use of the special construct STRICT-CARDINALITY, taking as argument an NKRL argument, or one of the AECS structures listed in the previous paragraph.

STRICT-CARDINALITY and STRICT-SUBSUMPTION have the following operational meanings:

- the presence of a STRICT-SUBSUMPTION operator forces the interpretation of the argument according to a 'no-subsumption' rule, thus requiring a perfect match (*see* point 1 before) on the type (NKRL entity, coord-branch, coord-tree, enum-tree, altern-tree) of the argument;
- the presence of a STRICT-CARDINALITY operator forces the interpretation of the argument according to a 'fixed-cardinality' rule, thus requiring a perfect match (*see* point 2 before) on the cardinality of the argument;
- the absence of any of the two special operators implies the 'subsuming' rule (*see* point 3 before), thus producing a successful match if the semantics of the query construct *is subsumed* by the semantics of the matched construct.

The algorithms that make use of the AECS query language to unify two AECS structured arguments are described in [Zarr96]. To illustrate intuitively what is expressed above, Table 3.65 gives some examples that refer to different modalities of matching the target AECS structure: `(ENUM chase_manhattan (COORD credit_lyonnais (SPECIF mediobanca_ merchant_bank) city_bank))`.

An example of high-level inference procedures, the transformations. The basic querying and inference mechanisms outlined in the previous subsections are used as building blocks for implementing all sorts of high-level inference procedures. For example, inference procedures which have been studied in depth in an NKRL context are the 'transformation rules', *see* [Zarr86a], [Ogon87].

In the database theory, the notion of 'transformation' is usually linked with that of 'semantic equivalence' between two queries: in a database context, two queries are considered as semantically equivalent if their answer is the same for all database states which satisfy a given set of integrity constraints. This notion is, therefore, used for operations of semantic query optimization. In an NKRL context, the notion of transformation acquires a wider significance.

NKRL transformations deal with the problem of obtaining a plausible answer from a database of factual occurrences also in the absence of the explicitly requested information, by searching semantic affinities between what is requested and what is really present in the repository. The fundamental principle employed is to transform the original query into one or more different queries which, unlike the transformed queries in a database context, are not strictly 'equivalent' but only 'semantically close' to the original one.

To give a very simple example, suppose that, working in the context of a hypothetical metadocument database about university professors, we want to pose a query like: 'Who has lived in the United States', even without an explicit representation of this fact in the repository – *see* in Section 3.443, the analogous example developed in a CYC context. If the repository contains some information about the degrees obtained by the professors, we can tell the user that, although we do not explicitly know who lived in the States, we can nevertheless look for people having an American degree. This last piece of information, obtained by transformation of the original query, would indeed normally imply that some time was spent by the professors in the country, the United States, that issued their degree.

Table 3.65 Examples of AECS unifications

- The query: (ENUM *?x* (STRICT-SUBSUMPTION (COORD credit_lyonnais mediobanca_ city_bank))) will succeed, binding *x* to chase_manhattan. Note that the STRICT-SUBSUMPTION operator concerns only the general structure of the coord-trees, and not the structure of the single coord-branches – in this case, (SPECIF mediobanca_ *merchant_bank*).
- The query: (ENUM *?x* (COORD credit_lyonnais (STRICT-SUBSUMPTION mediobanca_) city_bank)) will fail because of the STRICT-SUBSUMPTION restriction that prevents mediobanca_ from matching a coord-branch, (SPECIF mediobanca_ merchant_bank).
- The query: (ENUM *?x* (STRICT-CARDINALITY (COORD credit_lyonnais mediobanca_))) will fail because of the STRICT-CARDINALITY restriction.
- The query: (STRICT-SUBSUMPTION (ENUM *?x* (COORD credit_lyonnais mediobanca_))) will succeed, binding *x* to chase_manhattan. Once again, the STRICT-SUBSUMPTION restriction concerns only the top-level structure of the enum-trees.
- The query: (ENUM *?x credit_lyonnais*) will succeed, binding *x* to chase_manhattan.
- The query: (STRICT-SUBSUMPTION (ENUM *?x* (STRICT-SUBSUMPTION credit_lyonnais))) will fail, due to the restriction: (STRICT-SUBSUMPTION credit_lyonnais).
- The query: (STRICT-SUBSUMPTION (COORD credit_lyonnais mediobanca_)) will fail.
- The query: (COORD credit_lyonnais mediobanca_) will succeed.

Transformation rules are made up of a left-hand side – i.e. the formulation, in NKRL format (search pattern), of the linguistic expression to be transformed – and one or more right-hand sides – the NKRL representation(s) of one or more linguistic expressions that must be substituted for the given one. A transformation rule can, therefore, be expressed as: A (left-hand side) $\Rightarrow$ B (right-hand side). The 'transformation arrow', '$\Rightarrow$', has a double meaning:

- operationally speaking, the arrow indicates the direction of the transformation: the left-hand side A (the original search pattern) is removed and replaced by the right-hand side B (one or more new search patterns);
- the standard logical meaning of the arrow is that the information obtained through B implies the information we should have obtained from A.

In reality, the 'always true' implications (noted as $B \rightarrow A$, where we assume that the symbol '$\rightarrow$' represents, as usual, the implication arrow) are not very frequent. Most transformations found in real-world applications represent what we could call 'modalized implications'. We will note them as $\Diamond (B \rightarrow A)$, that means 'it is possible that B implies A'. '$\Diamond$' is the usual modal operator for 'possibility', which satisfies the relation $\Diamond p = \neg\blacklozenge\neg p$ with respect to the second modal operator, '$\blacklozenge$ = necessity'. An example of modalized transformation is given by the transformation t1 in Table 3.66, which allows us to deal with the informal example above about 'university professors', by using an inference engine based on the FUM module (*see* [Zarr86a] for details). As we can see, the antecedent and consequent of t1 are formed by search patterns, slightly simplified here for clarity's sake. Transformation t1 says: 'If someone (x) receives a title from an official authority by means of an official document, then it is possible that he has been physically present at that moment in the place (k) where the authority is located.' This rule, for example, is not always valid in the case of a university degree (it could be obtained from a correspondence school, etc.). Nevertheless, it is possible to see that in this case the semantic distance between an 'always true' implication and a 'modalized' one is not too important as it becomes possible, at least in principle, to change t1 into a true transformation by the addition of a few constraints on the variable p, for instance the 'disequation': '$p \neq$ *<obtainable_by_correspondence_degree>*'. More examples, and a complete 'theory' of transformations, can be found in [Zarr86a].

Table 3.66 A simple example of the 'transformation' rule

```
t1) EXIST   SUBJ  var1:(var2) ⇒   RECEIVE SUBJ    var1
                                          OBJ     var3
                                          SOURCE  var4: (var2)
                                          MODAL   var5

      var1     =    <human_being>
      var2     =    <location_>
      var3     =    <title_>
      var4     =    <authority_>
      var5     =    <official_document>
```

Final considerations about the functioning of the query subsystem of the 'standard' NKRL prototype. Returning to the general architecture of Figure 3.48, we can see that a search pattern may be generated from outside the system when it directly represents, in a deductive retrieving style, the NKRL translation of a query issued by the user – this corresponds to the basic mode of functioning of the query subsystem of an NKRL prototype. But in some cases, it may also be generated automatically from inside the system during the execution of some classes of inference procedures.

Let us consider, in fact, what happens to a search pattern corresponding directly to a user's NL query when, having used this pattern to ASK the central knowledge repository, the user obtains no answer – i.e. the unification of the pattern with the metadocuments failed – or when, having recovered some information, the user would like to know more. In such cases he can consider, as a first hypothesis, being in a situation where the NKRL image of the information that could supply a plausible answer effectively exists in the repository, but it may be difficult to retrieve and recognize. Under this hypothesis, the user will ask the query system to automatically transform the initial search pattern by substituting it with another 'semantically equivalent' pattern, *see* above.

Unfortunately, the problems associated with the practical utilization of this type of approach are not only technical (construction of appropriate inference engines) but concern mainly the way of i) discovering the common sense rules that constitute the real foundation of the transformation procedures, and ii) formalizing them so that we can obtain a sufficient degree of generality. These two activities can be executed *a priori* only to some extent because the knowledge engineers find difficulty in predicting all the possible practical situations. Concretely, the transformation rules are established often *a posteriori*, by abstracting and formalizing some procedures empirically found in order to solve particular 'cases'. This is why the possibility of having recourse to case-based reasoning (CBR) techniques (*see* [Kolo92], [Wess94], etc.) in an NKRL context has often been evoked. Given that the 'rules', when they exist, are normally of a more economic use than 'cases', the CBR procedures could be utilized not only for providing the users with a sophisticated and up-to-date problem-solving modality but also for blazing a trail towards the creation of a practical set of transformation rules to be stored in the rule base. These rules will then subsume all the different concrete 'cases' used empirically to set up a useful solution.

Implementation notes: NKRL and RDF

The usual way of implementing NKRL until recently has been by making use of a three-layered approach: Common LISP + a frame/object-oriented (commercial) environment + NKRL. In the framework of the CONCERTO European project, the decision has been taken to realize a new version of NKRL, implemented in Java and RDF-compliant (RDF = resource description format), *see* [Zarr99b]. Given the importance that all the 'metadata' issues (RDF included) have recently acquired thanks to the impressive development of the Internet – *see also* Section 3.434 – it may be of some interest to examine some of the problems brought forth by this decision of the CONCERTO consortium. Metadata is now synonymous with 'machine-understandable knowledge-describing Web "resources"' (*see* [Boll98]), where a resource may concern all sorts of multimedia documents, texts, videos, images, and sounds.

RDF [LassO99] is a proposal for defining and processing WWW metadata that is developed by a specific W3C (World Wide Web consortium) working group. The model, implemented in XML (eXtensible markup language), makes use of directed labelled graphs (DLGs) where the nodes, that represent any possible Web resource (documents, parts of documents, collections of documents, etc.), are described basically by using attributes that give the named properties of the resources. No predefined 'vocabulary' (ontologies, keywords, etc.) is in itself a part of the proposal. The values of the attributes may be text strings, numbers, or other resources.

The first, general problem we had to solve for the implementation of the XML/RDF-compliant version of NKRL concerned the very different nature of the RDF and NKRL data structures. The first – modelled on the 'traditional' ontologies – are *dyadic*, i.e. the main RDF data structure can be assimilated to a triple where

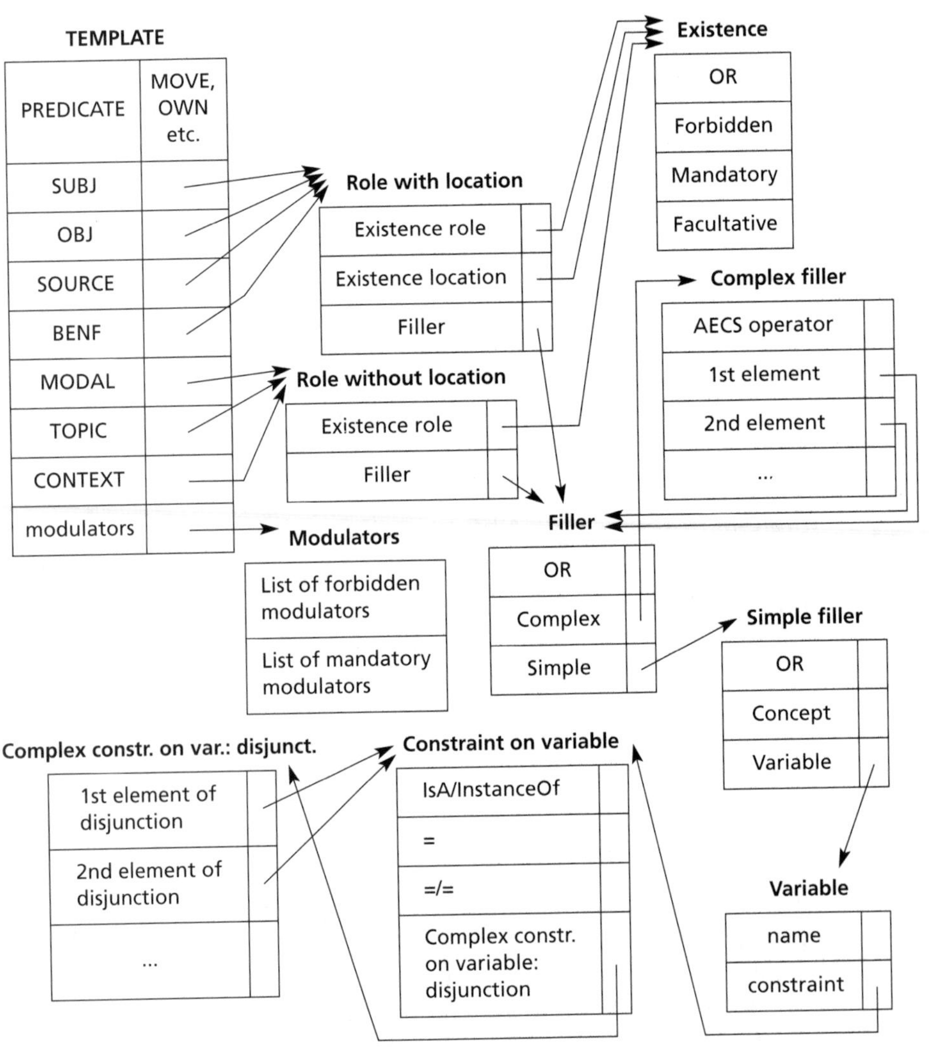

Figure 3.52 General structure of an NKRL template according to a 'binary' view

two resources are linked by a binary conceptual relation under the form of a property. We have seen on the contrary that the basic building block of the NKRL descriptive and factual structures is a complex *threefold* relationship associating a symbolic label, a predicate, one or more roles and the corresponding fillers (arguments of the predicate). To assure the conversion into RDF format, the NKRL data structures have been represented as intertwined binary 'tables' – *see* Figure 3.52 which describes the RDF-compliant, general structure of an NKRL template. For comprehensibility's sake, this figure has been considerably simplified and it does not take into account the hierarchical relations between templates or the relationships between templates and occurrences.

More specific problems have concerned the (still limited) choice of knowledge representation tools that are associated with RDF. To give an example, let us [LassO99] consider the solutions that, making use of the *containers* – RDF tools for describing collections of resources, *see* [LassO99] – we have adopted in order to reproduce the semantics of the AECS sublanguage illustrated above. We recall here that i) AECS operators are used to build up expansions (structured arguments) like those included in Tables 3.60 and 3.62 above; ii) AECS includes four operators: the disjunctive operator (`ALTERNative` = A), the distributive operator (`ENUMeration` = E), the collective operator (`COORDination` = C), and the attributive operator (`SPECIFication` = S). We recall also that the semantic difference between `COORD` and `ENUM` is that, in a `COORD` expansion list, all the elements of the expansion take part (necessarily) together in the particular relationship with the predicate defined by the associated role. As an example of the use of COORD, let us consider the simple situation illustrated in Table 3.67, where two persons, John and Peter, have been admitted *together* to hospital. In an ENUM list, on the contrary, each element satisfies the same relationship with the predicate, but they do this separately: (`ENUM john_ peter_`) should mean that the two persons have been admitted to the same hospital (`hospital_1`), but separately.

Table 3.67 A simple example of use of the COORD(ination) AECS operator

```
c6) EXIST SUBJ  (COORD john_ peter_): (hospital_1)
                [begin]
                date-1: 2-june-1999
                date-2:
```

AECS includes four operators; RDF, on the contrary, defines three types of containers:

- 'bag', an unordered list of resources or literals, used to declare that a property has multiple values and that no significance is associated with the order in which the values are given;
- 'sequence', Seq, an ordered list of resources or literals, used to declare that a property has multiple values and that the order of these values is significant;
- 'alternative', Alt, a list of resources or literals that represent alternatives for the (single) value of a property.

Of these, only Alt presents a precise coincidence with an AECS operator, obviously, ALTERN; moreover, we have at our disposal only *three* container constructions to represent *four* NKRL operators. We can note, however, that the use of a Bag construction is an acceptable approximation to represent the semantics of COORD. For example, in [LassO99], the use of Bag is associated with the representation of the sentence: 'The committee of Fred, Wilma and Dino approved the relation.' As the editors of this report say, '...the three committee members *as a whole* voted in a certain manner...' This situation corresponds in NKRL to a COORD situation. As a first conclusion, we can state then that:

- the ALTERN constructions (a disjunction between the arguments of the constructed complex filler) are described making use of the RDF container Alt;
- the COORD constructions (an unordered list of elements of the conceptual hierarchy) are represented making use of the RDF container Bag.

With respect to the RDF representation of the ENUM and SPECIF constructions, we make use of a 'liberal' interpretation of the semantics of Seq containers. Seq introduces an order relation between the elements of a list. We have already seen that the operator SPECIF introduces a 'partial order' relationship of the type (SPECIF e_i p_1 ... p_n), where the element e_i necessarily appears in the first position of the list, while the order of the residual elements p_1 ... p_n (the 'properties' or 'attributes' associated with e_i) is, on the contrary, indifferent. We can include these properties in an (implicit) Bag, and insert e_i and this Bag in a Seq list. The same solution has been adopted for the ENUM operator, with the (only) difference that an explicit enum identifier appears in the first position of the Seq list. Note that a previous solution, *see* [Jacq99], where ENUM was represented making use of the RDF 'repeated properties' has been abandoned because it could lead to an unacceptable proliferation of final RDF structures. We can say then that:

- for the SPECIF constructions, we use the RDF operator Seq followed directly by the elements of the SPECIF list. Of these, the elements representing the 'properties' are to be considered as inserted into a Bag; to simplify the RDF code, this Bag construction is conceived as an 'implicit' one, and the Bag operator is not expressly mentioned;
- the ENUM constructions are coded by using a Seq container where the first element is the identifier enum.

As an example, let us consider, in Table 3.68, the RDF representation of occurrence c6 of Table 3.67. In general, the RDF text associated with each predicative occurrence is composed by several tags, all nested inside the <CONCEPTUAL_ANNOTATION> tag and belonging to two different namespaces, rdf and ca. The first namespace describes the standard environment under which RDF tags have to be interpreted. The second namespace describes specific tags defined in the context of an application, in this case, the CONCERTO project. For example, the tag <ca:instanceOf>Templatei</ca:instanceOf> is used to denote that the predicative occurrence is an instance of the template identified by Template_i. The other tags specify the various roles of the predicative occurrence, together with the associated value. The tag <ca:subject> specifies, for instance, the role SUBJ of c6. The code li that appears in the Bag translating the COORD list of Table 3.67 means 'list item', and it was chosen in RDF to be mnemonic with respect to the corresponding HTML term.

Table 3.68 The RDF representation of a predicative occurrence

```
<?xml version="1.0" ?>
<!DOCTYPE DOCUMENTS SYSTEM "CA_RDF.dtd">
<CONCEPTUAL_ANNOTATION>
    <rdf:RDF xmlns:rdf="http://www.w3.org/1999/02/22-rdf-syntax-ns#"
    xmlns:rdf="http://www.w3.org/TR/1999/PR-rdf-schema-19990303#"
    xmlns:ca="http://projects.pira.co.uk/concerto#"
       <rdf:Description about="occ3">
       <rdf:type resource="ca:Occurrence"/>
           <ca:instanceOf>Template2.31</ca:instanceOf>
           <ca:predicateName>Exist</ca:predicateName>
       <ca:subject rdf:ID="Subj2.31" rdf:parseType="Resource">
          <concerto:filler>
            <rdf:Bag>
                <rdf :li rdf:resource="#john_"/>
                <rdf :li rdf:resource="#peter_"/>
            </rdf:Bag>
          </concerto:filler>
          <concerto:location>hospital_1</concerto:location>
       </ca:subject>
       <ca:listOfModulators>
             <rdf:Seq><rdf:li>begin</rdf:li></rdf:Seq>
       </ca:listOfModulators>
       <ca:date1>02/06/1997</ca:date1>
    </rdf:Description>
  </rdf:RDF>
</CONCEPTUAL_ANNOTATION>
```

3.46 Lexical approaches to the construction of large KBs

A consensus has emerged in the past few years concerning the assertion that some sort of large electronic repositories of linguistic-oriented knowledge, such as the most sophisticated electronic dictionaries and thesauruses, could be considered as an at least initial form of realistic, very large knowledge bases embodying general world knowledge.

This belief is based on some undisputed arguments, such as the fact that these advanced repositories contain substantial information about the semantics and pragmatics of natural languages, i.e. about important components of any general, common sense knowledge. But this position is also in strong agreement with some more controversial, recent suggestions in the knowledge representation field (*see* [Yoko95a]), which advocate the direct utilization of natural language as the best possible knowledge representation language ever created – *see* [Iwan93], [Iwan94]. It is possible to affirm, in fact, that all the 'artificial' knowledge representation languages produced until now – such as those examined in the previous sections of this chapter – are limited in some way, and suitable only for some specific type of applications. Natural language, on the contrary, constitutes surely the most universal, cheap and flexible knowledge representation tool – even if we can remark immediately that NL representations are difficult to exploit in any sort of computerized environment.

We will limit ourselves here to a very short description of two well-known projects, WordNet and the EDR Electronic Dictionary, which exemplify particularly well this new tendency towards the construction of successful, large repositories of knowledge.

3.461 WordNet

WordNet (*see* [MillG93], [MillG95], [Fell98]) has been defined humorously by its author, George A. Miller, as 'a poor man's CYC'. Developed at Princeton University, it consists of an online lexical database containing around 120 000 English word-sense pairs. While conventional dictionaries are built around individual words, in WordNet English nouns, verbs, adjectives and adverbs are organized into sets of synonyms (synsets). A synset is assumed to contain all the words that lexicalize a given 'concept'; a synset can then be considered as a sort of 'lexicalized' concept, and the synsets can be linked by simple sorts of semantic relations. To give an intuitive example, the verbs 'buy' and 'purchase' can be considered, to a large extent, as synonyms: these two verb forms are then part of a synset that can be informally denoted by a sentence such as 'obtain or acquire by means of a financial transaction'.

In more formal terms, WordNet defines the 'vocabulary' of a given language (here, English) as a set of pairs $w_{i,j} = (f_i, s_j)$, where the 'form' f_i is a string over a finite alphabet, and the 'sense' s_j is the element pertaining to a given set of meanings (synset) that the form can be used to express. A 'word' in English is defined as a form to which it is possible to associate at least a sense within the vocabulary: the 'dictionary' is an alphabetical list of words. In [MillG93], Miller makes use of the concept of 'lexical matrix' – see Table 3.69 – to emphasize the phenomena of 'polysemy' and 'synonymy' that can affect words defined as before: in this table, words corresponding to word forms f_1 and f_2 are synonyms (e.g. 'plank' and 'board', when both refer to a piece of timber); word (word form) f_2 is also polysemous (e.g. 'board', which can also mean a group of people assembled for some purposes). WordNet contains more than 118 000 different word forms and more than 90 000 different word senses, or more than 166 000 $w_{i,j}$ pairs.

Table 3.69 The lexical matrix

Word senses	xWord forms f_1	f_2	f_3	...	f_n
s_1	$w_{1,1}$	$w_{1,2}$		...	
s_2		$w_{2,2}$			
s_3			$w_{3,3}$		
...				...	
s_m					$w_{m,n}$

As already stated, synonymy plays a central role in WordNet; the sets of synonyms, such as {board, plank} and {board, committee}, are included in curly brackets and correspond implicitly, as already stated, to lexicalized concepts. 'Implicitly' means that the presence of a particular synset does not explain what the corresponding concept can represent, but simply announces the fact that such a concept must exist. In WordNet, the assumed definition of synonymy is a weakened definition of the classical one, which states that two expressions are synonymous if the substitution of one for the other never changes the truth-value of a sentence in which the substitution has been made. The weakened version makes synonymy relative to a context: two expressions are synonymous in a linguistic context C if the substitution of one for the other in C does not change the truth-value. Accordingly, the substitution of 'plank' for 'board' will seldom alter truth-values in a carpentry context, but there are other contexts where that substitution is totally inappropriate, e.g., in a context where 'board' means 'a person's meals, provided regularly for money'. To deal with situations like the last one, where appropriate synonyms do not exist for this new meaning of 'board', synsets including a single member associated with a short gloss in natural language are introduced. Therefore, we will find in WordNet the two synsets: {board, plank} and {board, 'a person's meals, provided regularly for money'}.

Anyway, the definition of synonymy in terms of substitutability adopted by WordNet makes it necessary to ground the system on nouns, verbs, adjectives, and adverbs – the so-called open-class words. In fact, words in different syntactic categories cannot be synonyms (cannot form synsets) because they are not interchangeable: nouns express nominal concepts, verbs express verbal concepts, and modifiers (adjectives and adverbs) supply ways to qualify those concepts. This means that word forms like 'back', 'right' or 'well' are interpreted as nouns in some linguistic contexts, as verbs in other contexts, giving rise to separate synsets. Note that the interface to the WordNet database provides inflectional morphology for each syntactic category: this means, for example, that if information is required for 'went', the system is able to return what it knows about the verb 'go'.

Generally speaking, WordNet is organized by semantic relations. Given that a semantic relation is an association between meanings, and since meanings can be represented by synsets, semantic relations are given in general as pointers between synsets, even if they can simply link single word forms. The semantic relations admitted by the system, including the central one of synonymy, are listed in Table 3.70, adapted from [MillG95].

Table 3.70 Semantic relations in WorldNet

Semantic relation	Syntactic category	Examples
Synonymy (similar)	N, V, Aj, Av	{pipe, tube} {rise, ascend} {sad, unhappy} {rapidly, speedily}
Antonymy (opposite)	Aj, Av, (N, V)	[wet, dry] [powerful, powerless] [friendly, unfriendly] [rapidly, slowly]
Hyponymy (subordinate)	N	[sugar maple, maple] [maple, tree] [tree, plant]
Meronymy (Part)	N	[brim, hat] [gin, martini] [ship, fleet]
Troponymy (Manner)	V	[march, walk] [whisper, speak]
Entailment	V	[drive, ride] [divorce, marry]

Note: N = *Nouns*; Aj = *Adjectives*; V = *Verbs*; Av = *Adverbs*

We will now add some comments on the semantic relations other than synonymy.

- *Antonymy*. Antonymy (opposing-name) is particularly difficult to define for nouns and verbs. For example, it may appear as reasonable to accept that [rise, fall] are antonyms, and so are [ascend, descend]; however, most people hesitate when asked if 'rise' and 'descend' or 'fall' and 'ascend' are antonyms. For this reason, antonymy is mainly considered in WordNet as a central organizing principle for adjectives and adverbs.
- *Hyponymy*. Hyponymy (sub-name) and its inverse, hypernymy (super-name), are transitive and asymmetrical relations between (in general) synsets. A concept represented by the synset {*x*, *x*', …} is said to be a hyponym of the concept represented by the synset {*y*, *y*', …} if native speakers of English can accept sentences built up using frames such as 'an *x* is a kind of *y*' (a 'maple' is a kind of 'tree'). Such relations represent the WordNet version of the ubiquitous inheritance relations; they provide the central organizing principle for nouns in WordNet.
- *Meronymy*. Meronymy (part-name) has as its inverse the holonymy (whole-name) relation. A concept represented by the synset {*x*, *x*', …} is said to be a meronym of the concept represented by the synset {*y*, *y*', …} if native speakers

of English can accept sentences built up using frames like 'an *y* has an *x* as a part', or 'an *x* is part of *y*'. The meronymic relation, reserved to nouns in WordNet, is transitive and asymmetrical; WordNet allows this relation to be specialized by distinguishing between 'component' parts, 'substantive' parts (*x* is the stuff that *y* is made of), and 'member' parts.

- *Troponymy*. Troponymy (manner-name) can be seen as the equivalent for verbs of the hyponymy (inheritance) relationship reserved to nouns. Hierarchies constructed using the troponymy relation are, however, much shallower than those built up using hyponymy.
- *Entailment*. In WordNet, entailment refers to a semantic relation between two verbs v_1 and v_2 that holds when the sentence 'someone v_1' logically entails the sentence 'someone v_2': 'snore' entails 'sleep' because the sentence 'he is snoring' logically entails the sentence 'he is sleeping'. We remind readers here that the logical entailment, or strict implication, means that a proposition *p* entails a proposition *q* if there is no conceivable state of affairs that could make *p* true and *q* false.

From an operational point of view, an XWindow interface allows a user to enter a word form and to select the appropriate syntactic category through a pull-down menu. He can then access the semantic relations that have been entered into WordNet for the corresponding word. For example, if the user has entered the word form 'leaves', he can access a noun menu (for 'leaf') and a verb menu (for 'leave'). The noun menu allows him to obtain i) the synonyms of 'leaf'; ii) the hyponyms, hypernyms and the sister nodes with reference to the inheritance hierarchy; iii) the meronyms and holonyms – no antonyms for 'leaf' are available. If the synonyms of 'leaf' have been requested, the system displays three synsets along with their immediate hypernyms: {leaf, leafage, foliage}; {leaf, folio}; {leaf, 'hinged or detachable flat section, as of a table or door; section, segment'}. The latter is an example of 'single' synset (no synonyms exist).

Lenat [Lena95b] directs several criticisms against WordNet from a 'conceptual' point of view – please consider, however, that the CYC system includes a WordNet browser that allows CYC's users to consult a WordNet in relation to the CYC ontology. Lenat criticizes, in particular, the insufficient number of semantic relations, the lack of common sense techniques for dealing with polysemy (see the well-known example of 'the pen is in the box' and 'the box is in the pen') and pronoun disambiguation, an understanding of concepts that sticks too strictly to an interpretation in terms of words and synsets – at least in particular contexts, 'JFK's assassination' or 'the first place one can remember calling home' represent plausible concepts. Lenat says that many of his comments apply similarly to Yokoi's EDR (*see* next subsection).

Note that a 'EuroWordNet' project (*see* [IdeN98]), begun in 1996 under the direction of the University of Amsterdam, is building a multilingual lexical database modelled on WordNet. It supports Dutch, Italian and Spanish.

3.462 *The EDR electronic dictionary*

The EDR dictionary is the result of a nine-year project led by the Japan Electronic Dictionary Research Institute Ltd (1986–1994). This project (a Japanese national project) was funded jointly by the Japan Key Technology Center and by eight private corporations: Fujitsu, NEC, Hitachi, Sharp, Toshiba, Oki, Mitsubishi and Matsushita. The aim was to develop a large-scale dictionary that could be neutral as far as possible with respect to linguistic theories, could be used effectively in computer processing, and could satisfy the following needs:

- supporting the development of powerful machine translation (MT) tools to allow the removal of the language barriers between Japan and the rest of the world;
- more generally, promoting the development of new tools for the Japanese language (such as tools for technical documentation, speech processing and language education) in order to keep up with the results already obtained in these fields for English and other Western languages.

EDR designers have conceived a dictionary that could, at least in principle, include all the information necessary for a computer to understand a natural language: the 'meaning' of a word, i.e. the 'concept' represented by this word, the grammatical characteristics of the word when it represents that concept, and the knowledge required in order for a computer to be able to understand that concept. Moreover, the data structures ('word dictionary') which represent the 'surface level' of a word (i.e. the morphological and syntactic information) must be completely separated from the data structures ('concept dictionary') handling the 'deep level' (i.e. the semantic information). Surface information is, in fact, strongly dependent upon a particular language, while semantic information in the form of a concept dictionary can be shared among the dictionaries of several languages. EDR is composed, therefore, of four types of dictionaries – word, concept, co-occurrence and bilingual – and of the EDR corpus – see Figure 3.53, derived mainly from [Japa93]. The content and the role of these dictionaries are as follows:

- The word dictionary includes i) the tools (morphological and syntactic information) necessary for determining the syntactic structure of each sentence, and ii) the tools (semantic information) which, for each word in a given sentence, identify all the possible concepts that correspond to that word. Semantic information constitutes, therefore, an interface between the word dictionary and the concept dictionary.
- The concept dictionary contains information on the 400 000 concepts listed in the word dictionary; one of its main functions is supplying the tools needed to produce a semantic (conceptual) representation of a given sentence. For example, the EDR conceptual representation of the sentence 'the elephant ate a banana' corresponds to:

  ```
  <<banana>> ← object – <<eat>> – agent → <<elephant>>;
  ```

  this type of representation evokes of course conceptual graphs, *see* Section

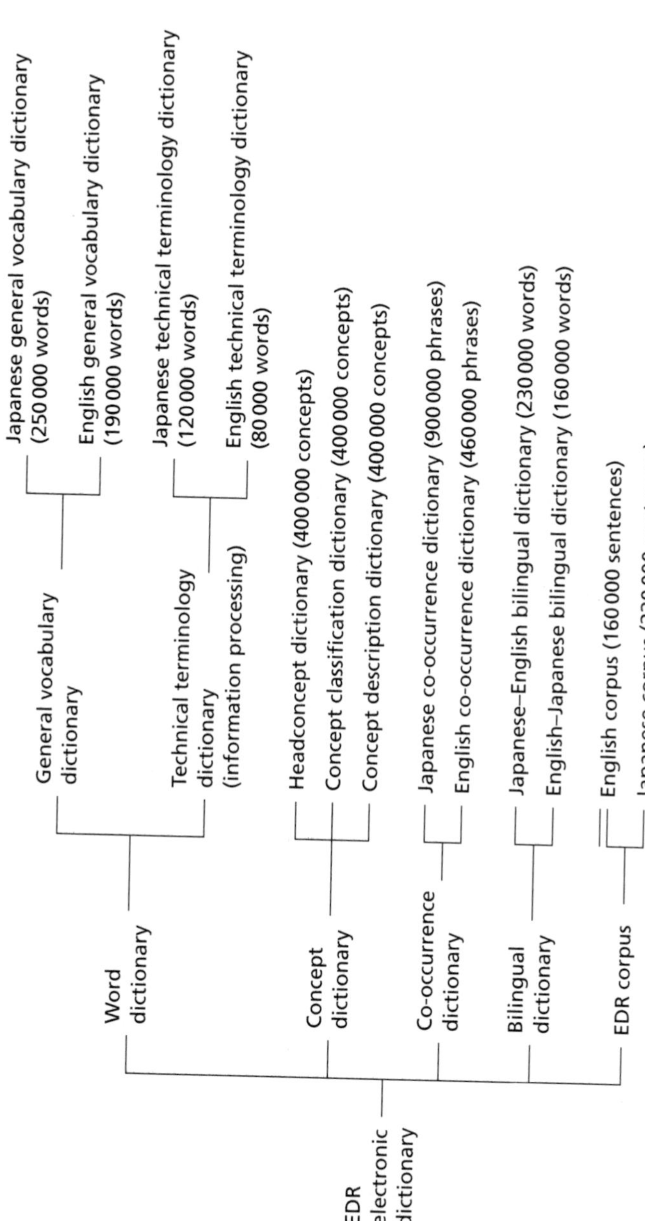

Figure 3.53 The structure of the EDR dictionary

3.451. The three components of the concept dictionary are: i) the headconcept dictionary, which describes information on the concepts themselves; ii) the classification dictionary, which shows the hierarchical relationships (super-sub relationships) between concepts, and helps the computer to find equivalent or similar concepts, or to compute the degree of similarity between concepts; iii) the description dictionary, which describes the (binary) conceptual links existing between concepts (for example, the 'agent' link between the concepts <<elephant>> and <<eat>> in the example before) and the methods for assembling several concepts to produce the final semantic representation. Information contained in the description dictionary seems, therefore, to be in some way similar to the NKRL templates, *see* Section 3.452. The combination algorithms are not, however, clearly described in [Japa93].

- The co-occurrence dictionary describes collocational information in the form of binary relations, and it is used mainly to select words in the target language when executing mechanical translation operations. It contains, in fact, information about surface relationships of a word with other words in a given language, such as the fact that the word 'repaired' can co-occur with the word 'car', but not with the word 'patient'. This can be used to avoid performing awful errors in the generation of the target sentence when trying to represent a given semantic content.
- The bilingual dictionary contains lists of correspondences between words in different languages. Several types of explanations are added, such as information on the situations in which the correspondence can be activated.
- The EDR corpus is a sort of usage database, created using machine-readable texts from newspapers and other published material such as encyclopaedias and educational texts. The corpus is used, for instance, when a word is detected which is not yet registered in the word dictionary: in this case, the corpus is used to extract its frequency of use and the grammatical information, in order to create a new dictionary entry.

The relationships between these dictionaries can be visualized as in Figure 3.54, slightly modified from Figure 2-2 of [Japa93].

In this figure, two concepts correspond to the Japanese word '*inu*': the concept of <<dog>> and that of <<spy>>. Each concept is represented by a hexadecimal concept identifier, such as '3bdc67' for <<dog>>. Correspondingly, two entries are created in the Japanese word dictionary, both characterized as 'Japanese nouns' (JN). Similarly, two concepts correspond to the English word 'dog', the concept <<dog>> and the concept <<follow>> (in expressions like 'He has been dogging me all day'). The corresponding entries in the English word dictionary will be characterized, respectively, as 'noun' and 'verb' (EV). <<follow>> is a specific concept ('concept classification entry') of <<spatial movement>>; <<spy>> is a specific concept of <<person>>. <<spatial movement>> and <<person>> are also linked by the 'agent' relation within a particular 'concept description entry'. As already stated, information in the co-occurrence dictionaries is used mainly for generation purposes.

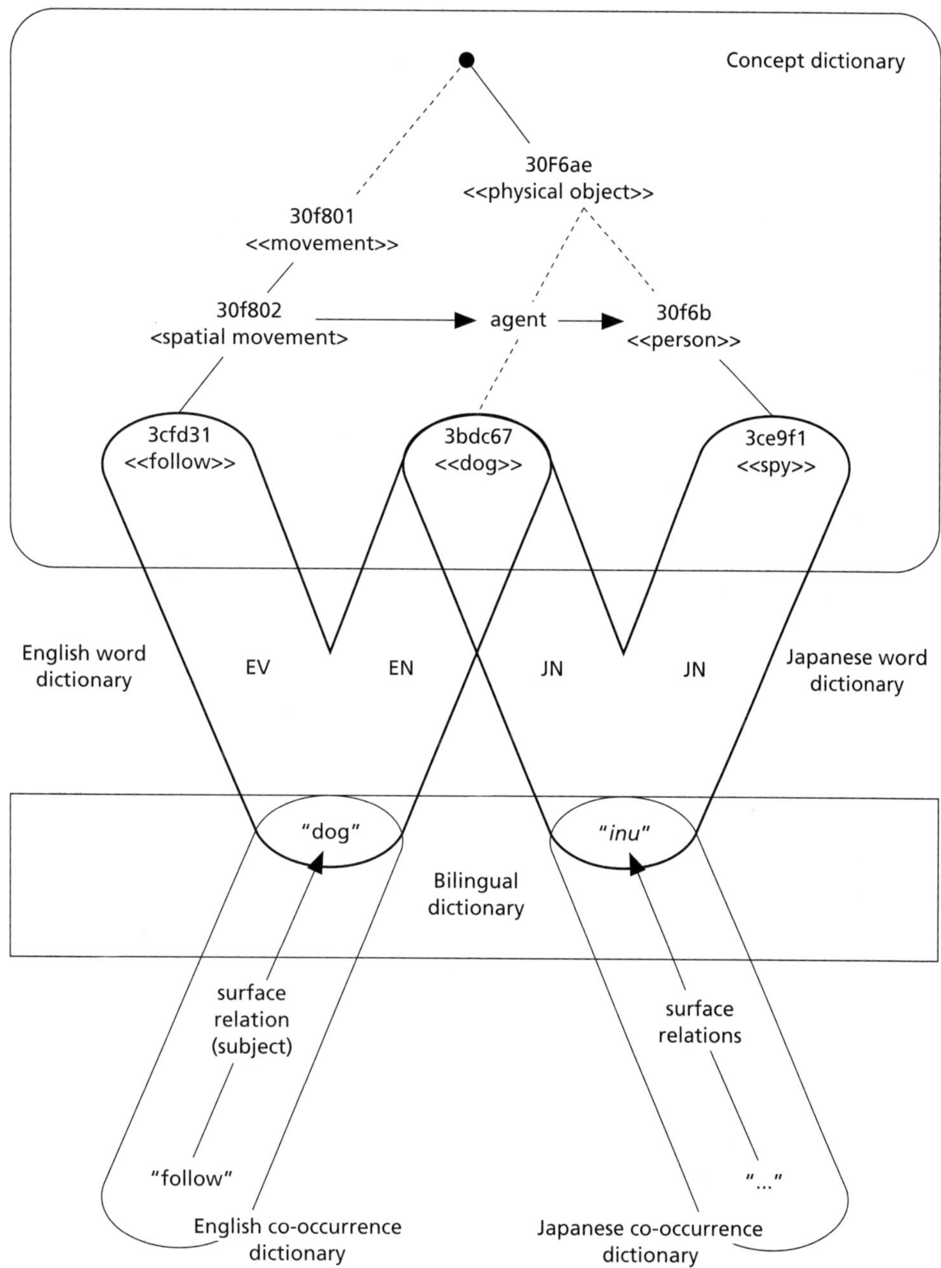

Figure 3.54 Relationships between the different components of the EDR electronic dictionary

Sales of EDR began in March 1995. Each of the EDR sub-dictionaries listed in Figure 3.53 was stored and sold as a CD-ROM. In [Yoko95b], Toshio Yokoi, the director of the EDR project, illustrates some general guidelines concerning the availability conditions. [Yoko95a] contains a description of the possible improvements that could be added to EDR (ellipsis and anaphora resolution, verification of compound propositions, etc.) and a discussion of the research activities necessary in order to transform the first EDR version into a 'real', large knowledge base. However, this new phase of the project seems to be frozen, perhaps indefinitely.

In [Feig94], Edward Feigenbaum and his co-authors remark that, even if the inspiring ideas of EDR are not particularly innovative – 'they have been in play since Quillian (mid-1960s) and Schank (late 1970s)' – the results obtained are particularly impressive from a practical point of view, given that '...most words and concepts currently encountered are already found in the dictionary', and 'EDR's pragmatic approach ... has allowed it to amass a significant corpus of concepts with significant coverage of the terms of natural language'.

3.47 Conclusions

The analysis of the characteristics of the systems described in the previous sections tends to suggest that an 'integral AI approach' is superior in a number of ways to the conventional DBMS approach, or even to the DBMS/KBMS approaches examined in the previous chapter. These points include the possibility of making use of really powerful knowledge representation schemata, a unified type of representation for both facts and rules, the presence of high-level inference capabilities, the absence of any type of mismatch problems, etc. It should be noted that the existence of these sorts of advantages, and their potential impact on the architecture of the next generations of information systems, are widely recognized, even inside the DB community. It will be sufficient to mention here M.P. Papazoglou's promotion of data models in the form of AI semantic networks to be able to question not only the 'extension' of the data (i.e. finding factual data such as the employees who have a yearly salary in excess of $50 000) but also their 'intension' (i.e. finding data concerning the abstract definition of an employee's status, whether he is a permanent employee or an employee under probation, for example) [PapaM95].

It is also evident, however, that for the time being at least these 'integral' systems are not in widespread use, not only in the general computer science world – and, in particular, in the commercial domain – but also within the AI and DB communities. It may be interesting trying to analyze the reasons for this and also to guess the probability of their being on the market within a reasonable interval of time: we can then find at least three sorts of general problems which affect all the solutions examined in this chapter. They are:

- *The great variety of AI knowledge representation models used in the 'integral approach' systems.* As already stated in the introduction, these AI models are used as a sort of general data model to express both the rules and the proper data. They are of vital importance for the IASs, and the absence of a clearly winning knowledge representation paradigm can only perplex potential users.

However, we can assume that this situation is, in practice, less critical than it could appear in the first instance. We can observe, for example, that at least some of the KR models used in the integral systems are very close to some sort of standard object-oriented representation: this is true, for example, for TELOS and CYC, in spite of the latter's move from a strictly frame-oriented to a logic-oriented approach. This fact is in good agreement with the tendencies towards the development of standard tools in the KR domain intended to favour the possibility of automating 'translating' among different KR formalisms. *See*, in this respect, the ARPA Knowledge Sharing Effort ([Nech91]) and the related initiatives that have led to the definition and implementation of canonical specification and description languages such as KIF ([Gene92], [Gene98]) or Ontololingua ([Grub93]). We can also mention here, in a knowledge base context, the 'generic frame protocol' (GFP) approach, which consists of an interface program for accessing knowledge bases stored in different frame representation systems (four at the moment), *see* [Karp95]. Problems with these sorts of standardization approaches concern, however, their strict adherence to the most 'traditional' forms of knowledge representation, such as ontologies structured according to the classical, object-centred, term-subsumption lines.

- *The complexity of the knowledge representation formalisms used in the integral approach systems.* This complexity implies – in a stronger mode than in the case of the 'traditional' DB systems where the data models are considerably simpler – the use of powerful knowledge acquisition tools for giving rise, safely and timely, to (very large) intelligent database systems. As is well known, in recent years there has been a shift of interest in the knowledge acquisition community from a strictly 'knowledge extraction' problematic (symbolized by the now infamous argument about the 'knowledge acquisition bottleneck') towards an approach of KA as 'modelling', *see* [Clan89], [Ford93]. In parallel, a lot of energy has been devoted in this community, especially in Europe, to the development of software engineering tools and methodologies – such as KADS, *see* [SchrG93] – for the conception of well-structured KBSs. It is not sure that these new orientations have produced some fundamental improvement in the availability of practical knowledge acquisition tools for populating large KBSs. In this respect, it is noticeable that, in at least three of the approaches mentioned in the previous sections – CYC, conceptual graphs and NKRL – preference has been given to some techniques proper to a discipline, extraction of information from natural language texts, which is often considered as marginal with respect to the main stream of the knowledge acquisition field. Some interesting progress has been accomplished in this domain recently, thanks mainly to the stimulus represented by the series of MUC (Message Understanding Conferences) organized by ARPA, *see* [Chin93], [MUC593], [MUC798]. It must be noted, however, that i) it is probably unrealistic to think of making use of this sort of technique for populating large fact databases *in a fully automated way*; ii) at least in their actual form, this type of technique is particularly useful in the context of (semi-) automatic creation of large fact databases: their immediate utility is more questionable for the production of rule bases, where real 'learning' techniques could be more adequate.

- *The integral systems provide only limited services for recovery, protection, integrity maintenance, concurrent access to distributed repositories, etc., if any is provided at all.* This is really distressing because, as we have already mentioned in the introduction, the implementation of the knowledge base versions of this sort of service is a necessary prerequisite for conceiving the 'integral approach' as commercially interesting. As a partial exception to the normal state of affairs we can mention TELOS which, not surprisingly, has been conceived in an AI milieu strongly influenced by the database and information retrieval practices. We should also remember here, on the contrary, some problems concerning the efficient exploitation of a huge knowledge base which seem to affect the first releases of CYC. These sorts of problems can be associated with a more general, well-known phenomenon characteristic of the AI field, i.e. the difficulty for the AI tools and architectures to scale up to support easy storage and retrieval in large KBSs, and to adapt themselves to provide services such as multi-user access or networked client-server operations.

In spite of the above remarks, we can be confident that the main, common characteristics of the systems examined in this chapter (unified type of representation for both facts and rules, excellent possibilities in the knowledge representation field, full inferencing, etc.) will also be present in at least the more advanced fraction of the commercial IDBSs of the future, such as those having their origin in an object-oriented context.

4 The latest developments

4.1 Introduction

The previous chapters have presented several approaches that have been proposed in both the database and artificial intelligence fields with the aim of defining and implementing intelligent database systems. Besides the approaches described before, researchers have investigated several other issues that have led to the development of systems that, even if they cannot be directly classified as 'intelligent', provide additional knowledge management techniques and reasoning capabilities in existing systems. For this reason, the last chapter of this book is dedicated to the discussion of such developments.

The developments we discuss are as follows:

- *Temporal databases.* Temporal databases directly support temporal knowledge at both the representation and query level. We consider them in this chapter because the ability to model and query temporal information improves the intelligence of the systems in performing advanced types of reasoning.
- *Ontologies.* Ontologies provide a specific representation of the world beings. Thus their usage makes systems aware of the semantics of a given application domain. Such knowledge can then be used for performing advanced reasoning.
- *Structured, semi-structured, and unstructured data.* Traditional database models support the representation of structured data, i.e. data whose structure is known in advance. Such an approach is quite restrictive for various advanced applications (for example, multimedia). For this reason, several approaches have been proposed to cope with unstructured and semi-structured data. Here, we review briefly the basic problems and we introduce XML, a semi-structured language that is becoming a standard in the context of information exchange.
- *Mediators.* Mediators represent one of the most promising approaches for integrating heterogeneous information. In this case, intelligence lies in the ability to hide the heterogeneous aspects of the various data sources, thus providing a homogeneous interface to client applications.
- *Multi-agent systems.* Multi-agent systems are computational systems in which two or more agents interact and work together to achieve some goal. In this case, the intelligence is implicit in the interaction and co-ordination activities that agents must be able to support in order to satisfy the stated goals.

- *Internet indexing and retrieval.* The Internet is becoming the largest 'database' available. Therefore, techniques have to be defined to deal with a wide number of heterogeneous sources, each hosted in specific locations of the Internet network. As for mediators, the development of Internet indexing and retrieval techniques overcomes the problems concerning the efficiency and the quality of retrieving information from heterogeneous sources, this time located all over the world.
- *Data mining.* Data mining refers to the process of non-trivial extraction of implicit, previously unknown, and potentially useful information from large amounts of data. In this case, the intelligence is implicit in the mechanisms used to infer new knowledge and in the ability to apply such mechanisms in an efficient way.
- *Medical and legal information systems.* These represent two good examples of application domains in which the satisfaction of the stated goals requires the integration of several techniques and approaches presented in this book. For this reason, this chapter ends with a short overview of both types of information systems.

We have neither the intention nor the space to cover in detail all the topics listed above. Rather, we will try in this chapter to give some basic notions about techniques and systems that may help in designing an intelligent system, providing several pointers to the existing scientific literature.

4.2 Temporal databases

Time is a fundamental aspect of all real-world phenomena since all events happen in specific instants of time and objects and their relationships are usually valid during specific temporal snapshots. The ability to model temporal information is therefore fundamental in several application contexts, such as banking, medical, scheduling, flight reservation, financial, and commercial applications.

In order to deal with time, a database management system should be able to adequately represent temporal knowledge and query it. Traditional DBMSs, however, do not provide the ability to represent data evolution along time, since they store only the values at the current time instant. Each time a value has to be modified, the old value is replaced by the new one. Thus, in traditional DBMSs, temporal data management can be realized only by application programs, with several problems in terms of efficiency and maintenance costs.

On the other hand, such problems are overcome by temporal database technology, whose aim is to provide a support to the storage and the management of information that is varying with time, in a way that is integrated with all the other DBMS components. In a temporal database, differently from traditional databases, data modifications are seen as new information to be inserted in the database without deleting old values. This means that the temporal information is completely integrated in the data model, with a clear semantics. This approach leads to several advantages in terms of efficiency, simplicity, and expressivity.

Several approaches have been proposed concerning temporal data models and temporal query languages. Most proposed data models and languages are temporal extensions of relational or object-oriented data models and languages. In the following, we first introduce the main concepts regarding time, then we briefly discuss data models and languages that have been proposed for temporal databases. For the latest 'temporal' developments in the artificial intelligence and knowledge representation fields, *see* the introductory sections of [Zarr98].

4.21 Basic concepts

There are several ways to think of time. First of all, different time structures can be devised. In particular, two different structural models are adopted for time: the linear model and the branching model. In the *linear model*, time is totally ordered. Thus it can be represented by a line, called the *temporal axis*. In the *branching model*, also called *model of the possible futures*, time is linear in the past, until the current instant; after that, time is divided into several different temporal axes, each representing a potential sequence of events. Such a model can therefore be represented as a tree, having as its root the current instant of time.

Structural models can also be classified depending on how the time is bounded (upper bounded, lower bounded, bounded) or unbounded. Currently, the most qualified thesis is that time is lower bounded by the so-called 'Big Bang' (i.e. the starting point of the universe, dated 12–18 billion years ago) and upper bounded by the so-called 'Big Crunch' (a non-precise instant in the future in which the universe will collapse). Finally, an additional classification is between models supporting an absolute notion of time (for example, '1 January 1996') and models supporting a relative notion of time (for example, '23 hours').

In the linear model, time can also be represented by considering different densities. In particular, we recall the following:

- *discrete model*. Under this model, time is isomorphic to the set of integer numbers. In such a model, each instant of time has a unique successor;
- *dense model*. Time is isomorphic to the set of rational numbers. In such a model, given two instants of time there always exists a finite number of instants between them;
- *continuous model*. Time is isomorphic to the set of real numbers. In such a model, given two instants of time there always exists an infinite number of instants between them.

The smallest temporal entities that can be represented in a model are called *chronon*. For example, in the discrete model, chronons are integer numbers, whereas in the continuous model, chronons are real numbers. Chronons can be aggregated to form different temporal granularities such as months, weeks, days, hours, and minutes. Even if time is continuous in nature, most temporal models adopt a discrete model, since it is simpler and can be implemented more easily.

In a DBMS context, two distinct temporal dimensions are typically considered: *validity time* and *transaction time*. The validity time of a fact is the time in which the fact has happened in the reality, independently of whether or not it has already been registered in the database. A validity time can also be collocated in the future and can be bounded or unbounded. On the other hand, the transaction time of a fact is the time in which the fact has been registered in the database. Usually, it is an interval whose lower and upper bounds represent the time in which a transaction has inserted the fact and a transaction has removed it from the database respectively.

Validity and transaction times are orthogonal dimensions, even if some correlations exist between them. For example, a fact can be registered as soon as it happens in the real world. In this particular case, validity time and transaction time coincide.

Recently, additional temporal dimensions have been introduced, such as the *decision time*, denoting the instant of time in which a certain event should have happened, and the *user defined time*. The semantics of the user defined time is known only by the user, unlike with other temporal dimensions. Such a dimension is quite easy to support in a DBMS and this is the reason why several DBMSs, such as DB2 [IBMC99a], [IBMC99b], and query languages, such as SQL2 [Melt93], support only this kind of time dimension.

Concerning data types by which temporal information can be represented, database management systems in general support some of the following types:

- *Instants.* These represent single chronons, thus they are useful to represent the instant in which a specific fact happens.
- *Temporal periods.* These represent the set of instants contained between two specified instants. For example, the expression 'May 1st, 1997' denotes a temporal period since the starting and ending chronons are known. A period can always be represented by a pair of attributes, assuming single chronons to be single values.
- *Temporal intervals.* An interval denotes a specific length of time, without precise starting and ending instants. For example, the expression 'one day' denotes a temporal interval. An interval can be characterized by an attribute assuming as value a number, representing the number of instants composing the interval.
- *Set of instants.* Often it is useful to represent a finite set of instants, not necessarily contiguous. This type is quite useful to represent the occurrence time of a fact that is repeated more than once.
- *Temporal elements.* A temporal element is a finite set of temporal periods and therefore represents a compact way to denote a set of instants not necessarily contiguous. Temporal elements are used mainly to represent the validity and transaction time of a given data item.

4.22 Temporal data models

Several data models have been extended to support the temporal dimension. Among them, we recall the entity relationship model, semantics models, and deductive models. Most of the proposals in the literature are, however, extensions of the relational or the object-oriented model. For this reason, in the following, we survey some of these proposals.

Temporal models can be classified with respect to the time dimensions supported by the model (in general, validity and/or transaction time), the way in which time is associated with relations or objects, and the way in which temporal attribute values are modelled. In general, with respect to the second aspect, time can be associated with relations and objects in several ways:

- Time is associated with each tuple, in the relational model, and with each object, in the object-oriented model.
- Time is associated with groups of attributes of a tuple or of an object.
- Time is associated with single attributes of a tuple or of an object.
- Time is associated with groups of tuples or objects. Such an approach is in general used by models only supporting transaction time, in order to identify the tuples or the objects that have been modified in the context of the same transaction.

Each solution has advantages and disadvantages. For example, associating time with a tuple or an object generates redundancy since the same value has to be repeated for each tuple or object. Redundancy further increases if time is associated with groups of tuples or objects. If time is associated with single attributes or groups of attributes, redundancy is reduced. The disadvantage of such a solution is that it is no longer possible to obtain relations in third normal form [Ullm89].

Concerning the representation of temporal attributes, we can identify the following choices:

- *Atomic values.* They are represented by values or sets of values, without internal structure.
- *Functions.* Attribute values are partial functions from the temporal domain to the set of legal values for the attribute.
- *Pairs.* Values are ordered pairs, or sets of ordered pairs, in which the first element is a legal value for the attribute, or a set of legal values, and the second element is an instant of time.
- *Triple.* Values are triples, or a set of triples, in which the first element is a legal value for the attribute, or a set of legal values, whereas the second and the third elements represent the interval in which the attribute is assigned to that value or set of values.

Note that if the time is assigned to a single tuple or object, the attributes can only assume atomic values or sets of atomic values.

A good classification of temporal data models is presented in [Ozso95]. The analysis of the existing models points out that most temporal models support only validity time (this is the case, for example, of the models presented in [Gadi88a], [Gadi88b], [LumV84], [Nava89], [Sard90], [Sege87], [Tans86]) whereas only a few models support transaction time, *see* [Jens91], [Lome89], and even fewer models support both, *see* [Aria86], [Jens94], [Snod87], [YauC91]. Moreover, in almost all relational models, time is assigned to the whole tuple [Jens91], [Jens94], [Lome89], [LumV84], [Nava89], [Sard90], [Sege90], [Snod87], thus obtaining third normal form relations. In those cases, attribute values are thus represented as atomic values. Among the temporal models assigning time to single attributes, we recall [Aria86], [Gadi88a], [Gadi88b], [Tans86]. In this case, attribute values have different types. For example, in the model presented in [Lore88], temporal attribute values are atomic; in the model presented in [Gadi88a], [Gadi88b], temporal attribute values are functions.

In the context of object-oriented models, time is mainly associated with single attributes whose values are modelled, in most cases, as partial functions on the temporal domain, see [Rose91], [WuuG92]. In specific cases, time is associated with objects [Kafe92], [Tans86], [WuuG92]. In this case, temporal values are often atomic.

4.23 Temporal query languages

A temporal query language must have additional properties to those generally provided by a traditional query language in order to consider temporal information in retrieval operations. In the following, we list the most significant properties that a temporal query language must support:

- The language should supply specific constructs for referring validity or transaction time within a query.
- Often, it is useful to identify the lower and upper bounds of the temporal period associated with a certain data item. In other situations, it could be useful to generate a period starting from two specified time instants or from an interval of a given length. Temporal query languages should support this aspect.
- The language should supply some predefined predicates for comparing instants, periods, intervals, and temporal elements.
- The language should supply mechanisms for temporal selection and projection depending on conditions concerning validity and transaction time.
- The language should support constructs for expressing temporal joins, i.e. constructs for relating different relations or objects based on conditions concerning validity or transaction time.
- The language should support aggregate functions concerning temporal dimensions.

A good classification of temporal query languages is presented in [Ozso95]. Most temporal query languages are extensions of query languages defined for traditional data models, mainly based on the relational model. This is the case of the languages presented in [Aria86], [Beec88], [Clif87], [KimW90b], [Sege90], [Lore88], [Nava89], [Rose93], [Snod94], [Sard90], [SuSY91], [Tans89].

4.3 Ontologies

Starting from the 1990s, ontologies have emerged as an important research topic investigated by several research communities, such as knowledge engineering, natural language processing, knowledge representation, knowledge represented through Internet technology, e-commerce – especially in defining standards for data exchange – information integration, and interoperability *(see* Section 4.5). As pointed out in [Pere99], ontologies aim to capture domain knowledge in a generic way and provide a commonly agreed understanding of a domain, which may be reused and shared across applications.

The word 'ontology' comes from philosophy, where it is used to describe the existence of beings in the world. In the AI context, several definitions have been proposed in order to assign to the term a more computational meaning. Among these definitions, *see* [Guar95], one of the most referenced in the literature is the one proposed by Gruber in 1993: 'An ontology is an explicit specification of a conceptualization' [Grub93]. This definition was modified by Borst in 1997. The new definition says: 'Ontologies are a formal specification of a shared conceptualization' [Bors97]. Studer and colleagues have presented an explanation of such definitions as follows [Stud98]: 'Conceptualization refers to an abstract model of some phenomenon in the world by having identified the relevant concepts of that phenomenon. Explicit means that the type of concepts used, and the constraints on their use, are explicitly defined. Formal refers to the fact that the ontology should be machine-readable. Shared reflects the notion that an ontology captures consensual knowledge, that is, it is not private to some individual, but it is accepted by a group.'

So several definitions of the word 'ontology' have been proposed, each providing complementary points of view of the same reality. In general, however, each definition agrees on the fact that an ontology should include a vocabulary of terms and some specification of their meaning.

Following the survey presented in [Pere99], the state of the art concerning ontologies can be described by considering the following aspects: ontology theoretical foundations, concerning the basic principles for defining and classifying an ontology; methodologies for constructing ontologies; and environments for ontology constructions. In the following, we look at all the previous aspects, concluding with some references to existing applications supporting the ontology building process.

4.31 Ontology theoretical foundations

Knowledge represented inside an ontology can be formalized by using five different components: classes, relations, functions, axioms, and instances. Classes, or concepts, are usually organized in taxonomies. Concepts are all the notions which are relevant for a given application domain. Therefore, they can be the description of objects, tasks, functions, actions, strategies, etc. Relations represent interactions between concepts and are defined as a subset of a cartesian product. Examples of relations are represented by: is-a, subclass-of, etc. A special case of relations is represented by functions, as for example 'Mother-of', 'Manager-of ', and so on. Instances represent specific instantiations of concepts whereas axioms are used to represent properties that concepts and instances have to satisfy.

Taxonomies may have several forms. For example, they can represent a simple tree [MillG90] or they can be organized according to several dimensions (thus, like a tree forest) [Bate94]. Moreover, there are a number of general classes of concepts that are represented in almost all the ontologies, such as things, processes, events, relations, and properties. In general, ontologies are quite similar in their upper levels. For example, the division of concepts between 'abstract' versus 'real' concepts is quite typical. Another typical subdivision concerns 'individuals' versus 'collections'. On the other hand, some important concepts are not modelled by all the ontologies. This is the case of temporal concepts. For example, ontologies like the Generalized Upper Model [Bate94], TOVE [Grun95], and CYC [Lena90] support simple concepts to represent time. On the other hand, other ontologies, such as GENSIM [Karp93], do not support this aspect.

A good ontology has to satisfy a set of properties, as pointed out in [Pere99]. In particular, it should be *clear*, meaning that it should provide an adequate documentation concerning its content; it should be *complete*, meaning that sufficient and necessary conditions are preferred over partial conditions; it should be *coherent*, permitting consistent inferences; *extendible*; and should provide *minimal ontological commitments*. The last property means that the ontology should make as few claims as possible about the world being modelled, in order to be possibly further specialized as required by the context. Additional properties concern the fact that classes should be disjoint, support (possibly multiple) hierarchies, be modular, and minimize the semantic distance between sibling concepts.

Several different types of ontologies have been proposed. The main trade-off that has been recognized in classifying them is that the more an ontology is *reusable*, the less the ontology is *usable* [Klin91]. Figure 4.1 illustrates such a consideration.

The most reusable ontologies are the so-called *Knowledge Representation Ontologies* [vanH97] that formalize knowledge in knowledge representation paradigms. An example is represented by the frame-ontology [Grub93], concerning frame-based languages and implemented in KIF [Gene92] (*see* Section 4.52). The second level is represented by *general/common ontologies*, including vocabulary concerning general aspects of each possible application domain. Typical aspects include time, space, behaviour, etc. The CYC ontology is an example of such types of general ontologies [Lena90b]. At the third level, we find *generic ontologies*, which are ontologies that can be reused across domains. Such ontologies often clearly define the meaning of the general relations and functions that an ontology should support. Mereology ontology [Bors97] is an example of a generic ontology. *Domain ontologies* provide terms and relationships concerning a given domain. For example, EngMath is an ontology developed for mathematical modelling in engineering [Usch96]. At the upper level, we find *application domain ontologies*, representing the required knowledge for modelling a specific application [vanH97].

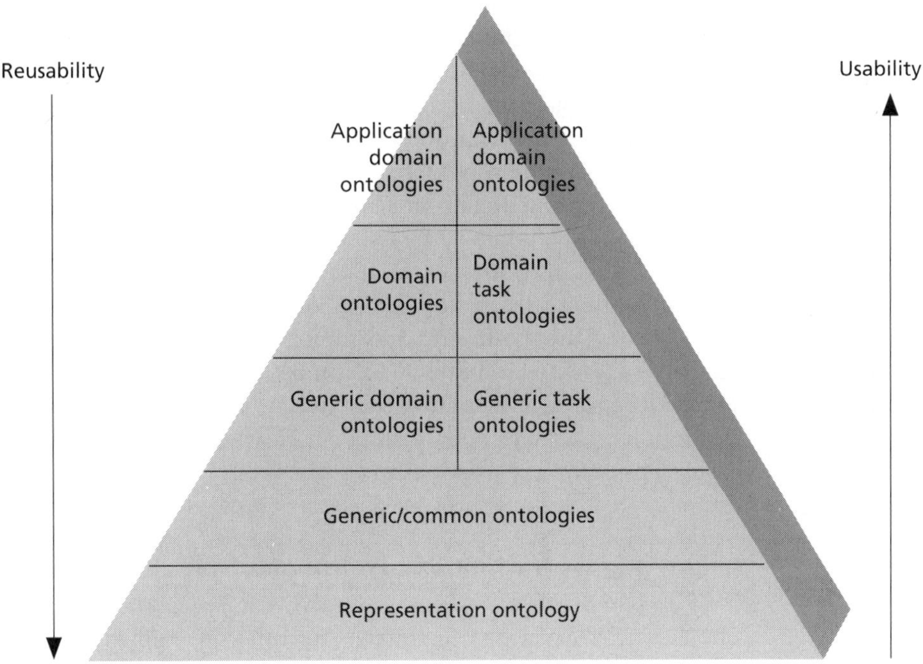

Figure 4.1 A hierarchy of ontology types

The last three levels of the proposed hierarchies, namely generic domain ontologies, domain ontologies, and application domain ontologies, concern the support of specific knowledge inside or across specific domains and in particular they represent static knowledge in a problem-solving, independent way. An orthogonal hierarchy can be defined concerning problem-solving knowledge. Ontologies of this type are classified into *generic task ontologies*, providing vocabularies of terms to be used to solve problems associated with specific tasks, that may or may not belong to the same domain [Mizo95], *domain-task ontologies*, i.e. task ontologies reusable in a given domain, and *application domain task ontologies*, supporting concepts and relationships used in specifying a given reasoning process in order to achieve a specific task [ChanB99].

All the ontologies already defined and belonging to the previously described hierarchy can be combined to define new ontologies for specific purposes. Of course, as we have already pointed out, the most usable ontologies are the less reusable ones, since they are very specialized for representing static knowledge and tasks of specific application domains. Note that ontology reuse and integration can be limited by the existence of different upper levels. On the other hand, ontologies with similar upper levels will be easier to integrate. In general, the usage of a mediation interface (*see* Section 4.52) could be useful for translating statements made in one ontology to another. To this purpose, *see* the work presented in [Camp95].

Several methodologies have been proposed for designing ontologies. Among these we recall Uschold's methodology [Usch96], Gruninger and Fox's methodology [Grun95], and the METHONTOLOGY framework [Gome98]. All these methodologies start the design process from the identification of the purpose of the ontology and the need for domain knowledge acquisition. Then, such knowledge is represented in some way (using a formal language under Uschold's proposal and using some intermediate representations for METHONTOLOGY). After this step, the ontology is constructed by using specific translators. In general, methodologies can be divided into two classes: those building the ontology by applying a bottom-up process, thus starting from single concepts and grouping them into more general concepts, and those building the ontology by applying a top-down process. Others, like those presented in [Usch96], [Grun95], apply a mixed approach.

Even if several methodologies exist, it is important to recall that no standard methodology has yet been proposed. However, all methodologies agree on the basic steps of the ontology building process.

4.32 Environments for building ontologies

The most representative languages for ontology representations are Ontolingua [Grub92], [Grub93], CycL [Lena90a], Loom [MacG91] and Flogic [Kife95]. Ontolingua is based on KIF (*see* Section 4.152) and on the frame ontology [Grub93]. It supports ontologies constructions by using three different approaches: by using KIF expressions, by using the frame ontology vocabulary, and by combining the previous two approaches. CycL is the language supported by the CYC knowledge representation system (*see* Section 3.4) and is a declarative and expressive language, similar to first-order calculus with extensions, including circumscription and unique names assumptions, and it may use the closed-world assumption when required. It also supports an inference engine. Loom is based on first-order logic and belongs to the KL-ONE family [BracR85d]. It provides an expressive model representation language and a powerful deductive engine. Finally, Flogic is an integration of frame-based languages and first-order predicate calculus, including object-based features.

Based on these and other languages, several tools have been proposed to support the ontology building process. Among these we recall the Ontology Server [Farq97], OntoSaurus [Swar97], ODE [Blaz98], Tadzebao and WebOnto [Domi98].

The Ontolingua system was developed in the early 1990s at Stanford University and is composed of a server and a representation language. The server provides a repository of ontologies that can be used to modify the existing ontologies, in different fields, and uses the available ontologies to construct new ones that can then be added to the repository. Connection with the server is provided by a standard Web interface and collaborative work is supported. Ontologies can be represented in various languages, such as Prolog, CORDA, IDL, CLIPS, and Loom.

OntoSaurus is a Web browser for Loom knowledge bases. It consists of two components: an ontology server that uses Loom as the knowledge representation system, and an ontology browser that dynamically creates HTML pages representing the ontology structure, that the user can edit.

ODE is an ontology construction tool that interacts with users at the knowledge level, providing several intermediate representations for ontologies that are independent from the language in which the ontology is implemented. The code is then automatically generated. To this purpose, several translators have been developed. This approach helps non-expert ontology builders in defining, implementing and validating ontologies.

Finally, Tadzebao is an ontology discussion tool, while WebOnto is a graphically oriented tool for constructing ontologies, providing collaborative browsing, creation, and editing tools.

4.4 Structured, semi-structured and unstructured data

Typical data stored in traditional DBMSs, such as relational or object-oriented ones, is *structured*, i.e. the schema is always specified and no data can be entered in the database that do not satisfy the format described by the schema. This approach is reasonable for traditional applications. However, it presents several limitations in modelling advanced applications. For example, by using structured DBMSs, it is very difficult to represent and query multimedia information that, in principle, is completely *unstructured*. On the other hand, several applications require the representation and the management of information for which a precise schema is not completely available even if some information about it is known, i.e. these data are *semi-structured*.

In both cases, the models and the architectures that have been developed for traditional DBMSs are no longer adequate and different models and systems have to be developed. In the following, we describe the main issues arising in defining such systems.

4.41 Multimedia database

The most important characteristic of a multimedia information system is the variety of data it must be able to support. Multimedia systems must have the capability to store, retrieve, transport, and present data with very heterogeneous characteristics such as text, images – both static and moving – graphs and sound. Moreover, multimedia data have large storage requirements. One single image usually requires several Kbytes of storage, whereas a single second of video can require several Mbytes of storage. Finally, the content of multimedia data is difficult to analyze and compare.

For all these reasons, the development of a multimedia system is considerably more complex than in the case of traditional information systems and cannot rely on the use of structured models. Conventional systems deal only with simple data types, such as strings or integers. On the contrary, the multimedia data model, query language and access and storage mechanisms must be able to support objects with a very complex structure [Baez99].

To this purpose, specific methods have been defined to identify and represent the content of multimedia documents, thus superimposing a sort of conceptual organization, providing semantic knowledge about the unstructured multimedia documents. This conceptual organization often consists of some sort of metadata, known as *features*. For example, in the case of images, typical features may be colour distribution, spatial relationships, or textures. Each multimedia object is therefore internally represented as a list of features, each of which represents a point in a multidimensional space. Multi-attribute access methods can be used to index and search for them [Baez99]. The extraction of features from multimedia documents can be either manual or automatic, but in general a hybrid approach is used, by which the system determines some of the values and the user corrects or augments them. Such values are usually obtained by comparing the document with some previously classified objects and it therefore cannot be precise. A weight is usually assigned to each feature value representing the uncertainty of assigning such value to that feature.

Since in a multimedia context data is no longer precisely represented, from the point of view of the query processing there is the need to express and execute similarity queries, according to which data are compared with distance measures. Moreover, different features can be given different weights in the same query to emphasize the relevance of specific features. All these characteristics require the definition of adequate query languages, indexing and optimization techniques suitable for the management of multimedia data [Baez99].

On the research side, several models for multimedia data have been proposed. These range from data models suitable for a particular data type, such as video data models [DayY95], [Esco95], [Gibb93], [Oomo93], to image data models [ChuW92], to general-purpose multimedia data models [Chri86], [Gibb91], [Ishi93], [Masu91], [Marc96].

From the point of view of commercial DBMSs, most DBMS-producers have started to introduce multimedia management capabilities in their most well-known products. For example, most of the current relational DBMSs support variable-length data types which can be used to represent multimedia data. The way these data are supported by commercial DBMSs is mostly non-standard in that each DBMS vendor uses different names for such data types and provides support for different operations on them (such as LOB, CLOB, BLOB). This type of representation is not always sufficient to deal with multimedia data since no interpretation, through the use of features, is provided. Moreover, in general, the operations that can be performed on such data by means of the built-in functions provided by the DBMS are very simple. Starting from these limitations, commercial DBMSs, such as ORACLE and Illustra, have introduced specific multimedia capabilities. For example, data cartridges provided by ORACLE support feature representation and query-by-content for text, spatial data, images, audio and video data. By using data cartridges, such data can be easily queried, together with traditional and structured data, inside SQL queries.

4.42 Semi-structured data

With the term semi-structured data we mean data which is not completely unstructured, such as images, sounds, and raw text. However, unlike traditional DBMSs, a precise schema is not completely available. This may be due to several reasons: the structure exists but it is not known, the user decides not to consider the structure, for example, for browsing purposes, the structure may be implicit, as in a formatted text, but not so rigid as in a traditional database, the schema often changes therefore it is ignored, and so on.

In general, semi-structured data are represented as a collection of objects. All models proposed for semi-structured data introduce some labelled graph to represent them. In such graphs, the nodes correspond to objects or values and the edges correspond to attributes. Of course, semi-structured data require specific query languages, update methods, indexing and optimization techniques. Up to now, few of these topics have been fully addressed. For a good introduction to semi-structured data, *see* [Abit97], [Bune97]. In all the proposed models, languages and techniques, the intelligence relies on the ability to deal with data without having complete information about them, guaranteeing similar performance to those achieved by traditional database management systems.

Among the proposals for modelling and accessing semi-structured data, we recall those presented in [Abit98], [Beer99], [Chaw98], [Deut99a], [McHu99], [McHu97], [PapaY99], [Suci98a], [Suci98b].

Among the proposed models and languages for semi-structured data, XML is assuming an increasing relevance [Brad98]. XML has emerged as a new standard for data exchange over the Web. The basic ideas underlying XML are very simple: tags on data elements identify the meaning of the data, rather than specifying how the data should be formatted (as in HTML), and the relationships between data elements are provided by simple nesting and reference. Web servers and applications encoding their data in XML can quickly make their information available in a simple and usable format and a high level of interoperability between applications is provided.

In order to understand the differences between HTML and XML, Table 4.1 presents an HTML text fragment and Table 4.2 presents an equivalent fragment of an XML document. Both documents deal with the representation of information about the books of a certain bookstore. For each book, information about the author, the title, the publication year, the ISBN number, and the price is maintained.

As we can see from the examples, the tags in the HTML documents are used to format the text. For example, the tag <UL> represents a list and the tag <LI> identifies each element of the list. On the other hand, in the XML documents tags have a semantic meaning, thus they associate a structure with the original information. In our example, the XML document points out that each book has a title, an author, a publisher, and a publication year.

From the point of view of DBMSs, the use of XML not only as a data exchange format but also as a format for the internal data representation guarantees high performance in supporting the efficient execution of expressive queries against

Table 4.1 An HTML document fragment

```
<UL>
<LI>
    Tom Evans. <BR>
    The Round Door <BR>
    1996. <BR>
    0-9546-0274-3. <BR>
    $23.00 <BR>
</LI>
<LI>
        Bill Eaton <BR>
        Creating Real Xml Applications <BR>
        1998 <BR>
        7-4562-0167-8 <BR>
        $35.00 <BR>
        A Look At How To Build Real Xml Applications <BR>
</LI>
```

Table 4.2 An XML document

```
<?xml version='1.0' encoding='UTF-8'?>
<!DOCTYPE Bookstore SYSTEM 'bookshop.dtd'>
<Bookstore>
    <Book>
        <Title>The Round Door</Title>
         <Author>Tom Evans</Author>
        <Year_Published>1996</Year_Published>
         <ISBN>0-9546-0274-3</ISBN>
         <Price>$23.00</Price>
        <Review>An Intriguing Tale Of A Round Door In A Wall</Review>
    </Book>
    <Book>
        <Title>Creating Real Xml Applications</Title>
        <Author>Bill Eaton</Author>
        <Year_Published>1998</Year_Published>
        <ISBN>7-4562-0167-8</ISBN>
        <Price>$35.00</Price>
        <Review>A Look At How To Build Real Xml Applications</Review>
    </Book>
<\Bookstore>
```

huge amounts of Web data. This ability is provided neither by HTML nor by traditional DBMSs, since typical information to be used in this context is semi-structured. The use of XML overcomes these limitations due to the fact that structure and data are stored in the same document. Indeed, the schema is defined together with data and may model irregularities that cannot be modelled in traditional systems. For example, it is possible to associate an atomic value with some data instances and a structured value with some other instances. In the context of XML documents, the concept of type is replaced by the concept of *document type definition* (DTD). A DTD resembles the concept of schema in traditional DBMSs, however it is much looser since irregularities can be easily modelled. The DTD for the document presented in Table 4.2 is presented in Table 4.3.

Table 4.3 An example of DTD

```
<!ELEMENT Bookstore (Book+)>
<!ELEMENT Book (Title, Author, Year_Published, ISBN, Price, Review)>
<!ELEMENT Title (#PCDATA)>
<!ELEMENT Author (#PCDATA)>
<!ELEMENT Year_Published (#PCDATA)>
<!ELEMENT ISBN (#PCDATA)>
<!ELEMENT Price (#PCDATA)>
<!ELEMENT Review (#PCDATA)>
```

On the research side, several approaches that have been proposed for semi-structured data are now being extended to deal with XML documents. Among the proposed approaches for modelling, querying, and efficiently accessing XML documents, we recall [Beer99], [Ceri99], [Deut99a], [McHu99a], [McHu99b], [Shim99], [GoldR99]. At the same time, all main DBMS producers are extending their products to obtain XML-compliant systems.

In general XML is used under two different modalities. Under the first, XML is just seen as a data exchange language. Therefore, under this point of view, traditional DBMSs are supplied with functionalities for extracting from a given XML document the specific information that will then be stored in tuples or objects. In this case, XML is just an interface language. On the other hand, XML documents can also be seen as new objects that must be stored and managed using specialized approaches. More precisely, current DBMSs supporting XML facilities are based on two main technologies:

- An XML adapter is used in front of a relational (or object-relational) database. This is the solution taken by ORACLE Corp. in Oracle 8i [Orac98] and by IBM Corp. in the XML extender for DB2 [IBMC99a]. The main advantage of this solution is that an existing technology (relational, object-relational) is used and extended to deal with XML. In this case, XML documents add a new logical level in data representation. This means that users see XML documents but such documents are stored by using a different reference model (for example, a set of related tables). The main disadvantages of this solution are the following:
  - the relational model cannot easily handle arbitrary XML data due to the intrinsic hierarchical nature of XML. This problem is partially overcome by object-relational technology;

  - building server-side applications based on data structures stored in a relational database requires that applications must have intimate knowledge of the physical implementation of the back-end databases and the protocol to access it, which is often proprietary. This could make server-side applications difficult to implement, maintain and modify.
- XML is the new reference model. This solution has been adopted by ObjectDesign Inc. [ObjeD98]. The main advantages of this solution are the following:
  - an XML-based store is constructed that can be manipulated using XML standards;
  - applications must be written with respect to the XML data model.

  The main disadvantage is that a new system, based on a new reference model, has to be acquired in order to deal with XML data, instead of extending an existing one with additional capabilities. In this respect, this solution could be more expensive and less portable than the previous one.

4.5 Mediators

Mediators represent one of the several approaches that have been proposed to deal with the problem of integrating heterogeneous information. In the following, we first review the motivations that have led to the development of mediator architectures, then we present the main aspects of the architecture itself. After that, we discuss how mediators can be used in a heterogeneous environment. We conclude with some short remarks on existing systems.

4.51 Motivation

A typical information system should cope with two main types of resources: data, representing specific instances and events, and knowledge, describing abstract classes, covering many instances. Data can be used to disprove knowledge. This duality is well reflected, from an architectural point of view, in the client-server architecture: the server supplies data, the client supplies application programs accessing such data and generating new knowledge for the user, often by applying sophisticated decision-making functionalities.

Such an approach suffers from two main shortcomings [Wied92]. First of all, data on the server, typically managed by a DBMS, is usually large in size and often lack the adequate level of abstraction required to successfully apply decision-making applications. Moreover, data often come from different sources, giving rise to heterogeneous environments. In this case, it is very difficult for application programs to cope with the complexity of the system. On the other hand, client-server architectures do not scale well as the number of services provided by the server grows. Indeed, while introducing a new client is easy if all the required services exist, if any change is needed in an existing service to accommodate the new client, a major maintenance problem arises since the other clients have to be inspected in order to understand how such change will impact on them.

From the previous discussion, it follows that typical two-layer architectures suffer from two main problems, the first mainly concerning lack of abstraction, required to generate knowledge from data, the second concerning architecture scalability. Mediators have been proposed to overcome such problems by introducing an intermediate layer in the typical client-server architecture. More precisely, mediators can be defined as software modules providing intermediate services, linking data resources and application programs. Such modules should be simple and small enough to be replicated eventually in the architecture.

The main functionality of mediators is to provide integrated information, without the need to integrate the data resources. As pointed out in [Wied92], the main tasks of a mediator can be summarized as follows:

- it supports the access and the retrieval of relevant data from multiple heterogeneous resources;
- it abstracts and transforms retrieved data to facilitate integration;
- it integrates and makes data homogeneous;
- it processes and integrates (i.e. it summarizes) data to increase the information density in the result.

4.52 Architecture

A typical mediator architecture is presented in Figure 4.2 [Wied97]. The architecture is horizontally divided into three layers: the client applications, the intermediate service modules, and the base servers. Such an architecture can also be vertically divided, depending on the different application domains mediation has to support. As pointed out in [MillG56], for each domain the number of servers should be limited to 7 ± 2. In general, all the functions that add value to data, and facilitate their conversion into knowledge, are assigned to mediators. In particular, different functionalities are assigned to the different architectural components as follows:

- data selection from persistent storage is assigned to the server;
- interaction with the user is performed by the client;
- integration of data from multiple servers and the transformation of those data to information is assigned to the mediators.

In a mediator-based architecture, two distinct interfaces can be distinguished, the first between mediators and applications (clients), the second between base resources (managed by the servers) and the mediators. For the second interface, several standards have already been defined, such as SQL [Melt93] for relational

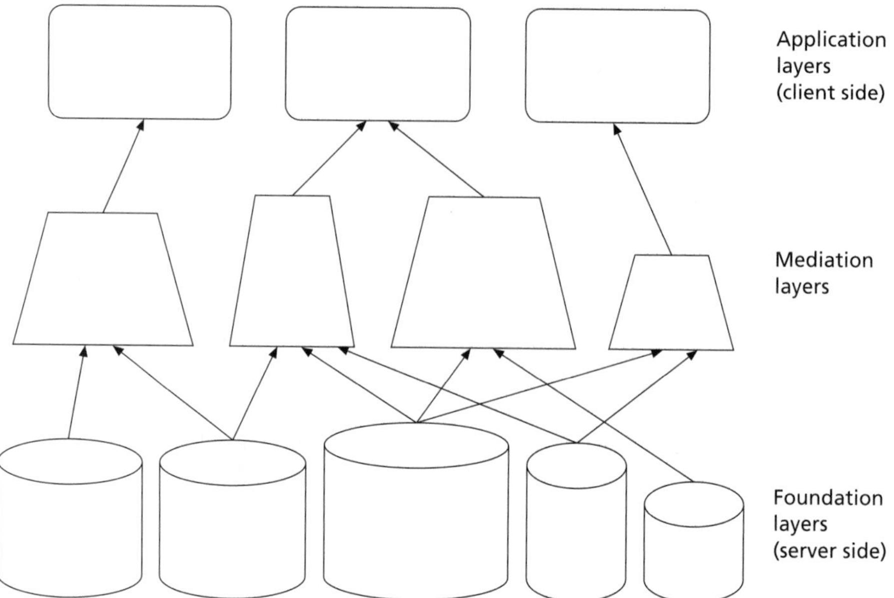

Figure 4.2 A mediation architecture

and object-relational data, and CORBA [ObjeM91] for object-oriented data. Concerning the interface between the application layer and mediators, agent languages such as KIF (knowledge interchange language) [Gene92] for content, and KQML (knowledge query and manipulation language) [Labo97], [Fini97] for complex requests, have been developed. We recall that KIF and KQML have been defined in the context of the ARPA knowledge sharing effort [Nech91], with the aim of defining the components of a standard agent communication language (ACL). In particular, ACL should be composed of three components: a vocabulary, an inner language, KIF, and an outer language, KQML. An ACL message is therefore a KQML expression in which the arguments are terms or sentences in KIF, formed from words in the ACL vocabulary. In particular, KIF is a prefix version of first-order predicate calculus with various extensions. On the other hand, KQML provides a linguistic layer in which context is taken into account. A valid alternative to such languages for exchanging information is represented by XML [Brad98] (*see* Section 4.4), which is becoming a standard for data exchange.

It is important to remark that mediators and applications need only a machine-friendly interface. Graphical user interfaces should be delegated to the application programs. The important aspect is that a language, on which mediators and application programs agree, must exist by which requests to the mediators and answers to the application programs can be represented.

4.53 Application of mediators to heterogeneous systems

Due to their nature, mediators have been successfully used in the context of heterogeneous databases, whose main goal is to integrate heterogeneous resources from heterogeneous database management systems. Heterogeneity may arise because of the data model used, the data types, and the data granularity of the data sources. Such sources could be structured databases, like relational and object-oriented databases, may contain semi-structured data, such as HTML and XML documents, or completely unstructured data, such as text and in general multimedia documents. In this context, mediators provide users with an integrated view of multiple sources, making the underlying data heterogeneity transparent.

The central problem in mediation is the identification of relevant resources for the client model and the retrieval and reduction of relevant data at the time of a client inquiry [Grav98]. This goal is achieved by three main functions: selection of data, translation of the user query into queries suitable for the underlying sources, and merging of the resulting data, avoiding redundancy and inconsistency. Through this entire process, the user should not be aware of the underlying heterogeneity. In order to support data selection, a fundamental task of the mediator is that of matching the client model to the resource model. The resource model can be available in an entity-relationship format, for example, whereas client models are typically hierarchical and related to a task set and a domain of interest, often represented by using a knowledge representation language. After this step, the user query should be decomposed into several queries, each converted into a suitable format for the underlying sources. After obtaining the results from the heterogeneous sources, an homogeneous result should be generated and presented to the user.

The overall process often relies on the use of *wrappers* [Roth95]. A wrapper is a simple software module whose aim is to standardize how information in legacy data sources is described and accessed. Wrappers also play an important role in query planning since they contribute, together with mediators, to determining their role in the query answering process. Thus wrappers export a common data model view of each source of data and provide a common query interface. After receiving a query, a wrapper translates it into a source-specific query or command, providing transparency to the user. The result of the query is then translated by the wrapper back from the underlying sources into the common data model or format. Figure 4.3 describes this approach.

A prerequisite in mapping the user model to the resource models is that the terminology used to describe objects and attributes matches. In order to formally model user application structure and available resources in the domain, *ontologies* are typically used (*see* Section 4.3). In general, the application ontology should be a subset of the resource ontology and techniques exist to perform such a match. Integration also requires operations to be performed on ontologies [Wied94a]. To this purpose, an ontology algebra has been defined [Wied94b], with the aim of matching and merging ontologies.

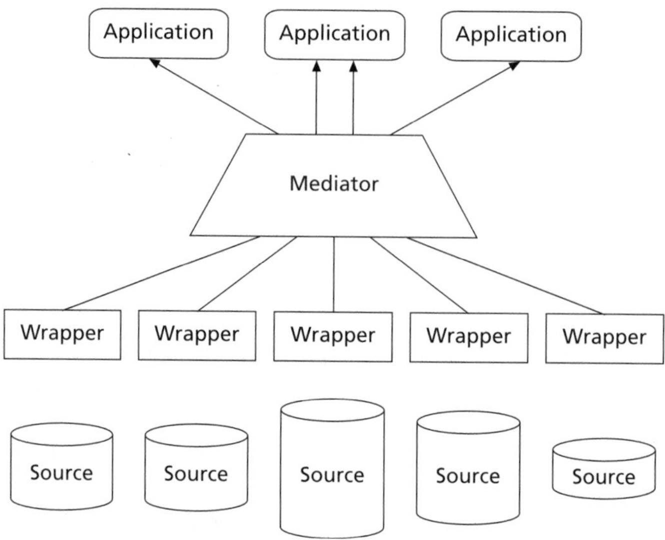

Figure 4.3 Role of wrappers in mediator architectures

4.54 Proposals

Several mediation approaches have been proposed. Among them is TSIMMIS, developed at Stanford [Garc97]. It offers a data model and a common query language that are designed to support the combination of information from different sources. It also offers tools for automatically generating the required components, i.e. mediators and wrappers. Another approach is represented by SIMS [Aren93]. This is an information mediator that provides a uniform language to express queries. It also provides mechanisms to determine which data sources have to be used in answering a query, how to obtain the designed information, and how to efficiently retrieve information. The application domain and the information sources are represented in Loom [MacG91], a hierarchical terminological knowledge representation language. We also recall Information Manifold [Kirk95], HERMES [Subr96], and GARLIC [Roth95]. HERMES proposes a mediator specification language where some literals explicitly specify parameters to be sent to the sources. GARLIC sees heterogeneous legacy data as instances of objects in a unified schema. GARLIC data models and programming interface are based on the ODMG standard [Catt96]. Each data source is associated with a wrapper. The use of constraint databases for interoperability and integration problems has been investigated in [ChomJ97], [ChenX99].

4.6 Multi-agent systems

Multi-agent systems are computational systems in which two or more, possibly heterogeneous, agents interact to satisfy a given set of goals. The area of multi-agent systems derives from distributed artificial intelligence. The main aim of this research area is that of developing computational models for 'constructing, describing, implementing, and analyzing the patterns of interaction and co-ordination in both large and small agent societies' [Less99]. To this purpose, techniques from several disciplines have to be combined. In the following, we describe the main issues in defining multi-agent systems and indicate some open problems. We refer the interested reader to the survey presented in [Less99], the special issues contained in [IEEE81], [IEEE91], the proceedings of the International Conference on Multi-Agents Systems, which is the main important conference in the field, and some books, [O'Har95], for additional information.

4.61 Main issues in designing a multi-agent system

Even though it is difficult to define precisely what an agent is, we can consider an agent as 'a self-contained program capable of controlling its own decision making and acting, based on its perception of its environment, in pursuit of one or more objectives' [Jenn96]. More specifically, an agent should be characterized by a number of key properties including *social ability*, referring to the ability to interact with other agents and/or humans; *autonomy*, referring to the control an agent should have over its own actions and internal state; and *reactivity*, referring to the ability of an agent to react to changes that occur in the agent state and in the environment.

With regard to the degree of co-operation supported, agents can also be classified as *benevolent* and *self-interested*. Benevolent agents work together in a co-operative way to achieve a common goal. On the other hand, self-interested agents have distinct goals but they may interact to advance their own goals.

One of the most important problems in multi-agent systems is how the agents co-operate. In general, the basic idea of a multi-agent system is that of having a single problem, which is in turn divided into several subproblems, each managed by a given agent. Subproblems are not necessarily distinct. For example, they can be overlapping, but different agents may have different methods or data to be used for obtaining a solution. This is the case for example of distributed situation assessment applications [Less99], where subproblems may correspond to data generated by different sensors and the regions to which sensors refer are not disjoint. Another example of non-independent problems concerns subproblems among which there exist some constraints. For example, as pointed out in [Less99], in a distributed expert system application involving the design of some product, assuming that each agent is responsible for the design of a given component (corresponding to a subproblem) there may exist several constraints concerning the design of the various components and the overall system must adhere to them. Non-independent subproblems can also be generated when an agent does not have enough local information or resources to solve a given task. In this case, it may require some help from some other agents.

Co-operation is also used to obtain reliable results in less time. This approach is typical in systems for fault analysis and diagnosis. In this case, different agents perform different forms of fault diagnosis, but solutions must be consistent and subproblems (i.e. fault detection) can be overlapping. However, each agent can use different algorithms to achieve the goal and can make mistakes – although it is quite difficult for two agents to make the same mistake. Therefore, co-operation provides an important way to exchange, for example, partial results, in order to reach an agreement about the detected faults in less time.

Co-operation can also be used to investigate the actual status of agents, recognizing for example which is working and who is solving a specific subproblem.

In general, co-ordination among agents requires reasoning about the nature of the subproblem interdependencies, the current status of problem solving, and the status of the network resources [Less99]. Bad co-operation usually leads to sub-optimal solutions or, in the worst case, to no solutions.

As pointed out in [Less99], several principles have to be followed in order to build a multi-agent system. Such principles can be summarized as follows:

- *Satisfaction criteria.* In general, there is no way to optimize all problem criteria at the same time, thus often an optimal solution does not exist or at least cannot be found by using a reasonable amount of resources. Therefore, satisfaction criteria for successful performance are adopted, based on the usage of a reasonable amount of resources, in order to obtain not the optimal solution but an acceptable one [Less81]. From this criteria, it also follows that there is not one single approach to organizing agent behaviour which will be good in all situations. In general, the best results are obtained by dynamically choosing a given strategy at run-time, based on the characteristics of the tasks that have to be executed.
- *Flexibility.* In a multi-agent system, agents must be able to achieve several goals and should not need too many details about them. This means that agents should be able to deal with uncertainty and incompleteness of their local databases. This also mean that multi-agent systems must be able to deal with uncertain and incomplete problem solving and must be able to reason about intermediate states of their computation.
- *Efficiency.* The co-ordination of large agent societies can benefit from an organization in terms of roles and responsibilities. Indeed, they significantly decrease the computational cost proper of co-operation, since they reduce the number of available options and constraints that need to be evaluated to take the right co-ordination decision.

4.62 Open problems

As pointed out in [Lass99], even if some aspects of multi-agent systems were investigated several years ago, there are still several problems. The first important problem concerns the definition of a high-level infrastructure, supporting the construction of multi-agent systems. Two approaches can be taken. The first concerns the definition of a set of operations and protocols for locating and communicating with agents. An example is given by KQML [Labo97]. Under this approach, the responsibility of what information to transmit and which protocol to use is left to the agent programmer. An alternative and extreme approach is to leave all co-ordination decisions to the framework, to be taken after an agent has described its needs and its co-ordination capabilities. Other important problems concern the design of multi-agent systems in which both benevolent and self-interested agents co-operate, the development of analysis techniques for predicting the performance of the system, and the development of learning techniques. All the previous issues make the multi-agent system design an important and active research direction in the development of intelligent systems.

4.7 Internet indexing and retrieval

The information available over the Internet can be seen as a very large database that has to be queried in an efficient manner. This task is made difficult by the variety of information. There are several sources, each containing different types of data (from structured documents to semi-structured and unstructured ones). Moreover, users in general want an integrated view of the result to enable them to better analyze the required information.

To this purpose, several tools have been developed to help with the retrieval of information on the Internet. Such tools can be classified into three main groups [Bert97]. The first represents indexing methods which became popular in the late 1980s and early 1990s, such as Gopher, Archie, and WAIS. The second group identifies search engines, providing an integrated view of a heterogeneous set of data sources. Finally, Internet agents belong to the third group.

4.71 Basic indexing methods

The relevance of searching for information through the Internet network was realized by the Internet community from the beginning. A good starting point for a new generation of Internet searching tools is represented by tools such as Archie, Gopher, Whois, and WAIS [Bowm94], [Cheo96]. Archie is a tool for performing searches in a distributed collection of FTP sites. Gopher is a distributed information system which supports hierarchical data collections and provides a simple text search interface. Whois is a tool for querying Internet sources about people and other entities (such as domains, networks, and hosts). WAIS is a distributed service supporting a simple natural language interface for finding information in Internet databases.

The indexing power of such tools greatly depends on the amount of information they use in the underlying indexing method. A first group of methods, including Archie, indexes only file names or menus, thus supporting a restricted set of queries. The second group of methods, including WAIS, Gopher, and WWW servers, provides full-text indexing of data located at individual sites. Finally, the third group of methods adopts solutions which are a compromise between the previous approaches. They represent some of the contents of the objects they index, based on selection procedures for including important keywords or excluding less important keywords. Wais++ belongs to this group.

4.72 Search engines or metasearchers

Search engines provide functionalities for searching a set of documents, stored at different Internet sites. Search engines are based on two types of techniques: *sequential search* and *inverted indexes*. Sequential search works well only when the search is limited to a small area. Most pattern-based search tools such as Unix's grep use sequential search. On the other hand, inverted indexes are a common tool in information retrieval systems. An inverted index stores in a table all word occurrences in the set of the indexes documents and indexes the table using a hash method or a B-tree structure. In general, inverted indexes are very efficient in terms of query evaluation but have a large storage occupancy, that in the worst case could be equal to the document size. To this purpose, several compression techniques have been proposed [Mehr90]. A typical problem arising with inverted indexes is that queries are successful only if words appear in the query with their correct spelling, otherwise an empty result set could be generated.

Examples of search engines are Glimpse [Manb94], Altavista (*http://www.altavista.com*), and Excite (*http://www.excite.com*). Among them, Glimpse allows word misspelling and supports a hybrid technique between the sequential search and the inverted index technique. The combination of these techniques guarantees low response time for most queries.

The intensive development of different indexing techniques for Web documents resulted in the definition of several heterogeneous search engines. In a way similar to what happened in heterogeneous databases, the appearance of several search engines has configured the Internet as the largest heterogeneous database. From this point of view, search engines are seen as heterogeneous document sources that should be integrated to provide a homogeneous view of the documents to the user, combining the potentiality of each source.

As with a mediator, the aim of a *metasearcher* is therefore that of simplifying the task of accessing multiple document sources over the Internet, usually represented by specific search engines [Grav98]. Some sources may contain text documents and support only simple searches by keywords, others may contain more structured documents (such as XML documents) against which some more semantically meaningful queries can be executed, in the style of relational languages. The problem is that the user does not want to see the heterogeneity of these sources. Rather, he/she wants to express the queries and obtain a result which is a combination of the results generated by all the sources involved in the query process.

Starting from the previous requirements, as pointed out in [Grav98], metasearchers can be seen as mediators with respect to a set of sources belonging to possibly different nodes of the Internet network. Thus, the architecture of metasearchers and mediators is quite similar. In both cases, wrappers have to be used to export the data model of each data source, providing a common query interface language. After receiving a query, the wrapper will translate it into the language characterizing the source, and wait for the result which will then be converted into the common data model and sent to the mediator.

In typical mediator architectures, a metasearcher architecture is complicated by several aspects. The first problem is the selection of the sources against which to execute the user query. Differently from mediator architectures, sources are typically represented by Web indexes that may charge for their use or may have a long response time. In both cases, a fundamental requirement for a metasearcher is that of contacting only the sources that could be useful in executing the query. If a source makes available all its content (this is typical for engines such as AltaVista), the metasearcher does not need any additional information about the source. However, this is not always the case. Often, sources may hide the information through a specific source interface. In this case, it is important that the source describes its content in some way, making available to the metasearcher all or part of the related information.

An additional problem concerns the interfaces and the capabilities of the various sources, which are usually quite different, both in their expressive power and in their syntax. Some sources may rely on simple *Boolean queries* [Baez99], whereas other sources may support the *vector-space retrieval model* [Baez99]. Boolean queries represent a simple retrieval model based on set theory and Boolean algebra. Queries expressed under this model have a clear semantics. A typical example of a Boolean query is the following: 'Find all documents containing the word "flower" and the word "shop"', to find all documents concerning flower shops. Under this modality the user specifies some terms and the engine is able to retrieve all the documents that exactly contain the specified term combination. In the second case, partial matching is applied. This means that some weights are assigned to terms that are then used to compute the degree of similarity between documents and the user query. Under this modality, documents containing not exactly the specified term combination but a similar one are also returned to the user. Additional problems are represented by the different approaches in dealing with stemming algorithms (i.e. algorithms for automatically dealing with the singular and plural of the specified words) and stop-words (i.e. algorithms for not processing words like 'the' in queries).

Due to the previous differences, it is important for a metasearcher to know the exact expressive power of each source, in order to submit to each of them a correctly executable query.

The final problem concerns how results obtained from the various sources can be merged. Here, the problem is that each source may apply different ranking algorithms and often these algorithms are not disclosed. This implies that often it is impossible for the metasearcher to further rank the results obtained by the various sources since it is not always possible to deduce a global ranking starting from the local ones.

Among the proposed metasearchers, we recall MetaCrawler [Selb89], SavvySearch (*http://guaraldi.cs.colostate.edu:2000/*), and ProFusion [Gauc96]. All of them provide support in querying multiple Web indexes but do not completely support all the tasks described above. In order to fully support such tasks, a group effort co-ordinated by Stanford's Digital Libraries and involving 11 companies and organizations proposed STARTS, a protocol for Internet retrieval and search that facilitates the task of querying multiple document sources [Grav97]. The protocol addresses and analyzes metasearch requirements and describes the facilities that a source needs to provide in order to help the metasearcher. If implemented, STARTS can really improve the implementation of metasearchers, enhancing the functionalities they can support.

It is also important to remark that the need to exchange data over the Internet has required the development of certain standards. XML represents the most promising approach for exchanging information on the Web (*see* Section 4.4) whereas RDF is becoming a standard for metadata representation and exchange [Lass99]. RDF (*see also* Section 3.452), developed by a specific W3C Working Group, is the result of an effort aimed at defining a foundation for processing metadata on the web. The model, implemented in XML, makes use of directed labelled graphs (DLGs) where the nodes, which represent any possible Web resource (documents, parts of documents, collections of documents, etc.), are described basically by using attributes that give the named properties of the resources. No predefined 'vocabulary' (ontologies, keywords, etc.) is in itself a part of the proposal. The values of the attributes may be text strings, numbers, or other resources. Initially, the model bore a striking resemblance to some early work on semantic networks, and the examples given of RDF annotations were, as usual, in the style of 'The individual whose name is X, email Y, is the creator of the resource Z'. In the latest versions of the RDF model and syntax specifications, new, very interesting constructs have been added. Among these, of particular interest are the 'containers' and the 'high-order statements'. Containers describe 'collections' of resources; the high-order statements can be used to make statements about other RDF statements.

4.73 Internet spiders

Besides indexing Web documents, another operation typically performed by the user on the Web is *browsing*, which is the ability to navigate from one document to another through the use of links. Typically, such links are inserted in the document by hand. This means that they have been predefined by the author of the document. However, in certain situations, it could be useful to browse a document not with respect to a set of predefined links but with regard to a set of similar documents, retrieved from the Web at browsing time. Such a functionality requires a combination of browsing and indexing capabilities in a single system. To this purpose, a new family of programs, often called *Web Robots, Internet spiders, or Internet agents*, has been proposed with the aim of providing more advanced search facilities [Cheo96]. The main goal of spiders is that of traversing the Web space by following hypertext links and at the same time retrieving and indexing new Web documents. Among the proposed Internet spiders are WWW Worm (*http://www.cs.colorado.com*), WebCrawler (*http://www.webcrawler.com*), Harvest [Bowm95], and WebGlimpse [Manb97].

Even if Internet spiders can help the user to obtain a quicker response from the Internet, at the current state of the art they have several limitations. First, their search mechanisms are often based on keywords; in some cases, keywords are not sufficient to get the right answer to a given question. Moreover, since they do not always provide the user with the ability to adequately personalize his/her requests, they often return several false hits. As pointed out in [Etzi95], Internet agents 'are similar to a taxi driver. They will take you to your destination (in this case, a particular location on the Web) but there they will drop you off and you are on your own. Furthermore, you may find that you are not at the destination that you wanted to reach'.

The main problem therefore revolves around the too-simple model by which the user requests are described. Internet Softbot represents a different approach to intelligently browsing and indexing the Web [Etzi95]. Differently from other systems, Softbot accepts high-level user requests and dynamically determines the corresponding sequence of Internet commands that should be executed to achieve the required goal. After that, Softbot executes the sequence. Typical commands contained in the sequence are `ftp`, `lpr`, `mail`, `ls`, `finger`, `netfind`. In summary, Softbot allows the user to specify the result required, leaving the decision of how and where to obtain it to Softbot. Thus, it provides a declarative approach to browsing and indexing the Web.

4.8 Data mining

Data mining refers to the process of non-trivial extraction of implicit, previously unknown, and potentially useful information from large amounts of data, stored in databases, data warehouses or other repositories, and transforming them into useful knowledge for the user [ChenM96a]. Such knowledge may identify patterns, associations, changes, and anomalies, explaining the behaviour of specific phenomena.

The problem of extracting useful knowledge from large amounts of data has been investigated in several computer science and mathematics contexts, such as AI, machine learning, visualization, statistics, information retrieval, neural networks, pattern recognition, probabilistic graph theory, and inductive logic programming. However, most of the proposed techniques are not directly usable for large amounts of data, for example because they do not scale well or they have unacceptable performance when applied to data stored on persistent storage, or because the type of knowledge obtained is not considered sufficiently useful. The main goal of data mining is to extend such techniques to deal with data stored in DBMSs, guaranteeing scalability and good performance. Moreover, traditional data analysis techniques are often assumption-driven, in the sense that a hypothesis is formulated and validated against data. On the other hand, data mining is discovery-driven, since previously unknown patterns have to be automatically derived from data.

Data mining is therefore an interdisciplinary discipline, combining results obtained in different contexts, and applying them to the case in which data are stored on persistent storage. Even if relational data represent the typical base for applying data mining techniques, it is important to note that data mining techniques for advanced data, such as spatial, temporal, and multimedia data, are currently being defined [Este97], [ChenX98], [ChenM96b], [Falo95], [HanJ97], [Zaia98].

In the following, we review the basic tasks performed by a data mining system, then we present some of the commercial tools available. We refer the reader to [ChenM96a] for a complete survey of data mining tasks.

4.81 Data mining tasks

A data mining system should perform several tasks by applying different techniques. In general, there is no technique which is better than the others; often the choice of a technique depends on the problem at hand and on the application domain. Therefore, most of the data mining tools on the market (around 40) support several data mining strategies. Such systems are quite sophisticated and versatile, both from the point of view of visualization techniques and the connection with the underlying DBMS. The main tasks performed by a data mining system can be classified as follows.

4.811 Class description

Class description provides a concise summarization of a collection of data, pointing out the properties distinguishing it from other data sets. Typical operations to be executed by the class description task include the generation of summary properties, such as count, sum, average, and other properties such as variance, quartiles, etc.

As an example, class description can be used to compare European with American sales of a given company, identifying the distinctive factors and presenting a overview. Note that class description is a typical task of a data warehousing system since it is the first step in analyzing large amounts of data and taking decisions based on them [Kimb96].

4.812 Association

The aim of the association task is to discover significant dependencies existing among data, i.e. to determine combinations of attributes that are more present in the database than others. More precisely, the primary goal of the association task is to generate *association rules* that are formally defined as follows. Let I be a set of items. An association rule is a rule of the form $X \Rightarrow Y$, where $X \subseteq I$, $Y \subseteq I$, $X \cap Y = \emptyset$. An association rule specifies that the presence of items X determines the presence of items Y. A *transaction* is a set of items such that $T \subseteq I$. Each transaction is assumed to be associated with an identifier. An association rule $X \Rightarrow Y$ has a support *level* c in a set of transactions T if the c% of transactions in T contains $X \cup Y$. It has a *confidence level* c in T if the c% of transactions in T containing X also contain Y. In general, it is useful to generate only the rules with a sufficiently high support.

In relational database terminology, the items are all the possible associations' 'attribute/values', transactions are tuples, and association rules specify that some values for some attributes determine some values for some other attributes.

The confidence level points out the 'strength' of the implication provided by the rule, whereas the support level provides information about the frequency by which the association is verified in the set of the considered transactions. In general, the algorithms for the detection of association rules determine only those rules having a support level higher than a given threshold, specified by the user.

Association is especially used in transaction data analysis, particularly for marketing and other decision-making processes. Typical problems that can be solved with association rules are, for example: given a database of purchase transactions where each transaction is a list of items, find all associations that correlate the presence of one set of items with another set of items. An example of discovered association is: '98 per cent of people who buy milk GoodMilk also buy cookies GoodCookies. Such rule is satisfied by the 60 per cent of the purchase transactions.' In this particular example, 98 per cent represents the confidence level whereas 60 per cent is the support level.

Note that the generation of all the rules having specific support and confidence levels can be very expensive. Therefore several techniques have been proposed for reducing these costs. Such techniques are based mainly on incremental algorithms. We refer the reader to [Mann94], [Park95], [Agra96], [Cheu96], [Agra93] for additional information.

As a final consideration, it is important to remark that association rules generated by association data mining tools are not always significant. Improvements of such techniques mainly concern the ability to group the items in hierarchical categories and to perform the mining at the various levels of the hierarchy [HanJ95], [Srik95].

4.813 *Classification*

Classification is a function determining whether an object belongs to a given class, chosen among a set of predefined classes, based on the values of some object attributes, i.e. based on a given *classification function*. The typical approach to constructing the classification function is the following. From the database, a set of tuples is extracted (*training set*). Each tuple is then associated with a given value called *label*. All tuples having the same label belong to the same class. The classifier, in order to understand the properties which are common to the elements of a given class, uses such labels. Starting from this information, classifiers construct a set of classification rules, which are then used to assign a label to each item in the database.

Classifiers have been investigated in several fields (statistics, machine learning, neural networks, and expert systems). Among the proposed techniques, *decision trees* have been defined in the context of machine learning and they are becoming a widely used technique for classification [Quin86]. Such trees are constructed starting from the training set and are then used to classify all the items. The leaves of the tree correspond to all the possible labels. Each internal node is associated with an attribute and has a child for each value that can be associated with that attribute. Often, single values are replaced by mutually disjoint conditions. The disjunction of all the conditions appearing in the children of a given node completely characterizes the domain of the attribute. This property guarantees that, given a certain item to be classified, there is always a single path from the root to a leaf. The conditions associated with the traversed internal nodes provide an explanation for the choice of that class.

As an example, consider the relation represented in Figure 4.4(a), containing some simple information about movies. Such information can be used as a training set to construct the decision tree presented in Figure 4.4(b). Such a tree can be used to classify additional data.

Main actor	Movie type	Label
Tom	Adventure	Success
Arnold	Comedy	Failure
Tom	Tragedy	Success
Bruce	Adventure	Success
Bruce	Tragedy	Failure
Arnold	Adventure	Success
Tom	Comedy	Success

(a)

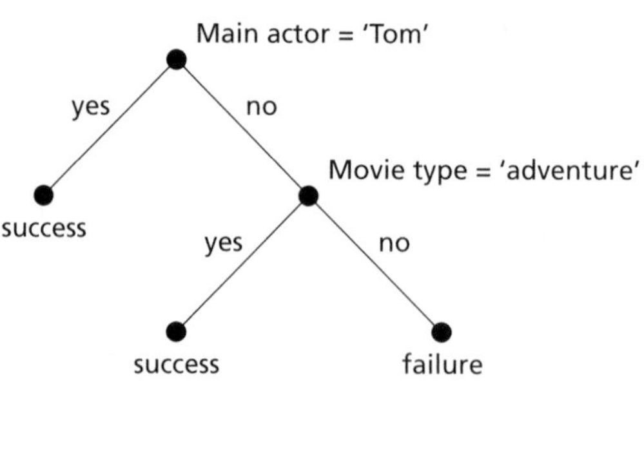

(b)

Figure 4.4 (a) A starting set of data; (b) A decision tree associated with the proposed data

4.814 *Prediction*

Prediction techniques predict the possible values of some missing data or the value distribution of certain attributes in a set of objects [Fayy96]. In general, such techniques apply some statistical analysis to determine the set of attributes that are relevant for the attributes whose values have to be determined. Then they predict value distribution based on the set of data similar to the set of selected objects. For example, the number of sold units of a given product can be predicted by considering the number of units sold for similar products.

Typical techniques used in prediction analysis are regression analysis, generalized linear modes, correlation analysis, decision trees, genetic algorithms, and neural networks.

4.815 *Clustering*

Clustering techniques partition a given set of objects into several object groups, in such a way that objects belonging to the same group are quite similar and objects belonging to different classes are quite different, with respect to some given similarity function. A good clustering method guarantees that inter-cluster similarity is low whereas intra-cluster similarity is high. As an example, clustering can be used to partition the customers of a given company with respect to their behaviour over payments.

Clustering techniques have been investigated mainly in statistics and they are often based on the use of neural networks and Bayesian network techniques [Chee96], [Jain88], [Fayy96], [Fish87].

Note that classification differs from clustering in that clustering techniques partition database items into non-predefined classes, such that the items contained inside a single class are more similar than objects belonging to different classes. On the other hand, classification techniques classify data according to some specific rule that is extracted from a previously classified data subset.

4.816 *Time-series analysis*

The aim of time-series analysis is to analyze large sets of time-series data to find regularities, such as similar sequences, sequential patterns, periodicities, trends, deviations [Fayy96]. In this context, the use of constraint databases for storing and managing the retrieved patterns seems quite promising.

As an example, time-series analysis techniques can be used to predict the income of a given company during the next year, starting from the incomes of previous years and the current customer payment situation.

4.82 Data mining tools

Data mining tools can be classified according to the types of techniques they support. The work reported in [Hall97] suggests classifying these tools as follows (*see* [Hall97] also for references to the specific tools):

- *Classification tools based on decision trees*: decision trees are quite simple to understand and clearly point out data correlations. However, such tools often generate too many rules and trees, making the result less understandable. Among tools based on decision trees are AC2, ALICE, C4.5, Clementine, Darwin, DataMine, DecisionSeries, Information Harvester, KATE, Knowledge Seeker, MineSet, ExpertRule Profiler, TOCLASS, taLogic/R, taMind, IS, delQuest, delWare, zWhy, YIELD.
- *Tools based on neural network techniques*: such tools are quite useful to generate valid statistical models for sparse, incomplete and non-linear databases. However, results are often difficult to understand. Among the tools based on neural networks techniques are Clementine, Rwin, DataBase Mining Marksman, DataBase Mining Workstation, DBProfile, DecisionSeries, IntelligentMiner, ModelMax, NeuralConnection, SkulPLAN.
- *Tools based on conventional statistical techniques*: these are very useful in scientific and engineering applications. They are more useful in the analysis of existing data than in the detection of previously unknown patterns. Among tools based on statistical approaches are Cornerstone, DATA, JMP, SAS, SPSS, SYSTAT.
- *Advanced visualization tools*: by using advanced multi-dimensional and animated visualization, relationships existing among data can often be detected. However, results have to be interpreted by an expert user. Among advanced visualization tools are AVS/Express, Clementine, Intelligent Miner, MineSet, NetMap, Parallel Visual, Explorer, Win Viz.
- *Tools based on fuzzy knowledge-extraction techniques*: these are quite useful in supporting clustering techniques. Only a few tools of this type are on the market, depending mainly on the fact that the underlying techniques have only recently been defined. Among the tools based on fuzzy techniques are DataEngine, FuzzyTech Business, Level5Quest.
- *Multi-strategy tools*: these tools support several different types of techniques and are therefore very useful in contexts in which it is not clear which approach will provide the better results. Among multi-strategy tools are Clementine, Darwin, DecisionSeries, Information Harvester, Intelligent Miner, MineSet.

Medical and legal information systems

As an example of application domains requiring the use of several techniques presented in this book, in the following we survey the basic problems underlying medical and legal information systems. The main issue in medical information systems is the ability to cope with heterogeneous types of (often non-structured) medical data and the ability to perform reasoning about them. On the other hand, in legal information systems there is the need to formally represent, often through ontologies, the legal domain in order to be able to perform legal reasoning.

4.91 Medical information systems

As well described in [Rami94], a medical information system is a system involved in the delivery of healthcare. This includes medical journal databases (bibliographic databases), clinical information systems for patient care, and medical research databases. Medical information systems are characterized by the management of heterogeneous data on which advanced reasoning has to be performed.

Data managed by a medical information system can be classified as follows:

1. demographic, identifying, and socio-economic data;
2. general, non-time-dependent data, such as research protocols, tumour registry information, and special patient needs;
3. problems or diagnoses, time-oriented data, for example assessment of disease progress;
4. data resulting from lab tests and x-rays;
5. therapies, including diets;
6. admission dates.

The previous types of data are generally organized into records, using two possible approaches. Records can be *event-based*, if they are stored in the system in chronological order, as they occur in time. The main goal of such systems is to provide a real-time display of clinical information. On the other hand, records can be *patient-based*. In this case, the system evolves as a result of user requests over time.

The management of all data described above requires the use and integration of advanced technologies and leads to the need for *intelligent medical systems*. Among the technologies that are already used in medical information systems and those that will be used soon, we note the following:

- In order to represent and reason about medical knowledge, specific ontologies have to be developed and made available.
- The need to represent temporal information also requires the use of temporal databases in order to be able to deal with time as an autonomous dimension.
- In order to support advanced reasoning, for example concerning diagnosis, deductive capabilities have to be used. To this purpose, deductive databases have already been used successfully in this context.
- The use of image data requires the support of multimedia database technology.
- Medical data is often distributed and not centralized in a single site. Therefore another important point is the development of heterogeneous distributed architectures, possibly based on mediation and/or multi-agent architectures.
- The need to analyze and learn from medical data (for example, for automatic diagnosing) also requires the use of advanced data mining techniques and decision support tools.

- Another important aspect is the development of user-friendly graphical interfaces.
- Active rules can be quite useful in alerting the system regarding entered data or to detect critical situations in some patients.

From the previous discussion it follows that, in order to build a medical information system, most of the technologies presented in this book have to be combined. Even if some intelligent (or partially) intelligent medical information systems have already been developed – *see* [Rami94] for some references – much more work has to be done in order to define a real system supporting all the features described above.

4.92 Legal information systems

Artificial intelligence techniques have been used in the legal application domain for several years. The use of AI techniques in law requires the development of a theory of law and a theory of legal reasoning. The first attempts to automate legal reasoning involved the creation of legal expert systems, containing knowledge and reasoning strategies, *see* [Aike95], [Aike96]. In such systems, knowledge is stored in the form of production rules. However, law cannot be well modelled as a series of defined deductive rules, but requires the modelling of *analogical reasoning*, by which existing and similar cases are considered and taken into account in order to solve a problem.

Starting from the previous considerations, another attempt to use AI techniques in law is based on the use of case-based reasoners, *see* [Aike95], [Aike96]. In such systems, one or more individual examples are stored in the system. The reasoner then tries to reach a conclusion by manipulating the existing cases. This approach overcomes some limitations of expert systems; however, it does not provide sufficient intelligence for dealing with uncertainty and similarity.

The legal community agrees on the fact that neither expert systems nor case-based reasoners are sufficient for representing and reasoning about legal knowledge since they do not view the legal problem from the right perspective. The approach based on production rules is typical of a formalist perspective. On the other hand, the use of cases is accepted by rule sceptics, 'regarding the multiplicity of human experience as requiring individual treatment of cases' [Aike96]. Another point of view sees law as a process of arguments that occurs between parties. Under this interpretation, a different law theory can be defined, known as *discourse theory of law*, that opens new perspectives in creating automated legal reasoning systems [Aike96].

Another criticism concerns the used techniques (production rules and case-based reasoners). Different techniques can be successfully integrated in expert systems and case-based reasoners to better support legal applications. Among them we recall [Aike95]:

- *neural networks*: their ability to match patterns can be used to match law cases with each other;

- *fuzzy logic-based systems*: fuzzy logic provides a formal framework for dealing with imprecision. Therefore, the extension of production rules with fuzzy logic seems a good approach for modelling uncertainty, typical of the legal application domain;
- *deontic logic-based systems*: deontic logic can be used to model the normative aspects of laws.

The design of legal ontologies plays another important role in the development of legal information systems. As pointed out in Section 4.3, the use of ontologies provides several benefits. In the legal domain, it provides the conceptualization of sharable building blocks of legal knowledge [Benc97], [Viss98]. Several legal ontologies have already been developed. Among them are LLD [McCa89], NORMA [Stam91], the Functional Ontology of Law [Vale95], and the Frame-based Ontology [VanK95], [Viss95]. An approach for structuring the content of a library of legal ontologies was presented in [Viss98].

As with medical information systems, legal knowledge is often not centralized. Rather, solving legal problems often requires the integration of information from multiple sources. Mediator and multi-agent systems can be used to this purpose – *see* [Viss97].

4.10 Conclusions

In this chapter, we have surveyed several developments, introducing new advanced capabilities in knowledge and data-based systems. From the presented approaches, it follows that, inside such systems, intelligence can be used for several purposes that can be summarized as follows:

- *Modelling capabilities for supporting the representation of non-traditional data*. Temporal databases, semi-structured and unstructured data modelling belong to this group. Ontologies can also be inserted in this group since they provide a formal representation of specific application domains, providing the right conceptualization over which applications can be developed.
- *Advanced architectural functions*, often requiring the management of heterogeneous data as well as co-operation and interaction between architecture components. Mediator and multi-agent systems belong to this group.
- *Ability to index, and retrieve (also non-traditional) data*. Data mining and Internet indexing and retrieval techniques belong to this group.

These techniques are often not used in isolation but, on the contrary, are often combined to support advanced applications. Medical and legal information systems are good representatives of such application domains.

There are several other techniques for intelligent data and knowledge representation and retrieval that have been developed that we have not surveyed. However, we believe that the approaches we have described are quite representative of what is needed for developing real intelligent information systems.

References

[Aber99] Abernethy, N.F., Wu, J.J., Hewett, M. and Altman, R.B. (1999) 'SOPHIA: A Flexible, Web-based Knowledge Server', *IEEE Intelligent Systems*, 14(4), 79–85.

[Abit87a] Abiteboul, S. and Hull, R. (1987) 'IFO: A Formal Semantic Database Model', *ACM Transactions on Database Systems*, 12, 525–565.

[Abit87b] Abiteboul, S. and Vianu, V. (1987) 'A Transaction Language Complete for Database Updates and Specification' in *Proc. of the Seventh ACM SIGACT-SIGMOD-SIGART Symposium on Principles of Database Systems*, San Diego (CA), May.

[Abit88] Abiteboul, S. and Vianu, V. (1988) 'A Transaction Language Complete for Database Updates and Specification' in *Proc. of the Eight ACM SIGACT-SIGMOD-SIGART Symposium on Principles of Database Systems*, Austin (TX), May.

[Abit89] Abiteboul, S. and Kanellakis, P. (1989) 'Object Identity as a Query Language Primitive' in *Proc. of the ACM SIGMOD International Conference on Management of Data*, Portland (OR), May–June.

[Abit90] Abiteboul, S. and Grumbach, S. (1990) 'COL: A Logic Based Language for Complex Objects' in F. Bancilhon and P. Buneman, eds, *Advances in Database Programming Languages*, pp. 347–377, ACM Press.

[Abit91] Abiteboul, S. and Vianu, V. (1991) 'Datalog Extensions for Database Queries and Updates', *Journal of Computer and System Sciences*, 43(1): 62–124, August.

[Abit93] Abiteboul, S., Lausen, G., Uphoff, H. and Waller E. (1993) 'Methods and Rules' in *Proc. of the ACM SIGMOD International Conference on Management of Data*, Washington (DC), May.

[Abit95] Abiteboul, S., Hull, R. and Vianu, V. (1995) *Foundations of Databases*, Addison-Wesley.

[Abit97] Abiteboul, S. (1997) 'Querying Semi-Structured Data' in *Proc. of the Int. Conf. on Database Theory*.

[Abit98] Abiteboul, S., McHugh, J., Rys, M., Vassalos, V. and Wiener, J.L. (1998) 'Incremental Maintenance for Materialized Views over Semistructured Data' in *Proc. of the Int. Conf. on Very Large Data Bases*, pp. 38–49.

[Abri74] Abrial, J.R. (1974) 'Data Semantics', *Data Base Management*, pp. 1–59, North Holland, Amsterdam.

[Afra94] Afrati, F., Cosmadakis, S., Grumbach, S. and Kuper, G.M. (1994) 'Linear vs Polynomial Constraints in Database Query Languages' in *Proc. of Second International Workshop on Principles and Practice of Constraint Programming*, Lecture Notes in Computer Science 874, Springer-Verlag.

[Agra93] Agrawal, R., Imielinski, T. and Swani, A. (1993) 'Mining Association Rules Between Sets of Items in Large Databases' in *Proc. of the 1993 ACM SIGMOD International Conference on Management of Data*.

[Agra96] Agrawal, A., Mannila, H., Srikant, R., Toivonen, H. and Verkamo, A.I. (1996) 'Fast Discovery of Association Rules' in U.M. Fayyad, G. Piatetsky-Shapiro, P. Smyth and R. Uthutusamy, eds, *Advances in Knowledge Discovery and Data Mining*, AAAI/MIT Press.

[Aike95] Aikenhead M. (1995) 'Legal Knowledge Based Systems: Some Observations on the Future', *Web Journal of Current Legal Issues*, 2.

[Aike96] Aikenhead M. (1996) al Intelligence, *Law Technology Journal*, 5(1): 13–18.

[AitK86] Ait-Kaci, H. and Nasr, R. (1986) 'Login: A Logic Programming Language with Built-in Inheritance', *Journal of Logic Programming*, 3: 185–215.

[AitK91] Ait-Kaci, H. (1991) 'An Overview of LIFE' in *Proc. of First International East/West Database Workshop*, Lecture Notes in Computer Science.

[AlAs93] Al-Asady, R. and Narayanan, A. (1993) 'More Notes on "A Clash of Intuitions"' in *Proc. of the Thirteenth International Joint Conference on Artificial Intelligence* – IJCAI/93, San Francisco: Morgan Kaufmann.

[Alhi99] Alhit, S.S. (1999) 'From the Unified Modeling Language (UML) to C++', www.devx.com.

[AlleF82] Allen, F.W., Loomis, M.E.S. and Mannino, M. (1982) 'The Integrated Dictionary/Directory System', *ACM Computing Surveys*, 14: 245–286.

[AlleJ83] Allen, J.F. (1983) 'Maintaining Knowledge About Temporal Intervals', *Communication of the ACM*, 26: 823–843.

[AlleJ84] Allen, J.F. (1984) 'Towards a General Theory of Action and Time', *Artificial Intelligence*, 23: 123–154.

[Alta89] Altair (1989) 'INRIA', *The O_2 Programmer's Manual* prototype Version 1.0, Dec.

[AlZo87] Al-Zobaidie, A. and Grimson, J.B. (1987) 'Expert Systems and Database Systems: How Can They Serve Each Other?', *Expert Systems*, 4(1): 30–37.

[AndrJ90] Andreoli, J.M. and Pareschi, R. (1990) 'LO and Behold! Concurrent Structured Processes' in *Proc. of International Conference on Object-Oriented Programming: Systems, Languages, and Applications.*

[AndrT87] Andrews, T. and Harris, C. (1987) 'Combining Language and Database Advances in an Object-oriented Development Environment', in *Proc. 2nd International Conference on Object-Oriented Programming Systems, Languages, and Applications*, Orlando (Florida), Oct. 4–8, 1987.

[Anwa93] Anwar, E., Maugis, L. and Chakravarty, S. (1993) 'A New Perspective on Rule Support for Object-Oriented Databases', in *Proc. of the 1993 ACM SIGMOD International Conference on Management of Data*, Washington DC, May 26–28.

[AptK82] Apt, K.R. and van Emden, M.H. (1982) 'Contribution to the Theory of Logic Programming', *Journal of the ACM* 29: 841–862.

[Aren93} Arens, Y., Chee, C.Y., Hsu, C.-N. and Knoblock, C.A. (1993) 'Retrieving and Integrating Data from Multiple Information Sources', *Int. Journal on Intelligent and Cooperative Information Systems*, 2(2): 127–158.

[Aria86] Ariav, G. (1986) 'A Temporally Oriented Data Model', *ACM Trans. on Database Systems*, 11(4): 499–527.

[Arta96] Artale, A., Franconi, E., Guarino, N. and Pazzi, L. (1996) 'Part-Whole Relations in Object-Centered Systems: An Overview', *Data & Knowledge Engineering* 20: 347–383.

[Atki89] Atkinson, M., Bancilhon, F., DeWitt, D., Dittrich., K., Maier, D. and Zdonik, S. (1989) 'The Object-oriented Database System Manifesto', in *Proc. of First International Conference on Deductive and Object-Oriented Databases (DOOD)*, Kyoto (Japan), Dec. pp. 4–6.

[Azza95] Azzam, S. (1995) 'Anaphors, PPs and Disambiguation Process for Conceptual Analysis' in *Proc. of the Fourteenth International Joint Conference on Artificial Intelligence* – IJCAI/95, San Francisco: Morgan Kaufmann.

[Baad91] Baader, F. and Hollunder, B. (1991) 'A Terminological Knowledge Representation System with Complete Inference Algorithm' in *Proc. of the Workshop on Processing Declarative Knowledge* – PDK-91 (Lecture Notes in Artificial Intelligence), Berlin: Springer-Verlag.

[Baad94] Baader, F., Buchheit, M., Jeusfeld, M.A. and Nutt, W., eds (1994) *Working Notes of the KRDBí94 Workshop, Reasoning about Structured Objects: Knowledge Representation Meets Databases* (Document D-94-11), Saarbrücken: Deutsches Forschungszentrum für Künstliche Intelligenz GmbH.

[Baad95] Baader, F., Buchheit, M., Nutt, W. and Jeusfeld, M., eds (1995) *Working Notes of the KRDB' 95 Workshop, Reasoning about Structured Objects: Knowledge Representation Meets Databases* (Document D-95-12), Saarbrücken: Deutsches Forschungszentrum für Künstliche Intelligenz GmbH.

[Baez99] Baeza-Yates, R. and Ribeiro-Neto, B. (1999) *Modern Information Retrieval*, Addison-Wesley.

[Bagn91] Bagnasco, C., Petrin, P. and Spampinato, L. (1991) 'Configuring with QUERELLE' in *Trends in Artificial Intelligence Proc. of the 2nd Conference of the Italian Association for Artificial Intelligence,* Ardizzone, E., Gaglio, S. and Sorbello, F., eds Berlin: Springer-Verlag.

[BalR93] Bal, R. and Balsters, H. (1993) 'A Deductive and Typed Object-Oriented Language' in *Proc. of 3rd International Conference on Deductive and Object-Oriented Databases* (DOOD), Phoenix (AZ), December 6–8.

[Bals93] Balsters, H., de By, R. and Zicari, R. (1993) 'Typed Sets as a Basis for Object-Oriented Database Schemas' in *Proc. of Seventh European Conference on Object-Oriented Programming (ECOOP'93).*

[Bane87] Banerjee, J., Kim, W., Kim, H.K. and Korth, H.F. (1987) 'Semantics and Implementation of Schema Evolution in Object-oriented Databases', in *Proc. of ACM-SIGMOD Conference on Management of Data*, San Francisco (Calif.), May.

[Bara94] Baralis, E. and Widom, J. (1994) 'An Algebraic Approach to Rule Analysis in Expert Database Systems' in *Proc. of the 20th International Conference on Very Large Data Bases, VLDB'94*, Bocca, J.B., Jarke, M., and Zaniolo, C., eds, San Francisco: Morgan Kaufmann.

[Bate94] Bateman, J.A., Magnini, B. and Rinaldi, F. (1994) 'The Generalized Italian, German, English Upper Model' in *Proc. of the 11th European Conference on Artificial Intelligence, ECAI'94, Workshop on Comparison of Implemented Ontologies.*

[Bati86] Batini, C., Lenzerini, M. and Navathe, S.B. (1986) 'A Comparative Analysis of Methodologies for Database Schema Integration', *ACM Computing Surveys*, 18: 323–364.

[Baud91] Baudinet, M., Niezette, M. and Wolper, P. (1991) 'On the Representation of Infinite Temporal Data and Queries' in *Proc. of the Tenth ACM SIGACT-SIGMOD-SIGART Symposium on Principles of Database Systems*, Denver (CO), May.

[Baue95] Bauer, M. (1995) 'A Dempster-Shafer Approach to Modeling User Preferences for Plan Recognition', *User Modeling and User-Adapted Interaction* 5(3–4): 317–348.

[Baue97] Bauer, M. (1997) 'Approximation Algorithms and Decision Making in the Dempster-Shafer Theory of Evidence – An Empirical Study', *International Journal of Approximate Reasoning* 17: 217–237.

[Beec88] Beech, D. and Mahbod, B. (1988) 'Generalized Version Control in an Object-oriented Database' in *Proc. of the International Conference on Very Large Data Bases*, pp. 14–22.

[Beer99] Beeri, C. and Tzaban, Y. 1999 'SAL: An Algebra for Semistructured Data and XML' in *Proc. of the Int. Workshop on World Wide Web and Databases (WebDB)*, pp. 37–42.

[Beie93] Beierle, C., Pletat, U. and Studer, R. (1993) 'Knowledge Representation for Natural Language Understanding: The LILOG Approach', *IEEE Transactions on Knowledge and Data Engineering*, 5: 386–401.

[Bein87] Bein, J., King, R. and Kamel, N. (1987) 'MOBY: An Architecture for Distributed Expert Database Systems' in *Proc. of the 13th International Conference on Very Large Data Bases, VLDB'87*, Stocker, P.M., Kent, W. and Hammersley, P., eds. San Francisco: Morgan Kaufmann.

[Benc97] Bench-Capon, T.J.M. and Visser, P.R.S. (1997) 'Ontologies in Legal Information Systems; The Need for Explicit Specifications of Domain Conceptualisations' *in Proc. of the Sixth International Conference on Artificial Intelligence and Law (ICAIL'97)*, Melbourne, Australia.

[Bene94] Beneventano, D., Bergamaschi, S., Lodi, S. and Sartori, G. (1994) 'Terminological Logics for Schema Design and Query Processing in OODBs' in *Working Notes of the KRDB' 94 Workshop, Reasoning about Structured Objects: Knowledge Representation Meets Databases* (Document D-94–11), Baader, F., Buchheit, M., Jeusfeld, M.A. and Nutt, W., eds, Saarbrücken: Deutsches Forschungszentrum für Künstliche Intelligenz GmbH.

[Berg95] Bergamaschi, S., Sartori, C. and Vincini, M. (1995) 'DL Techniques for Intensional Query Answering in OODBs' in *Working Notes of the KRDB' 95 Workshop, Reasoning about Structured Objects: Knowledge Representation Meets Databases* (Document D-95–12), Baader, F., Buchheit, M., Nutt, W. and Jeusfeld, M., eds, Saarbrücken: Deutsches Forschungszentrum für Künstliche Intelligenz GmbH.

[Bert89] Bertino, E., Negri, M., Pelagatti, G. and Sbattella, L. (1989) 'Integration of Heterogeneous Database Applications Through an Object-oriented Interface'. *Information Systems*, 14 (5): 407–420.

[Bert92] Bertino, E., Negri, M., Pelagatti, G. and Sbattella, L. (1992) 'Object-oriented Query Languages: the notion and the issues', *IEEE Trans. on Knowledge and Data Engineering*, 4 (3): 223–237.

[Bert93a] Bertino, E., Damiani, M., Randi, P. and Spampinato, L. (1993) 'An Advanced Information Management System' in *Proc. of the IEEE Workshop on Research Issues in Data Engineering Interoperability Among Multidatabase Systems*, Vienna, April.

[Bert93b] Bertino, E., Martino, L. (1993) *Object-Oriented Database Systems – Concepts and Architectures*, Addison-Wesley.

[Bert97] Bertino, E., Ooi, B.C., Sacks-Davis, R., Tan, K.L., Zobel, J., Shidlovsky, B. and Catania, B. (1997) *Indexing Techniques for Advanced Databases*, Kluwer Academic Publishers, Chapter 6.

[Bert00a] Bertino, E., Guerrini, G. and Merlo, I. (2000) 'Trigger Inheritance and Overriding in an Active Object Database System', *IEEE Transactions on Knowledge and Data Engineering*, 12 (4).

[Bert00b] Bertino, E., Catania, B., Laradi, D., Marin, B. and Zarri, G.P. (2000) 'Repository Management in an Intelligent Indexing Approach for Multimedia Digital Libraries' in *Foundations of Intelligent Systems – Proceedings of the Twelfth International Symposium on Methodologies for Intelligent Systems, ISMIS, 2000*, Berlin: Springer-Verlag.

[Bjor89] Bjornerstedt, A. and Hulten, C. (1989) 'Version Control in an Object-oriented Architecture' in *Object-Oriented Concepts, Databases, and Applications*, W. Kim and F. Lochovsky, (eds), Addison-Wesley, pp. 451–485.

[Blac87] Black, A. *et al* (1987) 'Distribution and Abstract Types in Emerald', *IEEE Trans. on Software Engineering*, SE-13 (1): 65–76.

[Blaz98] Blazquez, M., Fernandez, M., Garcia-Pinar, J.M. and Gomez-Perez, A. (1998) 'Building Ontologies at the Knowledge Level Using the Ontology Design Environment' in *Proc. of the 11th Workshop on Knowledge Acquisition, Modelling and Management.*

[Bobr77] Bobrow, D. and Winograd, T. (1977) 'An Overview of KRL, a Knowledge Representation Language', *Cognitive Science*, 1: 3–46.

[Boll98] Boll, S., Klas, W. and Sheth, A. (1998) 'Overview on Using Metadata to Manage Multimedia Data' in *Multimedia Data Management – Using Metadata to Integrate and Apply Digital Media*, Sheth, A. and Klas, W., eds, New York: McGraw Hill.

[Bonn94] Bonner, A.J. and Kifer, M. (1994) 'An Overview of Transaction Logic', *Theoretical Computer Science*, 133: 205–265.

[Booc92] Booch, G. (1992) *Object-Oriented Analysis and Design with Applications*, Addison-Wesley.

[Booc98] Booch, G., Rumbaugh, J. and Jacobson, I. (1998) *The Unified Modeling Language User Guide*, Addison-Wesley.

[Borg84] Borgida, A., Mylopoulos, J. and Wong, H.K.T. (1984) 'Generalization/ Specialization as a basis for Software Specification' in *On Conceptual Modelling, Perspectives from Artificial Intelligence, Databases, and Programming Languages*, Brodie, M.L., Mypopoulos, J. and Schmidt, J.W. (eds), pp. 87–114.

[Borg92] Borgida, A. (1992) 'From Type Systems to Knowledge Representation: Natural Semantics Specifications for Description Logics', *International Journal of Intelligent and Cooperative Information Systems* 1: 93–126.

[Borg93] Borgida, A. and Brachman, R.J. (1993) 'Loading Data into Description Reasoners' in *Proc. of the 1993 ACM SIGMOD International Conference on Management of Data – Special Issue of ACM Sigmod Record*, 22(2): 217–226.

[Borg98] Borgida, A., Chaudri, V. and Staudt, M., eds (1998) *Proceedings of the KRDBí98 Workshop, Innovative Application Programming and Query Interfaces* (Swiss Life Technical Report), Zürich: Swiss Life Information Systems Research Group.

[Bors97] Borst, W.N. (1997) *Construction of Engineering Ontologies*, PhD Thesis, University of Twente, Enschede.

[Boss93] Bossi, A., Bugliesi, M., Gabbrielli, M., Levi, G. and Meo, M.C. (1993) 'Differential Logic Programming' in *Proc. of the Twentieth ACM Symposium on Principles of Programming Languages.*

[Boss94] Bossi, A., Gabbrielli, M., Levi, G., and Meo, M.C. (1994) 'A Compositional Semantics for Logic Programs', *Theoretical Computer Science*, 122: 3047.

[Bowm94] Bowman, C., Danzig, P., Manber, U. and Schwartz, M. (1994) 'Scalable Internet Discovery: Research Problems and Approaches', *Communications of the ACM*, 37(8): 98–107.

[Bowm95] Bowman, C., Danzig, P., Hardy, D., Manber, U., and Schwartz, M. (1995) 'The Harvest Information Discovery and Access System', *Computer Networks and ISDN Systems*, 28(1–2): 119–125.

[BracG76] Bracchi, G., Paolini, P. and Pelagatti, G. (1976) 'Binary Logical Associations in Data Modelling' in *Modelling in Data Base Management Systems*, pp. 125–148. North Holland, Amsterdam.

[BracR79] Brachman, R.J. (1979) 'On the Epistemological Status of Semantic Networks' in *Associative Networks*, Findler, N.V., ed, New York (NY): Academic Press.

[BracR83a] Brachman, R.J. (1983) 'What IS-A Is and Isn't: An Analysis of Taxonomic Links in Semantic Network', *IEEE Computer* 16(10): 30–36.

[BracR83b] Brachman, R.J., Fikes, R.E. and Levesque, H.J. (1983) 'KRYPTON: Integrating Terminology and Assertion' in *Proc. of the Second National Conference on Artificial Intelligence – AAAI/83*, Cambridge (MA): AAAI Press/MIT Press.

[BracR84] Brachman, R.J. and Levesque, H.J. (1984) 'The Tractability of Subsumption in Frame-Based Description Languages' in *Proc. of the Fourth National Conference on Artificial Intelligence – AAAI/84*, Cambridge (MA): MIT Press/AAAI Press.

[BracR85a] Brachman, R.J. and Levesque, H.J. (1985) 'A Fundamental Tradeoff in Knowledge Representation and Reasoning' in *Readings in Knowledge Representation and Reasoning*, Brachman, R.J., and Levesque, H.J., (eds) San Francisco: Morgan Kaufmann.

[BracR85b] Brachman, R.J. (1985) '"I Lied about the Trees" Or, Defaults and Definitions in Knowledge Representation', *AI Magazine* 6(3): 80–93.

[BracR85c] Brachman, R.J., Pigman Gilbert, V. and Levesque, H.J. (1985) 'An Essential Hybrid Reasoning System: Knowledge and Symbol Level Accounts in KRYPTON' in *Proc. of the Ninth International Joint Conference on Artificial Intelligence – IJCAI/93*, San Francisco: Morgan Kaufmann.

[BracR85d] Brachman, R.J. and Schmolze, J.G. (1985) 'An Overview of the KL-ONE Knowledge Representation System', *Cognitive Sciences*, 9: 171–216.

[BracR85e] Brachman, R.J., Fikes, R.E. and Levesque, H.J. (1985) 'KRYPTON: A Functional Approach to Knowledge Representation' in *Readings in Knowledge Representation*, Brachman, R.J. and Levesque, H.J., eds, San Francisco: Morgan Kaufmann.

[BracR91] Brachman, R.J., McGuinness, D.L., Patel-Schneider, P.F., Resnick, L.A. and Borgida, A. (1991) 'Living with CLASSIC: When and How to Use a KL-ONE-Like Language' in *Principles of Semantic Networks*, Sowa, J.F., ed., San Francisco: Morgan Kaufmann.

[Brad98] Bradley, N. (1998) *The XML Companion*, Addison-Wesley, Reading (Mass.).

[Bran93] Branding, H., Buchmann, A., Kudrass, T. and Zimmermann, J. (1993) 'Rules in an Open System', in *Proc. of First International Workshop on Rules in Database Systems.*

[Brant93] Brant, D.A. and Miranker, D.P. (1993) 'Index Support for Rule Activation', in *Proc. of the 1993 ACM SIGMOD International Conference on Management of Data*, Washington DC, May 26–28.

[Brei89] Breitl, R. *et al* (1989) 'The GemStone Data Management System' in *Object-Oriented Concepts, Databases, and Applications*, W. Kim, and F. Lochovsky (eds), Addison-Wesley, pp. 283–308.

[Bres85] Bresciani, P., Franconi, E. and Tessaris, S. (1985) *Implementing and Testing Expressive Description Logics: A Preliminary Report (TR 9502-16),* Povo di Trento: Istituto per la Ricerca Scientifica e Tecnologica (IRST).

[Bres94] Bresciani, P. (1994) 'Uniformly Querying Knowledge Bases and Data Bases' in *Working Notes of the KRDB' 94 Workshop, Reasoning about Structured Objects: Knowledge Representation Meets Databases* (Document D-94–11), Baader, F., Buchheit, M., Jeusfeld, M.A. and Nutt, W., eds, Saarbrücken: Deutsches Forschungszentrum für Künstliche Intelligenz GmbH.

[Bres95] Bresciani, P. (1995) 'Querying Databases from Description Logics', in *Working Notes of the KRDB' 95 Workshop, Reasoning about Structured Objects: Knowledge Representation Meets Databases* (Document D-95–12), Baader, F., Buchheit, M., Nutt, W. and Jeusfeld, M., eds, Saarbrücken: Deutsches Forschungszentrum für Künstliche Intelligenz GmbH.

[Brew87] Brewka, G. (1987) 'The Logic of Inheritance in Frame Systems' in *Proc. of the Tenth International Joint Conference on Artificial Intelligence – IJCAI/87*, San Francisco: Morgan Kaufmann.

[BrodA93] Brodsky, A., Jaffar, J. and Maher, M. (1993) 'Toward Practical Constraint Databases' in *Proc. of the 19th International Conference on Very Large Data Bases*, Dublin (Ireland), August.

[BrodA95] Brodsky, A. and Kornatzky, Y. (1995) 'The LyriC Language: Querying Constraint Objects' in *Proc. of the ACM SIGMOD International Conference on Management of Data*, San Jose (CA), May.

[BrodA99] Brodsky, A., Segal, V.E., Chen, J. and Exarkhopoulo, P.A. (1999) 'The CCUBE Constraint Object-Oriented Database System' in *Proc. of the ACM SIGMOD International Conference on Management of Data*, pp. 577–579.

[BrodM88] Brodie, M.L. (1988) 'Future Intelligent Information Systems: AI and Database Technologies Working Together' in *Readings in Artificial Intelligence and Databases*, Brodie, M.L., ed, San Francisco: Morgan Kaufmann.

[Brog90] Brogi, A., Mancarella, P., Pedreschi, D., and Turini, F. (1990) 'Composition Operators for Logic Theories' in *Proc. of Symposium on Computational Logic.*

[Bruc75] Bruce, B. (1975) 'Case Systems for Natural Language', *Artificial Intelligence*, 6: 327–360.

[Buch93] Buchheit, M., Donini, F.M. and Schaerf, A. (1993) 'Decidable Reasoning in Terminological Knowledge Representation Systems', *Journal of Artificial Intelligence Research* 1: 109–138.

[Buch94] Buchheit, M., Donini, F.M., Nutt, W. and Schaerf, A. (1994) 'Terminological Systems Revisited: Terminology – Schema + Views' in *Working Notes of the KRDB' 94 Workshop, Reasoning about Structured Objects: Knowledge Representation Meets Databases* (Document D-94-11), Baader, F., Buchheit, M., Jeusfeld, M.A. and Nutt, W., eds, Saarbrücken: Deutsches Forschungszentrum für Künstliche Intelligenz GmbH.

[Bugl92] Bugliesi, M. (1992) 'A Declarative View of Inheritance in Logic Programming' in *Proc. of Ninth International Conference on Logic Programming.*

[Bugl94] Bugliesi, M., Lamma, E. and Mello, P. (1994) 'Modularity in Logic Programming', *Journal of Logic Programming*, 19: 443–502.

[Bune82] Buneman, P., Frankel, R.E. and Nikhil, R. (1982) 'An Implementation Technique for Database Query Languages', *ACM Transactions on Database Systems*, 7: 164–186.

[Bune97] Buneman, P. (1997) 'Semi-Structured Data', Tutorial at *ACM SIGART-SIGACT-SIGMOD International Conference on Principles of Database Theory.*

[Bunt94] Buntine, W.L. (1994) 'Operations for Learning with Graphical Models', *Journal of Artificial Intelligence Research* 2: 159–225.

[Byon95] Byon, J. and Revesz, P.Z. (1995) 'DISCO: A Constraint Database System with Sets' in LNCS 1034: *Proc. of the 1st International CONTESSA Database Workshop, Constraint Databases and their Applications*, pp. 68–83.

[Caca89] Cacace, F., Ceri, S., Crespi-Reghizzi, S., Tanca, L. and Zicari, R (1989). *The Logres Project: Integrating Object-Oriented Data Modeling with a Rule-Based Programming Paradigm*, Technical Report TR 89-039, Politecnico di Milano.

[Camp95] Campbell, A. and Shapiro, S. (1995) 'Ontologic Mediation: An Overview' in *Proc. of the Workshop on Basic Ontological Issues in Knowledge Sharing*, pp. 16–25.

[Capo98] Capobianchi, R., Mautref, M., van Keulen, M. and Balsters, H. (1998) 'An Architecture and Methodology for the Design and Development of Technical Information Systems' in *Foundations of Intelligent Systems – Proc. of the Ninth International Symposium on Methodologies for Intelligent Systems, ISMIS'96* (Lecture Notes in Artificial Intelligence 837), Berlin: Springer-Verlag.

[Cata95] Catania, B. (1995) 'Bottom-up Rewriting Methods for Datalog and Extensions: a Survey', PART 1, *Ingenierie des Systèmes d'Information*, 3(6): 637–676.

[Cata96] Catania, B. (1996) 'Bottom-up Rewriting Methods for Datalog and Extensions: a Survey', PART 2, *Ingenierie des Systèmes d'Information*, 4(3): 287–331.

[Catt96] Cattel, R. (1996) *Object Database Standard: ODMG-93*, San Francisco: Morgan Kaufmann.

[Catt97] Cattel, R. (1997) *The Object Database Standard: ODMG 2.0*, San Francisco: Morgan-Kaufmann.

[Ceri89] Ceri, S., Gottlob, G. and Tanca, L. (1989) 'What You Always Wanted to Know About Datalog (And Never Dared to Ask)', *IEEE Transactions on Knowledge and Data Engineering* 1: 146–166.

[Ceri90] Ceri, S., Gottlob, G., and Tanca, L. (1990) *Logic Programming and Databases*, Springer-Verlag, Berlin (Germany).

[Ceri96] Ceri, S., Fraternali, P., Paraboschi, S. and Tanca, L. (1996) 'Active Rule Management in Chimera', in *Active Database Systems: Triggers and Rules for Advanced Systems* (J. Widom, S. Ceri, eds), Morgan Kaufmann Publishers, San Francisco (Calif).

[Ceri99] Ceri, S., Comai, S., Damiani, E., Fraternali, P. and Paraboschi, S. (1999) 'XML-GL: a Graphical Language for Querying and Restructuring XML Documents' in *Proc. of the International World Wide Web Conference*, Canada.

[Cham96] Chamberlin, D. (1996) *Using the New DB2 – IBMs Object-Relational Database System*, Morgan Kaufmann Publishers, San Francisco (Calif).

[ChanA82] Chan, A., Danberg, S., Fox, S., Lin, W.T.K., Nori, A. and Ries, D. (1982) 'Storage and Access Structures to Support a Semantic Data Model', in *Proc. of the 8th International Conference on Very Large Data Bases*, pp. 122–130.

[ChanB99] Chandrasekaran, B., Josephson, J.R. and Benjamins, V.R. (1999) 'Ontologies: What are they? Why do we need them?', *IEEE Intelligent Systems and Their Applications*, 14(1): 20–26, special issue on ontologies.

[ChanC73] Chang, C.C. and Keisler, H.J. (1973) *Model Theory*, North-Holland.

[Char91] Charniak, E. (1991) 'Bayesian Networks Without Tears', *AI Magazine* 12(4): 50–63.

[Chau98] Chaudhri, V.K., Farquher, A., Fikes, R., Karp. P.D. and Rice, J.P. (1988) *Open Knowledge Base Connectivity 2.0.3 – Proposed.* Menlo Park, CA: SRI International (http://www.ai.sri.com/~okbc/spec/okbc2.html).

[Chaw98] Chawathe, S.S., Abiteboul, S. and Widom, J. (1998) 'Representing and Querying Changes in Semistructured Data', in *Proc. of the International Conference on Data Engineering*, pp. 4–13.

[Chee96] Cheeseman, P. and Stutz, J. (1996) 'Bayesian Classification (Autoclass): Theory and Results', in U.M. Fayyad, G. Piatetsky-Shapiro, P. Smyth, and R. Uthutusamy, eds, *Advances in Knowledge Discovery and Data Mining*, AAAI/MIT Press.

[Chei92] Chein, M. and Mugnier, M.-L. (1992) 'Conceptual Graphs: Fundamental Notions', *Revue d'Intelligence Artificielle*, 6: 365–406.

[ChenA00] Cheng, A.M.K. and Chen, J.-R. (2000) 'Response Time Analysis of OPS5 Production Systems', *IEEE Transactions on Knowledge and Data Engineering*, 12: 391–409.

[ChenM96a] Chen, M.S., Han, J. and Yu, P.S. (1996) 'Data Mining: An Overview from a Database Perspective', *IEEE Transactions on Knowledge and Data Engineering*, 8(6): 866–883.

[ChenM96b] Chen, M.S., Park, J.-S. and Yu, P.S. (1996) 'Data Mining for Path Traversal Patterns in a Web Environment', in *Proc. of the 16th International Conference on Distributed Computing Systems.*

[ChenP76] Chen, P. (1976) 'The Entity-Relationship Model: Towards Unified View of Data', *ACM Trans. on Database Systems*, 1(1): 9–36.

[ChenW89] Chen, W. and Warren, D.S. (1989) 'C-logic of Complex Objects', in *Proc. of the Ninth ACM SIGACT-SIGMOD-SIGART Symposium on Principles of Database Systems*, May.

[ChenW91] Chen, W. (1991) 'Declarative Specification and Evaluation of Database Updates', in *Proc. of the Int. Conference on Deductive and Object-Oriented Databases*, Munich (Germany), December.

[ChenX98] Chen, X. and Petrounias, I. (1998) 'A Framework for Temporal Data Mining', in *LNCS 1460: Proc of the 9th International Conference on Database and Expert Systems Applications*, pp. 796–805, Springer Verlag.

[ChenX99] Cheng, X., Dong, G., Lau, T. and Su, J. (1999) 'Data Integration by Describing Sources with Constraint Databases', in *Proc. of the International Conference on Data Engineering*, pp. 636–643.

[Cheo96] Cheong, C. (1996) *Internet Agents*, New Riders – Macmillan Publishing.

[Cheu96] Cheung, D.W., Han, J., Ng, V. and Wong, C.Y. (1996) 'Maintenance of Discovered Association Rules in Large Databases: An Incremental Updating Technique', in *Proc. of the International Conference on Data Engineering.*

[Chin93] Chincor, N. and Hirschman, L. (1993) 'Evaluating Message Understanding Systems : An Analysis of the Third Message Understanding Conference (MUC-3)', *Computational Linguistics*, 19: 409–449.

[ChomJ95] Chomicki, J. and Kuper, G. (1995) 'Measuring Infinite Relations', in *Proc. of the Fourteenth ACM SIGACT-SIGMOD-SIGART Symposium on Principles of Database Systems*, San Jose (CA), May.

[ChomJ97] Chomichi, J. and Revesz, P.Z. (1997) 'Constraint-Based Interoperability of Spatiotemporal Databases', in *Proc. of the International Symposium on Large Spatial Databases*, pp. 142–161.

[ChomN57] Chomsky, N. (1957) *Syntactic Structures*, The Hague: Mouton.

[Chri86] Christodoulakis, S., Theodoridou, M., Ho, F., Papa, M. and Pathria, A. (1986) 'Multimedia Document Presentation, Information Extraction, and Document Formation in MINOS: a Model and a System', *IEEE Transactions on Office Information Systems*, 4(4): 345–383, October.

[ChuW92] Chu, W.W., Ieong, I.T., Taira, R.K. and Breant, C.M. (1992) 'A Temporal Evolutionary Object-Oriented Model and its Query Languages for Medical Image Management', in *Proc. of the International Conference on Very Large Data Bases.*

[Clan89] Clancey, W.J. (1989) 'The Knowledge Level Reinterpreted: Modeling how Systems Interact', *Machine Learning*, 4: 285–292.

[Clif87] Clifford, J. and Corker, A. (1987) 'The Historical Relational Model (HRDM) and Algebra based on Lifespan', in *Proc. of the International Conference on Data Engineering*, pp. 528–537.

[Cloc81] Clocksin, W.F. and Mellish, C.S. (1981) *Programming in PROLOG*, Berlin: Springer-Verlag.

[Clue89] Cluet, S. *et al* (1989) 'Reloop, an Algebra-Based Query Language for an Object-oriented Database System', *Proc. of First International Conference on Deductive and Object Oriented Databases (DOOD)*, Kyoto (Japan), Dec. 6–8.

[Codd79] Codd, E.F. (1979) 'Extending the Database Relational Model to Capture More Meaning', *Journal of the ACM*, 31: 743–760.

[CoheB89] Cohen, B. (1989) 'Merging Expert Systems and Databases', *AI Expert*, 4(2): 22–31.

[CoheP98] Cohen, P., Schrag, R., Jones, E., Pease, A., Lin, A., Starr, B., Gunning, D. and Burke, M. (1998) 'The DARPA High-Performance Knowledge Bases Project', *AI Magazine* 19(4): 25–49.

[Coll94] Collet, C., Coupaye, T. and Svensen, T. (1994) 'Naos: Efficient and Modular Reactive Capabilities in an Object-Oriented Database System', in *Proc. of the 20th International Conference on Very Large Data Bases (VLDB)*, Santiago (Chile), September 12–15.

[Colm73] Colmeraurer, A., Kanoui, H., Pasero, R. and Roussel, P. (1973) *Un Système de Communication Homme-machine en Français* (Rapport de recherche), Marseille: Groupe d'Intelligence Artificielle de l'Université Aix-Marseille II.

[Colm82] Colmeraurer, A. (1982) 'PROLOG and Infinite Trees', in *Logic Programming*, Clark, K.L. and Tärnlund, S.-A., eds, London: Academic Press.

[Cons94] Constantopoulos, P., Jarke, M., Mylopoulos, J. and Vassiliou, Y. (1994) *The Software Information Base: A Server for Reuse* (Report DKBS-TR-94-1), Toronto: Department of Computer Science of the University of Toronto.

[Coop87] Cooper, G.F. (1987) *Probabilistic Inference Using Belief Network is NP-hard* (Technical Report KSL-87-27), Stanford (CA): Medical Computer Science Group of Stanford University.

[Coop92] Cooper, G.F. and Herskovits, E. (1992) 'A Bayesian Method for the Induction of Probabilistic Networks from Data', *Machine Learning* 9: 309–347.

[Dahl66] Dahl, O.J. and Nygaard, K. (1966) 'SIMULA – An Algol-based Simulation Language', *Communications of the ACM*, 9(9).

[Dami90] Damiani, M. and Bottarelli, S. (1990) 'A Terminological Approach to Business Domain Modelling', in *Database and Expert Systems Applications – DEXA'90*, Tjoa, A.M. and Wagner, R., eds, Wien: Springer-Verlag.

[Dami92] Damiani, M., Randi, P., Bertino, E. and Spampinato, L. (1992) 'The AIMS Project: An Information Server Architecture Integrating Data, Knowledge, and Multimedia Information', in *Proc. of the First International Conference on Enterprise Integration Modelling Technology*, South Carolina, June.

[DasS92] Das, S.K. (1992) *Deductive Databases and Logic Programming*, Addison-Wesley International.

[DayW97] Day, W.B. (1997) 'Expressive Applications of Constraint Logic Programming', *Artificial Intelligence Review* 11: 427–452.

[DayY95] Day, Y.F., Dagtas, S., Iino, M., Khokhar, A. and Ghafoor, A. (1995) 'Object-Oriented Conceptual Modeling of Video Data', in *Proc. of the IEEE Conference on Data Engineering*, pp. 401–405.

[Daya96] Dayal, U., Buchmann, A. and Chakravarthy, S. (1996) 'The HiPAC Project', in *Active Database Systems: Triggers and Rules for Advanced Systems* (J. Widom, S. Ceri, eds), Morgan Kaufmann Publishers, San Francisco (Calif).

[Delc88] Delcambre, L.M.L. and Etheredge, J.N. (1988) 'A Self-Controlling Interpreter for the Relational Production Language', in *Proc. of the 1988 ACM SIGMOD International Conference on Management of Data*, Special issue of ACM SIGMOD Record, 17(3): 396–403.

[Delc89] Delcambre, L., Waramahaputi, J. and Etheredge, J. (1989) 'Pattern Match Reduction for the Relational Production Language in the USL MMDBS', *ACM Sigmod Record* 18(3): 59–67.

[Deli79] Deliyanni, A. and Kowalski, R.A. (1979) 'Logic and Semantic Networks', *Communications of the ACM* 22: 184–192.

[deMa88] de Maindreville, C. and Simon, E. (1988) 'Deciding Whether a Production Rule is Relational Computable', in *Proc. of Second International Conference on Database Theory.*

[Demp67] Dempster, A.P. (1967) 'Upper and Lower Probabilities Induced by a Multivalued Mapping', *Annals of Mathematical Statistics* 38: 419–449.

[Derr93] Derr, M., Morishita, S. and Phipps, G. (1993) 'Design and Implementation of the Glue-Nail Database System', in *Proc. of the ACM SIGMOD International Conference on Management of Data*, Washington (DC), May.

[Dert90] Derthick, M. (1990) *An Epistemological Level Interface for CYC* (Tech. Rep. ACT-CYC-084-90), Austin (TX): MCC.

[DeutP91] Deutsch, P.L. (1991) 'Object-oriented Software Technology', *IEEE Computer*, 24(9): 112–113.

[Deut99a] Deutsch, A., Fernandez, M. and Suciu, D. (1999) 'Storing Semistructured Data with STORED', in *Proc. of the ACM SIGMOD International Conference on Management of Data*, pp. 431–442.

[DeutA99b] Deutsch, A., Fernandez, M., Florescu, D., Levy, A. and Suciu, D. (1999) 'XML-QL – A Query Language for XML', in *Proc. of the Int. World Wide Web Conference*, Canada, http://www.w3.org/TR/NOTE-xml-ql/.

[Deux90] Deux, O. *et al* (1990) 'The story of O2', *IEEE Trans. on Knowledge and Data Engineering*, 2(1):, 91–108.

[Deva91] Devanbu, P.T. and Litman, D. (1991) 'Plan-Based Terminological Reasoning', in *Proc. of the Second International Conference On Principles of Knowledge Representation and Reasoning – KR'91*, San Francisco: Morgan Kaufmann.

[Deva93] Devanbu, P.T. (1993) 'Translating Description Logics to Information Server Queries', in *Proc. of the Second Conference on Information and Knowledge Management, CIKM'93*, New York: ACM.

[Diaz91] Diaz, O., Paton, N. and Gray, P. (1991) 'Rule Management in Object Oriented Databases: a Uniform Approach', in *Proc. of the 17th International Conference on Very Large Data Bases (VLDB)*, Barcelona (Spain), August 12–15.

[DiEu94] Di Eugenio, B. (1994) 'Action Representation for Interpreting Purpose Clauses in Natural Language Instructions', in *Proc. of the Fourth International Conference On Principles of Knowledge Representation and Reasoning – KR'94*, Doyle, J., Sandewall, E. and Torasso, P., eds, San Francisco: Morgan Kaufmann.

[Domi98] Domingue, J. (1998) 'Tadzebao and WebOnto: Discussing, Browsing, and Editing Ontologies on the Web', in *Proc. of the 11th Workshop on Knowledge Acquisition, Modelling and Management.*

[Doni91] Donini, F.M., Lenzerini, M., Nardi, D. and Nutt, W. (1991) 'Tractable Concept Languages', in *Proc. of the Twelfth International Joint Conference on Artificial Intelligence – IJCAI/91*, San Francisco: Morgan Kaufmann.

[Dow184] Dowling, W.P. and Gallier, J.H. (1984) 'Linear-Time Algorithms for Testing the Satisfiability of Propositional Horn Formulae', *Journal of Logic Programming* 1: 267–284.

{Doyl91] Doyle, J. and Patil, R.S. (1991) 'Two Theses of Knowledge Representation: Language Restrictions, Taxonomic Classification, and the Utility of Representation Services', *Artificial Intelligence* 48: 261–297.

[EDRE93] (1993) *EDR Electronic Dictionary Technical Guide*, Tokyo: Japan Electronic Dictionary Research Institute Ltd.

[Elka93] Elkan, C. and Greiner, R. (1993) 'Book Review of D.B. Lenat and R.V. Guha, *Building Large Knowledge-Based Systems: Representation and Inference in the Cyc Project*', in *The Commonsense Reviews*, Stefik, M.J. and Smoliar, S.W., eds, special section of *Artificial Intelligence*, 61: 41–52.

[Elli95a] Ellis, G. (1995) 'Compiling Conceptual Graph', *IEEE Transactions on Knowledge and Data Engineering*, 7: 68–81.

[Elli95b] Ellis, G., Levinson, R., Rich, W. and Sowa, J., eds (1995) *Applications, Implementation and Theory* (Lecture Notes in Artificial Intelligence 954), Berlin: Springer-Verlag.

[Esco95] Escobar-Molano, M.L. and Ghandeharizadeh, S. (1995) 'A Framework for Conceptualizing Structured Video', in *Proc. First Int. Workshop on Multimedia Information Systems*, pp. 95–110, Arlington, Virginia, September.

[Este97] Ester, M., Kriegel, H.-P. and Sander, J. (1997) 'Spatial Data Mining: A Database Approach', in Lecture Notes in Computer Sciences *1262: Proc. of the 5th International Symposium on Advances in Spatial Databases*, pp. 47–66, Springer Verlag.

[Ethe87] Etherington, D.W. (1987) 'Formalizing Nonmonotonic Reasoning Systems', *Artificial Intelligence* 31: 41–85.

[Ethe88] Etherington, D.W. (1988) *Reasoning with Incomplete Information*, San Francisco: Morgan Kaufmann.

[Etzi95] Etzioni, O. and Weld, D.S. (1995). 'Intelligent Agents on the Internet', *IEEE Expert*, 10(4): 45–49.

[Fahl79] Fahlman, S.E. (1979) *NETL: A System for Representing and Using Real-World Knowledge*, Cambridge (MA): The MIT Press.

[Falo95] Faloutsos, C. and Lin, K.-I. (1995) 'FastMap: A Fast Algorithm for Indexing, Data Mining and Visualisation of Traditional and Multimedia Datasets', in *Proc. of the ACM SIGMOD International Conference on Management of Data*, pp. 163–174.

[Farg86] Fargues, J., Landau, M.-C., Dugord, A. and Catach, L. (1986) 'Conceptual Graphs for Semantics and Knowledge Processing', *IBM Journal of Research and Development*, 30: 70–79.

[Farq97] Farquhar, A., Fikes, R. and Rice, J. (1997) 'The Ontolingua Server: A Tool for Collaborative Ontology Construction', *Int. Journal of Human-Computer Studies*, 46(6): 707–728.

[Fayy96] Fayyad, U.M., Piatetsky-Shapiro, G., Smyth, P. and Uthurusamy, R. (1996) *Advances in Knowledge Discovery and Data Mining*, AAAI Press/The MIT Press.

[Feig94] Feigenbaum, E.A., Friedland, P.E., Johnson, B.B., Penny Nii, H., Schorr, H., Shrobe, H. and Engelmore, R.S. (1994) 'Knowledge-Based Systems Research and Applications in Japan, 1992', *AI Magazine*, 15(2): 29–43.

[Fell98] Fellbaum, C., ed. (1998) *WordNet, An Electronic Lexical Database*, Cambridge (MA): The MIT Press.

[Fens98] Fensel, D., Decker, S., Erdmann, M. and Studer, R. (1998) 'Ontobrocker: Or How to Enable Intelligent Access to the WWW' in *Proc. of the 11th Banff*

Knowledge Acquisition for Knowledge Based systems Workshop, KAW'98, Calgary: Department of Computer Science of the University.

[Fike85] Fikes, R. and Kehler, T. (1985) 'The Role of Frame-Based Representations in Reasoning', *Communications of the ACM* 28: 904–920.

[Fini97] Finin, T., Labou, Y. and Mayfield, J. (1997) 'KQML as an Agent Communication Language', in J. Bradshaw, ed., *Software Agents*, AAAI/MIT Press, Menlo Park, CA.

[Fish87] Fisher, D. (1987) 'Improving Inference through Conceptual Clustering', in *Proc. of the 1987 AAA Conference.*

[Ford93] Ford, K.M. and Bradshaw, J.M., eds (1993) *Knowledge Acquisition as Modeling*, New York: Wiley.

[Forg82] Forgy, C.L. (1982) 'Rete: A Fast Algorithm for the Many Pattern/Many Object Match Problem', *Artificial Intelligence* 19: 17–37.

[Forg95] Forgy, C.L. (1995) 'The OPS Languages: An Historical Overview', *PC AI* 9(5), 16–21.

Frenkel, K.A. (1990) 'The European Community and Information Technology', Communications of the ACM, 33: 404–410.

[Frey98] Freytag, B., Decker, H., Kifer, M. and Voronkov, A., eds (1998) *Transactions and Change in Logic Databases*, Lecture Notes in Computer Science 1472.

[Frid97] Fridman Noy, N. and Hafner, C.D. (1997) 'The State of the Art in Ontology Design – A Survey and Comparative Review', *AI Magazine*, 18(3): 53–74.

[Frid00] Fridman Noy, N., Ferguson, R.W. and Musen, M.A. (2000) 'The Knowledge Model of Protégé – 2000: Combining Interoperability and Flexibility' in *Proc. of the 12th EKAW Conference, EKAW' 2000*. Berlin: Springer-Verleg.

[Gadi88a] Gadia, S.K. (1988) 'A Homogeneous Relational Model for a Temporal Database', *ACM Trans. on Database Systems*, 13(4): 418–448.

[Gadi88b] Gadia, S.K. and Yeung, C.S. (1988) 'A Generalized Model for a Relational Temporal Database', in *Proc. of the ACM SIGMOD International Conference on Management of Data*, pp. 251–259.

[Gaed95] Gaede, V. and Guenther, O. (1995) 'Constraint-based Query Optimization and Processing', in *Constraint Databases and their Applications*, Lecture Notes in Computer Science 1034, Springer-Verlag.

[Gall83] Gallaire, H. and Lasserre, C. (1983) 'Metalevel Control for Logic Programming', in *Logic Programming*, Clark, K.L. and Tärnlund, S.-A., eds, London: Academic Press.

[Garc97] Garcia-Molina, H., Papakonstantinou, Y., Quass, D., Rajaraman, A., Sagiv, Y., Ullman, J., Vassalos, V. and Widom, J. (1997) 'The TSIMMIS Approach to Mediation: Data Models and Languages', *Journal of Intelligent Information Systems*, 8: 117–132.

[Gare79] Garey, M.R. and Johnson, D.S. (1979) *Computers and Intractability. A Guide to the Theory of NP-Completeness*, San Francisco: Freeman and Co.

[Gatz92] Gatziu, S. and Dittrich, K. (1992) 'SAMOS: an Active Object-Oriented Database System', *IEEE Data Engineering Bulletin*, special issue on active databases, 15(4): 23–26, December.

[Gauc96] Gauch, S. and Wang, G. (1996) 'Information Fusion with ProFusion' in *Proc. of the World Conference of the Web Society (WebNet'96).*

[Geha96] Gehani, N. and Jagadish, H.V. (1996) 'Active Database Facilities in Ode', in *Active Database Systems: Triggers and Rules for Advanced Systems* (J.Widom, S. Ceri, eds), Morgan Kaufmann Publishers, San Francisco (Calif).

[Gene92] Genesereth, M.R. and Fikes, R.E., eds (1992) *Knowledge Interchange Format – Version 3.0 Reference Manual* (Report Logic-92-1), Stanford (CA): Computer Science Department of Stanford University.

[Gene98] Genesereth, M.R. and Fikes, R.E., eds (1998) *Knowledge Interchange Format (KIF) – Working Draft of Proposed American National Standard* (NCITS – T2/98-004), Stanford (CA): Computer Science Department of Stanford University.

Genesereth, M. and Ketchpel, S. (1994) 'Software Agents', *Communications of the ACM*, 37(7): 48–53.

[Ghan93] Ghandeharizadeh, S. *et al* (1993) 'On Implementing a Language for Specifying Active Database Execution Models', *Proceedings of the 19th International Conference on Very Large Data Bases (VLDB)*, Dublin (Ireland), August 24–27; Goldberg, A. and Robson, D. (1983) *Smalltalk-80: the Language and its Implementation*, Addison-Wesley.

[Gibb91] Gibbs, S. (1991) 'Composite Multimedia and Active Objects' in *Proc. Int. Conf. on Object-Oriented Programming: Systems, Languages, and Applications*, October.

[Gibb93] Gibbs, S., Breiteneder, C. and Tsichritzis, D. (1993) 'Audio/Video Databases: an Object-Oriented Approach' in *Proc. 9th International Conference on Data Engineering*, pp. 381–390.

[GoldR99] Goldman, R., McHigh, J. and Widom, J. (1999) 'From Semistructured Data to XML: Migrating the Lore Data Model and Query Language' in *Proc. of the International Workshop on World Wide Web and Databases (WebDB)*, pp. 25–30.

[Gome98] Gomez-Perez, A. (1998) 'Knowledge Sharing and Reuse' in *The Handbook of Applied Expert Systems*, Liebowitz, J., ed., Boca Raton (FL): CRC Press LCC.

[Grah90] Graham, P. (1990) 'Using the RETE Algorithm', *AI Expert* 5(12): 46–51.

[Grei80] Greiner, R. and Lenat, D.B. (1980) 'RLL: A Representation Language Language' in *Proc. of the First National Conference on Artificial Intelligence – AAAI/80*, Cambridge (MA): AAAI Press/MIT Press.

[Grav97] Gravano, L., Chang, C.-C. K., Garcia-Molina, H. and Paepcke, A. (1997) 'STARTS: Stanford Proposal for Internet Metasearching' in *Proc. of the ACM International Conference On Management of Data (SIGMOD'97).*

[Grav98] Gravano, L. and Papakonstantinou, Y. (1998) 'Mediating and Metasearching on the Internet' in *Bulletin of the IEEE Computer Society Technical Committee on Data Engineering.*

[Grec90] Greco, S., Leone, N. and Rullo, P. (1990) 'COMPLEX: an Object-Oriented Logic Programming System', *IEEE Transactions on Knowledge and Data Engineering*, 4(2): 344–359.

[Grub92] Gruber, T.R. (1992) 'ONTOLINGUA: A Mechanism to Support Portable Ontologies; Knowledge Systems Laboratory', KSL-91-66, November.

[Grub93] Gruber, T.R. (1993) 'A Translation Approach to Portable Ontology Specifications', *Knowledge Acquisition*, 5: 199–220.

[Grum94] Grumbach, S. and Su, J. (1994) 'Finitely Representable Databases' in *Proc. of the 13th ACM SIGACT-SIGMOD-SIGART Symposium on Principles of Database Systems*, Minneapolis (MN), May.

[Grum98] Grumbach, S., Rigaux, P. and Segoufin, L. (1998) 'The DEDALE System for Complex Spatial Queries' in *Proc. of the ACM SIGMOD International Conference on Management of Data*, pp. 213–224.

[Grun95] Gruninger, M. and Fox, M. (1995) 'Methodology for the design and evaluation of ontologies' in *Proc. of the Workshop on Basic Ontological Issues in Knowledge Sharing*, held in conjunction with IJCAI'95.

[Guar94] Guarino, N., Carrara, M. and Giaretta, P. (1994) 'An Ontology of Meta-Level Categories', in *Proc. of the Fourth International Conference on Principles of Knowledge Representation and Reasoning (KR'94)*, Doyle, J., Sandewall, E. and Torasso, P., eds, San Francisco: Morgan Kaufmann.

Guarino, N. and Giaretta, P. (1995) 'Ontologies and Knowledge Bases: Towards a Terminological Clarification' in N.J.I. Mars, ed., *Towards Very Large Knowledge Bases: Knowledge Building & Knowledge Sharing*, pp. 25–32. IOS Press, Amsterdam, NL.

[Guha90a] Guha, R.V. and Lenat, D.B. (1990) 'Cyc: A Midterm Report', *AI Magazine*, 11(3): 32–59.

[Guha90b] Guha, R.V. (1990) *The Representation of Defaults in Cyc* (Tech. Rep. ACT-CYC-083-90), Austin (TX): MCC.

[Guha91a] Guha, R.V. and Lenat, D.B. (1991) *Comparing Cyc to other AI Systems* (Report ACT-CYC407-91), Austin (TX): MCC.

[Guha91b] Guha, R.V. (1991) *Contexts: A Formalization and Applications* (Tech. Rep. ACT-CYC-423-91), Austin (TX): MCC.

[Guha93] Guha, R.V. and Lenat, D.B. (1993) 'Re: CycLing Paper Reviews', in *The Commonsense Reviews*, Stefik, M.J. and Smoliar, S.W., eds, special section of *Artificial Intelligence*, 61: 149–174.

[Guha94] Guha, R.V. and Lenat, D.B. (1994) 'Enabling Agents to Work Together', *Communications of the ACM*, 37(7): 127–142.

[Gyss91] Gyssens, M. and Gucht, D.V. (1991) 'A Comparison between Algebraic Query Languages for Flat and Nested Databases', *Theoretical Computer Science*, 87: 263–286.

[Haas90] Haas, L.M. *et al* (1990) 'Starburst Mid-Flight: as the Dust Clears', *IEEE Transactions on Knowledge and Data Engineering*, 2(1): 143–160.

[Hall97] Hall, C. (1997) 'Data Mining Tools', *Data Management Strategies*, Cutter Information Corp.

[Hamm81] Hammer, M. and McLeod, D. (1981) 'Database Description with SDM: A Semantic Database Model', *ACM Trans. on Database Systems*, 6(3): 351–386.

[HanJ95] Han, J. and Fu, Y. (1995) 'Discovery of Multiple-Level Association Rules from Large Databases, in *Proc. of the 21st International Conference on Very Large Data Bases*.

[HanJ97] Han, J., Koperski, K. and Stefanovic, N. (1997) 'GeoMiner: A System Prototype for Spatial Data Mining' in *Proc. of the ACM SIGMOD International Conference on Management of Data*, pp. 553–556.

[HansM89] Hansen, M.R., Hansen, B.S., Lucas, P. and van Emde Boas, P. (1989) 'Integrating Relational Databases and Constraint Languages', *Computer Languages*, 14(2): 63–82.

[HansE89] Hanson, E.N. (1989) 'An Initial Report on the Design of ARIEL', *ACM Sigmod Record* 18(3): 12–19.

[Hans92] Hanson, E.N. (1992) 'Rule Condition Testing and Action Execution in Ariel', in *Proc. of the 1992 ACM SIGMOD International Conference on Management of Data*, San Diego (Calif), June 2–5.

[Haut92] Hautamäki, A (1992) 'A Conceptual Space Approach to Semantic Networks', in *Semantic Networks in Artificial Intelligence*, Lehmann, F., ed., Oxford: Pergamon Press.

[Harr84] Harris, L.R. (1984) 'Experience with INTELLECT: Artificial Intelligence Technology Transfer', *The AI Magazine*, 5(2): 43–50.

[Haye79] Hayes, P.J. (1979) 'The Logic of Frames' in *Frame Conceptions and Text Understanding*, Metzing, D., ed., Berlin: de Gruyter.

[Heck95] Heckerman, D., Geiger, D. and Chickering, D.M. (1995) 'Learning Bayesian Networks: The Combination of Knowledge and Statistical Data', *Machine Learning* 20: 197–243.

[Heck96] Heckerman, D. (1996) *A Tutorial on Learning with Bayesian Networks – Revised Version* (Technical Report MSR-TR-95-66), Redmond (WA): Advanced Technology Division of Microsoft Corporation.

[Hefl99a] Heflin, J., Hendler, J. and Luke, S. (1999) *SHOE: A Knowledge Representation Language for Internet Applications* (Tech. Rep. CS-TR-4078), College Park (MA): Department of Computer Science of the University of Maryland.

[Hefl99b] Heflin, J., Hendler, J. and Luke, S. (1999) 'Coping with Changing Ontologies in a Distributed Environment', in *Proc. of the AAAI-99 Workshop on Ontology Management*, Menlo Park (CA): AAAI.

[HeinJ94] Heinsohn, J., Kudenko, D., Nebel, B. and Profitlich, H-J.(1994) 'An Empirical Analysis of Terminological Representation Systems', *Artificial Intelligence* 68: 367–397.

[HeinN87] Heintze, N.C., Jaffar, J., Lassez, C. *et al* (1987) 'Constraint Logic Programming: a Reader' in *Proc. Fourth IEEE Symposium on Logic Programming*, September.

[Herz91] Herzog, O. and Rollinger, C.-R., eds (1991) *Text Understanding in LILOG – Integrating Computational Linguistics and Artificial Intelligence*, Berlin: Springer-Verlag.

[HillG91] Hillebrand, G.G., Kanellakis, P.C., Mairson, H.G. and Vardi, M.Y. (1991) 'Tools for Datalog Boundedness' in *Proc. of the Tenth ACM SIGACT-SIGMOD-SIGART Symposium on Principles of Database Systems*, Denver (CO), May.

[HillP94] Hill, P. and Lloyd, J.W. (1994) *The Godel Programming Language*, Cambridge, MA: MIT Press.

[Hopp93] Hoppe, T., Kindermann, C., Quantz, J.J., Schmiedel, A. and Fischer, M. (1993) *BACK V5 Tutorial and Manual* (KIT Report 100), Berlin: Department of Computer Science of the Technische Universität.

[Howa87] Howard, H.C. and Rehak, D.R. (1987) 'KADBASE – A Prototype Expert System-Database Interface for Integrating CAE Environments' in *Proc. of the Sixth National Conference on Artificial Intelligence* – AAAI/87, Cambridge (MA): AAAI Press/MIT Press.

[Howa89] Howard, H.C. and Rehak, D.R. (1989) 'KADBASE: Interfacing Expert Systems with Databases', *IEEE Expert*, 4(3): 65–76.

[Hull87] Hull, R. and King, R. (1987) 'Semantic Database Modeling: Survey, Applications, and Research Issues', *ACM Computing Surveys*, 19, 201–260.

[Hust94] Hustadt, U. (1994) 'Do We Need the Closed-World Assumption in Knowledge Representation?' in *Working Notes of the KRDB'94 Workshop, Reasoning about Structured Objects: Knowledge Representation Meets Databases* (Document D-94-11), Baader, F., Buchheit, M., Jeusfeld, M.A. and Nutt, W., eds. Saarbrücken: Deutsches Forschungszentrum für Künstliche Intelligenz GmbH.

[Hwan93] Hwang, C.H. and Schubert, L.K. (1993) 'Meeting the Interlocking Needs of LF-Computation, Deindexing and Inference: An Organic Approach to General NLU', in *Proc. of the Thirteenth International Joint Conference on Artificial Intelligence – IJCAI/93*, San Francisco: Morgan Kaufmann.

[IBMC99a] IBM Corp. (1999) *DB2 Universal Database – XML Extender Administration and Programming – Version 7.*

[IBMC99b] IBM Corp. (1999) *Technical Guide,* http://www-4.IBM Corp., 1999.com/software/db2/ extenders/xmlext/library.html.

[IdeN98] Ide, N., Greenstein, D. and Vossen, P., eds (1998) *Special Issue on EuroWordNet- Computers and the Humanities*, 32(2-3).

[IEEE81] IEEE Comp. Society. (1981) 'Special Issue on Distributed Problem Solving', *IEEE Trans. On Systems, Man, and Cybernetics*, 11(1).

[IEEE91] IEEE Comp. Society. (1991) 'Special Issue on Distributed Problem Solving', *IEEE Trans. On Systems, Man, and Cybernetics*, 21(6).

[IllU] Illustra Information Technologies, Oakland (Calif), *Illustra User's Guide*, Release 2.1.

[Ishi93] Ishikawa, H., Suzuki, F., Kozakura, F., Makinouchi, A., Miyagishima, M., Aoshima, M., Izumida, Y. and Yamane, Y. (1993) 'The Model, Language and Implementation of an Object-Oriented Multimedia Knowledge Base Management System', *ACM Transactions on Database Systems*, 18: 1–50.

[Iwan93] Iwanska, L. (1993) 'Logical Reasoning in Natural Language: It Is All about Knowledge', *Minds and Machines*, 3: 475–510.

[Iwan94] Iwanska, L. (1994) 'Talking about Time: Temporal Reasoning as A Problem of Natural Language' in *Knowledge Representation for Natural Language Processing in Implemented Systems – Papers from the 1994 Fall Symposium*, Ali, S., ed., Menlo Park (CA): AAAI Press.

[Jack90] Jackendoff, R. (1990) *Semantic Structures*, Cambridge (MA): The MIT Press.

[Jaco92] Jacobson, (1992) *Object-Oriented Software Engineering – A Use Case Driven Approach*, Addison-Wesley.

[Jacq99] Jacqmin, S. and Zarri, G.P. (1999) *Preliminary Specifications of the Template Manager* (CONCERTO NRC-TR-4). Paris: CNRS-CAMS.

[Jaff94] Jaffar, J. and Maher, M.J. (1994) 'Constraint Logic Programming: A Survey', *Journal of Logic Programming* 19(20): 503–581.

[Jain88] Jain, A.K. and Dubes, R.C. (1988) *Algorithms for Clustering Data*, Prentice Hall.

Japan Electronic Dictionary Research Institute Ltd. (1993) *EDR Electronic Dictionary Technical Guide*, Tokyo.

[Jark84a] Jarke, M. and Vassiliou, Y. (1984) 'Coupling Expert Systems with Database Management Systems', in *Artificial Intelligence Applications For Business*, Reitman, W., ed., Norwood (NJ): Ablex.

[Jark84b] Jarke, M., Clifford, J. and Vassiliou, Y. (1984) 'An Optimizing PROLOG Front-End to a Relational Query system', in *Proc. of SIGMOD'84*, Yormark, B., ed., special issue of ACM SIGMOD Record, 14(2): 296–306.

Jeffcoate, J. and Guilfoyle, C. (1991) *Databases for Objects: the Market Opportunity*, Ovum Ltd.

[Jenn96] Jennings, N.R. and Woldridge, M. (1996) 'Software Agents', *IEEE Review*, pp. 17–20, January.

[Jens91] Jensen, C.S., Mark, L. and Roussopoulos, N. (1991) 'Incremental Implementation Model for Relational Databases with Transaction Time', *IEEE Trans. on Knowledge and Data Engineering*, 3(4): 461–473.

[Jens94] Jensen, C.S., Soo, M.D. and Snodgrass, R.T. (1994) 'Unifying Temporal Models via a Conceptual Model', *Information Systems*, 19(7): 513–547.

[Kaba90] Kabanza, F., Stevenne, J.M. and Wolper, P. (1990) 'Handling Infinite Temporal Data' in *Proc. of the Ninth ACM SIGACT-SIGMOD-SIGART Symposium on Principles of Database Systems*, Nashville (TN), April.

[Kacz86] Kaczmarek, T.S., Bates, R. and Robins, G. (1986) 'Recent Developments in NIKL', in *Proc. of the Fifth National Conference on Artificial Intelligence – AAAI/86*, Cambridge (MA): MIT Press/AAAI Press.

[Kafe92] Kafer, W. and Schoning, H. (1992) 'Realizing a Temporal Complex-Object Data Model' in *Proc. of the ACM SIGMOD International Conference on Management of Data*, pp. 266–275.

[Kand97] Kandzia, P.-T. and Schlepphorst, C. (1997) 'DOOD and DL – Do We Need an Integration?' in *Intelligent Access to Heterogeneous Information – Proceedings of the 4th KRDB Workshop*, Baader, F., Jeusfeld, M.A. and Nutt, W., eds, Aachen: Department of Computer Science at the University of Technology (RWTH).

[Kane90] Kanellakis, P.C., Kuper, G.M. and Revesz, P.Z. (1990) 'Constraint Query Languages' in *Proc. of the Ninth ACM SIGACT-SIGMOD-SIGART Symposium on Principles of Database Systems*, Nashville (TN), April.

[Kane94] Kanellakis, P.C. and Goldin, D. (1994) 'Constraint Programming and Database Query Languages', Technical Report CS-94-31, Brown University, Providence (RI).

[Kane95] Kanellakis, P.C. (1995) *Constraint Programming and Database Languages: a Tutorial* in *Proc. of the Fourteenth ACM SIGACT-SIGMOD-SIGART Symposium on Principles of Database Systems*, San Jose (CA) May.

[Kapp94] Kappel, G., Rausch-Schott, S. and Retschitzegger, W. (1994) 'Beyond Coupling Modes: Implementing Active Concepts on Top of a Commercial OODBMS', *Proc. of International Symposium on Object-Oriented Methodologies and Systems*, Palermo (Italy), September 22–24; Lecture Notes in Computer Science N.858 (E. Bertino, and S. Urban, eds).

[Karp93] Karp, P.D. (1993) 'A Qualitative Biochemistry and Its Application to the Regulation of the Trytophan Operon' in L. Hunter, ed. *Artificial and Molecular Biology*, pp. 289–325, AAAI Press.

[Karp95] Karp, P.D., Myers, K.L. and Gruber, T. (1995) 'The Generic Frame Protocol' in *Proceedings of the Fourteenth International Joint Conference on Artificial Intelligence – IJCAI/95*, San Francisco: Morgan Kaufmann.

[Kess96] Kessel, T., Schlick, M., Speiser, H.-M., Brinkschulte, U. and Vogelsang, H. (1996) 'C3L++: Implementing a Description Logics System on Top of an Object-Oriented Database System' in *Knowledge Representation Meets Databases – Proceedings of the 3rd KRDB Workshop*, Baader, F., Buchheit, M., Jeusfeld, M.A. and Nutt, W., eds, Aachen: Department of Computer Science at the University of Technology (RWTH).

[Khos91] Khoshafian, S. (1991) 'Modelling with Object-Oriented Databases', *AI Expert*, 6(10): 27–33.

[Kier90] Kiernan, G., de Maindreville, C. and Simon, E. (1990) 'Making Deductive Databases a Practical Technology: A Step Forward', in *Proc. of the 1990 ACM SIGMOD International Conference on Management of Data*, Atlantic City (NJ), May 23–25.

[Kife89] Kifer, M. and Wu, J. (1989) 'A Logic for Object-Oriented Logic Programming (Maier's O-logic Revisited)' in *Proc. of the Eighth ACM SIGACT-SIGMOD-SIGART Symposium on Principles of Database Systems*, May.

[Kife95] Kifer, M., Lausen, G. and Wu, J. (1995) 'Logical Foundations of Object-Oriented and Frame-Based Languages', *Journal of the ACM* 42: 741–843.

[KimW90a] Kim, W. (1990) *Introduction to Object-Oriented Databases*, The MIT Press, Cambridge (Mass).

[KimW94] Kim, W. (1994) 'UniSQL/X Unified Relational and Object-Oriented Database System', in *Proc. of ACM-SIGMOD Conference on Management of Data*, Minneapolis (Minn.), May 24–27.

[KimW84] Kim, W. *et al* (1984) 'A Transaction Mechanism for Engineering Design Databases', in *Proc. of the International Conference on Very Large Databases*, Singapore, August.

[KimW89a] Kim, W., Ballou, N., Chou, H.T., Garza, J. and Woelk, D. (1989) 'Features of the ORION object-oriented database system' in *Object-Oriented Concepts, Databases*, and Applications, W. Kim, and F. Lochovsky (eds) Addison-Wesley, 251–282.

[KimW89b] Kim, W., Bertino, E. and Garza, J.F. (1989) 'Composite objects revisited', *Proc. of ACM-SIGMOD Conference on Management of Data*, Portland (Oreg.), May 31–June 2.

[KimW90b] Kim, W., Garza, J.F., Ballou, N. and Woelk, D. (1990) 'Architecture of the Orion Next-Generation Database System', *IEEE Trans. on Knowledge and Data Engineering*, 2(1): 109–124.

[Kimb96] Kimball, R. (1996) *The Data Warehouse Toolkit*, John Wiley.

[Kirk95] Kirk, T., Levy, A.Y., Sagiv, Y. and Srivastava, D. (1995) 'The Information Manifold' in *Proc. of the AAAI Spring Symposium Series.*

[Klin91] Klinker, G., Bhola, C., Dallemagne, G., Marques, D. and McDermott, J. (1997) 'Usable and Reusable Programming Constructs', *Knowledge Acquisition*, 3: 117–136.

[Knig89] Knight, K. (1989) 'Unification: A Multidisciplinary Survey', *ACM Computing Surveys* 21: 93–124.

[Kola88] Kolaitis, P. and Papadimitriou, C. (1988) 'Why Not Negation by Fixpoint?' in *Proc. of the Seventh ACM SIGACT-SIGMOD-SIGART Symposium on Principles of Database Systems*, Austin (TX), May.

[Kolo92] Kolodner, J.L. (1992) 'An Introduction to Case-Based Reasoning', *Artificial Intelligence Review*, 6: 3–34.

[Koub94] Koubarakis, M. (1994) 'Foundations of Indefinite Constraint Databases' in *Proc. of Second International Workshop on Principles and Practice of Constraint Programming*, Lecture Notes in Computer Science 874, Springer-Verlag.

[Kowa79] Kowalski, R.A. (1979) 'Algorithm = Logic + Control', *Communications of the ACM* 22: 424–436.

[Kowa82] Kowalski, R.A. (1982) 'Logic as a Computer Language', in *Logic Programming*, Clark, K.L. and Tärnlund, S.-A., eds, London: Academic Press.

[Kram91] Kramer, B.M., Chaudhri, V.K., Koubarakis, M., Topaloglou, T., Wang, H. and Mylopoulos, J. (1991) 'Implementing TELOS', *ACM SIGART Bulletin*, 2(3): 77–83.

[Kris89] Krishnamurty, R., Naqvi, S. and Zaniolo, C. (1989) 'Database Transactions in LDL' in *Proc. of The North American Conference on Logic Programming.*

[Krus91] Kruse, R., Schwecke, E. and Heinsohn, J. (1991) *Uncertainty and Vagueness in Knowledge-Based Systems*, Berlin: Springer-Verlag.

[Kupe00] Kuper, G.M., Libkin, L., and Paredaens, J. (2000) *Constraint Databases*, Springer Verlag.

[Labo97] Labou, Y. and Finin, T. (1997) 'Semantics and Conversations for an Agent Communication Language' in Huhns and Singh, ed, *Readings in Agents.* Morgan Kaufmann.

[LassJ90] Lassez, J.L. (1990) 'Querying Constraints' in *Proc. of the Ninth ACM SIGACT-SIGMOD-SIGART Symposium on Principles of Database Systems*, Nashville (TN), April.

[Lass99] Lassila, O. and Swick, R. (1999) *Resource Description Framework (RDF) Model and Syntax Specification*, Technical report, W3C.

[Lehm92] Lehmann, F., ed. (1992) *Semantic Networks in Artificial Intelligence*, Oxford: Pergamon Press.

[Lena83] Lenat, D.B. (1983) 'EURISKO: A Program That Learns New Heuristics and Domain Concepts', *Artificial Intelligence*, 21: 61–98.

[Lena95] Lenat, D.B. (1995) 'Steps to Sharing Knowledge', in *Towards Very Large Knowledge Bases*, Mars, N.J.I., ed., Amsterdam: IOS Press.

[Lena98] Lenat, D.B. (1998) *The Dimensions of Context-Space*, Austin: Cycorp.

[Lena84] Lenat, D.B. and Brown, J.S. (1984) 'Why AM and EURISKO Appear to Work', *Artificial Intelligence*, 23: 269–294.

[Lena86] Lenat, D.B., Prakash, M. and Shepherd, M. (1986) 'CYC: Using Common Sense Knowledge to Overcome Brittleness and Knowledge Acquisition Bottlenecks', *AI Magazine*, 6(4): 65–85.

[Lena90a] Lenat, D.B., Guha, R.V., Pittman, K., Pratt, D. and Shepherd, M. (1990) 'CYC: Toward Programs With Common Sense', *Communications of the ACM*, 33(8): 30–49.

[Lena90b] Lenat, D.B. and Guha, R.V. (1990) *Building Large Knowledge Based Systems*, Reading (MA): Addison-Wesley.

[Lena91a] Lenat, D.B. and Feigenbaum, E.A. (1991) 'On the Threshold of Knowledge', *Artificial Intelligence*, 47: 185–230.

[Lena91b] Lenat, D.B. and Feigenbaum, E.A. (1991) 'Reply to Brian Smith', *Artificial Intelligence*, 47: 231–250.

[Lena95b] Lenat, D.B., Miller, G.A. and Yokoi, T. (1995) 'CYC, WordNet, and EDR: Critiques and Responses', *Communications of the ACM*, 38(11), 45–48.

[Less81] Lesser, V. and Corkill, D.D. (1981) 'Functionally-Accurate Cooperative Distributed Systems', *IEEE Trans. on Systems, Man, and Cybernetics*, Special Issue on Distributed Problem Solving, 11(1): 81–96.

[Less99] Lesser, V.R. (1999) 'Cooperative Multiagent Systems: A Personal View of the State of the Art', *IEEE Trans. on Knowledge and Data Engineering*, 11(1): 133–142.

[Leun88] Leung, Y.Y. and Lee, D.L. (1988) 'Logic Approaches for Deductive Databases', *IEEE Expert*, 3(4): 64–75.

[Leve84] Levesque, H.J. (1984) 'Foundations of a Functional Approach to Knowledge Representation', *Artificial Intelligence* 23: 155–212.

[Leve85] Levesque, H.J. and Brachman, R.J. (1985) 'A Fundamental Tradeoff in Knowledge Representation and Reasoning (Revised Version)', in *Readings in Knowledge Representation*, Brachman, R.J. and Levesque, H.J., eds, San Francisco: Morgan Kaufmann.

[Leve86] Levesque, H.J. and Brachman, R.J. (1986) 'Knowledge Level Interfaces to Information Systems', in *On Knowledge Base Management Systems*, Brodie, M. and Mylopoulos, J., eds, Berlin: Springer-Verlag.

[Leve87] Levesque, H.J. and Brachman, R.J. (1987) 'Expressiveness and Tractability in Knowledge Representation and Reasoning', *Computational Intelligence* 3: 78–93.

[Leve88] Levesque, H.J. (1988) 'Logic and the Complexity of Reasoning', *Journal of Philosophical Logic*, 17: 355–389.

[Levi92] Levinson, R.A. (1992) 'Pattern Associativity and the Retrieval of Semantic Networks', *Computers and Mathematics with Applications*, 23: 573–600.

[Levy93] Levy, A.Y., Mumick, I.S., Sagiv, Y. and Smueli, O. (1993) 'Equivalence, Query-Reachability, and Satisfiability in Datalog Extensions' in *Proc. of the Tenth ACM SIGACT-SIGMOD-SIGART Symposium on Principles of Database Systems*, Washington (DC), May 1993.

[Levy96] Levy, A.Y. and Rousset, M.-C. (1996) 'The Limits on Combining Recursive Horn Rules with Description Logics', in *Proc. of the Thirteenth National Conference on Artificial Intelligence – AAAI/96*, Cambridge (MA): AAAI Press/MIT Press.

[Lieu96] Lieuwen, D., Gehani, N. and Arlein, R. (1996) 'The Ode Active Database: Trigger Semantics and Implementation', in *Proc. Twelfth IEEE International Conference on Data Engineering*, New Orleans (LA), February.

[Lind95] Lindsay, B. (1995) 'DB2 Comon Server: Technology, Progress and Directions' in *Proc. of the 21st International Conference on Very Large Data Bases*, Zurich (Switzerland), August.

[Lloy87] Lloyd, J.W. (1987) *Foundations of Logic Programming*, 2nd edition, New York: Springer-Verlag.

[Lome89] Lomet, D. and Salzberg, B. (1989) 'Access Methods for Multiversion Data' in *Proc. of the ACM SIGMOD International Conference on Management of Data*, pp. 315–324.

[Lore88] Lorentzos, N.A. and Johnson, R.G. (1988) 'Extending Relational Algebra to Manipulate Temporal Data', *Information Systems*, 13(3): 289–296.

[LouY91] Lou, Y. and Ozsoyoglu, Z.M. (1991) 'LLO: an Object-Oriented Deductive Language with Methods and Methods Inheritance' in *Proc. of the ACM SIGMOD International Conference on Management of Data*, Denver (CO), May.

[Luko95] Lukose, D., Mineau, G., Mugnier, M.-L., Möller, J.-U., Martin, P., Kremer, R. and Zarri, G.P. (1995) 'Conceptual Structures for Knowledge Engineering and Knowledge Modelling', in *Supplementary Proceedings of the 3rd International Conference on Conceptual Structures: Applications, Implementation and Theory*, Ellis, G., Levinson, R., Rich, W. and Sowa, J., eds, Santa Cruz (CA): Department of Computer and Information Sciences of the University of California.

[LumV84] Lum, V., Dadam, P., Erbe, R., Guenauer, J., Pistor, P., Walch, G., Werner, H. and Woodfill, J. (1984) 'Designing DBMS Support for the Temporal Dimension' in *Proc. of the ACM SIGMOD International Conference on Management of Data*, pp. 115–130.

[MacG87] MacGregor, R.M. and Bates, R. (1987) *The LOOM Knowledge Representation Language* (Technical Report ISI/RS-87-188), Marina del Rey (CA): USC/Information Science Institute.

[MacG91a] MacGregor, R.M. (1991) Inside the LOOM Classifier', *SIGART Bulletin*, 2(3): 70–76.

[MacG91b] MacGregor, R.M. (1991) 'The Evolving Technology of Classification-Based Knowledge Representation Systems', in *Principles of Semantic Networks*, Sowa, J.F., ed., San Francisco: Morgan Kaufmann.

[Maie86] Maier, D. (1986) 'A Logic for Objects' in *Proc. of Workshop on Foundation of Deductive Databases and Logic Programming.*

[Maki77] Makinouchi, A. (1977) 'A Consideration of Normal Form of Not-Necessarily-Normalized Relations in the Relational Data Model' in *Proc. of the International Conference on Very Large Data Bases*, pp. 447–453.

[Manb94] Manber, U. and Wu, S. (1994) 'GLIMPSE: A Tool to Search through Entire File Systems' in *Proc. of the 1994 Winter USENIX Technical Conference*, pp. 23–32.

[Manb97] Manber, U., Smith, M. and Gopal, B. (1997) 'WebGlimpse – Combining Browsing and Searching' in *Proc. of the 1997 USENIX Technical Conference.*

[MancS88] Mancarella, P. and Pedreschi, D. (1988) 'An Algebra of Logic Programs' in *Proc. of Fifth International Conference on Logic Programming*, Los Angeles (CA), February.

[MancS89] Manchanda, S. (1989) 'Declarative Expression of Deductive Database Updates' in *Proc. of the Ninth ACM SIGACT-SIGMOD-SIGART Symposium on Principles of Database Systems*, May.

[Manl90] Manley, J., Cox, A., Harrison, K., Sirett, M. and Wells, D. (1990) *KBMS1 A User Manual*, Information System Centre Hewlett-Packard Laboratories.

[Mann94] Mannila, H., Toivonen, H. and Verkamo, A.I. (1994) 'Efficient Algorithms for Discovering Association Rules' in *Proc. of AAAI Workshop on Knowledge Discovery in Databases.*

[Marc96] Marcus, S. and Subrahmanian, V.S. (1996) 'Foundations of Multimedia Database Systems', *Journal of the ACM*, 4(3): 474–505.

[Mark54] Markov, A. (1954) *Theory of Algorithms*, Moscow: USSR National Academy of Sciences.

[Mart98] Martin, P., Powley, W. and Zion, P. (1998) 'A Metadata Repository API', in *Proc. of the KRDB'98 Workshop, Innovative Application Programming and Query Interfaces* (Swiss Life Technical Report), Borgida, A., Chaudri, V. and Staudt, M., eds, Zürich: Swiss Life Information Systems Research Group.

[Masu91] Masunaga, Y. (1991) 'Design Issues of OMEGA, an Object-Oriented Multimedia Database Management System', *Journal of Information Processing*, 14: 60–74.

[Maye88] Mayer, B. (1988) *Object-oriented Software Construction*, Prentice-Hall.

[McCaJ80] McCarthy, J. (1980) 'Circumscription – A Form of Non-Monotonic Reasoning', *Artificial Intelligence* 13: 27–39.

[McCaJ87a] McCarthy, J. (1983) 'Some Expert Systems Need Common Sense', *Annals of the New York Academy of Sciences*, 426: 129–137.

[McCaJ83a] McCarthy, J. (1987a) 'Application of Circumscription in Formalizing Common Sense Knowledge', in *Readings in Non-monotonic Reasoning*, Ginsberg, M., ed, San Francisco, Morgan Kaufmann.

[McCaJ87b] McCarthy, J. (1987b) 'Generality in Artificial Intelligence', *Communications of the ACM*, 30: 1030–1035.

[McCaJ87c] McCarthy, J. and Hayes, P.J. (1987) 'Some Philosophical Problems from the Standpoint of Artificial Intelligence', in *Readings in Non-monotonic Reasoning*, Ginsberg, M., ed., San Francisco: Morgan Kaufmann.

[McCaJ93] McCarthy, J. (1993) 'Notes on Formalizing Context', in *Proc. of the Thirteenth International Joint Conference on Artificial Intelligence – IJCAI/93*, San Francisco, Morgan Kaufmann.

[McDeJ81] McDermott, J. (1981) 'R1: The Formative Years', *AI Magazine* 2(2): 21–29.

[McDeJ93] McDermott, D. (1993) 'Book Review of D.B. Lenat and R.V. Guha, *Building Large Knowledge-Based Systems: Representation and Inference in the Cyc Project*', in *The Commonsense Reviews*, Stefik, M.J. and Smoliar, S.W., eds, special section of Artificial Intelligence, 61: 53–63.

[McHu97] McHugh, J., Abiteboul, S., Goldman, R., Quass, D. and Widom, J. (1997) 'Lore: A Database Management System for Semistructured Data', *SIGMOD Record*, 26(3): 54–66.

[McHu99a] McHugh, J. and Widom, J. (1999) 'Query Optimization for XML' in *Proc. of the International Conference on Very Large Databases.*

[McHu99b]

[Mehr90] Mehrotra, R. and Tsakalidis, A. (1990) 'Data Structures' in *Handbook of Theoretical Computer Science*, vol. A, pp. 301–341, Elsevier Science Publishers.

[Melt93] Melton, J. and Simon, A.R. (1993) *Understanding the New SQL: a Complete Guide*, Morgan Kaufmann Publishers, San Francisco (Calif).

[Mena93] Menaglio, P. and Moizi, M. (1993) '*A DB Hook for a Knowledge Representation Language: Version 2*' (Report AIMS 4-93), Milano: Quinary SpA.

Meo, R., Psaila, G. and Ceri, S. (1996) 'Composite Events in Chimera', *Proceedings Fifth International Conference on Extending Database Technology*, Avignon (France), March 25–29, Lecture Notes in Computer Science N.1057 (P. Apers, and M. Bouzeghoub and G. Gardarin, eds).

[Mett88] Metthey, J. and Cotta, J. (1988) 'ESPRIT: Trends and Challenges in DB Technology', in *Proceedings of the 1988 International Conference on Extending Database Technology – EDBT'88* (Lecture Notes in Computer Science no. 303), Berlin: Springer-Verlag.

[Mili95] Mili, H. et Pachet, F. (1995) 'Régularité, génération de documents, et Cyc', *Revue d'Intelligence Artificielle*, 9: 139–164.

[MillD86] Miller, D. (1986) 'A Theory of Modules for Logic Programming' in *Proc. of IEEE Symposium on Logic Programming.*

[MillG56] Miller, G. A. (1956) 'The Magical Number Seven ± Two', *Psych. Review*, 68: 81–97.

[MillG90] Miller, G.A. (1990) 'WORDNET: An On-Line Lexical Database', *Int. Journal of Lexicography*, 3–4: 235–312.

[MillG93] Miller, G.A., Beckwith, R., Fellbaum, C., Gross, D., Miller, K. and Tengi, R. (1993) *Five Papers on WordNet* (Revised CSL Report 43), Princeton: Computer Science Laboratory of the University.

[MillG95] Miller, G.A. (1995) 'WordNet: A Lexical Database for English', *Communications of the ACM*, 38(11): 39–41.

[Mine93] Mineau, G.W., Moulin, B. and Sowa, J.F., eds (1993) *Conceptual Graphs for Knowledge Representation* (Lecture Notes in Artificial Intelligence 699), Berlin: Springer-Verlag.

[Mins75] Minsky, M. (1975) 'A Framework for Representing Knowledge', in *The Psychology of Computer Vision*, Winston, P.H., ed., New York: McGraw Hill.

[Mins87] Miranker, D. (1987) 'TREAT: A Better Match Algorithm for AI Production Systems', in *Proceedings of the Sixth National Conference on Artificial Intelligence – AAAI/87*, Cambridge (MA): MIT Press/AAAI Press.

[Mizo95] Mizoguchi, R., Vanwelkenhuysen, J. and Ikeda, M. (1995) 'Task Ontology for Reuse of Problem Solving Knowledge' in N.J.I. Mars, ed., *Towards Very Large Knowledge Bases: Knowledge Building & Knowledge Sharing*, pp. 46–57, IOS Press, Amsterdam, NL.

[MontD97] Montesi, D., Bertino, E. and Martelli, M. (1997) 'Transactions and Updates in Deductive Databases', *IEEE Trans. on Knowledge and Data Engineering*, 9(5): 784–797, September/October.

[MontL90] Monteiro, L. and Porto, A. (1990) 'A Transformational View of Inheritance in Logic Programming', in *Proc. of Seventh International Conference on Logic Programming*, February.

[Moon89] Moon, D.A. (1989) 'The Common Lisp Object-oriented Programming Language Standard' in *Object-Oriented Concepts, Databases, and Applications*, W. Kim, and F. Lochovsky, (eds), Addison-Wesley, 49–78.

[MUC593] (1993) *Proceedings of the Fifth Message Understanding Conference* (sponsored by Advanced Research Projects Agency, ARPA), San Francisco: Morgan Kaufmann.

[MUC798] (1998) *Proceedings of the Seventh Message Understanding Conference – MUC-7* (sponsored by Advanced Research Projects Agency, ARPA), http://www.muc.saic.com/proceedings/muc_7_proceedings/overview.html

[Mugn98] Mugnier, M.-L. and Chein, M., eds (1998) *Conceptual Structures: Theory, Tools, and Applications* (Lecture Notes in Artificial Intelligence 1453), Berlin: Springer-Verlag.

[Mylo90a] Mylopoulos, J., Borgida, A., Jarke, M. and Koubarakis, M. (1990a) 'TELOS: Representing Knowledge About Information Systems', *ACM Transactions on Information Systems*, 8: 325–362.

[Mylo90b] Mylopoulos, J., Borgida, A., Jarke, M. and Koubarakis, M. (1990b) *TELOS: A Language for Representing Knowledge About Information Systems, Revised* (Report KRR-TR-89-1), Toronto: Department of Computer Science of the University of Toronto.

[Mylo91] Mylopoulos, J. (1991) *Conceptual Modelling and TELOS* (Report DKBS-TR-91-3), Toronto: Department of Computer Science of the University of Toronto.

[Mylo94] Mylopoulos, J., Chaudhri, V.K., Plexousakis, D. and Topaloglou, T. (1994) 'Adapting Database Implementation Techniques to Manage Very Large Knowledge Bases', in *Knowledge Building and Knowledge Sharing*, Fuchi, K., and Yokoi, T., eds, Tokyo: Ohmsha; Amsterdam: IOS Press.

[Nado92] Nado, R. and Fikes, R. (1992) 'Saying more with Frames: Slots as Classes', in *Semantic Networks in Artificial Intelligence*, Lehmann, F., ed., Oxford: Pergamon Press.

[Napo97] Napoli, A. (1997) *Une introduction aux logiques de description* (Rapport de recherche no. 3314), Rocquencourt: Institut National de Recherche en Informatique et Automatique (INRIA).

[Nava89] Navathe, S.B. and Ahmed, R. (1989) 'A Temporal Relational Model and a Query Language', *Information Sciences*, 49: 147–175.

[Naza92] Nazarenko-Perrin, A. (1992) 'Causal Ambiguity in Natural Language : Conceptual Representation of "parce que/because" and "puisque/since", in

Proc. of the Fifteenth International Conference on Computational Linguistics – COLING 92, Nantes, France, August.

[Naza93] Nazarenko, A. (1993) 'Representing Natural Language Causality in Conceptual Graphs: The *Higher Order Conceptual Relation Problem', in Conceptual Graphs for Knowledge Representation (Proc. of the First International Conference on Conceptual Structures)*, Mineau, G.W., Moulin, B. and Sowa, J., eds, Berlin: Springer-Verlag.

[Nebe88a] Nebel, B. (1988) 'Computational Complexity of Terminological Reasoning in BACK', *Artificial Intelligence* 34: 371–383.

[Nebe88b] Nebel, B. and Von Luck, K. (1988) 'Hybrid Reasoning in BACK', in *Methodologies for Intelligent Systems 3*, Ras, Z.W. and Saitta, L., eds, Amsterdam: North-Holland.

[Nebe90a] Nebel, B. (1990) *Reasoning and Revision in Hybrid Representation Systems* (Lecture Notes in Artificial Intelligence, vol. 422), Berlin: Springer-Verlag.

[Nebe90b] Nebel, B. (1990) 'Terminological Reasoning is Inherently Intractable', *Artificial Intelligence* 43: 235–249.

[Nech91] Neches, R., Fikes, R., Finin, T., Gruber, T., Patil, R., Senator, T. and Swartout, W. (1991) 'Enabling Technology for Knowledge Sharing', *AI Magazine*, 12(3): 36–56.

[Newe82] Newell, A. (1982) 'The Knowledge Level', *Artificial Intelligence*, 18, 87–127.

[Niez92] Niezette, M. and Stevenne, J.M (1992) 'An Efficient Representation of Periodic Time' in *Proc. of International Conference on Information and Knowledge Management.*

[Nils80] Nilsson, N.J. (1980) *Principles of Artificial Intelligence*, Palo Alto (CA): Tioga Publishing Company.

[Norr94] Norrie, M.C., Reimer, U., Lippuner, P., Rys, M. and Schek, H.-J. (1994) 'Frames, Objects and Relations: Three Semantic Levels for Knowledge Base Systems', in *Working Notes of the KRDB'94 Workshop, Reasoning about Structured Objects: Knowledge Representation Meets Databases* (Document D-94-11), Baader, F., Buchheit, M., Jeusfeld, M.A. and Nutt, W., eds, Saarbrücken: Deutsches Forschungszentrum für Künstliche Intelligenz GmbH.

[Norv92] Norvig, P. (1992) *Paradigms of Artificial Intelligence Programming: Case Studies in Common Lisp*, San Francisco: Morgan Kaufmann.

[ObjeD98] Object Design Inc. (1998) 'An XML Data Server for Building Enterprise Web Applications', White Paper, *www.odi.com/Object Design Inc.*

[ObjeM91] Object Management Group. (1991) 'The Common Object Request Broker: Architecture and Specification', OMG Document 91.12.1, OMG and X/Open, distributed by QED-Wiley, Wellesley MA.

[Ogon87] Ogonowski, A. (1987) 'MENTAT: An Intelligent and Cooperative Natural Language DB Interface', in *Proc. of the 7th Avignon International Workshop on Expert Systems and Their Applications*, vol. 2, Paris: EC2&Cie.

[O'Har95] O'Hare, G. and Jennings, N., eds (1995), *Foundations of Distributed Artificial Intelligence*, Wiley Inter-Science.

(Omo93] Oomoto, E. and Tanaka, K. (1993) 'OVID: Design and Implementation of a Video-Object Database System', *IEEE Tran. on Knowledge and Data Eng.*, 5: 629–641.

[Orac92] Oracle Corporation (1992) *Oracle 7.0. SQL Language – Reference Manual.*

[Orac98] Oracle Corporation (1998) XML support in Oracle 8i and Beyond, White Paper, http:// www.technet.oracle.com/.

[Ozso95] Özsoyoglu, G. and Snodgrass, T. (1995) 'Temporal and Real-Time Databases: A Survey', *IEEE Trans. On Knowledge and Data Engineering*, 7(4): 513–532).

[Padg92] Padgham, L. (1992) 'Defeasible Inheritance: A Lattice Based Approach', in *Semantic Networks in Artificial Intelligence*, Lehmann, F., ed., Oxford: Pergamon Press.

[PapaM95] Papazoglou, M.P. (1995) 'Unraveling the Semantics of Conceptual Schemas', *Communications of the ACM*, 38(9): 80–94.

[PapaY95] Papakonstantinou, Y., Garcia-Molina, H. and Widom, J. (1995) 'Object Exchange Across Heterogeneous Information Sources' in *Proc. of the Eleventh International Conference on Data Engineering*, Los Alamitos (CA): IEEE Computer Press.

[PapaY99] Papakonstantinou, Y. and Vassalos, V. (1999) 'Query Rewriting for Semistructured Data' in *Proc. of the ACM SIGMOD International Conference on Management of Data*, pp. 455–466.

[Pare92] Paredaens, J. and Van Gucht, D. (1992) 'Converting Nested Algebra Expressions into Flat Algebra Expressions', *ACM Transactions on Database Systems*, 17(1): 65–93.

[Pare94] Paredaens, J., Van den Bussche, J. and Van Gucht, D. (1994) 'Towards a Theory of Spatial Database Queries' in *Proc. of the 13th ACM SIGACT-SIGMOD-SIGART Symposium on Principles of Database Systems*, Minneapolis (MN), May.

[Park95] Park, J.-S., Chen, M.-S. and Yu, P.S. (1995) 'Efficient Parallel Data Mining for Association Rules' in *Proc. of the* 4th *International Conference on Information and Knowledge Management.*

[Pate84] Patel-Schneider, P.F. (1984) *Small Can Be Beautiful in Knowledge Representation* (Technical Report 660), Palo Alto (CA): Fairchild Laboratory for Artificial Intelligence.

[Pate89] Patel-Schneider, P.F. (1989) 'Undecidability of Subsumption in NIKL', *Artificial Intelligence* 39: 263–272.

[Pear88] Pearl, J. (1988) *Probabilistic Reasoning in Intelligent Systems: Networks of Plausible Inference*, San Francisco: Morgan Kaufmann.

[Peck88] Peckham, J. and Maryanski, F. (1988) 'Semantic Data Models', *ACM Computing Surveys*, 20(3): 153–189.

[Pelt89] Peltason, C., Schmiedel, A., Kindermann, C. and Quantz, J. (1989) 'The BACK System Revisited' (KIT Report 75), Berlin: Technische Universität.

[Pere99] Pérezand, A.G. and Benjamins, V.R. (1999) 'Overview of Knowledge Sharing and Reuse Components: Ontologies and Problem-Solving Methods' in *Proc. of the IJCAI'99 Workshop on Ontologies and Problem-Solving Methods.*

[Piss94] Pissinou, N., Snodgrass, R.T., Elmasri, R., Mumick, I.S., Özsu, M.T., Pernici, B., Segev, A., Theodoulidis, B. and Dayal, U. (1994) 'Towards an Infrastructure for Temporal Databases: Report of an Invitational ARPA/NSF Workshop', *ACM Sigmod Record*, 23(1): 35–51.

[Plai84] Plaisted, D. (1984) 'The Occur-Check Problem in Prolog', *New Generation Computers* 2: 309–322.

[Post43] Post, E.L. (1943) 'Formal Reductions of the General Combinatorial Decision Problem', *American Journal of Mathematics* 65: 197–268.

[Pota96] Potamianos, S. and Stonebraker, M. (1996) 'The POSTGRES Rule System' in *Active Database Systems: Triggers and Rules for Advanced Systems* (J.Widom, S. Ceri, eds), Morgan Kaufmann Publishers, San Francisco (Calif).

[Pott88] Potter, W.D. and Trueblood, R.P (1988) 'Traditional, Semantic, and Hyper-Semantic Approaches to Data Modelling', *IEEE Computer*, 21(6): 53–63.

[Pott89] Potter, W.D., Trueblood, R.P. and Eastman, C.M. (1989) 'Hyper-Semantic Data Modelling', *Data & Knowledge Engineering*, 4: 69–90.

[Pott93] Potter, W.D., Kochut, K.J., Miller, J.A., Gandham, V.P. and Polamraju, R.V. (1993) 'The Evolution of the Knowledge/Data Model', *International Journal of Expert Systems, Research and Applications – Special Issue on AI and Databases*, 6: 39–81.

[Quin86] Quinlan, J.R. (1986) 'Induction of Decision Trees', *Machine Learning*.

[Rami94] Ramirez, J.C.G., Smoth, L.A. and Peterson, L.L. (1994) 'Medical Information Systems: Characterization and Challenges', *Sigmod Record*, 23(3): 44–53.

[Reim95] Reimer, U., Lippuner, P., Norrie, M. and Rys, M. (1995) 'Terminological Reasoning by Query Evaluation: A Formal Mapping of a Terminological Logic to an Object Data Model', in *Working Notes of the KRDB'95 Workshop, Reasoning about Structured Objects: Knowledge Representation Meets Databases* (Document D-95-12), Baader, F., Buchheit, M., Nutt, W. and Jeusfeld, M., eds, Saarbrücken: Deutsches Forschungszentrum für Künstliche Intelligenz GmbH.

[Reit80] Reiter, R. (1980) 'A Logic for Default Reasoning', *Artificial Intelligence* 13: 81–182.

[Reit83] Reiter, R. and Criscuolo, G. (1983) 'Some Representational Issues in Default Reasoning', in *Computational Linguistics*, Cercone, N.J., ed., Oxford: Pergamon Press.

[Ring88] Ringland, G.A. (1988) 'Structured Object Representation – Schemata and Frames', in *Approaches to Knowledge Representation: An Introduction*, Ringland, G.A. and Duce, D.A., eds, Letchworth: Research Studies Press.

[Ritc84] Ritchie, G.D. and Hanna, F.K. (1984) 'AM: A Case Study in AI Methodology', *Artificial Intelligence*, 23: 249–268.

[Robi65] Robinson, J.A. (1965) 'A Machine-Oriented Logic Based on the Resolution Principle', *Journal of the ACM* 12: 23–41.

[Robi82] Robinson, J.A. (1982) 'Expressing Expertise through Logic Programming', in *Introductory Readings in Expert Systems*, Michie, D., ed., New York: Gordon and Breach.

[Rose91] Rose, E. and Segev, A. (1991) 'TOODM – A Temporal Object-Oriented Data Model with Temporal Constraints' in *Proc. of the International Conference on the Entity Relationship Approach.*

[Rose93] Rose, E. and Segev, A. (1993) 'TOOSQL – A Temporal Object-Oriented Query Language' in *Proc. of the Int. Conf. on the Entity Relationship Approach.*

[Ross94] Ross, K.A., Srivastava, D., Stuckey, P.J. and Sudarshan, S. (1994) 'Foundations of Aggregation Constraints' in *Proc. of Second International Workshop on Principles and Practice of Constraint Programming*, Lecture Notes in Computer Science 874, Springer-Verlag.

[Roth95] Roth, M.T. and Schwarz, P. (1995) 'Don't Scrap It, Wrap it! A Wrapper Architecture for Legacy Data Sources' in *Proc. of the 23rd International Conference on Very Large Databases (VLDB'95)*, pp. 266–275.

[Rous75] Roussel, P. (1975) *PROLOG, Manuel de Référence et d'Utilisation*, Luminy: Groupe d'Intelligence Artificielle de l'Université Aix-Marseille II.

[Roye93] Royer, V. and Quantz, J.J. (1993) *Deriving Inference Rules for Description Logics: A Rewriting Approach into Sequent Calculi* (KIT-REPORT 111), Berlin: Technische Universität.

[Rumb91] Rumbaugh, J. *et al* (1991) *Object Oriented Modeling and Design*, Englewood Cliffs, N.J., Prentice Hall.

[Rupa91] Ruparel, B. (1991) 'Designing and Implementing an Intelligent Database Application: A Case Study', *Expert Systems with Applications*, 3: 411–430.

[Sand86] Sandewall, E. (1986) 'Non-Monotonic Inference Rules for Multiple Inheritance with Exceptions', in *Proc. of the IEEE* 74: 1345–1353.

[Sard90] Sarda, N. (1990) 'Extensions to SQL for Historical Databases', *IEEE Trans. on Knowledge and Data Engineering*, 2(2): 220–230.

[SchiK94] Schild, K. (1994) 'Tractable Reasoning in a Universal Description Logic', in *Working Notes of the KRDB'94 Workshop, Reasoning about Structured Objects: Knowledge Representation Meets Databases* (Document D-94-11), Baader, F., Buchheit, M., Jeusfeld, M.A. and Nutt, W., eds, Saarbrücken: Deutsches Forschungszentrum für Künstliche Intelligenz GmbH.

[SchiK95] Schild, K. (1995) *A Tractable Query Language for Knowledge and Data Bases Based on a Universal Description Logic and Logics of Programs* (PhD thesis), Saarbrücken: Deutsches Forschungszentrum für Künstliche Intelligenz GmbH.

[SchiU89] Schiel, U. (1989) 'Abstractions in Semantic Networks: Axiom Schemata for Generalization, Aggregation and Grouping', *ACM Sigart Newsletter* (107): 25–26.

[SchmA94] Schmiedel, A. (1994) 'Semantic Indexing Based on Description Logics', in *Working Notes of the KRDB'94 Workshop, Reasoning about Structured Objects: Knowledge Representation Meets Databases* (Document D-94-11), Baader, F., Buchheit, M., Jeusfeld, M.A. and Nutt, W., eds, Saarbrücken: Deutsches Forschungszentrum für Künstliche Intelligenz GmbH.

[SchmH75] Schmid, H.A. and Swenson, J.R. (1975) 'On the Semantics of the Relational Data Model' in *Proc. of the ACM SIGMOD International Conference on Management of Data*, pp. 211–223.

[SchmS89] Schmidt-Schauss, M. (1989) 'Subsumption in KL-ONE is Undecidable', in *Proc. of the First International Conference On Principles of Knowledge Representation and Reasoning – KR'89*, Brachman, R.J., Levesque, H.J. and Reiter, R., eds, San Francisco: Morgan Kaufmann.

[Scho92] Scholl, M.H., Laasch, C., Rich, C., Schek, H.-J. and Tresch, M. (1992) *The COCOON Object Model* (Technical Report 211), Zurich: Department of Computer Science of ETH.

[SchrU91] Schreier, U., Pirahesh, H., Agrawal, R. and Mohan, C. (1991) 'Alert: an Architecture for Transforming a Passive DBMS into an Active DBMS', in *Proc. of the 17th International Conference on Very Large Data Bases (VLDB)*, Barcelona (Spain), September.

[Schu89] Schubert, L.K. and Hwang, C.H. (1989) 'An Episodic Knowledge Representation for Narrative Texts', in *Proc. of the First International Conference On Principles of Knowledge Representation and Reasoning*, Brachman, R.J., Levesque, H.J. and Reiter, R., eds, San Francisco: Morgan Kaufmann.

[Sege87] Segev, A. and Shoshani, A. (1987) 'Logical Modelling of Temporal Data' in *Proc. of the ACM SIGMOD International Conference on Management of Data*, pp. 454–466.

[Sege90]

[Selb89] Selberg, E. and Etzioni, O. (1989) 'Multi-service Search and Comparison using the MetaCrawler' in *Proc. of the 4th International WWW Conference.*

[Sell88] Sellis, T., Lin, C.-C. and Raschid, L. (1988) 'Implementing Large Production Systems in a DBMS Environment: Concepts and Algorithms', in *Proc. of the 1988 ACM SIGMOD International Conference on Management of Data – Special Issue of ACM Sigmod Record*, 17(3): 404–412.

[Sell93] Sellis, T., Lin, C.-C., and Raschid, L. (1993) 'Coupling Production Systems and Database Systems: A Homogeneous Approach', *IEEE Transactions on Knowledge and Data Engineering* 5: 240–256.

[Shaf76] Shafer, G. (1976) *A Mathematical Theory of Evidence*, Princeton (NJ): Princeton University Press.

[Shet98] Sheth, A. and Klas, W., eds (1998) *Multimedia Data Management – Using Metadata to Integrate and Apply Digital Media*, New York: McGraw Hill.

[Shim99] Shimura, T., Yoshikawa, M. and Uemura, S. (1999) 'Storage and Retrieval of XML Documents Using Object-Relational Databases' in *Proc. of International Conference on Databases and Expert Systems Applications (DEXA)*, pp. 206–217.

[Ship81] Shipman, D.W. (1981) 'The Functional Data Model and the Data Language DAPLEX', *ACM Transactions on Database Systems*, 6: 140–173.

[Shmu93] Shmueli, O. (1993) 'Equivalence of Datalog Queries is Undecidable', *Journal of Logic Programming*, 15: 231–241.

[Shor76] Shortliffe, E.H. (1976) *Computer-Based Medical Consultations: MYCIN*, New York: American-Elsevier Publications.

[Simo92] Simon, E., Kiernan, J., and de Maindreville, C. (1992) 'Implementing High Level Active Rules on Top of a Relational DBMS', in *Proc. of the 18th*

International Conference on Very Large Data Bases (VLDB), Vancouver (Canada), August 23–27.

[Skuc93] Skuce, D. (1993) 'Book Review of D.B. Lenat and R.V. Guha, *Building Large Knowledge-Based Systems: Representation and Inference in the Cyc Project*', in *The Commonsense Reviews*, Stefik, M.J. and Smoliar, S.W., eds, special section of *Artificial Intelligence*, 61: 81–94.

[Skuc95] Skuce, D. (1995) 'Conventions for Reaching Agreement on Shared Ontologies', in *Proc. of the 9th Banff Knowledge Acquisition for Knowledge-Based Systems Workshop*, Gaines, B.R. and Musen, M., eds, vol. 1, Calgary: Department of Computer Science of the University.

[SmitB91] Smith, B.C. (1991) 'The Owl and the Electric Encyclopedia', *Artificial Intelligence*, 47: 251–288.

[SmitJ77] Smith, J.M. and Smith, D.C.P. (1977) 'Database Abstractions. Aggregation and Generalization', *ACM Trans. on Database Systems*, 2(2): 105–133.

[Smol87] Smoliar, S.W. (1987) 'Book Review of J.F. Sowa, *Conceptual Structures: Information Processing in Mind and Machine*', *Artificial Intelligence*, 33: 259–266.

[Snod87] Snodgrass, R.T. (1987) 'The Temporal Query Language Tquel', *ACM Trans. on Database Systems*, 12(2): 247–298.

[Snod94a] Snodgrass, R.T. (1994) 'Overview of the Special Section on Temporal Database Infrastructure', *ACM Sigmod Record*, 23(1): 34.

[Snod94] Snodgrass, R.T., Ahn, I., Ariav, G., Batory, D.S., Clifford, J., Dyreson, C.E., Elmasri, R., Grandi, F., Jensen, C.S., Kafer, W., Kline, N., Kulkanri, K., Leung, C.Y.T., Lorentzos, N., Roddick, J.F., Segev, A., Soo, M.D. and Sripada, S.M. (1994) 'TSQL2 Language Specification', *ACM SIGMOD Record*, 23(1): 65–86.

[Snod95] Snodgrass, R.T., ed. (1995) *The TSQL2 Temporal Query Language*, Dordrecht: Kluwer Academic Publishers.

[SohC89] Soh, C.-K., Soh, A.-K. and Lai, K.-Y. (1989) 'KBASE: A Customizable Tool for Building dBase Compatible Knowledge-Based Systems', *Advanced Engineering Software*, 11(3): 136–148.

[SohC92] Soh, C.-K., Soh, A.-K. and Lai, K.-Y. (1992) 'An Approach to Embed Knowledge in Database Systems', *Engineering Applications of Artificial Intelligence*, 5: 413–423.

[Sowa84] Sowa, J.F. (1984) *Conceptual Structures: Information Processing in Mind and Machine*, Reading (MA): Addison-Wesley.

[Sowa86] Sowa, J.F. and Way, E.C. (1986) 'Implementing a Semantic Interpreter Using Conceptual Graphs', *IBM Journal of Research and Development*, 30: 57–69.

[Sowa91] Sowa, J.F. (1991) 'Toward the Expressive Power of Natural Language', in *Principles of Semantic Networks*, Sowa, J.F., ed., San Francisco: Morgan Kaufmann.

[Sowa93] Sowa, J.F. (1993) 'Book Review of D.B. Lenat and R.V. Guha, *Building Large Knowledge-Based Systems: Representation and Inference in the Cyc Project*' in *The Commonsense Reviews*, Stefik, M.J. and Smoliar, S.W., eds, special section of *Artificial Intelligence*, 61: 95–104.

[Sowa95] Sowa, J.F. (1995) 'Distinctions, Combinations, and Constraints', in *Proceedings of the IJCAI'95 Workshop on Basic Ontological Issues in Knowledge Sharing*, Skuce, D., ed., Ottawa: Department of Computer Science of the University of Ottawa.

[Sowa99] Sowa, J.F. (1999) *Knowledge Representation: Logical, Philosophical, and Computational Foundations*, Pacific Grove (CA): Brooks Cole Publishing Co.

[Spee95] Speel, P.-H. (1995) *Selecting Knowledge Representation Systems* (Thesis Universiteit), Enschede: University of Twente.

[SpJo87] Sparck Jones, K. and Boguraev, B. (1987) 'A Note on a Study of Cases', *Computational Linguistics*, 13: 65–68.

[Srik95] Srikant, R. and Agrawal, R. (1995) 'Mining Generalized Association Rules' in *Proc. of the 21st International Conference on Very Large Data Bases.*

Srivastava, D. (1992) 'Subsumption and Indexing in Constraint Query Languages with Linear Arithmetic Constraints', *Annals of Mathematics and Artificial Intelligence.*

[Sriv94] Srivastava, D., Ramakrishnan, R. and Revesz, P.Z. (1994) 'Constraint Objects' in *Proc. of Second International Workshop on Principles and Practice of Constraint Programming*, Lecture Notes in Computer Science 874, Springer-Verlag.

[Star98] Starr, B., Chaudhri, V.K., Farquhar, A. and Waldinger, R. (1998) 'Knowledge-Intensive Query Processing', in *Proc. of the 5th KRDB Workshop (KRDB'98)*, Borgida, A., Chaudri, V.K. and Staudt, M., eds, Zurich: Swiss Life Information Systems Research.

[Stee94] Steels, L. and McDermott, J., eds (1994) *Perspectives in Artificial Intelligence*, New York (NY): Academic Press.

[Stef93] Stefik, M.J. and Smoliar, S.W., eds (1993) *The Commonsense Reviews – Eight Reviews of B. Lenat and R.V. Guha, 'Building Large Knowledge-Based Systems' and E. Davis, 'Representation of Commonsense Knowledge'*, special section of *Artificial Intelligence*: 61 (1).

[Stro86] Stroustrup, B. (1986) *The C++ Programming Language*, Addison-Wesley, Reading (Mass).

[Stud98] Studer, R., Benjamins, V.R. and Fensel, D. (1998) 'Knowledge Engineering, Principles and Methods', *Data and Knowledge Engineering*, 25 (1-2): 161–197.

[Subr96] Subrahmanian, V.S. *et al* (1996) 'HERMES: A Heterogeneous Reasoning and Mediator System', available at http://www.cs.umd.edu/projects/hermes/overview/paper.

[Suci98a] Suciu, D. (1998) 'Semistructured Data and XML' in *Proc. of the Int. Conf. on Foundations of Data Organization.*

[Suci98b] Suciu, D. and Vossen, G. (1998) 'Special Issue on Semistructured Data', *Information Systems*, 23(8): 517–519.

[SuSY83] Su, S.Y.W. (1983) 'SAM*: A Semantic Association Model for Corporate and Scientific-Statistical Databases', *Information Sciences*, 29: 151–199.

[SuSY91] Su, S.Y.W. and Chen, H.M. (1991) 'A Temporal Knowledge Representation Model OSAM*/T and its Query language OQL/T' in *Proc. of the Int. Conf. on Very Large Data Bases.*

[Swar97] Swartout, W., Patil, R., Knight, K. and Russ, T. (1997) 'Towards Distributed Use of large-Scale Ontologies' in *Spring Symp. Series on Ontological Engineering*, pp. 33–40, Stanford, AAAI Press.

[Tans86] Tansel, A.U. (1986) 'Adding Time Dimension to Relational Model and Extending Relational Algebra', *Information Systems*, 11(4): 343–355.

[Tans89] Tansel, A.U., Arkun, M.E. and Ozsolyoglu, G. (1989) 'Time-by-Example Query Language for Historical Databases', *IEEE Trans. Software Eng.*, 15(4): 464–478.

[Tayl76] Taylor, R.W. and Frank, R.L. (1976) 'CODASYL Database Management Systems', *ACM Computing Surveys*, 8(1): 67–103.

[Teor86] Teorey, T.J., Yang, D. and Fry, J.P. (1986) 'A Logical Design Methodology for Relational Databases using the Extended Relationship Model', *ACM Computing Surveys*, 18: 197–222.

[Topa89] Topaloglou, T. and Koubarakis, M. (1989) *An Implementation of TELOS* (Report TR-KRR-89-8), Toronto: Department of Computer Science of the University of Toronto.

[Tour86] Touretzky, D.S. (1986) *The Mathematics of Inheritance Systems*, London: Pitman.

[Tour87] Touretzky, D.S., Horty, J.F. and Thomason, R.H. (1987) 'A Clash of Intuitions: The Current state of Nonmonotic Multiple Inheritance Systems', in *Proc. of the Tenth International Joint Conference on Artificial Intelligence – IJCAI/87*, San Francisco: Morgan Kaufmann.

[Tsic76] Tsichritzis, D. and Lochovsky, F. (1976) 'Hierarchical Database Management: A Survey', *ACM Computing Surveys*, 8(1): 105–123.

[Tsur84] Tsur, S. and Zaniolo, C. (1984) 'An Implementation of GEM – Supporting a Semantic Data Model on a Relational Back-end' in *Proc. of the ACM SIGMOD Int. Conf. on Management of Data*, pp. 286–295.

[Tsur88] Tsur, S. (1988) 'LDL – A Technology for the Realization of Tightly Coupled Expert Database Systems', *IEEE Expert*, 3(3): 41–51.

[Ullm89] Ullman, J.D. (1989) *Database and Knowledge Base Systems*, vol. I and vol. II. Computer Science Press.

[Usch96] Uschold, M. (1996) 'Building Ontologies: Towards a Unified Methodology', *Expert Systems*.

[Vald87] Valduriez, P. (1987) 'Join Indices', *ACM Transactions on Database Systems*, 12: 218–246.

[vanE76] Van Emden, M.H. and Kowalski, R.A. (1976) 'The Semantics of Predicate Logic as a Programming Language', *Journal of the ACM* 23: 733–742.

[vanH97] Van Heijst, G., Schreiber, A.T. and Wielinga, B.J. (1997) 'Using Explicit Ontologies in KNS Development', *Int. Journal of Human-Computer Studies*, 46(2/3): 183–292.

[VanK95]

[Vela88] Velardi, P., Pazienza, M.T. and DeGiovanetti, M. (1988) 'Conceptual Graphs for the Analysis and Generation of Sentences', *IBM Journal of Research and Development*, 32: 251–276.

[Verm98] Vermesan, A.I. (1998) 'Foundation and Application of Expert System Verification and Validation', in *The Handbook of Applied Expert Systems*, Liebowitz, J., ed., Boca Raton (FL): CRC Press LCC.

[Vila86] Vilain, M. and Kautz, H. (1986) 'Constraint Propagation Algorithms for Temporal Reasoning', in *Proc. of the Fifth National Conference on Artificial Intelligence – AAAI/86*, Cambridge (MA): AAAI Press/MIT Press.

[Viss97] Visser, P.R.S. (1997) 'Towards Distributed Legal Information Systems: A Discussion of Ontology Mismatches' in *Proc. of the Tenth International Conference on Legal Knowledge-Based Systems*, pp. 43–53.

[Viss98] Visser, P.R.S. and Bench-Capon, T.J.M. (1998) 'Ontologies in the Design of Legal Information Systems; Towards a Library of Legal Domain Ontologies, *Conference on Applied Ontology*, Buffalo University, NY, USA, pp. 76–85.

[Wegn87] Wegner, B. (1987) The Object-oriented Classification Paradigm' in *Research Directions in Object-Oriented Programming*, B. Shriver, and P. Wegner (eds), The MIT Press, Cambridge, Mass., pp. 479–560.

[Wess94] Wess, S., Althoff, K.-D. and Richter, M.M., eds (1994) *Topics in Case-Based Reasoning* (Lectures Notes in Artificial Intelligence 837), Berlin: Springer-Verlag.

[Wido96a] Widom, J. (1996) 'The Starburst Rule System' in *Active Database Systems: Triggers and Rules for Advanced Systems* (J. Widom, S. Ceri, eds), Morgan Kaufmann Publishers, San Francisco (Calif).

[Wido96b] Widom, J. and Ceri, S. (1996) 'Introduction to Active Database Systems' in *Active Database Systems: Triggers and Rules for Advanced Systems* (J. Widom, S. Ceri, eds), Morgan Kaufmann Publishers, San Francisco (Calif).

[Wied80] Wiederhold, G. and El-Masri, R. (1980) 'Structural Model for Database Design' in *Entity-Relationship Approach to Systems Analysis and Design*, North Holland, Amsterdam.

[Wied94a] Wiederhold, G. (1994) 'Interoperation, Mediation, and Ontologies' in *Proc. of the International Symposium. on Fifth Generation Computer Systems (FGCS'94)*, Workshop on Heterogeneous Cooperative Knowledge-Bases, vol. W3, pp. 33–48, ICOT, Japan.

[Wied94b] Wiederhold, G. (1994) 'An Ontology Algebra' in *Proc. of the Monterey Workshop on Formal Methods.*

[Wied97] Wiederhold, G. and Genesereth, M. (1997) 'The Conceptual Basis for Mediation Services', *IEEE Expert*, pp. 38–47.

[Wile87] Wilensky, R. (1987) *Some Problems and Proposals for Knowledge Representation* (UCB/CSD Report no. 87/351), Berkeley (CA): University of California Computer Science Division.

[Will88] Williams, T. and Lambert, S. (1988) 'Expressive Power and Computability', in *Approaches to Knowledge Representation: An Introduction*, Ringland, G.A. and Duce, D.A., eds, Letchworth: Research Studies Press.

[Wins87] Winston, M.E., Chaffin, R. and Herrmann, D. (1987) 'A Taxonomy of Part-Whole Relations', *Cognitive Science* 11: 417–444.

[Wood75] Woods, W.A. (1975) 'What's in a Link: Foundations for Semantic Networks', in *Representation and Understanding – Studies in Cognitive Science*, Bobrow, D.G. and Collins, A., eds, New York: Academic Press.

[Wood91] Woods, W.A. (1991) 'Understanding Subsumption and Taxonomy: A Framework for Progress', in *Principles of Semantic Networks*, Sowa, J.F., ed., San Francisco: Morgan Kaufmann.

[Wrig93] Wright, J.R., Weixelbaum, E.S., Brown, K., Vesonder, G.T., Palmer, S.R., Berman, J.I. and Moore, H.H. (1993) 'A Knowledge-Base Configurator that Supports Sales, Engineering and Manufacturing at AT&T Network Systems', in *Proc. of the Fifth Innovative Applications of Artificial Intelligence Conference*, Cambridge (MA): MIT Press/AAAI Press.

[WuuG92] Wuu, G.T.J. and Dayal, U. (1992) 'A Uniform Model for Temporal Data Retrieval' in *Proc. of the Int. Conf. on Data Engineering*, pp. 584–593.

[YauG91] Yau, C. and Chat, G.S.W. (1991) 'TempSQL – A language Interface to a Temporal Relational Model', *Information, Science and Technology*, pp. 44–60.

[Yoko95a] Yokoi, T. (1995) 'The Impact of the EDR Electronic Dictionary on Very Large Knowledge Bases', in *Towards Very Large Knowledge Bases*, Mars, N.J.I., ed., Amsterdam: IOS Press.

[Yoko95b] Yokoi, T. (1995) 'The EDR Electronic Dictionary', *Communications of the ACM*, 38(11): 42–44.

[Zaia98] Zaiane, O.R., Han, J., Li, Z.-N., Chee, S.H. and Chiang, J. (1998) 'MultiMediaMiner: A System Prototype for Multimedia Data Mining' in *Proc. of the ACM SIGMOD Int. Conf. on Management of Data*, pp. 581–583.

[Zani83] Zaniolo, C. (1983) 'The Database Language GEM' in *Proc. of the ACM SIGMOD International Conference on Management of Data*, pp. 207–217.

[Zarr86a] Zarri, G.P. (1986) 'The Use of Inference Mechanisms to Improve the Retrieval Facilities from Large Relational Databases', in *Proc. of the Ninth International ACM Conference on Research and Development in Information Retrieval*, Rabitti, F., ed., New York: ACM.

[Zarr86b] Zarri, G.P. (1986) 'Constructing and Utilizing Large Fact Databases Using Artificial Intelligence Techniques', in *Expert Database Systems – in Proc. from the First International Workshop*, Kerschberg, L., ed., Menlo Park: Benjamin/Cummings.

[Zarr90] Zarri, G.P. (1990) 'Expert Databases: The State of the Art' in *Proc. of the Second International Conference on Expert Systems Applications – EXPERSYS'90*, Gouardères, G., Liebowitz, J. and White, M., eds, Gournay-sur-Marne: IITT-International.

[Zarr92a] Zarri, G.P. (1992) 'Semantic Modeling of the Content of (Normative) Natural Language Documents', in *Actes des douzièmes journées internationales d'Avignon 'Les systèmes experts et leurs applications' – Conférence spécialisée sur le traitement du langage naturel*, Paris: EC2 et Cie.

[Zarr92b] Zarri, G.P. (1992) 'The 'Descriptive' Component of a Hybrid Knowledge Representation Language' in *Semantic Networks in Artificial Intelligence*, Lehmann, F., ed., Oxford: Pergamon Press.

[Zarr94] Zarri, G.P. (1994) 'A Glimpse of NKRL, the "Narrative Knowledge Representation Language", in *Knowledge Representation for Natural Language Processing in Implemented Systems – Papers from the 1994 Fall Symposium*, Ali, S., ed., Menlo Park (CA): AAAI Press.

[Zarr95a] Zarri, G.P. (1995) 'An Overview of the Structural Principles Underpinning the Construction of "Ontologies" in NKRL', in *Proc. of the IJCAI'95 Workshop on Basic Ontological Issues in Knowledge Sharing*, Skuce, D., ed, Ottawa: Department of Computer Science of the University of Ottawa.

[Zarr95b] Zarri, G.P. (1995) 'Knowledge Acquisition from Complex Narrative Texts Using the NKRL Technology', in *Proc. of the 9th Banff Knowledge Acquisition for Knowledge-Based Systems Workshop*, Gaines, B.R. and Musen, M., eds, vol. 1, Calgary: Department of Computer Science of the University.

[Zarr96] Zarri, G.P. and Gilardoni, L. (1996) 'Structuring and Retrieval of the Complex Predicate Arguments Proper to the NKRL Conceptual Language', in *Proc. of the Ninth International Symposium on Methodologies for Intelligent Systems, ISMIS'96* (Lecture Notes in Artificial Intelligence 837), Berlin: Springer-Verlag.

[Zarr97a] Zarri, G.P. (1997) 'NKRL, a Knowledge Representation Tool for Encoding the "Meaning" of Complex Narrative Texts', *Natural Language Engineering – Special Issue on Knowledge Representation for Natural Language Processing in Implemented Systems*, 3: 231–253.

[Zarr97b] Zarri, G.P. and Azzam, S. (1997) 'Building up and Making Use of Corporate Knowledge Repositories', in *Knowledge Acquisition, Modeling and Management – Proceedings of EKAW'97*, Plaza, E., Benjamins, R., eds, Berlin: Springer-Verlag.

[Zarr98] Zarri, G.P. (1998) 'Representation of Temporal Knowledge in Events: The Formalism, and Its Potential for Legal Narratives', *Information & Communications Technology Law – Special Issue on Models of Time, Action, and Situations*, 7: 213–241.

[Zarr99a] Zarri, G.P. (1999) 'Knowledge Management', in *Wiley Encyclopedia of Electrical and Electronics Engineering*, J. Webster, ed., New York: John Wiley & Sons.

[Zarr99b] Zarri, G.P. (1999) 'Metadata, a "Semantic" Approach', in *Database and Expert Systems Applications – in Proc. of the 10th International Conference, DEXA'99* (Lecture Notes in Computer Science 1677), Bench-Capon, T., Soda, G. and Min Tjoa, A., eds, Berlin: Springer-Verlag.

[Zdon90] Zdonik, S. (1990) 'Object-oriented Type Evolution' in *Advances in Database Programming Languages*, F. Bancilhon and P. Buneman, (eds) Addison-Wesley, pp. 277–288.

Index